SECURITY STUDIES IN SOUTH ASIA: CHANGE AND CHALLENGES

SOME OTHER RCSS PUBLICATIONS

- CBMs in South Asia: Potential and Possibilities (RCSS, 2000);
- Confidence Building Measures in South Asia (RCSS, 1999);
- *Ethnicity and Constitutional Reform in South Asia* (Manohar, 1998);
- *Regional Economic Trends and South Asian Security* (Manohar,1997);
- *Diplomacy and Domestic Politics in South Asia* (Konark, 1996);
- *Nuclear Non-proliferation in India and Pakistan: South Asian Perspectives* (Manohar, 1996);
- *Refugees and Regional Security in South Asia* (Konark, 1996)

RCSS Newsletter

A quarterly bulletin is published containing reports on RCSS activities as well as work of other centres and institutions involved in South Asian strategic studies, as available. The newsletter also features articles of contemporary interest to the countries of the region, and an 'article annotation service'.

RCSS Policy Studies

12. Defence Expenditure in South Asia: India and Pakistan (May 2000)
11. Defence Expenditure in South Asia: Bangladesh and Sri Lanka (April 2000)
10. Defence Expenditure in South Asia: An Overview (March 2000)
9. Sectarian Conflict in Pakistan: A Case Study of Jhang (January 2000)
8. Politics and Theatre (September 1999)
7. Proliferation of Small Arms and Politics in South Asia: The Case of Bangladesh (May 1999)
6. The Politics of Violence and Development in South Asia (May 1999)
5. New Evangelical Movements and Conflicts in South Asia: Sri Lanka and Nepal in Perspective (December 1998)

Fellowship in South Asian Alternatives (FISAA) Monograph

- *Water, Power And People: A South Asian Manifesto on the Politics and Knowledge of Water* (1997), collaborative venture of the Fellowship in South Asian Alternatives.
- *The Nuclear Debate: Ironies and Immoralities* (1998), A monograph of the Fellowship in South Asian Alternatives.

Others

- *Directory of Individuals and Institutions Engaged in South Asian Strategic Studies* (1998).

Security Studies in South Asia: Change and Challenges

Edited by

DIPANKAR BANERJEE

REGIONAL CENTRE FOR STRATEGIC STUDIES
COLOMBO

MANOHAR
2000

First published 2000

ISBN 81-7304-363-9

Published by
Ajay Kumar Jain for
Manohar Publishers & Distributors
4753/23 Ansari Road, Daryaganj
New Delhi 110 002

Typeset by
Kohli Print
107 Radhey Shyam Park
Delhi 110 051

Printed at
Print Perfect
A-23, Mayapuri, Phase II
Delhi 110 064

Contents

Preface 7

Introduction 9

Nation-State, Security Studies and the Question of Margins in South Asia
JAYADEVA UYANGODA 15

Emerging Environmental Concerns in South Asia
SHAUKAT HASSAN 25

Security Studies in India: Recent Trends and Future Directions
P.R. CHARI 41

Security Studies in India: Continuity and Change in the Post-Cold War Era
W. LAWRENCE S. PRABHAKAR 59

Post-Cold War Security Studies in India: Continuity and Change
V.R. RAGHAVAN 79

Security Studies in Pakistan: Current Trends and Future Directions
ZAFAR IQBAL CHEEMA 91

Post-Cold War Security Studies in Pakistan: Continuity and Change
RASUL BAKHSH RAIS 111

Governance and National Security: Pakistan—a Case Study
KHALID MAHMUD 131

Security Studies in Bangladesh:
Continuity and Change
DILARA CHOUDHURY 145

Trends in Security Studies in Nepal:
Recent Trends and Future Directions
DHRUBA KUMAR 159

Internal and External Factors in
Security Studies in Sri Lanka
SUGEESWARA P. SENADHIRA 193

List of Contributors 207

Index 211

Preface

The Regional Centre for Strategic Studies has constantly attempted to understand the state, nature and potential of security studies in South Asia. The object is to identify the foundations, sketch the plans and define the outlines over which a superstructure may be built. This has been a steady and a methodical process. A number of projects were carefully designed to facilitate the process. The first, was the preparation of a compendium of scholars, institutions and research establishments engaged in strategic studies in and on South Asia. Research for this was undertaken in 1995 and a directory was published in 1998. This remains by far the most significant work on the subject till date helping network South Asian scholars and institutions. A related work has been a project on security studies in Asia. Its aim was to identify security issues that were gaining relevance in the changing circumstances among scholars and policy makers in the region.

A part of that process was a seminar held in July 1998, at Ahungalla in Sri Lanka to exchange views on the nature and state of security studies in South Asia. This conference brought together leading scholars of the region. Preparation for the conference was comprehensive. Scholars came prepared with competent papers and discussions ranged over a wide canvas. A number of new and salient points emerged and were widely debated. This book includes selected papers from that conference. Though not originally conceived to lead to a publication, the nature and importance of the subject and the quality of some of the papers presented merits their dissemination to a wider audience. The hope is that this will then generate a debate in the region. Understandably some of the articles may not be comprehensive. The book itself is not carefully structured with individual authors discussing issues that they viewed as important in their context. Yet topics raised are important enough to be seriously considered.

Three major issues emerged during this debate. One, was the new concept of security that is slowly coming to the fore in the world and its understanding and impact on South Asia. Two, a general bemoaning of the fact that security studies have received so little attention in South Asia and therefore, lacked both focus and direction. The consequence being that though all countries faced severe security challenges, very little intellectual input has been devoted to understand their nature and character or methods to deal with them. Third, was a general agreement that new issues were arising that affected security of the citizens of the state and which could be broadly put under a category of human security. But, there was neither an agreement on the scope and terminology, nor on the specific issues that needed to be put in this purview. The papers included in this compendium attempt to capture some of this debate and the dilemmas.

In the coming decades of the next century these issues will emerge as major questions facing South Asia. This book is a small initial step in developing a better understanding.

DIPANKAR BANERJEE
Executive Director
Regional Centre for Strategic Studies
Colombo

Introduction

A major question confronting students of strategic studies today, is what constitutes national security? What is it that is most important for a nation to protect and for which it needs to evolve strategies? Are state borders and frontiers the most crucial and which must be defended against all forms of external aggression and influence and at all costs? Or, are there other issues or core values, or questions affecting directly the concerns and interests of the citizens of a state that are more immediate and vital and those which can often brook no delay?

There are no clear answers to these questions yet or perhaps even in the near future. Nation states continue to be the building blocks of the international system. It is still almost the sole framework on which laws are framed. State sovereignty is the principle on which international relations are built. Citizens' loyalties still rest almost entirely on their respective nations and it is with this that they most clearly identify. Increasing the influence and power of respective states dominate elite thinking and forms the basis of national interests. People are still ready and willing to lay down their lives for the defence of the 'motherland' and to preserve national core values. These are unlikely to change fundamentally in the next couple of decades especially in Asia. Yet, there are also perceptible changes, both real and relevant.

Change is coming in atleast two dimensions. One, nations are now ready and willing to give up some part of their sovereignty to larger groupings of like minded states in order to enhance collective self interest. In an increasingly competitive world, individual nations feel that their interests and well being can be best enhanced through collective action. Hence there are attempts to come together, politically or economically or both. The European Union is but an advanced example. While this coming together is at an advanced and higher level of the state, down below there is often a coming apart. This is due to a greater consciousness of ethnic identities and through this an attempt to address their immediate concerns that largely determine their futures. Big multi-ethnic states in particular are often seen as distant entities incapable of responding to the needs of distant communities. Large pluralistic states increasingly resort to the use of force to keep them within the fold, not always with success after the cold war. As a consequence, ethnic assertions are giving rise to new nation states. From some 40 countries at the end of the Second World War, there are today 188 sovereign members of the United Nations, a few having emerged in the last decade. In a sense this reflects the urge for individual identity and need for human security at the expense of national security. This is a major challenge to governments around the world to which the strategic community has as yet no clear answers.

It is this new perception of human security that is the second important factor of change affecting one's thinking on security today. In this view it is argued that individual aspirations and their fulfilment are more important than defence of national borders. The Soviet empire collapsed when the people felt a palpable sense of deprivation even as the nation's borders were perhaps then the most secure. In the developing world, the deprivation of basic human needs is so overwhelming that to many of its citizens the larger glory of the nation remains an irrelevant consideration. Their security is linked to food, environment and personal samety above all else. The question then is what constitutes human security? Mahbub ul-Haq defined security in this context eloquently, and interpreted it to incorporate:

- Security of people, not just security of territory.
- Security of individuals, not just security of their nations.
- Security through development, not through arms.
- Security of all the people everywhere—in their homes, in their jobs, in their streets, in their communities, in their environment.[1]

This too poses a major dilemma. If one were to expand the concept of security to include every aspect of human needs and their fulfilment, then for practical purposes it may lose all meaning. It becomes too amorphous and general a term to merit any clear understanding or develop a basis for serious analysis. In a sense this is a dilemma that is the concern of this book.

The ten articles collected here represent many of the facets of this argument and in their separate ways attempt to reconcile these

[1] Mahbub ul-Haq, 'New Imperatives of Human Security', RGICS, Paper No. 17, New Delhi, 1994, p. 1

contradictory trends. Jayadeva Uyangoda addresses the question of 'margins in South Asia' and their relevance to nation states and security studies. The dominant paradigm of security studies, according to him is based on the 'centre's of modern nation states' leaving the 'margins' outside its purview. Central to this theme is a belief in the inviolability of the geographically defined territorial borders to the point of fetishism. To the extent that even the most basic needs of structural changes at the periphery is seen as threatening the stability and integrity of the state and must be resisted at all costs. Consequently, security studies then focus entirely on this elite perception to the exclusion of real and live causes threatening 'security'.

The next essay by Shaukat Hassan examines the environmental concerns in the security debate, an issue that is rapidly emerging as a major question of the present particularly in the developing world. How does one define environmental security? If the environment is defined as the physical space surrounding human beings, anything that threatens it, and therefore in turn threatens the livelihood of the people or their existence and well being, poses a threat to security. Shaukat places environmental security in the realm of unconventional threats as one of its principal constituents. He examines the major issues at stake, which he identifies as: poverty, population, energy needs and sustainable development. The scope for conflict in South Asia over these issues is indeed great, both between and within states. He argues that it is time that security studies focused on some of these issues, especially on adequate supply of food, sufficient and clean water, dealing with environmental pollution and the threat of weapons of mass destruction.

P. R. Chari's essay next focuses on recent trends in security studies in India. He carries out a comprehensive analysis of the state of security studies in the country and advances four propositions. One, that national security cannot be divorced from regional or global security. Two, individual security cannot transcend national sovereignty. Three, he discusses the permanent versus evolutionary threats to national security. Fourthly, he examines traditional versus comprehensive approaches to national security and emphasizes its dynamic nature. Finally, he highlights the need for a comprehensive and collective approach to national security. An interesting conclusion of his report is the research agenda that he outlines for the country and the region.

The next paper by Lawrence Prabhakar emphasizes continuity and change in security studies in India in the post-cold war era. Continuity is provided by the traditional outlines of security studies, such as ensuring territorial security, providing for internal integrity against low-intensity conflict and proxy war and dealing with terrorism. Changing phenomena are the nuclear strategic questions including concepts of deterrence and stability. His approach is more focused on the traditional dimension of security, a view widely prevalent in India at present. He too, outlines key areas that merit further study on security in India.

Zafar Cheema's paper on security studies in Pakistan is centred on the intense threat perception from India and how to cope with that threat, first through conventional military capability and now through nuclear deterrence. His study admirably traces the historical evolution of strategic thinking in Pakistan. Then traces the different and relevant approaches to security from the traditional, strategic military, non-conventional nuclear, diplomatic and then to the various forms of non-traditional approaches. The article is rich with insights into the different institutions and structures that shape security policy and thinking in the country today.

The second paper from Pakistan is by Professor Rasul Bakhsh Rais, examining continuity and change. He begins by attempting to redefine national security in the context of the 'wideners', such as 'common security' and 'human security' and outlines briefly the current global debate. He argues that in Pakistan the need to secure the 'physical base' puts a large onus on the military dimension. Hence, the domain of security studies remains focused on traditional perspectives. Interestingly, the three topics specifically identified by him as future security studies agenda for the country includes, nuclear deterrence, confidence-building measures and the 'wideners'.

The third eassy from Pakistan by Khalid Mahmud emphasizes the importance of governance and its links to national security. He deplores the lack of public debate on the multi-dimensional problem of national security in the country. A consequence of which is the over-emphasis on military security that has impoverished the nation and in turn aggravated its security concerns. He traces the origin of many of the current security threats to the inability of the state to address fundamental problems of development in a multi-national state such as Pakistan. He ends with a call to adopt Mahbub ul-Haq's approach for a basic change in the concept of security.

Continuity and change is again the theme from Bangladesh in the paper written by Dilara Choudhury. She too, calls for a review of security paradigms to focus on development as an important theme. Security studies in Bangladesh after its independence, according to her, focused essentially on strategic issues and not on development. This may appear curious, considering both the nature of its independence and the circumstances under which it found itself in the early years. There was no external threat perception to be concerned about, yet heavy defence expenditure and a high state of readiness exacted a toll that was not easy to bear for such a country. In addition, environmental degradation today poses the major security threat. Geopolitical realities bind its security concern to India. Both these pose a challenge to the nation on which inadequate consideration has been directed till now.

Dhruba Kumar presents a comprehensive analysis of recent trends and future directions of security studies in Nepal. The sudden change in Nepal's condition to that of a state sandwiched between two nuclear powers somewhat hostile to each other is yet to be fully understood. Yet, there is a consciousness of the threat to it should a nuclear war result in its vicinity. To examine this situation in a proper perspective, his article traces the history of security studies in Nepal over the last nearly 200 years. He examines next the four identifiable situations affecting state security: leadership inefficiency, economic disarray, ethnic revivalism and the incipient Maoist insurgency. From an examination of these factors, he evolves a security paradigm for Nepal.

The final article is by Sugeeswara Senadhira reflecting on the internal and external factors in security studies in Sri Lanka. He examines the conceptions of security from the perspective of a small island nation. Next, he traces the internal factors and particularly the ethnic conflict. The external factors affecting the internal conflict and finally, the paradigm of security studies in the country.

There is a common theme that runs through the different papers, even though the book is not structured and inspite of the fact that there is virtually no interaction between the security communities in the subcontinent. These may be identified as three inter-related themes. One, is a continuation of the 'realistic' approach to security, which dominates thinking and discourse in institutions and universities. At the same time there is an underlying acceptance that this is not an adequate framework for analysis and there is something substantial that is missing. Two, the restricted nature of the security discourse that continues to be limited to support state policies through sponsored institutions. This prevents a real debate and is against the spirit of analysis and objective thinking. This, thus, opens up considerable space for autonomous institutions to explore these areas. Finally, there is a near-universal acceptance that non-traditional issues of security and in particular the concept of human security needs further elaboration and formulation in the region.

This raises a number of questions and opens up a large research agenda. First, the questions of which only a few need to be identified. Can the states move away from the 'realist' paradigm of security thinking and develop alternate approaches that would address the fundamental questions of security for the region? One's understanding of human security is indeed flawed, notwithstanding the attempts by a few pioneers in the field. Could a cohesive approach be made to understand this and then set it in a regional perspective to operationalize the idea? How does one link defence and development questions? Could a regional approach towards comprehensive and cooperative security emerge in the region and how might this be pursued?

The tasks immediately at hand are obvious and can brook little delay. Three tasks that are probably the most necessary and relevant need only be identified. First, is the attempt to understand and develop the idea of human security in South Asian context. To put together the fledgling separate ideas into a comprehensive whole and in a regional context. Second, is to discuss the possibilities of evolving a comprehensive and cooperative security approach for the region that would develop alternate thinking and address human security considerations. Third, is to initiate annual meetings amongst South Asian 'Think Tanks' and strategic thinkers in order to develop a cohesive approach in South Asia.

DIPANKAR BANERJEE
Executive Director
Regional Centre for Strategic Studies
Colombo

Nation-State, Security Studies and the Question of Margins in South Asia

JAYADEVA UYANGODA

'Like in most other regions of the world', says the introduction note of this conference, 'debate and research on security in South Asia have traditionally focussed, essentially, on the nation state and external threat perception. Security studies in the region have also remained isolated in nature, and uni-dimensional and military oriented in approach.' As an outsider to the discipline of security studies, I share this concern. In this article, I will try to elaborate this concern through a critique of the nation state and nation state politics in South Asia. The main thrust of that critique is towards constructing a plea on behalf of the margins of the nation state: Give space to margins of the nation and the state in social science commitment.

Let me begin by making a somewhat generalized observation about nation state and its margins. Creation and marginalization of margins of the 'nation' has been one of the most pervasive practices of the modern nation state. South Asia's history of modernity is also a history of increasingly violent encounters between the centres and margins of the nation and the state. In the dialectic of the practice of marginalizing the margins, the nation state has also brought margins to the centre of its own problem of continuing historical validity.

Sri Lanka dramatically represents this particular historical predicament of the nation state. And indeed, Sri Lanka's political agenda today is largely decided through the dynamics of the war taking place between the centre and the margin. To add to the irony of it, what would happen today in the geographical margins—in the battlefield in Wanni jungles—can shape the political agenda of the centre tomorrow.

Even a cursory glance at counter-state insurgencies, rudimentary as well as protracted, developed in India, Pakistan, Bangladesh,

Bhutan and Nepal, would open our eyes to one incontrovertible fact about the modern South Asian state. Armed insurgencies against the state are the rule among ethno-political politics in social formations that are marginalized and excluded from the centre of 'nation- space'.[1] Politics of power usually functions within a logic of inclusion and exclusion. But politics of modern state power is particularly vicious in its inclusion-exclusion logic, because unlike the pre-modern state, the modern state is grounded on an extremely rigid set of conceptual as well as material resources.[2] Sovereignty, territory, national security, citizenship and political loyalty are concepts which are as inflexible and overwhelming as South Asia's huge bureaucracies, large standing armies and powerful planning commissions. To give just one example, the notion of sovereignty as understood and practised by the modern South Asian state is simply Austinian, even Hobbesian in its application. Otherwise, how could most South Asian states have turned their territorial margins into graveyards of small 'nation' communities?

The nation state, in its most pernicious form, demands not only the loyalty and obligation of the individual citizen, but also the total surrender of communities; the terms of which are defined at the centre, by the centre and for the centre. Any attempt at renegotiating these terms of the political contract by the margins, at the margins and for the margins would be immediately perceived as disintegrationist, separatist or anti—state strivings.

A Detour

It is a social law of power that marginality of the marginalized can be felt, experienced and understood only by the marginalized. Marginalizers cannot comprehend the phenomenology of marginality. The ontologies of the marginalizer and the marginalized rarely meet. This social law of margins is acutely present, in a variety of forms and at a multiplicity of sites, in power relations within the nation state.

Let me anthropologize this law of social margins of the state by referring to two of my personal experiences which are, of course,

[1] Homi Bhabha's essay, 'Dissemination: Time, Narrative, and the Margins of the Modern Nation', in *The Location of Culture* (London and New York: Routledge, 1994).

[2] Jayadeva Uyangoda, 'Biographies of a Decaying Nation-state', in Mithran Tiruchelvam and C.S. Dattathreya (eds.), *Culture and Politics of Identity in Sri Lanka* (Colombo: ICES, 1998).

infinitely insignificant compared with the events of the nation state that happen every day throughout South Asia. Sometime last year, in 1997, I was on my way to Chennai from Calcutta on an Indian Airlines flight. Seated next to me was a middle aged, well dressed man who, as I learnt, was an Indian citizen from the state of Meghalaya. He told me that he was a senior official of the State Bank of India, working in Nagaland. He was flying to Chennai with his family to escape the ferocious winter in Nagaland. He started telling me how he and family would be treated in southern India as 'foreigners' and he was prepared to accept that indignity, because the Meghalayan people would very often encounter this particular treatment in the rest of India. Once in Delhi, he told me, some one—a proper Indian citizen—asked him where he was from. He had said from Shillong.

The immediate response that came from his interlocutor was: 'What do you think about the Tigers? Do you think they will really go for a separate state?' or something to that effect. The proper Indian had confused Shillong with Ceylon, although he inadvertently referred to a factor commonly shared by both Shillong and Ceylon, ethnic insurgencies. Many a times, this senior Indian bureaucrat from the margins of India has been treated as a foreigner in India; as a Chinese visitor, as a Tibetan refugee, and in the most unlikely case a Ceylonese.

This politically very articulate man told me how Indian citizens from north-eastern states of India are constantly being treated by 'authentic' Indian citizens as foreigners, as non-Indians. As I gathered from him, many 'proper' Indians cannot come to terms with the fact that there can be 'Chinese-looking Indians'. In fact, he told me, quite stoically, that most mainstream Indians he knew of did not understand how people from north-east felt when they were perceived, in perfectly casual and chance encounters, as non-Indians and foreigners.

In encounters like this, there is very little sense one can make by saying that national integration and nation building are incomplete projects in India. Nation building is actually complete, because it has created the margins, in the geographical margins of the modern Indian state. It has also created a cruel casualness about marginalization of communities, which is so powerfully present in the practices of the nation state during the past fifty years.

Let me cite another example, from Sri Lanka. Not long ago, I was driving in Colombo with a friend who happened to be a member of the Tamil community. When we were approaching a military check point, we were signalled to stop. A soldier on duty asked for our identity cards. Having briefly examined my ID, the soldier asked a question which was quite innocent as far as his world view was concerned: 'You all are Sinhalese, aren't you?'

This was one of those profound moments when a young man in military uniform, carrying an automatic gun, radically deconstructed the Sri Lankan nation state and all its conceptual attributes—ethnicity, nation, language, citizenship, national unity and integration. This was also a revealing ethnographic moment for an academic interested in security as well as insecurity studies the extraordinary link established between the citizenship and the physical appearance of the individual. The 'security' which I felt as a member of the majority Sinhalese community and the 'insecurity' experienced by my friend as a member of the Tamil minority community are not just individual experiences.

There is a profoundly complex relationship between the centre and the margins of the nation, that has been inscribed in our bodies, in our skin complexion, in our shape of the skull and in the way we speak the 'official' language. What would have happened if the marginality of the margined was exposed at that moment of ensuring the nation's security? It was a moment when the margined had to hide his own identity behind the identity of an 'authentic' citizen. Who, except the margined, would have felt the enormity of violence of that moment?

As demonstrated in the anecdotes I just related, the nation state has a centrifugal innocence, the violence of which could be felt and experienced only by those in the margins. Insensitivity to margins is a perfectly uninnocent, that means, acutely violent, practice of the modern nation state.

But who would have comprehended, in the process of post-colonial state formation, this practice of violence and violation of communities in the margins of the state? Believers in the sanctity of the majoritarian nation state have repeatedly and consistently demonstrated a particular incapacity to even sense that marginalization of communities would eventually threaten the very foundations of the centre that is created through institutions specific to the modern state. Theoretically, refined constitutional mechanisms, developmentalist public policy, elaborate bureaucratic control and highly mobile military, might lead to subtle practices of exclusion. The individual experience of an Indian or a Sri Lankan, existentially located in the margins, is only a microcosmic representation of the practice of the modern state, a practice which can be discerned as a specific pathology of nation state politics.

SECURITY STUDIES AND THE NATION STATE

I don't think I am going to say anything new when I make the claim that the dominant paradigm of security studies is foregrounded on the sanctity of the centres of modern nation state. This argument has been made by many critics of the discipline of security studies. The point I wish to make as an addendum to that critique is that the sanctification of modern nation state and its centres is an academic practice, based on a certain historical fallacy concerning the eternity of this particular form of the state, which is history-specific.

The only exception to this sanctity rule is, as repeatedly demonstrated in Indo-Pakistan relations, is the perception that the breaking up, or at least weakening, of one nation state would serve the security interests of the other. The irony is that at the heart of South Asia's security studies is this particular exception. Insecurity of nation states and their centres constitutes the core of security regimes, as well as security studies. As far as India-Pakistan axis is concerned, one elementary, yet paramount, point comes to the fore: The security studies cannot liberate itself from the prison house of the nation state, so long as it fails to de-sanctify the borders of the nation state.

Central to the South Asian nation state as well as South Asian security studies, is a belief in the inviolability of the geographically defined territorial borders of the 'nation'. Bundled together within the geography of the territory are a host of anxieties concerning the survivability of the nation. Fixed territory is a defining characteristic of the modern state; but fetishism of territorial borders has been a particularly generic practice of the South Asian nation state since its formation, as demonstrated in the border wars between India and Pakistan and India and China. Indo-China relations, Indo-Pakistan relations, Indo-Nepal relations, Indo-Bangladesh relations—are key words in South Asian security studies. They are also a discourse of territorialized geographies.

The anxieties of insecurity are so embedded into the very being of the majoritarian nation state, that the demands for structural reforms of the state, pointing to the re-constitution of the existing mode of power sharing, are easily viewed as representations of disintegrationist desires that warrant resistance, denunciation and de-legitimization. Most of the social science inquiry in South Asia is an accomplice to this project of the state.

South Asia's social science disciplines that deal with the state and the nation have largely evolved as biographical sites of the nation state. For instance, for the political science inquiry, if there was any 'vision' for the future, it has been primarily conceptualized within the framework of nation building and political modernization. All the epistemological tools of this inquiry were defined by a practice of hyper-historicization of the nation state. What it means is, that, the form of the state which South Asia inherited from its encounter with Europe has been accepted as an eternal, natural form of political association. Even a casual encounter with young foreign service officials of South Asian states would be a tremendous experience to realize how the political consciousness of the cadres of the state has been totally shaped by a belief in the naturality of the territorially rigid nation state. And no wonder that many researchers in the field of security studies have a longing to consult retired foreign service officials.

The disciplinary agenda of security studies in South Asia is, in a sense, an enunciation of elite anxieties about territorial borders. In each state, there are powerful communities of coalitions that share and are animated by these anxieties. They have transformed those anxieties into public policy, defence strategies and quasi-theoretical categories of nation. In my own thinking, de-sanctification of territorial borders would open up unprecedented possibilities for a new paradigm of security for South Asia.

Flexible borders and the state should not be treated as a privileged synthesis, exclusively reserved for advanced capitalist nations. Backward capitalism in South Asia has made a fetish of territorial borders, within as well as between states. Under the logic of globalization, flexible movement of human and material capital among nations would enable South Asia to reap benefits from a new historical opportunity for rapid capitalist growth. But, who will explore into these new historical possibilities? Economists and planners, like security studies experts, continue to see the world through the prism of the state with strictly demarcated territorial boundaries.

My argument is that the social science preoccupation, including that of security studies, should cease playing this intellectual role of being an accomplice to a dying form of the state—the majoritarian nation state. Yet, intellectual liberation from the nation state is not an easy thing. There are two fundamental reasons for this difficulty.

Firstly, the counter nation state discourse has essentially emerged from among the communities of the margins and therefore, that discourse finds no legitimacy whatsoever in the mainstream political or social science thinking. Counter nation state practices have also been horridly violent, profoundly anti-liberal and astonishingly heartless, just like the practices of the nation state.

The nation state has, at least, the conceptual apparatus of rule of law and liberal democracy that can be easily deployed to veil its horrendous practice.

Secondly, our basic theoretical categories in political science and international relations, from which security studies derives its ideational sustenance, are so outdated in a historical sense that they simply cannot cope with the organic new developments within the nation state. We need to just look at the way in which the entire intellectual worldview of our undergraduates, who study political science and international relations, is shaped.

Almost all text books privilege the existing form of the state, with no critical insights into the alternative possibilities of political association among communities in a mode other than the nation state's present form. Students, some of whom may later become experts in security studies or join the foreign service, are seldom taught that states are history-specific political formations. Their political consciousness is totally de-politicized when it comes to the possible alternative forms of the state.

It is not an accident that there are no political science or international relations text books used in our undergraduate studies, written from the perspectives of the margins. The marginalized, paradoxically, don't write political science or IR text books. They write mostly propaganda tracts and formulate emotionally appealing slogans. Rarely do they withstand the rigorous test of social 'scientific' interrogation. Indeed, their critique is a critique of despair, of irrationality and of arms, which cannot enter university teaching curricula.

Liberating Security Studies

I think, the problem with security studies, at least partly, is that one is a discursive prisoner of the nation state narrative of human fate. One doesn't realize that one is a prisoner, because one doesn't see an alternative world outside. As a result, one doesn't even possess a political language to re-imagine an alternative form of the state. When I make the statement that security studies should cease to be an accomplice to the crimes of the nation state, which I have described elsewhere as a dying historical form of political association, I have to stop there and feel bewildered. Because, I have no access to a discursive resource base, which should enable me to verbalize my thoughts. I can only make an outrageous and hugely scandalous claim about political history of humankind: The nation state, as a historical form of political association, has come to an end. South Asia exemplifies this fascinating and profoundly exciting moment in the history of state formation. The emerging forms of the state are not yet clear. One can either wait and accept what may come or make an intervention in shaping its form and content.[3]

A dispassionate look at the politics in South Asia may enable one to understand some rudimentary forms and embryonic formations of the possibilities of the future state in the region. One is the formation of mono-ethnic mini states. This is one of the most disquieting scenarios for the academic community of security studies in South Asia; yet it is in the historical horizon. Its villainous heroes are already there all over South Asia and they are probably, in a quasi-Hegelian sense, unconscious tools of history.

Another is the transformation of the existing states into confederations of semi autonomous 'republics', in which the notion of state sovereignty would be radically de-centred. I use the term 'republics' in a slightly Aristotelian sense, to denote and accommodate the emergence of civil society as the most vibrant sphere of political action and activity in South Asia. A third is the transformation of the present group of states in South Asia into a fully or semi-antagonistic, hyper militarized entities. Recent developments in the Indian and Pakistani nuclear politics give some credence to this scenario, with which the security studies community might feel exceedingly comfortable.

I don't think the discipline of security studies has an autonomous space of its own. Its space is defined and determined by nation state politics. But if the practitioners of security studies are serious about the legitimacy and relevance of their own vocation, I suppose there are two options. One is, to abandon the discipline altogether. The second, more sensible one, is to move away from its nation state centrism in order to:

[3] When I teach political thought to undergraduate students, I occasionally feel that the greatness of political thinkers from Machiavelli to Marx was precisely the fact that they did not simply wait in uncertainty till new forms of the state evolved through war, violence and conflict. They intervened to shape the shape of the emerging state. But who are we to undertake such grand historical projects?

- Recognize the nation state in its present form as a historically contingent phenomenon.
- Acknowledge that politics during the past fifty years has changed the state and that the state has brought the margins to the centre of the process of change.
- Return to some of the old notions of the state to re-imagine the state as a flexible political association of sovereign communities and not as a trans-historical, unchangeable entity imprisoning human destinities.

Emerging Environmental Concerns in South Asia

SHAUKAT HASSAN

Two words have become ubiquitous these days: 'Environment' and 'Security'. While these words are not new, their meaning and importance have certainly broadened. This is reflected in the frequency of domestic and international conferences, seminars and workshops on the subject matter. There is also some confusion in the usage of these terms. The issue is further complicated when these two words are linked together into a phrase called 'environmental security.' What exactly is environmental security? How do environmental concerns take on a security dimension? Since environmental issues have existed ever since man began imposing his demands on nature, why are such concerns a matter of urgency today?

This article seeks to answer these and related questions in the light of recent developments in South Asia. In order to make the article more manageable and focused. I shall be exploring these issues in the context of Bangladesh which is a good test case.

A Working Definition

How one defines an environmental issue depends on how one perceives it. It may be argued that many of the problems which the countries of South Asia suffer from these days have existed in this region for quite some time, but they were never really addressed as such. Only in recent decades are these being labeled as environmental problems. Some of these problems have worsened over time and become quite acute, such as the depletion of forest resources due to high demand for timber and fuelwood, pollution of waterways from effluents, and resultant health hazards.

Their linkages are even less understood, which makes it difficult for government officials to handle them. Is the depletion of fisheries an environmental problem? Does overpopulation have any impact on the health of the environment? Is dislocation of human communities, either internally or across international borders, the cause or the effect of environmental degradation? These and similar questions require a clear understanding for proper policies to be formulated.

Given this uncertainty, two types of tendencies can develop. One tendency would be to adopt a minimalist approach and define environmental problems as those that are concerned primarily with ecology, and related issues such as agriculture and irrigation. While this approach may provide greater focus, however, it is too narrow and leaves out important concerns normally associated with the environment.

The other tendency would be to adopt a maximalist approach and view the environment as constituting both the ecological and the human domains and their interactions, and therefore, would include a much wider array of concerns ranging from, say, social space, human health and recreation, to climatic change. Such a definition would obviously broaden the scope of inquiry, making focused policy formulation a more difficult task. Both kinds of thinking appear to permeate government ministries which deal with environmental issues either directly or peripherally.

For the present purpose, however, I shall define environment simply as the layman understands it: Physical space on which one depends for one's livelihood. For the farmer this may mean his land, water bodies, forests and other habitats which he requires for the survival of his family and his livestock. For the city folk, this may mean the parks and lakes they use for their recreation, the urban air that they breathe, the water that they drink, etc.

Changing Concepts of Security

The fundamental shift in security perceptions that has been observed in recent decades is the transition from 'conventional threats to security' to 'unconventional threats to security'. Thus, for example, defence treaties and alliances in South Asia are a thing of the past. Notwithstanding the reported eleven nuclear tests that rocked the subcontinent recently and the continuing concern with conventional arms race and, now, the renewed possibility of a nuclear arms race between India and Pakistan, there has been for sometime a region-wide universal concern with unconventional threats to security which are primarily internal to each country.

These unconventional threats include religious fanaticism, ethnic cleansing, human rights violation, burgeoning impoverishment, secessionist activities, etc. Most of these arise from non-military activities of individuals and communities seeking defence, preservation and promotion of particular lifestyles and livelihoods. They are generally cumulative and usually not perceived as threats to national security until it is too late. What has been observed within this region, as also elsewhere, is that governments have, more often than not, failed to respond to the legitimate demands and aspirations of various segments of society; in instances where governments did respond, it was either too little or too late.

Looming large among these unconventional threats is the threat to the environment and its repercussions on human and other biotic communities. The massive degradation of the environment is today an unchallenged fact, and has caused widespread alarm. The ecological health of each country in the region is an issue which has affected all communities, rich and poor, urban and rural, and all ethnic or social groups. That resource scarcity resulting from environmental degradation may lead to conflict is, of course, not new. The root of all major conflicts among communities and nations throughout history has been the competition over territories and resources.

Even today, the logic of influencing or controlling the allocations of the environmental resources of the non-industrial world is predicated on the argument that they constitute the 'shadow ecology' of the economies of the handful of industrial countries.[1] What is new, however, is the fact that competition over increasingly diminishing resource access and use causes measurable stress among contending groups and communities; this leads to responses by aggrieved communities which may range from forced but peaceful population dislocation to outright conflict. Thus, while some scholars have challenged the suggestion that environmental stress directly leads to the breakdown of security and to violent conflict,[2] others have shown that environmental stress

[1] Jim MacNeill, Pieter Winsemius, Taizo Yakushiji, *Beyond Interdependence: The meshing of the world's economy and the earth's ecology* (New York: Oxford University Press, 1991), p. 159.

[2] Daniel Deudney, 'The Case Against Linking Environmental Degradation and National Security,' *Millennium: Journal of International Studies*, Vol. 19, No. 3 (1990), pp. 461-76.

is a significant variable and that environmental degradation does ultimately lead to conflict and to the breakdown of social cohesion and national unity.[3]

Recent studies by the Centre for Conflict Studies, University of Toronto, have concentrated on 'environmental scarcity' rather than on 'environmental security'. These studies have focused on the relationship between environmental scarcity and conflict. While the attempt to establish a direct causal link between resource scarcity and conflict still remains somewhat murky, sufficient case studies have been examined to suggest that there *is* a link between environmental scarcity, social change and conflict.[4]

Given widespread poverty among an increasing number of Asian and African countries, there is, therefore, growing urgency today to explore the linkages between resource use, environmental degradation and poverty. It would therefore be useful to define environment as comprising both the ecological and human domains, and to define environmental security as the measure of sustainability of the biotic resources of the planet.[5] In any case, whatever the approach adopted, governments are now increasingly focussing on the people, their economic and environmental rights, and their rights to a decent life and a prosperous future. The rights of future generations, however, tend to be crowded out. How is environment linked to security?

Environmental issues become identified as threats to national security by their increasing importance as factors underlying social instability, clashes between communities, breakdown of civil order and other forms of strife. Thus when the construction of a hydroelectric plant inundates farmlands, or homesteads or sacred burial grounds; or if traditional forests are mowed down and replaced by exportable timber plantation to satisfy a particular export market; or if access to certain resources is skewed in favour of any special group, this inevitably creates social strife between those who stand to benefit and those who suffer, thus compromising national security.

[3] Shaukat Hassan, 'Environmental Issues and Security in South Asia', *Adelphi Papers*, 262. The International Institute for Strategic Studies (London, Autumn 1991).

[4] Thomas Homer-Dixon, 'Environmental Scarcities and Violent Conflict: Evidence from Cases', *International Security*, Vol. 19, No. 1 (Summer 1994), pp. 10-14.

[5] Shaukat Hassan, 'Sustainable Development, Environmental Security and Disarmament Interface in South Asia: A Concept Paper', in D.D. Khanna (ed.), *Sustainable Development* (Delhi: Macmillan India Limited, 1997), pp. 457-74.

Environmental issues get identified as threats to regional or international security when their effects undermine the social, economic and ecological health and well-being of neighbouring countries. If industrial pollution from one country undermines the fragile mountain ecology of another country, thereby undermining the latter's tourism industry which is a major source of its foreign exchange earning; or if unilateral withdrawal of water from international rivers causes havoc to agriculture or to pisciculture in lower riparian states; or if radiation leaks from nuclear testing is carried by winds into neighbouring states thereby affecting the health of its nationals, then the possibility of bilateral conflict increases and regional security stands compromised.

One can therefore define environmental insecurity as the sense of fear, anxiety, danger from violence, and social and economic injustice arising from environmental decline. And environmental decline may either be triggered by natural climatic phenomena like floods and droughts, or by human developmental activities.

Environmental insecurity may, thus, breed environmental conflicts unless there is timely intervention both at the governmental and social levels.

Some Major Issues at Stake

POVERTY

Despite governmental attempts over many decades to eradicate poverty, it is still the scourge of South Asia. In some countries, as much as fifty per cent or more of the population is below the poverty line. This means that an unacceptable portion of the population of this region is at the subsistence level. The continued existence of poverty, therefore, is a reflection of livelihood unsustainability, which some may broadly equate with environmental unsustainability. In this sense, the measure of poverty is also the measure of livelihood insecurity.

Apart from poverty itself, defined in terms of a minimum daily caloric intake, there are several other dimensions of poverty identified by the impoverished themselves. Associated with poverty are issues such as powerlessness, vulnerability, physical and social isolation, security, self-respect and dignity. These issues have never been a part and parcel of policy interventions; which have focussed primarily on income and consumption measures of poverty. The primary reason why this has been so is that the poor in South Asia were not consulted. Many governmental policies fail because they are of the government, by the government and for the government, and not of the people, by the people or for the people, notwithstanding government assertions to the contrary.

For poverty alleviation policies to succeed, the stakeholders, who in this case are the impoverished, must be identified, and they should be drawn into the process of policy formulation so that policy ownership is broadened. The participation of, and dialogue with, other social groups would further widen the constituency for reforms, and the resultant policies grounded on reality are more likely to be implemented and sustainable in the long term. Without constructive engagements of affected communities in the policy process, experts level dialogue is likely to be a dialogue of the deaf. Since poverty remains rampant throughout South Asia, current governmental policies have obviously failed; this calls for review, reassessment and recasting of policy interventions along the lines delineated above.

POPULATION

The next major crisis that this region is wrestling with is how to contain the still-high population growth rate. Apart from China, this region is home to the largest density of mankind. The population base is already so large that it will require a few years before the effects of an integrated, multi-pronged policy intervention to reduce the growth rate are felt. But time is a resource which the subcontinent is likely to run out of, unless matters are handled urgently.

What is very important to note, however, is that the pace of environmental change in the subcontinent has shot up drastically in recent decades, and it is likely to increase further as the region industrializes. With rising population, socio-economic activities have multiplied and human-induced environmental change has significantly increased. Although the rate of population growth in some countries has fallen, if national statistics are to be believed, even at the current rates of growth, the pace of economic activities and technological interventions is on the course of a head-on clash with the region's natural systems; generating its own security dilemma.

The actual physical impact of population growth will differ between localities depending on, among other factors, the existing population base and density, population carrying capacity and the activities of the people of the particular region. There is therefore the need to understand the concept of carrying capacity in the context of basic human needs, developmental aspirations, the sufficiency and vitality of ecosystems and biodiversity of the region. One also has to be sensitive to intangible components such as human values, attitudes and behaviour conditioned by historical, socio-cultural, political and economic forces impacting on that region.

The threats generated by population pressures are manifest throughout the subcontinent. Irrespective of countries, they include urban squalor, unemployment, depletion of life-sustaining resources, declining quality of life, violence and breakdown of social order. As the population increases, the man-land ratio deteriorates leading to resource exhaustion. Competing use of land has already led to a shortage of agricultural land, destruction of forests, encroachment of habitats, real estate crisis and greater migration.

The latter will create additional burden on receiving countries, while repatriation of income of migrants will force the price of land to go up further. Already, farmers find it more lucrative to sell their lands rather than till it for agriculture. Poverty is often closely related to population growth, and the disappearance of traditional life styles and rural unemployment are important factors that force migration.

An ever-increasing number of people also means greater consumption and generation of waste. Today, South Asia's urban environment is rife with air pollution, faecal contamination of drinking water, hazardous wastes with poor or no disposal facilities, substantially reduced social space, and crime. These consequences of burgeoning population have undercut human health and quality of life, administrative capacities and services of municipalities, law and order, and social cohesion and justice.

Thus, regional governments in the not too distant a future will be hardpressed to even reconcile between the current rate of population growth and the demands it will generate. The question facing security analysts and government officials is: Can the subcontinent's natural systems satisfy the demand for foodgrains, fossil fuels, forests, fish and water, if the population growth is not brought under control, or even reversed?

ENERGY NEEDS

The transformation of the subcontinent's landscape into millions of zones of economic activities of varied kinds has already created a massive demand for energy which by and large remains unfulfilled. Since the countries of the region have embarked on the path of industrialization, future energy needs will far exceed the present generation capacity planned. Apart from the issue of generating adequate energy levels, the issue of its type and the impact on the environment should also be of concern.

The high rate of mining of coal, a recent venture in Bangladesh, will increase its use as a source of energy will undoubtedly produce considerable atmospheric pollution. The construction of barrages and the damming of rivers to produce hydroelectric power have caused painful repercussions on affected communities, including the loss of agricultural lands and homesteads. An important source of protein in the subcontinent is fish.

The generation of hydel power has caused massive aquatic dislocations which has adversely affected fish production; in some cases, the changes in water temperature and turbidity have reduced the nutrient content, which in turn has led to depletion of specific categories of fish species. This has directly affected the livelihood of fisherfolk. Unless the production of meat and the buying capacity of the poor are improved, loss of animal protein due to reduction, and in some places destruction, of fish species will exacerbate the health of millions who are already below the poverty line.

Among other sources of energy, wind and solar energy are considered to be clean and promising alternatives. However, the technology for mass production is still not available, nor have governments invested sufficient resources to explore its availability and viability. Nuclear energy, on the other hand, is too costly and if not properly monitored, too dangerous. Given the weaknesses of the economies of the subcontinent, it will be years before nuclear energy becomes universally viable in the region.

And finally, the most widespread source of energy in rural areas are forest produce and dung. Unless affordable alternative sources are made available to the poor, deforestation will continue unabated. The use of dung in domestic households is also removing an important biofertilizer from use in agricultural lands. The Bangladesh government has recently announced its desire to gradually ease out synthetic fertilizers to the extent possible and supplant them with locally available animal dung.

SUSTAINABLE DEVELOPMENT

A major challenge facing the regional countries today is how to choose appropriate development strategies for their people. One thing that is absolutely clear is that despite a half century's development efforts and activities, except for a small segment of the population the people of this region are poorer than before. While the high population growth rates may have eaten up much of the fruits of development, how much actual benefit was reaped from the various developmental strategies is still highly debatable.

The ecological, social and political costs are however quite clear. The consensus emerging from the grassroots is that fifty years of development have only led to a new form of colonialism, a new form of dependence, which is even more destructive than the old form. Far from revitalizing the regenerative capacities of the people, the mainstream paradigm of development has destroyed 'the very immune system that they had developed . . . throughout the ages'.[6] Many minority ethnic communities have lost their sustainable ways of life, and the subcontinent has lost, or is losing, its rich diversity.

And yet, development as we have come to understand over the years, that is, developmental ideas and strategies handed down to us by the West continue to shape our policy. The trouble with this elitist perception of development is that while such a paradigm safeguards the interests of the industrially advanced countries, it perpetuates the dependence of the non-industrialized countries of the region on the former. It does nothing for the teeming masses of South Asia who continue to languish in poverty. What is equally scary is that far from breaking the Western stranglehold on developmental thinking and strategies, they are being consolidated under the garb of globalization.

This post-cold war phenomenon—globalization—raises many additional concerns. Are the people of the subcontinent going to be players or victims in this globalization process? Are they equipped to play by Western rules and hold their own? Or, are they to emulate Western thinking and follow leads provided by the industrial states? Will indigenous ideas and ways of thinking count? What role will non-governmental organizations play in this globalization process? Will they serve as external agents of intervention in the policy making processes in underdeveloped countries?

If current strategies of development continue, it is highly unlikely that development will be sustainable. Consumption of grain, fish and water has already reached unsustainable levels; forests and grasslands are getting increasingly scarce; the burning of fossil fuels has already exceeded availability, and yet spiraling human demands seem to know

[6] Majid Rahnema, Victoria Bawtree, *The Post-Developmental Reader* (London: Zed Books, 1997).

no bounds. For South Asia to have sustainable economies, the population growth rate must be drastically reduced. So that human births and deaths are in balance; the natural rate of soil replenishment through silt must equal soil loss due to flooding, erosion or salinity; tree cutting should be balanced by tree planting; fish caught both inland and offshore should not exceed sustainable yields of fisheries; the number of cattle on a range should not exceed the latter's carrying capacity; tapping of groundwater should not exceed the natural rate of recharge of aquifers; carbon emissions and carbon fixations should be in balance; and the number of plant and animal species lost due to human intervention should not exceed the rate at which new species evolve.

In short, if South Asia's consumption exceeds the sustainable yield of the region's ecological endowment, then sustainability will collapse and security issues will dramatically rise.[7] This reality faces the present generation. For future generations, survival conditions will worsen if timely and proactive measures are not taken now in order to safeguard their equity.

Resource Constraints

The scarcity of resources—both renewable and non-renewable—is no longer a theoretical possibility but a reality in the subcontinent. The ratio of human demand and resource supply is worsening as populations increase. To assume that technology intervention on its own can restore balance may require a leap of faith, since the governments of the region do not have access to the required types of technologies nor the absorptive capacity to make any qualitative difference in the lives of their peoples. Scarcities, therefore, have to be dealt with by adopting social and political strategies, and urgently.

There are at least three ways of looking at resource scarcities. The first would be to look at scarcities which are demand-induced. As the region's human population increases, human activity will multiply, leading to growth in per capita economic product. This means that consumption of the region's renewable and non-renewable resources will also rise. Population and demographic factors therefore become an important consideration when looking at scarcity from the demand side.

[7] For additional discussion on sustainable development, see *World Resources: A Guide to the Global Environment*, 1992-3, Chapter 1.

The second approach would be to look at scarcity from the supply side. This type of scarcity is especially evident with regard to land, water and energy. The availability of good cropland, for instance, is a perennial problem throughout most of the subcontinent because of, among other things, land degradation. A recent study of the state of Bihar, where land is perceived to be very scarce and therefore the most sought-after resource, reveals certain trends which by and large reflect the general trends throughout South Asia.[8] There, permanent pastures and grazing lands have decreased over the last thirty years primarily due to human encroachment.

The percentage of land put to non-agricultural uses has been increasing over the years due to industrial and infrastructural growth. The percentage of barren and uncultivable land shows an upward trend, and this is due to a combination of factors such as floods, spread of salinity and top-soil depletion. Good agricultural lands are owned by rich landowners usually residing in cities. This type of land in some cases is left uncultivated; in other cases it has been subdivided into smaller parcels thereby making them uneconomical for agricultural use. There is no substantial net increase in the total quantity of agricultural land to meet Bihar's land demand. Whatever meagre gain there has been due to improved agricultural policies and techniques or government's reclamation efforts, has been nullified by land lost due to degradation of one sort or another. The upshot has been to target cultivable waste land, fallow land and forests, which is worsening the environmental problems facing Bihar. This scenario, with variations here and there, is generally applicable across the subcontinent.

The third type of scarcity is structurally-induced. It is caused by factors closely associated with social and cultural values of the people, the way the society is organized and the administrative system that is in place. In the economically underdeveloped societies of South Asia, social relationships are usually structured in such a way as to create inequitable access to, and use of, resources. Structurally-induced scarcity results as much from government policy interventions in the form of planning and management, as from policy non-interventions such as government's unwillingness for whatever reason to seriously pursue equitable land reform or land reclamation measures.

[8] Shaukat Hassan, 'Resource Scarcity and Acute Conflict: The Case of Bihar' (unpublished, 1996).

Scope for Conflict

What emerges from the above discussion is that the scope for conflict within the state and between states in South Asia is immense. Within the state, the clash of interest often leading to violent conflict between the landowners and agricultural labour, between farmers and industrialists, between the urban and rural communities, between the privileged and the under-privileged is increasingly emerging along environmental fault lines.

Some traditional resource-based clashes such as that over the ownership or possession of agricultural land or water bodies are turning into serious conflicts; others are new collisions. Conflicts over fishing rights are frequent. Fights over grazing land is a common phenomenon. Competition over forest resources regularly pit local inhabitants against timber contractors. Water scarcity fights are evident not only between states within a country—such as that over the waters of the Cauvery river between the states of Karnataka and Tamil Nadu[9]—but also within smaller communities where water for domestic and agricultural use is increasingly hard to come by either because of depletion in groundwater level or because of salinity intrusion. Food shortages either due to insufficient planting or failed crops or price hikes have caused famines, some of which turned into riots, in South Asia. If not a direct factor, food shortages have contributed to the collapse of at least one government in the subcontinent.

The Capacity of the State

We can discount the possibility that the state will wither away soon. It will continue to exist as long as there is the psychological need of nations to maintain segregated existence, which in turn will require a delimited territorial identity. Governments must also exist because human societies need institutions which must play regulatory and distributive roles. The current challenge is to reach a national consensus on what should be the government's role and on setting limits on it. At a minimum, a government must play the role of a facilitator and guarantor of security of the people and their territory.

However, increasingly, the capacity of governments in the subcontinent to deliver essentials is the subject of considerable concern. The

[9] Shaukat Hassan, 'Resource Scarcity and Acute Conflict: The Case of the Cauvery' (unpublished, 1996).

demands on the state are so large and the time frame for it to react to meet those demands is so less that dissatisfaction about governmental performance is widespread. As scarcities intensify, disadvantaged groups will focus on narrow survival strategies thereby reducing their interaction with civil society. Elite groups will also compete and at the same time try to weaken the state in order to maximize their gain.

Resource scarcities lead to reduced economic productivity and a fall in tax intake of revenues to the state. Thus, with increasing demand for social goods and services and decreasing revenues, the net result will be weakened state capacity. The ability of a people to adapt by employing social ingenuity may reduce the burden on the state, but ultimately what will matter is state performance.

If the performance gap widens, as is increasingly the case in South Asia, then the legitimacy of the state will be in question, and the state will be seen as having failed to be representative of or responsive to society. In that case, decreased legitimacy of the state will undermine social cohesiveness and increase opportunities for challenger groups to emerge. The effect of both these types of outcome is likely to be civil violence.

The capacity of the South Asian state may be judged in more ways than one. The quality of political leadership is an important factor. The trend appears to be the replacement of political leaders who have a national outlook by those with parochial concerns. Environmental and other worries within local communities are giving rise to leaders who arrive at the national stage through coalition politics. Once there, a fatal combination of ignorance of national and international issues and their linkages, pedestrian outlook, and preoccupation with the demands of their local constituency, results in poor leadership. They are generally unable to locate the demands of the specific constituency in the larger national context.

The administrative and governance structures are also generally flawed in the context of present needs. Decision making power is centralized; local and national consultations on important issues are unheard of; and the importance of partnership building is not understood. A lack of trained personnel, improper and inadequate infrastructure, and insufficient funds also plague South Asian governmental institutions.

In the specific case of environmental concerns, governments are making all the right noises and even going through the motions of policy formulation, but effective implementation of those policies is far from being guaranteed. While structures of environmental governance range from the rudimentary to the more serious kind, the continuing problems of inadequate budget, untrained and uninterested officials, and ad hocism undermine the credibility of their publicly expressed concerns about the environment. Their approach to solving environmental problems more than often appears to be cosmetic and publicity-driven than genuine.

Where there is a serious attempt, lack of conceptual clarity often results in muddled policies which are difficult to carry out. Environmental policies which cut across several ministries require a high degree of coordination which is not always forthcoming. And, monitoring of policies implemented is usually half-heartened because there is no clear perception as to which ministry or department is responsible for which component of the program.

What Are The Security Concerns of The Future?

Environmental issues will continue to demand greater attention from the governments and the peoples of South Asia. Even if the birth and death rates were in balance, the level of productive output that would be required to achieve a decent standard of living for all, would exact a lareg toll on the region's ecological base and its life-support systems. Among the challenges that this region must face are: How to reconcile the demands of this huge mass of people with the finite resources of the land, how to attain zero population growth rate, and how to prevent wasteful consumption?

Meanwhile, the possibility of conflict is high because the resources that are necessary to support even the current populations are fast becoming scarce. Water tables are receding, forests are diminishing, farmlands are being converted to non-farm use, fish stocks are getting reduced, and population is spreading. But the problem of overpopulation tops it all. Given these realities, what are the security concerns of the future?

Security specialists might do well to direct their attention to four areas. First, the problem of adequate supply of food. Increasing population means per capita land will decrease while demand for food will increase. With the majority of the population of the subcontinent already in poverty, starvation and famine may well be round the corner unless proactive measures are taken. The political ramifications and potential for violence are too scary to contemplate.

Scientific and technological interventions such as high yield varieties, efficient irrigation systems, bio-fertilizers and the like will significantly enhance food production, but will not resolve the impending disaster. National priorities will have to be reorganized to reflect the importance of food, and strategies of food production may require subcontinental rather than single-country planning. A million things need to be done to ensure sustainable food security, and signing a regional document on food security is only the first step.

The second concern is water security. In the pre-industrial stage demand for water was confined primarily to the agricultural and domestic sectors. Today, things are not what they used to be. Water requirement in agriculture, in industry, in transport and for domestic use has increased dramatically, and it will become more and more difficult to sustain supply if adequate steps are not taken soon. It appears that the total quantum of water in the region will remain adequate for the future as well, but the difficulty is with distribution. An integrated regional water plan with distributive mechanisms incorporated into it might even out the current simultaneous overabundance and scarcity of water. Good regional and local planning is essential, which in turn requires farsighted leadership willing to form water partnerships across the subcontinent.

The third insecurity will be caused by pollution. Pollution will only increase from here on. Pollution of rivers, other inland water bodies and sea coasts is on the rise. Pollution of land from dumping of domestic and industrial waste, and foreign nuclear waste is spreading. Pollution of air due to automobile emissions and industrial outlets is not lagging behind either. The effects on human health are well documented in the Western world. The cost to society is manifold.

It includes the cost of maintaining an adequate health care system with properly trained doctors and nurses, the cost of labour lost to the productive sectors of the economy due to ill-health, as well as social and psychological stigma attached to an idle member of a society. Strict emission standards and environmental legislation will have to be uniformly applied throughout the region, and provision for damage from pollution will have to be agreed to.

The fourth insecurity results from the possession of weapons of mass destruction, such as nuclear weapons. The recent nuclear tests are a wake-up call to all, suggesting that twenty-five years of 'peace' in the subcontinent may well have ended. Apart from the actual fear of a regional nuclear holocaust, nuclear weapons create serious environmental concerns.

They generate toxic wastes which are difficult to dispose and are certainly very costly. Toxic wastes as well as nuclear weapons storage sites pollute the ecology of the region by adulterating the land, aquifers and water tables. Radiation associated with weapons testing can also maim people for life, both in the vicinity and beyond. Large tracts of land are requisitioned and put to non-productive use such as building test sites, firing range, depots, waste dumps, etc. In addition, forests are often cleared to acquire more land, and quite often communities are dislocated who often find themselves as economic misfits in their new locations. The people of the subcontinent cannot and should not remain nonchalant to the adverse effects of nuclear weapons production, storage, transport and deployment.

Conclusion

While the insecurities discussed in the foregoing are not the only serious ones, they are likely to be the immediate ones, any one of which will have considerable repercussions for security and peace in the region. The study of environmental security has not been seriously undertaken in the region. As environmental issues become more prominent, questions of justice, equality and human rights will require serious attention. The Research Centre for Strategic Studies might consider launching a special long term multinational research programme on environmental security and its policy impact.

Security Studies in India: Recent Trends and Future Directions

P. R. CHARI

It is proposed to evaluate here, security studies in India within the larger regional and global framework, which requires speculation on recent changes in the international security system, and present trends in strategic literature. The current state of security studies in India and the conceptual issues involved would then be noticed in overview. Finally, an agenda for future research would be explored.

The Global Setting

The post-cold war world evolved after the Soviet Union dissolved and the Warsaw Pact disintegrated. This led some Western analysts to announce the victory of the United States in its pyrrhic struggle with the Soviet Union.[1] That conclusion was extended to a victory of Western liberal thought over communism and the transformation of Russia from a cause into a country.[2] And, further, to the triumph of democracy over dictatorship; freedom of thought over controlled media; market forces over command economies; and so on.

Traditionally, a Western bias has dominated strategic literature, where over 90 per cent emanate, mostly, from American and a few European academic and research institutions. Two examples can be cited. Firstly, describing the British withdrawal in the early seventies from east of Suez as creating a 'vacuum' in the Indian Ocean region.

The possibility that regional countries could work out their own inter-relations and power equations did not inform this conceptual framework. Secondly, designating *pax Atomica* imposed on Europe

[1] Francis Fukuyama, *The End of History and the Last Man* (London: Hamish Hamilton, 1992).

[2] Bruce D. Porter, 'A Country Instead of a Cause: Russian Foreign Policy in the Post-Soviet Era', *The Washington Quarterly*, 15, No. 3 (Summer 1992).

during the cold war as the 'long peace' in the world. This failed to appreciate that the East-East contentions were equally, if not more, signi-ficant during the cold war. Besides, a transference of East-West and East-East rivalries had occurred into Third World regions, wherein tensions were already subsisting for a melange of historical, territorial, ethnic, and religious reasons. This, too, did not receive adequate attention.[3]

Proceeding further, post-cold war international security issues display not only elements of closure, but also continuity and change. American-Russian tensions have abated. But, in spite of their mincing steps towards formalizing START-II and promises to reduce their respective nuclear arsenals, the commitment to the ultimate goal of nuclear disarmament is not reassuring. China has become a revisionist element in the international security system. Sino-US relations have acquired the same part-cooperative and part-competitive character that had distinguished the US-Soviet cold war relations.

The end of the cold war did not presage an end to violence in the international system. This was dramatised by the Gulf War in 1990-1; the crises in Yugoslavia, Somalia, and Rwanda; the Taiwan Straits imbroglio in 1996, and again Iraq in 1998. Wars between states are conceivable in the Third World, but their locus has decisively shifted from inter-state to intra-state conflicts. This reflects a 'decompression effect' arising from the resurgence of sub-nationalism, and is reflected in both ethnic upsurge and religious fundamentalism. SIPRI has computed that: 'In 1996 there were 27 major armed conflicts in 24 locations around the world. . . . All but one of the conflicts recorded for 1996 were internal, that is, the incompatibility concerned control over the government or the territory of one state.'[4] The present condition of security studies in India can be surveyed against this backdrop.

Security Studies in India

Their genesis is traceable to the establishment of the Institute for Defence Studies and Analyses in 1965, in order to stimulate public

[3] Robert J. McMahon, *The Cold War on the Periphery: The United States, India and Pakistan* (New York: Columbia University Press, 1994).

[4] Margareta Sollenberg and Peter Wallensteen, 'Major armed conflicts', in *SIPRI Yearbook 1997: Armaments, Disarmament and International Security* (Oxford: Oxford University Press, 1997), p. 17.

debate on defence issues in India. The Ministry of Defence funds the Institute and its publications have a wide circulation in academic and military circles. Over the years the Institute's contribution to the nuclear debate has attracted much attention. But its earlier work on the basic questions underlying national security and defence administration was largely instrumental in demystifying these issues.

The Institute's journal could not be sustained; but its main vehicle, *Strategic Analysis*, however, focuses on current defence and strategic issues. Over the years its annual publication, *Asian Strategic Review*, discusses significant defence-related problems and updates statistical information of relevance to them. Occasional papers on strategic issues are also published.

The other journals devoted to security studies are the *Indian Defence Review*, which publishes articles on organisational, technical and strategic issues and the *USI (United Services Institute) Journal*, which is the oldest publication in South Asia devoted to security matters. Apart from these journals there are others of military and professional interest; prominent among them are *Defence Manager* (College of Defence Management) and *Trishul* (Staff College).

Articles on security matters do appear occasionally in journals devoted to international relations, such as *India Quarterly* (Indian Council of World Affairs), *IIC Quarterly* (India International Centre), *International Studies* (School of International Studies), *China Quarterly* (Institute of Chinese Studies) and *South Asian Studies* (Indian Council for South Asian Cooperation).

The common problem facing these journals is the familiar one of immense difficulty in procuring papers of adequate quality for publication. This reflects five unfortunate realities pertaining to strategic studies in India.

First, the paucity of quality teaching institutions. International relations and security studies are still young disciplines in India. Until recently, international relations was taught as a sub-discipline of modern history or political science. Security studies are yet to develop as a sub-discipline of international relations, while the military and defence studies departments established in several universities after the sixties are of very poor standard. Insistence on teaching in Hindi and regional languages has further detracted their quality: this is exacerbated by the lack of books and instructional materials even in translation. Together, these issues have restricted academic training in security studies only to the disarmament and area studies departments in the

School of International Studies of the Jawaharlal Nehru University in New Delhi, and a few departments of international relations in the country.

Yet another anomaly is the concentration of security-oriented academic and research institutions in New Delhi, which explains their exaggerated concern with Pakistan, less with China, and far less with the other South Asian countries. The few institutions that are outside New Delhi have yet to make their impress on the national scene, and provide a sub-regional perspective on Indian security issues.

Second, a habit of conformity afflicts academicians in the security arena. The belief is deeply embedded that such issues impinge on national interest/security; consequently, questioning the actions or decisions taken by the government-of-the-day would tantamount to being unpatriotic, even anti-national. Unquestioning support of the government's policies is hardly conducive to serious or dispassionate academic enquiry which, naturally, reflects in their quality.

The situation in the media is even more parlous. Journalists belonging to the *genre* of foreign affairs and defence correspondents are almost wholly dependent on official sources for information. They are aware that access to even this paltry information would be denied if they criticize the government's policies or actions. These habits of conformity are hardly conducive to independent thinking.

Third, the lack of serious personal reflection (with some exceptions), by those who have worked in the defence apparatus. This gains salience because of the government's reluctance to share information—except on banalities—with outsiders. First hand information about the defence decision-making processes regarding weapons selection and acquisition, defence planning and budgeting, organisational issues like reform of the Ministry of Defence/Services Headquarters/ command structures and so on is therefore sparse.

A large number of memoirs are available, incidentally, to describe the experiences of armed forces officers in the Sino-Indian and Indo-Pak wars and other military operations. But their common weakness, with some exceptions, is their self-justificatory or self-exculpatory nature and failure to illumine the larger strategic or defence issues involved.

Fourth, a hiatus prevails between scholars and practitioners in this policy-oriented discipline. The reasons are easily discernible. Scholars view practitioners' writings as being largely empirical in nature and lacking a theoretical foundation. Practitioners view scholarly writings as being 'academic', and being insufficiently rooted in ground realities.

The government, however, does make some ritual efforts to harness academia into the policy process by funding studies on specific issues by scholars. But little is known of their fate or influence on policy-making. Also, both these communities in India work in water-tight compartments during their professional lives. This is unlike the situation in the United States and some other democracies where movement does take place between government and academia.

Instances of scholars becoming practitioners for some years are rare in India and practically non-existent in the security area. So are cases of practitioners enjoying a spell in academia. Academics are invited no doubt to speak at civilian and military instructional establishments. But such contacts are limited. Fortunately, a healthy new development has occurred in recent years, in that, civilian and military officers are being encouraged to acquire higher academic qualifications.

The synergy available in bringing together scholars and practitioners could be effectively harnessed for proceeding with studies relating to the internal and non-military sources of insecurity. For their optimization they could bring together a range of practitioners—civil servants, police officials, military personnel, and academics from various disciplines—strategic studies, political science, sociology, psychology and social anthropology.

Finally, focussing on the current state of the art, apart from a plethora of studies obtained in India on nuclear and arms control issues, such as accounts of its various conflicts since independence, there is a paucity of politico-military studies on India's tension-ridden relations with its neighbours, or its interests in the Indian Ocean region.

Little attention has also been paid to theoretical concepts underlying security studies; alternative approaches to national security, especially its internal/newer/non-military dimensions; linkages between defence and development, particularly the problem of defence conversion; and reforming the structures—civil, military, and military-industrial—required to grapple with the security issues of the post-cold war era. Admittedly, these are large generalizations. Exceptions can be discovered to all these assertions. But this statement provides a backdrop to delineating the underlying conceptual issues and drawing up a future research agenda on India's security concerns.

CONCEPTUAL ISSUES

The following propositions can be discussed:

- *The inability to divorce national security from regional and global security*

An essential Indo-centricity defines South Asian security as the tension existing between India's natural weight in the regional polity and its neighbours' resistance to India's alleged 'hegemonistic' ambitions. Furthermore, insecurity in one part of the subcontinent can affect others. Examples can be multiplied. The LTTE's armed struggle against the Sri Lankan government has spilt over into Tamilnadu with horrendous results. Insurgency in India's north-eastern states has spilt over into Myanmar, Bangladesh and Bhutan. Ethnic conflicts, too, can transcend national boundaries. Hostile neighbours can use subversive means to exacerbate them and further their perceived national interests; consequently the resolution of ethno-political instabilities places a premium on regional military and economic cooperation.

Similarly, the flow of narcotics into eastern India from the Golden Triangle, and from Afghanistan via Pakistan has created serious internal security problems in north-east India and the states of Kashmir, Punjab, Maharashtra and Gujarat respectively. The reality is that drug trafficking is linked to the arms trade and international terrorism, and the anti-social (mafia) elements involved are rapidly entering the governance processes. These problems are becoming common to the region. They require regional solutions, like cooperation in intelligence sharing and undertaking joint operations against drugs/arms smuggling.

At another level, an engagement with the international community is imperative to manage the 'global commons' that comprise the common heritage of mankind. They embrace issues like global warming; loss of bio-diversity; water and air pollution and the increasing pressures on land, water, forests and marine resources.

This range of non-military threats to national security has manifested itself in river water disputes within and between states in South Asia. They could enlarge to the exploitation of the exclusive economic zones as well. A contention is observed here, between the refusal of developed countries to stop their wasteful use of natural resources and the need for the developing countries to exploit them for meeting the demands of their growing population.

Energy security through assured access to fossil fuels is becoming another area of international contention. Over 70 per cent of the world's proven oil and 40 per cent of its natural gas reserves occur in the Gulf states and around the Caspian Sea. 'One survey estimates that the demand for energy will double over the next ten years, while another forecasts the need for triplication in energy capacity over the next fifteen years. The *Economist* provides the more conservative estimate of a 9 per cent annual growth in power capacity, assuming a 6 per cent growth in GDP.'[5] The pressure on oil and gas supplies from this region therefore will rapidly increase over the years.

Some 69 per cent of India's current power generation of around 85,000 MW is derived from fossil fuels. India's dependence on foreign (largely Gulf) fossil fuel is apparent, and will increase in the future. Proposals also exist for extending pipelines to India from Oman by a sea-route via Afghanistan to Pakistan and then into India. But these proposals cannot be proceeded with unless Indo-Pak relations improve radically, which seems unlikely at the present juncture. The possibility therefore of securing oil and gas supplies from Bangladesh/South-East Asia needs more serious exploration. An element of cooperative reciprocity is clearly underlined here for seeking regional solutions to these problems of energy security.

- *Individual security cannot transcend national sovereignty*

Can the individual's right to security supersede the state's prerogative to national sovereignty in defined circumstances? All states enjoy the right to establish their own form of government and pursue their preferred social and economic policies. Outside powers have no right to interfere, although they could encourage or persuade a state to abide by generally accepted global norms. Incidentally, the United Nations' Charter guarantees 'the right to life, liberty and the security of property' [Article 3], and commits the world organisation to promote 'universal respect for, and observance of, human rights and fundamental freedoms' (Article 55). The UN members are also pledged 'to take joint and separate action' to achieve these purposes (Article 56).

Inclusion of human rights into the concept of individual and national security highlights the danger of over-extending their ambit.

[5] Geoffrey Kemp and Robert E. Harkavy, *Strategic Geography and the Changing Middle East* (Washington Brookings Institution Press, 1997) p. 377.

The nexus between human rights issues and the larger questions of war and peace, and/or the threat to national security must be firmly established in the first place. Thus, including individual security within this framework 'should be tempered therefore with pragmatic understanding of what can be remedied by the state and what must remain in the domain of society'.[6] These are questions and dilemmas of growing future relevance to South Asia.

The problem then arises: Should a state be neutral if a neighbouring state grossly offends global norms? More graphically, if a state proceeds with a policy of 'ethnic cleansing' should the world community intervene? Or observe an attitude of benign indifference and non-interference? Should states intervene only if their own security is affected? No obvious answers are available here; consequently this conundrum enters the area of speculation on just and unjust wars.[7] It also enters the debate on state 'responsibility', 'legitimacy' and the need to codify international norms on 'humanitarian interventionism' and international criminal justice, to deal specifically with the difficult area of 'war crimes'.

- *Permanent versus evolutionary threats to national Security*

Both facets of this argument can be argued. The need to bring order into an 'anarchic' international system emphasizes the need for hierarchy, polarity and the inviolability of nation states. In this 'realist' paradigm the state must optimize its military power for assuring itself maximum security from external threats. Its adversaries are expected to act likewise: Thus the dead weight of history dominates this paradigm. But this static form militates against the verity that social and political processes are continuously fermenting in the polity. The concept of national security should evolve similarly.

Apropos, a bipolar world order distinguished the cold war era. But a multipolar balance of power is a more 'natural' structure of the international system, which existed before the Second World War. The strengthening of polycentrism after the cold war's demise reflects a return to this more complex reality.

In the case of India, the decade of conflicts—1962-71—highlighted

[6] P.R. Chari, 'Newer Sources of Insecurity: The Crisis of Governance in India', *RCSS Policy Studies 3* (Colombo: Regional Centre for Strategic Studies, January 1988), p. 2.

[7] Michael Walzer, *Just and Unjust Wars* (New York: Basic Books, 1977).

the external threat from China and Pakistan and its collusive nature. The eighties stressed the internal threats to India's security arising from militancy in Punjab and Kashmir, apart from the north-east. They had their origins in domestic politics and in difficult identity crises, but were indubitably exacerbated by Pakistan, which perceived them as targets of opportunity. After the recent tests, the nuclear dimension of Indo-Pak and Sino-Indian security relations has reached centre stage. The conclusion is possible that conceptualizing India's national security is a dynamic enterprise and needs constant review.

- *Traditional versus comprehensive/collective approaches to national security*

Security studies can be delimited to questions relating directly to war and peace. The social and political factors underlying them can also be comprehensively studied. The narrow view is founded on beliefs that national security is concerned with military threats and the use of military force to counter them. Analyses of threats, responses thereto, and their effect on the national, regional and international system thus become matters of relevance. The study of inter-state conflicts and tension-prone regions assumed great significance in this milieu due to the danger of a catalytic nuclear war being ignited between the superpowers.

The conflictual situation existing between India and Pakistan, besides the tensions and instabilities arising from a plethora of internal conflicts in India, became priority areas for investigation within this paradigm of national security. To justify its five nuclear tests, for instance, the Indian government drew attention to the 'deteriorating nuclear environment in India's neighbourhood'. Hence, these tests were needed to 'provide reassurance to the people of India that their national security interests are paramount and will be promoted and protected'.[8] The nuclear threat from China and Pakistan was thereby posited.

But this traditional concept does not address the complexity of national and regional security issues. This is true at one level. But 'the current threats to national security in India largely arise from non-military causes like cross-border movements of population; ethno-

[8] Prepared statement by Principal Secretary to Prime Minister reproduced in *The Hindu*, 12 May 1998, and all major Indian newspapers of even date.

political, socio-economic, and communal-religious politics; terrorism, with its seminal linkages to money-laundering operations, and drugs/arms smuggling; environmental degradation, spawning its related problems of deforestation and desertification; internal migration; chaotic urbanization; and so on'.[9] These security threats lie in the internal polity but have a close bearing on regional/global security. And the military instrumentality is of limited value to meet these threats though recourse to it may become unavoidable to curb any ensuing violence.

Further, the narrow view of security does not reflect the realities underlying national and regional security within the international system. Issues like the struggle for resources embedded in the pursuit of energy security, food security and, more lately, environmental security. Apart from that, the security implications of regional global problems associated with overpopulation, such as, environmental degradation and resource depletion; forced migrations; international terrorism; ascendancy of non-state actors in drugs, arms, money-laundering and financial crime organisations; and the growing linkages between governance and international security, reflect the more complex verities of international security.

The concept of comprehensive security further highlights the need for a cooperative approach being adopted to assure national security. Apropos, the cold war superpower relationship included elements of both cooperation and competition within the central strategic balance created between them; they had to 'manage' a relationship, which neither could dominate nor avoid. This logic can be extended to the nuclearized Indo-Pak relationship and to Sino-Indian relations. Moreover, with the ascendancy of economics in the international system, the need for regional cooperation is emphasized. Bilateral/regional security issues, like cross-border migration due to natural disasters or population movements in search of a better quality of life, can also be resolved by cooperation between the originating and destination countries.

Cooperative security's basic premise is that conjoint efforts by nations can ensure national security more effectively than conflict. According to this view, military strength and 'the correlation of force' between nations lose their primacy. Instead, the focus shifts to regional and sub-regional cooperation, confidence-building measures,

[9] Op. cit., n. 7, p. 2.

and Track II diplomacy. The concept of cooperative security does not preclude efforts to ensure national defence. Nor can it mitigate the competition for power and influence in the world. But it discourages intervention in the internal affairs of neighbouring countries: This is of especial relevance to ensuring national security in South Asia.

The conclusions reached by two important reports are relevant here.

> An important task of constructive international policy will have to consist in providing a new, more comprehensive understanding of 'security' which would be less restricted to the purely military aspects. In the global context, true security cannot be achieved by a mounting build-up of weapons—defence in the narrow sense—but only by providing basic conditions for peaceful relations between nations, and solving not only the military but also the non-military problems which threaten them.[10]

> A more effective way to ensure security is to create positive processes that can lead to peace and disarmament. It is essential to create an irreversible process with such a momentum, that all nations cooperate for their common survival. Acceptance of common security as the organising principle for efforts to reduce the risk of war, limit arms, and move towards disarmament means, in principle, that cooperation will replace confrontation in resolving conflicts of interests.[11]

The caveat can be entered now that over-stretching the concept of national security would eviscerate that term of all meaning. As perceptively noticed: 'Once anything that generates anxiety or threatens the quality of life in some respect becomes labelled a "security problem", the field risks losing all focus. Such an agenda is conceivably rich, and is certainly inclusive, but it can also be off-puttingly vague'.[12] Besides, inclusion of all manner of problems into security concepts would become wholly unmanageable unless a plausible link is established with national security as, for example, strife over access to water and natural resources.

[10] *North-South: A programme for survival, Report of the Independent Commission on International Development Issues* (London: Pan Books, 1980), p. 124, also called the Willy Brandt report.

[11] *Common Security: A programme for disarmament, The Report of the Independent Commission on Disarmament and Security Issues* (London: Pan Books, 1982), pp. 7-8, named the Olaf Palme report.

[12] Lawrence Freedman, 'International Security: Changing Targets', *Foreign Policy* (Spring 1998), p. 53.

An Agenda for Research

The following subjects are suggested seriatim, but in no particular order, for inclusion in a research agenda for security studies in India: This could also be extended to South Asia.

- The belief is common in India that theory is irrelevant in dealing with practical matters like security. Further, as astutely observed: 'Theory is represented as a product the West can afford, but which India, thrown as it was into an unforgiving and hostile post-colonial world, cannot. Represented in this way, theory appears as an evasion of social responsibility and to that extent as anti-national'.[13] No discipline can effloresce however without being premised on a body of theoretical knowledge.

Thus, the application of concepts like comprehensive security, co-operative security, common security, newer and/or non-military sources of insecurity to the Indian situation would be profitable. Clearly, a large number of sub-disciplines and case studies are involved here. This must include threats to the nation state from resurgent sub-nationalism. How these sources of insecurity in India might influence South Asia, and how such insecurities within the region might impinge on India also require investigation.

Further, comprehensive security, for instance, requires issues like environmental security, resource depletion, the linkage between social and climate change, urbanization, and problems of governance being investigated at micro and macro levels. The issue of environmental security, for instance, could be studied in relation to the construction of large dams, or by focussing on particular dams, and the consequential ecological and human rights problems they generate.

Discerning the linkages between the problems of governance and internal security is of especial importance in India. The criminalization of politics has transformed now into the politicisation of crime in many parts of the country and requires greater scholarly attention. But the caveat must be reiterated that the relevance of these studies to national security must initially be firmly established.

Similarly, studies on cooperative security could focus on its national, regional and global dimensions. This could include the traffic in small

[13] Kanti Bajpai, 'International Studies in India: Bringing Theory Back Home', in M.S. Rajan (ed.), *International and Area Studies in India* (New Delhi: Lancers Publishers, 1997), pp. 41-2.

arms and explosives and/or drugs, money laundering and so on, that could be countered by cooperation between nations. Further, the problem of migration into India from Sri Lanka and Bangladesh, either forced or voluntary and how it could be mitigated is another cooperative security issue needing urgent scholastic attention. These studies could be extended to the cooperative measures envisaged by SAARC that have a nexus with security, and further extended to sub-regional cooperation.

At the same time, the interactions existing between global, regional and national security threats require more adequate research, e.g. the linkages between small arms and drugs trafficking from Afghanistan into Pakistan and thereafter into India; or from the Golden Triangle into north-east India via Myanmar. How are these nefarious activities financed? How does this traffic affect the governance processes in border states? And, how does it affect sub-regional security? A multi-thematic approach would need to be pursued to derive a holistic policy to deal with these threats.

It could also be more rigorously investigated whether the pursuit of national security in India has any ideological basis. Indian scholars have explained Pakistan's anti-Indian obsession as reflecting its seminal need to assert an Islamic identity. Can this logic be extended to a concept of Indian security premised on the growing influence of Hindu nationalism in India? Does its anti-Pakistan fixation reflect a need to assert its Hindu identity? Besides, the ideological basis to India's interests like seeking a non-discriminatory world order, general and complete disarmament, and economic justice had been founded on Nehruvian idealism. Has this ideology been appropriated by the BJP-led coalition to justify its realpolitik approaches?

• The history of pre- and post-independent India reveals several instances of its military intervention in other countries. The British Indian armed forces were extensively employed in different parts of the world; indeed, they were expressly designed to pursue Britain's imperial interests abroad.

After independence India has provided its armed forces for numerous UN peacekeeping operations. Documenting their experience opens up a rich field for more detailed research. The political and military lessons available therefrom would be of general applicability to future peacekeeping operations.

Equally, India intervened for humanitarian and realpolitik reasons in East Pakistan (1971), Sri Lanka (1987) and the Maldives (1988).

Several Indian, Pakistani, Bangladeshi and Sri Lankan scholars have addressed these episodes from different national perspectives. But, it has been perceptively noted that 'clear examples of what is called "humanitarian intervention" are very rare. Indeed, I have not found any, but only mixed cases, where the humanitarian motive is one among several'.[14] Whether Indian interventionism was 'humanitarian' or guided by realpolitik or other reasons can be researched.

Two sub-themes concerning these interventions bear investigation. Firstly, they have often recoiled on the intervener. Apropos, India's training and equipping of the Mukti Bahini had exacerbated the insurgencies in north-east India and the law and order situation in West Bengal and Bihar. And India's training and assistance to the LTTE facilitated the latter's violent *entree* into Tamilnadu politics.

Is this situation particular to South Asia, or has it been replicated in other regions? Secondly, it could be reasoned that the intrusion of an external intervener would unite the fractious groups opposing central authority in any country. In practice, the opposite has occurred and militant groups have fought and destroyed each other. Why has this occurred? Both these issues in the empirical experience merit greater academic attention.

● Literature recognizes South Asia, along with the Middle East, north-east Asia and, now, Central Asia to be tension-prone regions in the world and a menace to international peace and stability. In this perspective, the recurrent crises in South Asia, that prominently feature India, need to be more adequately researched.

Thus Indo-Pak relations have been crisis-prone despite an absence of conflict since 1971. Atypically, there were two crises in 1984 arising from India's occupation of the Siachen glacier, and Pak allegations that an Indian attack upon Kahuta was imminent. The latter crisis resurfaced in 1985 and 1986. A serious military crisis occurred in 1986-7 ensuing from the Brass tacks exercise. This recurred in 1990 following a precipitated deterioration in the internal security situation in Kashmir.

Further, the Indo-Pak crisis was associated with the Bombay bomb blasts (1993), forcible occupation of the Hazratbal mosque by militants (1993 and 1996), and destruction of the Charar-e-Sharif shrine (1995). The crisis-prone relationship between India and Pakistan has become more hazardous now after their recent nuclear tests. Similarly,

[14] Op. cit., n. 7, p. 101.

there were tensions in the eighties between India and Nepal on the Trade and Transit Treaties; with Bangladesh on the Chakma refugees' issue; and Sri Lanka concerning the rights of its Tamil population. These crises require more detailed study in the light of the crisis literature available.

Besides, the several internal crises relating to sectarian strife in India could also be researched. The caste-based conflict in northern India, leading to recruitment and maintenance of private armies, is a phenomenon that needs particular attention from a sociological perspective. The implications for communal violence from resurgent Hindu fundamentalist parties coming to power at the Centre and in several states also require closer attention.

A subject of perennial scholarly interest is the violent ethno-political movements in north-east India and Kashmir (continuing) and the communal-religious conflicts in Punjab (since quietened). These conflicts are embedded in difficult crises of identity that can change over time and get either de-constructed or re-constructed. For this reason, a multi-disciplinary approach needs to be followed to comprehend these conflicts, and this approach would enhance their value.

It is common for South Asian governments, including India, to divert public attention from their domestic inadequacies by declaring that external forces have exacerbated ethno-political or communal-religious violence. This is the ubiquitous doctrine of the 'foreign hand'. The truth in such matters is worth pursuit to discover how far external and how far internal factors are responsible for these situations. Is a role possible for external powers to resolve them? How should it be exercised? This is an area of research that has not been investigated but could be profitably guided by the experience of other conflict-ridden regions.

• Finally, the military aspects of India's security—conventional and nuclear—must be included within a future research agenda for security studies. The nuclear tests conducted recently by India and Pakistan have moved both countries further up the nuclear ladder. There are several areas in consequence that are worth exploring.

The armed forces maintained by India are among the largest in the world. This is true for the three services. The manner in which their future growth might occur now requires attention in the light of recent advances in military technology presaging a 'revolution in military affairs'. How will this influence force structuring decisions by India and its likely adversaries? Simultaneously, the opportunities available for reducing the strength of the armed forces after India's declaration that it is a nuclear weapon power is worth consideration. This has obvious implications for controlling the defence budget.

Reform in the decision-making apparatus pertaining to defence, especially in the weapons acquisition process are two issues pertaining to the higher direction of defence that could be considered afresh. Besides, the need for establishing credible and adequate command and control arrangements is imperative, particularly in the light of India's nuclear weaponization. What also needs greater investigation is the changes resultantly required in the pattern of civil-military relations. These arrangements have remained unaltered for the last 50 years.

Coming thereafter to military sociology, the changes in the social base for recruitment of officers and men over the years bear scrutiny. What has been their role in society as modernizing or integrative factors? What has been their influence in domestic politics, especially in areas where ex-servicemen numbers are sizeable, like the Punjab-Haryana-Himachal Pradesh area, or the Garhwal/Kumaon hills?

The Confidence Building Measures (CBMs) that India has established with its neighbours is another area of perennial interest. Current studies suffer from two major lacunae. First, studies in this area have been obsessively concerned with the Indo-Pak confrontation and have focussed therefore on military CBMs. These studies should be extended to India's other South Asian neighbours, and also to China. Second, more attention could be devoted to non-military CBMs. For instance, extension of the Indus Waters Treaty—one of the few successful non-military CBMs in the Indo-Pak case—which had partitioned the waters of the Indus river basin into a spatial development plan for the better exploitation, could receive attention.

This brings one to the nuclear dimension, which has reached centre stage after the recent nuclear tests. Why had India observed restraint for so long, and why did it finally give it up could be investigated. How far did the earlier state of non-weaponized deterrence keep the peace in South Asia, and will its current nuclear situation stabilize or destabilize Indo-Pak and Sino-Indian relations? The implications of India's nascent weaponization and whether the firebreak between weaponization and deployment can be maintained is a subject of obvious research significance. It has been urged that a minimum deterrent posture would be viable and credible for India vis-à-vis China and/or Pakistan.

The nuclear doctrine that would underpin this posture and the command and control arrangements needed require close attention, especially to evaluate whether the warheads could be stored separately to prevent an accidental nuclear exchange. These and other issues in contention could be identified for exploration in bilateral or trilateral Track-II dialogues with the United States, China and Pakistan.

Lastly, there are specific issues that could be researched like the conditions under which India could enter the CTBT; its policy approaches towards the FMCT; the legal framework to clothe India's demonstrated restraint in transferring nuclear and missile technology; the technical parameters of a firebreak separating weaponization and deployment of missiles; the verification measures needed to strengthen the Biological Weapons Convention; and how India might negotiate with the nuclear weapon powers to achieve the elimination of nuclear weapons.

It bears recognition that epochal events like the end of the cold war, disintegration of the Soviet Union, and China's shifts of its core relationship from the Soviet Union to the United States and then to a position of equi-distance between them, have seminally perturbed the international system. But, they were not clearly foreseen by either the practitioners or scholars of international security before they occurred. Conceptual issues also gain recognition or currency in harmony with the obtaining international situation. In the light of these varied issues, any research agenda cannot obviously remain static, but must recognise newer security concerns as they arise from time to time.

Security Studies in India: Continuity and Change in the Post-Cold War Era

W. LAWRENCE S. PRABHAKAR

The end of the cold war and the emergent period constitutes a transition in the global security structure. In one sense it constituted the victory of Western liberal democracy over totalitarian communism with its accompanied effects like the triumph of individual rights, civil society, the market and so on.

Yet, in another sense, it had exposed the fragile foundations of the state structure in the Third World, that had hitherto been 'frozen' as a unified structure due to the greater persistence of external threats to it, in some cases held intact due to the competing largesse of the super powers.

The dominance of the realist paradigm (with its extended corollary neo-realism) in the academic theory of international relations, has been largely due to the Western (mainly the United States) predominance of the scholarship of the discipline. State making in the Western experience has been a unique evolutionary phenomenon, as contrasted to the spasmodic developments in the Third World.

Neo-realism posits for a state-centric analysis of security. Essentially, the focus was on (a) units of analysis—the sovereign state, (b) the state behaviour—assumed as rational, and (c) the nature of the inter-national system as anarchic.[1] Neo-realism in its Western ethno-

[1] Abraham Itty, 'Towards a Reflexive Security Studies in South Asia', in Marvin G. Weinbaum and Chetan Kumar (eds), *South Asia approaches the Millennium: Re-examining National Security* (Boulder, Colo: Westview, 1994), p. 19. Also the related literature in Barry Buzan, *People, States and Fear* (Boulder, Colo: Lynne Rienner, 1991); Mohammed Ayoob, *The Third World Security Predicament: State Making, Regional Conflict and the International System* (Boulder, Colo: Lynne Rienner, 1995); Edward Kolodziej, 'What is Security and Security Studies. Lessons

centric focus assumed that the state in its domestic order was politically stable, liberal and democratic in its governance, socially cohesive, and economically progressive and growth oriented and therefore, it was a stable and relatively homogenous entity in its internal order. Its threats and challenges were external, impinging on its territorial integrity and sovereignty.

It had envisaged a national security complex that would factor and account all threats and challenges diagnostically and in a prognostic perspective. The national security complex, thus required a predictive ability and a policy oriented enterprise, that constituted the multiple inputs of economy, technology, policy and strategy into a framework, namely, strategic studies.[2]

Strategic studies in its essence was national in character and was tailor-made for the state-centric and inter-state issues of security. The end of the cold war in its unpredictable manner belittled the prognostic value of strategic studies and instead, opened up a new agenda that would comprehensively account for both military and non-military factors in the security of the state.[3]

The post-cold war era has now witnessed a shift from strategic (national) to security studies, having both transnational and international ramifications.[4] This shift has now reversed the priorities of security studies, away from the earlier central strategic questions to the emergent security predicament of the Third World.[5]

The regional character of global security has opened up a new agenda of substantive security issues, based on each regions unique features, to be debated in the post-cold war era. The post-cold war security of Third World states is in the context of the foundations of their statehood.

---

from the Cold War', *Arms Control*, Vol. 13, No. 1 (April 1992); Stephen M. Walt, 'The Renaissance of Security Studies, *International Studies' Quarterly* (1991) pp. 211-59.

[2] Lawrence Freedman, 'International Security: Changing Targets', *Foreign Policy* (Spring 1998), p. 51.

[3] Edward Kolodziej, 'Whither Security Studies After the Cold War', in Stephen Cohen and Kanti Bajpai, *South Asia after the Cold War—International Perspectives* (Boulder, Colo: Westview, 1993), p. 19.

[4] Freedman, op. cit., p. 52.

[5] Mohammed Ayoob, *The Third World Security Predicament: State Making, Regional Conflict and the International System* (Boulder, Colo: Lynne Rienner, 1995), Chap. I, Concepts and Definitions.

The Third World is in a constant struggle in the process of transforming their juridical statehood to effective statehood, accelerating social and economic development industrialization; endeavouring to achieve, the compatible levels of growth, in health, education, sanitation standards and attempting to meet the rising political, civic, economic, and social expectations of the populace.

The Third World, in its different geographical locales and specific historical circumstances, has been confronting internal security challenges emanating from ethnic conflict, sectarian crises, racial tensions, imbalances of socio-economic development, rising population, and the increasing degradation of the environment. Besides, it has to contend with inter-state disputes that has resulted in frequent wars, etc.

The cumulative effect of such pressures and challenges led Third World regimes to seek refuge in building huge military establishments and hardware at the expense of the populace, with the apparent purpose of 'state security', but actually achieved regime security. The cold war and its corollary of regional military alliances had paved the way for massive infuse of military and civilian aid, that actually built the state security apparatus in the Third World without concomitant human development.

The Indian security predicament is the reflection of Third World realities aggravated by the post-colonial aberrations of internal challenges to its integrity and external threats to its sovereign boundaries.

This article endeavours in its attempt to (a) understand the framework of Indian security perspectives that anchor the thought and policy process of security, (b) analyse the substantive issues that constitute the menu of security studies, in terms of its elements of continuity and change, and (c) identify the role and significance of policy and academic research, and study of security studies in India, with a view to chart the emerging agendas and issues in research.

The Framework of Indian Security Perspectives

Indian security perspectives are rooted in a specific time-spatial context of South Asian history and geographical realities. The dominant Indian perspective has been that the South Asian system is Indo-centric, reflected by its antique civilizational complex, the geographical domain of India in South Asia with its contiguity with all

South Asian states, bestriding the Indian Ocean to the south, China to the east, Central Asia to the north, and West Asia to its west. This has endowed for itself a hegemonic role in the region and it beckons commensurate credence to its big power position in the region. Colonization and its aftermath are specific historical aberrations to its civilizational past.

The second important Indian perspective is its assumed internal integrity and consolidation, justifying its eminence of greatness through the centuries. The Indian social and cultural system though diverse, had always been one of unity in a pluralistic environment. Despite its pacifist, non-aggressive character, India had been the foci of many an aggression, conquest, domination and colonialism. Its uniqueness rested in the fact that its assimalationist character absorbed the diverse contours or other cultures into its own synthesis without breaking down.[6]

Indian statehood in its sovereign political existence since 1947, had perceived a sense of siege and attempts of aggression and violation of its territorial integrity and sovereignty. Its perceived vulnerability of territory since 1948 had gone along with the internal secessions and subnational challenges articulated on ethnic, lingual, communal and regional lines, both peaceful and violent from time to time. The crisis in Punjab, Kashmir, the north-east and in Tamil Nadu for sometime reflected the pressures on the Indian body politic.

The third significant perspective is that of an Islamic-Chinese-Western siege against India, which is regarded as neo-colonial and imperialist.[7] The combination of the perceived external siege and its internal vulnerabilities has been an important Indian security predicament. India's wars with Pakistan in 1948, 1965 and 1971, and with China in 1962 and the near war conditions in 1955, 1987 and 1990 are defined as challenges to its external sovereignty and security.

This argument is buttressed by the fact that India's internal problems of insurgency in the north-east in the 1960s, the militant terrorism in Punjab and the current situation in Kashmir are all inspired and abetted by India's hostile neighbours attempting to weaken its internal fabric prior to the next round of conventional war.

[6] Jawaharlal Nehru, *The Discovery of India* (New Delhi: Oxford University Press, 1982), p. 88.

[7] Stephen P. Cohen, 'The Structural Dimensions of Conflict in South Asia', *RCSS Policy Papers #2* (Colombo: Regional Centre for Strategic Studies, 1997), p. 3.

The framework of Indian security perceptions has three stages.

- The cold war years saw India's policy of non-alignment as the macro strategy of security pursued, maintaining an equidistant position from the superpowers with concrete gains in economic and military assistance from both the former Soviet Union and the United States. It ensured India's credible conventional strength and therefore regional military superiority in conventional terms against Pakistan, and an effective conventional deterrent against China in the light of its disastrous experience in 1962. The 1980s saw the growth of Indian military power from a minimalist perspective to maximalist strategic response.

  The earlier minimalist response to the traditional threat perspective was the ability to fight a 'one and half wars'. Indian military capability equipped it to fight a full-scale war with Pakistan and a border holding operation against China, till a superpower diplomatic or military intervention ensued.

  The maximalist strategic response was an extended power posture for a three full and three half wars, which included a full-scale conventional war against Pakistan, latent nuclear weapons and IRBM capabilities, land based war with China, naval power in Indian ocean, proximate island intervention and defence of maritime zone. These strategic responses were projected for acquisition from 1989-2000.[8]

  This strategic projection based on a hypothetical power posture was formulated taking into account the emergent missile threats from Pakistan, Iran, Saudi Arabia and possible threats from the Central Asian republics. These hypothetical postures however, did not materialize since the end of 1980s, due to the economic difficulties and the subsequent restructuring of the Indian economy.

- The second phase commences with the collapse of Soviet power in 1991 and India's loss of a credible strategic partner. Indian security environment drifted from its early determinism of the 1980s, to being wavering in the 1990s. This phase saw the increase in the proliferation of low intensity conflicts in Punjab and Kashmir and the

[8] Raju G.C. Thomas, 'The Growth of Indian Military Power: From Sufficient Defence to Extended Deterrence', in Sandy Gordon and Ross Babbage, *India's Strategic Future: Regional State or Global Power* (New Delhi: Oxford University Press, 1992), pp. 42-4.

compounding effect of which was felt in the 1987 Sri Lankan peace keeping mission fiasco. The changes in Indian leadership, political instability and resultant economic crisis, the gulf war and its shocks to the Third World, especially India in the aftermath of Iraq's defeat, led to serious re-think in the prevalent strategic and security perspectives of the nation.[9]

The economic reforms and the consequent liberalization process had a favourable impact on India, with sustained rate of growth albeit, for a short period. This phase also witnessed sincere attempts by India for conflict resolution with Pakistan through Prime Ministerial level talks; exchange of heads of state/government visits to China and the progress by the joint working groups of China and India.

But the gravity and plurality of threat perceptions proliferated due to the accelerated missile threats in India's neighbourhood; namely, Pakistan, Iran, and Saudi Arabia, and Pakistan's articulation of acquiring 'strategic depth' with the Islamic Central Asian states.

Similarly the Chinese expansion of its strategic reach into neighbouring Myanmar, viewed in the aftermath of the Chinese crackdown of the Tibetan nationalists and militants between 1987-9 indicated a renewed Chinese offensive in the region.[10]

- The third phase can be identified with the 'Mutual Nuclear Brinkmanship' (MNB) act of India and Pakistan, in the conduct of their respective nuclear tests in May 1998. This phase is characterized as the Indian deterministic response to the gravity of threats emerging overtly out of the Sino-Pakistan nuclear and missile collaboration efforts.

This phase commenced with the promise of the Bharatiya Janata Party (BJP) to conduct a strategic defence review, constitute the National Security Council of India along with corresponding changes in the higher defence organization and most significantly the induction of nuclear weapons.

The BJP's decision to go nuclear in an overt fashion, reflects the signal changes that were occurring in the subcontinent, which ranged from the escalation of insurgency in Kashmir, the test firing of the

[9] Ravi Rikhye and Pushpainder Singh, 'External Threats and India's Conventional Capabilities: Perspectives till 2010', in Bharat Karnad, *Future Imperilled: India's Security in the 1990s and Beyond* (New Delhi: Viking, 1994).

[10] Raju G.C. Thomas, 'The Melancholy Chapter of Tibet', *Christian Science Monitor* (22 October 1987).

Ghauri missile by Pakistan to the overt expansion of Chinese military presence in Myanmar, the construction of naval facilities in the Coco Islands by the Chinese and their reach to the Andaman Islands. These were the emerging threat perceptions India had to contend with. The above perceptions and the BJP's strategic defence review, led to the decision to go nuclear and weaponize its nuclear capabilities.

SUBSTANTIVE ISSUES IN INDIAN SECURITY STUDIES

In the light of the derivation of Indian security perspectives, it would be proper to analyse the substantive issues in Indian security studies.

India's strategic culture has always been an issue of regular debate both within the country and among the security studies scholars abroad, who have specialized on India. It has been repeatedly pointed out that the inadequacies in Indian security policy and its responses are reflected in the lacunae of a credible and categorical strategic culture.

India's strategic planning has always been absorptive, defensive and inward looking. It has lacked a focussed, directed and offensive approach,[11] which has had a direct impact on the nature and dynamics of its security policy formation. The defensive nature in strategic culture goes with the characterization of India as a 'weak-strong' state.[12] The weak-strong hypothesis is one of the paradigms of Indian security perspectives that articulate the mutual nature of internal and external vulnerabilities.

This strategic approach had repeatedly exhibited the tendency to favour synthesis amid decisive actions, a process of compromise, reconciliation of opposing views and doctrines, and accommodation of diverse interests.[13] Hence, the strands of synthesis, compromise, and reconciliation had always produced a defensive, inward looking culture. Indian strategic culture thus allowed for the deft employment of moral and ethical norms to reinforce its policy stand, often justifying its weaknesses as well as its exploits.

[11] George K. Tanham, *Indian Strategic Thought: An Interpretative Essay* (Santa Monica: Rand, 1992).

[12] Lloyd and Suzanne Rudolph, *In Pursuit of Lakshmi: The Political Economy of the Indian State* (Chicago: Chicago University Press, 1987), alternatively quoted in Sandy Gordon, *Domestic Foundations of India's Security Policy*, in Sandy Gordon et al., *India's Strategic Future* (Delhi: Oxford University Press, 1992), p. 11.

[13] Maroof Raza, *Low Intensity Conflicts: The New Dimensions to India's Military Commitments* (Meerut: Karthikeya Publishers, 1995), pp. 54-8.

Secondly, these lacunae have impacted on the arrangement and structure of the higher defence organization. What had been hitherto lacking was an integrated policy and planning organization, that would holistically consider the varied inputs into the security policy process. The Parliament mandated the creation of the National Security Council in 1990 as an integrated effort to analyse and factor security threats and challenges.

This systemic inadequacy prevalent till date, is due to the resistance of the political and bureaucratic elite to changes; the turf protection by the bureaucracy of its interests; unfamiliarity of functioning in an integrated decision making system and familiarity of the political and bureaucratic elite to ad hoc decisions.

Strategic and organizational culture are vital ingredients to a viable and vibrant security policy process of India. India's security policy had always been subject to political direction in the name of civilian control over the military. This trend has been inimical to the security interests of the nation. The sidelining and the lack of a meaningful involvement of the military in the inputs of the security policy process, has pushed the Indian security into pitfalls of confusion and the lack of clarity in responses.

Similarly, the Indian security policy is also devoid of an intellectual-academic pluralist contribution, that is essential to provide the due variety of inputs and balance into an integrated security policy process. It is hoped that the National Security Council when constituted would fill the void.[14] This Council would perhaps be the most appropriate forum, given its statutory status and the flexibility of constitution, to consider an integrated effort in conducting studies on Indian security, taking into consideration the multiple inputs of both military and non-military aspects of security. The various security regimes are elaborated further thematically, providing an agenda for study and analyses.

Military-Strategic

The primary security regime for consideration is the military-strategic perspective. The predominance of the military related security chal-

[14] Kapil Kak, 'Management of India's Security and Higher Defence—I', *Strategic Analysis* (New Delhi, June 1998), p. 335

lenges persists and would continue, pending a comprehensive resolution of all outstanding disputes and challenges.

Apart from the traditional concerns of arms build-up, arms race, and arms trade, etc., the emergent post-nuclear tests period would focus on the nuclear theology in South Asia; the implications of nuclear weaponization; the size, scope and mission objectives of the nuclear deterrent force, employment doctrine declaratory postures; the integration of the command, control, communication, computation information and intelligence (C4I2) assets; potential for early warning systems, etc. Besides, the economics of investing in a nuclear arsenal, their maintenance and the essential safeguards are all issues that deserve priority of study, analyses and debate.

The implications of the international non-proliferation security regimes, viz., the NPT, CTBT and the FMCT would be factored into the security studies agenda. The post-nuclearization phase would also focus on the reorganization of the Indian armed forces, in terms of pruning manpower in relation to costs and the adaptation of mechanization to the existing formations, is yet another element of debate.

At the next level the military responses to trans-national threats of narcotics, small arms proliferation, narco-terrorism and possible forms of nuclear-terrorism, are the new emerging challenges that warrant for fresh innovative approaches of resolution. The predominant challenge that the Indian armed forces would be contending in the next two decades would be the phenomenal wide-spectral challenges that would range from the contingencies of high intensity conflict (nuclear-chemical-biological) to the medium (regular conventional war) and the endemic low intensity conflicts.

In the backdrop of these expanding challenges and proliferating threats, the Indian armed forces are struggling with their serious shortfall in manpower and the poor recruitment results that show an alarming slide. New assignments in the emergent order would mean additional formations and appropriate training and specific mission oriented deployments. The tasking of the army divisions to constant internal 'aid-to-civil' duties, has had its fatigue on the preparedness of these formations. The reconstitution of some infantry divisions into a task force for specialized operations of combating low intensity conflicts is an urgent imperative.[15] The military-strategic security regime has opened up new vistas for study and debate.

[15] Raza, op. cit., pp. 75-7.

- *The nuclearization process*

This has several serious implications on the armed forces, that includes the war-fighting strategy in nuclear-biological-chemical environments, to the question of development and deployment of battlefield nuclear weapons or tactical nuclear weapons of sub-kiloton range, besides, the counter-strike and counter-value options against potential nuclear threats. Thus, both strategic and tactical, issues concerning civil defence measures have enormous significance.

The expanding scope of internal security threats that has gained the form as low intensity conflicts, opens up the flank for an irregular conflict interspersed with a conventional round of fighting. If the Pakistani articulation of the Islamic Central Asian 'Strategic Depth' materializes, then India would have to contend a steep escalation of low intensity hostilities in the Kashmir valley, with the possible induction of some 50,000 Afghan mujahideen irregulars in their cause of 'Jihad' in Kashmir. This could be followed with a major assault by the combined forces of Pakistan and an Islamic multinational force. This is a possible reality in the light of 'internationalization' of the Kashmir issue.[16]

The issue of increased defence spending in the context of nuclear weaponization, with the raising of new formations in the Army, stalled earlier due to resource constraints, has now become vital in the changed circumstances; continued modernization plans; the cumulative effect of the sanctions on the economy and its pressure on the defence sector are vital issues of the future debate.

- *Political threats to security*

The emergence of political threats to security have resulted from the problems of governance and the complications in the state-making process.[17] These threats to security are: (i) secessionist movements bordering on militancy (ii) ethnicity and related conflicts (iii) social and sectarian conflicts.

All the above typologies have gained momentum in the faltering process of governance that has now decayed, due to high levels of

[16] Rikhye, op. cit., p. 113.

[17] P.R. Chari, 'Newer Sources of Insecurity: The Crisis of Governance in India', *RCSS Policy Papers #3* (Colombo: Regional Centre for Strategic Studies, 1998), pp. 5-7.

corruption, blatant violation of the constitutional norms and safeguards, criminalization of politics, and the nexus between the political elite and drug traffickers, arms smugglers and other criminal elements.

The extent of the threat is evidenced by the fact that the police forces of the Indian states lack the resolve and the means to tackle this criminal epidemic.

- *Secessionist movements and its impact on the Indian polity*

These have been well documented as studies in their political, constitutional, economic aspects and studies on Indian federalism. The character and the scope of secessionist demands are gaining a separatist tendency bordering on political violence, while the Indian approach has primarily been integrationist and accommodationist. The external support to such movements through small arms smuggling (like the mysterious Purelia arms drop), nexus between the Naxalite groups and the international terrorist and militant movements, and in some cases their covert involvement in the subterranean narcotics networks, have alarming implications and are grave security threats.

- *Ethnicity and related conflicts*

This is yet another dimension that reflects the failure of the Indian state to pacify the political and economic demands of the contending groups. The Jharkhand, Uttarakhand and the Bodoland agitations reflect the ethnic and sub-ethnic demands on the state. The geo-strategic location of these areas near the Indian borders and their possible contagion with external powers, has now raised new problems. India's experience in tackling these problems using the force has been in vain, though the offer of economic inducements has ameliorated the situation. In cumulative assessment, India's ethnic problems reveal the crisis of governance.[18]

A related internal security vulnerability to the issue of sub-nationalism is the linking of human rights to the secessionist demands of the group. In the cases of both the Sikh and Kashmiri secessionist agenda, the highlighting of the human rights as part of their demands which attracted considerable international attention, and provided them with a high profile visage in the Western political and media circles,

[18] Ibid., pp. 6-7.

thus distorting ground realities. Such an exercise has raised grave security concerns that challenge the sovereignty and legitimacy of the Indian Union.

- *Social and sectarian movements*

These movements have accentuated in recent times as serious challenges to effective governance. The politics of caste and religion has heightened the level of civic strife wrecking the fragile body politic. Fundamentalism has now adopted the extremes of the 'bomb culture', that has wrecked the tranquillity of the southern states. With the growing political amnesia and the ineptitude of the police forces, once again the intervention of para-military forces to tackle these anarchical tendencies have come to the fore.

The agenda of studies in the political threats to security would encompass the crises of governance; the culture of political violence; the changing nature of political culture; the criminalization of politics; the failing prospect of stable governance either by a dominant party or a coalition of parties, reflecting on the growing amnesia within the political parties and the rampant rise of corruption, are the emergent issues that draw focus.

- *Economic threats to security*

The economic dimension of threats to security, are basically internal. At the macro level the Indian government has been struggling with budgetary deficits; adopting a lopsided subsidies programme that has not effectively addressed the panacea; its ineptitude to tackle the 'parallel economy'; its rising defence expenditure and the prospect that the future price hikes are inevitable and more painful; the prospect of a cumulative sanctions regime that is likely to have its adverse effects on the financial markets; the continuing slide of the value of the Indian Rupee are some of the indicators and emerging threats to economic security. Three areas of this challenge need focus in the context of its seriousness.

The cumulative budgetary deficits faced by the Indian government and the prospects of a blockage of the international financial assistance on one hand, besides the linking of economic and financial assistance to the pruning of the Indian defence budgetary outlays and organization, have a very serious impact on the overall security posture of the country. This is a serious issue, when the pressures to 'roll back' the Indian nuclear programme are indiscriminately linked to international economic assistance.

Energy security is another vital dimension in this paradigm. India's energy deficits are burgeoning with its population growth, and with it, linked the growing dependence on the West Asian oil and natural gas imports. Indian keenness to participate in the Central Asian oil explorations and its interest in oil pipeline project connections to the country reflects the gravity of the situation. India's serious competitor for the mega oil and natural gas reserves in Central Asia in the coming century would be China.

Demography and the steep rise in population is yet another vulnerability in the dimension of India's internal security threats, the burgeoning urban increase in population and its environmental consequences is another factor. A more serious threat emerges from the cross-border spillage of population, in the form of migrants in India's north-east, besides the economic refugees and in some cases, environmental refugees, reflect the multi-dimensional nature of the problem.[19] Whilst, its overlapping consequences reflect the trappings of the security predicament of India in conjunction with its growing crisis in governance.

- *Social and cultural threats to security*

The social cohesion and cultural pluralism of India, has always been a remarkable source of its strength and resilience. Its social, ethnic and lingual diversities have always been cushioned in this matrix. Hindu fundamentalism has emerged as the dominant alternative to the secular political orientation.

The BJP has projected a 'national pattern of governance', which seem to adapt to the current vagaries of the fluid political situation, but the real agenda of its other communal associate organizations, like the Vishwa Hindu Parishad (VHP),the Bajrang Dal, the Rashtriya Swayamsevak Sangh (RSS) and the Shiv Sena, is the dominant projection of the Hindutva as an ideological and political alternative to the prevalent dispensation. This move would alienate the minorities. The politics of

[19] K.S. Subramaniam, 'The National Security Scenario: Some issues and approaches', *Indian Defence Review*, Vol. 11 (2), April-June 1996, p. 41.

religious and cultural alienation of the minorities in India is the avowed objective of this communal quartet.

There are two long-term aspects to the growth of the BJP and Hindu revivalism. Irrespective of electoral vagaries their intermediate objective is the imparting of the 'Hindu' imprint into the national agenda in domestic, economic, civic, educational, foreign and security policies of the country, this is in tune with their version of the 'swadeshi' (nationalist).

The second aspect is that the BJP's political presence and mileage has actually levered additional pressure on the Indian state, which is already in the siege of multiple ethno-linguistic, religious, and separatist movements.[20] The implications of a dominant majority questioning the basic foundations of India's constitutional polity pose a fundamental challenge to the prevalent domestic political and social paradigm having very serious ramifications on the future of the Indian polity.

- *Ecological threats and transnational threats to Indian security*

The nature of ecological threats to the physical security of the Indian territory and its implications are transnational. The India-centric domain of South Asia has its complications. While the potential of ecological related threats to conflict is episodic, their gravity in the context of resource depletion, conflicts over sharing of river waters within the polity, the consequences of acid rain, the over exploitation of fishing grounds and overgrazing of pasture lands with attendant implications, are some of threats that have the potentials to affect the security and tranquillity within the country and in its inter-state relations. The ecological approach to Indian security demands a subcontinental approach of regional co-operation in a comprehensive framework covering all issues.

The second issue in the ecological agenda, is the opportunistic exploitation by the industrialized powers of the ecological activism of the Third World ecological non-governmental movements, whose dissent and protest over mega-industrial projects in the region attracts considerable criticism and pontification, this amounts to ecological aggression.[21]

[20] Shekhar Gupta, 'India Redefines its Role', *Adelphi Papers #293* (London: International Institute of Strategic Studies, Oxford, 1995), p. 20.

[21] Rikhye, op. cit., p. 116.

The prospect of the Kashmir or the Jharkhand movements to 'go green' on their secessionist demands and appeal for international humanitarian intervention to save their ecology against the ravages of the Indian government, is a good possibility for international intervention in the name of 'green rights' and human rights of the groups.

Transnational threats have emerged due to the direct or indirect Indian intervention in the neighbouring South Asian countries, resulting in the spill-over of illegal migrants and economic refugees.[22] The narcotics-arms smuggling nexus transiting through India from the Golden Crescent and the Golden Triangle, has ravaged the socio-economic lives of the people in the transit states of Maharashtra, Gujarat and Punjab in the north-west and Assam, Meghalaya and Mizoram in the north-east.

This problem is reinforced by the crisis of governance that now afflicts the Indian polity. The nexus between the local criminals, the politicians and the narcotics mafia has hindered attempts to combat the menace by the police forces.

- *Technological threats to Indian security*

The emerging dimension in the range of security threats in the Third World is the prospect of technological obsolescence in the face of the rapid technological innovation and the dynamics of the market. The advocates of interdependence argue that the autarkic technological policies are outdated due to the enormous benefits of interdependence. The politics of technology transfer/sharing however is not unbiased; it is wrought with its own contradictions.

The post-nuclear test period has its own challenges to the Indian access and acquisition of Western hi-technology. The fears of the technological vulnerability are factored on the following realities

The Indian military battle order is predominantly of ex-Soviet origin in terms of hardware, tactics, doctrine, etc. The defeat of Iraq, whose battle formations resemble India, has provoked serious rethink on the deployability of hardware and software, viz., the tactics and doctrine.

The ongoing revolution in military affairs, skilfully extrapolates the cutting edge of technology and finds its most appropriate employment. Indian technological quests are likely to increase. These would include hybridization of advanced electronics systems to prevalent

[22] Chari, op. cit., p. 10.

platforms, synergism of the existing systems with reinforcements, and acquisition and colloborative ventures.

The second threat prospect emerges from the pace of technological advancement of China and its seemingly vast access to advanced dual-use hi-tech from the West. The offer of hi-tech to China comes uninterrupted while being of restricted access to India, as a penalty imposed for its recent adventurism.

Role of Policy Research and Academic Research in Security Studies

Policy research in security studies is perhaps one of the excellent endowments that the country has in its possession. Given the substantial thrust in India's higher education and the quality of its institutions, the Indian expertise in this field has been good. In terms of repute and professionalism, the Indian think tanks have done their bit in terms of quality, scholarship and commitment.

Pre-eminent among the think tanks and policy research institutions in India is the United Services Institution of India (USI), modelled after the Royal United Services Institute of-the U.K. The USI has been in the field of defence and strategic studies research for over a century. Its expertise in national security studies research in India is considered premier and professional

The USI publishes a journal which focusses on wide spectrum of issues including articles on military, operational, and doctrinal aspects of strategy. The USI has a series of publications such as monographs, proceedings of lectures, seminars, etc. Its recent focus has been in the evaluation of military and non-military sources of threat to Indian security.

The Institute for Defence Studies and Analyses in New Delhi, established as an autonomous society in 1966 (in the aftermath of the Sino-Indian war of 1962) has been functioning as a premier institute in policy-related research in security studies.

It has been endowed annually by the grants of the Ministry of Defence, the Ministry of External Affairs, and the Department of Atomic Energy and by collaborative efforts of other national and international institutions. Its primary mandate is for the government of India and acts as a centre for research and studies.[23] Earlier the Institute was

[23]*Annual Report*—Institute for Defence Studies and Analyses, New Delhi, 1996-7.

publishing the quarterly IDSA Journal along with the monthly periodical journals, viz., 'Strategic Analyses and Strategic Digest'. The journal was discontinued and in its place the Institute publishes the 'Asian Strategic Review', which discusses significant security and defence issues with statistical updates, besides, the Institute publishes its monographs and occasional papers.

The Centre for Policy Research was established in the year 1973 as an autonomous society to conduct research in all aspects of public policy in India. The centre has its national security studies policy division and has produced some of the best available research in the fields of India's national security on a variety of themes, from nuclear weapons to technology control policies, to the futuristic perspectives of security policy.[24]

The Centre for the Study of Developing Societies is another premier institute of international repute. The Centre has been examining the comprehensive aspects of India's security in critical and alternate perspectives, that have focussed on the economic, social and ecological dimensions. The Centre's journal 'Alternatives' is of critical scholastic repute in alternate thinking on a host of issues. The Centre for Policy Research and the Centre for the Study of Developing Societies have been focussing on the critical and alternate studies.

The recently established institutes of study and research in security studies are, the Institute for the Study of Peace and Conflict, which has been conducting policy studies on military and non-military aspects of security; the Institute has recently published research monographs on these issues. The Delhi Policy Group is the other institute of recent origin and has been working in the area of Conflict Resolution and in Confidence Building Mechanisms.

The 'Indian Defence Review' is a professional quality journal in defence and strategic affairs. Its comprehensive scholarship and critical analysis in national and international security affairs is well known.

The Ministry of Defence has its staff colleges and institutes that train the military professionals in the higher direction of war. The premier institutions are the Defence Services Staff College (DSSC) in Wellington in south India, the National Defence College, New Delhi, the National Defence Academy at Khadakvasala in western India, the School of Combat at Mhow in central India are the institutions that train the officer cadres in the various aspects of combat.

[24] Centre for Policy Research—Report, 1996-8.

The significant inputs of these institutions are in their study programmes. The DSSC offers an M.Sc degree in Defence Science and the programme is affiliated to the Department of Defence and Strategic Studies, University of Madras. Besides, the DSSC also has academic collaborative programmes in pre-doctoral (M.Phil.) and Doctoral (Ph.D.). The officer candidates are exposed to the academic environment of civilian academic scholarship in national security studies and in international relations. The National Defence College in New Delhi is another premier training institution that offers training for officers at a higher level.

The DSSC publishes the journal 'Trishul', which is a bi-annual publication. It is perhaps one of the journals, along with the 'Combat' (published from the School of Combat, Mhow), that carry articles on national and international security, drawn from both civilian and military authorship.

The university centres and departments and the affiliated colleges in India have academic degree/research programs in Defence and Strategic Studies. Academic research has always been 'pure research', mainly because of academic scholastic requirements and partly because the academic programmes have very little to do with either the 'Policy' or the 'Operations' dimensions in India. The other significant reason is the apparent cloak of secrecy and confidentiality that covers all matters of national security in India.

Prominent centres and departments in defence and strategic studies in India are Allahabad, Pune, Madras, Osmania University in Hyderabad, Gorakhpur, Punjabi University in Patiala, and Meerut, to name a few, which have full-fledged teaching and research programmes.[25] The academic curricula in these university centres are still in tune with the cold war milieu and require complete reorientation by encompassing the expanded scope of the post-cold war changes. The need for a comprehensive overhaul in concept and methodology of security studies is indispensable for any meaningful pursuit of academic research in this field.

The significant issues in security studies that are in vogue in the various academic centres, policy institutions and the military training centres are that they are compartmentalized. The lack of an integrated perspective is evident. Given the interdependent nature of the security

[25] National Congress for Defence Studies, Report, 1994.

studies with its diverse implications, the need in India is to evolve integrated perspectives that would eclectically key in the intellectual-academic-policy-operations dimensions into a framework that would address the emergent issues and problems in a holistic manner. Secondly, the absence of 'lateral mobility' between policy and the academia, fails to effectively synergize the potential of the conceptual framework of the academia's specialist expertise to apply in the field of policy analysis.[26]

The constitution of the National Security Council of India would perhaps instil coherence and integration of the diverse perspectives of policy, intelligence, analysis, and operations with the academia into the emergent agenda of security studies

In conclusion the foregoing analysis has endeavoured to map out the state of security studies enterprise in India and to summarise it in the following propositions.

- Indian security studies have been in a state of transition since the end of the cold war and have encountered a shift from a 'autarkic' to an emergent state of 'interdependence', in both conceptual as well as in policy dimensions. This interdependence is currently prevailing, as the nature of security threats are more regional and transnational and the knowledge base to perceive, analyse, and correlate, demands a multidisciplinary perspective and approach.
- The changing foci of security, demands the employment of prognostic approaches of mapping future threats, that would effectively factor the long-term perspectives and challenges. There is also a greater need to evolve an integrated pattern of thinking. The ad hocism of the past should never be an excuse for the emergent threats, simply because they are no longer simplistic and zero-sum in nature, but rather more complex with a menu for inter-related disasters, if they are not adequately tackled.
- While policy research has been able to analyse and provide a very effective trend analysis. Academic research and teaching on the other hand, has not been able to innovate on what can be termed as the emergent paradigm on the new dimensions of Indian security thinking. The methods of reverse analysis and the effective utility of

[26] K. Subrahmanyam, 'Academic Contribution to National Security Policy Formulation in India', in K. Subrahmanyam, *Perspectives in Defence Planning* (New Delhi: Abhinav Publishers, 1973).

prognostic studies are still to be applied. The need of the hour is the autonomy of academic research and the lateral mobility between the policy officialdom, the policy analyst, the military, the media, and the academia. For the age of secrecy is now rendered transparent, by the 'cutting edge of information technology'. India has to come a long way!

Post-Cold War Security Studies in India: Continuity and Change

V.R. RAGHAVAN

At the turn of the century, the world is going through an unprecedented change in ideas of warfare and its relevance in human affairs. One is witness to a revolution in ideas, technology, social and political structures, and economic imperatives which rightly bring into question the meaning of security. The notion of national security itself is changing to absorb the new driving forces that are now operating across the globe. Security studies as understood for five decades and more since World War II, are being viewed in a new light. It would not be an exaggeration therefore to wonder, if the absolute values placed on the concepts of security since 1945, are entirely applicable at the turn of the century.[1]

In some ways the focus of research in security studies is already shifting to cope with the ever-emerging new, and rapidly widening range of threats to security. The Third World or the world of developing countries, is more affected than others by the changed dimensions of security. No continent is free from armed conflicts involving the developing states. Latin America, Africa, Southern Europe, Middle East, South Asia and East Asia are all seething with armed conflicts of different kinds. The Indian subcontinent is no exception to this trend. It is in some ways more affected by the post-cold war conflicts than others. The geo-strategic location of the subcontinent, in fact, makes this conflict-prone zone critical to regional and international stability.

The continuing conflicts, their management by successive governments, their impact on society and the future conflict possibilities have influenced Indian strategic and security thinking. The end of the cold

[1]Richard Smoke, *National Security and the Nuclear Dilemma* (New York: Random House, 1984).

war has given a fillip to this process. The emerging world order of control regimes which favour the developed nations, of nuclear elitism, of monopolies have all impacted on security studies in India. The range and scope of security studies in India after the cold war offer a unique insight, into the outlook of the country about its security imperatives.[2]

INDIA AND THE COLD WAR

It is a strange paradox that India, which tried to remain non-aligned in the geo-political alignments of the cold war, was most affected by it. The cold war emphasis of the US on the policy of containment of the Soviet Union and Pakistan's decision to be part of that policy, led to raising the levels of conflict in the subcontinent. That conflict, not unexpectedly, assumed an ideological and communal dimension with a wide range of adverse consequences to both countries. China's war with India, and India's substantial linkages with Soviet Union to build effective armed forces, are too well known to need repetition. These major security challenges to India's sovereignty were clearly linked to the cold war standoffs of the major powers. The ideological conflict based on Pakistan's pursuit of the 'two-nation theory' brought about the consequences of long lasting and disruptive internal conflicts in India, in Punjab and Jammu and Kashmir, during the 1980s and 1990s.

The Soviet involvement in Afghanistan and the impact of the Afghan struggle on India, is not adequately appreciated till date. The impact of the massive flow of Afghan refugees into Pakistan, the availability of small arms in huge quantities, and the exponential role of narcotics consequent to that conflict, has been very substantial on India. Its impact has been felt in all internal conflicts in India. In the 1990s, the nuclear dimension added to the region by China, through its technical support to Pakistan, continues to be a major factor. The pressures on India from the NPT and CTBT regimes, a fallout of the cold war constructs of security, pursued by the permanent members of Security Council, who are also the Nuclear-5 influenced Indian security thinking significantly.[3]

India, as an independent nation, was thus born into the cold war

[2] Edward Kolodziej, in Cohen and Bajpai, *South Asia After the Cold War* (Boulder, Colo: Westview, 1993).

[3] Shekhar Gupta, 'India Redefines its Role', *Adelphi Papers 293*, 1995.

and could not but be affected by the bipolar nature of that confrontation. India attempted to reduce the impact of the cold war bipolarity through the Non-Aligned Movement and the Group of 77. These two organizations helped in reducing threats in the international dimensions but, did little to offset the adverse security impact of cold war in the region. India's continuing conflict with its western neighbour was only one facet of the security problem. The secessionist movements in north-east, supported for years by China, and the costs of sustaining a military response on the second front, i.e. with China, were major security challenges faced by India. These were not entirely free from influences of the bipolar cold war interface.

The paradox was that while super power rivalry affected Indian interests, Indian security interest did not materially influence the super powers relationship, which influenced the global balance during the cold war.[4] The super powers also made a distinction between the conflicts in regions of vital importance, i.e. the Third World. Indeed, the super powers imperatives of arms exports, spheres of influence and trading preferences considerably influenced conflict in South Asia. India had to cope with its security challenges simultaneously in the cooperative and competitive mode of super power rivalry.

Strategic thinking during the cold war had made a significant shift from the efficient conduct of war toward the threat of war. It laid greater emphasis on deterrence, crisis management and risk manipulation. Victory over the opponent took second place to surviving as a nation. Strategic thinking also became abstract and speculative.[5] The influence of cold war strategic thought on Indian security thinking was, therefore, considerable. Cold war values placed on deterrence through nuclear weapons and their linkage with a major power status, greatly influenced Indian thought.

The attempt to retain a measure of autonomy in the military as well as the technological arena, required both skill and determination. India reflected both to a considerable degree, in the development of its nuclear and missile capabilities enabling it to adopt a stand on the NPT and CTBT related issues, indicate both the compulsions of emerging threats in the region and the desire to seek autonomy from

[4] Rasul Baksh Rais, in Weinbaum and Kumar, *South Asia Approaches the Millennium: Reexamining National Security* Boulder, Colo: Westview, 1995).

[5] Hedley Bull, 'Strategic Studies and Its Critics', in *Power, Strategy and Security* edited by Knorr (New Delhi: Asian Books, 1983).

the cold war bipolar arrangements, that were seen to be constricting India's security options. The Chinese example of linking nuclear capability with international stature was not lost on India. The super powers contributed no less to this Indian perception by their responses towards China.

India After the Cold War

The cold war ended less than a decade ago. It is too soon to come to conclusions about the geopolitical world order which would emerge. The end of the Soviet Union as a strategic entity does not necessarily create conditions for lasting peace. The fundamental elements of conflicts in and around India, have not been changed by the end of the cold war. The removal of the cold war template has not changed either the scope or the intensity of conflicts, which India has been subjected to by the cold war. On the other hand, the removal of super power interest in the Third World conflicts, has led to their gaining strength and continuing to flare longer than is good for international stability.

The post-cold war era has coincided with the emergence of new threat dimensions. The external and military threats to a nation's territory have receded. The costs of a military adventure through an overt war are now prohibitive. Such actions are also no longer sustainable in the post-cold war era. The compulsion to seize territory for obtaining resources is no longer the driving force. Control over resource-rich areas through trade, alliance, economic cooperation and interdependence is now possible without recourse to wars. At least in the Third World, wars are no longer an economic proposition, even if the maintenance of large armed forces is still possible at considerable costs.[6]

External threats have been replaced in the Third World by internal dissent, and claims to autonomy and ethnic recognition by sub-national entities. These claims are forcefully being pushed through armed conflict. India and South Asia are uniquely affected by this. India is unique in the region by virtue of sharing a border with each of the SAARC states—other than the Maldives—while none of the others share a border with each other. This coincidence is compounded by the presence in each of the states of the region of population segments which have ethnic and communal linkages with population elements in the others. The circumstance is fraught with the possibilities of

[6] V.R. Raghavan, *India's Need for Strategic Studies* (Delhi Policy Group, 1996).

political exploitation of the sentiments of exclusivity through ideological, armed, financial and other support. The South Asian states have also faced internal conflicts which have in most cases been supported from outside.

The increase in non-military threats to security in South Asia and in India have also become manifold. The widespread and long-lasting ethnic conflicts, the flow of unlimited quantities of small arms have already been alluded to. These are closely linked to the trade in narcotics, whose production areas straddle India both from the east and west. This is made worse by the nexus between crime syndicates and politicians, making-counter measures extremely difficult to initiate and implement. There are the additional threats of currency and financial crimes. These are made nearly impossible to be tackled by the information technology revolution, and the international nature of electronic money transactions in a globally-linked economy. As if these were not enough, in South Asia, India faces trade barriers which are more a reflection of cold war animosities than of economic necessities.

The states in South Asia inclusive of India, are also facing a transition from political stability to instability. The political ruling class in India during the cold war, was influenced by a liberal western background and an understanding of the nation's essential needs to work through regional and international linkages. A tacit shift of priorities has led to the emergence of a whole new class of leadership, which is not only wholly driven by its local political imperatives unrelated to international and regional needs, but, which is aware of its political strength through electoral arithmetics. Security is far from the thoughts and perceptions of the new ruling class, which has its feet firmly planted in local political calculations. This new development has led to national security to be viewed in relation to the security of the ruling class or clique.

Even during the cold war, Third World security was a different construct than that of the developed nations. Security in the Third World, 'does not simply refer to the military dimension . . . but to the whole range of . . . of a state's existence which are already taken care of in the more developed states ... for example, the search for internal security of the state through nation-building, the search for secure systems of food, health, money and trade. . . .'[7] It is not surprising

[7] Caroline Thomas, *In Search of Security: The Third World in International Relations* (Boulder, Colo, 1987).

therefore, that, security in the Third World is now attempted to be articulated, 'in relation to vulnerabilities that threaten to, or have the potential to, bring down or significantly weaken state structures, both territorial and institutional, and regimes which preside over these structures and profess to represent them internationally'.[8]

The emerging pattern of interventionism by the developed nations in the Third World, is a disturbing development from India's point of view. When combined with the developed world's actions to retain its dominant economic and military position, Indian fears of its being deliberately targeted as a potential world power, find many takers in the country. There are fears expressed by Indian security analysts on the dangers to the probability of a true multipolar balance of power emerging, as the new millennium begins. There are in fact fears of a new cold war beginning if the US nuclear policy of engaging China on one hand, and a containment policy through a China-specific ballistic missile defence on the other, goes ahead. Indian security studies portray that a US-China cold war would have serious consequence for India and the South Asian region. A new US-China axis shows signs of emerging after the Indian nuclear tests, as seen from the communiques issued after the visit of President Clinton to China. This is being seen to have the potential of further complicating the security scenario in South Asia, even more than in the cold war.

POST-COLD WAR SECURITY STUDIES

Security studies in the post-cold war period have indicated a new strategic situation. The importance of military power is seen to have declined in international relations.[9] It is no longer the sole source of power in statecraft. It is also now recognized that a re-examination is overdue in the way national security and international relations are viewed. There is a new belief evolving that national security be examined in a broader context, including non-military threats and domestic security issues. There is a need now to look at security not as the sole or most important goal, but one amongst many values, whose relative importance can vary from country to country and situations. Security studies need to shift the emphasis from the military to

[8] Mohammed Ayoob, *The Third World Security Predicament* (London: Boulder, 1995).

[9] J.L. Gaddis, *The US and the End of Cold War* (New York: OUP, 1992).

economic stability and welfare. Indeed, a tradeoff between security and economic factors is an area which requires a greater than ever focus. The relationship between national security and the internal situation in a state, is another factor requiring study. Citizens of a state are unlikely to be concerned with national security if there is anarchy, food shortages and absence of governance.[10]

There is also a need to look more closely at the objectives of security. The cold war security studies emphasis on the means of security, is no longer adequate to the requirements of the larger goals of security. One needs to ask are the military means in themselves adequate to guarantee security. The objectives of military security policy are rarely discussed in governments, even if it is sometimes questioned in deciding foreign policy. The goal of 'enhancing' security is often considered to be an absolute need. The theoretical basis of this absolute assumption is rarely looked at in national security studies.

It is useful to look at the security study thrusts in the US which influenced the situation which now prevails in South Asia to a large extent. The realist school of international relations had led the security studies in the US for 50 years. The end of the cold war, evoked a response from this school, which reflected its inability to see the emerging global security environment. In a short time after the break-up of the Soviet Union, the realist approach to international relations came up with the cry of new threats to the US security. That the US security can no longer be viewed as different from that of the rest of the world was a conclusion which remained beyond the dominant security study thought in the US.

The domination of the realist-neorealist beliefs in international security studies requires a corrective. A new set of beliefs based on cooperative security instead of 'leading the world' by the US is essential. The view that, 'There is only one approach to international relations . . . the approach (which) for want of a better terminology is power politics . . .' is now a fallible one.[11] Power in itself is an unrecognizable entity in the post-cold war world. It can hardly be expected to serve the needs of the next millennium, unless the new world order is to be based, once again on the cold war notions of security. In this context one may well ask whether the new nuclear uncertainties in

[10] World Bank, The State in a Changing World, *World Development Report*, 1997.

[11] Colin Gray, *Strategic Studies: A Critical Assessment* (Westport, 1982).

South Asia were a cause, or, was it the effect of the Nuclear-5's policies of nuclear proliferation? Did security studies view arms control and non-proliferation as the means to a safer world or as ends in themselves? The global implications of information technology and of economic interdependence are likely to impact as much on the developed states as on the Third World.

There is need, therefore, to rethink the fundamentals of security studies. Even more necessary is the need to redefine security. Is security to be seen as the need of a single powerful state or system, on the assumption that it would then ensure the security of others? The security needs of other states which seek the well-being of their people rather than the domination of others, are no less important to the security of the powerful states. The contradiction in the inevitable growth of multipolarity of powers and the beliefs of a single powerful state, which views its security as more vital than that of the world, is another area in need of closer examination.

Security Studies in India: After The Cold War

The Indian security studies viewpoint in the 1990s has over-whelmingly perceived the US as hegemonic. Every security analyst of repute, has viewed Indian security as being adversely affected by the US attempts to browbeat India into accepting a permanent secondary power position. This perception has also not been helped by the initiatives of the US State Department and its officials. It is ironic that what was seen in India as its responsible international conduct in matters of security, in nuclear weapons restraint, in the UN peacekeeping operations and above all in opening the Indian economy to a global interaction, were reciprocated by forcing an unequal and discriminatory security arrangement on it. Whether on the issue of J&K, or on matters nuclear, or in instances of arms aid and nuclear technology to Pakistan, Indian security studies could not but identify a continuous US bias. The end of the cold war and the advent of the Clinton administration—a Democratic Party President who was expected to be responsive to Indian needs—appeared in the Indian context to have brought about a new cold war involving India.

The main question in the security studies arena in India for the last six years has been whether there is really a new security era based on an equitable world order? The collapse of the Soviet Union had made a dramatic impact on Indian defence needs. India attempted to ensure peace with China, through an agreement with it, on settling the border issue peacefully. The US initiatives on Kashmir, its ineffective determination of Pakistani nuclear weapons programme, and the US policy on China all had an impact on India. Chinese technological and military assistance to Pakistan not only grew but from the Indian point of view, evoked no response from the US.

Indian security studies community could thus draw only one conclusion. The world's most powerful democracy preferred to compromise the interests of the world's largest democracy, for gaining an economic advantage in China. Thus, the security study thrust in India developed a not-unnatural preference for responding to the new cold war with the old cold war solution of becoming a nuclear weapons state. That argument has carried the day, as proved by the events in May 1998. The consequences of the skewed post-cold war security outlook of the US and of its 'realist' security studies focus, has in no small measure contributed to the new nuclear uncertainties at the turn of the century.

Indian security concerns, consequent to developed states' and specially the US post-cold war policies, have been articulated in no uncertain language. In external threats, China's actions relative to nuclear technology transfers to Pakistan and its own force modernization is an important threat. The anxiety over deployment of sea-borne nuclear weapons in the Indian Ocean and doubts over tactical nuclear weapons in Central Asia, are other threats. The thaw in India's relations with China have not led to a corresponding Chinese response relative to Pakistan. The inability of the SAARC to forge a regional solidarity while other regions are progressing towards it, e.g., ASEAN, NAFTA, APEC, etc., is worrisome. The unwillingness of the US to consider India as a factor in its strategic planning, is another cause for security concern.

Internally, a long list of security concerns have influenced security perceptions. These include first, the erosion of the legitimacy of plural societies and multi ethnic states, as seen from the break-up of the Soviet Union and Yugoslavia. Second, heightened economic aspirations of the Indian society, which are beyond the resource capacity of the Indian state to meet. Third, the emergence of sub-regional and ethnic centrifugality. Fourth, the social and political reaction to these trends by the majority Hindu community. Fifth, the overspill of ethnic conflicts in the South Asian region into India is seen as a matter of serious concern.[12]

India has claimed itself to be a nuclear weapons state since its tests in May 1998. How will this affect security studies in India? The response in the media, after the tests, was remarkable for the speed with which a balanced view emerged on the relevance of nuclear weapons. In the span of a few months after the tests, the views of the pro-bomb strategic analysts are already being questioned. Even those national newspapers which had taken a strong nationalist position on India going overtly nuclear, have started to balance their comments. The growing public doubts expressed in the media, in public debates and the letters to the editors of national and regional dailies, is having an impact. While a decade-long critique of anti-India-US policies has had an impact on the people, who inform themselves through the print media and TV, the need for restraint and caution in India's nuclear weapons policies are a prominent feature of the post-test public discourse. The whole range of new security studies, based on the presence of nuclear weapons in the Indian subcontinent, is now going to take off. The questions of nuclear weapons strategy, of deterrence, of arsenal size, et al., is just beginning and would take some time evolving into an Indian nuclear thought.

Indian security studies have been strong in identifying the fact that there are no more autonomous states at the turn of the century. Even the sole superpower is no longer in a position to operate autonomously and requires to build consensus and cooperative arrangements to secure its interests. This has led to conflicts in some parts of the world becoming of little or no concern to the major powers. The South Asian conflicts, i.e. Punjab, Tamil, Chakma, Pathan and others do not interest the powers as issues in need of resolving. If Kashmir has taken the fancy of the US and some other powers, it is consequent to the nuclear tests in the subcontinent.

The need to retain autonomy over the security dynamics, therefore, became a critical need for India. In both its technical and military needs the compulsion to obtain, retain and expand autonomy for controlling the security dynamics, was forcefully articulated in the

[12] J.N. Dixit, 'India's Security Concerns and Their Impact', in *Indian Foreign Policy: Agenda for the 21st Century,* Foreign Service Institute (New Delhi: Konark Publishers, 1997).

India's post-cold war security studies. It is of course debatable whether India's interests and its autonomy over security issues have enhanced or been reduced by the nuclear tests. It is, however, important to note that the Indian security outlook is shifting from the traditional defence of national borders, to the more important defence of national interests. The gap in the perceptions on security, however, remains in the understanding of the criticality of economic and political stability in national power.

The nuclear weapons status of the Indian subcontinent would inevitably make more complex the management of conflict and military risks. Now that nuclear weapons are a reality in India, a range of measures are required to be put into place both to make the conflict thresholds stable, and to reassure the states in the region. Nuclear weapons-related CBMs would be the first such measure. India would also need to put into place measures which would demonstrate its resolve to prevent an arms race and its ability to manage the nuclear capability responsibly.

It is possible for SAARC states to play a part by initiating dialogue, facilitating discussions, creating fora where meetings can take place, in and outside the governments, and through media coverage. More than anything else, security studies groups can take up the issue of nuclear weapons and their impact on peace and conflict management as applicable to the region. A corpus of security studies thought, relative to the region's needs, is a shortcoming which needs to be corrected. Exchange of thinkers, research facilities, and the encouragement of a regional security outlook is now an urgent need. The creation of regional security studies programmes in universities, collaborative studies between 'Think Tanks' and creation of a South Asian Security Studies Centre under the aegis of SAARC would now be appropriate.

The security studies community academia, think tanks and NGOs in India are all going to have to face up to the economic, domestic, and non-military threats to security. It will not happen because the P-5 or G-8 have issued their high-handed and one-sided diktats to India on the nuclear tests. Such demands from the developed states will only help strengthen the unfavourable opinion in India and other Third World states of the failure of the single track 'realist' approaches to security. The change in opinion in India on nuclear weapons will come because the real meaning of security in its widest context of human development, economic growth, political stability, individual safety and well being shall soon be viewed as not having been secured by nuclear weapons.

Security studies in India will need to reckon with the weight of arguments on economic and political security. A decisive outcome in war becomes the first casualty in a condition of nuclear balance.[13] The choice of war is now no longer available to the major nations of the subcontinent to resolve their problems. Indian security analysts still advocating the cold war logic of military route to security, will in due course, need to take into account the limits of military and nuclear weapons power. Inevitably, the security debate in India would shift focus to the larger meaning of security in the post-cold war era. It is heartening to see that the process has begun.

[13] Robert Jervis, *The Meaning of Nuclear Revolution* (Cornell University Press, 1989).

Security Studies in Pakistan: Current Trends and Future Directions

ZAFAR IQBAL CHEEMA

Traditionally, security studies in Pakistan have primarily focused on the military and strategic issues, such as, an intense threat perception from India and how to cope with it through conventional military capability, and eventually a nuclear deterrent posture. The scope of security studies has however, widened beyond traditional approaches after the demise of Soviet Union and the end of the cold war. None the less, the emergance of the new pattern is almost inapplicable in South Asia because the cold war paradigm and conflict-relationship between India and Pakistan is still intact. Moreover, the overt demonstration of nuclear weapons capabilities by both states in May 1998 has had a diabolical influence on the South Asian security: While it has transformed ambiguous deterrent relationship into a weaponized deterrence regime, its overall impact on deterrent stability has yet to crystallize.

Historically, the growth and development of security studies in Pakistan has been very slow especially in the initial years after independence. With the passage of time, the pace of its development accelerated but remained incompatible with the security needs in the real sense. Security studies in Pakistan have exceedingly drawn on Western paradigms and data to address its security issues and that of South Asia.

Security studies in Pakistan have been based upon historical-realist approach, having more relevance with humanities than with social sciences.[1] A major obstacle in the way of development of the field has been the complete dominance of the military with its martial law

[1] Shireen M. Mazari and Ayaz Naseem, 'The Development of Defence and Strategic Studies As a Social Science Discipline in Pakistan', in S.H. Hashmi, ed., *The State of Social Sciences in Pakistan* (Islamabadi: Quaid-i-Azam University, 1989), p. 224.

regimes, over civilian inputs. Problems of indigenization of Security Studies have also significantly contributed to its slow development. Indigenization includes the use of national language, sources of data, dependence on national experts for analytical and policy-making process, and the need for methodological reorientation.[2]

For many years since its inception Pakistan remained essentially a bureaucratic polity with military's dominance that established the authoritarian character of the state.[3] The occasional imposition of martial law further aggravated the problem. As a result, security studies could not be institutionalized.

In the Third World as a whole, institutional role in security studies could not be established. Role of national leaders remained pre-eminent because they made policies in congruence with their personal perceptions.[4] In Pakistan, the institutional development and inducement for civilians to engage in security matters was further reduced in the military regime of General Ayub Khan. Decision-making was vested in an oligarchy.

The individuals' role from the civil sector was also not enough to influence decisions of military leaders. Sisson and Rose in their study of decisional structures and processes that characterized the separation of Bangladesh, describe that Pakistan's decision making core was small, and composed almost exclusively of politically inexperienced and uninformed military personnel.[5] General Yahya Khan felt no need to solicit political advice and cooperation. They suggest that decision making in Pakistan was unsystematic, ad hoc, minimalist, passive and reactive.[6]

Zulfiqar Ali Bhutto succeeded Yahya Khan as the leader of the new Pakistan after the secession of Bangladesh. During the Bhutto era, the nature of regime did somewhat change, but the characteristic bureaucratic structure remained. However, the overall situation did not change partly because Bhutto added two contradictory dimensions to it: The populist and the feudal. Bureaucracy retained its traditional control

[2] Yogesh Atal, 'The Call for Indigenization', *International Social Sciences Journal*, 33: 1 (1981), pp. 192-3.

[3] Inayatullah, 'Social Sciences in Pakistan: An Evaluation', in S.H. Hashmi, ed., op. cit.

[4] Pervaiz Iqbal Cheema, *Pakistan's Defence Policy 1947-58* (London: The Macmillan Press, 1990), p. 68.

[5] Richard Sisson and Leo Rose, *War and Secession: Pakistan, India and the Creation of Bangladesh* (Berkeley: University of California Press, 1990), p. 278.

[6] Ibid.

over academic and research institutions, which were not many. He however, tried to change the system by building up an arrangement of greater civilian control and establishing some kind of accountability of the military. In his aspiration to re-organize the decision making process, he set up the Higher Defence Organization (HDO) which continues until today.[7]

With the passage of time, some institutions were established to promote the field of security studies and enhance the level of their inputs in the decision making process. Apart from these, a few individuals also started working in this field. From late 1980s onwards, the civilian institutional inputs increased partly due to the gradual development of a nuclear weapons capability, and partly due to the functional differentiation of professional expertise. The political architect of Pakistan's nuclear weapons capability was a civilian—Z.A. Bhutto. Security studies for the last few years are seriously concerned with the proliferation of nuclear weapons capabilities in India and Pakistan. Since the end of the cold-war, world focus has shifted to economic security and development, while South Asia is still deeply involved in the traditional approach to security studies. Non-military instruments of power and influence have been neglected with little or no attention paid to the role of economic, industrial and monetary policies.

The state is no more a unitary and coherent actor as is generally perceived. Its role has been modified due to the world-wide revolution in communications and information technology, giving rise to many non-state players. NGOs are becoming stronger and many of them are able to even push around the larger groups.[8] This has resulted in a situation of confusion, with reasons to believe that diffusion of power from nation state may mean more conflict.[9]

This consideration merits recognition in the field of security studies and as such importance should be given to non-state actors, having the capacity to influence security matters. In today's age of economic competition, the security and political stability of a state are directly related to its economy, thus making economic security a vital ingredient in security studies.

[7] Details of the Higher Defence Organization will be provided in the subsequent parts of the article.

[8] Jessica T. Mathews, 'Power Shift', *Foreign Affairs*, 76: 1 (January/February 1997), pp. 51-2.

[9] Ibid., p. 64.

Although terrorist activities, sectarian violence and ethnic conflicts are gradually increasing; these do not figure much in the various security dimensions of Pakistan. Another issue, causing concern is the environment. Environmental changes, according to Thomas Horner—Dixon, can be a cause of acute conflict.[10] In this context, the environment becomes an important subject of contemplation in security studies.

Traditional Approaches to Security

Pakistan security is a victim of traditional as well as non-traditional threats. At the global level, the end of the cold war offered a unique opportunity to address challenges, such as, population explosion, development and poverty, environmental degradation, and arms proliferation. However, in case of Pakistan, the traditional threats to its security are still perceived dominant and, therefore, traditional approach to deal with this problem is pervasive. Ironically, when the international community is assigning low priority to such an approach, Pakistan is forced to ascribe it high priority, primarily because of the Kashmir dispute and attendant problems with India.

Strategic Military Approach

Initially, the 1948 war with India over Kashmir, growing rivalry and mistrust compelled Pakistan to maintain a high conventional military capability. To realize this objective, Pakistan adopted a two pronged approach: It joined Western sponsored alliances for a protective strategic equilibrium against India, and gradually modernized its own conventional military capability to deal with threat contingencies, where Western support against India could not be forthcoming. Pakistan joined Western sponsored alliances SEATO (1954) and CENTO (1955), and signed a Mutual Defence Agreement with the U.S. (1959) for the realization of the above policy objectives.

From 1954-5 until 1962, the Pakistan armed forces although quantitatively smaller than India, were equipped with more sophisticated arms and better trained. However, the Sino-Indian war of 1962 brought profound changes in the regional strategic environment. The U.S.

[10] Thomas F. Horner-Dixon, 'On the Threshold', *International Security*, 16: 2 (Fall 1991), pp. 76-116.

strategic support for India against China, without regard to Pakistan's security imperatives, drifted the latter towards developing friendly relations with China. The development of closer Sino-Pakistan relations generated misgivings in the West, especially the U.S.

The U.S. imposition of an arms embargo against Pakistan during the 1965 and again in 1971 wars with India, brought a tangible change in Pakistan's defence policy. The reliance on alliances ended and the concept of self-reliance dominated the mind-set of defence policy makers. In support of this policy, a defence production division was set up in 1973, to encourage the indigenous production of arms and ammunition. The Wah ordinance factory was expanded and modernized with three new ordinance factories.

By the mid-1970s, Pakistan sought technical and financial assistance from China. A Heavy Forge Foundry was set up in 1978 and a Heavy Rebuild Factory in 1979, both with the Chinese help. The Pakistan Aeronautical Complex was established at Kamra comprizing of the Mirage Rebuild Factory in 1978, with assistance from France, and F-6 Rebuild Factory in 1981, with Chinese assistance.[11]

NON-CONVENTIONAL APPROACH (NUCLEAR OPTION)

In December 1971, Pakistan was divided, defeated and demoralized. Its leadership, while assessing the causes of defeat in the 1971 Indo-Pak war, concluded that conventional military disparity against India was one of its determinant factors because most of the weapon systems were imported. The U.S. arms embargo led Pakistan to find its own avenues for defence against its traditionally hostile neighbour. The drive for strong defence forced Pakistani policy makers to review their nuclear policy and develop a nuclear weapons capability. President Zulfiqar Ali Bhutto who later assumed the office of Prime Minister, played the decisive role in the formulation of this policy. Nuclear deterrence was thought to be the only viable option against any likely aggression.[12]

The Indian nuclear explosion in May 1974 served as a catalyst, and strengthened the argument of nuclear hawks in Pakistan. Prime Minister Zulfiqar Ali Bhutto stated in the National Assembly of

[11] Hasan Askari Rizvi, *Military and Politics in Pakistan* (Lahore: Progressive Publications, 1987), p. 205.

[12] Steve Weissman and Herbert Krosney, *The Islamic Bomb* (New York: Times Book, 1983), pp. 42-5.

Pakistan that Indian nuclear capability had qualitatively changed the situation, and India could resort to nuclear blackmail. Hence, the government became serious about the nuclear weapons option. Pakistan signed an agreement with France in March 1976, for the procurement of a plutonium reprocessing plant. This deal was made possible when Pakistan accepted all the safeguards required by France and IAEA.

But the US interpreted this as an effort on the part of Pakistan to acquire nuclear weapon capability, and thus, a potential threat to its non-proliferation policy. The then Director of United States Arms Control and Disarmament Agency stated that Pakistan's real interest in acquiring the reprocessing plant was to match India's nuclear capacity.[13] Eventually, the Franco-Pakistan agreement on the reprocessing plant was cancelled due to the U.S. pressure.

Realizing the problems in reprocessing plant deal, Pakistan put into operation its second option to go nuclear, namely, the uranium enrichment plant. In early 1984, Dr. Abdul Qadeer Khan announced that the uranium enrichment plant at Kahuta had succeeded in producing enriched uranium. After that announcement, Pakistan defence policy makers began asserting their nuclear weapons capability.

The Presslar amendment proved counter-productive and increased Pakistan's reliance on nuclear deterrence. However, Pakistan's nuclear deterrence was based upon a policy of ambiguity. The winter 1986-7 Brass tacks and 1990 Kashmir crises convinced Islamabad, that, one of the reasons why the eyeball-to-eyeball confrontation with India did not escalate into military conflict, was the existence of an elementary form of nuclear deterrence. After 11 and 13 May 1998 nuclear explosions by India, Pakistan was forced to follow suit. Since then, deterrent stability ensuring the absence of a nuclear conflict between traditional adversaries is and must be the primary focus of security studies.

Diplomatic Approach

Diplomacy has been an important determinant for addressing Pakistan's security problems. Since its independence, Pakistan has been relying on bilateral as well as multilateral diplomatic options for the

[13] Samina Ahmad, 'Franco-Pak relation II', *Pakistan Horizon*, Vol. XXXI, No. 1, 1978, pp. 35-70.

fulfillment of its security and foreign policy objectives. It actively participates in the regional and international forums to raise issues of conflict with India for their solution. Since the 1948 Kashmir conflict, it has heavily relied upon the U.N. role in the resolution of the dispute with India and recurrently invoked the U.N. Security Council Resolutions on Kashmir, which promised the right of self-determination to the people of Kashmir. It has vigorously pursued that policy at all the diplomatic forums since then.

The reliance upon Western alliances in the mid-1950s to meet its security requirements against India, was indicative of the primacy of diplomatic approach in the search for security alternatives. In the absence of a strong U.S. influence vis-à-vis India in the mid-1960s, Pakistan demonstrated willingness to accept Soviet mediation in the aftermath of the 1965 war with India. Soviet mediation led to signing of the Tashkent Declaration. After its dismemberment in December 1971, Pakistan signed the Simla Agreement with India in July 1972, which secured the release of prisoners of war and the withdrawal of their respective forces to pre-war locations. It also converted the Kashmir cease-fire line into a *Line of Control*.

Under the most adverse circumstances, the Simla Agreement was a reasonable trade-off from the Pakistani perspective. The Agreement is however, being differently interpreted by India and Pakistan: India highlighting its exclusive bilateral dimension, whereas Pakistan rejects such a narrow interpretation. According to Pakistani perspective, the Agreement does not preclude her from raising the Kashmir dispute at other international fora, especially when the Simla Agreement has not led to a resolution in the last 27 years.

NON-TRADITIONAL APPROACHES

- *Economic approach*

The 1990s have seen a major shift from the realist view of security to new essentials 'as enhanced importance of economics in national security'[14]. Governments and the public have increasingly perceived and reacted to economic issues as security issues. States became

[14] Donald C. Hellman 'Economics and Security', *Security Studies in 1990*, Richard Shultz, Roy Godson and Ted Greenwood, eds. (New York: Brassey's [US], 1993), pp. 303-26 (308).

increasingly vulnerable to international economic developments.[15] Economic factors are being used as means for achieving state policy that effects national security and welfare. The rise of multinationals was viewed as a challenge to the national state as the primary international actor. Today this issue is seen less in terms of eclipse of the state and more in terms of how to employ state power to control and regulate co-operation, on behalf of national economic interests.

In the 1980s, despite the U.S. assistance, Pakistan's economic performance remained bleak, and the budget to GDP ratio was at 8.2 per cent in 1986-7. However, the Pakistan trade deficit was brought down to 5.04 per cent of the GDP, to sign a second structural adjustment agreement with the IMF.[16] During the time of the caretaker government of the Mr. Moeen Qureshi, Pakistan signed the third structural adjustment agreement, Social Action Programme (SAP); the most significant being a rapid tariff reduction as per requirement of new international trade regime.

The 1994-5 budget was a major departure from the IMF conditionalities for several reasons. Firstly, it was an effective opposition to the IMF imposed conditions after 1993-4 budget, which lead to a consensus in the country on gradual import tariff reduction.[17] Secondly, negotiations with the IMF enabled the PPP government to apply the consensus till the next budget, driven by the policy of appeasement. However, in the 1995-6 budget, the government's arms were twisted by the IMF, which delayed the release of the second tranche of SBA facility. In 1996-7, an understanding was reached between the IMF and PML (N) government, for the fourth extended structural adjustment facility (ESAF) fund package.[18] The options available to the government at present are no different than in the past, i.e. resort to short and long term borrowing and seek concessional credits from the IMF.[19]

• *Environmental approach*

Environmental problems have gained immense importance in the post-cold war scenario, due to the growing concern with the prospects and

[15] Ibid., p. 309.
[16] *The Dawn* (Karachi), 15 February 1997.
[17] *The Dawn* (Karachi), 19 August, 25 and 28 September 1997.
[18] Ibid.
[19] *The Dawn* (Karachi), 29 September 1997.

implications of environmental changes, and relatively decreasing importance of the state centric view of security. There are two fundamental approaches to the concept of environmental security inherent in the current literature.[20] One interpretation holds that environmental degradation and resource depletion could be a threat to the survival of the state, causing conflict and violence within the country. The phenomena could also escalate to transnational levels. The second approach deals with the threat that environmental change can pose to the security of the individual.[21]

Pakistan faces grave environmental problems, rapid population growth (average ranging from 2.4 to 2.8 per cent per year since 1970s) and with GDP growth of 6 per cent, have put tremendous pressure on Pakistan's natural resources. Expansion in industrial production and urbanization has also led to increased level of water and air pollution, which has caused serious health problems. A recent study attempted to evaluate environmental cost in Pakistan and put the estimates of environmental damage at US $ 1 billion to US $ 2.1 billion per year or 2.6 to 5.0 per cent of GDP at 1992 values.[22] The linkage between environmental degradation and poverty alleviation is becoming clear day by day. Pakistan stands at the crossroads in terms of structural reforms that would reincarnate developmental economics in comparison to the current economic practices.

In the beginning, various governments in Pakistan did not demonstrate full awareness of the importance of environmental security. Some policies were initiated by, as late as, the 1980s, to incorporate environmental concerns into its policy planning framework. Environmental legislation concerning the establishment of Pakistan Environment Protection Agency was undertaken. In 1988, it began to design a comprehensive national conservation strategy. Proposed investments in the environmental undertakings are incorporated in the 8th Plan (1993-8).[23]

In addition to the present environment-friendly economic policies,

[20] *The Muslim* (Islamabad), 26 August 1993. Also see 'future of Indo-Pak Trade', A.M. Khusro, *Indian Express* (New Delhi), 23 October 1991.

[21] Daniel Deudney, 'The Case against linking Environment at degradation and National Security', *Millennium* 19, No. 3 (Winter 1990).

[22] Ibid., p. 488.

[23] Brandon C. Valuning, 'Environmental costs in Pakistan: The economy-wide impact of environmental degradation'. Unpublished background paper for Pakistan 2010 Report (Washington, DC: World Bank, Asia Technical Department, 1995).

various efforts have been made to raise awareness among government institutions. The national conservation strategy of 1992, helped in the establishment of NCS implementation unit in the Environment and Urban Affair Division (EUAD), and the creation of an Environmental Section to elucidate environmental concerns in economic and development planning. The Sustainable Development Policy Institute (SDPI) was set up on the basis of national conservation strategy, to provide economic and policy analysis for sustainable economic development.[24] At the provincial level, environmental cells have been created in the respective planning and development projects.

- *Arms control and disarmament approach*

The overt postures of India and Pakistan about nuclear weapons since May 1998 and their delivery systems, have sparked a full-fledged nuclear and missiles arms race. Arms control and disarmament offers an alternative to proliferation and its potential hazards. Arms control encompasses unilateral, bilateral and multilateral measures, designed to diminish the risk of conventional and nuclear weapons. Pakistan adopted a pragmatic policy regarding nuclear arms control. It offered India a number of proposals to establish a non-nuclear regime. It initiated a South Asian nuclear weapon-free zone proposal to the UN General Assembly in November 1974.

In the 1980s, Pakistan offered six specific measures for regional arms control and disarmament, which include a joint India-Pakistan renunciation of the acquisition of nuclear weapons (1978); mutual inspection of nuclear facilities (1979); simultaneous acceptance of full-scope safeguards (1979); simultaneous accession to the NPT (1979); a regional nuclear test ban treaty (1987) and a multilateral conference under UN auspices on nuclear non-proliferation in South Asia.[25]

In June 1991, Nawaz Sharif asked for a meeting of the five powers to discuss the nuclear issue in South Asia and in 1993, a proposal for a zero missile regime in South Asia was proposed by Pakistan. All these proposals have been rejected by India on the plea that it does not regard non-proliferation of nuclear weapons as regional issues. From India's perspective, proliferation of nuclear weapons is an inter-

[24] Hartwig D.C. Haen, 'Agricultural Development and Environmental Protection: Some key issues of potential relevance to Pakistan', *The Pakistan Development Review* 32: 4, Part I (Winter 1993), pp. 501-21(50).

[25] Ibid.

national issue, which should have a linkage with time-bound global disarmament.

INSTITUTIONAL INPUTS

- *Security decision-making in Pakistan*

Defence planning and decision-making mechanism had been the sole domain of the military up to 1971 in Pakistan. The experience of 1971 war forced the ruling elite to institutionalize the defence decision making process because in this war, the three services of Pakistan fought differently, without much inter-force coordination. The lack of coordination amongst the army, air force and navy had badly affected the performance of Pakistani forces. However, the end of martial law and takeover by Z.A. Bhutto relatively decreased the influence of the army in the making of national policy.

- *Reorganization of decision-making mechanism*

In 1974, a study was undertaken by the Bhutto Government to evaluate the defence decision-making process and coordination amongst the armed forces. An official document named *White Paper* on Higher Defence Organization was prepared, which laid emphasis on civilian control over Pakistan's defence decision-making process and armed forces.[26] According to the *White Paper*, the national defence policy was no longer a military affair alone. The evolution of the national defence policy and its administration required an effective political control at the top with a number of institutions set up for professional advice on which military decisions could be based.[27] The military bureaucracy agreed on civilian control but it confined strictly to political leadership alone.

- *Structure of higher defence organization*

The *White Paper* recommended the establishment of Defence Council (DC), Defence Committee of the Cabinet (DCC) and Joint Chiefs of Staff Committee (JCSC).[28]

[26] Government of Pakistan, *White Paper on Higher Defence Organization* (Islamabad: Ministry of Defence, 1976).

[27] Ibid.

[28] Ibid.

All these three institutions are functioning since 1976. The first two are civilian bodies while the third is the highest military institution headed by chairman JCSC (CJCSC). The Defence Council is chaired by the Prime Minister, and its important members include Ministers of Defence, Foreign Affairs, Finance, Interior, States and Frontier Regions, Information and Broadcasting, the chairman JCSC, the three Service Chiefs, and Secretaries of Defence, Foreign Affairs, Finance and Interior. The Prime Minister is assisted by the Minister for Defence who is responsible for military preparedness, defence planning, civil defence and the defence industries.

The Defence Council's functions include the determination of general strategy and defence policy and force goals, and their coordination with the actions of other ministries and to supervize the conduct of war.[29] However, the main responsibility of the Defence Council is defence planning and military preparedness. It is also responsible for the development of Pakistan's arms industry.[30] The civil service head of the Defence Ministry is the Secretary Defence, who is ex-officio member of the DCC and DC. The Defence Ministry is composed of the Defence Division, Defence Production Division, the Joint Chiefs of Staff Committee, and three armed services headquarters.[31]

The Defence Committee of the Cabinet (DCC) is the executive organ of the HDO, which provides decisive inputs towards national defence through frequent meetings and consultations. DCC is presided over by the Prime Minister and includes Ministers for Defence, Foreign Affairs, Finance, and Interior, CJCSC, the three Chiefs of Staff, Secretaries of Defence, Finance and Foreign Affairs. The main function of the DCC is the executive supervision of military policy and national defence. As compared with the DC, the DCC is a narrower body, though it includes more or less the same participants except a few.

JCSC is the highest military body whose chairman serves as Principal Staff Officer to the Prime Minister.[32] Military planning, coordination, and integration amongst the three armed services were the main objectives, which led to the creation of JCSC in 1976.[33] The JCSC was

[29] Ibid.

[30] John Keegan, *World Armies* (London: Macmillan Publishers, 1979), op. cit., p. 447.

[31] Ibid.

[32] Government of Pakistan, *White Paper on Higher Defence Organization*.

[33] Ibid.

charted to be responsible for preparing joint strategic and integrated logistic plans, providing the strategic direction to the armed forces, periodically reviewing the role, size and shape of the three services, advising the government on strategic communications, and industrial mobilization plans, and formulating and reviewing defence plans.[34]

ACADEMIC INPUTS

• *Institutions*

There are many academic and policy research institutions involved in research on security-related issues. These institutions provide an analytical assessment of the concerned problems with the objective to work out alternative options and provide inputs for future policy planning. These institutions include: Pakistan Institute of International Affairs (PIIA), Karachi, Institute of Strategic Studies, Islamabad (ISS), Institute of Regional Studies (IRS) Islamabad, Department of Defence and Strategic Studies (DSS), Quaid-i-Azam University, Islamabad, National Defence College (NDC), Islamabad, and Foundation for Research on International Environment, National Development and Security (FRIENDS), Rawalpindi.

All these institutions function as independent, apolitical and non-profit organizations. The National Defence College is a combined armed forces institution, which works under the Joint Chiefs of Staff Headquarters. Additionally, there are five centres of excellence, four in the provincial capitals and one in Islamabad. Each of these centres are associated with a University as follows: Centre for North American and African Studies, Quaid-i-Azam University, Islamabad; Centre for Central Asian Studies, Peshawar University, Peshawar; Centre for European Studies, Karachi University, Karachi; Centre for Middle Eastern Studies, Baluchistan University, Quetta; and Centre for South Asian Studies, Punjab University, Lahore.

• *National Defence College*

National Defence College is a premier military institution of the Pakistan Armed Forces sponsoring degree-oriented professional training in defence and strategic studies, and war studies. The courses at

[34] Government of Pakistan, *White Paper on Higher Defence Organization*.

the National Defence College are reserved for the senior cadre of the three armed services, with a limited civilian attendance. The research output of the college, though restricted (not available for public consumption), is high quality literature on vital issues on security studies in Pakistan.

- *The Pakistan Institute of International Affairs*

This is the oldest research institute of Pakistan, established in August 1947, with the aim to facilitate understanding of issues in international affairs, and to promote analysis through research, seminars, and discussions. Its research output is published in the form of books, monographs, and periodicals. The Institute publishes its journal named *Pakistan Horizon* which deals with topics relating to politics, international affairs, economics and foreign policy. These topics are dealt from different perspectives and dimensions of international politics and security. The institute is an independent, non-political and non-profit think tank.

- *Institute of Strategic Studies, Islamabad*

The Institute of Strategic Studies (ISSI) established in 1972, is one of the important institutions, which is promoting broad-based and informed public debate on vital strategic issues affecting Pakistan and the international community as a whole. For the promotion of public understanding of strategic issues, a multi-disciplinary approach to strategy, peace and security is adhered. The institute initiates studies, discussions and analyses based on published and unpublished sources of information. It establishes and maintains liaison with other similar institutes and arranges seminars and conferences on strategy, peace and security. It also publishes a quarterly journal *Strategic Studies*, Islamabad papers, monographs, booklets and books covering a variety of subjects. Being relatively the oldest think tank in Islamabad, it plays an advisory role to various government departments, especially the Ministry of Foreign Affairs, on need basis.

- *Institute of Regional Studies, Islamabad*

The Institute of Regional Studies was established in 1982 with the aim to promote an understanding of the South Asian regional issues. The major focus of the Institute is foreign and internal affairs, economy, socio-cultural and security-related issues of states in South Asia, South

West Asia, Central Asia and Indian Ocean region. The Institute also assists other official and non-official establishments, agencies and institutions in carrying out studies and analyses of strategic issues. Moreover, the Institute analyses not only the external security problems but also those of internal security. Its publications include periodical and quarterly journals, monographs and books, etc.

Regional Perspective is a periodic study that deals with important regional issues in larger perspective involving Pakistan and its neighbouring states. *Regional Studies* is a quarterly journal of the Institute that focuses on regional, extra-regional and internal sources of insecurity using a multi-disciplinary approach. *Focus* and *Spotlight* are its periodic publications respectively, with focus on particular issues in one or more of regional countries. It also publishes *Selections from Regional Press*, comprising from regional newspapers and periodicals, which not only provides different perceptions about a particular development in the region but also helps scholars to analyze different issues. In addition, it publishes monographs and books on topical issues for wider dissemination.

- *Department of Defence and Strategic Studies*

The Department of Defence and Strategic Studies was established at the Quaid-i-Azam University, Islamabad in 1980 with a view to facilitate scholars to study the strategic studies as a professional discipline and thereby, create a think tank for the country. Its objective was to train analysts, authors and critics for providing expertise and policy-oriented inputs. At present it is offering M.Sc. and M.Phil. courses. It is providing theoretical as well as professional understanding of problems of peace and security. Besides teaching, the Department frequently arranges seminars on national and international topics of vital importance. It provides the students and teachers an exposure to the new developments in strategic studies and helps in creating an academic culture.

War is studied as a social and political phenomena, tracing a linkage between war and politics and analyzing its causation patterns vis-a-vis existing theories. For the better comprehension of international wars and politics, balance of power theories are discussed with reference to various case studies. Students are taught advance courses like theories of contemporary strategy, economics of defence and dynamics of foreign and defence policies in which theoretical basis of strategic planning and policy formulation are discussed. Besides, optional courses are available under three different categories (1) Area Studies (2) Conflict Studies (3) Military Science and Art. Different courses on six areas namely South Asia, West Asia Central Asia, Latin America, Africa and East Asia/Pacific are offered.

These courses focus on political, economic, geographic and psychological description of respective areas. Super powers' interests and policies in the respective areas are discussed to understand the linkage between the defence and foreign policies of regional states, and comprehend the ground realities of their strategic dynamics.

Some regional peculiarities are also studied, like the nuclearization of South Asia, and the kind of deterrent relationship between India and Pakistan, and its impact on regional and global political order. The dynamics of conflicts are studied through traditional and contemporary approaches. These include the study of revolutionary warfare, war and strategy in Islam, conduct of war and international law, nuclear proliferation, arms control and disarmament and crisis management. Revolutionary warfare, its techniques and tactics, and transformation from rural to urban warfare are analyzed.

Nuclear weapons have changed the nature of strategic studies altogether and giving a new look to strategic literature. Nuclear proliferation versus non-proliferation debate is emphasized from both the perspectives. New approaches to security, including arms control and disarmament, and crisis management along with their conceptual and theoretical base are highlighted as alternatives for resolving the core issues that were potentially destabilizing. These approaches are not only applicable to South Asia, but are also of greater importance to achieve crisis stability in the region. Such issues are being discussed with a view to create better understanding of Pakistan's geo-strategic realities, especially with the possession of nuclear weapons by both India and Pakistan.

The department has made a significant contribution by developing a community of experts equipped with academic and professional knowledge in strategic and security studies, and analytical ability to evaluate national, regional and international strategic environment.

• *FRIENDS, Rawalpindi*

The Foundation for Research on International Environment, National Development and Security (FRIENDS) was established in 1991 at Rawalpindi. The FRIENDS undertakes research on domestic, regional and global issues which promote the cause of peace and stability. It also undertakes various academic and field-oriented socio-economic developmental activities in collaboration with different national and international organizations. It undertakes research on both aspects of security, traditional and non-traditional. For example the Foundation is not only carrying out research on security through elimination of core conflicts, arms control and disarmament, but also on international environmental and ecological issues.

Besides being the associate of the United Nations' Department of Public Information (DPI), FRIENDS also works in close collaboration with number of academic institutions, NGOs and centres situated the world over. Since 1991, FRIENDS has arranged more than 85 national, regional and extra-regional seminars, discussions and colloquia on issues ranging from domestic politics to problems of international security. Its publications include a quarterly *National Development and Security*, a monthly *FRIENDS Perspective*, and has produced more than 25 books and monographs. Their quarterly journal '*National Development and Security*' includes research articles on subject relating to national development, security and international issues. The '*FRIENDS Perspective*' discusses topical issues of national, regional and international importance. Books published by FRIENDS are based either on proceedings of different seminars or authored by individual writers. Broadly, these books deal with issues pertaining to international affairs, regional, extra-regional opportunities for security, nuclear disarmament, elimination of weapons of mass destruction, control of conventional and light weapons.

- *Islamabad Policy Research Institute*

Islamabad Policy Research Institute has been recently established as an autonomous, non-profit and research-oriented advisory body with a grant from the Ministry of Information and Media Development (Government of Pakistan). It aims to carry out studies, discussions, research and analysis to promote informed understanding of the vital political, economic and strategic issues having a direct bearing on Pakistan. Additional objectives are to assist and guide official and non-official organizations in carrying out professional studies, and establish liaison with similar institutions at the national and international level for exchange of views.

- *Institute for Policy Studies*

Institute for Policy Studies was established in 1979 as autonomous research organization with the objective to stimulate policy debate on a variety of national and international issues. It specially focuses on Pakistan's policy with reference to South, Central and West Asia, and the Muslim World. Though not formally affiliated, the institute has inclinations towards the Jamat-e-Islami of Pakistan.

- *Individual inputs*

There are few scholarly contributions on security studies in Pakistan. Aslam Siddique's very valuable contribution, *Pakistan Seeks Security*, is not only out-dated but perhaps out of publication as well. A wide gap follows. Pervaiz Iqbal Cheema, a professor of International Relations at Quaid-i-Azam University Islamabad, has succinctly analyzed Pakistan's defence policy issues and behaviour. He has also contributed in *Brasstacks and Beyond: Perception and Management of crisis in South Asia* along with Kanti Bajpai, P.R. Chari, Stephen Cohen and Sumit Ganguly. This work mainly deals with crisis management during Brasstacks crisis of 1986-7 in both theoretical and practical perspectives. Dr. Hasan Askari Rizvi, Professor of Political Science, Punjab University, Lahore, has made valuable contribution in the field of civil-military relations in Pakistan. General (Retd.) Mirza Aslam Beg is another important security analyst whose main interest lies on development and security at national, regional and global level. Maleeha Lodhi, Rasul Bakhsh Rais, Tanvir Ahmad Khan and Syed Rifaat Hussain have also made useful contributions.

Newspapers in Pakistan have recently generated a high quality debate on national security issues, especially *The Dawn*, *The News*, and *The Nation*. However, notwithstanding the bright analyses they offer, most of the inputs are shortsighted in its very nature because its written to meet deadlines, even if the events discussed have never fully unfolded. Daily journalism is just a first draft of history, which has to be revised many times over once the full length of truth comes to light. Unfortunately, the journalistic tradition in Pakistan does not refer to meticulously researched and dispassionate studies after the events have fully unfolded, but restricts itself to just the daily accounts.

FUTURE DIRECTION OF SECURITY STUDIES

The May 1998 nuclear explosions by India and Pakistan have profoundly changed the nature of security in South Asia. The non-weaponized deterrence between India and Pakistan, which existed for more than a decade, has been irrevocably transformed into weaponized deterrence. In the aftermath of nuclear explosions, new dynamics have been unleashed with unpredictable consequences for peace and security in the South Asian region. The atomic explosions has initiated a new debate, that whether India and Pakistan would be able to live in peace with nuclear weapons and would nuclear weapons provide the requisite security and stability?

The issue is divisive of course, with both nuclear lobbies, pro and anti-bomb, projecting their own viewpoints. Apparently, nuclear deterrence seems to have decreased the chances of conventional war in South Asia. This line of argument has been undertaken by many South Asian and Western scholars. Devin Haggerty, for example, suggests:

> the two countries continue to feel their unusual assortment of imperatives towards conflict like insurgency in Kashmir, but nuclear weapons capability introduces a new set of incentives to cooperate.
>
> Among these is the desire to avoid mutual devastation, the fear of escalation is thus, factored into political calculations: faced with this risk, states are more cautious and prudent than otherwise they would be.[35]

Some Indian analysts have also viewed this dimension in a similar way. The most prominent pronouncement was made by General K. Sunderji, when he was asked whether India and Pakistan would have refrained from three wars they fought in 1948, 1965 and 1971, had both of them possessed minimum nuclear deterrence. Sunderji categorically stated: 'These wars would not have occurred'.[36] He went on to add: 'If Bangladesh had to come about, it would have come about by other means and not by Indian military intervention'.[37]

The opponents of nuclear weapons argue that both India and Pakistan are infant nuclear powers without a comprehensive system of command, control and communications. Peter D. Feaver argues that arms race's future direction is dangerous as well as costly.[38] A nuclear command and control is a necessity as the system can be prone to accidental or unauthorized use. A system optimized against accidental or unauthorized use however runs the risk of not being readily available for authorized use, especially after a surprise attack. This is a

[35] Afzal Mahmood, 'After the Nuclear stand-off', *Dawn* (Karachi), 12 June 1998.

[36] Ibid.

[37] Ibid.

[38] Peter D. Feaver, 'South Asian Nuclear Stand-Off: What people should really worry about?' *Dawn* (Karachi), 10 June 1998.

dilemma: Making sure nuclear weapons are ready for use when needed but do not detonate accidentally or by any unauthorized person.[39]

During 50 years of cold war experiment, the US and the former Soviet Union adopted technical fixes like coded locks buried inside the warheads, and administrative measures like the two men rule. These steps went far to reduce the nuclear security problems. India and Pakistan have proven that they have the ability to detonate nuclear device, but they are neophytes when it comes to nuclear security.[40]

For India-Pakistan analysts, the relationship between Moscow and Beijing in the 1970s can be a role model for future Islamabad-Delhi relationship. The former USSR and China refrained from war because of their nuclear capabilities. The former USSR had overwhelming nuclear superiority over China, but it avoided an attack on China due to the fear of retaliation.[41] There is an urgent need for both India and Pakistan to have direct and reliable dialogue to avoid any miscalculations. The institution of nuclear-related security and confidence-building measures would go a long way to ensure strategic stability.

[39] Ibid.

[40] Ibid.

[41] Zafar Nawaz Jaspal, 'Matching response was inevitable', *The Scenario* (Islamabad, June 1998), pp. 24-5.

Post-Cold War Security Studies in Pakistan: Continuity and Change

RASUL BAKHSH RAIS

The traditional paradigm of security studies that is premised on external military threats, is not capable of fully explaining the national security problems of post-colonial Third World states, like Pakistan. The threats it faces are more complex, varied in character, and emanate from diverse sources, which are external as well as internal. There are a number of domestic issues pertaining to the process of state-formation and nation-building that fall within the category of threats to national security, as they increase vulnerability of the state and its vital institutions to fatal decay and disintegration.

Therefore, as an argument, in the case of late developers, national security analysis must use broader canvas to cover the whole range of issues and threats, and not just the security of the borders. The disintegration of the Soviet Union has raised the possibility that nation states can collapse from within. Also, the phenomenon of failed and failing states, which is more due to bad governance than any external threat, compel us to explore new approaches to comprehending national security problems of Third World regions.

The discourse on security in Pakistan has still to break free from its conventional mind-set. The field remains dominated by state-centric geopolitical conceptions of threats focusing on essentially military responses to challenges on the borders, primarily from India. Academic scholarship and defence policy analyses continue to ignore 'new thinking' about national security issues with very few exceptions.[1] It

[1] Saba Gul Khatak, 'Security Discourses and the State in Pakistan', *Alternatives* 21 (1996), pp. 341-62; Rasul Bakhsh Rais, 'Security, State, and Democracy in Pakistan', in Marvin G. Weinbaum and Chetan Kumar, *South Asia Approaches the Millennium: Re-examining National Security* (Boulder: Westview Press, 1995), pp. 63-78.

would be necessary to examine the factors that have prevented a re-examination of security from a holistic perspective. The perceptions of Indian threat that are held, both at the popular as well as elite levels, have to a great extent contributed to the military dominant view of national security policy.

Although these perceptions have undergone a change over the past 50 years from reversing partition of the British Empire to establishing a hegemonic security regime in the region, India continues to occupy central position in the security calculations of Pakistan.[2] The memories of communal conflict before and after the partition set the two peoples and states on a confrontational path that led to three wars. The bitter legacy of these wars further strengthened antagonism between the two countries. The unresolved, and potentially explosive territorial question of Kashmir, the dominant posturing of India and the agenda of the right wing Hindu leaders may continue to sustain traditional views of national security in Pakistan.[3]

Redefining National Security

The significant changes in the world power relations following the end of the cold war have generated a fresh debate about conceptualizing security. The debate is essentially between the traditionalists and

[2] Agha Shahi, *Pakistan's Security and Foreign Policy* (Lahore: Progressive Publishers, 1988); Noor A. Hussain, 'India's Regional Policy: Strategic and Security Dimensions,' in Stephen Philip Cohen, *The Security of South Asia* (Urbana and Chicago: University of Illinois Press, 1987), pp. 24-49; Hasan-Askari Rizvi, *Pakistan and the Geostrategic Environment* (New York: St. Martin's Press, 1993); S.M. Burke and Lawrence Ziring, *Pakistan's Foreign Policy: An Historical Analysis* (Karachi: Oxford University Press, 1990); G.W. Choudhury, *Pakistan's Relations with India, 1947-66* (London: Pall Mall Press, 1968).

[3] Aslam Siddiqi, *Pakistan Seeks Security* (Lahore: Longmans, Green, Pakistan Branch, 1960); Pervaiz Iqbal Cheema, *Pakistan's Defence Policy, 1954-58* (Basingstoke: Macmillan, 1990); Rais Ahmad Khan, Rasul B. Rais and Khalid Waheed, eds., *South Asia: Military Power and Regional Politics* (Islamabad: Islamabad Council of World Affairs, 1989); K. Subrahmanyam, *Indian Security Perspectives* (New Delhi: ABC Pub. House, 1982); K. Subrahmanyam, 'India's Security Challenges and Responses: Evolving a Security Doctrine', *Strategic Analysis*, Vol. 11, No. 1 (April 1987), pp. 6-15; Mohammed Ayoob, 'India in South Asia: The Quest for Regional Predominance', *World Policy Journal*, Vol. 7, No. 1 (Winter 1989-90), pp. 107-33; Mohammed Ayoob, 'India as regional hegemony: External Opportunities and Internal Constraints', *International Journal*, Vol. 66 (Summer 1991), pp. 420-48; Bharat K. Wariavwalla, 'Security with Status: What Motivates India's

their challengers who offer a more inclusive definition of security. Both the new and old schools of thought on security studies, have different theories of state, society and individuals and their interactive relationships.

The traditionalists have strong roots in political realism and its variant of neo-realism. They explain security dilemma exclusively in terms of an anarchical world that the nation states have formed. The power structure that the anarchy has imposed compels each state to seek survival through acquiring and maintaining reasonable degree of military capabilities.[4] Security, therefore, would depend largely on how successful a state is in defending itself against a potential aggressor.

The traditionalists view relations among states as coercive, because they involve threat or use of force to achieve political objectives. In the competing world of sovereign states, notions like distribution of capabilities, balance of power, equilibrium and deterrence play a key role in the management of security. In the classical security studies, the state is the primary level of analysis and a unitary actor, threats are external, mainly from other states; and, the means to defend against them are essentially military in nature.[5]

This 'narrow' view of security has come under increasing attack after the fall of communism and disintegration of the Soviet Union. Edward Kolodziej has argued that security studies cannot be confined to issues of military threats and force structures. All those societal, economic and political factors, that support and sustain military capabilities, have to be brought into focus. In his view, the disintegration of the Soviet Union resulted more from economic and techno-scientific underdevelopment than from the erosion of military power. The military strength of the West didn't play a direct role except pushing the Soviet Union to an unaffordable level of arms race, which

---

Security Policy', in W. Thomas Wander and Eric H. Arnett (eds.), *The Proliferation of Advanced Weaponry: Technology, Motivation, and Responses* (Washington, D.C.: AAAS, 1992); Douglas C. Makeig, 'War, No-war and the Indo-Pakistan Negotiating Process', *Pacific Affairs*, Vol. 60, No. 2 (Summer 1987), pp. 271-94

[4] Edward A. Kolodziej, 'Wither Security Studies After the Cold War?', in Kanti P. Bajpai and Stephen P. Cohen (eds.), *South Asia After the Cold War: International Perspectives* (Boulder: Westview Press, 1993), p. 16.

[5] Colin S. Gray, 'New Directions for Strategic Studies: How Can Theory Help Practice'? *Security Studies*, Vol. 1, No. 4, 1994, pp. 610-35; 'Global Security and Economic Wellbeing: A Strategic Perspective', *Political Studies*, Vol. 42, No. 1, 1994, pp. 25-39; John Chipman, 'The Future of Strategic Studies Beyond Grand Strategy', *Survival*, Vol. 34, No. 1, 1992, pp. 109-31.

its weak domestic political and economic institutions could not sustain.[6]

What is important to learn from the collapse of the Soviet security structure is that military power is necessary but not sufficient to maintain a legitimate security system. Economic and political measures, a responsive state apparatus with roots in the civil society and satisfaction of societal demands, are no less important in ensuring stability at home and supporting a condition of deterrence against external foes.

The new thinking on security represents an inclusive approach. It has brought into discourse concepts like 'common security' and 'human security'. What Barry Buzan, et al. call 'wideners' conceptualize security in an extended sense. Their definition of security includes security of individuals, groups, and international system. Horizontally, they extend the conception of security to political, economic, social and environmental issues.[7] The new meanings and understanding of security rests on the philosophical ideas of liberalism of the late eighteenth century.[8] The cold war politics, bipolar structure of power, military alliances and confrontation between the two superpowers had overshadowed liberal principles by giving prominence to state-centric geopolitical thinking of security.

The classical political liberalism of the last century, placed rights and sovereignty of the individual above all other considerations. The theory of natural rights of man, supported the view that state couldn't violate them under any pretext. The contractual nature of civil society and a system of governance based on consent, further institutionalized individual rights that the state had primary responsibility to protect and expand. The international liberalism of the post-cold war period has re-focused on the individual as a subject of international politics, by pulling him from the periphery to the centre of an emerging international civil society.

However, the security of the individuals or communities that are members of the civil society, cannot be discussed as a separate category from the state itself.[9]

A state, in order to legitimize authority, must ensure protection to the individuals and groups against threats of physical injury, economic

[6] Kolodziej, p. 23.

[7] Barry Buzan, Ole Waever and Jaap de Wilde, Security: *A New Framework for Analysis* (Boulder: Lynne Rienner Publishers, 1998), pp. 2-5.

[8] Emma Rothschild, 'What is Security?', p. 54.

[9] Kolodoziej, p. 35.

deprivation, violation of fundamental rights, social rank and status.[10] Against the traditionalist view of security that focuses only on war and military force,[11] Barry Buzan et al. argue that non-military threats and issues, if they become sufficiently securitized, can be legitimate subjects of security.[12] They define securitization as an extreme form of politicization when 'an issue is presented as an existential threat, requiring emergency measures and justifying action outside the normal bounds of political procedure'.[13] Securitization of an issue can take place within the formal institutions of the state or in the civil society.

However, before an issue becomes securitized it must be accepted as a plausible threat to the vital interests of the society; and it must become the subject of public debate and state action. In this scheme, any issue can qualify as the subject of security, if it is seen posing 'an existential threat with a saliency sufficient to have substantial political effects'.[14] Keeping in view the new dimensions of threat that may securitize an issue, Buzan et al. extend the security studies agenda beyond the military to environmental, economic, societal and political sectors.

The traditionalists reject such an inclusive definition of security on the grounds that, bringing a dizzying array of issues into the debate, will render the concept of security meaningless. Conceptualization of security beyond the military threats, use of force or strategic doctrines of defence and deterrence would make it stretched and incoherent to be applied as a useful tool of analysis. Although the inclusivists take such a critique seriously, they insist that not all issues would fall within the parameters of security. Nor will the quality of threat presented by each issue be the same or demand equal attention.

They try to resolve the problems of incoherence and elasticity by disaggregating security into five sectors, i.e. military, environmental, economic, societal and political, and by establishing rigorous criteria of securitization.[15] Mohammed Ayoob, though himself a neo-realist,

[10] Barry Buzan, *Peoples, States, and Fear* (Boulder: Lynne Rienner, 1991, revd.), pp. 18-35.

[11] Stephen M. Walt, 'The Renaissance of Security Studies', *International Studies Quarterly*, Vol. 35, No. 2, 1991, pp. 211-39.

[12] Barry Buzan et al., *Security: A New Framework for Analysis*, p. 4.

[13] Ibid., pp. 23-4.

[14] Ibid., p. 25.

[15] Buzan et al., op. cit.

addresses the question of elasticity by suggesting the primacy of politics. In his analysis, issues of identity, politics of group conflict, and state and nation-building processes, define the security dilemma of Third World countries.[16] Further details on this subject will be explored later in this article.

The security predicament of Third World countries, like Pakistan, is much more complex than the traditional concept of security can explain. External threat perceptions must be attended to, but an exclusive focus on territorial dimension of security would obscure more varied threats emanating from internal contestations of power, identity, legitimacy and other forms of conflicts.[17]

Secondly, in a politically less integrated society, that Pakistan is, security as a concept and policy evokes different images and reactions from different sections, such as, ethnic groups, political institutions and the military elite, within the state. In the transformative phase of the post-cold war era, when the notions of security are undergoing radical redefinition, these elements can no longer be ignored in understanding the security predicament of post-colonial states.

The Western paradigm of security that has been cast by the experiences of democratic, industrialized nation-states, which are 'internally pacified',[18] does not gel with the peculiarities of South Asian countries. Moreover, the historical process of state formation, central features of the state, underdevelopment of political institutions, and the essential relationship between the state and society is at variance in the developing world.

[16] Mohammed Ayoob, *The Third World Security Predicament: State Making, Regional Conflict and the International System* (Boulder: Lynne Rienner, 1995).

[17] Brian L. Job, ed., *The Insecurity Dilemma: National Security of Third World States* (Boulder and London: Lynne Rienner Publisher, 1992); Ken Booth (ed.), *New Thinking About Strategy and International Security* (London: Harper Collins Academic, 1991); Edward E. Azar and Chung-in Moon (eds.), *National Security in the Third World: The Management of Internal and External Threat* (College Park, Md.: Center for International Development and Conflict Management, University of Maryland, 1988); Nicole Ball, *Security and Economy in the Third World* (Princeton: Princeton University Press, 1988); Caroline Thomas, *In Search of Security: The Third World in International Relations* (Boulder: Lynne Rienner, 1987); Barry Buzan, *People, States and Fear: The National Security Problem in International Relations* (Brighton: Wheatsheaf, 1983).

[18] Anthony Gidden, *The Nation State and Violence* (Berkeley: University of California Press, 1987), pp. 3-4.

The primary difference is that the Western states have achieved a satisfactory level of political integration. They have developed a system of governance based on representative legitimacy, and popular participation. This has enabled them to resolve or significantly reduce the potential of internal threats to the state and its institutions. Therefore, whatever be the ideological inclinations of an elected regime in a western democracy, it may not face the problems of legitimacy, mass agitation or revolutionary upheaval.

Contrarily, the internal aspects of security cannot be excluded from any meaningful analysis of national security of Third World states, where the imperatives of state-building quite often come in conflict with the popular aspirations for political representation or regional autonomy demands of diverse ethnic groups.[19] It is believed that institutions based on consensus, political participation, citizenship rights and consent of the governed determine the degree to which a state can be 'weak' or 'strong',[20] and not on the coercive means available to a particular regime.

Therefore, in this analysis, the issue of democratic development or the broader questions of national integration, and human rights, can't be divorced from the holistic perspective of national security that must involve both the territorial defence as well as the larger issues of societal security.

However, the military dimension remains crucial because failure to defend the physical base of the state, domestic political institutions or an elected regime, would wipe out the political and societal elements of security. However, raising of a territorial security apparatus, even in conventional sense, must be based on consent and not on coercion, because such an enterprise requires valuable economic resources that

[19] Mohammed Ayoob, 'The Security Problematic of the Third World', *World Politics*, Vol. 43 (January 1991), pp. 265-73.

[20] Caroline Thomas explains state strength and weakness in terms of institutional capacities, which she differentiates as despotic-arbitrary, and infrastructural effectively exercised through the institutions. Caroline Thomas, 'Southern Instability, Security and Western Concepts: On an Unhappy Marriage and the Need for a Divorce', in *The State and Instability in the South*, edited by Caroline Thomas and Paikiasothy Saravanamuttu (New York: St. Martin's Press, 1989), pp. 182-8; Michael Mann identifies infrastructural power with the ability of the state to implement its decisions and 'penetrate civil society'. Mann, 'The Autonomous Power of the State: Its Origins, Mechanisms and Results', in Job A. Hall (ed.), *States in History* (Oxford: Basil Blackwell, 1986), p. 113.

other sections of the society must make available, postponing their welfare. While, heavy investment in the military might, run the risk of tilting the institutional balance against the political forces, where the supremacy of civilian institutions has yet to be established.

In Pakistan, progress on essential issues, like sharing of political power, forming a representative authority structure, and obtaining political consensus, has been frequently stalled by military's intervention in politics. The military regimes rule through outright repression or by forming narrow-based oligarchies of powerful elite. Such authoritarian recourse to state formation and structuring of political order has perpetuated societal fragmentation, which exposes the state to a variety of ethnic and communal or sectarian strife, and foreign intervention.

On the other hand, institutionalization of democratic politics, popular participation and wider representation of all groups in political power would significantly enhance capacity of the state to mediate internal conflicts. Strong centralized or hegemonic state apparatus offers no viable option for welding together the ethnically diverse and socially incohesive peoples into a nation.

The demise of the Soviet Union is a classical case of preponderant military power disintegrating from within. Therefore, the national security analysis of Pakistan must focus on the issues of democratic development, nation-building and internal threat conditions, and place at the centre of future security agenda of Pakistan.

Focus of Security Studies

An overview of writings and research on Pakistan's security published during the past eight years would show that the field continues to be dominated by the traditionalist perspectives.[21] Here, it would be prudent to explain in detail what is the substance of security studies, and what are the important elements that have not found any meaningful expression. In this critique of the major themes of security studies, one would raise the question of their relevance to Pakistan's security dilemma and attempt to explain why they remain the focus of security debate in the country.

[21] Much of the debate can be seen in the following publications: *Pakistan Defence Journal, Strategic Studies, Journal of Regional Studies, Pakistan Horizon*, and *Strategic Perspectives*.

• *Territorial dimension*

The security studies in Pakistan mainly focus on the defence of the territory against an external threat, which requires essentially military means to deter. Such a formulation of security dilemma contains all the elements of realist perspective on international security. The phenomenon of war, structure of military forces, threat and use of force central of this kind of analysis, have been accepted uncritically as the sole and legitimate focus of security studies by the Pakistani analysts. It is understandable that a country in the geopolitical situation of Pakistan and with a troubled legacy of conflict with India, would not overlook the external elements of threat. That also explains why most of the Pakistanis look at interstate relations as coercive, force-oriented, differentiating states in terms of enemies and friends.

However, excessive preoccupation with external threats in the complex security environment of Pakistan, not only overlooks other important dimensions of security, but also the threats emanating from a variety of domestic sources. At best, the traditionalists by dealing only with the territorial aspect focus on a part or fragment of a much wider security problem.[22]

There are two reasons why the Pakistani security experts give too much attention to the territorial defence of the state, ignoring other threats that may erode the structure of the state from within. First, the transfer of social science knowledge and its methodology to the colonial territories, then established a pattern of imitation in all disciplines, including security studies. This made the local knowledge in social sciences flawed, as the Western methodologies and epistemology that was applied was not attuned to address the local social realities

The field of security studies has an imprint of Western paradigm on it because of technological factors, teaching of military history and contemporary doctrines of warfare. For instance, a cursory look at the curricula of international relations, defence and strategic studies in Pakistani universities would show that, the imitator model is deeply ingrained.[23] Therefore, the latent biases in thinking, writing, research

[22] Agha Shahi, *Pakistan Security and Foreign Policy* (Lahore: Progressive Publishers, 1998); Zulfiqar Ali Khan, *Pakistan's Security: The Challenge and the Response* (Lahore: Progressive Publishers, 1988).

[23] Shireen M. Mazari and Ayaz Naseem, 'The Development of Defence and Strategic Studies as a Social Science Discipline in Pakistan', in S.H. Hashmi, *The State of Social Sciences in Pakistan* (Islamabad: Quaid-i-Azam University, 1989), pp. 219-28.

and teaching in security studies prevent the traditionalists from looking at complex internal conflict situations, like ethnicity, sectarianism, and religious and ethnic terrorism.

Secondly, the conception of the state in Pakistan was taken as a complete event that occurred in 1947 with the partition of British India. At once, the event transformed it into an entity, a regional actor with an international personality in the juridical sense. But in political sense, state in Pakistan as in other parts of South Asia must be seen more as a process than a finished product.

The process of state-making is difficult; strength and might involve frequent use of force to overcome resistance from the internal 'enemies' of the state. In establishing a link between state-making and the use of force, one's imagination becomes colored by the experience of the Western state in its early form. While looking at the contemporary nation state in the West, one forgets that it went through internal conflicts over issues of group identity, political power and territorial dominance in order to achieve national consolidation. In the formative years, a vast number of rival nationalities were amalgamated into larger nations by force.

The process of state formation was violent as the military means of settling disputes, acquiring power and redefining nationhood were widely practised and accepted then. The intrusive international system that is now known at the end of the second millennia, with such a density of interactions and ideas of international civil society, didn't exist at that point. It was only after the peace of Westphalia in 1648, that they established a degree of mutual recognition as states and the idea of inviolable nationhood based on coerced or real homogeneity of language, culture and ethnicity began to take roots. Therefore, the question is, how the national security model of post-consolidated nation states, can be applicable to post-colonial state nations that have to address the issues of national integration or nation-building in a different international setting.

Pakistani academics as well as policy practitioners in the field, have blindly followed the precepts of Western security paradigm without paying any attention to the peculiarities of the Pakistani state, its internal components and the politics of power and identity. The history of conflict with India, the centrality of the Kashmir dispute to their confrontation and military deployment patterns suggest that security of the borders and external challenges can not, and should not be ignored. But such a narrow conception of security and exclusive approach may only partially explain the security dilemma of the country. Internal dynamics of security that pertain to ethnicity, sectarianism, and the larger issues of insufficient state capacity are no less important in fully comprehending the security problems of Pakistan.

- *Military orientation*

Here, two issues come to fore. First, the neglect of societal and political aspects of security, and second the dominant role of the retired military officers and diplomats in shaping the security discourse in Pakistan. What is meant by societal and political factors and how they influence national security is best explained by Mohammed Ayoob, in one of his recent works on security, convincingly argues that the security problem of Third World countries is rooted primarily in the politics of identity, legitimacy and nation-building.[24] Pakistan is a transitional polity, where growth of democratic civic culture has been relatively slow and still remains below the threshold level of genuine participatory democracy.[25] Ideas of constitutional government, democracy, participatory politics, and popular sovereignty have been introduced since the colonial times, and they figure prominently in public discourse on politics. But these ideas and democratic practices have yet to be fully institutionalized, and a pattern of peaceful transfer of power through periodic elections has yet to be established.

Also, the question of subordinating the military and civil bureaucracy to the elected representatives remains undefined and unsettled. Therefore, military is not just another institution of the state that carries out a defence strategy formulated by the various departments of the government after deliberations. Its views, particularly on national security, are rather not only heard, but also fully respected. It is also pertinent to mention that on three fundamental issues of security, i.e. Indian threat, Kashmir dispute, and nuclear status, there is a sort of national consensus in Pakistan.

However, consensus in countries like Pakistan is not entirely the function of interaction among a large number of institutions and groups, but reflect a tacit understanding among the oligarchy. Therefore, claims of having achieved consensus on any issue may be superficial at

[24] Ayoob, *The Third World Security Predicament.*

[25] Rasul Bakhsh Rais, *State, Society and Democratic Change in Pakistan* (Karachi: Oxford University Press, 1997).

best, because of the lack of grass-root social support and inadequate political channels of articulating alternative visions. Silence may not be considered a measure of support to an officially dominant view.

The security problem both in military and extended sense concerns the entire population, and therefore, can't be left only to the oligarchy. In mature democratic polities, non-military, academic and policy-oriented independent think tanks and forums dominate security discourse. Most of the institutions that study and debate security issues in Pakistan are headed by retired military officers or diplomats.[26] This is true of government-funded institutions as well as those established privately.

The publication of journals, organizing seminars, conferences, lectures, and bringing out research reports, are important means of shaping the security debate. Many prominent retired military officers and diplomats also contribute regular columns to the English language dailies. Because of official patronage and due to the false notion that only soldiers can understand the security problems of a country, the debate on security has often been one-sided. The retired ambassadors, military generals and brigadiers are not sufficiently exposed to the debates in different social sciences or trained in the academic tradition. They are not flexible enough to come out of the uni-dimensional approach to security.

There are voices of dissent in Pakistan that have begun to question the rationale of too much concern with military security and its fundamental assumptions,[27] but they are few, disorganized, and equally uni-dimensional in their approach to national security. They take a totally opposite view of military security and swing too far on the side of human security. Their views are based on untutored variants of liberal political thinking. The problem is that independent, civil society-based institutions have not developed in the country.

It is only recently that some non-governmental organisations funded by the Western countries have begun to challenge the military domi-

[26] For decades, two of the more known institutions, Institute of Strategic Studies and Institute of Regional Studies have been headed by the retired military officers or diplomats. Private, non-governmental type institutions—Islamabad Council of World Affairs, FRIENDS, PASDA—are also headed by former diplomats and military generals.

[27] Late Dr. Mahbub ul-Haq founded the Centre for Human Development and started publishing an excellent report on human development in South Asia. He popularized the discourse on tension between development and military security.

nant view of national security.[28] Even being in their initial stage of development, they have made important contribution to the security discourse by introducing social development, human rights and women, and environmental issues to the debate. But unfortunately, the NGOs themselves have a 'hidden interest', like the military's, in promoting their own vision of national security. This involves allocation of greater resources to their causes and advancement of careers.[29] This new phenomenon is essentially a part of the international civil society project of the liberal internationalists, and fits well into the ideology of the new world order.

In Pakistan, the Western-sponsored NGOs face problems of credibility, as they largely transfer the biases of the donor agencies and countries. Thus, they are vulnerable to the images of Western 'outposts', which their opponents, particularly from the right political spectrum unfairly affix on them. Also, the alternative views of national security that are being promoted by the NGO networks have a limited audience. Historically, nowhere in the world has this sector of the society produced any scholarship that could match the quality and rigor of the academy. The NGOs that are organized and oriented to help civil society institutions or evolve models of appropriate development, are poor substitute for the academic institutions.

Therefore, the major responsibility lies with the academia. The members of the academic community with specialization in the security studies could, perhaps, play a greater role in influencing the security discourse than they have done so far because of their weak institutional and intellectual base. A critical re-examination of the national security problem in its wider sense by the academia, more focused research and analysis on societal and political factors that impinge on security, and the flourishing of independent policy-oriented institutions may help balance the old debate.

- *State-centric*

The security studies in Pakistan emulating the Western patterns are centred on the security of the state that is threatened by another state, India. Placing the state, or nation, higher than any other actor or

[28] Shahrukh Rafi Khan, 'Five reasons for restraint', *The News* (Rawalpindi), 23 May 1998; Anees Jillani, 'Avoiding a ruinous path', *The News*, 22 May 1998.

[29] Rothschild, op. cit., p. 80.

entity in Pakistan is, therefore, not different from other countries. In Third World regions, role of the state in society and in an individual's life, is much greater than in the Western democracies where the role of the state in public life has somewhat diminished.

Even in the West, the state continues to remain a primary unit of analysis in the literature on security and international politics. Although references to human and environmental security are becoming more frequent in the post-cold war period, no paradigmatic shift is visible in the mainstream thinking. The only change that has occurred is in the areas of defence spending, reciprocal arms reduction and reformulation of threat. This is more a reflection of a new relationship between Russia and the West, than a radical departure from the traditional thinking on security issues.

The state-centric model postulates that the system of sovereign, self-governing states places a high premium on state capabilities, in order to pursue self-defined national interests, and influence external security environment in its favour. The issue of state capabilities is, however, debatable. Accumulation of coercive power in relation to a perceived external adversary doesn't explain the larger issue of state capabilities. In the words of Azar and Moon, these types of capabilities fall in the category of 'hardware'.

Any analysis of state capabilities in the Third World, as elsewhere, must focus on 'software' issues. By this, they mean three things, i.e. legitimacy, integration and policy capacity.[30] In a similar vein, Ayoob does not divorce the issue of national capabilities from political capacity and institutional coherence. He argues that 'primitive accumulation of power' and use of coercion for nation-building would be counter-productive in the Third World.[31]

One must be sensitive to the compulsions of pushing this process and to the need to complete the nation-building project in the shortest possible time-frame; but there are risks that the national state could turn out to be an oppressor and violator of fundamental rights. As is evident from the number of internal conflicts in the region, national state can be a threat to the lives, interests and rights of the individuals.

[30] Edward E. Azar and Chung-in Moon, 'Legitimacy, Integration and Policy Capacity: The 'Software' Side of Third World National Security', in Edward E. Azar and Chung-in Moon (eds.), *National Security in the Third World: The Management of Internal and External Threats* (College Park: University of Maryland, Center for International Development and Conflict Management, 1988), pp. 77-101.

[31] Ayoob, *The Third World Security Predicament*, op. cit., pp. 21-2.

Therefore, the larger issue of national security in Pakistan and other Third World countries, must bring into focus the problems of state-society relations, quality of the stateness and various patterns of interactions between individuals, groups and the political authority.

• *Indian threat*

India constitutes the central theme of security studies in Pakistan. Almost all studies on defence and foreign policy of Pakistan argue that India poses a major threat to national security. Why India is at the centre of Pakistani threat perceptions is not hard to understand, as some factors have already been alluded in the beginning. Explanations of hostility between the two countries is at variance in the literature. Among these, four need to be mentioned here.

First, India, it is asserted, did not accept the partitioning of British India in good faith. It tried to cripple Pakistan before it could consolidate its statehood by denying canal waters for irrigation, refusing to hand over Pakistani share of the military hardware and currency reserves.[32] In the writing of national histories, both the countries have cultivated negative images of each other. Unquestionably, India is depicted as an adversary that has a hidden agenda of destroying Pakistan, or at least, weakening it to the extent that it would submit to the Indian hegemony in the region.

Second, the Kashmir dispute figures prominently in the Pakistani security perspectives. It is presented as a concrete evidence of Indian bad faith. According to Pakistani versions of the problem, accession of the state to India is in dispute that can only be resolved through a plebiscite under the United Nations resolutions.[33] It is widely acknowledged that the Kashmir dispute has been a catalyst of confrontation between the two countries and a source of friction and conflict for about half a century. The security studies in Pakistan present Kashmir as a core issue and an unresolved problem of the partition of the subcontinent.[34] It is asserted that without resolving this dispute, no progress

[32] Pervaiz Iqbal Cheema, *Pakistan's Defence Policy, 1947-58* (Houndmills: Macmillan Press, 1990).

[33] Suroosh Irfani (ed.), *Fifty Years of the Kashmir Dispute* (Muzaffarabad: University of Azad Jammu and Kashmir, 1997).

[34] Ibid.

can be made in improving relations with India, including liberalization of bilateral trade.[35]

Third, there is a bitter legacy of three wars, 1948, 1965, and 1971. The last war that resulted from Indian military intervention in former East Pakistan, now Bangladesh, reconfirmed Pakistani fears about Indian intentions of reshaping the geopolitical map of South Asia. The humiliating defeat and surrender of the Pakistani forces had a profound effect on the strategic thinking in Pakistan. Civil and military leaders of Pakistan reached three definite conclusions that have defined security policy of the country since then: That Pakistan could not rely on Western 'allies' to defend itself; that the international system was too weak to defend a small state against the aggression of a major regional power; that Pakistan had to take a nuclear route to security against India. Both the prognoses of the security dilemma and its remedy became firmly grounded in the old-fashioned geopolitical thinking.

Fourth, the history of conflicts between the two countries has generated its own dynamics both in domestic politics, as well as in foreign and defence policies. India as a major factor in Pakistani security calculations, is heavily politicized, that complicates any meaningful process of rapprochement. Right wing groups with religious orientation in both the countries have acquired street power and threaten the ruling coalitions of dire consequences, if they dared compromise well-established positions on the Kashmir issue.

Bitterness of the past has laid up so many field-mines that can derail all sincere efforts in restoring normalcy in India-Pakistan relationship. One such problem is covert warfare, in which both the countries are engaged against each other. India is alleged to be operating a large network of subversion, sabotage and state terrorism, something that India also blames Pakistan for. This is symptomatic of deep hostility, fear and hatred that have persisted well over half a century.

- *Nuclear equation*

Among the politicians, Z.A. Bhutto was the first to articulate the issue of nuclear deterrence in 1968 in his book, *Myth of Independence*. He argued that India, with its nuclear edge, would blackmail Pakistan if it

[35] Tahir Amin, *Mass Resistance in Kashmir: Origins, Evolution and Options* (Islamabad: Institute of Policy Studies, 1995).

restricted or suspended its own nuclear programme.[36] The underlying assumption was that Pakistan's nuclear capability would off-set the several critical advantages in conventional forces that India had over Pakistan. In his passionate pursuit of the bomb, he disregarded the financial and technical difficulties in acquiring nuclear capability for the country. He remarked 'Pakistanis will eat the grass but make the bomb'.[37] When he took over power in December 1971, within two months, he launched the nuclear programme.

National security against India and an ambition to build Pakistan as an important regional player in the Muslim world motivated Bhutto to seek a nuclear deterrence.[38] All other successive regimes, both military and civilian, have continued developing and expanding various elements of nuclear power capability.

Writings and research on the nuclear question have focused on five aspects—discriminatory character of non-proliferation regime; supplementing of conventional inferiority with nuclear capability; minimal deterrence; parity with India, and regional power status. Pakistani writers on the subject have questioned the credibility of non-proliferation regime. They consider its constituent elements, NPT, CTBT as discriminatory and monopolistic. It is asserted that the non-proliferation regime did not prevent Israel or India from acquiring nuclear capability.

In the case of Israel, much of the materials and technological know-how was transferred from France and the US. Most of the writings support the official view that Pakistan should not sign these treaties until India has done so. But the position on signing the CTBT seems to be changing in the wake of American-sponsored sanctions, both against India and Pakistan. Pakistan has announced that it would sign the CTBT next year after sanctions have been lifted.[39]

One of the major factors that pushed Pakistan to testing nuclear devices on 28 May, was the assessment that India, after having com-

[36] Zulfikar Ali Bhutto, *The Myth of Independence* (London: Oxford University Press, 1969), p. 153.

[37] Bhutto made 'grass eating statement' in 1966, in the wake of 1965 war with India. See Hamid Jalal and Khalid Hasan (eds.), *Awakening the People* (Bhutto, 1966-9 speeches), Pakistan Publication, Rawalpindi, no date, p. 21 (speech at Larkana, Sind, 29 December 1966).

[38] Ashok Kapur, *Pakistan's Nuclear Development* (London: Croom Helm, 1987); Maj Gen D.K. Palit and P.K.S. Namboodiri, *Pakistan's Islamic Bomb* (New Delhi: Vikas Publishing House, 1979).

[39] *Nation*, 4 October 1998.

pleted a series of nuclear tests on 11 and 13 May, would sign the treaties, leaving Pakistan vulnerable to more severer pressures, if it delayed testing of its capability.[40]

It is generally argued that nuclear weapons of Pakistan would compensate for its conventional military inferiority, and in the long run, bring down the heavy defence burden that is 5.2 per cent of the GNP. This shows only a perfunctory knowledge of nuclear strategy. Weapons of mass destruction that might target population centres of the adversary with much larger destructive counter-value capacity cannot supplement the conventional forces.

The question is, what will Pakistan's response be, if India launched a conventional attack? Will Pakistan respond by using nuclear weapons? No rational decision-maker would risk the destruction of the country by retaliating by nuclear weapons to a conventional attack. Holding a first-strike threat against a nuclear-armed adversary may lose credibility, if the war fighting capability were ignored.

Therefore, weak or absolutely inferior conventional forces will limit Pakistan's choices to using or losing nuclear weapons. Neither of this will be a prudent choice. Such a decision will have to be taken under very tense circumstances within very limited time. Nuclear weapons may compensate for conventional inferiority only if Pakistan decides to develop and deploy tactical nuclear weapons, which at the moment is a distant possibility. If and when Pakistan succeeds in this venture, it will create a different set of problems, pushing both India and Pakistan into higher levels of nuclear arms race and expose them to higher probability of nuclear exchanges.

Minimal deterrence forms the third theme in the Pakistani writings on nuclear weapons capability. It is suggested that Pakistan would avoid the nuclear arms race with India and maintain only limited numbers of weapons. Minimal deterrence cannot be understood without explaining concepts of sufficiency, survivability and second-strike capability. Therefore, it is suggested that Pakistan should attempt to achieve sufficient nuclear weapons capability, that its decision-makers would consider enough to prevent India from committing aggression; that it should be able to survive the first Indian strike, and be able to launch a retaliatory counter-attack against the Indian targets.

[40] Nasim Zehra, 'The case for a Pakistani nuclear explosion', *The News*, 15 May 1998; Mirza Aslam Beg, 'Indian Nuclear Intimidation', *The News*, 21 May 1998; Farooq Hasnat, 'Should Pakistan go nuclear?' *The News*, 20 May 1998.

It is a widely held view among the Pakistani analysts that Pakistan's nuclear capability would deter India, and introduce an element of stability in the security relations in South Asia. Those who are critical of Pakistan's nuclear programme, question nuclear weapons on moral and economic grounds and have very little to argue against the larger issue of deterrence.

The issue of parity with India has been one of the dominant themes in the foreign policy writings on Pakistan. There is little or no explanation of this fuzzy concept. It is primarily a rhetorical stance that reflects a general sentiment for equal treatment. Since the nuclear testing on 28 May, the government leaders and the popular press have repeatedly asserted that a balance of power has been restored between India and Pakistan.[41] Leaving aside other components of the balance of power, they focus on the possibility of a rough nuclear parity with India.

The number game, as it is evident from the history of the US-Soviet strategic relations, is not relevant. It is argued that India and Pakistan have sufficient numbers, delivery vehicles and kill potential to effectuate a stable balance of terror or Mutually Assured Destruction (MAD). This is an optimistic scenario that seems to have been drawn in time of national euphoria. Real dangers or possibilities of a better future will emerge later, once the dust of nuclear testing has settled in the subcontinent. The members of security community in Pakistan have greater responsibility than ever before to reflect on the issue of nuclear deterrence and how it could be stabilized. At present, research and reflection on the nuclear power related security themes is both inadequate and limited.

Future Security Agenda

- *Nuclear deterrence*: As suggested above, theory of nuclear deterrence and under what condition it would work and what could cause its failure need to be the subject of future studies. The nuclear horses of India and Pakistan are out of the barn and they can not be expected to be forced back. The issue of minimal deterrence, its basic assumptions, technological components, command and control system are some of the areas in which Indian and Pakistani experts can work together

[41] Prime Minister's address on radio and television, *Nation* (Islamabad), 29 May 1998; Sardar F.S. Lodhi, 'India's Nuclear Thunder', *Nation*, 31 May 1998.

- *Confidence-building measures*: Nuclear deterrence has introduced a new element into very hostile relationship that exists between India and Pakistan. There is urgent need to study and devise sensible and workable arms control proposals and confidence-building measures.
- *Holistic approach to security*: It is time to have a second look at the geopolitical conceptions of security and include threats from within the domestic environment. The contemporary research on national security issues should open up to the perspectives of 'wideners'.[42] The new agenda must address the following issues: Environmental security, ethnic and sectarian conflict, the human dimension, governance, political capacities of the state and economic crisis. These are the problems that may define the security of Pakistan in the coming years and decades.

[42] *Survival*, Vol. 31, No. 6, 1989; *Current History*, May 1995.

Governance and National Security: Pakistan—a Case Study

KHALID MAHMUD

Arguing their case for the abolition of state, nineteenth century anarchist ideologues had pointed out, that, while quite often in history, standing armies had failed to defend a country, spontaneous resistance of the people had eventually forced the foreign invaders to quit. The all-powerful state apparatus, which Lenin had predicted would 'wither away' once the means of production and distribution were socialised, however, went from strength to strength, more so in the socialist world, arrogating to itself the sole responsibility for the security of the people.

The collapse of the Soviet Union has brought to fore the question of the relevance of war-machines to a country's peace, harmony and stability. Nonetheless, the post-cold war era has not witnessed the much desired departure from militarism. The power-blocs contention has been replaced by pursuit of hegemony by the sole superpower. Neither the military alliances, the most conspicuous of them being the NATO, have been disbanded, nor the scores of military bases around the world—from Cuba to Saudi Arabia, have been wound up.

The Arms Trade

The arms trade is perhaps the most lucrative business in the world, as more and more sophisticated weapons are being developed, produced and sold. While the 'more equal than others' elite countries have assumed the prerogative to set the rules of the game and stop others from acquiring a strategic capability, that they have pronounced as the 'forbidden fruit' for upstarts, regional bullies could yet manage to flourish so long as they were not on the wrong side of the global overlords.

The ruling elites in the Third World have by and large followed the role model of their erstwhile colonial masters or neo-colonial mentors. But, above all, it has been handy for them to subscribe to the view that building a war machine is the only guarantee for safeguarding national security.

Their perception of threat to national security does not go beyond the possibility of a military invasion, and thus, if there is no real enemy flexing its muscles, nothing can stop them from creating one to legitimize their spendings on raising troops and buying arms. The people have been fed on cliches, such as, if there was no country there would be no question of development, implying thereby that defending the territory, and not the people, was the principal task of national security.

A dangerous by-product of glorifying the men-in-uniform as the saviours of the nation has been the rise of Bonapartist tendencies. Pakistan, among others, being a victim of what has mockingly been described as 'an army conquering its own country'. Seizure of political power by the armed forces has been greatly facilitated by the abject failure of the political leadership to deliver, more precisely, the unwillingness or the inability of the elected governments to bring about a significant improvement in the quality of life of the populace.

Nonetheless, the people have learnt from experience that a military-run administration is not necessarily better qualified for efficacious governance, apart from being least responsive to popular aspirations. The fact that popular upheavals, such as the 1968-9 mass movement in Pakistan, that forced the military rulers to abdicate political power, has to an extent contributed towards some checks and balances on the culture of militarism. Nevertheless, it has not yet been possible to muster popular support for a drastic reduction in military spending.

National Security

In Pakistan there has hardly been a meaningful public debate on the multi-dimensional problem of national security. And opinion leaders have, by and large, been prone to accepting the officially promoted line that the nation would eat grass, rather than weaken its military capability. Needless to say, the insecurity syndrome has been accentuated by the formidable military build-up of the belligerent 'big brother' across the border.

Ironically, whenever there has been a suggestion to cut the defence expenditure by mutual agreement between the two neighbours, New Delhi has always held the position that India cannot be equated with Pakistan, since it has to reckon with other sources of threat to its national security. To argue for a unilateral downsizing of the armed forces, or opting out of the arms race in the region, without a corresponding Indian gesture, is therefore no less than asking for the moon.

In the aftermath of India's nuclear explosions, followed by a prompt rejoinder from Pakistan, the arms race in the region has assumed alarming proportions. Some observers see it as a point-of-no-return, since the enormous cost at which the two countries have acquired the 'big bomb', calls for justifying it as the right decision; while others are hopeful that a 'strategic parity' may impel the two countries to opt for a quid pro quo.

On the face of it, a doomsday scenario awaits whatever little hope there has been of diverting resources from guns to development, and letting the common people at some stage have a more tangible reward for their toil and sweat, than illusions of national honour and glory. However, it may not yet be a hopeless cause, if India and Pakistan were to agree to some damage control mechanism, and declare a moratorium on the nuclear race.

Now that militarism has acquired a degree of legitimacy more than ever before, and the people in both the countries have been overwhelmed by a chauvinistic tide, holding a brief for a non-military approach to national security is indeed a tall order. Nevertheless, the fact remains that equating security with military capability is an over-simplified, short-sighted view of the problem. And, if a country was spending the lion's share of its resources on buying arms and equipment and raising combat divisions, while allocating meagre funds for the welfare of the people, it is from a long-term perspective, engaged in a counter-productive exercise.

An expatriate Pakistani scholar, recently on a visit to Islamabad, spoke to a select audience of intellectuals on the multi-dimensional problem of national security. The security of a country, he argued, does not hinge on the prowess of its fighting force, but calls for popular resistance to any manifestation of foreign domination. The people must have a sense of belonging to their country, the motivation to defend the national interest, and the will to act in unison in the face of an external threat, in order to rally round forces in defence of national security. Some eminent economists have been pleading for a higher priority to investment in human resources, saying that the so-called 'social sector' has been more a showpiece than a catalyst for change.

GOVERNANCE

The mode of governance in the country has been under fire for lop-sided priorities. If the lot of the common man is no better than it was a decade ago, and there has been no visible improvement in the quality of life of the people, then, there must have been something wrong with the mode of governance, critics have said. In the 50 years of post-independence governance, benefits of whatever development or prosperity was achieved, did not trickle down to the masses, who are, as they were under colonial rule, condemned to be the underdogs forever. To add insult to injury, the 'have-nots' are often told by their spiritual mentors, that destiny is pre-determined.

Nothing could be more humiliating for an independent, sovereign nation, than the bitter reality that it has not managed to eliminate either mass poverty, or mass illiteracy. The bulk of the people live below the poverty line, have no access to schools, hospitals, electricity or even clean drinking water. Even more depressing is their hereditary servitude to feudal lords, the tribal chiefs and the evil gentry who exercise writ in the countryside. Ironically, education has been the most conspicuously neglected area of development. On the one hand, the ruling elite has been constantly harping on the imperative of facing up to the challenge of twenty-first century, and on the other hand, it continues to show an utter disregard for breaking the shackles of ignorance and social backwardness.

Paucity of resources has been a handy alibi for non-performance. People in power have often been saying that the country did not have enough financial resources to spend more on education, indicating their order of priorities for development. Nonetheless, the fiction of scarcity of resources, standing in the way of a national campaign for eradicating illiteracy, has been exposed by significant achievements in several Third World countries, in particular Sri Lanka.

While the regime has refused to divert more resources to education, whatever little is being spent on sustaining an obsolete, moribund system of education is virtually being wasted on buildings and bureaucrats. The rot of education in the country has been so disastrous, that, even the ex-President was impelled to publicly acknowledge that there was no longer any system of education in the country.

Why is the ruling elite so callously indifferent to the collapse of the education system, is partly explained by the facility that the privileged classes have to send their children abroad, initially, for higher education and now, even for schooling. While the landed gentry and the bourgeoisie have plenty of money, the top bureaucrats have the expertise to manipulate grants for their sons and daughters.

Regardless of what percentage of the foreign educated young men and women are willing to return home to contribute to nation building, the new generation of well-off Pakistanis seem to be drifting away from the national ethos. It is common these days for young people to scornfully dismiss their country as not worth living in. The growing inclination to disown the country is perhaps the most serious threat to national security.

If the 'have-nots' have no cause to identify themselves with a country, which does not give them a fair deal, and the 'haves' have been enticed away by the glamour of money and power to abdicate their national identity, one is heading for a structural breakdown. Rhetoric alone is not enough to invoke patriotism, or motivate the people to rally to the support of a national endeavour, be it an economic crisis, or an external threat.

Why should people fight for a cause which has no real meaning for them. Despondency among the people may not have reached the stage where they would say 'a plague on both your houses', but a sense of betrayal is manifest in the attitude of the common man towards the system of governance in the country.

Most people would say politicians are a bunch of scoundrels, are corrupt to the core and power hungry. Something drastic will have to be done to change this image. Any government, which is incapable of convincing the people that corruption in high places is only an aberration, and no one has the prerogative to be treated as 'more equal than others' is liable to suffer a serious credibility crisis, no matter how spectacular its electoral campaign may have been. And, in case the people do not have a modicum of peace and security in their day to day lives, they would be right to question the wisdom of spending, year after year, the bulk of what the country earns in sustaining a military establishment.

That a mighty military power, like the Soviet Union, turned out to be an 'elephant with feet of clay', has comprehensively brought home the message that if the people are alienated from the system and there is no motivation for them to identify themselves with the country, its national security cannot be safeguarded by the armed forces. Erosion of the system from within is far more serious a threat to national security, than external aggression.

A sense of belonging to the country, is to an extent the outcome of birth, family ties and the cultural milieu, but the level of expectation of the citizens from the motherland is a crucial factor. The constant outflow of economic migrants, some of whom eventually forsake for good their native lands for a decent living abroad, underscores the delusion of a national identity exclusively based on emotional ties.

The poor, ignorant and socially depressed people are hostages of the circumstances of their existence, like dumb, driven cattle. Their habitual allegiance to the system is neither a conscious choice, nor a behavioural pattern that could be taken for granted in the wake of social awareness. Sources of discontent, discord and friction, even if the process of social awakening is belated and slow, cannot be prevented for long from giving rise to divisive and disruptive tendencies.Sentiment of deprivation often finds expression in lawlessness and violence.

One has over the years witnessed in Pakistan the emergence of what has been termed as the 'Kalashnikov culture'. Gun running, drug trafficking, armed robberies, kidnapping for ransom have been some manifestations of the breakdown of the law and order system.

To attribute the phenomenon to the fall out of the Afghan war has been a handy explanation. There is no denying the fact that the Pakistani society has borne the brunt of confronting the 'evil empire' in Afghanistan. Apart from millions of Afghan refugees, who have swelled beyond manageable proportion, the population of illegal residents in the country creating sanctuaries for criminals, weapons and drugs have also found their way to breed mafias and racketeers. Nonetheless, the man primarily responsible for inviting disaster and jeopardiszing Pakistan's national security, was none other than military dictator Zia-ul-Haq, who fancied himself as a 'crusader of Islam', destined to extend his writ to Central Asia.

THE BIRTH OF ISLAMIC FUNDAMENTALISM

Easy access to weapons of all kinds to anyone who could afford to buy them in the open market, and a lucrative drug traffic that produced black money in abundance, were not Zia-ul-Haq's only gifts to the nation. He was also responsible for sowing the seeds of religious fanaticism and sectarian strife. The crusaders who had converged on

Afghanistan from various parts of the Muslim world, refused to leave when the war was over.

The Zia-ul-Haq regime was a perfect host to them, and they had the facility to pursue their unfinished agenda of fighting the 'infidels' elsewhere in the region. Meanwhile, a mushroom growth of indigenous religious fanatics had also given rise to militant groups, initially campaigning for 'Islamization' of the legal and political system in the country, but subsequently promoting conflicting sectarian causes.

To sponsor Islamic fundamentalism was handy for Zia-ul-Haq to rationalize his authoritarian regime, and he did everything possible to patronize the lobby willing to proclaim him the 'Caliph', with a divine mandate to rule over the Muslims.

Nonetheless, what he had contrived as a self-defence mechanism, turned out to be a recipe for sectarian warfare, as rival gangs of religious fanatics, joined in by hardened criminals, unleashed a reign of terror to liquidate one another. Target killings were followed by indiscriminate bombings, as the prophets of hate and violence did not hesitate to attack even the places of worship to settle scores with the rival sects.

Sectarian warfare, some analyses said, was facilitated by extra-territorial connection of the rival factions. Money and arms, it was pointed out, were readily available from foreign sources to conduct a proxy war on the Pakistani soil. But, nevertheless, the 'fodder for the cannon' was provided by the 'madrassas', the countless schools being run by one or the other religious group.

The 'madrassas' have flourished, largely because of the subsidy they are getting since Zia-ul-Haq days from the government's 'zakat' fund, albeit some of them are known to be the recipients of donations from abroad, including grants from foreign governments. The madrassas have no legitimacy as a parallel system of schooling and its graduates are hardly qualified to do any job, other than spreading the message that they have been tutored to project the 'gospel truth'.

But, thousands of young boys, mostly from a poor, rural background, enrolled every year and joined the 'army of faithfuls', reared in a culture of bigotry and intolerance. Interestingly enough, the hard core of the Taliban in Afghanistan, comprises products of Pakistani madrassas. No wonder some opinion leaders in Pakistan have warned against promoting the Taliban in the Afghan power struggle, as they see the rise of the fundamentalist outfit as a potential threat to the country's stability.

SECTARIAN VIOLENCE

How to contain sectarian violence has been a subject of public debate in Pakistan. Critics have said the law-enforcing agencies, infested with corruption and incompetence, neither have the will, nor the capability to cope with terrorism. A more incisive approach to the problem has suggested that the lack of political will has forestalled decisive action, as successive governments, fearing a religious backlash, have been reluctant to crackdown on the sources of sectarian violence. The madrassas, it has been said, are the hotbeds of sectarian strife, providing a support system to the militants engaged in terrorist activities, and the government will have to take the battle to the 'lion's den' in order to salvage a modicum of peace and harmony in the society.

To view the problem of sectarian violence as merely a question of law and order, would be superficial and short-sighted. Fortunately, the sectarian conflict, notwithstanding the no-holds-barred strategy of violence and terror adopted by the rival militant groups, has failed to draw the ordinary people into the battle, saving the society from a massive turmoil. The militants are by and large not seen as warriors for a religious cause and their actions have had no popular endorsement, but the end result of their hate campaign has been a degree of polarization on sectarian lines.

Affiliation to a religious sect has historically been a marginal factor in determining political loyalties or social linkages. 'Sunnis' and 'Shias', the two principal religious sects in Pakistan, who are being pushed into an antagonistic posture by extremists in both the camps, have traditionally been living in peace and harmony with one another. Mohammad Ali Jinnah and Zulfiqar Ali Bhutto, both had Shia antecedents, but were yet able to establish their political authority as outstanding mass leaders among a pre-dominantly Sunni population. It goes without saying that Pakistan can ill-afford a Sunni-Shia divide, as it would amount to a virtual paralysis of the organs of state power, where followers of both the sects are well represented.

Pakistan is a multi-national state. The fact was acknowledged in the 1940 Pakistan Resolution which had called for the establishment of a federation of provinces. Unlike India, the provinces in Pakistan were not reorganized on linguistic basis in the aftermath of independence, but the existing four provinces more or less represent the principal nationalities, the Punjabis, Pukhtuns, Sindhis and the Baloch.

In the chequered political history of the country, the operative norm has been to centralize power and treat the provinces as the appendages of the centre. Prior to the first military takeover in 1958, when the federal system of governance was practically scrapped, centre-province relations were among the bones of contention that had stalled the process of constitution making. The power struggle that saw the dismissal of a Prime Minister and the dissolution of the Constituent Assembly, was described by analysts as the manifestation of the ruling 'Punjabi-Mohajir' clique's unwillingness to transfer power to the Bengali majority.

In the backdrop of a civil-military oligarchy taking control of the levers of power, the Bengalis who were outsiders in the establishment, were denied majority representation in the compromise constitutional arrangement, while the smaller provinces of West Pakistan were forced to abdicate their separate identity and become part of the Punjabi-dominated one unit. History is replete with instances of ethnic minorities being given an unfair deal, and driven by the feelings of deprivation, turning bitter and hostile. But, ironically enough, it was perhaps an unprecedented development that a majority held in bondage was alienated from its own country.

To give the devil his due, it was Gen. Yahya Khan, to whom Ayub had transferred power, following the army's refusal to bail him out from the 1968-9 popular uprising, and who subsequently had the dubious distinction of presiding over Pakistan's break-up and who made the first significant move to undo the historic wrong done to the 'oppressed nationalities'.

In his drastic reform package, Yahya Khan conceded the principle of 'one man-one vote'; establishing representation on the basis of population, and thereby giving Bengalis 54 per cent seats in the National Assembly, while he abolished one unit to restore the former provinces of West Pakistan. He has also been accredited with holding the first-ever general election in Pakistan in 1970, universally acclaimed as fair and free, albeit some critics have said, the military ruler was misled by intelligence reports that no political party was in a position to secure majority.

Nonetheless, when the moment of truth arrived, Yahya Khan refused to transfer power to the majority party, precipitating a mass rebellion among the Bengalis. The Awami League's six-point charter, the plank on which it had contested the 1970 election and won a landslide victory, was denounced as a recipe for secession.

The Pakistani historians have by and large been prone to ascribing

Pakistan's break up in 1971 to Indian military intervention. It was external aggression, they have said, that dealt a death blow to the country's territorial integrity. Unfortunately, only a small but outspoken minority of intellectuals has had the vision to underscore, that the security of a nation is, in the final analysis, determined by the degree of allegiance and belonging of the people to its raison d'etre. Separatist tendencies are an expression of discontent with the mode of governance, and cannot be neutralized by use of force.

The Indians had intervened and succeeded in cutting Pakistan down to size, primarily because, the process of alienation of the Bengalis had reached a point-of-no-return, and the entire populace was willing to welcome the foreign invaders, rather than cooperating with the national army, which had earlier let loose a reign of terror to subdue the insurgents.

The task of nation-building, often confused with state-building, was grossly overlooked in Pakistan, as has been the case elsewhere in the Third World. The will to live together, is, according to social scientists, the crucial element in the formation of a nation. In countries where people speak different languages, or belong to various ethnic or cultural groups, going an extra mile is required to create a feeling of oneness.

Nevertheless, the ruling elite's prescription for national unity has been uniformity, rather than unity in diversity. While centralization of power, resources, and decision-making has been vigorously advocated as necessary for national integration, voicing of regional aspirations has been branded as divisive and anti-national.

Grievances of Minorities

The smaller nationalities have had a long list of grievances, basically arising out of uneven economic development of the regions and their inequitable share in the country's power structure. Separatist tendencies were manifested in the rise of regional forces, some of which went as far as to preach secession. The most serious threat to national integrity, in the aftermath of East Pakistan breaking away to found Bangladesh, was the 1974 insurgency in the province of Balochistan. Following the dismissal of the provincial government, headed by the National Awami Party (NAP), which the then Prime Minister Zulfiqar Ali Bhutto had charged with subversion, Baloch nationalists took to mountains and fought the Pakistan Army for more than a year.

The Baloch nationalists, by and large led by tribal sardars, have over the years split into feuding factions, and their politics has degenerated into jockeying for a share in the booty. Nonetheless, Baloch nationalism is still a factor to be reckoned with, though it does not any longer have the facility to find foreign sponsors, like it had in the heyday of cold war.

The Pukhtun nationalism, spearheaded by the pre-independence associates of the Indian National Congress in the NWF province, has had a mixed bag of fortunes. Though politically handicapped because of their opposition to the partition of the subcontinent in 1947 and therefore, sitting ducks for an 'anti-Pakistan' label, the Pukhtun nationalist elements were able to stay in business by projecting themselves as the defenders of a Pukhtun identity.

Raising in the process the 'Pukhtunistan' demand, which, in the absence of a clearly spelt out agenda, was given different meanings at different times—from independence to autonomy—to suit their convenience, the Pukhtun nationalists made no bones about describing their Afghanistan connection as a fraternal bond of language and culture. Ironically, the forces of history, and not a deliberate design of the votaries of 'one-country one-nation', has checkmated the advance of Pukhtun nationalism.

The enterprising Pukhtuns have over the years seized whatever opportunities were available in the country, to prosper and conspicuously outgrow the under dog syndrome. They are now not only in business, trade and industry, but also shareholders in political power. And some analysts are prone to describing the country's power structure as 'Punjabi-Pukhtun partnership'.

An equally significant development has been the extraordinary social mobility of the Pukhtuns, which has impelled them to travel and explore possibilities of earning a livelihood in all parts of the country. While a substantial number of Pukhtuns have set-up business, or secured jobs everywhere, more so in the metropolitan city of Karachi, where they outnumber all ethnic groups barring the Mohajirs (the refugees from India), the process of their economic and social integration with the rest of the country has rendered Pukhtun nationalism an obsolete plank for mustering popular support.

Compounded by the arrival of millions of post-independence refugees from India, the problem of regionalism and ethnicity in the province of Sindh has been a far more intricate and explosive phenomenon than elsewhere in the country. The Sindhis, largely captives of a feudal mode of production and a medieval system of governance, were tied to the land, the landowners, and the 'pirs' (spiritual overlords). The immigrants on the contrary, dynamic and socially more advanced, were able to fill the vacuum in business and jobs created by the en masse migration of Sindhi Hindus, and virtually take control of the urban centres, in particular Karachi.

The massive inflow of settlers in Sindh, mostly urdu-speaking people from UP and Bihar, critics said, was a deliberate policy adopted by the first Prime Minister Liaquat Ali Khan, himself an urdu-speaking refugee, designed to create a constituency for himself and his displaced fellow politicians. The heavy concentration of immigrants created immense problems of economic and cultural adjustment.

On the one hand, the growing population of settlers, facilitated by a constant inflow of refugees, gave rise to a sense of insecurity among the Sindhis, prompting Sindhi nationalists to express the fear that the Sindhis may be reduced to a minority in their own homeland. On the other hand, ethnic cleavage was accentuated because the settlers were, either unwilling, or unable to identify themselves with the Sindhi language and culture, projecting themselves as a distinct entity, and eventually demanding recognition as the 'fifth nationality' in Pakistan.

The rise of the Mohajir Qaumi Movement (MQM) as the champion of Mohajir rights, signalled the outbreak of an ethnic strife, degenerating into a free-for-all politics of violence and vendetta, as the MQM, initially patronized by Zia-ul-Haq regime to settle scores with the Peoples' Party, turned into a Frankenstein monster, like the LTTE in Sri Lanka. The MQM which holds total sway over Karachi, and runs a formidable network of terror and coercion, has survived a head-on collision with the state apparatus, including the army.

The MQM has at one time or the other, campaigned for a separate mohajir province; albeit, it has also been accused of harbouring a design to split Karachi from Pakistan and make it an independent city state. The MQM agenda, pronounced as well perceived, has obviously spread alarm and despondency among the Sindhis.

The outspoken Sindhi nationalists, rallied round to the cause of Sindh's unity at one stage, holding out an olive branch to the Mohajirs, saying, as the Sindhi nationalist patriarch G. M. Syed had put it, 'we have to come to terms with the Mohajirs, since we cannot throw them in the Arabian sea'. Ironically, the Sindhi nationalist forces had also explored secessionist options, as they saw the Sindhis as a perpetual underdog in a 'Punjabi dominated state'.

The Sindhis have had a marginal presence in the country's power structure until the advent of Zulfiqar Ali Bhutto. They had no representation in the armed forces, not even among the ranks, only a handful of persons in top bureaucratic positions, and little influence in political decision-making.

The Mohajirs were not the only settlers in Sindh; Punjabis and Pukhtuns had also migrated in large numbers to seek jobs and set-up business enterprises. But, what the Sindhi nationalists termed as loot and plunder, was the 'grabbing of choicest lands' by Punjabi bureaucrats and army officers in the fifties, around the newly-built Ghulam Mohammad Barrage on Indus river. G.M. Syed, the high priest of Sindhi nationalism, went as far as to demand the creation of a 'Sindhudesh', which he said was the only course to 'liberate' the Sindh nation from the slavery of Punjabis.

Long spells of military rule had meant total exclusion of Sindhis from the power structure. And, analysts pointed out, that it could have alienated the Sindhis to a point-of-no-return. Nonetheless, the 'Bhutto factor' has been the saving grace for the federation of Pakistan. The meteoric rise of ZAB as a national leader did more than anything else to retrieve a sense of belonging and participation among the Sindhis, by letting them have the pride that a Sindhi politician could also call the shots among the Punjabis.

The ability of the Peoples' Party, under the leadership of Bhutto's daughter, to survive as a political force in the post-ZAB era and sustain a support base in different parts of the country, has been a significant unifying factor. No wonder, the Sindhi nationalist forces have always drawn a blank in electoral politics when pitted against the PPP.

CONCLUSION

In his recently published report on human development in South Asia, Dr. Mahbub ul-Haq, renowned Pakistani economist and a former Finance Minister, has projected a doomsday scenario of the process of development in the region. In a nutshell he says, 'South Asia is fast emerging as the poorest, the most illiterate, the most malnourished, the least gendre sensitive—indeed the most deprived region in the world. Yet it continues to make more investment in arms than in the education and health of its people'.

In his view the divergence between economic growth and human development is greater in Pakistan than most other countries. Over two-thirds of Pakistan's adult population is illiterate, 60 million people do not have access to health facilities, 67 million people are without safe drinking water, and 89 million people are deprived of basic sanitation facilities. Yet, he says, Pakistan carries a heavy military burden. There are nine soldiers for every one doctor and three soldiers for every two teachers.

Dr. Haq strongly advocates a change in the basic concept of security. The essence of real security, he says, lies in safeguarding the people, not just safeguarding the borders. But, this is a lesson not yet learnt in South Asia. Despite their grinding poverty, the countries of the region invest heavily in their armies, and the social and human cost of this spending is enormous.

To illustrate, the cost of arms vis-à-vis the cost of urgently needed social services, the report points out that, for the purchase of each battle tank, 4 million children can be immunized. If one Mirage 2000-5 is not purchased, it would be possible to extend primary school education to 3 million children and each submarine purchased means denying safe drinking water to 60 million people.

Security Studies in Bangladesh: Continuity and Change

DILARA CHOUDHURY

Security studies of Third World countries, especially of the weak states did not dominate the research conducted by Western scholars. Most scholars from developing countries allege that since international security was captivated by the doctrine of East-West confrontation, the traditional international literature mostly dealt with well-established concept of Western security. Such a paradigm called for military preparedness of a country in order to deal with the threats emanating from outside the state borders. As long as the external aggression could be deterred, a country's security, i.e. preservation of its 'core values', were supposed to be protected as well.

This concept fitted well into developed countries' security conceptualisation. Since these countries did not suffer from any nation-building and state-building malaise, due to centuries of development, their 'external orientation, positive links with systemic security, and the correspondence of state security with alliance security—the situation in the Third World has been radically different from that at the heart of the global strategic system that includes North America, Europe, and Japan'[1].

Consequently, a search for a new concept of security came to the fore in the 1970s. The concept of security for Third World countries was widened and used in political sense. Since security means a state's instinct to ensure the survivability of the state, Third World countries' security predicaments seem to be forthcoming more from their internal rather than external sources. In this concept, 'security-insecurity is defined in relation to vulnerabilities, both internal and external—that threaten or have the potential to bring down or weaken state structures, both territorial and institutional, and governing regimes'. Though this kind of definition suffers from entanglement of a regime's security issues with those of the state, it nevertheless serves the purpose of security studies of Third World countries in a comprehensive manner.

Barry Buzan, for example, pointed out how political turmoil and economic underdevelopment 'may pose threats to a country's independence and sovereignty'. The 'core values', whose threats were previously thought to be coming from military aggression alone.

So 'while still largely concerned with the security of the state, security studies have, with the growing democratization of both international and national societies and the end of the era of acute bipolar military confrontation, been liberated from narrow strategic confines. And, increasingly begun to focus on more comprehensive definitions of its ambit: Preservation of the political system, economic and political well-being of all sections of the people, as well as external security that encompasses military, economic, food, energy, environment and political dimensions'.

Concepts like comprehensive security have emerged and have been adopted as the appropriate paradigm, by several states and a growing number of analysts.

Bangladesh being a weak and developing country also suffered from the classic security predicaments of Third World nations. After an initial period of incoherence and lack of consensus regarding the security issues of the country, there have been substantive changes during successive regimes while having continuity for its search for a viable security paradigm. Despite this need for a well-conceived security doctrine, there is an acute paucity of intellectual resources in the field of security studies in the country. Nevertheless, a number of studies were done in the late 1980s and 1990s, to identify the sources of insecurity facing Bangladesh.

With this end in view, attempts would be made in this paper, first, to outline briefly the initial state response to what were thought to be national security threats emanating from outside the country rather than inside.

Secondly, the issues in which the primacy on domestic situation came to the fore; how the internal dimension of security, such as brutal poverty, dismal socio-economic scenario, rising external debt and foreign aid dependency, environmental degradation, natural disaster, rising unemployment and ethnicity problem in the Chittagong Hill Tracts became paramount in the Bangladesh's security calculus, would be appraised.

Finally, Bangladesh's endeavours to deal with the impact of regional and global variables, which profoundly influence the internal dimension of security, would be critically analysed. The article concludes with Dhaka's continued search for a coherent and consensus list of security issues in the midst of continuity and change.

Security Studies in The Formative Phase

The main emphasis of security studies in Bangladesh, immediately following its inception—although not overtly military hardware based—seemed to have been strategic rather than internal. Bangladesh emerged at a time when the superpower rivalry in the subcontinent had not yet diminished. The major powers, the United States, the Soviet Union and the Peoples' Republic of China and the three regional powers—India, Pakistan and Bangladesh remained engaged in shifting and sometimes conflicting patterns of inter-relationship, 'in spite of the apparent international stability and balance achieved by bipolar or multipolar politics, the inherent weakness of the earlier stages to plague the new relations between nations'.

As a result, Dhaka adopted a two pronged approach. On the one hand, it signed the India-Bangladesh Treaty of Friendship and Co-operation of 1972, which kept it heavily titled towards Indo-Soviet bloc; on the other hand, it made non-alignment as the corner stone to deal with the country's security concerns.

However, unlike the majority Third World countries in post-World War II era, Bangladesh did not anticipate external military aggression. Strategically, such threats could emanate only from India. The treaty and friendly relations with New Delhi were to counter such possibility. In case of any other military threat or entanglement in superpowers' rivalry in the region, it counted on India's military strength rather than building up its own military.

As a result, during the initial period there was no increase in the Defence Budget of the country. It seems that the regime had no clear-cut defence strategy, as the then Prime Minister Sheikh Mujibur Rahman neither totally disbanded the regular military nor raised national para-military forces as stated in his famous six-point programme. Moreover, Sheikh Mujibur Rahman's deep-seated mistrust of the military, somewhat contributed to such thinking. This strategy met with severe internal criticism, as a substantial number of people considered it to be a policy of 'subservience' to New Delhi, which did not serve the vital national interest of the country. There was also deep-seated suspicion that it was meant for regime security in order to deal with radical ultra-left elements that were increasingly posing threats to its ability to stay in power.

Dhaka's concerns about the dire socio-economic needs of the country also got top priority among the policy planners of Bangladesh. But there was no clear-cut understanding about its security dimension. This is discernible from the fact that there was no intellectual discourse on the subject during this period. In sum, Dhaka seemed to have been unable to identify the actual sources of its insecurity.

The trend continued following the change of regime. There was a renewed emphasis on the socio-economic development of the country, but, both Zia and Ershad perceived strategic security threats from across the borders and as such clear-cut security strategy was formulated. As a result, along with diversification of the foreign policy options, there was a steady increase in the Defence Budget. The deterrence doctrine, i.e. in case of an external aggression the army should be able to deter the aggression for a period of time before United Nations could intervene, seemed to be the logic behind this military buildup by an economically impoverished Bangladesh.

However, there was scepticism about the actual rationale behind country's security strategy. In particular, the increase in the defence budget during the Ershad regime has been cited by political analysts as a ploy by the former president to consolidate his hold on his principle constituency, namely, the military. As a consequence, the internal dimension of the country's security threats remained unaddressed.

It was only in the late 1980s, after a number of studies, as mentioned earlier, highlighted the security predicaments of Third World countries, that Bangladesh began to seriously identify its peculiar security needs. Even with regard to Dhaka's strategic threats, a number of scholars suggested a 'nations-in-arms' strategy, rather than continuing with a military build up. It should, however, be noted that despite such policy advocacy, the military expenditure in Bangladesh continues to grow.

This trend is due to the scepticism about the applicability of 'nations-in-arms' strategy, in the context of the volatile and dissensious nature of Bangladesh's politics. Nevertheless, there has also been a profound transformation in security studies in Bangladesh, in which emphasis is now more on the internal rather than strategic. Some of the internal sources of insecurity has had intellectual attention both by scholars as well as the NGOs. Now the discussion continues on those security issues confronting Bangladesh in 1990s.

POLITICAL DIMENSION

The basic and fundamental issue of security deals with the question of survival. As such, there is a growing awareness in the country about the very survivability, not in terms of military hardware, but in the organic survival of its population. Bangladesh with a territory of only 54,000 sq. miles, a population of 120 million, low literacy rate, foreign aid dependency, rising debt services, and a per capita income of only US $ 170.00, needs to telescope hundreds of years of development in decades. This gigantic task cannot be achieved if there is no political stability. But unfortunately political stability has eluded the country ever since its inception. The causes are rooted in the disfunctional nation-building process. It has been aptly noted by a reputed analyst that 'central to Bangladesh's political instability are its relentless dissensions on core national issues and the resultant political crisis and instability. Problems are certainly associated with the process of nation-building'.

Nation-building process should not have any hindrance in a country like Bangladesh, whose population enjoys a near unanimous homogeneity in terms of language and religion. Despite this, the country has remained divided on vital national issues. As a result even with the return of democracy after years of military and semi-military rule in 1991, the much needed cohesion and institutionalization of the democratic process has been eluding. Instead, politics of hartal has taken precedence over constitutional politics. It is evidenced by the fact that during the previous BNP regime, the major opposition led by the Awami League staged as many as 243 hartals to meet their demands. The hartals and the prolonged boycotting of parliament by the opposition, thus undermined the efficacy of the political institutions and gave rise to extra-constitutional politics.

With the return of the Awami League to power in June 1996, after couple of years of acute political turmoil, it was expected that the overall political and economic situation of the country would improve. But belying such hopes, Bangladesh seemed to be heading towards another spat of political instability. Within two years the main opposition BNP had also resorted to similar tactics previously taken by Awami League. It has so far gone for 12 hartals, intermittently boycotted parliament and resorted to various extra-constitutional procedures.

The government, on the other hand, instead of reaching for compromise and consensus on various issues, has injected politics of instability by allowing two opposition MPs to cross the floor and join the administration. This was an act of alleged violation of the constitutional spirit, which adversely affected democratic institutions, namely the Parliament and the judiciary.

Lack of governance has further exacerbated the country's inability to deal with the most serious security problem, namely the insurgency in Chittagong Hill Tracts (CHT), in an effective manner. The protracted low intensity conflict, allegedly sustained by the neighbouring country India, has been debilitating for the country. Several rounds of talks were held between the Parbattya Chattagram Jana Sanghati Samity (PCJSS) and the National Committees, established by former President Ershad, during 1985-90 and 1991-6, proved inconclusive.

However, within one year of coming to power, the Awami League managed to sign a peace accord with the PJCSS. Unfortunately, signing of the peace accord instead of accelerating the national healing process, has further exacerbated the stand-off between the government and the opposition. The opposition maintained that the accord had been signed to 'please' India and help it to control the cross-border insurgency between Assam/Tripura and Bangladesh. It was alleged that the accord was done as a quid pro quo for the Ganges Water Sharing Treaty and belied the 'Gujral Doctrine', on the grounds that impinged on the sovereignty and political independence of the country.

It is, thus, easily discernible that without political stability, Bangladesh is unable to deal with the issues threatening the 'core values'.

Economic Dimension

Need for Bangladesh's economic development had been identified as one of the foreign policy objectives since it was born in 1971. Sheikh Mujibur Rahman, as early as in 1972, had emphasized at a news conference in London, that Dhaka would accept economic assistance from any source, including the US if there were no political strings attached. (His foreign minister Abdus Samad Azad had previously announced that Dhaka would not accept any aid from the US because it was tainted.) His statement underlined the need for economic development for the country where about three-fourths of the population lived below the poverty line.

Lacking the resources to generate rapid socio-economic growth, Bangladesh, from the outset, sought large-scale economic assistance from the developed countries. At that time it was not identified as a source of insecurity. Rather, it was ranked after the national security issues were made clear, i.e. protection of sovereignty, political independence and territorial integrity. This is how economic development was viewed.

But even after years of independence, sadly, Bangladesh has been ranked as 144 out of 177 countries in terms of Human Development Index. The report also gives a dismal picture about the socio-economic conditions of the people. Despite huge injection of foreign aid and Bangladesh's recent endeavours to attract foreign investment through reforms and structural adjustment, the economy has remained agrarian, absorbing 55.[illegible]7 per cent of the total work force of the country and contributing 4[illegible] per cent of its total GDP. Most people are engaged in a bare survival struggle.

Obviously, when the people remain engaged in a struggle for survival, concepts like state-structure, its sovereignty or territorial integrity mean very little in their psyche. Moreover, economic underdevelopment exposes a country like Bangladesh to the manipulation of international economy. Whereas the extreme debt and foreign dependency put a limit to state autonomy. Foreign aid, loans and grants from international funding agencies are considered essential for development but when such agencies are able to formulate policies curtailing the autonomy of the supreme decision-making body of the country, then the question of its sovereignty and political independence do come under question.

One very encouraging development has been that the dismal economic situation of the country has been identified as a serious threat to its security. A number of studies have been made in this regard. The government of Bangladesh has also undertaken several measures through bilateral, regional and multilateral efforts to boost the economy.

Environmental Degradation and Security

Linkage between environmental issues and national security in Bangladesh came to the attention of the policy planners only in the 1990s. The West, especially the United States, had begun to realize the environmental dimension of security since late 1970s and the outcome of it had been the Earth Summit in Rio de Janerio. There is now substantial literature, which points out the linkage between environmental degradation and scarcities, as the potential threats to social as well as inter-state conflicts. All these studies show that environmental degradation and scarcities can have two-fold impact: First, environmental issues enhance inter-state conflicts; and second, it can have devastating consequences on the economy and polity of a nation. Looking from this perspective, Bangladesh's national security is threatened by environmental issues in multifarious ways, three of which are discussed below.

Land scarcity and ethnic conflicts: The runaway population growth in Bangladesh is the principle threat to the country's renewable resources.

Though the country has a brilliant record of bringing the population growth rate down from 3.1per cent to 2.1 per cent , 'the United Nations predicts that Bangladesh's current population of 120 million will reach 235 million by the year 2025. At about 0.08 hectare per capita, cropland is already desperately scarce. Population density is 785 per square kilometer (in comparison, the population density in the adjacent Indian state of Assam is 284 per square kilometer).

Because all the country's good agricultural land has been exploited, population growth will cut in half the amount of cropland available per capita by 2025. Flooding and inadequate national and community institutions for water control, exacerbate the lack of land and the brutal poverty and turmoil it endangers. Moreover, environmental degradation, population pressure and unequal access to resource are increasingly causing scarcity of renewable resources. For a weak state like Bangladesh, it can be a national security nightmare in terms of migration or expulsion, ethnic conflicts, decreased economic productivity, deprivation conflicts and even coups d' etat.'

Environmental change and flooding: Bangladeshis are the worst victims of the varying change in Himalayan eco-system. Devastating yearly floods cause havoc both in terms of economy and human misery. About 18 to 19 million people are affected by floods every year, most of whom are the wretched, landless poor. Obviously, besides the economic devastation the chances of trans-district or trans-national migration become more heightened, which again cause both social and inter-state conflicts.

For centuries, Bangladesh has lived with yearly floods. They have actually been always welcomed in the area because they renew the land with silt deposits are needed for the country's intensive agriculture. 'The floods are essential to maintain fertility of the soils, to replenish the groundwater and soil moisture for the winter season, to help maintain the extensive fisheries, to provide plentiful water to the monsoons crops. In normal years, floods do all these without causing havoc.'

But the recent devastating floods are happening not 'due to the fragile seismic structure and ecosystem of the Himalayas with which human society has lived for ages' but due to increased human activities. Increased pressure of population and need for food and fuel have caused alarming deforestation in the Himalayas. It is predicted that within the next 25 years, the Himalayas would become bald. As it is the fragile seismic structure and ecosystem of the Himalayas, as reported by the Centre for Science and Environment (CSE), cause enormous siltation down stream, and now with deforestation and unchecked water flow as well as soil erosion, the problems have compounded and become manifold. Besides, other human activities in the upstream and downstream are causing unprecedented flooding in Bangladesh.

The impact of climate change: Another environmental factor, which is causing concern, is the effect of climate change on Bangladesh. Ironically, Dhaka's contribution to climate change, due to global warming, is minimal. Exhensive use of fossil fuel mostly by the West, in its quest for rapid industrialization, precipitated an increase of pollutants into the atmosphere, thus causing global warming. This is anticipated to increase global mean surface air temperature in relation to 1990 about 2 °C by 2100. The average sea level is expected to rise as a result of thermal expansion of the oceans and melting of glaciers and floes. There would be an increase in the sea level of about 50 cm from the present to 2100.

The atmospheric imbalance is apprehended to cause acute climatic conditions in the country, such as, intensity of cyclonic and associated storm surges, flooding and salinity of land, and drought conditions, all within a span of 25 years, leading to widespread loss of food grain production, affecting 56 per cent of the population. Security of Bangladesh in the context of the environmental issues confronting the country, thus, seems to be at peril if proper steps are not taken in time.

Use of narcotics: Illegal trafficking of narcotics through Bangladesh and other internal factors have caused unprecedented abuse of drugs, mostly by the youth during the last two decades. Bangladesh's proximity to the Golden Triangle, Golden Crescent and the Golden Wedge has contributed to the use of this country for trafficking of drugs. It is evident from intelligence records that international drug traffickers started using the territory of Bangladesh as a corridor for trafficking narcotics and drugs produced in India, in the Golden Wedge and in the Golden Triangle, from the very beginning of the last decade. The movement of drugs through Bangladesh's territory resulted in the development of an internal market as well. The abuse of heroin and some chotropic substances are partly a direct consequence of such 'in transit traffic'.

The present drug epidemic in Bangladesh is an after-effect of the liberation war of 1971, which includes economic break down; lack of discipline in every sector of national life; violence and delays in academic programmes in almost all the major educational institutions; scarcity of employment everywhere; frustration among the educated younger generation; political instability; social disintegration; rapid urbanisation; massive migration of people from rural to urban areas; influence of western culture and breakdown of families in the urban population.

At present 'Phensidle'—the trade name of Codeine phosphate mixed syrup for cough suppressant—a highly popular drug in use in Bangladesh. Though there is a ban on its production but it is manufactured in India and smuggled into the country in large quantity. Heroin of the brown variety is trafficked through the western, northern and eastern borders. White powder heroine is transported through Bangladesh for international markets. The use of drugs by the young generation is corrupting institutions, retarding socio-economic development, and endangering state security. The money and the man-power needed to deploy advanced equipment for border control in order to close the gap in the security systems, thereby thwarting the threats posed by the drug-runners and smugglers, are simply beyond the reach of Bangladesh's national capabilities.

Geo-Political Realities

Despite Bangladesh's geo-strategic location, its importance in regional and extra-regional politics is somewhat minimal. Dhaka has little room of manoeuvrability, geo-strategically, in the context of its India dominated geo-political realities. It is surrounded by India from three different sides, with an outlet through the Bay of Bengal, access through which is also heavily dependent on New Delhi. This 'tyranny of geography', thus, undermines the national security of Bangladesh. As such, most of the external vulnerabilities stem from across the border. Policies formulated in New Delhi have direct bearings on Dhaka's security concerns. In the context of Bangladesh's weak state status and consequent vulnerabilities, New Delhi's behaviour affect its political independence and sovereignty in varying forms.

New Delhi is fully aware of Dhaka's need to co-operate with India on vital issues, like sharing of common rivers' water, especially the Ganges, environmental issues and so on. On the other hand, New Delhi also needs Bangladesh for geo-strategic reasons. Most important of which is the cross border insurgency between Bangladesh and Assam and Tripura. A friendly Bangladesh serves New Delhi's national security in the context of the protracted insurgency in the north-eastern provinces as well as the socio-economic development of the area.

So the impetus for a mutually beneficial relationship can serve the interests of both countries. After all, if there is no co-operation, then environmental degradation and its devastating consequences alone would cause unprecedented security threats to both India and Bangladesh. Who can save the situation when 'by the year 2020, there will be 220 million Bangladeshis and one billion Indians competing for land and jobs. Without policies on population and migration, and flood and river control in the next few years, there will be clashing nationalities and ethnic groups on the borders of India and Bangladesh, perhaps on a greater scale than in Yugoslavia, Armenia, and Azerbaijan'.

But unfortunately, New Delhi's policies towards its smaller neighbours, including Bangladesh, has been considered 'bullish,' and has failed to generate confidence among its neighbours. Many security analysts feel that most of Bangladesh's security threats that have originated from across the border have been due to New Delhi's deliberate policies to keep Bangladesh internally vulnerable, so that it can be pressured. Such apprehensions have been heightened with the advent of BJP-led government in New Delhi.

A number of issues need to be resolved in order to minimize Dhaka's national security threats emanating from its geo-political environment. First, the sharing of water of the common rivers, especially the Ganges. Though there is still no permanent agreement on how to augment and share the water of the Ganges, Dhaka, after years of ad hoc and intermittent periods of no agreements, has managed to sign an agreement covering a period of 30 years on 10 December 1996.

While the opposition alleges that the agreement has not enhanced the flow of the water in any significant way the government maintains that it is a fair agreement. It should be noted that this was done in the context of the 'Gujral Doctrine'. The present BJP-led government has pledged to uphold the treaty, but its viability is under question in the context of Advani's rhetoric, with India going nuclear in May 1998.

Second, the huge trade gap between the two countries. Bangladesh's official annual imports (which does not include the huge smuggling across the borders) from India now amounts to about US $ 1.5 billion, while the exports to India are just around US $ 70 million. During the recent secretary-level talks held in Dhaka, New Delhi asked it to 'sell transit and port facilities' in order to correct the trade imbalance but only got assurances for the measures which would really promote economic co-operation and reduce the trade imbalance—like 'zero-tariff', removal of existing non-tariff barrier or setting up of joint venture industries on buy-back basis.

Third, the issue of illegal immigrants from Bangladesh into the north-eastern states of Assam and Tripura. According to the present Indian government, there are about one crore alleged Bangladeshi illegal immigrants and BJP's manifesto called for a previous 'push-back' policy. Since coming to power, however, the BJP-led government in a subtle change, has called for the identification of these so-called foreigners so that they can be provided some services but there are apprehensions in Bangladesh that under this garb even Indians belonging to minority communities would be pushed back.

Fourth, the insurgency in the north-eastern provinces of India. Bangladesh's location makes it an important factor in India's attempts to control the situation in Assam and Tripura. A friendly Bangladesh would serve India's interests. Actually, this was one of the reasons why India gave all-out support to Bangladesh's liberation war. Lastly, Dhaka should maximize its security interests vis-à-vis New Delhi's likely change of attitude toward its smaller neighbours since its nuclear explosions in 1998.

By conducting nuclear tests and thereby provoking Pakistan to follow suit, New Delhi feels a kind of isolation by the international community. By antagonizing Pakistan, China as well as Myanmar, India, at present, cannot afford to antagonize any other regional country. Its pressure on Bangladesh on insurgency and other issues would be less since it would not be able to divert troops from the borders of Pakistan and China into its north-eastern provinces. Therefore, Dhaka has now the unique opportunity and advantage vis-à-vis both India and Pakistan. But the fact of the matter is, despite Dhaka's all-out endeavours and New Delhi's present uneasy situation, the former's policies would most likely create very little impact on the latter.

This has been evidenced by the outcome of Bangladesh Prime Minister's much trumpeted visit to New Delhi to play a peace-maker's role. There are speculations now that the purpose of her visit was to inform Indian Prime Minister Vajpayee about Dhaka's intention of signing Status of Advanced Forces Agreement (SAFA) with the United States. Moreover, its inability to extract any concession on trade, joint ventures, ratification of Mujib-Indira 1974 Border Agreement, financial assistance for the development of Chittagong port, and the so-called immigrants issue, continues to make Bangladesh's external security threats more poignant.

From the above discussion it is discernible that security studies in Bangladesh have undergone profound changes. The security managers are more concerned with non-military issues such as political stability, economic development and environmental issues. This is not to say that the military-hardware-based security dimension is less significant. What is significant is that a number of security threats emanating from the internal dimension, some of which have cross-border ramification, are now more menacing threats to the state's survival as an independent and sovereign country. In this respect, Dhaka needs to formulate comprehensive national, regional and multilateral policies, in order to tackle the complex and multifarious threats originating both from outside as well as inside the country.

Trends in Security Studies in Nepal: Recent Trends and Future Directions

DHRUBA KUMAR

A defining moment for the South Asian realists has arrived, with the onset of nuclear reality and its consequent implication on security studies. As the concepts of balance of power and deterrence have become the focus of the policy statements emanating from India and Pakistan after their spectacular nuclear tests in May 1998, militarism in South Asia has essentially become synonymous to security. Stephen Walt may perhaps be proven true in this pernicious atmosphere created by the nuclear reality, along with several realist and neo-realist advocates of security studies in South Asia.

Although the South Asian realists, like Walt, agree that the external military threat is not the only source endangering national security they, however, tend to treat it as the most ominous problem around which statecraft revolves. Accordingly, Walt has defined security studies as the 'study of threat, use and control of military force' in relation to a specific policy that a state adopts, 'in order to prepare for, prevent, and engage in war'.[1] Notwithstanding a harsh critique of the concept of military primacy in the field of security studies and its primarily external orientation in conceptualizing the threat, this tendency has invariably influenced the perceptions of strategic elite responsible for the national security management of the state.[2]

The realist paradigm that has been predominantly influential in the

[1] Stephen M. Walt, 'The Renaissance of Security Studies', *International Studies Quarterly*, June 1991, pp. 12-13. For some discourses on security studies, particularly, in the West, also see John Chipman, 'The Future of Strategic Studies: Beyond Even Grand Strategy', *Survival*, Spring 1992, pp. 109-31; and, Joseph Nye and Sean Lynn-Jones, 'International Security Studies: A Report of a Conference on the State of the Field', *International Security*, Spring 1988, pp. 5-27.

[2] Edward A. Kolodziej, 'Renaissance in Security Studies? Caveat Lector! *ACDIS Occasional Paper*, September 1991.

development of security concepts and strategies in relation to military programmes, drawn up with the objective of defending territorial integrity and national sovereignty, appears to have been derived from the Darwinian notion of the survival of the fittest. The studied disregard that India has shown towards the concerns of its neighbours, while detonating the nuclear fuse, can be understood in this context.

The momentous change in the Indian strategic posture, particularly against China, has driven a message home to Nepal reminding it about its geopolitical tragedy. India's official articulation of China as the 'number one enemy' has instantly changed the strategic configuration across the Himalayas with the possibility of tension escalation as well as the renewal of hostility across the border.

Assertion by India of its nuclear weapons power status has now changed the status of Nepal to a landlocked state sandwiched between the two nuclear weapons powers with profoundly articulated enmity. Given this nuclear reality, the role of these two protagonists could perhaps be, counter targeting each other in the future.

Even in the absence of a direct conflagration, it would be imperative for them to engage in contingency planning with likely nuclear use. Their counter force targeting across the Sino-Indian border would make Nepal's situation worse, as the perception of itself being indirectly hostage to the nuclear forces of either India or China becomes a reality. Nepal would not be in a position to ignore the existence of nuclear weapons or their planned deployment, even if these weapons of mass destruction are supposedly meant for deterring the antagonist than their actual use. But their use in the case of deterrence failure can never be discounted or ruled out in totality.

Concerns like the nuclear fallout and radiation effects have distinctly emerged in Nepal. Even if these are remote possibilities, nonetheless the possibility exists. The Nepali concern over the Indian and the Chinese nuclear weapons has two aspects. One is the fear that if war, even in the distant future, breaks out but does not involve Nepal, the possible use by either of the protagonists of the nuclear weapons would create an inescapable situation with harrowing consequences. The second is that any deployment of nuclear weapons in its closer proximity represents a long-range threat (in the case of the use of tactical weapons). The existential threat, therefore, is the most critical concern for Nepal despite the fact that it has hostility-free relations with both neighbours.

Although, it can also be safely assumed that the possible border skirmishes between India and China in the future would never cross the Rubicon set by the past historical precedence, the certainty is there that the intensity of fighting would never be the same as it was before. Notwithstanding the technological calibre that the Chinese and the Indian armed forces might possess, war in conventional footings would be highly disastrous, there is also no guarantee that the future Sino-Indian war would only confine to the high Himalayas.

In the case of determined assault by China from across the Chumbi Valley down to the Chicken Neck in the Siliguri corridor, eastern Nepal would immediately be enveloped as a war zone by India, through the invocation of the July 1950 Treaty and Nepal will have to bear the brunt of the Sino-Indian conflict. As Nepal is considered a territory (and a state) falling within the Indian security perimeter, it may not be spared, as before, in the case of the Sino-Indian war in the future. The Indian confidence boosted by the possession of nuclear weapons may make the Nepali position miserable in the bilateral context if and when the Indian leadership desires so.

One can further contemplate on the deteriorating security situation of Nepal endangered by the Indian nuclear tests. It has yet to reassess its own position against the challenges emanating simultaneously from the worsening internal as well as external situation. Internally, the leadership infirmities, along with the economic downturn, have become one of the grievous challenges questioning the governmental credibility and the viability of the state. Externally, a strategy shift has occurred with the declaratory policy of India now being a nuclear weapons power.

What would be the best available strategic imperative for Nepal when it is confronted with an external milieu bordering on the possible military escalation and the continuation of the arms race? Here, the strategic imperative does not mean a military one, because the military option for Nepal is a no option. The national strategy is defined as encompassing diplomatic, economic and political means; the broad spectrum available to the state to achieve its objectives and to enhance the state's capability to face and manage challenges.

Security a la Carte

Defining security studies in the context of Nepal is an uphill task. Nepali literature, is devoid of material that systematically defines security issues and discusses the nature of threat. There are no centres of learning in Nepal where security studies are pursued with a full-blown programme. Actually, the need to 'know thy enemy' never occasioned.

The perception that Nepal is encircled by two giant neighbours is realistic enough to lead its security elite to determine the future of relations with them through diplomacy rather than military preparedness. Notably, Nepal has not fought a war since 1816. And defence through military offense is never a choice for a state like Nepal even in its present form, which has about US $ 4 billion GDP and US $ 180 per capita income. Its armed forces of 50,000 and US $ 50 million defence budget in itself appears a wasteful exercise. The Royal Nepal Army does not even have a 24 hours conventional defence capability of its home territory whenever the crunch comes.

There exists, however, a small body of writings on the subject in relation to security affairs of the state. Piecing together the essence of these writings is difficult because most of these writings have treated security at contextual level while delving on the details of Nepal's foreign policy. Nonetheless, these studies are useful in understanding the Nepali mindset and in pointing out the security dilemma of Nepal which stems from an existential threat. The existential threat is the issue most debated and discussed both in the policy-making and academic circles.

Its origin goes back to the *Dibya Upadesh* of the first Shah King Prithvi Narayan Shah of modern Nepal who had laid down the measures to be undertaken for the national defence. With a suggestion that Nepal is a 'gourd between two rocks', he had advocated a defensive strategy for the state best suited for the preservation of its territorial integrity. Continuation in maintaining friendship with both the neighbouring states—India and China—was the foci of his strategic principle. But he was more suspicious of the southern neighbour (the expansionist British East India Company) against which the national defence was directed.[3]

This pattern of security thinking has continued even today. There is a broad agreement among the national security managers in Nepal that the dynamics of relationship between India and China underlie the basic ingredient of Nepali geopolitics. Central to the geo-strategic thinking in Nepal, therefore, is the structure of relations between its

[3] L.F. Stiller, S.J., *Prithiwinarayan Shah in the Light of Dibya Upadesh* (Ranchi, Bihar: The Catholic Press, 1968).

two giant neighbours. Tension between the strong and the strategy of the weak had been pivotal in formulating policies of national survival in its historical context.[4]

This flawed policy of balance of power did not work to the Nepali advantage in the long run, particularly it could not withstand the severe tests during the panchayat regime. The foremost reason behind the failure of this strategy was the legitimacy crisis of the regime, which was, at the most, exclusionary in its performance, that had also attempted to infuse a sense of legitimacy crisis with the crisis of the state, and had deliberately identified monarchy with the state. This brought about a context in which leadership or a regime's insecurity was primarily treated as a national security concern.

However, regime insecurity had always been treated as exogenous. For the traditional leadership and strategic elite who have continued to hold their sway over the Nepal state, threat to security has always emanated from India. It is not only in the geostrategic context that the threat has been inculcated and interpreted. The challenge to national integrity of Nepal has also been underlined by some commonalities fostered by religiosity and culture, in generating the psychological fear of absorption with the civilizational centre, that is, India.

The irony, however, is that the traditional strategic elite of Nepal, irrespective of their being the Shahs, the Ranas, the Thakuris, etc., have never failed in claiming their genealogical lineage or their ancestry back to Chittor or Mewar (Rajasthan) of India, to establish their gentility over the rest of the Nepalis. But their psyco-cultural motivations are particularly geared to prove their differences between the hill Hinduism and the plains Hinduism, as a factor in contributing to inter-state conflicts. Celebrating nationalism has become a driving force behind the drawing of a political boundary and in defining identity explicitly in relation to the traits and quality of the other state, even though there is much in common with each other.

While seeking to define and articulate a more coherent strategic identity, the cultural root to the formation of the Nepali state provides a basis to present the Shah dynasty as a force of national unity. Quite often the monarchy in Nepal has been presented as a saviour 'Without which the country would have lost its existence as an independent and sovereign state'. Arguments, thus, put testify that in the history of

[4] Leo E. Rose, *Nepal: Strategy for Survival* (Berkeley: University of California Press, 1971).

Nepal monarchy symbolizes the nation that has preserved its national identity even in a 'situation in which even God might fail'.[5]

Similarly, a review of the Nepali history and society has led another scholar to conclude: 'Remove monarchy and there is no state, and minus the state, there is no nationalism'.[6] Perhaps, this scholar has in mind the dynastic legitimacy of monarchy in the Nepali state in its juridical foundation, while giving a spirited rendition to the monarchy as a unifying force in Nepal, than all other forces working towards assertion of their socio-political niche.

Therefore, the slogan '*Hamro Raja Hamro Desh Pran Bhanda Pyaro Chha*' (we love our king and our country more than our life) had been officially advocated as a course of national unity throughout the panchayat era. This cultural root had tried to instill a strategy culture, wherein, national security revolved around the safety and security of the institution of monarchy in Nepal.

Thus, geography, history, culture and the regime being the crucial factors in the formation of the Nepali state, have influenced the strategic or security thinking in Nepal. More prominently, the type of political regime that Nepal had in the past, particularly in the recent past between 1960 and 1990, which in the words of Lok Raj Baral, had a 'close parallel to the Spanish regime under Franco',[7] had shaped a strategic culture in Nepal in reaction to the factors mentioned above.

The 'land-military complex' provided the rationale to the formation of the Nepali state, that led to the development of a bureaucratic-authoritarian regime under a monarchy, whose personal fulfilment and status defined the security imperatives for the country, with a hand-picked oligarchy working in close contact with the monarchy at the Palace Secretariat.[8] Security, therefore, was much of a taboo in

[5] Ganesh Raj Sharma, 'Monarchy and the Democratic Development in Contemporary Nepal', in Kamal P. Malla (ed.), *Nepal: Perspectives on Continuity and Change* (Kirtipur: Centre for Nepal and Asian Studies, 1989), p. 365.

[6] Prayag Raj Sharma, 'Nation-Building, Multiethnicity, and the Hindu State', in David N. Gellner et al. (eds.), *Nationalism and Ethnicity in a Hindu Kingdom: The Politics of Culture in Contemporary Nepal* (Amsterdam Harwood Press, 1997), p. 482.

[7] Lok Raj Baral, *Nepal: Problems of Governance* (New Delhi: Konark Publications, 1993), p. 4.

[8] Rishikesh Shaha, 'Patrimonial Elites in Nepal: Their Identity, Role and Character', in his *Essays in the Practice of Government in Nepal* (New Delhi: Manohar, 1982); Mahesh C. Regmi, *King and Political Leaders of the Gorkhali Empire*, 1768-1814 (Hyderabad: Orient Longman, 1995); and Ludwig F. Stiller, S.J. *The Rise of the House of Gorkha* (Kathmandu Ratna Pustak Bhandar, 1975).

Nepal. Whatever debates took place concentrated on the need of political stability as a security imperative And political stability within the state was viewed only possible through denial of democracy and pluralism while maintaining 'equidistance' with India externally, by proposing a non-provocative defence strategy of declaring Nepal to be a 'Zone of Peace'.

As the concept of the zone of peace was closely identified with the shrill rhetoric originating from the establishment, it had drowned the possibility of any healthy and objective debates on the issue. The concept was explained as a sacred omen proclaimed by the king, on the auspicious occasion of his coronation in 1975. Thereby, attempts at considering its policy contents and implications never seriously occurred publicly. Criticism of the concept, though rare, was never tolerated. Those indulging in the academic discourse over the issue were clearly blamed as anti-monarchists. Voices which were not in conformity with the stilted official line were systematically marginalized. Therefore, the zone of peace could never become a public policy and died prematurely after the political change in Nepal in 1990.

Lessons From History

What has history taught one? Colonialism in the Indian subcontinent had not absorbed Nepal In fact, the present day international border of Nepal had been arrived at through negotiations with British India, after the Sugauli Treaty in 1816. It has no major territorial disputes with either of its neighbours (save the presently ensuing negotiations over the status of Kalapani area between Nepal and India, that lies in the tri-juncture of Sino-Indian and Nepali border in western Nepal). It has never faced the challenge of physical extinction, because it would be a liability more than an asset for any power attempting to do so.

But it does not mean that since Nepal survived as a challenge-free state in the past it would continue to do so in the future. The challenges it faced in its external milieu were caused by its landlocked state, changing correlation of forces in its neighbourhood, and the ambition of India, in maintaining a status quo in its relationship with Nepal, which it had tried to change meaningfully. Such a challenge has been reinforced again with the demonstrated power potential by India through nuclear tests, leading to the possibility of tension escalation across the Sino-Indian border.

The momentous truth is that the Chinese military disposition towards India has changed along with India's nuclear power status. It is, however, not clear whether this change in their strategic orientation would make their relations to evolve peacefully, competitively, or conflictually. Nepal is no doubt now in a situation to think seriously over the nuclear reality, in reassessing its position before imparting any policy in its relations with both the nuclear weapons powers. It should also realize that the underlying temptation to use the mystic 'China card' can no longer be a psychological threat to India in its policy maneouvre. Defining ties with the neighbours in positive terms would both be credible and acceptable.

It may also lead to help mitigate any underlying suspicion about Nepal and avoid misunderstanding. For Nepal, its role in conflict prevention bilaterally between India and China with constructive and active engagement is more important now than remaining passive as in the past.

The bitter lesson of history which the domestic political vulnerability of the leadership was one of the key factors in determining its approach to foreign and security policies, including a policy of brinkmanship, to survive in power. When threatened internally by the mass uprising that almost coincided with the economic blockade imposed by India leading to economic difficulties, the gap in the national security thinking was clearly demonstrated, when the Nepali leadership linked its failure to manage domestic challenges with foreign machination.

King Birendra's appeal to the international community at the ninth Non-Aligned Summit Conference in Belgrade on 5 September 1989, exemplified the security dilemma of the state, where the people's demand for democracy had threatened the regime's survival, closely linked with the monarchical order.

In the words of King Birendra, there is a 'distinct need for a more effective mechanism by which security and survival of small states may be guaranteed under international law . . . Because, small states are susceptible to many forces beyond their control, be it an onslaught of mass communication or the threat of gunboat diplomacy. . . . While the strong ones can pursue the goals of economic, technological and military powers, the weaker and vulnerable countries have to constantly struggle for bare survival.'[9]

King Birendra's raising of alarm for state security, in fact, his

[9] *The Rising Nepal*, 6 September 1989.

concern for the security and stability of the panchayat regime and the plea for the refrain from the perceived external interference in support of the movement for democracy in Nepal from India, sums up the context in which 'security, stability and status'[10] of the Nepali state was defined.

While conceptualizing security of the Nepali state the India factor, perhaps, looms larger than others in military, economic and political dimensions. Particularly, Nepal's socio-economic dependency on India, notwithstanding its claims of decreasing trade dependency ratio-wise, has opened up other vulnerabilities. The Indian stakes in Nepal reinforced through bilateralism (treaties and agreements) from mutual security arrangement to water resources sharing treaties have tied Nepal boundlessly with the Indian interests. India is, therefore, in a position to influence the course of Nepali politics internally, and constrain as well as complicate the latter's diplomatic endeavours externally.

These are some of the most important issues on which Nepal will have to tread cautiously in the future. There had been some instances in which Nepal's extensive external ties with countries other than India were substantially less influential in bridging the Nepal-India differences. Neither internationalization of bilateral issues involving India nor diversified dependency had rescued Nepal from the Indian ire. Fundamental to India's external relations in South Asia would be a stringent bilateralism irrespective of SAARC or sub-regionalism. The likely implication for Nepal, therefore, is that India would remain a perennial external threat whenever the former fails to manage relations with the latter.

But this Indian threat, as a matter of fact, is relational to Nepali domestic politics that has assumed increasing importance after restoration of democracy in 1990. As different political parties have shown their tendency to stress on different priorities on the execution of foreign policy, in and out of the government, they have created a chaotic direction in foreign policy pursuit, opening the door for manipulation and manoeuvre by external forces. This is certainly an indication of domestic political instability, leading to the weakening of the state and national resilience, thereby producing unforeseen challenges and uncertainty to the question of the nation's future

[10] Muni in his seminal work has used this phrase (borrowed from George Liska) while defining the objectives of Nepal's foreign policy. See S.D. Muni, *Foreign Policy of Nepal* (Delhi: National, 1973).

These are, indeed, some traditional security concerns for a country like Nepal situated in a very complicated geostrategic landscape, with a national leadership in transition and yet to be consolidated democratic order. Ensuring the continuation of a democratic order, with a prudent leadership sensitive to the domestic challenges, requires a reversal of their role in defining security in terms of threat emanating from external forces. Choices open to a small, weak and vulnerable state like Nepal in its external realm are very unattractive.

Nepal can neither opt for unilateral military defence nor enter into a strong alliance with either of the nuclear weapons powers in its vicinity, nor ensure security guarantee because these can all be suicidal. These policies can also lead to an uninvited confrontation. History, evidently stands against the renewal of such a motivation.[11]

This suggests that a small state like Nepal should look beyond the confines of security defined in military terms. The fundamental reality thus, is that Nepal is neither in a position to fight nor preserve its territorial integrity and independence through military means, nor would it have any ally to fight on its behalf.

Primacy of Politics: The Missing Link

The preceding sections discuss the evolution of security conception in Nepal and the historical experiences leading to the security dilemma of the state in the context of its external milieu. Articulation of external hostility, perhaps, was the best policy for the leadership then to impart on a policy of regime consolidation, with bureaucratic expansion and administrative control in the course of state building.

The development of Nepal as a unitary state, with the accumulation of state power by the centralized authority of monarchy, had excluded society at large in the course of the functioning of the state, except in the context of extraction and control. State making in Nepal, as elsewhere, was largely a military enterprise. Though defined as national unification and political integration, it was, nevertheless, the military conquest that has shaped the present day Nepali state's identity. Hence the military as the coercive instrument of state power has a role both in internal and external security maintenance. And the excessive reliance on this traditional coercive institution, even during

[11] Nepal's imports of arms from China in mid-1988 was not only interpreted as a breach of agreement entered with India in 1965, it also created misunderstanding leading to the Indian imposition of economic blockade against Nepal in March 1989.

the panchayat period, had weakened the societal factors making the state a fragile entity in overall context.

This fragility has been the cause and consequence of a preoccupation with the physical security of Nepal's territory and its ruling elite. For the sake of clarity it should be noted here, that, despite the maintenance of a strong coercive capacity, the panchayat regime disturbingly lacked the elemental institutional capacities which Mann describes as the 'infrastructural power' or 'capacity through the realm', to derive support and consent to the regime.[12] Mann's definition of infrastructural power is closer to Buzan's understanding of the 'institutional expression of state', with popular support to exercise the state power in governance.

In the absence of a legitimating popular support, the imposed institutions could lose their authority that was reflected in the very origins of the panchayat system. Despite the widespread identification among the people with the 'idea of the state',[13] the institutional atrophy of the panchayat system, combined with its exploitative and repressive role, produced defiance, alienation as well as a low socio-political cohesion threatening the domestic realm.

Precisely speaking, security studies, as Richard Betts has noted, is 'everything that bears on the safety of a polity'.[14] The 'boundary problem' of such an all inclusive definition of security has been narrowed down by Mohammed Ayoob, by the use of 'vulnerable-invulnerable continuum' framework, in defining security specific to the Third World states.[15] Accordingly, Ayoob defines security in relation to 'vulnerabilities that threaten, or have the potential, to bring down or significantly weaken state structures, both territorial and institutional, as well as the regimes that preside over these structures and profess to represent them internationally'.[16]

So long as other phenomena ranging from economic performance and environmental damages does not directly impinge on the question of the survival of the state in territorial or other forms, these have been

[12] Michael Mann, 'The Autonomous Power of the State', in John A. Hall (ed.), *State in History* (Oxford: Basil Blackwell, 1986), p. 113.

[13] Barry Buzan, *People, States and Fear* (Brighton: Harvester Press, 1983), Chapter 2.

[14] Richard K. Betts, 'Should Strategic Studies Survive?,' *World Politics*, October 1997, p. 9.

[15] Mohammed Ayoob, 'The Security Problematic of the Third World' (review article), *World Politics*, January 1991, pp. 257-83.

[16] Ayoob, p. 259.

excluded from the vulnerability component of the continuum defined above. Also, there are four other crucial vulnerabilities, critical to the survival and security of Nepal as a viable state in the future. These relate particularly to the problem of governance, in which the national leadership under democracy has to consider a role in democratic consolidation. The newer sources of insecurity in Nepal are socio-political in nature, which could effect a dimensional change in the constitutive principles of Nepali state in the future.

To make the problems of security understandable in the case of Nepal within its social milieu, four situations are identified to describe factors leading to further vulnerabilities, compounding insecurity of the state. These are the systemic erosion of the state caused by the leadership inefficacy, the economic disarray, the ethnic revivalism, and the Maoist insurgency. For the sake of convenience, I treat these issues separately.

A Question of Leadership

It would be peculiar to state here that the formidable challenge to state security being caused by the political leadership, described as a challenge of governance; is actually, the challenge to governance. Within the past eight years of democracy in Nepal (1990-8), the country has had two elected Parliaments and seven Prime Ministers. In the second Parliament from 1994 onward, the making and unmaking of governments have produced five Prime Ministers under different political setups. Parliamentarians have invested their time and energy in toppling governments one after another, making such exercises most dangerous and expensive than the periodic elections.

The irony of democracy, according to the former Minister of Parliamentary Affairs, Narahari Acharaya, is that the day a person is elected as a Prime Minister, the parliamentarians will start thinking about his alternative and begin unfolding their tantrums to replace him. The crux of the problem for the political stability in Nepal lies with the parliamentarians and their greed and grandeur, for which they have started a process of criminalization of politics for their self-aggrandizement. As a consequence, Nepal has a record-breaking number of ministers within the past three-and-a half-years, with five-time changes of government, one after another.

Out of the 265 members in Parliament, 121 (45.7 per cent) were lucky enough to become ministers. Within this review period, 55 (65.5 per cent) of the 84 Nepali Congress legislators have become ministers, 26 (29.2 per cent) of the 89 CPN-UML legislators had enjoyed ministerial portfolios, before its break-up in February 1998. Also, 20 (100 per cent) of the Rashtriya Prajatantra Party (RPP) legislators have become ministers, along with three (100 per cent) from the Sadbhavana Party (Terai based) and 3 (100 per cent) from independent legislators. Between 1996 and 1997, Nepal had the largest cabinet of 48 ministers.

It has also set a record of appointing 4 cabinet rank ministers without portfolio. This trend has been aptly defined by the political observers as patrimonialism generating cleavages within and outside the political parties.

The politicization of bureaucracy as well as the police forces, has been a trend setting development in Nepali politics, eroding the ethics conversant with the rule of law and enhancing the prospects of political corruption. Political parties have, thus, nourished corruption as the norm of the political process.

Particularly, political parties have done nothing within the past few years of democracy, except to involve themselves in corrupt practices, because of the ensuing political instability and uncertainty leading to the concern for impending election. Every successive government formed after 1994, set a target to commence election under its supervision. It not only led to the development of a single agenda to amass election funds through manipulation of the state purse for the party, personal or 'private regarding', but also encouraged strategies to be adopted to win election through fair as well as foul means.

Scandals about corruption are a media blitz, that blemishes the credibility of political leadership. The erstwhile panchayat era is known as the 'golden age' of corruption. Out of 22 major cases of corruption recorded so far, besides gold, idol and drug smuggling, 18 were committed between 1974 and 1989 (King Birendra's era).

Of the rest of the four largest scandals, namely the RNAC-Dhamija deal, fertilizer deal, telephone distributions, and the sugar and petroleum deals, all the major political parties' leaders were found indulging in corrupt practices. Corruption, malpractices and criminal activities are so deeply entrenched and protected by the government that its public disclosure would threaten it with extinction.[17] The government has never felt it necessary to clarify how the financial irregularities,

[17] See the interview of former Finance Minister Rabindra Nath Sharma, who made no disclosure but admitted that if he were to name the person he would be dead the next day. *Deshanter Weekly*, 19 April 1998.

which, according to the Public Accounts Committee of the parliament, has risen to the tune of Rs. 50 billion in the shape of unsettled account, can be settled.

Parliament in Nepal has become a problem for democratic consolidation and challenge to governance. Records reveal that there were very few occasions during which serious discussions are held on issues of national importance. Usually, the partisan interests of the political parties—both ruling and opposition—have guided the parliamentary proceedings and legislation like the tax-free vehicles' imports and increasing perks and privileges to the parliamentarians were passed unanimously, rather than passing of the bills in the interest of the people.

There are instances when the ruling party had even passed bills unilaterally to avoid stiff opposition during the past 13 parliamentary sessions. Such unconstitutional and undemocratic behaviour shown by the political parties in Nepal have left the question of democratic consolidation unattended. Sadly, under the advantage of democratic legitimacy, the political leaders in Nepal are functioning as 'protection racketeers', with the sanctity of the governments formed under their party flags as organized criminals.[18] This contention has been substantiated by the politicians' self-confession that the governments' functioning in Nepal are under the grips of mafia.[19]

These are signs of systemic erosion of democratic ethos, making consolidation of political order more difficult. Since consolidation is equated with the process of institutionalization and political stability, the patrimonial-type of leadership (more pronounced under democracy) has a reverse impact on the entire process of democratic consolidation. A schism has therefore, developed in Nepal, questioning the viability of democracy itself, because of the governmental unaccountability and irresponsibility.

Although, there are no squabbles on the transfer of power from one to another elected government, the political parties are, however, seen

[18] The notion of 'protection racketry' and 'organized crime' have been borrowed from Charles Tilly's work 'War-making and State-making as Organized Crime', in Peter B. Evans, Dietrich Rueschemeyer and Theda Skocpol (eds.), *Bringing the State Back In* (London: Cambridge University Press, 1985), pp. 169-71.

[19] The contents of Nepali newpapers are spread with the interviews given by various politicians on the subject irrespective of their political leanings, particularly, the national weekly and news magazines in the first half of 1998 have covered reports on the issue.

to have been working at variance to the need of democratic consolidation. Evidently, the Communist Party of Nepal (CPN-UML in its previous form), has not completely reconciled with the parliamentary system. On the other hand, the RPP is widely viewed to have been functioning as a royalist party because of being a party formed by the former panchayat elite. The Nepali Congress as a masses party instrumental in bringing in political change in Nepal, has now become thoroughly faction-ridden. Thus, it has lost the required political vision in pursuit of its democratic mission.

To summarize, all the major political parties who had already enjoyed governance and power in one form or another, within the past 8 years of multiparty democracy in Nepal, of which the Nepali Congress has been in power for nearly seven years in the form of a majority, coalition and minority governments, are particularly to be blamed for ensuing political instability and weakening of the state.

THE ECONOMIC MALAISE

Irrespective of what the government claims, Nepal is in economic disarray, which will be difficult to surmount in the context of continuing political uncertainty created by the governing elite. Figuring out what has happened to the Nepali economy is possible if one were to look at the cold facts.

When a country's indebtedness increases by more than 200 to 250 per cent of its total export trade earnings or the debt servicing ratio crosses 20 per cent of the total exports (according to the IMF classification), that country reaches the point of economic breakdown. Nepal's position on these matters, for example, in 1994-5 was more than 600 per cent on the former and the debt-servicing ratio in that particular fiscal year was exactly 35 per cent. Yet, Nepal still has not declared the state bankrupt.

Nepal is a state that has long been driven by the philosophy 'borrow and prosper'. And, it has survived throughout the past 45 years, to be exact, with a policy of becoming rich on steroids (continuous flow of foreign aid). Foreign loans as a component of external cooperation was at its lowest before 1970, hovering around US $ 2 million. By 1987, the debt burden was still under US $ 1 billion, which accelerated to more than US $ 2.5 billion by 1996. The figure now stands at around US $ 3 billion. With the depreciation of the Nepali currency following the rapid crunch in Indian currency after the nuclear test,

Nepal is facing a problem of renewal in its economy with sluggish exports and mounting imports.

Economic malaise and growing dependency are also described as twin factors impeding democratic consolidation in Nepal. Nepal is one of the least developed and the poorest of countries in the world, where socio-economic anomalies are widespread. Poverty characterizing the national economy has increased, encompassing more than 70 per cent of the people below poverty line, even though the official figures run between 42 to 49 per cent. The destitute and deprived are the features of national life.

Even the urban centres, where most of the capital is invested, are hit by lopsided growth. Most dangerous is the fact that the Nepali economy is highly penetrated, controlled by a handful of local business elite and foreigners, namely the Indians. Nepal is also an economic unit where resource transfer in the name of development cooperation in the past 45 years, has shown no signs of improvement in its infrastructural base.

Actually, only 15 per cent of the population are beneficiaries of the foreign aid received. Foreign aid has helped the Nepali authorities to expand their control and coercive power. As a consequence, Nepal is the only country in South Asia where there are more soldiers and police force than doctors and health centres. According to Mahabub ul-Haq, there are more soldiers (35) per doctor in Nepal.[20]

Again the problem of resource transfer through foreign aid in the post-cold war world is no longer a free-lunch. According to Nepal's Auditor General's Report 1997, foreign aid (both in terms of grant and loan) is tied up to the extent that the government is obliged to appoint technical advisers of the donors' choice to become a legitimate recipient.

A major chunk of the aid—30 per cent on road projects, 37 per cent on irrigation, and 39 per cent on tourism development projects—constitutes the expenditure on advisory services. Besides, the failure of many project undertakings, with the tenure of some projects extended ten times the original planned period of six months, the advice of a consultant, has largely been responsible for raising the project cost.

The problem of economic development has been revealed by the scarcity of funds that the government has not been able to garner

[20] Mahabub ul-Haq, *Human Development in South Asia* 1997 (Karachi: Oxford University Press, 1997).

at the moment. Besides the government has not been able to disburse more than Rs. 6 billion for developmental works in the first seven months of the fiscal year 1997-8, out of the total allocated amount of Rs. 34 billion. Never before has the national economy been in such a sorry state.

The ever-widening economic and social disparities are recorded in official reports. The report published by the National Planning Commission is a testimony to the economic woes the country is facing.[21] The human development indices tabulated in both the human development report and the 49 nations ESCAP survey report published in April 1997, classify Nepal at the near bottom of the country survey. The indigenously produced report on human development in 1998 suggested that the economic structure of Nepal was largely characterized by the semi-feudalistic pattern of development, where low agricultural productivity prevails.[22]

In essence, poverty alleviation has been a crucial component of Nepal's economic development efforts since the first five-year plan (1956-61) was conceived. The basic objective then was to 'raise production, employment, standard of living and general well-being throughout the country, thus opening out to the people opportunities for richer and more satisfying life'. The conceptual framework behind the ninth plan (which is still under consideration after a lapse of a year) too lies in reformulating policies to reinforce poverty alleviation programmes and employment generating schemes, in a situation where the incidence of poverty is increasing.

In 1998, for the first time in Nepali history, deaths due to famine increased to more than 400. Thus, the widening economic disparities have already proved the failure of preceding eight five-year plans. This has led to a situation in Nepal, where the government has not been able to instill a sense of belonging among the people nor does it care about any issue which is not directly related with its particular political interests. As a consequence, the flow of economic migrants to India, especially in the form of seasonal or permanent settlers, is on the rise.

Therefore, when the government or the state fails to provide even the subsistence needs of the people and secure their right to live within their motherland, a simple and decent life, to expect nationalism or the

[21] Central Bureau of Statistics, *Nepal: Living Standard Survey Report 1996* (Kathmandu: National Planning Commission Secretariat, 1996).

[22] NSAC, *Nepal: Human Development Report 1998* (Kathmandu: Nepal South Asia Centre, 1998).

struggle for the independence of the state, cannot be expected from them.

Ethnic Revivalism: How could the people identify with a state that has been thoroughly exploitative, repressive and 'gangrened' by clan politics, rooted in primordial kinship and the exclusive ethnic solidarity? What would be the state of affairs in a country where the core issue of national integration has never been addressed through the development of a political culture of tolerance, accommodation and consensus? And what would be the final consequence of the bureaucratic-authoritarian governance, that has functioned with a singular tendency to maximize the leadership autonomy; with one's own self-proclaimed goal of political stability through control and coercion and the co-opting of the like minded social elite, in a society where political competition was considered as sin till recently?

The fueling of the ethnic grievances, as a consequence, are the responses to such a deprivation which is emerging as a crucial issue challenging state cohesion. As a matter of fact, ethnic demands are not new realities, but its assertions are. The tension it has created and the debates rendering the dusting off of piles of documentary evidences to the historicity of the ethnic problems, are sufficient to put the Nepali state into an ethnic abyss. Till recently the Nepali state has fared much better on the ethnic issue in comparison to its neighborhood; but, for how long, is the question that most people are concerned with.[23]

Would there be an ethnic backlash in Nepal as experienced elsewhere or would the ethnic groups continue to press for a systemic hearing of their demands, and strive for recognition under the constitutional arrangement? As elsewhere in the Third World, ethnicity in Nepal is also articulated against the 'mononoethnic tendency' expressed by the state. A common perception prevalent among the 'indigenous people', popularly known as *Janajatis* in Nepal, is that they have been systematically marginalized by the Hinduized regimes, irrespective of the political system, in different time frame.

Under democracy (after 1990), the *Janajatis* reorganized themselves

[23] Lok Raj Baral, 'Ethnicity and Constitutional Reform in Nepal', in Iftekharuzzaman (ed.), *Ethnicity and Constitutional Reform in South Asia* (New Delhi: Manohar, 1998), pp. 84-107; Krishna B. Bhattachan, 'Ethnopolitics and Ethnodevelopment: An Emerging Paradigm in Nepal'; and Dilli Ram Dahal, 'Ethnic Cauldron, Demography and Minority Politics: The Case of Nepal', both in Dhruba Kumar (ed.), *State, Leadership and Politics in Nepal* (Kathmandu: Centre for Nepal and Asian Studies, 1995).

to put their demands for social justice and equality more forcefully. The impulses of aspiration and expectation that have guided them to ask for a fair deal under democracy have, however, been belied by the political reality. Three consecutive events have turned their expectations towards desperation.

Firstly, when the 'multilingual, multicultural, and multiethnic' Nepal constitutionally became a Hindu state and the Nepali language declared a *lingua franca* of the country, the manufactured myth of social harmony continued to be reinforced again under democracy. Activities jeopardizing this said harmonious relation subsisting among the peoples of various castes, tribes and communities undermining the sovereignty and integrity of the state, were considered impervious.

Secondly, the imposition of Sanskrit as a compulsory study at the primary level as well as broadcasting of news bulletin by Radio Nepal in that language at the expense of other recognized language of the community further antagonized the *janajatis*.

Thirdly, the policy adopted by the National Election Commission to block the participation of the non-Hindu ethnic group as political parties to contest national elections, was seen as the hammering of the last nail in the coffin of ethnic harmony. Many mongoloid Nepalis feel it is but a Hindu revivalism under democracy, induced politically by upholding the process of harmonizing Nepali culture in persuance of the ideals of the erstwhile panchayat system, 'eutai desh, eutai bhasha, eutai bhesh' (one nation, one language, one dress), which fly in the faces of the champions of secularism and socialism (as professed by the largest party, the Nepali Congress, throughout its struggle for democracy in Nepal).

Against this background, ethnic identity has indeed surfaced with a new impetus both in opposition to the policies of the state, and as a conscientious striving at identifying the national ethos in a non-Hindu social formation.[24] There are several groups demanding the rights for the mongoloid people, particularly on the issue of political participation as an organized party. One of the major grievances of this group is that, except one, none is recognized as a political party, under the pretext that they were fomenting religious and sectarian interests.

[24] According to Smith, the politics of ethnonationalism everywhere has been fueled by the triple process of the purification of culture, universalization of closeness and territorialization of memory. See Anthony D. Smith, 'Culture, Community and Territory: The Politics of Ethnicity and Nationalism', *International Affairs*, July 1996, pp. 488-9.

Contrarily, the Tarai based Hindu Sadbhavana Party, with explicit sectarian tendencies and forewarning Nepal to meet the same fate as Sri Lanka, has been recognized by the National Election Commission and registered as a political party to contest elections. This overt discrimination at the political level is interpreted by the mongoloid groups as a testimony to the Hindu high caste's refusal to comply with the demands for power sharing, equity, and justice under democracy in Nepal.

As militancy on the part of the ethnic groups has increased, it has led them to gradually challenge the very constitutive principles of the Nepali state. The Nepali state since 1769 has been premised on the idea of the political primacy of a Hindu monarchy, imperative of national unity through declaring itself a Hindu state, designation of Nepali as a national language and Gorkhali eliticism.[25] Criticism to this constitutive principle of the Nepali state came from no less a person than the former Prime Minister B.P. Koirala (1959-60) who died struggling for democracy in Nepal.

> He said, the objective of Prithvi Narayan Shah and his immediate successors was just expansion of the Gorkha state. To say that was a campaign for national unity and provide historical justification would be absolutely incorrect. At least, the sense of Nepali nationalism was absent at that time. Nepali nationalism was latter day historical construct.
>
> The expansion of the Gorkha state was not a campaign for national solidarity, nor were the rulers of Gorkha inspired by Nepali nationalism; nor the machinery of the Gorkha state expansion, Gorkha soldiers or officers were nationalists. Gorkhali kings had launched the victory campaigns and their characters were that of victors, not of national leaders; due to which they maltreated the vanquished kings and people. Still the Newars of Kathmandu have nourished that wound.[26]

The logic behind B.P. Koirala's argument was that nationalism as a composite whole can only flourish under democracy. The Nepali nationalism, manufactured only after the Sugauli treaty with the British in 1816, was phoney, because, ever since the Nepali monarchs have not been able to leave their characteristics of a victor. Whenever people raise their voices for their rights in the nation, they are

[25] Dhruba Kumar, *Nepali State and Politics: Inevitable Crisis and Harrowing Transition* (a book-length study report submitted to the Centre for Nepal and Asian Studies for publication, 12 December 1997).

[26] B.P. Koirala, 'Rastra-Rastriata Ra Prajatantra' (Nation, Nationalism and Democracy) (Varanasi: Tarun Prakashan, 1978).

'ruthlessly suppressed by the monarchy'. For B.P. Koirala, nationalism actually originated in Nepal spontaneously, during the 1950-1 revolution.

For the first time in the Nepali history, people made a collective effort for a cause that did not only change the political regime but also united the Nepali people, thus shaping Nepali nationalism. Earlier, the Kot massacre (1846) had also led to political change and the rise of Jang Bahadur, whose family ruled Nepal for 104 years till February 1951. Hence the Royal coup of 15 December 1960, accordingly, was not only basically undemocratic but also anti-national. Abolition of the sovereign rights of the people can never be said to be a step towards nationalism.

Nepal in the 1990s awaits a rethinking and reassessing over the philosophy underlined in BP's work on democracy and nationalism. A policy encompassing the feelings of different communities could be the only way out from the presently ensuing ethnic morass for Nepal, that may contribute towards democratic consolidation. Denial of democracy, even under a democratic constitution, would make the problem intractable by ultimately threatening the national cohesion.

Maoist Movement

A development that has presently sensitized the Nepali political scene is the violent Maoist movement, launched for the emancipation of people from the holds of a 'feudalist, comprador bourgeois multiparty system', and transform the power structure of the country from the hands of 5 per cent bourgeois of the total Nepali population.[27] The 'People's War' is launched by an extreme faction of the Communist Party of Nepal (UPF), who had won 9 parliamentary seats in the 1991 General Election and had become the third largest opposition party between 1991 and 1994.

Though their sudden turn to the politics of violence seemed inexplicable, they had, however, never reconciled with the parliamentary system and claimed to have participated in the electoral system to wreck the citadel from within. So far the insurgency has claimed

[27] In two of his recently published 'interviews' from underground, Dr. Babu Ram Bhattarai, as the commander of the guerrilla movement, accused the government of insensitivities to the United People's Front's 40-point demands placed before the then Prime Minister Deuba on 4 February 1996. See the *Himalaya Times*, 27 April 1997; and the *Spotlight*, 21 March 1997.

217 lives, of which, 140 are Maoists, 58 innocent civilians and 19 police personnel.[28] The situation at the time of writing is that political violence has spread gradually from some of the most under-developed districts to those comparatively developed, as well as some districts adjoining the Indian border in the south.

The fragility of the Nepali government at the centre has been a reason why the Maoists have succeeded in spreading a fear psychosis around the country, by virtually creating a statelessness situation in some 18 districts, where local elections are yet to be held and the normal administrative functions established.

Although there are only eight districts completely affected by the Maoist movement, presently there are eleven other districts affected partly, and some ten more districts where the potential of the spread of insurgency is acutely felt. If the trend persists, it is widely speculated that the government in Nepal would not be able to hold elections in some thirty districts in the 1999 General Elections.

The feature of the insurgency is that the institution of monarchy has become its prime target and the establishment of a republican state its objective. Within the framework of the republican state, the Maoists have advocated the rights to 'self-determination' by conceding the rights to secession, and the establishment of a separate and free state by the *Janajatis* (indigenous people). The inclusion of ethnic issues and the rights to self-determination by the Maoists,[29] as the *raison d'être* for the people's war, can be understood as a strategy to widen the canvas of struggle, through the formation or attempted formation of a broad coalition of interests against the state, at a time when some ethnic groups like the Khambuwan Mukti Morcha (Khambuwan Liberation Front) have started their public support to the Maoist cause.

The coalition of ethno-nationalism and the Maoist exhortation of the 'Total War' against the state, is theoretically a possibility as the target of both groups is the state that has wronged them. The attempt to mobilize different types of people by exploiting their nationalist sentiments, have a fair chance of success for the Maoists.

That nationalism, in whatever form, has been an undercurrent in the Maoist mobilization strategy, the broadening of its influence among the masses, in comparison to the declining influence of the elected governments on the people, cannot be denied. Again the possibility of

[28] *Rising Nepal*, 17 June 1998; *Kathmandu Post*, 17 June 1998.
[29] *The Mahima Weekly*, 14 February 1998.

each supporting the other's cause, even tacitly, cannot be ruled out. However, a formal coalition of interests between the Maoists and various ethnic groups at this juncture is difficult to anticipate.

One of the prominent reasons for the ethnic groups' apparent hesitation in supporting the wholesale violence wrecked by the Maoists is that the former has yet to evolve and consolidate an umbrella organization to form a singular political platform to take indisputable decisions.

Another reason for not doing so, is that, Nepal has been constitutionally a 'multilingual and multi-ethnic' state that has theoretically opened up avenues in articulating legitimate ethnic grievances. The cropping up of ethnic demands in democratic Nepal can understandably be explained as taking advantage of the new social and political opportunities open to the disadvantaged groups.

Fortunately, ethnic separatism is not the demand it faces. Moderation is still the currency through which both the government and ethnic groups can reach satisfactory resolutions to the problems they face. Likewise, there is room for negotiation between the government and the Maoist groups, to settle their differences instead of accusing each other of barbarity and brutality.

Would the government take up the issue seriously? As is well known, it depends primarily on the state's response to the ethnic demands in the future. Again, to go back to the moot question of the possibility of a coalition between the Maoists and the ethno-nationalists to breed political violence in Nepal, much depends on the democratic state's relationship with the society it governs.

A prerequisite for the state to be stable and functional in response to the needs of society, is to form a broad coalition of interests in state-society relations in order to build a socio-political cohesion. The disruption of the very fabric of the socio-political cohesion, in whatever form, and the state's continued neglect for remedying the ills could lead to further instability by opening new vulnerabilities to the question of regime/state survival.

In theory, political disruption in the absence of social cohesion could provide a fertile ground for breeding insurgencies or even revolutions, aimed at completely transforming social, economic and political structures of the state with massive violent upheavals. Social discontent that has become a reality in Nepal, along with the systemic failure of successive governments have provided a situation for breeding insurgencies. Although, it may not necessarily lead to the breakdown of democratic order by precipitating revolutionary prospects, it may succeed in discrediting the government and erode its legitimacy if it fails to cope with the internal stresses caused by the rising social dissent.

The situation now prevailing in Nepal is that disillusionment is increasing. Indeed, the people feel betrayed by the political parties, while the immobility of the government has made the country's situation pitiable. Actually, Nepal today is facing unimaginable problems in history. But, not all the problems are historical, rather they are created by the governmental lethargy under democracy. Governments in Nepal have failed not because they have not been able to perform in accordance to the 'high expectations' of the people, their failure is related to the destruction of democratic sanctity, with the criminalization of politics for personal advancement.

People had simple expectations that the political parties, after a long and arduous struggle for democracy will, at least, govern with accountability. The simmering discontent towards the political parties and the political leadership in general is, therefore, the cause and consequence of the growing sense of betrayal. Unless politics becomes responsible, Nepal may experience continued instability and economic hardships.

It is one thing to celebrate democracy and quite another, to recognize the way it operates in Nepal, which tends to marginalize the ordinary people while pampering the wealthy, privileged and the powerful. The main threat to the Nepali state and the democratic regime does not come from the Maoist insurgencies or political dissent of different forms, but rather from the failure of the government and the political parties controlling it, to guarantee all its citizens access to their bare necessities. The complexities of the ferment below the high politics of making and unmaking of the government at the centre, can expand if left unattended.

No matter how the Maoist insurgencies operate, the government will have to tackle this problem properly and soon in order to avoid further destabilization and destruction, which, however, cannot be anticipated at the moment. The strength of the Maoist insurgency is directly proportionate to the relative weakness of the government. So long as the government remains unconcerned with political violence and treats it simply as a law and order situation, and does not seek political solutions to the problems by addressing their demands collectively or segmentally (concerned with distributive justice and economic upliftment of the wretched), the phenomenon will remain.[30]

The Threat and The Concept of Security

The purpose in outlining these issues is to raise a question about who and what actually threatens the security of Nepal. Is it because Nepal being a small, weak, resource-poor and a landlocked state, now surrounded by the nuclear weapons powers, its national security has been inescapably jeopardized? Or is it because of the fact that Nepal is functioning as an appendage to the Indian economy, it has lost autonomy in decision-making and, thus, increasingly becoming insecure? Is the security of a state identified only with territorial integrity and all the traditional attributes of being a state?

Central to the security/insecurity of Nepal is the quality of political leadership it possesses. Unfortunately, Nepal is yet to possess a leadership that works. In assessing the challenges facing the country, the political parties themselves have become one of the most crucial factors in debilitating the state under democracy. In fact, the actual threat that Nepal is facing at the moment is the consequence of non-performance of the government, leading to heightened political discontentment and public alienation.

The dissatisfaction on the part of the people is caused by the immobility of the government and the excessive zeal of the politicians to serve their petty interests rather than their dissatisfaction with the political system. The chronic political instabilities leading to a growing social discontent and economic decline have impeded national coherence, with severe vulnerabilities. Other things remaining the same, the leadership infirmities and its inefficacies have been largely responsible in opening up vulnerabilities to the state and the threat arising not only as a challenge to authority, but also questioning the viability of the state.

What this articlele tries to explain is that the leadership in Nepal, in its historical development, had upheld security in preservation of its political interests. Even when defined narrowly to serve the interests of the incumbent ruling groups, the leadership had conscientiously tried to limit challenges to its interests, both from internal and external forces because it had never compartmentalized domestic threats

[30] Dhruba Kumar, *Nepali State and Politics*, Chapter 3.

entirely from the influence of the external powers. But Nepal under democracy is perceptively an exception to that rule.

The leaders in Nepal today are unhindered by the threat to a system called democracy, which has universal support and domestically, they have sensitized the peoples' feeling towards it. Having lived for long under the trauma of an undemocratic system, the people believe that they have actually won democracy in Nepal, after a hard struggle and enduring a lot of suffering. Externally, the leaders have a floating bank in support of the 'strengthening democracy projects' in Nepal, with money pouring in from abroad.

Nepal is a recipient of US $ 32,235,789, aimed at strengthening democracy projects between 1990-6,[31] apart from foreign aid on favourable terms. Besides, there are many NGOs and INGOs involved in making democracy thrive in Nepal. Democracy in Nepal is, therefore, taken care of from abroad. The international environment, guaranteeing the process of democratization in the post-cold war era, has become both, a source of financing democracy and development while freeing the leaders of a country like Nepal to indulge in kleptocracy and not work for democracy.

So, what are the vulnerabilities for a state placed in a situation of present day Nepal? Ayoob, while arguing about the basic characteristic of security for a state like Nepal, has emphasized on the internal dimension of the problems emanating in the process of state making, in which the role of the leadership is pivotal. However, insecurity/security of a state like Nepal is not the consequence of state-building or caused by the attempts at democratic consolidation, but the contrary. According to Ayoob, the political realm is fundamentally shaped by the political leadership, who command the authority to deliver goods and services to the people within a defined territory, and, therefore, becomes a primary referent of security.

But when a political leadership works against the primary function of the state as an accumulator and distributor, that leadership becomes a real threat to the security interest of people and the state. Primarily, the leadership role is that of preventer of conflict and this cannot be done by avoiding challenges. The leadership inertia in Nepal is the basis for complicating the domestic problems emanating from ethno-nationalism and the Maoist insurgencies.

There are records of some aborted political decisions to deal with

[31] *Development Cooperation Report* (Kathmandu: UNDP/Nepal, 17 January 1997).

the Maoists repressively. Likewise, the leadership has shown a lapse in managing diversity and practice a policy of inclusion and empowerment through decentralization of state apparatuses. Bureaucracy which is a wing of the government to implement political decision, has virtually come to a grinding halt due to the political uncertainty.

Thus, the socio-economic problems have compounded due to the increasing disparities and sharply pronounced social inequalities. Besides, abject poverty has characterized the Nepali society, with acute disparities in distribution of wealth and income. According to official statistics, only 3.7 per cent of the national income is received by the bottom 20 per cent of the Nepali households, whereas the top 10 per cent is endowed with 50 per cent of the pie.

Similarly, 69 per cent of the landholdings are less than 1 hectare in size, and 88 per cent are below 2 hectares.[32] The 'land-military complex' that dominated the course of state formation in Nepal 230 years ago, has continued, supplemented by a new political class with vested interests in maintaining the status quo by conspiring 'to place Nepal's economy in its prolonged stage of stagnation'; to be ultimately entangled with the spider web of smuggling, black marketing, commission brokerage and corruption.[33]

The political leaders under democracy have encouraged this trend to continue. No efforts are being made to systematically curb the prevailing economic malaise. The deepening crisis and the disparities are perhaps one of many reasons fueling ethnic demands and Maoist insurgencies. In the same vein, a majority of the rural population, especially the poor peasants, dalits, untouchables and the landless workers, abandoned by the state in its socio-economic programme, have developed a feeling that the government has continued to be exclusionary, exploitative and repressive.

However, they have yet to organize themselves into a powerful pressure group, in the absence of a common ideology providing them with an organizational base. The dependency of the rural peripheries on the urban centres for bare survival is stratified, as the hierarchy of the social system has developed an unending patron-client type of

[32] Central Bureau of Statistics, *Nepal: Living Standards Survey Report 1996*, Vols. I and II, Kathmandu: National Planning Secretariat, 1997.

[33] Devendra Raj Panday, 'The State of Political Economy', in Malla (ed.), *Nepal: Perspectives on Continuity and Change*, p. 276; and 'HMG/Nepal, Bartaman Arthik Sthisthi' (Current Economic Situation) (Kathmandu: Ministry of Finance, 25 May 1990), p. 34.

relationship at the local level. At the same time, the state itself has forged a similar relationship with the dominant political-economy of the region and, beyond. Thus, under the procedural democracy based on the elected representation system, the masses are remembered periodically, their popular participation limited to the casting of votes and forgotten till the next round of election is scheduled

Trading poverty has been a 'trademark' of an enterprising cottage industry in Nepal, in which the leadership has its share. The broadly framed donor-recipient nexus has pushed Nepal into the bottomless pit of dependency rapidly eroding its sustainability any chances of national renewal. The condominium of national political elite and the aid agencies has led to a situation in which the national leadership has become more loyal and responsible to the wishes of the donors, for their own sustenance and legitimacy to be in power, than the desires of the people they represent.

The need of external dependency has so profoundly influenced the leadership thinking, that the country's development programme in the name of poverty alleviation, has been made solely dependent on foreign aid, which has historically enlarged and expanded poverty in Nepal rather than alleviating it. As a recent survey report shows, donors are least desirous in preferring local needs but rather pushing their global agenda of liberalization, marketization, privatization and homogenization, which, however, do not cater to the interests of the poor.[34]

Instances such as the unilateral cancellation of Arun III project by the World Bank in 1995 (on which Nepal had already spent US $ 60 million on feasibility studies) show that the country is not in a position to negotiate with the donors on its own terms and preferences. As the country works on the donor-driven development agenda, the relevance of the projects to the indigenous needs is the least considered fact. A National Planning Commission report in 1994 had indicated that most of the projects implemented were contrary to local demands.

These projects designed by donors, absorb 50 per cent of the total assistance amount by way of remuneration and perks to the expert consultants appointed by the donors themselves. While 20 per cent is spent on expense head of 'training abroad', and 20 per cent

[34] Krishna B. Bhattachan, 'Nepalese Perception of European Donors' Approach to Poverty Reduction in Nepal' (unpublished). Comparative Study of European Aid for Poverty Reduction *Collaborative European Research Project*, 31 July 1997.

on technical learning and the balance 10 per cent on local project site.[35] As a consequence of the leadership inefficacy in determining the destiny of the state, Nepal is put in a helpless and hapless situation where representative institutions (in whatever shape they are) are falling apart and public accountability has disappeared, and national resilience disrupted.

The state in Nepal is gradually disintegrating, not physically, but psychologically. The pervasive societal frustrations, growing tensions and uncertainty have created a situation that may ultimately lead to the breakdown of even a semblance of authority, leading to anarchy.

A Security Paradigm for Nepal

Construction of a security paradigm for a state in the position of Nepal is neither ambiguous nor ambitious. Among many states in the Third World laden with a situation like Nepal, perhaps, Nepal is the most secure. The examples of Buddhist Cambodia and Muslim Afghanistan come to mind when geostrategic challenges to Nepal are considered. Within South Asia when almost all the states are wrecked by ethnic conflicts with continuing armed struggles for secession and self-determination, Nepal until recently, remained relatively free from such troubles. On the external front, Nepal's territorial integrity has continued to be maintained by an unwritten understanding between India and China (Treaty on Tibet 1954) to honour the interests of these two powers across the Himalayas, the violation of which by either would certainly be adverse to the *status quo*.

Despite this, the Nepali case is underlined with chronic socio-political instability and underdevelopment, along with the challenges of regime legitimating and economic development. However, with a transitional democracy in the 1990s, Nepal has successfully overcome, although superficially, the regime legitimating challenge, which is universally acknowledged.

In understanding the imperative of security for Nepal, the role of the state or the political leadership that claims to be legitimate representative of the state requires to be explained in proper perspective. As the state or the leadership asserts itself to be, the repository of the people' power, particularly under a democracy, the concept of governance actually becomes a function of state character and capacity, which in turn constitute a function of politics.

[35] *Kathmandu Post*, 21 April 1994.

Governance primarily associated with the technical fixtures of administrative and managerial competence without concern for history, practice, and the theory of the state as agent in the development process, is an inadequate explanatory tool in understanding the nature of the state and politics in Nepal. Managerial skills and administrative power to control and coerce are also attributes of some cruel authoritarian regimes.

Some states that have failed politically in the recent past, Indonesia, for example, have developed sophisticated measures to derive legitimacy as well as means to accelerate the pace of economic development of a familial and patrimonial regime. Ultimately, it proved to be bad governance.

The point is, governance is not synonymous to a strong government with centralized authority to manage a chaotic society. Disorder and anarchy could be dangerous but the most threatening aspect of the experience of Third World states, including Nepal, remains their history littered with bloody handiworks of strong centralized states.

Similarly, bad democracy with misuse of authority cannot endure governance, because the problems of governance would be intertwined within democracy whenever the constitutional liberalism would be foiled by the leadership. Hence, governance under democracy cannot be achieved, endured and maintained through social exclusion.

Nepali history of the past has been of social exclusion. The term in its normative sense connotes a process 'through which individuals or groups are wholly or partially excluded from full participation in the society in which they live'.[36] The leadership's behavioural pattern which is crucially influenced by the concept of *afno manchhe* (one's own men), is widespread in practice. At the most, around ten thousand people are the real beneficiaries of this so-called 'democratic system' in Nepal. While they live in one of the poorest countries of the world, they enjoy a very high standard of living, comparable to the West. What about the rest of the 21 million people? No answer is in sight, but one need not be a Marxist to detect this reality in Nepal.

The situation in Nepal is, therefore, becoming much insecure with the continuation of a policy of social exclusion, jeopardizing the

[36] This generic definition of social exclusion is provided in the works of European Foundation. Basically the term has its French origin which is attributed to Rene Lenoir whose publication *Les Exclus: Un Francais Sur Dix* in 1974 popularized the idea in social studies. The term now is used to refer to various types of social anomaly ranging from economic, social to political sphere.

inherent constitutional liberalism under democracy and by the leadership's refusal to practise a policy of social inclusion. To recall Ayoob again, such a policy posture of the Nepali state has widened the vulnerabilities from within its social, economic and political sphere, and from without, as a consequence of the changing power configuration in South Asia.

The state or the leadership should be prepared to mitigate challenges of social disruption emanating from different quarters, such as the Maoist insurgency, with the adoption and implementation of a decentralized administrative structure and by opening up avenues of participation through negotiations. If not, it would be sheer fantasy to expect the government to face these external challenges successfully.

Social inclusion could form the basis for upholding a collective national identity in contributing to national resilience, as it carries the sense of integrative and distributive justice. The underlying motive of social inclusion is to break out from exclusion caused as a consequence of the formation of group monopoly, thereby generating social inequalities.

Attempts to reverse this trend can arrest the growing social disruption to a considerable extent. The need of the hour for Nepal is to reduce, if not eliminate, the domestic vulnerabilities caused by the social-political fragmentation. The nationalities problem as underlined in the ethnic demands and the problems of distributive justice, fomenting the Maoist insurgency, require urgency to be resolved. In the case of failure to solve these problems, Nepal will 'remain vulnerable to dismemberment, intervention, instability and internal conflict in ways not normally experienced by states in harmony with their nations.'[37]

These factors overlay the security sensitivities of the Nepali state for the present and in the future. The denial of democracy through social exclusion could cost Nepal dearly, as witnessed in the Kashmir conflict for India, and Jaffna for Sri Lanka. These cases have been reflected in the conscience of the destitute and deprived in Nepal.

For the past 230 years the Nepali leaders had done great disservice to the ethnic group of the nation in the name of national unity and territorial integrity. The process called the project of nation-building was actually nation-destroying.[38] Ultimately, national unity enforced

[37] Barry Buzan, *People, States and Fear*, p. 47.

[38] Walker Connor, 'Nation-Building or Nation-Destroying?', *World Politics*, April 1972, pp. 319-55.

through the use of coercive apparatus of the Nepali state is bursting at the seams, as a consequence of conscious attempts at forging territoriality and ethnic sovereignty by some mongoloid groups in Nepal. Given the context of the emergence of 'Gorkhaland' and a provision for a separate Himanchal state in India, it can undoubtedly be assumed that a mongoloid territoriality could be a possibility for Nepal in the future.

When viewed in the context of the state in ferment and attempts at reshaping the traditional boundaries of the state, there are no theoretical premises on which one can rule out the possibility of convergence of interests, between the ethnic and the Maoists, in forming a broad coalition in reconstituting the Nepali state. As secession and self-determination become a new religion in the political discourses and actions of the dissent, how would the Maoist insurgency and ethnic demands reflect in the future is difficult to foresee at the moment. The converging forces of interests to challenge the historicity of the Nepali state is, however, there to see at the moment, in that, the future of the Nepali state would not be the same as it is now.

The foremost issue confronting the leadership in Nepal today is how to arrest this trend and avert the possibility of further social disruption and its future consequences. Embracing the policy of social inclusion can be a significant move towards this end.

The leadership should desist from the temptation to use coercive forces under the pretext of maintaining law and order, in its attempts to eliminate political challenges, even though these appear to be extra-systemic. Such a move would be a process wholly preoccupied with subjugating the people, instead of assimilating them under a democratic process. Cases elsewhere have shown that state repression has generated extremism, with irreconcilable political division between the rulers and the ruled, and opened up political space for coalition between the forces in contempt with the state.

In a situation where the leadership has a low level of credibility with evident political uncertainty, any repressive measures undertaken could be suicidal. The state's policy of possessing territory but dispossessing the people living within, can no longer be regarded as the security of the state. Circumstantial evidences have led to entrench a feeling among the people that the Nepali state does not exist other than in its predatory form.

Education has crumbled, services have disappeared, population has increased, with decreasing agricultural productivity. The debt burden has increased with shrinking development activities, casteism and political intolerance are on the rise whereas the state as a facilitator is stagnant. This horrendous condition is living testimony to the Nepali state's 'unity in diversity' and national harmony, preserved as a 'garden of four caste and thirty-six varna'.

Albert Camus once wrote, 'I rebel, therefore, we exist'. The present day Nepali leadership is a product of a ceaseless rebellion against a system, that had wronged the people of Nepal. Alas, the leadership is the most despicable term among the people of Nepal today.

In the words of a member of the Upper House, Jagadish Sumsher Rana (Nepali Cogress), 'We've been raping the country. . .' under democracy. So whence the threat to security of Nepal? Is the Maoist rebellion unconstitutional or extra-systemic? Or the growing ethnic demands a conspiracy in destabilizing democracy and the state? Instead, would the leadership in Nepal be ever amenable to the fact, that, failure in governance has been a factor critical to destabilization and cause of state insecurity? Despite following the usual practice of suppression and denial of legitimate rights to the people, would the leadership shift its policy approach towards cooperation, coordination and genuine participation through social inclusion?

The popular lexicon of the post-cold war security studies—common, cooperative, and comprehensive security—requires to be tested in the domestic context, wherein, the leadership will have to extensively forge a societal relationship with substantial dialogue in upholding the fundamental state interests. The generic meaning of these terms is inclusivity, national resilience and societal well-being, primarily in promoting the state interests.

It requires the state or the leadership to facilitate an environment to create a condition for intensive domestic negotiations between and among the diverse interest groups, by recognizing the possibilities of convergence of interests as a means of resolving domestic problems with assurance, reciprocity and commitment. Security challenges emanating from domestic discourse must not be seen in zero-sum terms. Because domestic security problems have no gainers, both the contending parties can be a loser, in case the problem remains unresolved.

This situation may also provide opportunities for external forces' to penetrate and engage in manipulation. The leadership has a responsibility in promoting an environment to build the capacity of the state to face the challenges emerging out of competitive priorities and interests. These could be both internal and external.

The security problems now experienced in Nepal are twofold. Firstly, the leadership has not been able to build authority in a competitive political environment due to its own folly. Secondly, the weakening of the leadership with declining credibility internally and externally, has reflected in the loss of the state's capacity to meaningfully use the available resources to sustain and preserve the broader national interests.

How would Nepal react to the rapidly changing strategic environment in South Asia, is a question out of bounds to be considered properly at the moment. The dynamics of South Asian politics and the conflict inherent in the course of state building in the region, is less understood by the leadership in Nepal, which is only versed in the tradition of accumulating power, prestige, and privilege.

It is, therefore, less likely that the Nepali state will unfold a process of transforming itself from a monopolistic centralized authority to a decentralized social formation, with its mediatory role contributing to enhancing social-political cohesion and building a multiethnic and pluralistic state. The security predicament of Nepal, therefore, will relate to internal fragmentation, characterizing violence in the absence of a visionary leadership.

Thus, in the future, security studies relating to Nepal, should be directed towards understanding the causes leading to the erosion of statehood, by situating the leadership within the context of the security problems of the state. Statehood for Nepal can be mediated through a policy of sustaining domestic social coherence, in order to build a political order; in which, the leadership role will be critical in transforming Nepal from juridical to effective statehood. Would the Nepali leadership rise to the occasion to face this challenge? The Frankesteinian libido influencing the leadership in Nepal may be least expected to do so.

Internal and External Factors in Security Studies in Sri Lanka

SUGEESWARA P. SENADHIRA

The sudden and dramatic disintegration of the Soviet Union also marked the end of the cold war resulting in significant developments in Asia, such as the disengagement of Russia from the region, a major readjustment of the US involvement and the rise of China as a major power. The latest development affecting regional security is the recent nuclear testing carried out first by India, and then by Pakistan.

These developments in combination with the rapid entrenchment of new concepts of economic interdependence, globalization and trade liberalization, the security concerns also underwent a rapid transformation.

In Sri Lanka, there were significant revisions in security policy in three different phases. First, the post-colonial period from independence in 1948 to the change of government in 1956, which was characterized by a pro-West policy. The second phase, from 1956 to 1983, witnessed the pre-eminence of the policy of non-alignment, with a little tilt either to the West or to the Communist block. Since 1983, the third and the current phase, Sri Lankan security concerns rallied around the ethnic imbroglio.

Conceptions of Security in Sri Lanka

As a small island-nation, Sri Lanka equates security to the safeguarding of national sovereignty and territorial integrity from military aggression, economic dominance or political intervention and interference, utilizing internal pressure groups opposed to the state due to ethnic, economic or ideological reasons. These pressure points include non-military aggressive measures, such as internal subversion, economic subversion and/or pressures and political coercion or pressures.

Since the eruption of the ethnic problem in Sri Lanka, with its external dimensions in the first part of the 1980s, external intervention has become the main concern of national security in the country.

Most Sri Lankan security analysts and researchers believe that the Indian intervention in Sri Lanka's ethnic problem, though at one stage it became beneficial to the country, resulted in a spring-board effect, unleashing an uninhibited wave of chain reactions severely damaging the well maintained balance of power.

The 'action-reaction syndrome', either preceding or following Indian intervention, (this is debatable), manifest in the Washington-London-Pretoria-Islamabhad-Tel Aviv combination being cultivated by President Jayewardene, was perceived by Indira Gandhi and later even Rajiv Gandhi, as a real threat to Inida's own security concerns.

Hence, the Sri Lankan security concept has further broadened, to include military or non-military threats and aggression, as well as intervention and interference affecting the wellbeing of the island state.

Internal Factors of Security Studies

• *Political crisis*

Post-independence Sri Lanka, then known as Ceylon, inherited the colonial concept of security from the departing British rulers. This made the ruling elite of the newly independent nation place, an unqualified faith in the Western block, believing that would safeguard the security of the state.

Explaining the pre-independence agreement signed with the United Kingdom on 11 November 1947, the first Prime Minister D.S. Senanayake made a significant statement in Parliament:

> I went to the length of preparing the draft of such an agreement to govern the relations between Ceylon and the United Kingdom, particularly in the matters of defence and external affairs, on lines which would be acceptable to the State Council. This method would, I suggested, assure the government of Britain of a friendly people and a friendly government, another Dominion on the sea and air routes to Australia and New Zealand. It will assure the government of Britain of naval and air bases that would dominate the Indian Ocean.[1]

[1] Parliament Hansard, November, 1947.

There were no major crises affecting national security and there was relative stability of the Sri Lankan state in the early decades after independence. However, the structural weaknesses inherited by the new state, saw the gradual rise in the social conflicts and political discontent plaguing successive regimes.The dissention that arose was directed at the state, seen as the target of attack.

After a gradual build-up for nearly a quarter century since independence, the first serious internal threat to the state came in 1971, when the Janatha Vimukthi Peramuna (JVP) or the People's Liberation Organization, unleashed an armed insurrection in an attempt to capture state power. The armed youths of the JVP challenged the legitimacy of the state, its social base and the institutions, by adopting violent means.

It was the first serious expression of the failure of the state to create a political and social consensus, that obviates the widespread use of internally generated violence and terror in political life. The JVP threat to the security of the state had exposed its fundamental political weakness of the state. In consequence, the state started to resort to regular and systematic use of coercive state power, in order to safeguard its security. National security, thus became the overwhelming concern of the state, with the security of the regime and its interest groups assuming top most priority. The gradual rise of authoritarian tendencies were evident in the increased use of emergency regulations and politicization of the bureaucracy for stringent social and political control of society, ostensibly for national security.

The authoritarian tendencies increased in magnitude with the resurgence of the JVP, in a much more powerful dimension in the late 1980s. It posed more pervasive security threats at all levels than in the first insurrection, in the sense, that it had developed a wider social base. The danger came when the tentacles of the JVP extended into the armed forces, the bureaucracy and even some established political parties. The only sphere where it failed to gain sufficient influential position was the labour movement, which was by and large, under the control of old Leftist movements like the socialist, Lanka Sama Samaj Party (LSSP) and the Communist Party (CP).

The prolonged and widespread use of violence and terror by the JVP brought the state machinery virtually to a halt by 1987. In order to undermine the strength of the state, the JVP forced the society as a whole to act as an accomplice and was at the same time used as hostage. This created a dilemma for the state in the performance of its security functions as identification of organizers and perpetrators of terror and violence, both against the state, its institutional structure, and also the civil society, became difficult.[2]

The state resorted to counter terror, which not only undermined the legitimacy of the state and its institutions responsible for order and peace, but also transformed the state into an instrument of insecurity at the levels of the individual and civil society.

The security of the state received a threat of an unprecedented level, when the government was forced to sign the Peace Accord with India in 1987 and invite the Indian Peace Keeping Force, so that the full strength of the Sri Lankan armed forces could be deployed to suppress the JVP.

- *Ethnic conflict*

The Sri Lankan state was not founded on a collective idea acceptable to the principal ethnic minority—the Tamils. At the time of independence of the new state, the majority Sinhala community as well as the minority Tamils, were represented by the elite of the two communities and a strong central authority was quite attractive to their leaders. Thus, the social and political issues pertaining to the vast majority of both communities were completely ignored and that became the foremost weakness of the state. That the Sri Lankan state was not founded on a collective idea acceptable to the Tamils manifested itself, first, as peaceful and non-violent protests and constitutional and legal challenges to the state and its institutions. The peaceful protests based on minority aspirations were treated as threats to the security of the state by the successive Sinhala-dominated regimes. The strong and high-handed Sinhalese reaction to these developments often took the form of ethnic violence against the Tamils.

As a result, in the latter part of 1970s, the Tamil struggle assumed the form of an armed separatist movement and the state was faced with a complex security problem, which assumed gigantic proportions within a short period. The firm establishment of the concept of a separate state for the Tamils, challenged the idea of the sovereignty of the Sri Lankan state. The challenge posed by Tamil militants, together with the covert support of India—first the southern state of Tamil Nadu and later the central government of India—exposed the weakness of the institutional structure of the Sri Lankan state.

[2] See M.G.A. Cooray, 'Security and Intervention: A Theoretical Overview', in Mahinda Werakea and P.V.J. Jayasekera, eds., *Security Dilemma of a Small State*, New Delhi: South Asia Publishers, 1995.

The ability of the state to conduct normal functioning of the society in maintaining law and order and establishing peace, became questionable when the Tamil struggle soon created a situation of civil war. Thus, ethnicity became the most crucial factor in the execution of the security functions of state with the state, represented largely by the majority Sinhala community and the Tamil separatists, projecting the two ethnic groups as sources of mutual insecurity.

- *Economic security*

A prerequisite for the security of the state is economic security, as economic development is a basic requirement to sustain security of any state. In the present context of globalization, security is determined by the international economic system, which exerts strong pressure on small states to adopt economic policies and programmes which would supplement their global economic strategies. To safeguard their security interests, dominant powers use various economic devices to increase the dependency of the smaller economies. Preservation of economic interests is accorded a very high priority in the agenda of dominant powers, that even military intervention to safeguard economic interests is regarded as a legitimate act.

After 1977, the World Bank and International Monetary Fund (IMF) gradually tightened their grip on economic policy decisions of Sri Lanka, by using the implementation process of the 'structural adjustment package' on hold. The protracted civil war in the north and east and the radical Marxist movement spearheaded by the JVP in the south, increased the insecurity of the state. This has pushed Sri Lanka to become a cog in the international arms trade, thus, further aggravating economic insecurity of the state.

The political authoritarianism and the militarization of the Sri Lankan society can be attributed to the vicious cycle of economic dependence, political instability, external coercion, inflation and spiralling prices, wage freezes and social tensions, as the state was forced to unleash ruthless suppressive measures to check rising threats to security.

- *Unrest in the south*

Two insurrections spearheaded by the JVP posed the most severe threat to the security of the state. Years of deprivation of political and economic participation by using numerous constitutional devices to undermine the democratic processes of government, weaken the democratic opposition, postpone elections and curtail freedom of expression, together with unemployment and denial of employment opportunities, were the basic reasons for the rebellion.

The threat to security reached an unprecedented level in 1987, with the JVP's attempts to undermine the loyalty of the armed forces in their role as guardians of state security. The seriousness of this threat to the state was one of the considerations behind the decision to deploy Indian troops under the Indo-Sri Lanka Agreement of 1987, so that the full military strength could be used to suppress the insurgency movement. However, the public feelings against the induction of foreign troops were exploited by the JVP to pose as the defender of the sovereignty of the state. India, itself, was sensitive to the situation that a strong anti-Indian terrorist movement was threatening the survival of the Sri Lankan state, which amounted to a new security concern for India because of both its external and internal implications. Thus, the internal threat to security snow-balled into a factor with external dimensions.

Despite the elimination of the JVP threat, the conditions which gave birth to youth insurrection have not been removed and the Sri Lankan state is still confronted with the complex inter-relationship between internal political crisis, generated by the southern militants and the different levels and dimensions of security.

- *Individual security*

The security of the individual suffered badly, in the vicious cycle of violence, when the Sri Lankan state was confronted with excessive violence. In its haste to safeguard itself, the state severely curtailed the individual freedom of civil society and ultimately undermined individual security itself. The situation further aggravated when anti-state movements too used violence and terror against the individual, as a means of destabilizing the state by perpetrating violence on the individual. Individual security eroded because in the indiscriminate use of violence by the state against the perceived threat to its own security, the individual was often considered a threat to the state, either because of passive acquiescence or active involvement in or else connivance with anti-state violence.

In its blind frenzy to suppress the JVP, the state agencies did not even spare those who were engaged in democratic and legal exposure of the excessive use of violence by the state. They were also treated as enemies of the state. The net result was that individual security reached its lowest ebb in the period between 1988-91, when a good part of the population became either victims or potential targets of violence from both the state and the armed militants.

Besides, the unprecedented militarization of the state, the new constitutional apparatus, emergency regulations, Prevention of Terrorism Act, emergency regulations, and the Indemnity Act were some of the formal mechanisms used by the regime in the exercise of the coercive power of the state. Although constitutional procedures were adopted to introduce these devices, their questionable use became a serious threat to individual rights. Violation of fundamental and human rights through informal and extra legal devices, such as the use of paramilitary units, armed administrative machinery for harassment, became common features of state terror.[3]

External Factors

Sri Lankan security was always linked to external factors. In the first few decades, Sri Lanka was a part of the Western defence treaties and the bogey of communism haunted the state so much so, that, Russian scientists were denied visas to visit this country in 1955 to study a solar eclipse.

Sri Lankan Tamil militants became a part of an international diaspora, which they use as a support base. With the help of that diaspora, the militants established working relationships with their counterparts across the borders. This chain was helpful for them to exchange information and technology and also for sharing expertise and resources. In the traditional national security perceptions, however, the main focus of attention has been on external threats to sovereignty and territorial integrity of the state. This is because of the highly complex linkages between the internal and external sources of insecurity. These linkages arise from several factors of which the most crucial is the structural conflict and the haphazard search for outside military and diplomatic support, not only causing security concerns for India but also providing the opportunity for intervention, violating Sri Lanka's sovereignty and territorial integrity.

External Factors of the Ethnic Problem

The ethnic problem in Sri Lanka reached a stage of chronic violence, following external intervention. General view of the South Asian researchers is, that the security of the region, by and large, depends on

[3] See P.V.J. Jayasekera, *Sri Lanka's Security Problem*, 1995.

India. Since India is the largest geopolitical entity in South Asia, its internal political, economic and socio-cultural stability adds to the general stability of South Asia.

However, lately there are signs that the Indian political system is under pressure, if not siege. The other societies in South Asia are also passing through a critical phase of political transition, in which the search for a more stable and viable system is being vigorously pursued, albeit with a local ideological flavour.

The smaller six member countries of South Asia have no problems among themselves, but each has a problem/problems with India. All the problems and tensions felt by the six are related to India which, at least for the moment, stands as an obstacle to better inter regional relations. As the largest state in South Asia, India must take the initiative to ease tension in the region, to reassure its smaller neighbours, and to move with them towards that paradise. With India lies the key.[4]

India Factor

The 1987 Indo-Sri Lanka Accord came after at least five years of covert intervention by India by way of training Tamil militants and exerting various pressures on the Sri Lankan state. The agreement was clearly enforced, using the coercive power by India. The 'Indira Gandhi doctrine' of creating an Indo-centric security regime in South Asia, was put forward forcefully, and in that context, few outside international forces who were disinclined to intervene in favour of Sri Lanka had to accept the Indian warning of 'hands-off South Asia'.

The internal crisis therefore, facilitated India's entry into the centre stage of Sri Lanka's national security problem. However, the scenario changed completely with the introduction of the 'Gujral doctrine' of non-interference taking firm root and institution of a new government in Colombo in 1994, which India saw as friendly.

Sri Lanka's hasty assurance to New Delhi in May 1998, that it did not oppose India becoming a nuclear power, further cemented the friendship.

External Economic Pressures

With the bad management of the economy since independence and the heavy burden of social security measures as free or subsidized rice

[4] Lt. Gen. A.I. Akram, *Security and Stability in South Asia*, 1987.

and bread in the first three decades and massive defence budget in the recent years, Sri Lankan economy has had to increasingly depend on external assistance. On the security side, the dependence on donors and the susceptibility to global economic changes have undermined the decision making power of the state. The World Bank and International Monetary Fund (IMF) introduced various packages and structural adjustment measures, without fully taking into account the peculiar social and economic context in Sri Lanka.

The failure of those measures further increased the debt burden and the forced diversion of potential funds from basic needs to sacrifices in social welfare, on the advice of World Bank/IMF, contributed to political instability in the country.

Regional Factor

Sri Lanka, during the last few decades, has undergone a transition from a state of relative security to one of chronic insecurity, which has become a deep-rooted structural malaise having its ramifications at all levels. A vicious cycle has developed where the insecurity of individuals, and of ethnic, social and political groups threatens the peace and order in society as a whole, and where the legitimacy of the state and of the regime has been challenged.

These internal threats and their external linkages have undermined the authority, sovereignty and territorial integrity of the state to a degree that has legitimized the use of state terror against individuals and ethnic and political groups. This internal crisis of security and its external linkages and spill over effects, have made Sri Lanka a security problem within the South Asian sub-system.

Security Studies

A unique feature in security studies in Sri Lanka is, that the security of the state has been identified in the post-colonial state in country, essentially as the security of the majority community. The reason for such identification, is the majoritarian character and Sinhala élitist control of the state. The security of South Asian states was directly linked to the superpower rivalry in the past.

In Sri Lanka, security studies was not a subject even among official, academic or non-governmental research groups until recently. There was no defence study group in the ministry of defence and external affairs in the post-independence period, barring the short tenure of Defence Secretary General Hamilton Wanasinghe, who appointed a five-man committee, comprising of five retired defence chiefs, two ex-army commanders, a retired chief of navy, a retired air force commander and former Inspector General of Police.

Defence analysts, security specialists and policy researchers, have unanimously agreed that the post-cold war years witnessed greater violence stemming from insurgency. Yet, there was no comprehensive analysis conducted though, there were serious attempts to develop a comprehensive theory to explain the phenomenon. There is an urgent need to address this problem in future studies on security.

While the foremost threat to the state came from the LTTE, which was heavily dependent on overseas sources for funds and arms, the policy and decision makers of the government did not fully recognize the LTTE threat coming from overseas. Many were not aware that one out of every four Sri Lankan Tamils lives overseas. Even widely travelled Sri Lankan diplomats see only a part of the threat.

Very few conceptualize the bigger global aspect. Neither the Ministry of Defence, nor the Ministry of External Affairs have yet conducted a comprehensive study on the LTTE international network and developed a comparable well thought out, comprehensive world-wide counter-strategy. There has been no in-depth analysis of the interactive forces at play, generating US $ 24 to 36 million per annum to procure weaponry for the LTTE.

The Sri Lankan national security apparatus has been slow in rising to meet existing trends and emerging threats. It is of paramount importance for defence and military thinkers, planners and bureaucrats of today, to develop the Sri Lankan intelligence, security and military structures to meet security challenges. This must be the corner stone of the national security policy of Sri Lanka.

Although an inter-ministerial committee for defence and foreign affairs has been recommended to address such issues, it has not taken off the ground completely. The committee was to comprise the secretaries of defence and foreign affairs, Director General of Foreign Affairs (Political), Director of National Intelligence Bureau (NIB), Director of Military Intelligence, Director of Information and relevant officials.

Accordingly, they were to meet periodically, (a) to assess the threat, (b) to review government progress, and (c) to task relevant agencies to produce and disseminate counter-propaganda. The corresponding inter-ministerial operations team was to monitor and rapidly respond to LTTE international procurement, funding and propaganda.[5]

SUB-ISSUES IN SECURITY STUDIES IN SRI LANKA

- *Ethnicity*: Tamils in Sri Lanka are only 18.5 per cent (inclusive of the up-country Indian Tamils comprising 6 per cent) of the total population of 18 million. The majority Sinhalese perceive the Tamils as a threat to their existence. This is because of the 65 million Tamils living in the south Indian state of Tamil Nadu. This phenomenon of double ethnicity or cross border affiliations, more particularly the resurgence of ethnicity, has complicated Sri Lankan security.
- *Terrorism*: Terrorism and its trans-state ideological, financial and technological linkages is perceived as the biggest and most potent source of threat to the Sri Lankan state. Terrorist groups, with trans-state links receive, procure and exchange weaponry from diverse sources, thereby contravening the established international arms control conventions and agreements. There is recent evidence to suggest that the suicide bomb technology has been transferred—copied or emulated— from the LTTE of Sri Lanka to the Kurdish PKK, Algerian FIS and the Punjabi Sikh militants.
- *Nuclearization*: The latest threat to South Asia is nuclear proliferation in the region. Although the Sri Lankan government did not protest over the recent nuclear tests, the threat to the region cannot be underestimated. In the event of the current campaign in Kashmir graduating into a conventional war between India and Pakistan, the threat of nuclear war in South Asia will assume increasing potence.
- *Illicit weapon transfers*: Although South Asia is moving heavily towards militarization, to date, 90 per cent of the weaponry in the region originate from outside. West, Central and South-East Asia, the Mid-East and Europe provide a source of conventional weapons to non-state entities. The arms pipe line of the semi-covert multi-national, anti-Soviet Afghan campaign, leaked profusely and continues to feed South Asia. Although the US and Soviet intelligence agencies have scaled down their operations in the region, domestic agencies have stepped up their activity.

[5] Rohan Gunaratna, *Sri Lanka's Ethnic Crisis and National Security*, 1998, Colombo.

- *Narcotics*: Heroin from the Golden Crescent and Golden Triangle feeds South Asia, a region with major transit routes to the West. Some 80 per cent of the heroin found in the US, originates from Myanmar, a state sharing a common border with India. In addition to the increase in consumption within the region, narcotic trafficking is a major source of revenue for South Asian militants, particularly groups with a trans-state reach. Sri Lankan Tamil militants are in the thick of drug trafficking, to raise funds for arms purchases.

In the 1980s, there were more than 400 Sri Lankan Tamils, mostly couriers, languishing in jails of Italy alone. The number of the total Tamils jailed for drug trafficking in Europe in the decade, was over 2,000 and according to Interpol estimates, only 10 per cent of the drug smugglers get caught; the number involved could be around 20,000.[6]

In recent years, as a result of globalization which made both trade and cultures transnational, security of states are under severe threat to meet several challenges originating from other states. Militancy and its terrorist face, together with crime, are moving in search of opportunities in acquisition of weapons, resources and safe havens. To prevent these from taking root, states have to be ever-watchful and constantly review legal and logistic loop holes and tighten the law.

CONCLUSION

The post-cold war threats to security and peace in South Asia, stem mainly from ethnic and religious conflicts. Other threats include nuclear proliferation, damage to ecology and environment, sharing of natural resources and expansion of narcotic transfers. Some of the domestic and transnational ethnic and religious extremists have cross-border, spring-board effects and they have manifested as dangerous insurgency and revolutionary movements. Considering the emergence of threats posed by those movements to domestic and regional security, the governments in the region should redefine their security concerns and change their strategies to meet those threats.

On the eve of the twenty-first century, South Asia is one of the most

[6] Personal communication, Ranatunge, Dushmantha, researcher on the Sri Lankan conflict, UK, 1997.

insecure geographic regions in the world. One of the overwhelming features of the region, is its vulnerability to armed conflict.

Security threats to the Sri Lankan state are no longer confined to national boundaries. They have spread across the borders. This transnational dimension can only be fought by bilateral as well as regional diplomatic and security arrangements. The government must give due importance to security research and the steps to develop expertise and skills to maximize security studies. There should be active coordination and a working arrangement between the military and civilian branches of the government, policy research and non-governmental organizations, and various other bodies involved in security research.

Two main factors affecting security of Sri Lanka, terrorism and political violence, will continue as long as socio-economic and political unrest persist and the flow of weapons into the region continues unabated.

A small nation state like Sri Lanka, with strong international relations, should systematically build a strong foreign policy, as diplomacy could be effectively used as a line of defence and security. The objective of foreign policy has to be the use of international exchange for the benefit of the state, while retaining as much autonomy as possible. The mismanagement of diplomacy was as responsible for the present security crisis of Sri Lanka as the mismanagement of the ethnic conflict. A consistent foreign policy foundation with India as a corner stone, is essential to safeguard security of the Sri Lankan state.

Contributors

P. R. CHARI, Director, Institute for Peace and Conflict Studies, New Delhi, India.

ZAFAR IQBAL CHEEMA, Professor, Defence & Strategic Studies, Quaid-i-Azam University, Islamabad, Pakistan.

DILARA CHOUDHURY, Professor, Department of Government and Politics, Jahangirnagar University, Savar, Dhaka, Bangladesh.

SHAUKAT HASSAN, Senior Program Officer in the Peace building and Reconstruction Programme, International Development Research Centre, Ottawa.

DHRUBA KUMAR, Senior Fellow, Centre for Nepal and Asian Studies, Tribhuvan University, Kathmandu, Nepal.

KHALID MAHMUD, Professor, Institute of Regional Studies, Islamabad, Pakistan.

LAWRENCE PRABHAKAR, Professor, Department of Political Science, Madras Christian College, Chennai, India.

V. R. RAGHAVAN, Lt. General (Retd), Director, Delhi Policy Group, New Delhi, India.

RASUL BAKHSH RAIS, Director, Area Study Centre for Africa, North and South America, Quaid-i-Azam University, Islamabad, Pakistan.

SUGEESWARA P. SENADHIRA, Associate Director of Regional Centre for Strategic Studies, Colombo, and Colombo Correspondent for *Newsweek*.

JAYADEVA UYANGODA, Senior Lecturer in Political Science and Director, Center for Policy Research and Analysis, University of Colombo, Sri Lanka.

Index

Acharya, Narahari 170
arms, illegal trade in 46, 50, 73, 1[illegible]1-[illegible], 204
Asian Strategic Review 43, 75
Awami League 149-50
Ayoob, Mohammed 115, 121, 124, 16[illegible], 184, 189
Azad, Abdus Samad 150
Azar, Edward E. 124

Bajpai, Kanti 108
Bajrang Dal 71
Bangladesh,
  climate change impact in 153
  environmental change and flooding in 152-3
  geo-political realities in 154-[illegible]
  land scarcity and ethnic conflicts in 152
  narcotics use in 153-4
  nation-building process in 149-50
  securities studies in
    continutiy and change in 145-57
    economic dimension 150-1
    environmental degradation and 151-4
    in formative phase 14[illegible]-9
    political dimension 149-50
Baral, Lok Raj 164
Beg, Mirza Aslam 108
Betts, Richard 169
Bharatiya Janata Party (BJP) 53, 64-5, 71-2, 155-6
Bhutto, Zulfiqar Ali 92-3, 1[illegible], 126-7, 138, 140, 143
Birendra, King 166, 171
Buzan, Barry 114-15, 146, 1[illegible]

CTBT 57, 67, 80-1, 127
Camus, Albert 191
Centre for Policy Research, India 75
Centre for Science and Environment (CSE) 153
Centre for Study of Developing Societies 75
Chari, P.R. 11, 41, 108
Cheema, Pervaiz Iqbal 108
Cheema, Zafar Iqbal 12, 91
China Quarterly 43
Choudhury, Dilara [illegible]2, 145
Cohen, Stephen 108
Combat 76
common security, concept of [illegible]2
Communist Party, Sri Lanka 195
Communist Party of Nepal 171, 173, 179
comprehensive security, concept of 50, 52, 146
Confidence Building Measures (CBMs) 56, 130
cooperative security, concept of 50-3
crime, politicisation of 52

Dawn, The 108
Defence Manager 43
Defence Services Staff College (DSSC), Wellington 75-6
Department of Defence and Strategic Studies, Quaid-i-Azam University, Islamabad 103, 105-6

Economist 47
Environment and Urban Affairs Division (EUAD) 1[illegible]
environmental issues,
  conventional threats to 26-7
  degradation of environment 27, 151-4
  insecurity 29
  security 25-9, 151-4

unconventional threats to 27
urban environment 31
working definition 25-6
Ershad, President 150

FMCT 57, 67
FRIENDS Perspective 107
Feaver, Peter D. 109
Focus 105
Foundation for Research on International Environment National Development and Security (FRIENDS), Rawalpindi 103, 106-7

Gandhi, Indira 194, 200
Ganguly, Sumit 108
global security, concept of 46-7, 53, 60
governance
and national security 134-44
importance of 12
Gujral Doctrine 150, 156, 200

Haggerty, Devin 109
Hassan, Shaukat 11, 25
Higher Defence Organization (HDO), Pakistan 93, 101-2
Hindu Sadbhavana Party 178
Horner-Dixon, Thomas 94
human security, perception of 10, 12
Hussain, Syed Rifaat 108

IIC Quarterly 43
India,
after cold war 82-90
cold war and 80-2
ecological threats 72-3
economic threats 70-1
energy security 71
ethnicity and related conflicts 69-70
non-aligned policy 63, 81
nuclearization process 68
population 71
secessionist movements impact on 69
security perception framework 61-5
collapse of Soviet power 63-4
Mutual Nuclear Brinkmanship act of India and Pakistan 64
policy of non-alignment 63
security studies in,
academic research in 74-8
conceptual issues 46-51
continuity and change in 59-90
ethno-political movements in 55
global security 46-7, 53
individual security 47-8
military aspects of 55-6, 67-74
national security 46-51, 53
national sovereignty 47-8
policy research role in 74-8
post-cold war era 59-90
recent trends and future directions 41-57
regional security 46-7, 53
research agenda for 52-7
strategic studies 43-5, 60
substantive issues in 65-7
theoretical concepts 45
security threats 68-74
social-cultural threats 71-2
social-sectarian movements 70
strategic culture 65
technological threats 73-4
transnational threats 72-3
India-Bangladesh Treaty of Friendship and Cooperation of 1972 147
India-Pakistan relations 54-5, 62, 64, 80-1, 125-6
India Quarterly 43
Indian Council of World Affairs 43
Indian Defence Review 43, 75
Indian Peace Keeping Force, in Sri Lanka 196
Indian security,
ecological threats to 72-3
economic threats to 70-1
ethnicity conflicts and 69-70
political threats to 68-9
secessionist movement and 69
see also India
social and cultural threats to 71-2
social-sectarian movements and 70
technological threats to 73-4
transnational threats to 72-3
Indira Gandhi doctrine 200

individual security 47-8
Indo-Sri Lanka Agreement of 1987 195, 198, 200
Institute for Policy Studies 108
Institute for the Study of Peace and Conflict 75
Institute of Defence Studies and Analysis, New Delhi 42, 74
Institute of Regional Studies, Islamabad 103-5
Institute of Strategic Studies, Islamabad 103-4
International Monetary Fund (IMF) 98, 173, 197, 201
International Studies 43
Islamabad Policy Research Institute 107
Islamic Fundamentalism 136-7

Janajatis, Nepal 176-7, 180
Janatha Vimukthi Peramuna (JVP) Sri Lanka 195-8
Jang Bahadur 179
Jayewardene 194
Jinnah, Mohammad Ali 138

Kalashnikov culture 136
Khambuwan Mukti Morcha (Khambuwan Liberation Front) 180
Khan, Abdul Qadeer 96
Khan, Ayub 92, 139
Khan, Liaquat Ali 142
Khan, Tanvir Ahmad 108
Khan, Yahya 92, 139
Koirala, B.P. 178-9
Kolodziej, Edward A. 113
Kot massacre, Nepal 179
Kumar, Dhruba 13, 159

LTTE 202-3
Lanka Sama Samaj Party (LSSP) 195
Lawrence, W. 59
Lenin, V.I. 131
Lodhi, Maleeha 108

Machiavelli 22
Mahbub ul-Haq 10, 12, 143-4, 174
Mahmud, Khalid 12, 13
Mann, Michael 169
Marx, Karl 22
military intervention, in other countires 53-4
minorities grievances, in Pakistan 140-3
Mohajir Qaumi Movement (MQM) 142
Moon, Ghung-in 124
Mujib-Indira 1974 Border Agreement 157
Mutual Nuclear Brinkmanship (MNB) act of India and Pakistan 64
Myth of Independence 126

NPT 67, 80-1, 100, 127
narcotics, trade and use of 46, 50, 73, 153-4, 204
Nation, The 108
National Awami Party (NAP) 140
National Defence Academy, Khadakvasala 75
National Defence College, Islamabad 103-4
National Defence College, New Delhi 75
National Development and Security 107
National Election Commission, Nepal 177-8
National Planning Commission, Nepal 175, 186
national security,
  definition of 12, 112-18
  governance and 131-44
  individual security and 47-8
  permanent *vs.* evolutional threats to 48-9
  regional and global security and 46-7, 53
  traditional *vs.* comprehensive/collective approach to 49-51
National Security Council of India 64, 66, 77
national sovereignty 47-8
Nepal,
  economy of 173-9
  ethnic revivalism 176-9
  leadership crisis 170-3, 189-91
  lessons from history 165-8
  Maoist movement in 179-83
  politics 168-73

security paradigm for 187-92
security studies in,
perception of 161-5
recent trends and future dimensions of 159-92
threat and security concept 182-7
Zone of Peace 165
Nepali Congress 170, 173, 177
Nepali nationalism 178-9
News, The 108
Pakistan,
future security agenda 129-30
governance and national security in 131-44
Islamic fundamentalism 136-7
minorities grievances in 140-3
sectarian violence in 138-40
security studies in 12, 91-144
academic inputs 103-10
arms control and disarmament approach 100-1
current trends and future directions 91-130
diplomatic approach 96-7
economic approach 97-8
environmental approach 98-100
focus of 118-29
future direction of 108-10, 129-30
Indian threat and 125-6
institutional inputs 101-3
institutions 103-8
military orientation of 121-3
non-conventional approach 95-6
non-traditional approach 97-101
nuclear programme and 126-9
post-cold war era 111-30
security decision making 101
state-centric analysis approach 123-5
strategic militiary approach 94-5
territorial dimensions in 119-21
traditional approaches 94
threat from India 125-6
Pakistan Environment Protection Agency 99
Pakistan Horizon 104
Pakistan Institute of International Affairs (PIIA), Karachi 103-4
Pakistan People's Party (PPP) 142-3
Pakistan Seeks Security 108
Parbattya Chattagram Jana Sanghati Samity (PCJSS) 150
People's Liberation Organization, Sri Lanka 195
politics, criminalization of 52
Prabhakar, Lawrence 11
Prabhakar, S. 59
Prevention of Terrorism Act, Sri Lanka 199

Qureshi, Moeen 98

Raghavan, V.R. 79
Rahman, Sheikh Mujibur 147, 150
Rais, Rasul Bakhsh 12, 108, 111
Rana, Jagadish Sumsher 191
Rashtriya Prajatantra Party (RPP) 171, 173
Rashtriya Swayamsevak Sangh (RSS) 71
Regional Perspective 105
regional security, concept of 46-7, 53
Regional Studies 105
Rizvi, Hasan Askari 108
Rose, Leo 92
Royal United Services Institute of UK 74

Sadbhavana Party 171
School of Combat, Mhow 75-6
security,
changing concepts of 26-9
comprehensive 50, 52, 146
conventional threats to 26-7
cooperative 50-3
definition of 10
diplomatic approach to 96-7
environmental 25-9, 151-4

global 46-7, 53
in Third World states 60-1, 117, 145-6
individual 47-8
national, *see* national security
non-conventional approach to 95-6
non-traditional approaches to 97-101
arms control and disarmament approach 100-1
economic approach 97-8
environmental approach 90-9
nuclear option to 95-6
regional 46-7, 53
state-centric analysis of 59-60, 123-5
strategic military approach to 94-5
threats,
conventional and unconventional 26-7
ecological 72-3, 151-2
economic 70-1, 150-1
political 68-9, 149-50
social and cultural 71-2
technological 73-4
transnational 72-3
traditional approaches to 94
unconventional threats to 27
ecurity studies,
agenda for research 52-7
continuity and change in 11-13, 59-90, 111-30, 145-57
environmental concerns in 11, 25-40
focus of 118-29
military orientation 121-3
state-centric issue 123-5
territorial dimension 119-21
freedom in 21-3
global setting 41-2
in Bangladesh 13, 145-57
in Formative Phase 147-9
in India 41-90
in Nepal 13, 159-92
in Pakistan 12, 91-144
in South Asia 15-23
in Sri Lanka 193-205
internal and external factors in 13, 193-205
nation state and 19-23
political dimensions 149-50
post-cold war studies 84-90, 111-30
trends in 11, 13, 41-57, 91-130, 159-92
Selections from Regional Press 105
Senadhira, Sugeeswara 13, 193
Senanayake, D.S. 194
Shah, Prithvi Narayan 162, 178
Sharif, Nawaz 100
Siddique, Aslam 108
Simla Agreement 97
Sisson, Richard 92
Social Action Programme (SAP), Pakistan 98
South Asia,
capacity of 36-8
conflicts in 36, 196-7
energy needs 31-2
environmental concern in 25-40
margins of 15-23
non-military threats to 83
population 30-1
poverty in 29-30
resource constraints in 34-5
demand induced scarcity 34
structurally-induced scarcity 35
supply side scarcity 35
security concerns 38-40
health care system 39
pollution 39
water scarcity 39
weapons of mass destruction 39-40
security studies in 15-23
see also specific country
South Asian Security Studies Centre 89
South Asian Studies 43
Spotlight 105
Sri Lanka,
conception of security in 193-4
external factors of security studies in
economic pressure 200-1
ethnic problem 199-200
India 200
regional factor 201
internal factors of security studies in
economic security 197
ethnic conflict 196-7

individual security 198-9
political crisis 194-6
unrest in south 197-8
security studies in 193-205
ethnicity and 196-7, 203
external factors 199-201
illicit weapon fransfer 203
internal factors 194-9
narcotics 204
nuclearization 203
sub-issues in 203-4
terrorism 203
Strategic Analysis 43, 75
Strategic Digest 75
Strategic Studies 104
Sugauli Treaty of 1816 165
Sunderji, K. 109
Sustainable Development Policy Institute (SDPI) 100
Syed, G.M. 142, 143

Tashkent Declaration 97
Trishul 43, 76

UML 171, 173
UN peacekeeping operations 53-4
USI (United Services Institute) Journal 43
United Services Institution of India 74
Uyangoda, Jayadeva 11, 15

Vajpayee, A.B. 157
Vishwa Hindu Parishad (VHP) 71

Walt, Stephen 159
Wanasingha, Hamilton 202
Warsaw Pact 41
World Bank 186, 197, 201

Zia-ul-Haq 136-7, 142, 148

The Regional Centre for Strategic Studies (RCSS) is an independent, non-profit and non-governmental organization for collaborative research, networking and interaction on strategic and international issues pertaining to South Asia. Set up in 1992, the RCSS is based in Colombo, Sri Lanka.

The RCSS is a South Asian forum for studies, training and multi-track dialogue & deliberation on issues of regional interest. All activities of RCSS are designed with a South Asia focus and are usually participated by experts from all South Asian countries. The Centre is envisaged as a forum for advancing the cause of co-operation, security, conflict resolution, confidence building, peace and development in the countries of the South Asian region.

The RCSS serves its South Asian and international constituency by: (a) networking programmes that promote interaction, communication and exchange between institutions and individuals within and outside the region engaged in South Asian strategic studies; (b) organizing regional workshops & seminars and sponsoring & co-ordinating collaborative research; and (c) disseminating output of the research through publications which include books, monographs and a quart-erly newsletter. The RCSS facilitates scholars and other professionals of South Asia to address, mutually and collectively, problems and issues of topical interest for all countries of the region.

Queries may be addressed to:

Regional Centre for Strategic Studies
2, Elibank Road
Colombo 5, SRI LANKA
Tel: (94-1) 599734, 599735; Fax: 599993; e-mail: rcss@sri.lanka.net
RCSS website: http:///www.rcss.org

PRICE DETERMINATION IN THEORY AND REALITY

LESSONS FOR LIBERALIZATION AND GLOBALIZATION POLICY

PRICE DETERMINATION IN THEORY AND REALITY

LESSONS FOR LIBERALIZATION AND GLOBALIZATION POLICY

FRED HABER

ATLANTIC PUBLISHERS AND DISTRIBUTORS

Published by
ATLANTIC PUBLISHERS AND DISTRIBUTORS
B-2, Vishal Enclave, Opp. Rajouri Garden, New Delhi-27
Phones : 5413460, 5429987

Sales Office
4215/1, Ansari Road, Darya Ganj, New Delhi-110 002
Phones : 3273880, 3285873, 3280451
Fax : 91-11-3285873
e-mail : info@atlanticbooks.com
www : atlanticbooks.com

ISBN 81-7156-851-3

This edition is published by arrangement with
The Americas Group, 9200 Sunset Blvd.,
Suite 404, Los Angeles, California 90069
U.S.A.

Typeset at
APD Computer Graphics, Delhi

Printed in India at
Mehra Offset Press, Delhi

ACKNOWLEDGMENTS

While the ideas in this book are those of the author—and any errors are also ultimately his responsibility—the project could not have been completed without the diligent and dedicated assistance of a number of other individuals.

- In the United States, I must thank Charles Goodman for his expert and careful editing of the final draft; Jamie Pfeifer for his colorful and original cover design; Desiree Vidal for her patient and skillful handling of all the typesetting requirements; and Godfrey Harris for his unfailing effort to render the text more readable and for taking care of all aspects of the production and presentation of this book.

- In Switzerland, I wish to extend my deep appreciation to Ernst Erdös, recently deceased, philosopher and sociologist of high standing, a close friend for many years. Our numerous discussions in the early nineties led to the conviction that the quasi-undisputed triumph of neo-liberalism had to be challenged by a basic critique of the theories supporting it and of their practical consequences for economic reality the world over. This endeavor, which resulted in the present book, was undertaken years before the weaknesses and failings of neo-liberalism had become evident in the economic crises that struck Southeast Asia, Russia, and other countries in 1997/98 and have since opened the eyes of many to the dangerous course economic history is taking when dominated by neo-liberal philosophy.

FRED HABER

CONTENTS

		PAGE NOS.
	Acknowledgments	*v*
1.	**Introduction**	**1—9**
2.	**The Market Economy**	**10—13**
3.	**The Formation of Price**	**14—34**
	Price Formation and the Optimum Allocation of Resources	20
	Consumer Behavior	21
	Perfect Competition	22
	Economic Reality	25
	Price Formation Becomes Price Determinatioin	32
4.	**Power or Economic Law**	**35—58**
	Power in the Economy	45
	The Measurement of Monopoly Power	53
5.	**Competition and Other Confrontations**	**59—80**
	The Competitive Struggle	59
	The Confrontation Between Producer and Wage-Earner	63
	A New Formulation of the Law of Value	69
	The Neoclassical View on Distribution	72

The Confrontation Between Producer and Supplier 77
The Confrontation Between Producer and Financier 78

6. The Dynamics of The Market Economy **81—107**
David Hume 81
Adam Smith 83
Thomas R. Malthus 85
David Ricardo 88
Karl Marx 91
Alfred Marshall 95
J.A. Schumpeter 98
Mark Blaug 103

7. Economic Growth and The Perspectives of The Market Economy **108—124**
The Perspectives of Economic Growth and Its Limits 116

8. The Process of Concentration in The Economy **125—135**

9. The Evolution of The Rate of Profit **136—141**

10. Liberalization and Globalization **142—145**
International Liberalization 143

Summary and Conclusion **146—156**

Footnotes 157—161

Bibliography 162—164

Index 165—174

1

INTRODUCTION

This book considers price as an expression of relationships of power. It presents a critical analysis of the market economy and of the theories that support it.

Theoreticians of political economics view a transaction in the market as a process of exchange. There are two principal schools of thought :

- **THE SCHOOL OF CLASSICAL ECONOMISTS** : According to their concept, exchange takes place between commodities of equal value. The process of exchange, therefore, represents a fair and correct transaction; there is no cheating, no overreaching. As a result, the act of exchange guarantees that both parties preserve their substance; however, it does not grant a profit.
- **THE SCHOOL OF NEOCLASSICAL ECONOMISTS** : According to their concept, commodities are exchanged so that both parties receive a commodity whose value or utility is greater to them than the value of the commodity they have given in exchange. According to this view, both parties obtain a profit.

Instead of barter, there can be a sale — the value of exchange of a commodity is replaced by its price. The process of exchange itself is not affected since the price of a commodity corresponds to its exchange value.

In real economic life, as well as in the theory of the economy, the price of a commodity or of a service occupies a central position. With the rise of market economies and the exchange of commodities under conditions of competition, price gains an even more special significance. The mechanisms of price formation and price determination are for the science of economics the object of basic study.

- The price of a commodity can be understood to be the expression of its value, where value is seen as an objective fact — the result of a performance, of labor, of the creation of value. This is called the theory of cost or labor value in classical economics.
- Price can also be understood as a subjective evaluation — the expression of an estimation of utility. This is called the subjective theory of value, or the theory of "marginal utility," by neoclassical economists.

In both cases, there are clearly defined, quantifiable economic factors (costs, utilities) that determine value and, with that, the price of a commodity.

However, a third view of the process of exchange can also be developed. According to this concept, the act of exchange and the resulting price express a relationship of power — in effect, the relative power of the contracting parties.

This third view accepts that exchange can be beneficial to both parties. It holds, however, that the distribution of the benefit is determined by the relative power of one party over another. In that sense, exchange can be seen as a sort of "zero-sum game" since what one party gains, the other loses. In short, the sum of gain and loss is zero.

Gain or loss is here defined as the amount above or below the amount obtained at a theoretical price. The theoretical price is considered to be the price that would result in the absence of the relative superiority of the power of one party over the other.

The higher the effective price as compared with this theoretical price, the greater the relative profit of the supplying party; the lower the price, the higher the relative profit of the receiving party and the greater the relative loss of the supplying party. The sum of profit and loss remains at zero.

The stronger one party becomes compared with the other, the more it can influence price to its own

> advantage. This book tries to demonstrate that the price of a commodity or service within the limits drawn by economic factors is determined by "conditions of power," and that price, in this instance, is the result of the relationships of forces and expresses them.

Power, in the sense it is used in this book, is not the exercise of raw, physical force. It is, as Max Weber stated it, "the chance to prevail even against resistance." Power is the capacity to control the means of its own exercise and the willingness to exercise those means.

Factors of power, among others, are as follows :

- Physical and psychic superiority;
- A superiority in knowledge;
- A lead in information;
- A higher organizational capacity;
- A greater efficiency;
- Relative scarcity; and
- The ownership of the means of production, or capital.

Power is also a matter of the dependence of one party on the act of exchange, of the relative importance this act has for it and of the availability of alternatives, as well as of the degree of scarcity of the offer or of the demand. Insofar as one party is capable of influencing the degree of scarcity, be it by controlling supply (*e.g.*, by monopoly, patent protection, trademark and so forth) or by acting on demand (marketing, sales promotion, advertising and more), it has the power to influence the price. It follows, then, that price expresses this power. In short, scarcity confers power, and power can also influence scarcity, even produce it.

With monopoly or monopsony (a monopoly of demand), we talk of monopoly power. Whether a seller controls supply or a buyer controls demand, the term monopoly is used in this book. Whenever scarcity is induced, the demand for promoting competition arises.

Adam Smith distinguishes between the market price of a commodity — the result of offer and demand under conditions of relative scarcity — and the "natural" price, which corresponds to the cost of production. For Adam Smith, competition forces the market price to adjust to the natural price. In our terms, competition should neutralize the influence of power on price.

In a constitutional political environment — with the freedom to contract in a market economy — power is only relative. In such a case, power manifests itself in that one party is more or less capable of making the other act, or abstain from acting, in accordance with its own will. The result of this permanent tug-of-war is the resulting price; the theater for this tug-of-war is the market, where the stronger party is able to determine the result — the price — to its own advantage and to the disadvantage of the weaker party. The market makes it possible to establish a balance between supply and demand, but it is a balance under conditions of the given relationship of power where the weaker party must more or less submit to the will of the stronger party.

Besides the community of interests of the parties in an economy — a community of interests that finds its expression in their interest in the size of the product of the economy — there is also a confrontation between the parties in the economy. Here, the profit of one causes loss to the other; while this does not exclude eventual compromise, it is a compromise determined by the relationship of power. After all, every buyer, tenant, borrower or employer wants to pay a price as low as possible for a given commodity or service; every seller, landlord, creditor or wage-earner wants to receive a price as high as possible.

On both sides, the pursuit of profit maximization — of maximum utility — is operating. Here it is a question of the *share* of the product — of the share of the cake obtainable out of the *total* product. So at the same time, and side by side with the common interests of the parties, there are also conflicting interests.

As John E. Roemer explains in his book on political economy, *A General Theory of Exploitation and Class*, for the neoclassical theory of political economy, there is a confrontation between man and nature; in this view, economy means an optimum allocation of scarce means to obtain a maximum of utility in the satisfaction of needs. In other words, it is the size of the product that counts!

Marxist theory, on the other hand, has put confrontation between man and man at the center of its analysis. It is a question of the *share* of the total product that the parties obtain; it is the problem of exploitation.

This book tries to put this confrontation in a wider context. Our analysis looks at several types of confrontations. Apart from the struggle between capital and labor, the confrontation between the producer (here understood as the supplier of commodities and services) and the consumer is examined. This is a complement to the former, since it determines the real wage. Then the confrontation between firms is investigated, *i.e.*, the struggle of competition, as well as the confrontation between producer and supplier (or subcontractor), and the confrontation between the producer and his financier.

This analysis is based on two assumptions:

- The pursuit of profit maximization
- The "imperfect market."

The first assumption concerns human behavior in economic life, the pursuit of maximum utility. This means simply that a man behaving rationally will, in his economic life, act to further his economic interests as much as possible. This does not imply that all his activities are determined exclusively by material interests. But within his economic activity, these will have precedence.

It is true that maximizing immediate profit cannot in every case be equated to maximizing utility. For one thing, short-term profit may interfere with a long-term goal, such as ensuring the existence of the firm. In our times, with the economy subject to frequent and rapid change, the short-term aspects are dominant (John Maynard Keynes). Who fails at the short term may not live to see the long term, as Arthur C. Pigou put it. Small and medium-sized firms will find it difficult to sacrifice short-term advantages to further their long-term interests. Big companies are in a better position to develop long-term strategies and maintain them. For such firms, maximizing profits for the long term means securing and developing market shares, reinforcing market leadership and establishing market dominance. Except for these qualifications, the principle of profit maximization still holds.

The second assumption on which we base our analysis concerns the market and its structure.

Classical economists — and even more so, the neoclassical economists — proceed on the assumption of a free market; that is, a perfect market with perfect competition. This market provides for a balance of supply and demand, of prices and quantities. Any deviation from this perfect market — such as cartels or monopolies — is considered an exception that does not alter the general rule.

It is only with the development of the theory of "imperfect competition" (Joan Robinson), or "monopolistic competition" (Edward H. Chamberlin), that economists have begun to take into account the inconvenient but undeniable realities of economic life. For Chamberlin, free competition on one hand and monopoly on the other are borderline cases of the market, which for the rest is characterized by monopolistic structures.

This book bases its view on the real economy where the actions of the players in the market decompose it into innumerable sections. In these sections the individual entrepreneur enjoys a more or less effective protection against competition, in particular against price competition, and conducts himself as a quasimonopolist. The entrepreneur favors this fracturing of the market since the competitive struggle in the form of price competition, given the problem of "fixed costs," impels the producer to favor output at almost any price and so tends to threaten his very existence. Companies that apply methods of product differentiation, of creating trademarks, of marketing and advertising, and that are promoting the image of their firm, are in a position to direct the competitive struggle away from price competition to other fields and to deal with competitors and consumers from a position of strength. In this case, competition is not abolished; it takes on other forms and another function. Instead of being a mechanism that restricts power, it becomes a mechanism to exert it and make it prevail.

When competition mutates from free competition to "power-determined competition," the instruments and methods of power are used not only to impose "monopolistic" prices and protect them, but also to raise prices while increasing the quantity of the products sold. This is achieved by revaluing the commodity supplied in the eyes of the consumer. In this way price loses its function as an expression of economic rationality. It becomes a premium for the successful use of power.

This evolution creates its own dynamics. Power leads to profits, and profits reinforce power. So a trend is put in motion to always get bigger, to create always more powerful enterprises. The result is an ever increasing degree of concentration in the economy by the effect of power.

Even if power is not identical with size and size is not always a means to power, size still is a very important factor in the manifold confrontations that a firm has to deal with on many fronts. Big and powerful enterprises have greater means to promote their growth, be they by their own development or by taking over other companies. The dynamics of economic development are such that the accumulation of capital leads to an ever greater concentration in and polarization of the economy and of society.

In summary, this book explores the following theme :

> The market economy has thus far proven its superiority over other forms of economic organization. In particular, it has proven itself superior to the various forms of centrally planned economies. Steering the economy by the market has proved itself to be more efficient, and

more capable of innovation and growth, than steering the economy by central planning.

Yet the market economy has not kept a number of its principal promises. It has not been able to prove that the pursuit of the particular interest of an individual leads to a maximum of satisfaction of all interests. The 'invisible hand'' does not guide the economy so that a maximum of utility is created at a minimum of cost; nor has the market economy demonstrated that optimum use of scarce resources is guaranteed. The "supercomputer," as Mark Blaug likes to describe the market, does not prevent market failure; it does not direct the economy so it will find its equilibrium. Poor utilization of resources and growing chronic unemployment mark the reality of the market economy of today and bear witness to the failings of the market mechanism. This mechanism is all the less capable of playing its role to neutralize power since it operates under the given conditions of the real economy and not under perfect competition in a perfect market.

This does not mean that there is no "normal" competition, no price competition anymore, no "normal" prices based on "correct" full-cost calculations. However, at the present stage of development in the market economy, these are less and less characteristic of it. This is true despite abandoning fixed prices on many-branded commodities and despite the rise of discounters of all sorts. Price competition today is basically a technique for gaining a larger market share.

This competition of displacement, side by side with quality competition, is gaining ground more and more. Price competition as a form of "free competition" has largely lost its function as the rational regulator of the economy. It no longer serves to establish an equilibrium between supply and demand, between cost and utility. Rather, it is used as a weapon in price fights; it is used, if need be, to destroy an existing equilibrium; it is deployed to conquer markets.

As an instrument of power in the strategy of competition, price no longer has the function of coordinating supply and demand; instead, it directs demand. It no longer has the function of informing about relative scarcities due to economic factors; instead, it expresses relationships of forces that are determined by relative power. Price does not control performance or the efficient use of scarce goods or of the means of production; instead, it directs this use in the service of a superior strategy.

Nevertheless, neoliberals act as if the concepts of neoclassical economists were still valid under the real conditions of today's economy — under the conditions of "power-determined competition." They believe that optimal results would be guaranteed if the market were left alone to function on its own, without any external interference. The "undisturbed" market, however, serves power and the powerful. Since power is prevailing in the market, since competition itself is put at the service of power, means other than those that promote competition must be developed to constrain power.

In short, this book attempts to expose the economic reality of today. It tries to contribute to an understanding of the complex reality of our economy, of the forces that drive and control it, and of the mechanisms that determine how it functions. This book can also serve to stimulate a discussion of methods and plans to improve the functioning of the economic system and its development.

2

THE MARKET ECONOMY

Before turning to the principal themes of this text — price and its formation — we want to define the environment in which prices are formed. This environment is the market. The system in which it functions is the market economy. Market economies are defined as systems where supply and demand are brought into balance by the mechanism of price. This determines what commodities in what quantities are to be produced and how the result of the production is to be distributed. Buying or not buying by the consumer decides the kind and quantity of the production.

The preconditions of a market economy are as follows :

- The right to private property in goods;
- The right to private property in the means of production;
- Freedom to contract;
- Freedom to trade;
- Free choice of profession;
- Free choice of workplace; and
- Freedom of consumption.

The functioning of the market economy rests on these further premises : that man acts in a rational manner, that he is guided by the profit motive and utility maximization, and further, that free competition is the norm and is not hampered or influenced by individuals, groups or the state.

In a market economy, decisions of the participants in the marketplace are determined by price. Prices bring supply and demand into balance. Prices, besides having the function of coordinating the forces in the marketplace, also provide information. In addition, prices control economic performance and its cost. And last, prices of goods and services, as well as those of the means of production (labor, capital and land), determine the distribution of incomes.

The demand for consumption goods and the supply of the means of production are determined by the concept of utility of the consumers — their aim : maximization of utility.

The demand for the means of production, production itself and the supply of consumption goods are determined by the expectations of profit of the producers — their aim : maximization of profits.

Changes in demand or supply cause changes in the price of commodities and changes in the use of the means of production.

The market economy is not just a means to exchange goods and services. It is really an economic system that — at least in principle — is regulated throughout by the market mechanism. In short, it is a system that controls itself.

Karl Polanyi describes and defines the market economy as follows :

> *A market economy is an economic system controlled, regulated, and directed by markets alone; order in the production and distribution of goods is entrusted to this self-regulating mechanism.*

Polanyi enumerates the premises on which such a system is based :

> *An economy of this kind derives from the expectation that human beings behave in such a way as to achieve maximum money gains. It assumes markets in which the supply of goods (including services) available at a definite price will equal the demand at that price. It assumes the presence of money, which functions as purchasing power in the hands of its owners. Production will then be controlled by prices, for the profits of*

> *those who direct production will depend on them; the distribution of the goods also will depend upon prices, for prices form incomes, and it is with the help of these incomes that the goods produced are distributed amongst the members of society. Under these assumptions order in the production and distribution of goods is ensured by prices alone.*

Polanyi then proceeds to describe the mechanism of self-regulation :

> *Self-regulation implies that all production is for sale on the market and that all incomes derive from such sales. Accordingly, there are markets for all elements of industry, not only for goods (always including services) but also for labor, land, and money, their prices being called respectively commodity prices, wages, rent, and interest. Interest is the price for the use of money and forms the income of those who are in the position to provide it; rent is the price for the use of land and forms the income for those who supply it; wages are the price for the use of labor power and form the income for those who sell it; commodity prices, finally, contribute to the incomes of those who sell their entrepreneurial services, the income called profit being actually the difference between two sets of prices, the price of the goods produced and their costs, i.e., the price of the goods necessary to produce them.*

Polanyi concludes and presents the result of the self-regulation :

> *If these conditions are fulfilled, all incomes will derive from sales on the market, and incomes will be just sufficient to buy all the goods produced.*[1]

Karl Polanyi has drawn a vivid picture of the self-regulating automaticity of the market economy. For him, it served as a starting point for a fundamental criticism of the system.

For us, his presentation permits the author to introduce the main theme of this book and to confront this model of the market economy with its reality. Our analysis starts with these questions :

> If price is the central element of control of the market economy, what actually determines the price of commodities and services, how are the prices of the means of production — labor, land and capital — really set and how does this affect the functioning of the economy itself?

3

THE FORMATION OF PRICE

Classical economists hold that the price of a commodity is determined by its value, and this, in principle, is determined by its cost of production.

Adam Smith assumes that production is carried out at constant cost; that means that the cost per unit is independent of the quantity produced. Therefore, the demand for a bigger or a smaller quantity has no influence on the "natural" price, but only on the quantity produced — in other words, the supply. Smith, however, distinguishes between the "market price," which at short term is determined by supply and demand, and the "natural price,"[1] which corresponds to the cost of production and on which the market price tends to align itself in the long run. It is the "effectual demand" — the "demand of those who are willing to pay the natural price of a commodity" — that determines the quantity of the supply.[2]

This theory — the "objective theory of value" — rests on assumptions that must be seen in their historical context. As noted, it assumes constant cost of production since this, at that time, was mainly the cost of labor. This, however, changed with the progress of industrialization to an ever greater degree. The increasing use of machinery and larger installations led to a continual increase in fixed cost, the cost of depreciation and interest on capital. The consequence of this was significant. With increasing output, cost per unit decreased!

Fixed cost does not change with the quantity produced. With

the growth of factories and larger enterprises, other fixed costs arose — the cost of management and administration, a greater part of sales cost, the cost of advertising and public relations, and the cost of research and development. Finally, even the cost of the personnel of production had fixed elements. Most important, instruction and training transformed labor into "human capital," and the organization of wage-earners made wage costs more and more constant. In this process, fixed cost became a substantial, if not the principal, part of the cost of production.

The variable costs of production, which, apart from the costs of raw material, energy and supplies, consist in the main of labor, are in principle proportional to the quantity produced. But, according to established but not uncontested theory, variable costs tend to rise with the increase of production beyond a certain point since the productivity of labor is thought to fall beyond this point. Another way to put it is that the cost of labor rises with the increase of demand for it.

Be that as it may, this assumption concerning the evolution of cost is basic to economic theory since without it the finding of solutions representing an optimum is not possible. To illustrate the evolution of cost or prices, note the diagram (Figure A) on following page. The horizontal axis records quantities of output. The vertical axis shows costs.

> The curve of piece cost initially falls because of the decrease of fixed costs and then, under the effect of increasing variable costs, rises.
>
> This cost curve shows the relationship between costs and quantities of supply, the supply curve.[3]

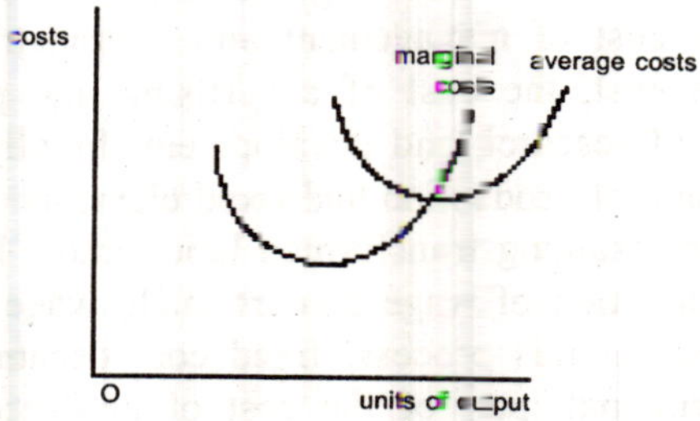

Figure A

Piece costs are shown by two curves :

One curve is depicting average costs, and the other curve is showing marginal costs (costs that arise from adding a single piece to production and are called direct costs).

As long as marginal costs are below average costs, the curve of average costs falls; when marginal costs are higher, average costs rise.

In a similar way the relationship of prices to quantities demanded is shown in Figure B. At a higher prices, smaller quantities are wanted; at lower prices, greater quantities are demanded. The course of demand is therefore represented as a falling curve (or a falling straight line).[4] A higher price, P_1, corresponds to a lower quantity, Q_1; a lower price, P_2, to a bigger Q_2.

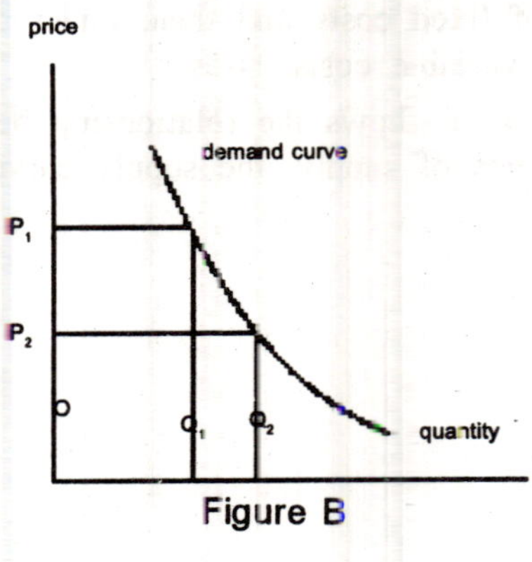

Figure B

The resulting price per unit of a commodity is shown in Figure C in the intersection of the curve of supply and the curve of demand.[5] This diagram shows that at the intersection of the two curves, *i.e.*, at a certain price, the quantities of supply and of demand are in balance.

Supply cannot accept a lower price for the same or a bigger quantity since this would be below the costs of production; a higher price for a smaller quantity would permit supply to increase to the point where the demanded quantity corresponds to that price. Since the curve of supply is not a horizontal straight line, as would be the case with constant costs, a different price results for each demanded quantity. Therefore, demand determines price indirectly by the amount of the commodity demanded.

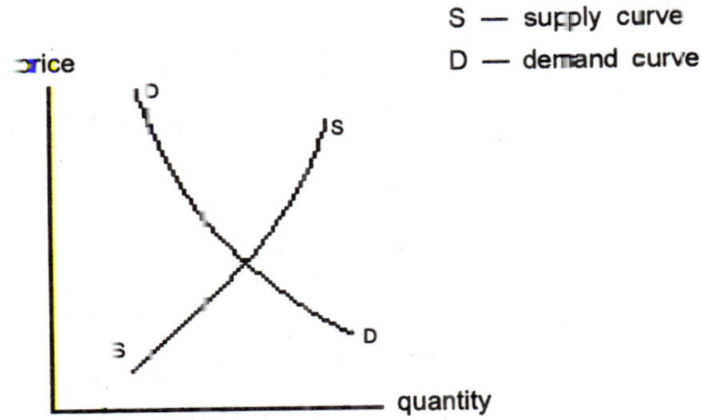

Figure C

For the determination of price, however, the question was posed : What determines demand, effective demand? The reply to this question was given at about the same time — but independently from each other — by three economists, Walras (Lausanne), Menger (Vienna), and Jevons (Manchester).

They made "the principle of diminishing marginal utility... the fundamental building block of a new kind of static micro-economics."[6]

The theory of marginal utility is based on the idea that with the additional quantity of a good being consumed, the satisfaction of want is diminishing (at saturation, this is equal to zero), and that consumer behavior is determined by the principle of "equalization of marginal utility."

Under marginal utility theory, it was understood what a consumer gains by a minimum increase in consumption of a given good. The equalization of marginal utility — according to the second law of Gossen — means that "a person maximizes his utility when he distributes his available money among the various goods so that he obtains the same amount of satisfaction from the last unit of money spent upon each commodity."[1]

Consequently, the marginal utility of a commodity depends on the quantity that is being consumed, which on the principle of equalization of marginal utility should be equal for all commodities consumed.

In other terms : The consumer tries to structure his consumption so that the last part of a commodity that he consumes offers the same utility to him as the last part of every other commodity. According to this theorem, a consumer gains a maximum of total utility — of satisfaction of his needs — when the marginal utility of all commodities he consumes is equal. As long as this is not the case, he consumes too much of one commodity, too little of another and does not maximize his utility. The consumer acts, according to this view, within the limits of his means, that is, of his income by equalizing marginal utilities. This conforms with the principle of utility maximization and maximizes his total utility by equalizing individual marginal utility.

With the theory of diminishing marginal utility and of the equalization of marginal utilities, demand was defined and quantified — at least for the theoreticians of marginal utility.

At the same time they were able to place the cost theory of price on a new basis and to eliminate the annoying fact of classical theory that explained value by costs. This disregards the fact that costs themselves were prices : They had explained prices by prices.

The neoclassical economists — the adherents of the school of marginal utility — also applied their principle of price determination to costs. The same mechanism that governs consumer behavior — the maximization of utility — determines the behavior of the producers and manifests itself as profit maximization. Mark Blaug explains that the principle of the equalization of marginal utility was not limited to consumer behavior but is effective everywhere that the required conditions are met :

> *[T]he principle at issue is that of maximizing marginal values : in dividing a fixed quantity of anything among a number of competing uses, ''efficient'' allocation implies that each unit of the dividend is apportioned in such a way that the gain of transferring it to one use will just equal the loss involved in withdrawing it from another. Whether we refer to allocating a fixed income among a number of consumer goods or a fixed outlay among a number of productive factors or a given amount of time between work and leisure, the principle always remains the same. Moreover, in each case the allocation problem has a maximum solution if and only if the process of transferring a unit of the dividend to a single use among all the possible uses is subject to diminishing results. In the theory of the household, an optimum situation obtains when the consumer has distributed his given income in such a way that the marginal utility of each dollar or purchase is equal; the ''law'' of diminishing marginal utility insures that such an optimum exists. In the theory of the firm, an optimum result is obtained when the marginal physical product of each dollar's worth of factor purchases is equalized : the ''law'' of diminishing marginal productivity plays the same role here as diminishing marginal utility in the theory of demand. Both examples are merely particular applications of the ''equimarginal principle.'' The whole of neoclassical economics is nothing more than the spelling out of this principle in*

ever wider contexts, coupled with the demonstration that perfect competition does under certain conditions produce equimarginal allocations of expenditures and resources.[2]

This means that the producer, like the consumer, has the task of supplying a given demand with available resources so as to achieve maximum utility, maximum profit.

To this effect he strives to allocate his factors of production in an optimum way. The price of his products, given by "effective demand," therefore also determines the price of his factors of production. He obtains a maximization of utility, *i.e.*, profit, by an optimum employment of the means of production — optimum in their composition (labor, capital, etc.) and optimum in the creation of utility for the consumer.

So the theory of marginal utility closes the circle : Prices are determined by utility and costs by obtainable prices, *i.e.*, also by utility. The problem of price determination becomes a problem of optimization and can be solved by mathematical methods, by the use of calculus. Walras arrives in this manner at his model of "General Equilibrium," which he develops with the use of mathematics.

PRICE FORMATION AND THE OPTIMUM ALLOCATION OF RESOURCES

While classical theory tries to establish the conditions for the growth of an economy, neoclassical economists place the problem of optimizing economic performance in the center of their concerns. Their model building tries to create a model of equilibrium, where equilibrium should be stable and apt to reproduce itself. This state of equilibrium must also be automatic, *i.e.*, equilibrium occurs by the self-controlling steering mechanism of the system, when changes of supply or demand affect prices or costs.

For the neoclassical economists, the accent lies on demand and not, as with the classicists, on supply — on consumer utility, not on costs to the producer. A subjective theory of value replaces the objective theory of the cost of labor. The "principle of maximization is extended from business firms to households."[9]

Curves of demand are derived from scales of utility, and curves of supply from marginal costs. The result of this model-building, the "General Equilibrium" of Walras, can be seen as the model of an economic mechanism that is based on profit maximization and on free, or rather "perfect," competition.

Walras investigates and furnishes the mathematical proof that under certain conditions the model represents an optimum situation. It is optimum in the sense of efficiency, meaning that a maximum of general satisfaction of needs results. It is also optimum in the sense that the factors of production — labor and capital — are used optimally, and that neither capital nor labor is unemployed. The Walras model is also stable in the sense that deviations from the state of equilibrium are corrected by the self-steering mechanism of the system, and that equilibrium is always restored by it. The essential precondition for the functioning of this self-steering mechanism is "perfect competition." In addition, the model is also based on another vital assumption : consumer behavior.

CONSUMER BEHAVIOR

The theory of "marginal utility and its equalization" presupposes a consumer who maintains a permanent — mainly unconscious — activity of optimization. This activity is exercised by a consumer who arrives at his judgment and his decisions in a sovereign manner, who processes all relevant information (under complete market transparency) and who manifests a purely rational, autonomous behavior, which cannot be influenced by the supplier of a commodity : truly a heroic assumption (Joseph Schumpeter, but also Helmut Arndt)!

If we consider, for example, that the consumer normally judges the quality of a commodity by its price (Blaug), we must conclude that the price of this commodity determines the estimation of utility and the expected satisfaction of the consumer, *i.e.*, determines his "effective demand" and not *vice versa*. So it is not demand that determines the price, but rather it is itself determined by it. This is an inversion of cause and effect; it invalidates the curve of demand of the theory of marginal utility and makes it inapplicable in such cases since a higher price does not result in a lower demand and possibly even in a higher demand.

This is not to say that the notion of the inverse relationship between prices and quantities is false or that the salable quantity of a commodity is not also determined by its price. It must, however, be understood that price in many cases also is understood as a mark of *quality*. In addition, price furnishes information, which goes beyond the one to be expected according to established theory — and even can be in contradiction to it — to influence the behavior of the consumer.

Under conditions of an extremely varied supply, where the consumer has to choose from a great number of similar, if not equivalent, commodities, and where he is not in a position to judge the quality, a higher price often is taken to express or promise higher utility and will, if no other more weighty reasons (such as a limited budget, etc.) prevail, induce the consumer to choose this commodity. In these cases, price competition is excluded.

But even apart from such cases, with the great variety of consumer goods — and in view of the difficulty of individual consumers to get complete and reliable information, judge qualities and compare prices correctly on their own — real market transparency is not assured. The consumer depends on information, and this he obtains principally from publicity. The task of advertising, however, is first of all the promotion of sales; it may be true that it can best meet this obligation if it disguises publicity as credible information. The reliability of information, however, must take second place behind the main purpose of advertising — the promotion of sales.

PERFECT COMPETITION

The conditions that govern the self-regulating mechanism of the economy involve "perfect competition" — a type of market structure characterized by

A. A large number of independently acting firms and buyers, each firm and buyer being sufficiently small to be unable to influence the price of the product transacted;

B. Homogeneous products, that is, products offered by the competing firms that are identical, not only in physical attributes, and are also regarded as identical by buyers who have no preference between the products of various producers;

C. Free-market entry and exit, that is, there are no hindrances to the entry of new firms or impediments to the exit of existing ones; and

D. Perfect knowledge of the market by buyers and sellers. In a perfectly competitive market, individual sellers have no control over the price at which they sell, the price being determined by aggregate market demand and supply conditions. Each firm produces such a small fraction of total industry output that an increase or decrease in its own output will have no perceptible influence upon total supply and, hence, price. Further, given the infinite cross-elasticity of demand between the homogeneous outputs of the competing sellers, no seller can increase his price above the ruling market price without losing all of his custom. Thus, the demand curve (Figure D) facing the firm will be a horizontal straight line at the ruling market price. As a consequence, marginal revenue (MR) equals average revenue (AR). The competitive firm is a price taker, accepting price as something completely outside its control, and will simply adjust its output independently to the most profitable level at that price; that is, the firm will continue to produce additional units of output so long as price (MR = AR) exceeds marginal cost. When these are equal, the firm will maximize profits.[10]

The following figure, taken from Collins (p. 382), shows the demand curve, d, forming a straight line at the ruling market price; the quantity of output at the optimum (Q[1]) in the long-run equilibrium lies on the lowest point of the curve of average piece cost, *i.e.*, at the intersection of this curve with the curve of marginal cost; at this point the average cost curve touches the demand curve tangentially.

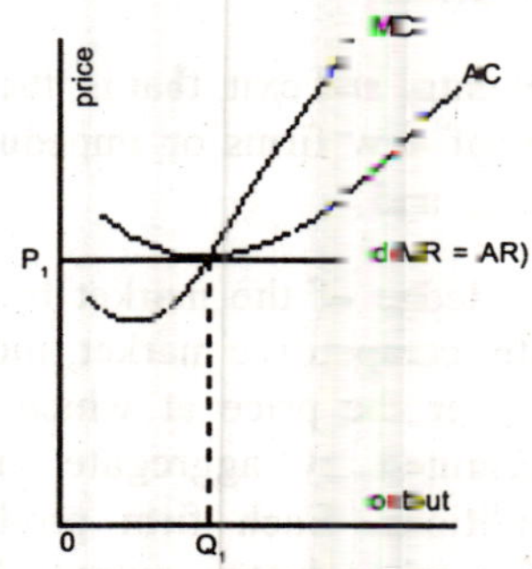

Figure D

In this model, firms accept the market price as given and adapt their output to this price to obtain a maximum profit. In other words, under conditions of rising marginal cost, firms increase their output to the point where their marginal cost corresponds to the market price (the intersection of the curve of marginal cost and the curve of market price). If marginal costs are above the market price, firms will reduce their output accordingly. When marginal cost is always above the market price, there is no intersection of these curves and the firms are not competitive and have to drop out of the market.

In this model, an equilibrium of price is reached based on complete market transparence and free access to and exit from the market. If the profit of this industry lies above or below that of other industries, there is an entry of new firms or a withdrawal of old firms from this market. Because of this, the rate of profit between industries is equalized and the "General Equilibrium" for the whole economy is realized with the result of a maximum satisfaction of needs at a minimum of cost for the entire economy.

In the eyes of its advocates, this model shows the mechanism at the base of the multitude of economic phenomena and allows observers to understand their functioning. It also proves the efficient economic performance of the system. "Perfect competition" accordingly offers a more efficient supply of the market than monopoly. Production is optimized by supplying *the* output that corresponds to the lowest piece cost. The consumer pays the goods at the price that corresponds to these costs. Allocation of resources and supply of the market are therefore at an optimum.

"General Equilibrium" also implies market clearance. Market clearance puts the economy in equilibrium when the produced quantities of commodities are completely absorbed by the market at equilibrium prices and when the available capital is completely invested just as the available labor is fully employed.

This model generally corresponds to the notion of the "invisible hand" of Adam Smith. This "invisible hand" is equipped with the attributes of omniscience (market transparency and consumer information), of omnipotence (the producing of equilibrium) and of all-bountifulness (optimum supply of the market); the essential attributes of divine power are ascribed to it.

This coronation of economic theory, however, poses the question of its relevance to economic reality since its assumptions are so restrictive that it hardly bears any resemblance to real-life economics and therefore cannot truly help to make it understood.

ECONOMIC REALITY

How does the optimality of allocation of resources really function? Can we talk of optimality in the use of the factors of production if in the industrial countries of Western Europe structural unemployment has grown to more than 10 per cent of the workforce?

If one considers that over one-tenth of the active population that is capable of and willing to work is condemned to idleness, not only as producers, but also as regular consumers and taxpayers, the pretended optimality of the allocation of resources cannot be affirmed, or only if the concept of "creative destruction," which Schumpeter has coined for capital, is also applied to labor or if we hold that there is need for 10 per cent unemployed to make the remaining 90 per cent work as hard as they should.

In brief, the model of a market mechanism bringing about the clearance of the markets does not correspond to the reality of the market economy; the mechanism of the market is not capable of guaranteeing full employment and the complete utilization of resources.

While this failure of the market — of the mechanism that controls it — concerns labor, capital is confronted with the problem that the struggle for maximizing profits, under conditions of "perfect competition," makes profits disappear.

This has already been demonstrated by theory, which explains that in a state of equilibrium, the market price obtained is equal to marginal cost. In the real economic world, the consequences of this fact are even more dangerous.

Technological development; the growth of markets, of the size of plants and firms; and new organizational and technical demands and opportunities make the share of "fixed cost," in proportion to total cost, rise continuously.

As explained earlier, fixed cost is not only the cost of capital, but also the cost of administration, organization and management, as well as the cost of research and development and a good part of the costs of sales, advertising and public relations. To some extent, even the cost of production personnel is fixed. Fixed costs are consequently not just "calculated costs"; they are to a great extent real expenses — or "out of pocket costs."

Fixed costs, however, "cry for saturation" (in Schmalenbach's term). That means fixed costs impel output to rise permanently to as high a utilization and occupation of productive capacities as possible, even at the consequence of lower prices.

As a result of technical innovations that are introduced at an ever accelerated pace, firms are obliged to make permanent adaptations. They increase their productive capacities to take advantage of the expansion of the markets resulting from technological development (means of transportation, telecommunications and the like) and from the extension of free trade — fom the removal of trade barriers (by common markets, the World Trade Organization [WTO] and similar organizations). So plants and enterprises are confronted with ever new, ever bigger optima of size. The lowest point of the curve of supply, its intersection with the curve of demand, is pushed ever lower if it is not becoming completely unattainable with constant direct cost and the continued lowering of fixed costs (see Figure E).

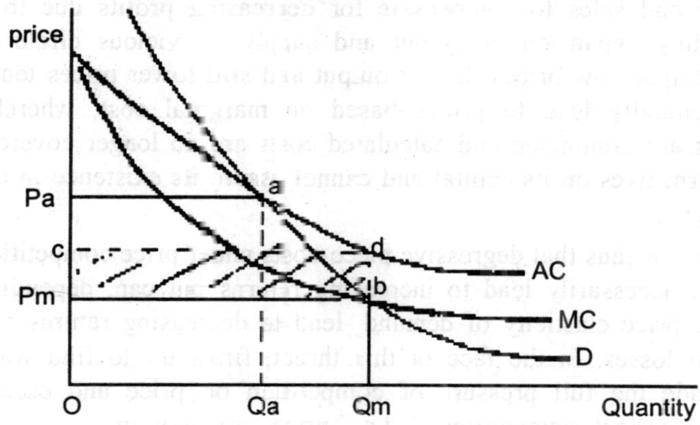

Figure E

AC	average cost
MC	marginal cost
D	demand
Pa	price at average cost
Pm	price at marginal cost
Qa	quantity at average cost

Qm	quantity at marginal cost
O Pa a Qa	turnover at average cost
O PM b Qm	turnover at marginal cost
PM c d b	overhead not covered by price at marginal cost

Because of this, the firm does not attain a point of saturation, the market does not attain equilibrium. Under the pressure of competition, or to exert pressure on competition, the firm expands its capacities of production, its size, ever further. Under conditions of price competition, the firm is obliged progressively to lower its sales price to let the market absorb its increasing production.

To compensate for lower prices, the firm tries to increase its sales ever further. So a process is put in motion for expanding output and sales to compensate for decreasing profits due to a preceding expansion of output and supply. A vicious circle of high output, low prices, higher output and still lower prices tends to eventually lead to prices based on marginal cost, whereby profits are eliminated and calculated costs are no longer covered. The firm lives on its capital and cannot assure its existence in the long run.

This means that degressive piece-costs under price competition do not necessarily lead to increasing returns but can, depending on the price elasticity of demand, lead to decreasing returns and to real losses. In the face of this threat, firms try to find ways to evade the full pressure of competition on price and escape from "perfect competition," *i.e.*, price competition.

They can meet their aim of maximizing profits for the medium and long term only if they divert competition away from the arena of price and fight it on other fronts. Quality, service, reliability and other factors — imagined or real — serve as sales arguments and help to develop a specific product or business profile in the face of competition. The aim is to render comparisons of commodities of equal usability and, in principle, utility more difficult and to make it impossible to quantify comparisons by comparing price.

In Contributions to Modern Economics,[11] Joan Robinson enumerates the principal forms the struggle of competition takes :

> *The assumption that price is the main vehicle for competition is a great oversimplification of reality. The main vehicles of competition may be summarized as :*
>
> 1. *Imitation of products.*
> 2. *Differentiation of products — and these may be in respect of qualities which affect practical usefulness or pleasure to the consumer, qualities which appeal to snobbishness or pseudo-scientific notions, or simple methods of packing and labelling articles.*
> 3. *Services of all kinds, prompt delivery, long credit.*
> 4. *Advertisement.*
> 5. *Pure salesmanship, in the sense of persuasiveness of travellers, etc.*
> 6. *Higher price — giving the impression of better quality.*
> 7. *Lower price.*

Joan Robinson also explains : "Product differentiation and advertising, which appeal to the consumer over the head of the retailer, appear to be as much an element in the struggle for strategic advantage between manufacturer and dealers as a vehicle of competition between manufacturers." Both aim to reinforce the position of individual producers in the face of their competitors.

Complete homogeneity and identity of the products of an industry exist only in rare cases : This may be true for fungible commodities negotiable on stock or produce exchanges (securities, raw materials, agricultural products and the like); with these goods, the market gets closest to the ideal form of "pure competition." With most products of industry, complete homogeneity is excluded by the process of production. Moreover, intentional product differentiation finds its expression and confirmation in proprietary brands. There, by definition, possibilities of precise comparison are not given. The proprietary article has its own specific profile, supported by product design and corporate identity. Each product of a supplier is fitted with unmistakable features that make any real comparison with other products impossible.

The decisive factor in this process is advertising. It long ago developed not just its function of providing information, but also that of causing seduction. It can best succeed in the latter role if such advertising is taken as information. One important task of advertising is product differentiation; beyond that it tries to shape demand if it does not create it altogether. Advertising consequently acts to awaken needs, to awaken the demand specifically for a given product.

As a result of this process, the market is segmented into as many individual markets as there are products. In these "individual markets" the producer becomes a monopolist.

This evolution that has displaced "perfect competition" (or what was taken for it) with "imperfect" or "monopolistic" competition was discovered in the 1930s at about the same time but independently of each other by Joan Robinson at Cambridge University in England and by Edward H. Chamberlin at Harvard University in the United States.

In *The Theory of Monopolistic Competition,* Chamberlin exposes the differentiation of products :

> *A general class of products is differentiated if any significant basis exists for distinguishing the goods (or services) of one seller from those of another. Such a basis may be real or fancied, so long as it is of any importance whatever to buyers and leads to a preference for one variety of the product over another. Where such differentiation exists, even though it be slight, buyers will be paired with sellers not by chance and at random (as under pure competition), but according to their preferences.*

Chamberlin goes on :

Differentiation may be based on certain characteristics of the product itself, such as exclusive patented features, trademarks, tradenames; peculiarities of the package ...singularity in quality, design, color or style. It may also exist with respect to the conditions surrounding its sale. In retail trade, to take only one instance, these conditions include such factors as the convenience of the seller's location, the general tone or character of his establishment, his way of doing business, his reputation for fair dealing, courtesy, efficiency, and all the personal links which attach his customers either to himself or to those employed by him. In so far as these and other intangible factors vary from seller to seller, the "product" in each case is different, for buyers take them into account, more or less, and may be regarded as purchasing them along with the commodity itself. When these two aspects are held in mind, it is evident that virtually all products are differentiated, at least slightly, and that over a wide range of economic activity differentiation is of considerable importance.

Chamberlin complains of the fact that economic theory consisted of two views : on one hand a theory of competition, on the other, a theory of monopoly. Products that are protected by patent or copyright were considered as monopolies. Products less distinctly profiled were considered as compatible with the competition. So the price of commodities protected by patents was explained by monopolistic profit maximization, whereas for trademarks the formation of price was represented in the sense of an equilibrium between offer and demand.

Chamberlin rejects this bipolar interpretation as well as the notion that monopoly and competition are mutually exclusive, or that competition is to be defined by the absence of monopoly and *vice versa*. Chamberlin rejects the statement that "where monopoly reigns, there is no competition." He states :

To say that each producer in an industry has a

monopoly of his own variety of product is not to say that the industry is monopolized. On the contrary, there may be very inter se competition within the industry, not of the sort described by the theories of pure competition to be sure, but different by virtue of the fact that each producer has a monopoly of his own variety of product. Thus every monopolist faces the competition of substitutes.[12]

PRICE FORMATION BECOMES PRICE DETERMINATION

The producer as supplier, according to Chamberlin, acts as a monopolist. A monopolist is defined as one who controls supply. The monopolist fixes prices above the "price of equilibrium" of pure competition and supplies a quantity below the equilibrium. In spite of slightly higher marginal cost (because of the smaller quantity produced) and the slightly smaller quantity sold, he realizes a bigger profit because of the higher price charged; he acts in conformance with the principle of profit maximization.

But Chamberlin also sees a further factor in the evolution of supply. In his enquiry into sales cost, especially the cost of advertising, he shows the influence of advertising on the quantity demanded (*i.e.*, to increase this quantity in spite of a higher price). He attributes the effect of advertising to two factors :

A. Imperfect knowledge; and

B. The possibility of altering people's wants by advertising or selling appeal.

Advertising increases a seller's market by spreading information (or misinformation), on the basis of which buyers' choices as to the means of satisfying their wants are altered. This is the equivalent, of course, to a change either in the shape or in the location of the demand curves for their products.[13]

Advertising affects demands, ...by altering wants themselves.... Insofar as selling methods are...not informative, they are manipulative.

Helmut Arndt deals with this aspect of advertising in *Markt und Macht* : He also does not admit the theory of monopoly price under the real conditions that prevail with the differentiation of products on the market. He explains that the supplier uses his power in the market to obtain higher prices for equal or even bigger quantities sold. He achieves this by increasing the esteem and evaluation of utility through advertising. This effects a displacement of the curve of demand to the right, to a higher price for a bigger quantity (see Figure F below).

This figure, derived from *Markt und Macht,* shows the effect on the growth of profit by a growth of demand, which takes place in spite of a higher price. It shows the effect on turnover, price and profit when the demand curve is shifted from D_1 to D_2 by advertising.

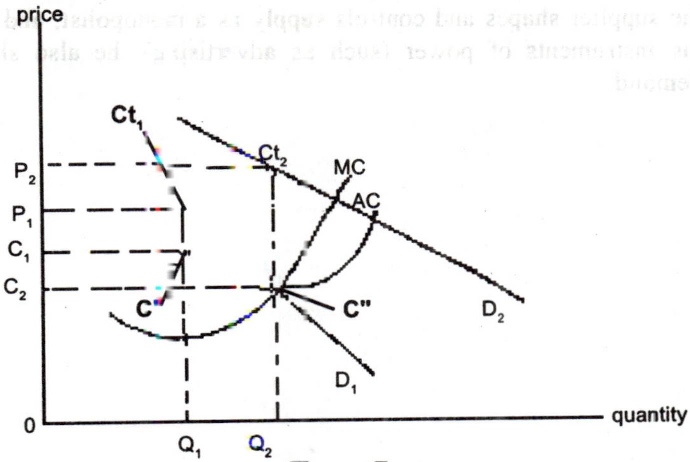

Figure F

MC — marginal cost
AC — average cost
D_1 — demand before shift
D_2 — demand after shift
Price rises from P_1 to P_2
Quantity increases from Q_1 to Q_2
Cost fall from C_1 to C_2
Profit rises from C_1P_1 Ct_1 C' to C_2 P_2 Ct_2 C"

The demand curve is shifted to the right, which gives, perpendicular to the intersection of the marginal cost curve with the average cost curve (at "C"), an intersection with the new demand curve D_2 at Ct_2 for the bigger quantity Q_2 at the higher price P_2.

Cournot's point of equilibrium Ct_p (giving the equilibrium of quantity and price at a monopoly price) has moved to Ct_2. In consequence, profit has grown from $C_1P_1Ct_1C'$ to $C_2P_2Ct_2C''$.

Such a change cannot be called "monopolistic"; this competitive situation is not just "monopolistic competition." A new term must be coined that takes into account the use of the "means of power" when profit is increased by a bigger quantity as well as by a higher price of the commodity sold. This type of competition could be called *power-determined competition.* Here the supplier shapes and controls supply as a monopolist, and with his instruments of power (such as advertising), he also shapes demand.

4

POWER OR ECONOMIC LAW

Under the same title used for this chapter, Böhm-Bawerk wrote an article in the economic journal *Zeitschrift für Volkswirtschaft, Sozialpolitik und Verwaltung*, published in Vienna in 1914. In the article, he takes issue with the representatives of the "Historical School" in Germany. Böhm-Bawerk argues against the notion that power, in the last analysis, determines the price of a commodity and accordingly the price of labor.

Böhm-Bawerk begins by explaining that economic theory was always oriented toward the discovery of the laws that govern the economy and "to claim for these laws the name and character of Natural Laws." By this he means that

> *just as the laws of purely natural phenomena perform independently of man's will and of human law in unalterable causation, there exist also in economic life laws against which the will of man and be it even the mighty will of the state are powerless; that even by artificial intervention of powers of society, the stream of economic life cannot be pushed out of certain paths, into which it is forced peremptorily by the power of economic laws.*[14]

Böhm-Bawerk explains that such a law was held to be the law of pricing — of offer and demand — against which even attempts of the almighty state to bring down the price of bread — prices set "against nature" in years of hunger — were condemned to fail. According to Böhm Bawerk, the same is true for the laws governing the remuneration of the factors of production : labor, land and capital, and for the distribution of the social product among the classes of society.[15]

Böhm-Bawerk then points to the "famous or ill-famed" theory of the wage fund of classical and post-classical economic theory. According to this theory, "the level of the wage of labor is held to be determined by a natural connection of downright mathematical imperative power, a connection that exists between the sum of capital available in the economy and disposable for wage payments, the so-called 'wage fund,' and the number of available workers." According to that theory, all the workers together cannot receive more (or less) than the wage fund, and the average wage of a worker results by

> *constraining mathematical necessity out of the division of the wage fund by the number of workers.... [According to this view] ...no action intervention, even strikes, can change anything, since the wage of successful strikers, artificially raised by a strike, will only leave a smaller part of the wage fund for the other workers, whose wages must necessarily fall, to compensate for the wage rise of the former; ...a general or average lifting of labor wages over the extent of the wage fund is something impossible.*

Böhm-Bawerk abstains from taking a clear-cut position on this extremely rigid wage-fund theory; he neither rejects it explicitly, nor does he openly accept it.

In view of the fact that the quantity attributed to the factors of production — capital and labor — is not fixed once and for all, it is difficult to accept the assumption of an invariable amount that is reserved for wage payments. Neither is it admissible to talk about the number of "available workers," since this is not fixed either; and, moreover, it is not clear whether these include the unemployed — the "industrial reserve army."

Böhm-Bawerk takes issue with representatives of the "Historical School" — who question whether economic laws had the quality of "Natural Law" and who point to "historical-legal categories" (the legal order, laws, social institutions, etc.). To this "social category," Stolzmann attributes a "decisive or at least very fargoing influence on the laws of distribution" (quoted by Böhm-Bawerk).[16] For Böhm Bawerk, the question is : How far does this influence go?

> *One must be an idiot today, if one would want to deny the effect social institutions and measures have on the distribution of goods; ...the existence of labor organizations with strike as their instrument of struggle, are not without influence on the formation of labor's wages... ; [on the other hand]...no reasonable man will be of the opinion, that "social regulation" is omnipotent and alone decisive.*[17] *...not that "natural" or purely "economic categories" on the one hand, and the "social categories" on the other, exert an influence at all on the laws of distribution can be the question today; since both of them do...the question can only be, how much influence they exert....the big problem that has yet not been solved to our satisfaction is the kind and the degree of influence that comes from both sides; to explain how much the one along with the other, or possibly against the other, is able to do.*[18]

Böhm-Bawerk states that the school of "marginal utility" has occupied itself with this problem, "to develop the laws of distribution under conditions of not just legal, but also factual free and fully effective mutual competition, that is, on the premise which excludes the superiority of one part, a state which one had chiefly in mind with the catchword of power." This precondition and the further simplifying one of the "exclusive reign of purely economic motives," the assumption of maximization of utility, of profit as a motive, have led the theory of marginal utility to the result that

> *every concrete factor of production in the process of distribution receives approximately so much as recompense for its participation in the process of production as the product or the increment of production represents,*

> *which according to the laws of distribution is owed to its participation in the process of production. The shortest expression this idea finds is in the well-known formula of the "marginal productivity" of the factors.*[19]

Böhm-Bawerk is conscious of the fact that this theory of distribution is only a "torso," a general theoretical framework within which only the theory of free competition is worked out. There remains a gap where the influence of social power has to be taken into account. This gap, to Böhm-Bawerk, is disturbing since

> In *our most recent economic development the impact of social means of power is ever more increasing. Trusts, cartels, pools, monopolies of all kind crowd in from one side, workers' organizations, with the means of power, of strike and boycott, from the other side into the formation of price and of the distribution...while at the time of the classical economists the theory of free competition could claim, not only to be the systematic basis of the whole, but at the same time the theory of the normal principal case, today the mass and importance of the phenomena for whose interpretation the theory of competition cannot anymore suffice, has perhaps already grown beyond that which even today can still be interpreted by the formula of free competition.*[20]

For Böhm-Bawerk, even the representatives of the "Historical School" have not filled this gap. He cites Stolzmann, who maintains "that not as the theory of marginal utility teaches, the purely economic conditions of the imputation, not the proportion that the individual factors of production contribute to the product of production, but the social relations of power decide over the distribution of the product of production between the landowner, the capitalist and the worker.... Power alone. .prescribes the size of the share. Not what factors of production contribute to the works of production but what men, who as owners stand behind the factors of production can according to the existing social relations of power enforce as recompense, that decides over distribution."[21]

This Böhm-Bawerk cannot accept. To him the essence of the problem is this :

> *[I]t is indeed a question of not less than of the scientific foundation of every rational economic policy. Since it is evident that an artificial intervention in economic processes can only make sense to start with, when the initial question can be answered in the affirmative, if power in face of the "natural laws" of the economic process can prevail to do anything at all ...that the aims and the limits of such interventions can only be marked off rationally, and the means to realize them only be chosen rationally, if one can form clear and true conceptions on the measure and the kind of influence, which can be accorded to "power" against the "natural" economic" process.*[22]

In other words The question is whether the character of "economic laws" can be assimilated to that of "natural law." The answer to this question is important since it decides whether intervention in the economic process by the state or other "social powers" makes sense and can have an effect.

The question of the "natural" character of economic laws can be answered positively only if it can be proved that "economic laws," such as they are formulated by economic science, are capable of explaining economic phenomena and the economic process without contradicting economic reality. If this proof cannot be furnished, the action of "factors of power," be it on the part of the state or "social forces," cannot be rejected on principle.

Böhm-Bawerk considers that "on the basis of the unanimous judgment of every expert in our days it can be established that power is an influential factor in the formation of price generally and in particular in the distribution."[23] Böhm-Bawerk poses the question : "If the influence of power makes itself felt within or against the economic laws on the price, if it there where it appears thwarts the price laws of the theory and interferes with them, or on the contrary, implements them?" And Böhm-Bawerk again makes the comparison with natural law, when "all the power of man over nature can only be exercised within natural law and by the strict implementation of the conditions posed by it." He concludes "on the question of price and distribution as well, 'power' works obviously not outside or against but within and by implementation of the economic laws on the price."

Böhm-Bawerk proceeds to show by examples — even where the power of one of the parties is obviously present, as in the case of usury or of monopoly — that it is the price formula developed by the economic theory of marginal utility that makes the process of price formation intelligible. He says that "the price at the intersection of offer and demand, there where equal quantities are offered and demanded, is establishing itself."[24]

Böhm-Bawerk also shows that even the monopolist by his conduct "merely creates conditions of a certain price level and quantity of sale that conform to price law, and not against the price law." He concludes, that "for the validity of the economic laws of price and distribution, because of the existence of social influences of power, we neither have to make a proviso, nor are we permitted to do it."[25]

He says further that "economic power cannot act on the relations of distribution otherwise, but through the medium of the categories of 'marginal utility' and subjective value." This is a daring statement indeed! If we consider that demand can be manipulated and supply controlled, the formula — that price is formed at the intersection of supply and demand — is empty as long as it does not say precisely how demand and supply are determined.

There is a fundamental difference between the view that marginal utility and marginal productivity determine supply and demand, and thus price, and the view that it is their relative scarcity that sets price if this scarcity is not determined by marginal utility and marginal productivity, and is being controlled and manipulated. Insofar as scarcity can be influenced by the supplier, insofar as the supplier can also influence demand, scarcity can be attributed to the action of power, expresses relationships of power.

> Scarcity itself represents power : Who controls scarce goods possesses power.

Böhm-Bawerk explains :

> *It is true that the effect of economic factors to begin with is essentially only limiting : the subjective estimation (of value) of the parties on the market at first really designates only upper and lower limits for the possible formation of price. But the "limiting" is strengthened towards "determining," if and where the marks limiting below and above are so numerous and so close to each other, that they narrow the latitude of the decision to a very narrow zone, or directly to a certain point, as this for instance, usually is the case with a lively and at the same time atomized mutual competition."*[26]

So limiting becomes determining, but only when the conditions of perfect competition are given.

Böhm-Bawerk says that apart from the position of power of the parties who negotiate, there is also "a different degree of skill in negotiating, in seeing through the position of the other party, of toughness, patience, of consideration of public opinion, of obstinacy or fear even with the same degree of objective 'power' shift the price to a quite different level of the price scale."[27] All these, however, are factors of an extra-economic nature that, in the terms this book, fall under the global notion of "factors of power." It is true that they do not necessarily all have to favor one party against the other; they can act in an opposite direction, the effect of these "forces," however, is expressed in the price that results.

Böhm-Bawerk summarizes his defense of the theory of marginal utility and declares it to be capable "under proper elaboration, to express the total influence of social power" and that it still remains true "that prices are limited by the subjective estimations based on marginal utility, and by this limitation are determined more or less precisely." Böhm Bawerk declares :

> *[T]he value of the goods of production rests on nothing else, but on the value of the products that originate from them, and in the last instance also the value of the factors of production on the quota of the product, that according to their contribution to production can be attributed to them.*[28]

This explanation of the value of the factors of production is incomplete, because it overlooks the fact that markets exist for them where offer and demand reign, where scarcities and power find their expression in price.

Let us now return briefly to our central problem, to the question of whether power in the face of natural law is able to accomplish anything at all. We have seen that Böhm-Bawerk, on the one hand, declares that "even in economic life there are laws, against which human will, and be it the will of the state, remains powerless." He says such a law was the price law of supply and demand, determined by marginal productivity and marginal utility. On the other hand, Böhm-Bawerk recognizes the importance of power and the fact that power must be taken to be an influential factor on the formation of price. We now want to see how Böhm-Bawerk tries to integrate power into economic law.

Böhm-Bawerk examines the case where competition is not fully effective on both sides, and "on the side of the employers restricted or excluded" by monopoly or by a coalition of the employers of one branch. Then, according to Böhm-Bawerk, the case of a monopoly of buyers is on hand. The monopoly price lies "between the value of labor to be bought, as an upper limit for the monopolistic employer, the value of the unsold labor for the worker himself as the lower limit. The upper limit is determined by the value of the product of the last worker, since the employer does not want to lose money, not even by the last worker hired by him and the wage for equal work cannot be measured unequally."[29]

This would mean that all the workers are remunerated at the lower wage rate of the last worker, and that the employer does not pay the labor of all the other workers according to their (higher) marginal productivity.

Böhm-Bawerk has (as shown by Mark Blaug) recognized this problem and has noted, as an argument against the theory of marginal productivity of the wage, that the worker — insofar as he is not the last worker — is nevertheless remunerated in accordance with the marginal productivity of the same, and is the object of exploitation. This argument is countered by J.B. Clark in *Distribution of Wealth*[30] who points out that the supposition was valid that every factor of production was homogeneous, that all parts of a factor were equally efficient and that the marginal productivity of labor was declining since more labor (power) was added to a given quantity of capital. The greater marginal productivity of a smaller number of workers was due merely to the fact that they were equipped with a greater amount of capital. The greater productivity of a smaller number of workers could therefore be just as well attributed to the productivity of capital.[31]

This sounds quite convincing but means that there exists no marginal productivity of labor at all, and no "just" wage in accordance with marginal productivity. Instead, there would be a homogeneous productivity of labor whose product in accordance with its equipment with capital goods would be bigger or smaller. How then is the wage to be determined? Since labor and capital are complementary goods the productivity of the one cannot be separated from the productivity of the other (Blaug). This is precisely the point of contention between capital and labor.

The producer will, as the case may be, set the upper limit of an acceptable wage in accordance with the expected return. This could lie above or below the average of the level of wages in his factory. But he will also take into account eventual repercussions that a deviation from the given level of wages could have on this level.

In this process of judgment and decision concerning the upper limit of the wage, the criterion of "marginal productivity" is only of limited importance.

As for the lower limit : Depending on the workers' potential to choose between jobs or to get a job at all, it will vary, as Böhm-Bawerk writes : "[F]or one, who has nothing to lose, the marginal value of the wage he could gain is so exceedingly high, that even an extremely low wage will have more weight than the enjoyment of leisure."[32] However, "the lower the monopolistic employers set the wage rate, the fewer workers they will acquire at this rate."[33] By that Böhm-Bawerk takes the supply of labor (power), like any other commodity, to be determined exclusively by economic factors.

Now, labor (power) is insolubly tied to the person of the worker. But the "production" of workers does not depend alone on economic factors. We have known this since Malthus. These are essentially factors outside the economy — birth rate, falling infant mortality, social habits, etc. — that in the real life of society result in a chronic oversupply of workers; and finally there is the "reserve army," the redundancy of workers caused by innovations in the process of production and by the accumulation of capital. This is the reason why classical economists had assumed that the level of wages again and again aligns itself on the level of subsistence. As a result, the mechanism that could lift the wage rate above subsistence level by limiting the supply of labor is blocked.

In other words : The oversupply of workers puts labor in a weak position and forces it to accept wages near subsistence level. When the monopoly power of the employer is confronted with unorganized labor competing for jobs, employees can determine the level of wages largely by their own will.

It is therefore not true that "if under these circumstances the wage rate by the 'power' of the monopolistic employer...is pushed below the level of marginal productivity, the...factors of the price formula, as developed by the marginal theory of value, will bring the price back to that level."

If there is unemployment, if unions are weak or nonexistent, the superiority of power of the employer and not marginal productivity will determine the level of wages within the limits set by history, by custom and by the general economic context. Even when power acts within the limits set by economic law, such as the price laws of supply and demand, it can, by controlling supply in the face of practically unlimited demand, prevail and determine the price.

When Böhm-Bawerk emphasizes that "even the most imperious dictate of power is not able to. .act against, but only within the economic laws of value, price and distribution, cannot abolish them, but only fulfill and confirm them...," he misses the point of the problem of power in the economy. The question put initially (power or economic law?) has thus not been answered.

An economic theory has to be developed that, basing itself on economic reality, makes just and adequate allowance for the effect of power and explains the functioning of the economy and the direction in which it evolves in these terms.

This brings us to Helmut Arndt, a German economist (professor at the Free University of Berlin), who specialized in research on concentration in the economy and the effect of power and its abuse.

POWER IN THE ECONOMY

Helmut Arndt analyzes in *Markt und Macht* the effect of power on the market and rejects the view that the market is governed by laws that exclude the influence of power.

In his preface he writes : "The market is not, as assumed by classical and neoclassical economists, an institution which because of a natural law prevents power and the abuse of power." He goes on : "[N]either is exploitation a consequence of natural necessity of the economy of the market, as many socialist authors assume."[34]

By that statement Arndt dissociates himself from the notion that the market is functioning in accordance with laws that have a quasi-automatic effect (such as being guided by the "invisible hand") and do not permit any abuse. He also rejects the view that they have consequences of "natural necessity," such as exploitation.

This is far from evident. Since Arndt rejects the quality of natural law when applied to the laws of the market, he also excludes the "natural" necessity of exploitation in and by the market economy. Since, however, the laws of the market do not "automatically" prevent the use of power and its abuse, in the face of the *actual presence* of power and the *absence* of *equivalent counter-power, i.e.*, in the real process of the market economy, power generally is effective and prevails. As Arndt put it : "[H]ouseholds just as enterprises...(can)...be exploited." Exploitation in the market economy may not be a necessity given by natural law, but it may well be a necessary consequence of the real functioning of the market economy.

Arndt further on decidedly rejects the model of "General Equilibrium," as well as the notion of an equilibrium in the economy at all. He also rejects the assumption of "perfect competition" of a "perfect market." He points to the fact that needs, as well as costs, are relative quantities and are apt to be manipulated.

Arndt poses the question : "Are the economic needs of the households as the costs of firms absolute or aren't they perhaps relative quantities and therefore magnitudes that can be manipulated by power?"

Under the heading : "Relativity of needs — relativity of values,"[35] Arndt writes : "Economic needs are neither constant, nor definitely predetermined by their nature."[36] "They can be changed and can be influenced, and by that they are parameters of action for one who possesses power over other parties in the economy."[37] Arndt goes on : "Economically relevant needs of man change with his age, with his environment, with the level of his income, the kind of goods offered on the market, and with the difference of their prices.... Neighbors and colleagues exert their influence on taste and fashion decides what we hold to be chic.... And new products that arrive on the market incite the economic agents to revaluations."[38]

Arndt points to the fact that economically relevant needs cannot be taken for granted, that they change and can be influenced, that advertising arouses new needs or activates existing ones. He writes : "He who disposes over authority or power, also can exert an influence on valuations and thereby on the economic needs of men." We here think of the "dictatorship of fashion." "Economic power in this sense is the capacity to force other parties in the economy to change their economically relevant needs." In other words, changing demand pushes the demand curve to the right.

Consumers can be made to pay a higher price for a commodity without reducing the quantity they demand. The increased expense for this commodity goes at the cost of the demand for other commodities. A displacement of demand takes place in favor of the "revalued" commodity, at the expense of other commodities.

In accordance with his realistic view of the economy, Arndt rejects the laws of Gossen that maintain that enjoyment declines with progressive satisfaction of needs (this may be true in certain cases, but not as a general "law"), and that the consumer maximizes his total enjoyment and utility by allocating his means in a way that equalizes their marginal utilities; he takes this view to be devoid of realism.

The theory of marginal utility that is based on these laws proceeds, according to Arndt, from "heroic assumptions," such as :

- Constancy of human needs;
- Maximization of enjoyment as the only aim of economic activity;
- Absence of qualitative differences in the satisfaction of needs;
- Insignificance of social phenomena;

- Unlimited divisibility of all products and of every satisfaction of needs;
- Satisfaction declining with the beginning of consumption; and finally, as Arndt declares, "[E]conomically relevant needs are not independent of prices."[39]

Arndt goes on to say : "Needs do therefore not only determine the level of prices, as the adherents of the theory of marginal utility presume, but the level of prices itself determines (economically relevant) needs."

Moving to the subject of costs, Arndt points to the relativity of costs and the relativity of valuations. He declares : "Costs are not less apt to change and apt to be manipulated than are needs. They are therefore just as little of use as a (absolute) standard, as the classical economists have been trying to do."[40]

Arndt shows that costs that are caused by the production of a good change with the evolution of the technology of production, and he adds : "[T]he costs which occur with the production of a good cannot — in an economy that evolves — be exactly established"; that, for example, the depreciation of machines and equipment, whose working life not only depends on their wear and tear, but on the pace of technological development, cannot be calculated with precision.

> *Nobody can safely predict how rapidly technological innovations will appear on the market, innovations that would render prematurely worthless machinery purchased now.... Just as developments on the market could render products manufactured on specialized machines unsalable, and depreciate these machines completely.*

And Arndt declares : "The costs that arise with the production of a good can be manipulated by the holder of economic power. If an enterprise obliges its suppliers to accept lower prices, it lowers by that its costs of raw materials (and supplies)."[41]

Arndt explains that even the cost of personnel is not an amount dictated by nature.

> *If trade unions do not exist, or are powerless...the level of wages is largely dependent on the power of the employer.... The individual worker is then not in a position to defend himself, if his wages — in spite of increased productivity of labor stay near the physiological minimum of existence. If, however, strong and independent unions exist, we could say as a countervailing power), wages can rise with the productivity of labor (or even beyond it).*[42]

Arndt concludes his exposition on costs :

> *The "socially necessary costs of reproduction" of a good are therefore not an amount imposed by nature. They change with the evolution of technology, they are ...subject to individual evaluation, and the evaluation by society, and can — within certain limits — be manipulated by whoever has the power to do so.*

Arndt also argues against the neoclassical model of the perfect market, of perfect competition. "[A] market where there exists only one price, where the goods that are traded are in every sense homogeneous; ...on a 'perfect market' there exists neither time nor space, nor material or personal differences."[43] So every market is imperfect when one of these criteria is not given. Since a perfect market does not exist in real life, and cannot even exist at all, "every market that exists in reality is imperfect."[44]

Arndt enumerates the imperfections : "[I]mperfect for reasons of time (markets at different times)...imperfect for differentiation in space...imperfect for differences in price, etc."[45] And Arndt concludes : "This way of thinking effaces differences that are of essential significance for the functioning of markets within their historical reality : the degree of competition and the extent of differences of power."[46]

Arndt thereby rejects essential elements of the neoclassical theory : Economic laws as natural laws, the theory of marginal utility and of marginal value, the perfect market, the model of

"General Equilibrium," and he furnishes the proof of the effect of power in the economy.

On the other hand, Arndt dissociates himself from the notion of the omnipresence of power and its effect in the economy. He writes in *Konzentration in der Wirtschaft* :[47]

> *If the problem of market domination and thereby the phenomena of monopoly (and monopsony, the monopoly of demand) is being considered from the point of view of economic power, it is not possible to consider every infringement of the "law of indifference" of William Jevons, and with that of the "equation of homogeneity" (Gutenberg) as a sufficient precondition for the formation of a monopoly such as it had been done — together with Sraffa — principally by Joan Robinson, Edward H. Chamberlin, or Robert Triffin.*

And Arndt continues :

> *As a result of preferences of customers (as Sraffa claims in his famous essay 'The Laws of Return under Competitive Conditions') every [!] firm within its own market and under protection of its proper borders... has a privileged position whereby it obtains advantages, which — if not in their extent, so still in their nature — resemble those which a common monopolist enjoys. In accordance with this thesis, which has been adopted by the authors of "monopolistic" or "imperfect" competition, there exists in real life, because and so far as every firm disposes of customer preferences, only "monopolies."*

Arndt continues : "If one proceeds from the position that every infringement of the equation of homogeneity" suffices to establish a monopoly, every firm would indeed not only possess the "monopoly of its output" (as Joan Robinson had formulated), but dispose over as many monopolies as it possesses "heterogenous goods." The difference between competition and monopoly, according to this theory, is completely effaced since it bases itself on a definition that no longer has anything to do with the original — and for the explanation of reality necessary — notion of monopoly.[48]

Arndt here rejects the notion of Sraffa, Robinson *et al.*, according to which there exist only gradual differences in the extent of a monopoly, and every economic agent appears to be a monopolist "without taking into account, if he can influence his sales or his supplies in a qualitative or quantitative way, if he ...has monopoly power or not." (But this is just what we consider to be the effort that every economic agent undertakes more or less successfully in using the means of power at his disposal.)

And Arndt concludes peremptorily : "For a theory that examines monopoly and monopsony from the point of view of power, a criterion, which manifestly effaces every distinction between power and powerlessness, there can be no use."[49]

It is astonishing that Arndt does not want to see — and by that closes his mind to the important realization — that it is precisely the omnipresence of power of every shade and its exercise in the economy that on one side acts on the formation of price, and on the other by these acts drives the market economy as well as the accumulation and concentration of capital ever further. Having characterized the perfect market as devoid of reality and having introduced "power" into the theory of the economy, Arndt fails to draw the necessary conclusions and to integrate the factor power in his analysis of the market economy.

Instead of exposing the fact that the factor of power is effective everywhere on the market as well as in the struggle of competition — and can have effects because of the imperfections of the market — Arndt returns to an opposition of monopoly and competition, of competition and power.

Thus Arndt robs himself of the opportunity to draw the conclusion that the results of the confrontation between the parties in the economy generally — and this holds equally for relations between, or confrontations of, producer and consumer, employer and wage-earner, producer and producer — are determined by power, and that the relatively greater power prevails.

It is the omnipresence of power in the economy that offers the more powerful a "power bonus" and makes them emerge from their confrontations stronger and more powerful. It is not true that occasionally one party or the other is successful, and that in the long run the results compensate each other. Neither does the mechanism of the market provide compensation or establish an equilibrium. In reality, an evolution results, which produces a trend, a trend to always more powerful and stronger units, to always stronger concentrations of power in the economy, and this is a necessary result of the formation of price and of competition, of the competitive struggle

This does not mean that in every single case an increase of power is guaranteed to the powerful company; even these can experience failures, and even a collapse of a powerful enterprise can occur.

In the tough struggle of competition, unadapted structures, insufficient or belated in reacting to changed conditions, and wrong decisions can have grave consequences from which great power and great size do not always protect. But this does not invalidate the trend shown.

It is essential to realize that it is not competition that constrains power, but that power asserts itself through competition and so reinforces itself.

For the evolution of the economy, it is irrelevant if a falling rate of profit really prevails and what this rate is on the average. The accumulation and concentration of capital are supported and financed by profits, that the enterprises that succeed in the competitive struggle realize; they are not limited by a theoretical average rate of profit.

THE MEASUREMENT OF MONOPOLY POWER

A.P. Lerner's essay "The Concept of Monopoly and the Measurement of Monopoly Power" analyzes monopoly and its power over price formation and profit. Lerner also looks at the possibility of measuring monopoly power. Lerner provides a definition of monopoly :

> *The exclusive right of a person, corporation or state to sell a particular commodity.*

This means in essence that "the monopolist — as distinguished from a seller in a competitive market — arbitrarily [can] decide the price of a commodity, leaving it to the buyers to decide how much they will buy at that price, or, alternatively, to decide the quantity he will sell, by so fixing the price as to induce buyers to purchase just this quantity."[50]

This means that the commodity the monopolist supplies encounters a falling price curve of demand — the lower the price, the bigger the quantity demanded, and *vice versa*; its elasticity of demand is smaller than infinite. When prices are raised, a smaller quantity of the offered commodity is demanded. This is in distinction to a pure competitive market where the elasticity of demand is infinite and a rise in price leads to the total loss of demand to the competition.

To maximize profit, monopolists will fix the price where profit per piece, multiplied by the salable quantity, will be the greatest. Lerner calls monopoly revenue "a levy upon the consumers that the monopolist is able to appropriate for himself purely [by] virtue of his restrictive powers qua monopolist."[51] Lerner explains that "the monopoly revenue per unit of output... is the excess of price over marginal cost, so that the mark of the absence of monopoly is the equality of price or average receipts and of marginal cost."[52]

Lerner then tries to define the degree of monopolization. He proceeds from the notion of the "single seller" — assuming that as the number of sellers increases, the degree of monopoly decreases. Lerner notes, however, that this does not actually work nor reveal its real effect : "[T]here may be a very high degree of monopoly...even where there are many sellers if one or two sellers control a sufficiently large proportion of total supply."[53]

It makes better sense to find out "how great a proportion of the total supply is controlled by one or a few individuals or organizations." Just as instructive, according to Lerner, is the size of the firm. But even this does not always convey the relevant information since

> *control by a single firm of 100 per cent of the supply of a commodity for which the demand is infinitely elastic (which will always be the case if there is some equally satisfactory substitute available at a constant price) is absolutely unimportant and has no economic significance, while a "partial" monopoly of a commodity for which the demand is inelastic may be able to raise price by reducing output and is clearly a much more effective case of monopoly.*[54]

Lerner concludes by saying that the extent of monopoly cannot be measured by statistical methods : "A man may have a considerable degree of monopolistic power, although he is in control of only a very small part of the supply of a commodity, if he is afforded some protection from the competition of the rest of the supply by the cost of transporting other supplies to this market...under these conditions the price of the commodity will be different in different places."[55]

It can be assumed, therefore, that commodities

> *having the same physical characteristics are not the same goods if they are at different places. Location is an essential and distinguishing characteristic of economic goods, and the only relationship between the prices of similar goods in different places is that which results from the possibilities of transforming the one good into the other by transporting it from the one place to the other...location is not the only variant of this kind,*

> *but rather the simplest species of a large genus, and is useful for a simplified exposition of the problem involved every specialized gradation of every particular quality of every commodity...as "distance," and the cost of changing the quality to a particular grade as the cost of 'transport.'*'[56]

To these qualitative variants Lerner adds

> *all the fictitious variations, such as are successfully imposed upon the minds of buyers by skillful advertising, as well as the tendencies of customer to buy from one seller rather than from another by sheer force of habit.... Here the "distance" is the fictitious difference in quality, or the goodwill of the customer, while the "transport costs" are the costs involved in overcoming the "goodwill" whether by reducing price or by counter-advertisement.*[57]

Lerner concludes that splitting up the concept of a commodity leads to a state where "every firm now becomes a monopoly.... In calling the same thing at different places different commodities, we have rejected the criterion of physical similarity as a basis for the recognition or classification of commodities and have put in its place the principle of substitutability at the margin."[58] Substitutability as a criterion also means that different commodities do not have to possess the same physical properties to substitute for each other. As a result Lerner redefines commodity, monopoly and competition in a new manner, noting that physical qualities, spacial and temporal positions are irrelevant now that we have the ultimate criterion of substitutability at the margin.

Lerner also proposes that references be made to "units of accommodation" instead of commodities. "There is no qualitative criterion of wants. Wants can only be considered as similar when the person who feels them displays equal concern for their satisfaction and thus shows them to be equal in quantity." Lerner, in short, dissolves the concept of the commodity (and services) and replaces it with the notion of accommodation. In doing this, monopoly and competition are separated from control over the supply of the commodity and are considered only in relation to the satisfaction of wants. As a result, commodities need no longer be viewed in physical terms — as, for instance, kilograms or calories — but can be evaluated by the subjective perception and judgment of the person concerned.

Exerting influence on this perception and judgment by a supplier of a commodity becomes of decisive importance in his struggle against his competition. By promoting sales through marketing programs, advertising, trademarks, public relations and the like, a firm builds up exclusivities and acquires a position of monopoly in the fight for the consumer. In this sense, advertising has long since outgrown its function to inform. It has taken on the task of fictitiously shaping the product.

Lerner then goes on to show how monopoly power can be measured. To do so, he compares "the amount of monopoly revenue with the total receipts, and [uses] this ratio as a measure of the degree of monopoly power." This allows Lerner to make "allowance...for the size of the industry or the firm."[59] As a result, he obtains values between zero — when perfect competition exists — and one — when all return is monopoly revenue. If the curve of cost is a horizontal line, and if the curve of demand is also horizontal, monopoly revenue is zero. This is a state of perfect competition. Under conditions of monopoly there is a divergence between marginal cost and average receipts, "and it is in the divergence between these...that the essence of monopoly is to be found."[60] In those cases where the cost curve is horizontal "the ratio of monopoly revenue to total receipts coincides exactly with the ratio of the divergence of price from marginal cost to price." It is this formula that Lerner proposes as a measure of monopoly power :

$$\frac{P - C}{p}$$

In this formula, P = price and C = marginal cost; the formula reads that Monopoly Power is equal to Price less Marginal Cost divided by Price. This formula appears to be the inverse of the formula Lerner proposed for the elasticity of demand. He explains that it "differs only in that [an] item's marginal cost replaces the item's marginal receipts. In equilibrium, marginal cost coincides with marginal receipts, so that our formula becomes identical with the *inverse* of the elasticity of demand. In this special case, we can find the degree of monopoly power via the elasticity of demand."[61] This means that the greater the elasticity, the smaller the monopoly power (and *vice versa*).

The formulas proposed by Lerner are instructive since they show clearly and help one to understand the connection of monopoly power and elasticity of demand, and their expression in price. The elasticity of demand determines the possibility of finding a substitute for a product. The greater this possibility is, the smaller the "distance" to other products; the smaller monopoly power, the closer monopoly price is to the price in equilibrium (*i.e.*, to marginal cost). In other words, as with every monopoly, the consumer has the possibility of defending himself by renouncing a product or replacing it.

Since "differentiated products" are only tendentially monopoly products, as they stand out against other products principally by their "profile," their replacement by similar but equivalent products is easier than with genuine monopoly products. The better this can be done, the smaller the monopoly power is.

On the part of the supplier, a great effort is undertaken to counter this possibility. The formula of Lerner reveals the success of these efforts.

What Lerner calls "marketing cost" and Chamberlin calls "sales cost," *i.e.*, the cost of selling, advertising, sponsoring, presentation, etc., not only serves to give the product in the eyes of the buyer its specific profile; it should also enhance the value of the product. Thereby the curve of demand (as we have seen) is moved to the right, to bigger quantities at an equal or higher price. The question is posed whether these sales costs, as Chamberlin proposes, should be counted as "costs of production" (they principally do not occur in production), or if they should be deducted from the sales price, as Lerner proposes, to obtain "net receipts." In our view, it may be better to compare these costs with the "increase in value" (or rather increase in price) caused by them since the value of a commodity, in the eyes of the buyer, is enhanced by them, and a higher price is the result. We therefore would take "sales cost" to be an investment in developing and maintaining market power.

Trademarks and brands show most clearly this type of monopoly by product differentiation and company profile. They serve to build up positions of power, which create conditions of competition that cannot be called just monopolistic. They may be characterized as "power-determined competition."

The theories of "monopolistic competition" (Chamberlin) and of "imperfect competition" (Robinson) have made clear that the reality of the market economy does not correspond to the neoclassical theory of the market and its functioning. This had to be revised to make it conform to the reality of the market economy. By designating it as "monopolistic," however, only one aspect of this reality is taken into account : raising price made possible by reducing supply (controlled by the monopolist). The other aspect, however, influencing the quantity of demand — the displacement *of* the demand curve to the right (and not just a movement on the demand curve) — is not being expressed by the term monopolistic. It is therefore justified to coin a new term that takes account of this aspect, and to introduce the term "power-determined competition."

5

COMPETITION AND OTHER CONFRONTATIONS

To this point, we have examined the market economy and different theories of value and price formation. We have seen how monopoly power is measured and have coined the term "power-determined competition." We now want to show the relationship of "economic partners" in the real economy and what effect they have on the formation of price and on the evolution of the economy.

THE COMPETITIVE STRUGGLE

The market economy, far from presenting a scene of peaceful cooperation, is actually a theater of conflict, of diverse confrontations. Several distinct confrontations arise, depending on the field where they take place. Take the competitive struggle between producers. In a given market, it is a struggle for sales, for customers, for market shares. The struggle is against competitors, a struggle to ensure and reinforce a firm's own existence.

For the producer, this struggle has two orientations : One is directed against fellow competitors; the other is directed against the consumer. Both orientations are closely connected. This struggle against competitors is fought mainly as *price competition.* It manifests itself clearly in comparative publicity, in the fight for space on sales shelves and generally in the competition of displacement where the goal is to supersede the competitor. But product differentiation and corporate identity are also forms of the struggle against a competitor.

Essentially, however, competition is a struggle for the mind and pocketbook of the consumer. Consumers must be convinced that the producer's product or service offers greater benefit, more utility — in short, a better relationship of price to utility — than those of their competitors. This fight *for* the customer is also a fight *against* him. This is best demonstrated by the fashion industry, by the "dictates of fashion." Fashion and its advertising not only court the consumer, they try to subdue him.

The producer and his helpmate, the advertising agency, exploit the quest for pleasure by the consumer. They want to make him feel not only fashionable, but "modern" when he submits to the dictates of fashion. At the same time the producer exploits the consumer's fear of shame, fear of being old-fashioned.

In other fields, the same struggle against the consumer can be observed. So all haggling over price is a struggle, and this by no means takes place only in the oriental bazaar. And finally advertising as well, insofar as it is manipulative, is a tool to make the consumer's act conform with the interests of the producer.

As shown earlier, the competitive struggle tries to avoid pure price competition whenever possible since it endangers profit. Instead, it uses product differentiation, the creation of brands, differences in design — qualities that are not quantifiable — and advertising to make difficult or impossible the rational, calculated comparisons of commodities and services. This should help to create a particular market for one's own product. In this market the supplier — as we have seen — is a monopolist; he enjoys the benefits of monopoly power and secures a monopoly rent for himself, as pointed out by Robinson, Chamberlin, Lerner *et al.*

Among the instruments of power the producer has at his disposal are trademarks (the brand), the company profile (corporate identity) and the physical presence in the market — if possible, an omnipresence in space and in time (*e.g.*, Coca Cola is everywhere, all the time). To create and reinforce their presence in the market, companies employ different forms and means of publicity in combination: advertising in newspapers and magazines, publicity on the radio and on TV, posters, direct mail, etc. It is obvious that for such campaigns, company size is of crucial importance. Only large companies can make full use of all available instruments of advertising, can employ strategies whereby the different instruments reinforce their effect mutually; size makes it possible to be omnipresent in the market, in public, in space and in time. So out of size grows power, and out of power grows bigger size; power yields profit, and profit further power — accumulation and concentration feeding each other.

The extent to which profiling and differentiation can be successful depends on the elasticity of demand of a product. At the same time elasticity itself is also determined by one's own power, by the effectiveness of using one's means of power such as advertising or by the power of competitors, which may constrain this power in part. Here also it is the relationships of power that determine the result, find their expression in price and with it in the "monopoly profit," the "bonus of power."

Free competition in the theory of classical and neoclassical economists has essentially the function of neutralizing power and optimizing the formation of price, *i.e.*, to determine price, which grants a maximum of satisfaction of needs at a minimum of cost. With that, the dynamics of the economy is thought to be ensured, technological progress and the development of productive force promoted.

Adam Smith saw free competition as the condition that forces producers to adjust the price of their products to their value, *i.e.*, their cost of production. Following these and similar considerations, the state by legislation tries to guarantee free competition (laws against price fixing, against monopolies, against the abuse of cartel power, etc.).

The dynamics of the development of the market economy — of the forces of production, technology and organization, released by competition — has, however, caused fixed costs to grow continuously. The ensuing price struggle (the main instrument of free competition) a price struggle unleashed and reinforced by increased output due to the attempt at better distribution of fixed costs, increasingly endangers the very existence of enterprises. To counter this, competition in the form of *price competition* is replaced by other forms, such as *quality competition,* but thereby competition loses ever more its function as the regulator of price.

Insofar as this is the case, the price of a commodity does not guarantee an optimum of satisfaction of wants at a minimum of cost; price ceases to be a reliable indicator of the value of a commodity and no longer exercises a reliable control over the optimal allocation of scarce resources, as it had been supposed to do in the past. To the extent that price competition is replaced by a competition of marketing and advertising, the danger arises of wasting scarce resources, of an always more critical misallocation of resources.

If, for instance, a firm makes use of advertising to draw even with a competitor (advertisement against advertisement, billboard against billboard), it may not achieve much more than to reestablish a situation that had prevailed before but at a much higher cost. By increasing its expenses for advertising, it may oblige its competitors to follow suit, and so, by and large, the situation before the campaign would be restored. It is not evident that all this expense brings an increase of utility to the consumer, that it increases value and that the relationship of expense to value has been improved. The fact that advertising — under the given conditions of the market economy — is necessary and useful, even indispensable, should not be questioned. However, we may question the usefulness of the "given conditions," the usefulness of the market economy, of monopoly prices, consumer manipulation and the wasteful use of resources.

Since advertising, as an instrument of power, can be dealt with by counteradvertising (after all, this is what the struggle of competition in large measure is all about) and may as a result lose its impact, the problem of wasteful expense is not resolved by the functioning of the market. It is legitimate to measure this situation against the claim of optimized price formation, of a maximum of satisfaction of needs at a minimum of cost.

To protect the consumer against power, legislatures have tried to promote competition, *i.e.*, price competition, and to prevent the rise of excessive concentrations of power. They have tried to intervene against cartels and trusts. They could not, however, change the trend toward further concentration of power and its progressively worldwide dimensions. The globalization of big corporations reduces the effectiveness of measures taken on a national level. It is therefore open to question whether the state by itself is capable of acting against such a powerful and elemental evolution and fighting it effectively, this the more so since the state itself cannot be considered to be a neutral institution; rather, it must be seen as expressing relationships of forces in society, and therefore these forces determine not only the state's ability, but also its will.

THE CONFRONTATION BETWEEN PRODUCER AND WAGE-EARNER

The object of this confrontation is wage levels and the terms of employment (working hours, working conditions, social-security contributions and possibly the rights of codetermination). In this confrontation, the two parties by necessity have contrary positions. While the wage-earner fights for a wage as high as possible and for advantageous terms of employment, the producer is interested in the highest possible yield of the "working power" at the lowest possible cost. He also wants the highest possible profit out of his investment in labor. Insofar as this profit depends on the productivity of labor, both parties may seem to have common interests; since, however, profits depend on the level of the wage, their interests are opposed. At the center of their confrontation, therefore, stands the wage.

The effective "distribution" of the national product takes place only when the wage-earner, as consumer, receives the equivalent of his wages in commodities (and services). In this sense, the struggle between the producer and the consumer is just as much a fight over the distribution of the value added by production as the struggle between producer and wage-earner. Concessions of the producer concerning the nominal wage rate can be brought to nothing if prices increase by the same amount.

Since wages are costs for the producer, and the cost of production is increased by a rise in wages, the producer will endeavor to pass the increase of the costs of his products on to the consumer. The extent to which he can actually do it is determined by the conditions of the market, the elasticity of demand and the relative power of the producer over the consumer. If a rise in wages results from an agreement between an association of employers and an association of wage-earners, and becomes binding for an industry, the rise can more easily be passed on in increased prices. So wage increases frequently have only a temporary effect on the situation of the wage earners and may not necessarily increase their buying power.

For the classical economist, the problem of a confrontation between the social classes is, in principle, not posed. According to Adam Smith, the "natural" price of labor — the wage — like the price of any commodity, is equal to the cost of producing that commodity. Accordingly, the economy produces the commodity labor (power) at the cost of producing labor. The cost of production corresponds to the cost of maintaining the existence of the worker; they are — in the long run — on the level of his minimum of existence, on his level of subsistence. This is due to an excessive supply of labor relative to the capital available.

To Adam Smith, capital represents an advance granted to labor for the time it takes to produce and sell a commodity; it is the wage fund. Since the means of this fund are limited, the number of jobs is also limited. For the long term, the level of wages is therefore equal to the minimum of existence; it cannot be lower since the worker otherwise would starve; it cannot, durably, be much higher since the competition of those looking for jobs will lower the wage to this level. As long as there is an oversupply of labor, an unemployed worker, looking for work, will be ready — in order not to starve — to lower the wage he demands to the level of his subsistence.

In the short run, wages could well be higher in Adam Smith's view if an increase of productivity increases profits; consequently more capital — a bigger wage fund — is at the disposal of the producer. Thereby the offer of jobs in relationship to demand is increased; the growth of the population — the supply of labor — falls behind. In the short run, the level of wages, according to Adam Smith, is determined by offer and demand; in the long run, however, it is determined by the subsistence level of the worker.

The determination of the price of labor, however, does not follow automatically the mechanism described. This price, even according to Adam Smith, is negotiated between the parties. This "bargaining," however, takes place under conditions that are favorable to the employer.

> *Employers being fewer in number, and able to hold out much longer. Moreover the law favors employers. Hence masters are always and everywhere in a sort of tacit, but constant and uniform combination, not to raise wages of labor above their actual rate.*[62]

So there is nevertheless a confrontation where the relationship of power finds its expression and is decided by means of power. In this sense, even for Adam Smith the conditions of power exert an influence on the price of labor, and on wages, and find their expression in it.

David Ricardo, an economist a generation after Adam Smith, takes the objective theory of value and develops it as *the theory of labor cost.* Relative prices of commodities are accordingly determined by the relative amount of labor necessary to produce them. This, however, is true only for goods that can be reproduced under conditions of free competition.

Goods that cannot be reproduced, goods in limited supply ("rare" goods), are sold at monopoly prices. These are determined by demand only. But Ricardo does not want to explain relative prices; he investigates the laws that determine the distribution of the product of industry (see Blaug).

For Ricardo, the cost of labor, the "natural" wage, also is on the level of subsistence of the worker since the supply of labor is bigger than the demand for it. This is due, on the one hand, to demographic pressure; on the other hand, it is a consequence of the accumulation of capital. Accumulation increasingly causes labor to be replaced by capital. As a result, workers are constantly made redundant.

The accumulation of capital, however, also causes the creation of new jobs and by that a greater demand for labor; this brings about a temporary rise in the "market" wage over the "natural" wage. The replacement of labor by capital and the following redundancy of labor then lower the offer of jobs and lower the wage again to the subsistence level of the "natural" wage. Ricardo, however, does not consider the minimum of subsistence as biologically determined, but as determined by history and custom. For Ricardo, in Schumpeter's interpretation, the "natural" wage is the wage that maintains the population on a stationary level, while the "market" wage, being higher, makes possible a growth of the population.

The difference between the value added to the product by labor and the wage is profit. This, according to Ricardo, finds its expression in the interest on capital. Interest is a consequence of the fact that production consumes time while the worker is in immediate need of his goods of consumption; he cannot wait for the completion and sale of the products of his labor. The employer advances, as Ricardo sees it, finished products to the worker; the sum of these advances constitutes the wage fund. In return, the employer receives the interest on capital. "[W]ho receives the interest is a matter of who can afford to do the requisite waiting."[63] For Ricardo, profits depend on "a high or a low wage." The rate of profit stands in direct relationship to the value of the marginal product (to the value of the last piece produced by capital and labor). Since the wage, in principle, remains constant (on the subsistence level), it is only profit that changes. Profit has the tendency to fall since the marginal productivity of labor is falling (this because of diminishing returns in agriculture) and marginal costs are rising. For Ricardo, "profits vary inversely with wages."[64] With a given cost of production and sales prices, the higher the profit, the lower the wage.

So the relationship of capital to labor contains an opposition of interests, a latent conflict. But this conflict is not fought out; it does not lead to a confrontation : It is regulated by the mechanism of the market.

It is remarkable that Karl Marx, in his theory of value, does not on principle diverge from this model. Marx has clearly recognized the division of society into classes, in antagonistic strata. Nevertheless, in his theory of surplus value, he does not grant trade unions, as representatives of the working class, a determining influence on the distribution of the product of labor. In his theory of value, Marx follows his "master," Ricardo, in the word choice of Schumpeter. For Marx, just as for Ricardo, the value of a commodity under free competition stands in direct relationship to the amount of labor embodied in a commodity; this is measured by the existing standard of efficiency of production. It corresponds to the "socially necessary amount of labor." This quantity both men measure in terms of hours of work, and both men reduce different qualities of labor to a single standard.

The value of a commodity represents its value of exchange. In the process of exchange, commodities of *equal value* are supposed to be exchanged against each other. For Marx, as for Ricardo, this theory of value is also valid for labor as a factor of production. Accordingly, the worker exchanges his labor (power) for the wage received. The value of his labor (power), just as the value of any other commodity, corresponds to the labor that has gone into its production, *i.e.*, the cost of the production of labor. These costs result in the value of the exchange of his labor (power).

Labor (power) performs work and produces goods, which as commodities have the value of the labor embodied in them. The value of these commodities, however, is greater than the value of the labor (power) since more *labor* has gone into their production, more hours of work are contained in them, than in the worker's *labor (power)*, in his wage. The difference between the value of his labor (power) and the value of the product of his labor Marx calls "surplus value." This distinguishes Marx essentially from Ricardo and the classical economists. While the latter call the part of the value that is above the wage profit, which accrues to capital, Marx designates it as surplus value, which is produced by the worker and is appropriated by capitalists. This expropriation Marx calls *exploitation*.

Exploitation, according to Marx, is not a result of cheating or robbing the worker.[65] It is the necessary consequence of the functioning of the economy under conditions of the capitalist market mechanism, under conditions of bourgeois property rights, the private ownership of the means of production. So the results of exchange, as Marx sees them, are entirely correct : All commodities, even labor (power), which is marketed as a commodity, are valued and exchanged after the same principle : the amount of labor they contain.

The worker receives the full value of his labor (power). Nevertheless there remains a profit since the capitalist, as the owner of the means of production, buys labor (power) but sells commodities, the product of labor. The worker is constrained to sell his labor (power); he cannot sell the product of his labor (power) since he does not dispose of the means of production and cannot himself employ his labor (power) for the production of goods. Accordingly, the worker cannot change the rate of distribution of the values created by him; he can only abolish exploitation if he changes the "relations of ownership." The confrontation, the class struggle between labor and capital, does not, according to Marx, have as its object the distribution of the product of labor. Its object is the ownership of the means of production since it is this ownership that appropriates the surplus value.

Against this view it can be argued that the theory of labor value is valid only under certain conditions. It "does not work at all outside the case of perfect competition."[66] It requires that labor is the only factor of production (of importance) and that labor is homogeneous, "is all of one kind," that no natural differences in the quality of labor and its efficiency have to be considered. Only within the narrow limits drawn by these restrictions would a theory of labor value, as a theory of exchange of commodities, be appropriate.

A NEW FORMULATION OF THE LAW OF VALUE

This deterministic formulation of the law of value is today being abandoned by Marxists such as John E. Roemer.

Roemer explains in *Analytical Foundations of Marxian Economic Theory*[67]

> *The labor theory of value of Marx, played a double role as a theory of exchange and a theory of exploitation. Marx's approach was to use the theory of exchange as a conduit to generate the theory of exploitation. Our approach is to reject the labor theory of value in its role as exchange theory, and reconstruct the theory of exploitation on a different basis.*[68]

For Roemer, the labor value embodied in a commodity is dependent on the market on "prices of equilibrium."

> *What distinguishes labor power from other inputs into production ..must be that its value (that is, the consumption...) does not enter as a technological datum, but is determined by social interactions.*[69]

Roemer declares :

> *A modern Marxian theory...should maintain the general concept that class struggle determines real wages...*[70] and...*the real level of consumption of workers as a class is determined by their power as a class relative*

> *to capital, and is not necessarily limited to subsistence... (as Marx had more or less maintained).*[71]

And Roemer writes :

> *The "law of value" is the name we shall give to the principle which says that the world of social relations regulates relations in the world of prices and commodities [This means that power relations determine prices.] I think this is the most fruitful interpretation of what Marx meant by the law of value.*[72]

The bundle of subsistence (bundle of goods that guarantees the existence of labor), which had been considered as a *datum* by the objective theory of value, a datum that determines the "value of labor power," cannot be ascertained before the "drama of exchange and production," *i.e.*, the circulation of capital. The producer must know which methods of production generate profit to determine the value of labor, and this can be done only after the market has chosen one method out of the many other technological models. Roemer discards the notion that labor equivalents exchange for each other on the market.

> *We do not define the value of labor power.... We lose the notion, therefore, of "fair" exchange on the labor power market....*
>
> *The laws of exchange are not "fair" in some sense of the exchange of some abstract equivalent : They are governed by competition and class struggle. Class struggle sets the distributional variable — whether this is to be thought of as the wage, the real wage bundle, the profit rate, labors' share, or the rate of exploitation in different models — and competition regulates prices to allow capitalist reproduction consistent with the distributional boundary condition of class struggle. [Or, more generally, competition and class struggle codetermine prices and wages.] The labor theory of value is discarded entirely as an exchange theory but is preserved as a measure of exploitation.*[73]

Roemer explains :

> *[C]orresponding to any given constellation of social relations...(indicated by a social variable which measures the intensity of exploitation) there exists a set of prices, profit rates, and commodity consumptions for workers, that realize...the social conditions (of the intensity of exploitation) as an equilibrium in the world of profits and commodities — in the sense that profit-maximizing production by capitalists can take place and reproduce the economy at those prices (because the rate of profit is equalized in all sectors), while every worker maximizes utility subject to his wage constraint.*[74]

If the rate of exploitation reflects the relative strength of both classes, the corresponding "reification" of the relative position of these classes appears in prices, wages and profit. This means that prices, wages and profits express power. Roemer's views can be summarized as follows :

1. The real level of consumption of workers as a class is determined by their power as a class relative to capital and is not necessarily limited to subsistence.
2. Exchange of labor power for the wage is not characterized as fair in the sense of an exchange of equivalents but as determined by class struggle.
3. The labor theory of value is preserved to define exploitation and is discarded as a theory of microexchanges. Roemer shares the concept of Marx that economic categories (price, wage, etc.) are reflections of social categories (labor, exploitation). He states : "The commodity-price veil placed over social relations is removed by seeing that class struggle and competition determine wages and profits and that the latter can exist only with social exploitation."
4. The Marxian 'law of value" states not that labor values determine prices, but that a given set of social relationships

is reified into a particular set of economic variables (prices, outputs, products) in such a way as to reproduce the system. This reification or realization process of social relationships into commodity relationships is the process by which value "regulates" price, or the law of value.

5. The rate of exploitation describes the social distribution of the product but does not describe precisely the allocation of any individual worker's labor time between him and the capitalist.[75] Roemer so replaces the special subsistence theory of wages by the general class theory of wages.

One is inclined to say that Marx discovered the social category of value behind the economic category of the price, and that Roemer discovered power behind value.

It must be said that Roemer limits his analysis to the effects of power on the determination of the price of labor (power), and does not treat the effect of power, and of the various means of power, as a factor in the determination of prices for all commodities (and services) in the economy in general.

THE NEOCLASSICAL VIEW ON DISTRIBUTION

Neither have neoclassical economists all treated the problem of distribution and the question of an eventual confrontation between producer and wage-earner in a uniform and unequivocal way. We have already discussed the argumentation of Böhm-Bawerk, one of the most prominent representatives of the Austrian School of Marginal Utility, and have seen that he accords priority to economic law but also concedes a certain latitude to the exercise of power.

Léon Walras himself has also recognized the effect of the "action of men" on the "determination of the distributive share ...on the rate of wages and of profits."

Blaug, explaining the Walrasian "General Equilibrium," writes :

We have shown that consumers with given money incomes maximize utility relative to prices ruling in the market so as to obtain the same marginal utility per dollar from every product they purchase. At the same time, producers maximize profits relative to factor and product prices by employing the factors of production in such quantities and proportions as to obtain the same marginal value product per dollar of factor outlays; this leads them in the long run to build plants of optimal scale, producing levels of output at which average costs are minimized and marginal supply prices are equal to the given demand price for the final product.... At the same time, however, the resulting demand prices of all industries in a particular factor market must equal the supply prices of the owners of factor services. The aggregate demand for all factors in any period must equal the incomes received by households from supplying factor services in the same period. This provides the household with the given incomes with which we started the analysis of consumer behavior, thus completing the circle.[76]

In this model Walras replaces the originally given assumed inputs (*e.g.*, incomes) by values determined by their marginal productivity. Factors of production are compensated for their products in accordance with their rareness relative to the demand of the consumers. The demand for factors of production is deduced from the expected demand of the consumers for the products of these factors. The prices of production performances and of consumer goods are in the same way determined by the demand of the consumers. The income of the factors of production is the result of the prices on the market of the goods of consumption.

For Walras, the wage — from the side of demand — is determined by its marginal productivity. This is measured by adding (or subtracting) the effect a single unit of the factor has on the aggregate result — when the quantities of the other factors remain constant.

If the supply of a factor of production is infinitely elastic, growing demand has no influence on price; *i.e.*, it does not have the effect of increasing its price. For the factor labor, this means a wage on the level of subsistence.

The theory of marginal productivity is, however, not, as often claimed, a theory of the *distribution* of the relative shares of national product; it is a theory of *demand* for a factor of production.[77]

And Walras declares : "The returns to productive agents are perfectly susceptible to human action."[78] So class struggle has much to do with determining the "distributive shares," with the rate of wages and of profits.

"Wages may be raised by reducing the numbers available for hire." Also, raising workers' efficiency, brought about by an increase of the capital with which they are working, has an influence on the level of wages. And last but not least, the exercise of bargaining power has its effect on the wage obtained. To determine wages in regard to profits (or interest on capital) only by the marginal productivities of labor or capital is also impossible since there is no specific marginal product of *one* factor of production considered in isolation from the other. The factors of production are complementary, the marginal product of one being the consequence of the marginal product of the other. Blaug explains, however : "[T]he normative function of rewarding factors in accordance with marginal productivity is to achieve efficiency in resource allocation."[79]

For the neoclassical economists, the primary economic problem was the search for conditions under which given productive performances could be allocated to competing applications with optimum results. This optimum means maximizing consumer utility. Maximizing utility and efficiency occupy the center of their concern. If, however, marginal productivity loses its decisive role in determining wages (and profits) — and is reduced to a theory of resource allocation — it thereby also abandons its claim to guaranteeing the optimum allocation of the factors of production. An optimum allocation aiming at a maximum of satisfaction of wants is abandoned since it is not the criterion of productivity that determines their price but the relationships of power.

If prices express scarcities — and if these are not the consequences of marginal productivities only but also caused by the effect of power — they furnish "wrong signals" (in the neoclassical sense) for the allocation of resources and do not guarantee efficiency. Besides, the theory of marginal productivity and that of optimized allocation of resources based on it would be valid only under conditions of a perfect market, of perfect competition. There, a multitude of independent suppliers and consumers are in the market, none of whom is able to influence the price of products that are homogeneous. There is free access to and retreat from the market, and complete information for suppliers and consumers is assured. All this takes place within the framework of a closed economic system and under full employment.

These conditions, however, in the real-life economy are not given. It is therefore inadmissible to claim an optimum of results for the functioning of the mechanism of *the real-life market* as neoliberals do and to suggest that they were guaranteed by an unhindered functioning of its mechanism. It is equally wrong to reject every intervention in its functioning by claiming that this impairs the optimum. In any case, it would not be correct to justify this claim by referring to Walras and to his model of "General Equilibrium."

The model designed by Walras was not — according to William Jaffe, translator and commentator of Walras — thought to be the image of the real economy, and neither is it its ideal example. It was the attempt to show that a "realistic utopia" (Blaug), a rational construct, a non-self-contradictory economic system could be designed on the basis of profit maximizing and perfect competition, a system that maximizes the welfare of society : an ideal construct, not a positive analysis of the economy of the market.

Summing up : In the confrontation between producer and wage-earner, the classical economists, the Marxists and the neoclassical economists have admitted the effect of power on the distribution of the national product; they have, however, failed to integrate power into the body of their theories.

One more word on power and the level of wages : To be less constrained in the exercise of power by unions, companies have displaced their plants to regions with a low level of workers' organization or to low-wage countries of the Third World. There they can fully enjoy the advantage of their size and their superior power.

Another way to draw full benefit from size has been the introduction of methods of "slender production." In this system a number of intermediary products are given out to be manufactured by subsuppliers. This offers the producer a number of advantages. The industry restricts the risks of production by transferring them to an outward supplier. So too with the system of "just in time" deliveries, a considerable reduction of space requirements and space costs is realized; capital requirements and costs are also reduced.

The subsupplier often is capable of producing more efficiently and cheaper. It can better adjust the size of its plant to specialized production than a big factory can do for all its intermediate products. It can also, in its limited sphere, take better advantage of specialization. Moreover, as a medium-sized or smaller enterprise, it can frequently make use of cheaper, unorganized labor and avoid one of the disadvantages of size.

To this is added a further factor in favor of "slender production." This concerns the relationships of power between the producer and its subsupplier. This leads to another scene of confrontation.

THE CONFRONTATION BETWEEN PRODUCER AND SUPPLIER

In the course of "slender production," a big company can make full use of the weight of its size in its relations with its suppliers. These suppliers are normally more dependent on their customer than he is on them. The big company can, to squeeze prices and keep them under control, make full use of the competition between its suppliers and make them pass on their cost advantages to itself. The bigger its demand, the bigger its weight as a customer.

Moreover, as a customer, the big company has the advantage of full information, of full price transparency. It alone knows all the prices offered and the sales conditions of the suppliers who are competing for its orders. While suppliers generally move in a more or less large zone of uncertainty with the prices they quote, they normally learn about the prices of their competitors from the more or less reliable information furnished by their customer.

The greater their specialization as suppliers, the bigger the share a customer takes of their total output, the greater their dependence on their customer, the greater their readiness — especially when not at full capacity — to go to the very limit of their possibilities (and occasionally even beyond them, as we have seen when discussing the problem of fixed cost). Suppliers make price and other concessions to keep the customer and gain his order, and to insure the occupation of their enterprise.

But even outside the field of slender production, the supply market offers great opportunities to exploit positions of power. This is not only true for the rather rare cases of monopsony; this very often determines the relations of producer and supplier as such.

It is the supply market where often the biggest opportunities exist for reducing cost. For this reason, big corporations make intensive market research in their supply markets, finding new sources of supply, making comparative price analyses, comparing terms, qualities. Concentration and use of power on the supply market are important tasks of up-to-date purchasing departments.

If we consider that expenses for raw materials, semifinished products and other outside supplies often amount to more than the total sum of wages a company pays, we can better estimate the importance of this market for maximizing profits.

Supply also involves the furnishing of machines and equipment. Here in real economic life, anything but market transparency reigns. Prices of machines and installations, to say nothing of construction, differ from country to country and even from case to case. Here again a big company has the advantage — via its subsidiaries — to have better information on prices and to make use of the best offer.

To conclude, we can say that the supply market offers manifold opportunities for the use of power and that the size of an enterprise there plays an important role as a factor of power.

THE CONFRONTATION BETWEEN PRODUCER AND FINANCIER

This confrontation, as far as credit is concerned (making allowance for the amount of credit, the duration, the collateral demanded, the terms of repayment), has as its principal object the rate of interest or the price of credit. The rate of interest also depends on the general level of interest in the economy.

We here disregard the factor of monetary stability since we are interested mainly in the relative level of the rate of interest. Apart from the factors mentioned, the price level of credit is determined by supply and demand.

Supply of capital or credit is furnished by savings of households and enterprises (including the forced savings in the form of payments to pension funds), by the creation of credit by credit institutions and by the deficit of national governments.

Demand consists of the need of producers and consumers for liquid funds and of the demand for speculative purposes.

> The higher and more urgent demand is in relation to supply, the *higher — ceteris paribus —* the rate of interest.

Within this framework we consider the level of interest, as the price of any commodity and service, as an expression of relationships of power. This is illustrated by consumer credit where interest rates frequently are twice as high as those of commercial credits, and this not only for reasons of greater risk and higher administrative expense. Particularly crass is the case of usury. According to Böhm-Bawerk, this is not due to relationships of power but to an extremely urgent need, whose satisfaction offers extremely high utility. The price of this extremely high utility then is an extremely high rate of interest. It serves as proof that price corresponds to utility, that the price is paid. If the price were now still higher, utility would logically be still greater. Such absurd reasoning can be explained only by the fact that "laws" that may be valid for "perfect competition" are applied where there is no trace of it.

But also in normal relations between the producer and his creditor, power is effective. Big companies benefit from better terms, lower rates of interest and lower charges than smaller firms, and this not just because of the smaller risk involved. A big credit customer will enjoy preferential treatment, just as on the market of supply He is also able, by better information on all the possibilities of financing, to keep the cost of credit lower than the smaller firm. An international corporation is better able to exploit the differences of interest levels between different markets. As a result, it may gain important advantages over competitors but also in the face of its creditors since it is better able to take advantage of the competition between them.

This shows that the credit market is far from being a "perfect market." On this market quasi-unlimited needs are confronted with relatively scarce means. This disproportion creates a basic differential of power between creditor and debtor, which also finds its expression in the rate of interest. It may well be generally true that the interest a producer is capable of paying for a sum of credit — in the long run — cannot be higher than the returns on the investment he has financed by this credit. But this does not mean that "marginal return" determines the rate of interest. Rather, the producer will choose out of its intended investments those whose expected profitability would not be lower than the rate of interest he has to pay. In real economic life, it is the rate of interest that determines investment, and in that sense, the expected returns, and not *vice versa*; this is due to the fact that capital in relation to demand is scarce.

And finally one remark on the general level of the rate of interest : To a great extent this also depends on the monetary policy of the state; discount rates, open market operations, regulations concerning minimum reserves of banks, policy concerning the money supply, all these exert an important influence on the rate of interest. Here the power of the state and its policy make themselves felt, be they in the sense of a policy of high interest or of cheap money, be they in defense of the stability of the currency and the maintenance of its value or to promote growth and to fight unemployment. And the choice between these alternatives also is determined by economic and social relationships of power.

In all these confrontations the effect of power on price has been demonstrated. In the confrontation with the consumer, power permits higher prices; in the confrontation with labor, it can result in lower wages; in the confrontation with suppliers, it can reduce the price paid for supplies; and in the confrontation with financiers, it can lower the price of credit.

As a result of these confrontations the profits of powerful firms continue to grow.

6

THE DYNAMICS OF THE MARKET ECONOMY

We have, so far, discussed the function of power and the effect of its use on the economy of the market. To better understand the functioning of the market economy, we must, however, look into its history and consider the analysis of leading economists concerning its dynamics. We want to see what makes the market economy an economy of growth and what are the factors determining its dynamics as seen by leading theoreticians. At the same time we shall, as in previous chapters, confront these theories with the reality of the economy.

The economy of the market is without question the most efficient and most dynamic form of economy that man has created — so far — in his struggle to ensure and improve his material existence. What now constitutes the vitality and dynamics of the market economy? What are its mechanisms favoring growth? Why was it superior over other economic systems? In his book *Theorists of Economic Growth — from David Hume to the Present,* W.W. Rostow presents and analyzes the theories of growth of a number of leading economic theoreticians from the beginnings of classical theory to our days.

DAVID HUME (1711 — 1776)

Hume developed "a reasonably coherent and consistent theory of the dynamics of growth."[80] "He linked manufactures and agriculture in a rather subtle way. It is the attractions of manufactured consumer goods that constitute the incentive for those in agriculture 'to increase their skill and industry.' "[81] Hume declared : "When a nation abounds in manufactures and mechanic arts, the proprietors of land, as well as the farmers study agriculture as a science, and redouble their industry and attention."

For Hume, it is the availability of the products manufactured that is the "necessary incentive for the exertion of proprietor and farmer (and the urban working class as well)" to increase their efforts.

Manufacture in turn is stimulated by "foreign trade [which] by its imports, furnishes materials for new manufactures; and by its exports, it produces labor in particular commodities, which could not be consumed at home." And Hume finds the dynamics of economic development in the "exploitation of comparative advantages"; this is what imparts drive to trade.

Output, for Hume, is "a function of labor, land, manufactures; the productivity of labor and land is determined by the scale of manufactures and the scale of manufactures is determined by the scale of trade, foreign and domestic, and the productivity increases provided by the exploitation of comparative advantage."[82] It is the merchant who as "miser," in contrast to the prodigal landlord, generates the required savings and supplies the capital; he "knows no such pleasure as that of seeing the daily increase of his fortune... [this is why] ...trade increases frugality...and frugality the expansion of trade."[83]

Reinvesting the profits of trade in further trade to exploit comparative advantages confers the expansionist dynamic to the system of Hume.

This reinvestment Hume takes to be ensured, as soon as "fermentation" sets in with the expansion of trade and the incentive of luxury goods provided by foreign trade. (Hume cites the impact of calicoes, imported colored cotton textiles from India, which caused a sensation in Europe furthered consumption, created new demand and led the industry to copy the product and improve its methods of production; this resulted in the rise of the

British industry of textiles and of textile machinery, which wanted to have its share of the new market.)

For Hume, foreign trade is the motor of economic development, trade that generates an evolution (import of luxury goods, incentive for greater efforts, for increasing productivity in agriculture and manufacturing). On the other hand, by exploiting comparative advantages, trade creates profits that, because of the parsimony and greed for gain of the merchants, are reinvested and so further expand trade and manufacturing, offering still greater profits.

This growth of the economy, however, is not unlimited. Hume declares : "The growth of everything, both in arts and in nature, at last checks itself."[84] The relative superiority of one trading partner over the other, which creates comparative advantages, the difference in capacity of performance between trading partners, is eventually eliminated and with it profitable foreign trade. Hume sees the problem as "rich country-poor country",[85] where the rich country first by its superior technique enjoys comparative advantages, against which the poor country can only set the advantage of lower wages. With the passage of time, however, the technological gradient is flattened out and with that the relative advantages, whereby profits and finally even foreign trade vanish. It would seem that this conclusion is rather the fruit of Hume's philosophy : The growth of everything...at last checks itself, and not the result of observation.

It is true that Hume lived before major technological innovations added a comparative advantage that in turn reinforced their financial superiority. This helped rich countries to evade the limits to growth predicted by Hume and to retain their lead.

ADAM SMITH (1723 — 1790)

Rostow explains that to Hume, capital formation (the mechanism of saving-investing) ' virtually appears as a by-product of the expansion of trade and the plow-back of the profits by the creative, but miserly merchant."[86] "In Smith, labor, land and capital are unambiguously the three factors of production, but the system is driven forward, as in Hume by the savings of the frugal, who are assumed to invest all their savings without leakage." For Smith, however, it is the manufacturer who is supposed to reinvest all his savings

"In Hume capital made possible the exploitation of regional or international relative advantages; in Smith, capital permits the widening of the market and, thereby the division of labor."[87] The division of labor increases productivity since it increases the workers' dexterity; it saves "workers' time as he concentrates on a single task rather than move from one task to another" and by "the invention of a great number of machines, which facilitate and abridge labor, and enable one man to do the work of many."

What is important for Adam Smith is change — development — and not the status of the economy. By that, Smith reveals himself to be not only the theoretician of growth, but its apostle.

Rostow summarizes Smith's arguments in "three fairly complex propositions" :

1. All savings are invested; the motive for saving is profit, taking account of risk; savings will rise with the level of income.
2. Increased investment is the basis for growth because it is required for (a) enlarging the market, (b) equipping labor to perform increasingly specialized functions and (c) raising wages above subsistence as necessary to induce the population to grow. This will increase effective demand and the scale of the market while also generating the labor necessary to supply the needs of the expanded market. Because savings-investments rise with the increase in income, a cumulative process is set in motion by an initial rise in the rate of investment.
3. However, the benign upward spiral is constrained. The rate of profit will decline as capital accumulates, income

rises and an economy approaches its "full complement of riches."[88]

The self-reinforcing process of growth, whereby increased capital investment makes possible the expansion of the market, which generates bigger profits and further investments, does not go on indefinitely. It is, according to Adam Smith, constrained by land and the climate of a country and by its situation with respect to other countries as well as by its laws and institutions.

However, history shows that the industrialized countries of the First World used Third World countries as suppliers of raw materials and of cheap labor; at the same time they inundated their markets with the products of their industries and condemned them to stagnation from which only a few countries have succeeded in escaping.

To the superior power of the producer in the face of its supplier and that of the producer in the face of its wage-earners was added their power in the face of their customers, which has marked the relations of the First and the Third Worlds. By these power relations, rich countries continued to enrich themselves at the expense of the poor and were able to maintain their lead and continue their growth.

THOMAS R. MALTHUS (1766 — 1834)

Thomas Malthus was one of the greatest economists of his time. Of particular interest is his work on the growth of population, on the conditions of growth and on its consequences for the economy and for society.

He sounded the alert on the dangers of overpopulation and on the need to restrain population growth to make further development of the economy and of society possible. We have seen that overpopulation was one of the factors that cause an oversupply of labor, which weakens and depresses the position of labor in the face of capital. The warnings of Malthus also enter in this context.

The theory of growth of Malthus is in the main based on the classical theory of Adam Smith.[89] But Malthus also makes allowance for noneconomic, institutional, moral and religious factors. Malthus examines the effect of the "variables" in the field of political economy, such as growth of population, formation of capital, land and its fertility, labor-saving inventions and the role of demand and supply in determining the rate of growth.[90]

Malthus wants to find the explanation for the difference in the rate of growth of various countries. He asks : "What are the ...stimulants to the creation and progress of wealth?" and he explains :

> *It is obviously true that there are many countries, not essentially different either in the degree of security which they can afford to property, or in the moral and religious instruction received by the people, which yet, with nearly equal natural capabilities, make a very different progress to wealth... If the actual riches of a country not subject to repeated violences and frequent destruction of produce, be not after a certain period in some degree proportioned to its power of producing riches, this deficiency must have arisen from the want of an adequate stimulus to continued production. The practical question then for our consideration is, what are the most immediate and effective stimulants to the creation and progress of wealth?*[91]

> *The three great causes most favorable to production are accumulation of capital, fertility of soil, and inventions to save labor. They all act in the same direction; and as they all tend to facilitate supply, without reference to demand, it is not probable that they should either separately or conjointly afford an adequate stimulus to the continued increase of wealth.*[92]

Only the growth of population can have this economic effect since it stimulates consumption. For Malthus, this is a question of effective demand. "[D]ynamic equilibrium in a growing economy requires endless correct proportioning and balancing of supply and demand." While he states that "increase of population is a powerful and necessary element of increasing demand," it is not a sufficient condition for the growth of wealth. Malthus points to the "natural tendency of population to increase beyond the funds destined for its maintenance" and declares "the slowest progress in wealth is often made where the stimulus arising from population alone is the greatest." Malthus asserts : "From high real wages...two very different results may follow : one, that of a rapid increase of population, in which case the high wages are chiefly spent in the maintenance of large and frequent families; and the other, that of a decided improvement in the modes of subsistence, and the conveniences and comforts enjoyed, without a proportionate acceleration in the rate of increase."[93]

For Malthus, "the cause of these different habits.. which make in one case... [the lower classes] unable or unwilling to reason from the past to the future, and ready to acquiesce, for the sake of present gratification, in a very low standard of comfort and respectability." while in the other, to "tend to... make them act as beings who look before and after, and who consequently cannot acquiesce patiently in the thought of depriving themselves and their children of the means of being respectable, virtuous, and happy' ; and he states : "Among the circumstances which contribute to the character first described, the most efficient will be found to be despotism, oppression and ignorance : among those which contribute to the latter character, civil and political liberty, and education." This is an important point : By defining the circumstances that determine labor's choice (either of present gratification or of looking "before and after"), Malthus uncovers political causes behind psychological reasons.

In one case oppression and ignorance paralyze labor and keep it in submission; in the other case, under conditions of civil and political liberties and by education, labor is permitted to develop its autonomy. In one case labor is powerless; in the other it can develop as a counter-power.

But finally,

when cultivation is pushed to its extreme practical

limits, that is, when the labor of a man on the last land taken into cultivation will scarcely do more than support such a family as is necessary to maintain a stationary population, it is evident that no other cause or causes can prevent profits from sinking to the lowest rate required to maintain the actual capital. But though this principle is finally of the greatest power, yet its progress is extremely slow and gradual; and while it is proceeding with scarcely perceptible steps to its final destination, the second cause (i.e., voluntary limitation of population growth) is producing effects which entirely overcome it, and often for twenty or thirty, or even 100 years together make the rate of profits take a course absolutely different from what it ought to be according to the first cause.[94]

Rostow comments : "Malthus' view of the stages and limits to growth is, in effect, an exercise in the relative power of his 'first' and 'second' causes...the first -the inexorable expansion of population up to the point where the means of subsistence, whatever the form of the economy, can maintain at best a stationary population at a minimum level" where population by "positive" checks, such as misery, sickness, vice and mortality, is kept in check, and the limits of economic growth are attained.

The second, on the contrary, could "to the extent that diminishing returns can be fended off, aided by benign preventive checks to the population" arrest this evolution at least for a long time. And Rostow declares that for Malthus, noneconomic factors play a greater role in the analysis of economic growth than for Adam Smith. The "population issue" introduced noneconomic variables, which are decisive for the direction evolution can take.

DAVID RICARDO (1777 — 1823)

Ricardo's view of the growth of the economy is marked by his theory of diminishing returns in agriculture and by his conception of the ground rent as a differential rent. Ricardo's theory of diminishing returns is based on the fact that the increase of population demanded an increase in the production of grain, and that this, in a fully developed country, can be achieved only by extending the cultivation of land to lands of lower quality, of lower yield.

With every increase of cultivation on lands of lower yield, the costs of production rise, as do the prices of the products of agriculture. With them, the ground rent (as differential rent for better lands) rises, as does the money wage (if it is assumed that real wages stay constant); the profit of capital (*i.e.*, the difference between cost and returns), however, falls.

This is equally the case if the fall of the marginal productivity (of land) is compensated by more labor, or by more capital, by extending the cultivation to more land of lower quality, or by a more intensive cultivation of better land. The ground rent rises, since it accrues as *differential rent* for all better, more productive land that can be cultivated at lower cost. It benefits from the rise of (the sales) price that is due to the higher costs caused by the cultivation of land of lower quality or by more expensive methods of production (according to Ricardo, one could see the differential rent to be a kind of farm rent, which a tenant would be ready to pay for lands of higher return).

For Ricardo, diminishing returns govern the products of agriculture and of mining, increasing returns governing the products of manufacturing. Ricardo declares :

> *The natural price of all commodities, excepting raw produce and labor, has a tendency to fall in the progress of wealth and population; for though on one hand, they are enhanced in real value, from the rise in the natural price of the raw material of which they are made, this is more than counterbalanced by the improvements in machinery, by the better division and distribution of labor, and by the increasing skill, both in science and in art, of the producers.*[95]

The race between diminishing returns in agriculture and

increasing returns in manufacturing plays a central role in Ricardo's view of the stages and of the limits of growth.

Ricardo sees a socially determined, rising natural wage as a possibility; a precondition, however, was a diminution of *demographic pressure*. "From manufactured commodities always falling, and raw produce always rising, with the progress of society, such a disproportion in their relative value is at length created, that in rich countries a laborer, by sacrifice of a very small quantity only of his food, is able to provide liberally for all his other wants."[96] As opposed to that, the market wage has the tendency to fall, because through technological progress workers become redundant; it is true that new employment is created, but again and again replacement by machinery follows, making workers redundant, "a technical unemployment that renews itself continuously."[97]

With that, money wages and even real wages are falling, which under the pressure of the increase of population, approach subsistence level if prices do not follow the evolution of costs. This may reduce the pressure on the rate of profit, but in the last instance technological improvements benefit mainly the ground rent, the landowner. We would say that the oversupply of labor due to demographic pressure and to technical unemployment puts labor in a weak position in the face of the employer; this makes the slope of power in favor of the employer steeper and prevents labor from successfully resisting the pressure on wages.

To summarize, we can say that :

> The classical economists see the merchant or the manufacturer as the agent of economic growth.

The condition of growth is the saving and reinvesting of profits, the transformation of income into capital, the accumulation of capital. Investments have the effect of expanding the market, of increasing productivity, and raise profits and reinvestment.

Profits accrue to the merchant from the exploitation of "relative advantages," to the manufacturer by the expansion of the market and of production, of the division of labor, and also from innovations.

The growth of population stimulates demand and ensures for production an increasing supply of the required labor. Uncontrolled growth, however, leads to stagnating wages and to the stagnation of progress.

Limits on growth in the economy result on the one hand from an uncontrolled growth of the population and on the other from diminishing returns of agriculture and the fall of the rate of profit, which restricts saving and reinvestment.

KARL MARX (1818 — 1883)

The *Communist Manifesto* declares :

> *The bourgeoisie has in its barely hundred years of class rule created more abundant and colossal forces of production than all previous generations put together. Subjugation of the forces of nature, machinery, application of chemistry to industry and agriculture, steamships, railways, electrical telegraphs, cultivation of whole continents, making rivers navigable; entire populations created (from the ground) — what previous century foresaw that such productive forces lay dormant in the womb of social labor?*[98]

The history of the last 150 years since the publication of this manifesto has in no way given the lie to this statement. Quite the contrary, and also in contrast to the historical perspectives of its authors and all other economists of their time, the pace of economic development has not only not slackened, it has accelerated.

If we take the "class rule of the bourgeoisie" in the economy to mean "economy of the market," as it by and large corresponds to the way it functions, then this quotation of Marx and Engels reflects their vision of the dynamics of the market economy. To Marx, these dynamics find their expression in the development of the productive forces. At a given level of their development, however, the mode of production, *i.e.*, the private ownership of the means of production, turns into fetters on further development.

> *In the social production of their life, men enter into definite relations that are indispensable and independent of their will, relations of production which correspond to a definite stage of development of their material productive forces. The sum total of these relations of production constitutes the economic structure of society, the real foundation on which rises a legal and political superstructure and to which correspond definite forms of social consciousness.* The mode of production of material life conditions the social, political and intellectual life process in general. *It is not the consciousness of men that determines their being, but, on the contrary, their social being that determines their consciousness. At a certain stage of their development, the material productive forces of society come into conflict with the existing relations of production, or — what is but a legal expression of the same thing — with the property relations within which they have been at work hitherto. From forms of development of the productive forces these relations turn into their fetters.*[99]

Marx undertakes to demonstrate this judgment scientifically and to lay bare the "laws of motion" of the capitalist economy. Starting from the "objective theory of value" of classical theory, Marx defines the value of a commodity — under perfect competition and in equilibrium — to be proportional to the amount of labor that is embodied in it (under the condition that it corresponds to the "socially necessary quantity of labor").[100]

Marx distinguishes between constant capital (machines, installations, raw material, etc.) and variable capital (labor, the sum of wages), and calls the "organic structure of capital" the relationship between constant and variable capital. He establishes the relationship of profit to total capital to obtain the rate of profit and puts profit in relation to variable capital to obtain the rate of surplus value, the rate of exploitation. Surplus value is the difference between two values : the value of labor and the value of the product of labor.

The value of labor is — like the value of every commodity — determined by the amount of labor embodied in it, *i.e.*, the labor necessary to ensure the existence and reproduction of the worker : "the number of labor hours it took and takes to rear, feed, clothe and house the laborer" and his family.[101]

The level of existence and reproduction varies cyclically around a socially determined "level of subsistence." It is always brought down again to this level by the existence of a chronic layer of unemployed, by the "industrial reserve army." This reserve army is not the result of Malthus' population growth, but of three displacements :

- The displacement of the peasant from his land by the big landowner;
- The displacement of the artisan by industry; and
- The displacement of the industrial worker by the machine.

Labor, however, does more work — expressed in hours of work — than is necessary for its reproduction; as a result, it creates a "surplus value." This surplus value is appropriated by the capitalist who, having bought the *labor (power)* through the mechanism of the market, has become its owner, and as the owner of the means of production (capital and labor), becomes the owner of their product, of the commodity that embodies the surplus value.

Marx characterizes the appropriation of the surplus value by the capitalist as exploitation since the worker does not receive the total product of the value he added, but only the value of his *labor (power)* that he sold to the capitalist. Marx combines this theory of exploitation with his theory of the accumulation of capital.

"The main part of the loot wrung from exploited labor... capitalists turn into capital, means of production." This corresponds roughly to the view of the classical economists that savings equal investments.

For Marx, capitalists are driven to save and invest, not just for psychological reasons (avarice, rapacity, greed) or moved by

Puritan ethics. They are driven by necessity since in a competitive economy, profits if reinvested make possible the expansion of production and the further growth of profits, make possible maximizing profits. Accumulation of capital thus results from the pursuit of profit, from the urge to maximize profit.

At the same time, however, the cumulative effect of the expansion of production causes the rate of profit to fall, a consequence of the rise of wages due to the increased demand for labor and also to the fall of price caused by the increased supply of commodities. As a result, the individual capitalist suffers a loss of profits and is forced to counteract this, to accumulate even more to compensate for these losses (a good example of the contradictions inherent in the capitalist system).

This compulsion to accumulate does not let the economy find an equilibrium before the surplus value has fallen to zero and accumulation has destroyed capitalism.

This is how Schumpeter presents the Marxian theory of the falling rate of profit.

In terms of the theory of value of Karl Marx, one reads : The accumulation of capital causes the "organic structure" of capital to change; it makes constant capital rise in proportion to variable capital (labor). Since only variable capital (labor) creates value and by that surplus value — constant capital is merely remunerated at its value — surplus value in relation to total capital is falling, and so does the rate of profit. It is the fall of the rate of profit that for Marx brings an end to the dynamic development of the capitalist economy, a dynamism based on the accumulation of capital.

And finally Marx develops the theory of the concentration of capital from his theory of accumulation; the tendency of the capitalist process to increase the size both of the industrial plants and of units of control, "the battle of competition is fought by cheapening commodities, (which) depends, *ceteris paribus,* on the productivity of labor...the larger capital beats the smaller... the increasing bulk of individual masses of capital becomes the material basis of an uninterrupted revolution in the mode of production itself,"[102] i.e., leading to a concentration of capital as result of the process of accumulation.

And Rostow, in this context, cites J.R. Hicks, who more than a century later argues

> *If the population can once be controlled, there is no need for the economy to go on expanding, in order that wages should be above subsistence level. Instead of land being the main fixed factor, so that (as in the Ricardian stationary state) surplus production is swallowed up in rent, it is labor that becomes the main fixed factor, so that surplus production can be made to go at least in large measure, to wages. This is an altogether different, and much more agreeable, picture. The stationary state is no longer a horror. It becomes an objective at which to aim.*[103]

ALFRED MARSHALL (1842 — 1924)

Alfred Marshall is the economist who discovered the importance of increasing returns (or rather decreasing cost) in the economy of our time, "the normal condition of many firms and sectors in an economy regularly absorbing new technologies." For them, "no single stable equilibrium position exists for price and output." When the marginal cost curve continues to slope downwards, "conventional micro-economics become inoperative."[104]

We have encountered this problem when discussing fixed costs and their effect on price formation (price at marginal cost, being below average cost, does not cover fixed cost).

On growth, Marshall wrote that although diminishing returns would eventually reassert themselves in the world economy, he did not believe that "diminishing marginal utility for real income [would] decree a stationary state from the side of demand... since British and other workers had still much to ask of the economic system."[105]

> *There seems to be no good reason for believing that we*

> *were anywhere near a stationary state in which there will be no new important wants to be satisfied; in which there will be no more room for profitably investing present effort in providing for the future, and in which the accumulation of wealth will cease to have any reward. The whole history of man shows that his wants expand with the growth of his wealth and knowledge.*

Nor does Marshall see stagnation as a threat caused by the decline of the "productivity of investment." In spite of a decline of interest rates in advanced industrial countries, he does not believe that "along with all the other determinants of saving," this decline would lead to a "cessation of investment and a stationary state."

He examines the prospects of labor and explores a range of variables bearing on the future of real wages, including hours of work, the effect of excessively high wages on the direction of investment, including investment abroad the positive and negative effects of labor unions, and an evaluation of income inequities" and concludes that "on balance there is no necessity, and therefore no moral justification, for extreme poverty side by side with great wealth."[106]

Marshall sees the dynamics of the system as follows :

> *[W]e saw the extra return of raw produce which nature affords to an increased application of capital and labor...tends in the long run to diminish...we have seen how man's power of productive work increases with the volume of the work that he does.... Every increase in the physical, mental and moral vigor of a people makes them more likely.. to rear to adult age a large number of vigorous children. Turning next to the growth of wealth, we observed how every increase of wealth tends in many ways to make a greater increase more easy than before. And lastly we saw how every increase of wealth and every increase in the numbers and intelligence of the people increased the facilities*

> *for a higher developed industrial organization, which in its turn adds much to the collective efficiency of capital and labour.*[107]

But Marshall has made an important contribution on a further question. On the problematics of "profit, saving, investment," he states that savings do not exclusively come from (retained) profits, that rent as well as the "earnings of professional men and hired workers are an important source of accumulation"[108] and have been all along. "The middle and especially the professional classes have always denied themselves much in order to invest capital in the education of their children, while a great part of the wages of the working classes is invested in the physical health and strength of their children."[109]

> *The older economists took too little account of the fact that human faculties are as important a means of production as any other kind of capital — and we may conclude, in opposition to them — ...that any change in the distribution of wealth which gives more to the wage receivers and less to the capitalists is likely, other things being equal, to hasten the increase of material production...and not retard the storing up of material wealth... From the national point of view the investment of wealth in the child of the working man is as productive as its investment in horses or machinery.*

Altogether, Marshall "saw no end to the operation of increasing returns, although he perceived the costs as well as the benefits of the complex process involved."[110] But the continued net progress of the system required, in his own famous image, that new trees rise in the forest as the great old trees reach their natural limits, "lose vitality, and one after another give place to others, which, though of less material strength, have on their side the vigor of growth." (To this Joan Robinson put the question : Why did Marshall not rather use the simile of the fish pond, a remark to which one can perhaps better subscribe today.)

For us, it remains to say that Marshall has freed the process of growth of the economy from its exclusive dependence on the mechanism of "profit, saving, investment." If "human capital" is just as important as material capital, if this is favored by a more equal distribution of income, a distribution at the cost of profits, then the fall of the rate of profit, and perhaps even its disappearance, may not necessarily mean the end of growth, the end of development as the classical economist had maintained.

J.A. SCHUMPETER (1883 — 1950)

Schumpeter was one of the most original economic thinkers of his time. Unlike the neoclassical economists, he undertook to integrate innovation in his theory of economic growth. Schumpeter sees the evolution of the economy as a process based on innovation, "a spontaneous and discontinuous process."[111] Starting from a "particular version of static equilibrium [a Walrasian ... system] in a state of circular flow," a system that "allows for incremental changes in technology" and is administered by "unimaginative managers," he proceeds to the fundamental problem of economic development :

> *Development in our sense is a distinct phenomenon, entirely foreign to what may be observed in the circular flow or in the tendency toward equilibrium. It is spontaneous and discontinuous change in the channels of the flow, disturbance of equilibrium, which forever alters and displaces the equilibrium state previously existing.*

This concept covers five cases :

1. The introduction of a new good — that is, one with which consumers are not yet familiar — or of a new quality of good.
2. The introduction of a new method of production, that is, one not yet tested by experience in the branch of manufacture concerned, that by no means need be founded upon a scientifically new discovery and can

also exist in a new way of handling a commodity commercially.

3. The opening of a new market, that is, a market into which the particular branch of manufacture of the country in question has not previously entered, whether or not this market has existed before.
4. The conquest of a new source of supply of raw materials or half-manufactured goods, again regardless of whether it has first to be created.
5. The carrying out of the new organization of any industry, like the creation of a monopoly position (for example, through trustification) or the breaking up of a monopoly position.''[112]

Schumpeter distinguishes principally between product innovation (1, 3, 5) and process innovation (2, 4), the former mainly affecting the price, the latter cost. Both, however, exert their influence on the position of the firm in the market and its position with its customers and competitors. Both create positions of power, and both influence the rate of profit.

Under the criterion of innovation, Schumpeter distinguishes two sectors of the economy : The one sector is the sphere of the ''circular flow system,'' where the ''General Equilibrium'' of Walras prevails. This sector is not completely static, so that ''year after year the same things happen.'' It allows for ''incremental changes in technology that displace the equilibrium point of the system so marginally as to permit new equilibrium positions to be reached from the old by 'infinitesimal steps,'' which ''unimaginative managers (as opposed to heroic innovating entrepreneurs) can deal.''[113]

In this circular sector, interest on capital accrues only in the sense that interest represents a premium of present as compared with future purchasing power.

The second sector is the true sector of innovation in the economy where spontaneous and discontinuous change constantly disturbs the equilibrium. It is the proper sector for development of the system. For Schumpeter, the motor of this development is the "creative entrepreneur." "Particularly creative individuals — entrepreneurs, as opposed to managers — were required to respond effectively to the potentialities for profitable innovation generated within the system."[114]

Schumpeter talks of "the lonely creativity demanded when an innovating entrepreneur, with imperfect information, steps off uncertainly into the dark to do something new.... Carrying out a new plan and acting according to a customary one are things as different as making a road and walking along it."

"To finance the early stage of their creative endeavors, the entrepreneurs require that capitalists grant them credit." Out of the profits innovation offers the entrepreneur can come interest on this credit.

Unlike the sector of static circular flow where "wages of management" are paid, the sector of innovation gives rise to profits as "excess of total receipts over total costs induced by innovation and its consequences for development throughout the system.... The consequences include a 'clustering' of entrepreneurship around the new innovation once truly pioneering entrepreneurs demonstrate profit possibilities, as well as 'creative destruction' of activities superseded and rendered unprofitable by the diffusing innovation. Capital investment and the expansion of wealth derive mainly from the plowback of profits associated with innovation."

The development of the economy, as seen by Schumpeter, moves in cycles. In his theory of business cycles, Schumpeter explains that booms and recessions are not deviations from the "normal" course of development of the economy, but the "form economic development takes in the era of capitalism."[115]

With his theory of business cycles, Schumpeter provides the connection between the innovative sector and the economy as a whole. According to this, the innovating sector drives and the circular-flow sector is driven by the ups and downs of booms and recessions. It is this movement that transmits the dynamics of economic development from the innovative sector to the sector of circular flow. By the business cycle, the "static sector" is forced into dynamics, since its outdated activities prove to be unprofitable and are displaced, *i.e.*, suffer "creative destruction," by the diffusing innovation, innovations that offer new opportunities of gain or opportunities to avoid loss.

For Schumpeter, it is the "heroic, creative entrepreneur" who is the motor of economic development. Its mechanism is that of the economy of the market, which by the sequence of boom and recession transmits the dynamics to the system as a whole. However, Schumpeter does not see the market as a mechanism; rather, he sees it as an organism that functions according to the laws of natural selection and the survival of the fittest. (This view may countenance a social-Darwinistic ideology that considers society as being governed by the "law of the jungle" and ignores other factors of importance, such as human consciousness and the human need and capacity for solidarity.)

In Capitalism, Socialism and Democracy, Schumpeter sums up his theory of growth for capitalism, *i.e.*, for the market economy, as follows :

> *Capitalism...is by nature a form or method of economic change and not only never is but never can be stationary. And this evolutionary character of the capitalist process is not merely due to the fact that economic life goes on in a social and natural environment which changes and by its change alters the data of economic action; this fact is important and these changes (wars, revolutions and so on) often condition industrial change, but they are not its prime movers. Nor is this evolutionary character due to a quasi-automatic increase in population and capital or to the vagaries of monetary systems of which exactly the same thing holds true. The fundamental impulse that sets and keeps the capitalist engine in motion comes from the new consumer goods, the new methods of*

production or transportation, the new markets, the new forms of industrial organization that capitalist enterprise creates.

And he explains : "The problem [is not] how capitalism administers existing structures, ...the relevant problem is how it creates and destroys them."[116]

This development, however, does not go on indefinitely. Schumpeter sees the end of capitalism, of the market economy, as coming from social developments and not from purely economic factors.

So Schumpeter does not see the dynamics of economic development as impaired by monopolistic practices. Restrictive methods, which limit production to maintain a high price, may well influence or exclude price competition. By that, however, competition itself is not eliminated. It takes on other forms : quality competition, sales promotion, the competition of new products and new methods, all factors that offer decisive cost and price advantages — methods that are much more effective than the price struggle.

Neither do 'vanishing opportunities to invest" put an end to the dynamic, to further development, neither the falling birth rate, nor the end of breaking in new lands to cultivation, nor a slackening off of technological progress. None of these sets limits on further development.

This may be due, rather, to a certain saturation (a decline of the marginal utility of new satisfactions) that could rob the dynamic evolution if not of its drive, then of its sense. For Schumpeter, it is not a failure of the system of the market economy, but its very achievements that bring about its end. Decisive for Schumpeter is the fact that entrepreneurship is becoming obsolete, that the function of the entrepreneur, by the development of the system, becomes superfluous.[117]

"Technological progress increasingly becomes the business of teams of trained specialists."[118] "The perfectly bureaucratized giant industrial unit not only ousts the small and medium-sized firm and 'expropriates' its owners, but in the end it also ousts the entrepreneur, and expropriates the bourgeoisie which in the process stands to lose not only its income but also, what is infinitely more important, its function."[119] It is the entrepreneur who for Schumpeter is not only the representative and standard bearer, but the very basis of the support of the system. Entrepreneurship is replaced by planning, the market economy by the socialist planned economy — a perspective that Schumpeter as a conservative thinker by no means welcomed but believed to be inevitable.

MARK BLAUG (1927—)

For Blaug, similarly to Schumpeter, the entrepreneur is the agent that drives the dynamics of the market economy. In *Economic History and the History of Economics,* Blaug investigates the function of entrepreneurship within the framework of the market economy. In the chapter "Entrepreneurship Before and After Schumpeter," Blaug declares that the "innovational process as a whole is the outcome of responses to market pressures."[120] Principal agent of these reactions is the entrepreneur.

Blaug declares : "If we fully understood the nature of industrial entrepreneurship and the conditions under which it flourishes, ...we would at long last be near to answering the great question with which economics began : what are the causes of the wealth of nations?"[121]

In that, Blaug follows Schumpeter; for him the entrepreneur is the key figure of the market economy. "[T]he function of entrepreneurship stands at the center of the functioning of a capitalist society.' For Blaug, industrial entrepreneurship means that "an individual takes the risk, to introduce a new method or a new product." Besides the function that private ownership of the means of production may involve, such as "the provision of financial capital, the employment and coordination of the factors of production, the management and administration of the entire enterprise..., [there is] the function and the ultimate power of making strategic decisions about investment."[122]

Blaug explains that

> *[the] existence of capital markets and the invention of the principle of limited liability (of the owner for his enterprise) makes it possible completely to separate the supply of financial capital from all the other functions.... Likewise, the hiring of inputs and the functions of routine management and administration can be almost completely delegated to salaried employees. That leaves the power of making fundamental decisions to invest or not to invest, to enter a new market or to leave an old one...as the only functions that cannot be hired off : a businessman need not be a "capitalist" or "manager," but he must be a decision-maker, whether he liked it or not. It is this function and this function alone that deserves the title "entrepreneurship."*[123]

Blaug here lets us gain a new vision of the factors of production. Since it is the entrepreneur who hires capital (and pays interest on it), hires labor (and pays wages) and uses land and pays rent these factors might just as well be seen as mere inputs in production with no claim on the value added.

The only really creative factor, the only one who creates a plus value according to this vision, is the entrepreneur. It is then logical — if the difference between the cost of production (supplies, capital, labor and land) and the price of the produced goods represents profit — that this should go to the entrepreneur.

By that, discussion of contributive shares, of marginal productivity and of the distribution of added value loses its sense. However, the question of what determines the rate of interest and the level of wages is not answered.

Utility and productivity aside, this can be seen to be due to the relationships of power between the agents in the economy.

Blaug refers to Richard Cantillon, who (20 years before Adam Smith) created economic theory and coined the term "entrepreneur" as distinguished from the capitalist. Cantillon realized that "discrepancies between demand and supply in a market create opportunities for someone to buy cheap and sell dear and that it is precisely this sort of arbitrage that brings competitive markets into equilibrium." He named people who take advantage of these unrealized profit opportunities "entrepreneurs, ...those who are willing to buy at a certain price and sell at an uncertain price."[124] Entrepreneurship for Cantillon is "a matter of foresight and willingness to assume risk, which is not necessarily connected with the employment of labor" or with staking one's own capital.

Blaug also cites Johann von Thünen *(The Isolated State,* 1850), who considers the gains of the entrepreneur to be the "returns for incurring those risks which no insurance company will cover because they are unpredictable."

The neoclassical theorists, such as Walras, had no use for the entrepreneur. "In the state of 'General Equilibrium,' every productive agent is rewarded according to his marginal product, ...the increment of output which is contributed by the marginal product of that agent."[125] When all productive agents (*i.e.*, the representatives of the factors of production) are paid their marginal products, there is no rest left, the total product is "exhausted." When perfect competition has done its work and we have reached a short-run and long-run equilibrium, labor receives "wages" in accordance with the marginal product of labor, capital receives "interest" in accordance with the marginal product of capital goods, but profits have been eliminated and the entrepreneur, as Walras said, "neither benefits nor loses."[126]

Blaug cites Mark Casson *(The Entrepreneur, an Economic Theory, 1982),* for whom "capitalism is simply an economic system that harnesses entrepreneurship to industrial decisions."[127] Casson defines the entrepreneur as "someone who specializes in taking judgmental decisions about coordination of scarce resources."

The entrepreneur consequently is somebody who benefits from a relative advantage in making decisions, an advantage due to his judgment and his readiness (or eagerness) to take decisions.

For Casson, the "profits of entrepreneurship are 'earned income' in the true sense of the term. In the short-run the entrepreneurs' reward is a 'rent of ability,' a temporary monopoly rent to superior judgment (in our sense, a power-determined gain), and in the long-run "a necessary compensation for the time and effort involved in identifying and making judgmental decisions."

Blaug explains :

> *Entrepreneurship may be a universal feature of all society, but capitalism provides a unique institutional setting to release the entrepreneurial spirit.... The technical dynamics of capitalism, which Marx attributed to the organizational invention of the factory, the despotic control of the workers by capitalists, and the restless urge of the bourgeoisie to save and invest, must instead be credited in large part to the institution of private property rights, which channels the entrepreneurial spirit into productive outlets where previously it remained locked into speculative and purely merchandising activity.*[128]

And by grasping the true nature of industrial entrepreneurship, Blaug thinks he can come "near to answering the great question : What *are* the causes of the wealth of nations?"

Here a critical comment on Blaug's (and Schumpeter's) presentation of the role of the entrepreneur is due : Because capitalism is based on the accumulation of capital and the exploitation of the worker, the role of the "organizational invention" of the factory, as the place of control over the worker and his work — a place where democracy as well as the market economy is excluded — cannot be minimized when judging the dynamics of capitalism. The role of the entrepreneur as the key figure of the market economy, as *the* creator of the "wealth of nations," has been unduly overdrawn by Blaug.

The entrepreneur undoubtedly plays an important role, not only in industry, but also in trade, in finance and even in science, in research, in the arts and in sports. Neither can it be denied that the economy is driven forward by people, a dynamic economy preferably by dynamic people. However, to find in the process of selection and confirmation of such individuals the *very basis* of the capitalist system may not take sufficiently into consideration the complex contexts and determinants of the economy and its development. It may reduce them in an oversimplifying manner to a rather narrow denominator, a rather narrow basis for a system as strong as the market economy. This could be the reason why Schumpeter's prognosis of the end of the capitalist system has — at least so far — proven to be wrong.

Blaug's dramatic presentation of the entrepreneur does not explain why an entrepreneur cannot be hired along with his entrepreneurial capacities, just as a manager or any other agent along with his specific qualities, nor why his "ultimate power of making strategic decisions" cannot be shared by a team of competent collaborators, as is often the case in real economic life. It does not explain why the entrepreneur must to this extent be singled out, the process of "creative activity" in many cases being the result of teamwork and of the contribution of a great number of agents. Apart from that, and not by mere chance, this being presented under the title of a famous treatise, the idea of Adam Smith turns up again, that the success of individual efforts results in the success of society, of the nation.

The point is that society is not a field of harmony of interests; that the "nation" does present antagonistic features; that conflicts of interest are fought out there; that in different ways and forms the gain of the one may cause the loss of the other; that the result of the effort of the individual can be as beneficial to the "wealth of the nation" as detrimental to it; and finally, that the market economy does not possess a mechanism that guarantees the former. And beyond these points, the question is : are dynamics, and be it the dynamics of the economy, in every case equivalent to progress, and do they result in the creation and increase of wealth for all?

7

ECONOMIC GROWTH AND THE PERSPECTIVES OF THE MARKET ECONOMY

We have now discussed a number of representative theories on the question of what is the cause of growth, of the dynamics of the economy of the market; where does it lead; and what are its prospects?

These theories differ insofar as they bear the mark of their times in two ways. On the one hand they are marked by the reality of their historical environment, by the respective states of development of their society and economy. This is the more so because of the dynamics of the market economy; both have undergone enormous changes. On the other hand, they also express the development of their science, a development that in its stages not only reflects the development of their "subject of research," but also the general development of scientific thought.

There are also basic differences in the theories developed due to a different conception of the world, a different philosophy if not ideology. If we very much simplify, we can say that for the classical economists, the growth of the economy occupied the center of the stage. Adam Smith may well be seen as an apostle of growth; for him, growth is identical with the increase of wealth. For the neoclassical economists, the problem of wealth presents itself differently. Central to them is the problem of optimization, an optimum employment and use of scarce resources to obtain a maximum of supply for society at a minimum of cost.

The classical economists see the creative and parsimonious merchant or manufacturer guided by his pursuit of gain, of maximizing profit, as the support of development and of the dynamics of the market economy. The neoclassical economists, in principle, can do without a personified support; to them, the interplay of supply and demand, determined by marginal productivity and marginal utility under conditions of perfect competition, produces an optimum of results, a "General Equilibrium." This corresponds to a balance between supply and demand, between prices and quantities and employs the factors of production — labor and capital — not only optimally, but also entirely and yields a maximum of subsistence at a minimum of cost. This equilibrium not only establishes itself automatically; it also, when disturbed, reestablishes itself by self-regulation.

For the classical economists, the mechanism of growth is based on "profit, saving, investing and more profit"; profit grows out of exploiting relative advantages (Hume) or out of specialization and the division of labor (Smith), and the additional gain from an expansion of the market and of production made possible by reinvesting. For the neoclassical economists, "General Equilibrium," *i.e.*, equilibrium under perfect competition, has no room for profit. The problem of growth is not posed.

The classical economists see the limits of growth and its end caused by the decline of relative advantages (Hume) and by the decline of the rate of profit. This is a consequence of the growth of capital in relation to labor and of an increased demand for labor, causing a rise of wages at the expense of profits (Adam Smith). It is accompanied by decreasing returns in agriculture and mining (Ricardo), but growth can also be impaired and potentially ended by an excessive growth of population (Malthus).

Decreasing returns in agriculture stand opposite to increasing returns in manufacturing, while scientific research and development of technology (in agriculture, and especially in manufacturing) figure as the most important factors in the struggle against diminishing returns. Growth, however, does not only depend on the expansion of production, of supply, but also on an increase of effective demand. This increase depends on the growth of population, which influences economic growth positively only if it is constrained by an act of volition (Malthus).

For Alfred Marshall, growth is determined by the capacity to save, which results from net income. It is therefore not just the profit of firms that makes investment and growth possible. Among the most important investments for Marshall are the investments in education and training (instruction) of the "children of labor"; therefore, the importance of an even distribution of incomes for the growth of the economy becomes apparent. Marshall also sees the cumulative effect of the increase of wealth, every increase making it easier to effect a further increase. However, it is also true that Marshall accepts that eventually diminishing returns will prevail.

Karl Marx builds a coherent theory that explains the laws that determine the functioning of the capitalist economy. Starting from the theory of labor value of his predecessor (Ricardo), according to which labor is the factor of production that creates value, and from the concept that commodities of equal value are exchanged against each other, Marx develops the theory of surplus value; according to this, labor creates more value than it consumes, the difference, surplus value, being embodied in the product of his labor, which, as a commodity, is the property of the capitalist, containing his profit. The theory of labor value serves Marx as the basis of his theory of exploitation. It is, however, possible to explain exploitation in the market economy in dispensing with the theory of labor value, in freeing the doctrine of Marx of the "ballast" of the theory of labor value. Then surplus value is seen to be due to capital as the scarce factor of production and labor in abundance. It is the scarce factor that attracts the surplus value the profit.

The further development of Marx's theory on the "laws of motion of capital," the law of accumulation, of concentration of capital, is thereby not affected. The dynamics of the market economy, for Marx, are based on the urge to accumulate capital (in pursuit of profit) and the compulsion to accumulate under the pressure of a falling rate of profit. This is due to the accumulation of capital, the increase of the "organic structure" of capital and the need to compensate this fall by increasing output, employing more capital and labor and thus trying to increase profit and drive the accumulation ever further. Accumulation, therefore, drives the dynamics of the system. The fall of the profit rate, however, continues and makes profits decline, reducing saving and investment, and by that further accumulation. As a result, growth butts against its limits, dynamics peter out. (Marx : "The mode of production becomes a fetter to further development of the means of production.")

Comparing this theory with actual developments in market economies, one realizes that Marx has not only underestimated the possibilities and capacities of the development of science and technology, but in particular the capacity of the market economy to make use of them and drive them ever further.

Marx had realized the problems of growth, of accumulation, feeding on the appropriation of surplus value but had overestimated the effect of competition on the rate of profit; he also held the equalization of the rate of profit to be a basic fact of the capitalist economy, while differences in the rate of profit (between industries and firms) are characteristic of the economy of the market in real life and are one of the causes that drive the process of growth.

For Schumpeter, innovation is central to economic development. He considers the capitalist economy, the market economy, to be a system of economic change; it is never stationary, never in equilibrium. The economic process is marked by spontaneous, discontinuous change. The engine driving development, the support of its dynamics, is the "heroic, creative entrepreneur," not necessarily the capitalist or the manager. The position of the entrepreneur in economy and society is founded on the process of selection, modeling, confirmation and promotion of the entrepreneur. The impulse that keeps development in motion comes from innovation, new consumer products, new methods of transportation and production, and new forms of industrial organization.

Schumpeter distinguishes between product innovation and process innovation, which are frequently connected with each other. Competition, for Schumpeter, is not only fought as price competition, but much more effectively as quality competition, a struggle between the qualities of products by innovations, by promoting sales, by marketing and advertising.

Schumpeter divides the economy in two sectors : the static sector of circular flow, which tends to equilibrium, and the dynamic, innovating sector, which is subjected to permanent revolution. Under the effect of business cycles, the change from boom to recession and back, the dynamics of the innovating sector transmit themselves to the static sector of circular flow. This sector is forced to adopt innovations or perish. Business cycles open new opportunities for gain to the circular sector; at the same time old methods are proved to be unprofitable and must be abandoned; a renewal of the economy takes place by "creative destruction."

The limits signaling the end of this development are not given by vanishing opportunities for investment, nor are they a consequence of price rigidities, of monopolistic practices; it is not the failure of the system that sets its limits, but its success. This evolution is the result of the loss of the functions of the entrepreneur. They are becoming more and more obsolete. Technological progress becomes the task of teams of professional specialists. Huge industrial and financial corporations displace not only the small and medium-size firms, they also replace the entrepreneur, replace entrepreneurship by planning and finally replace the market economy by a planned economy. "The end of the entrepreneur becomes the end of the system"; here Schumpeter underlines not so much economic, but in particular, social and political factors.

This Schumpeter thesis, a thesis of great consistency, has at least for the medium term been disproved by history, by the real development of the economy and of society. Capitalism and the market economy have proved to be much more viable, to have much more vitality than Schumpeter (writing in 1942) had suspected, the socialist alternative on the contrary much more difficult to realize.

Equating capitalism and entrepreneurship so completely may have been responsible for this misjudgment. The function of the entrepreneur has in reality been very successfully taken over by the new manager, and teams of "professional specialists" also have been put to serve enterprising dynamics.

And even the social basis of the market economy has so far proved to be much wider and stronger than Schumpeter had suspected. Growth, as we have seen, depends on investment, on innovation, on competition and on the human support.

Investments are financed out of retained profits, out of nonconsumed incomes and out of credits. In all, credits play a decisive role in financing investments. Investments, therefore, do not depend on a single source of finance, such as on realized profits, even if these directly or indirectly (as a condition for granting credits) play an important role. More important, however, are expectations, expected profits. The readiness to invest is decisively determined by the gain an investment is expected to bring.

The prospect of gain to a great extent depends on the cost of financing, that is, on the rate of interest on credits. Since profits are the difference between "expense and return," the rate of interest as a determining cost is an important if not decisive determinant for an investment to be made. So it is the rate of interest that determines profits.

Insofar as profits are increased at the expense of wages, a change of distribution affects consumption, affects effective demand of wage-earners as well as their capacity to save. As a result, demand is reduced, and so are demand prices, whereby the prospects for gain by suppliers are impaired. They turn to additional exports and to gaining a larger share of the home market at the expense of foreign competitors to compensate for these losses. A great part of the enterprises, especially the smaller ones, however, will not be able to realize such compensations.

The confrontation of the producer and the wage-earner over the distribution of the added value therefore has effects on promoting growth insofar as it may result in greater profits. But it may have effects on restraining growth by reducing wages and lowering effective demand, consumption and prices.

If the prospects of gain offered by an investment are found to be insufficient as compared with other possible uses of capital, funds disposable for investments are employed elsewhere. They tend to flow into diverse channels of speculation (real estate, stock exchanges, etc.) and thus reduce available capital and augment the scarcity of capital needed for investments. This scarcity leads to price increases for capital, to a rise of interest rates, and so a number of innovations and other investments, because of expectations of insufficient returns, are not realized. Investments are reduced, the dynamics of growth is hampered.

The relative scarcity of capital and its higher price impede the creation of new jobs, this the more so since new places of work, because of technological progress, increasingly require higher investments per place of work. As a consequence, a growing part of the available workforce stays unoccupied, condemned to unemployment. This development, according to neoclassical and neoliberal theory, is supposed to produce a process by which the oversupply of job seekers depresses the level of wages and by that lowers the curb of profitability of jobs sufficiently to permit increasingly the creation of new jobs.

A precondition for such a development should be a "flexibilization" of wages and of working conditions, meaning a lowering of the standards attaching to each. Lowering wages may at first increase the prospects of gain, but this probably only temporarily since a lower cost of labor, under the pressure of competition, often is followed by a lowering of sales prices. Lower wages can therefore not generally be considered as apt to promote growth; in addition, lower wages do not stimulate the introduction of labor-saving innovations and so do not promote future development.

On the other hand, a lowering of interest on capital would facilitate the realization of investments and promote the growth of the economy. Lowering the price of capital for investment would require a "flexibilization" of the credit system as well as restrictions on speculation (*e.g.*, by special taxes) to impede the drain on capital it causes.

Flexibilizing wages or flexibilizing capital, lowering the cost of labor, or reducing the cost of capital, favoring the creation of new jobs or maintaining a high value of money by high interest rates and scarce capital — these alternatives are, or should be, the object of the confrontation between capital and labor. Insofar as government by its economic, financial and fiscal policies is in a position to determine the choice of these alternatives, influencing government actions is of importance. The extent of this influence in one or the other direction is determined by the relationships of power; the economic policy that results is their expression.

Innovations reinforce the effect that investments have on the growth of the economy, on the dynamics of its development. Innovations also are a most effective means to increase profits. Product innovations create (at least temporarily) protected markets, higher profits, and offer protection against competition. Process innovations serve to reduce cost and increase productivity, help to gain an advance on competitors. It can be assumed that innovations in most cases change the "organic structure" of capital, cause a displacement of labor by capital; production becomes more capital intensive. As a consequence, "fixed costs" are rising and the pressure to increase production, output and turnover is increased.

The mechanism that transmits the compulsion to invest and forces the introduction of innovations is the mechanism of the economy of the market, the mechanism of competition. It causes successful innovations to be rewarded and those that are noninnovating to be punished.

Competition creates an impulse to follow suit since the alternative is to "grow or perish." Not every form of competition, however, nor the fierce intensity of the competitive struggle, necessarily favors the introduction of innovations and the realization of investments. A tough price fight can rob firms of the means they require to invest. With unbridled competition, the "leap into the uncertain," which innovation often means, could appear to involve excessive risks. Big investment projects, those that require long periods for planning and execution, often depend on the protection that a certain form of monopoly status can grant to an enterprise (Schumpeter). In these cases, but also conceivably as a more general possibility, the pressure to innovate normally due to competition is replaced by planned growth.

Support of the dynamics is man; man as Hume's merchant, as Smith's manufacturer, as Schumpeter's entrepreneur or even as Marshall's worker's child.

Finally, however, when we return to the "starting point of political economy," we must pose the crucial question : Does growth in itself always mean progress, advancement of the "wealth of nations" meaning wealth for all?

THE PERSPECTIVES OF ECONOMIC GROWTH AND ITS LIMITS

Rostow distinguishes three perspectives developed by the theoreticians of economic growth.

One perspective is determined by the decreasing returns and rising prices of basic materials (food and raw materials). The second perspective is based on a possible failure of the economic system, its incapacity to provide sufficient effective demand and to prevent excessive and long-duration unemployment. The third perspective foresees the necessity to restrain growth to maintain and preserve the "quality of life." The first perspective is that of Ricardo and Malthus, who saw that the growth of population made necessary the use of land of lesser yield, involving higher cost of cultivation, an inevitable consequence of economic growth and a cause of its limitation.

The second perspective, high and chronic unemployment in a state of equilibrium of the economy, had been developed by John M. Keynes in the wake of the Great Depression of the thirties. This perspective today, after the collapse of the Soviet Union and the end of an economic boom that had practically eliminated unemployment, has gained new actuality with periodic recessions and a high and growing rate of unemployment in the economies of Western Europe.

The third perspective, already envisaged by classical economists in the context of the threatening exhaustion of natural resources, has been brought to new actuality by the work of the "Club of Rome," by the authors of *The Limits to Growth* (Meadows *et al.*). They establish the need to end "quantitative growth," not only because of the exhaustion of natural resources, but also to protect our living space, our environment, against man and his technology; the problem of reconciling the requirements of ecology with those of the economy, however, is still largely unresolved. To these three perspectives a fourth should be added.

It may be assumed that economic growth continues within a foreseeable space of time in spite of problems of ecology and in spite of the progressive exhaustion of natural resources. Neither the fall of the "rate of profit" nor diminishing returns in agriculture and primary production need in the foreseeable future set limits to growth.

Apart from the fact that a fall of the rate of profit as a trend for the entire economy has not been proved, for the dynamics of economic development, the average rate of profit of the economy is not relevant; what counts for further development is the amount of profit and its rate among leading firms; the rest of the economy is forced to follow.

It is the leading firms who, by their position of power and their financial might, are capable of financing innovations or acquiring them by takeover and introducing them into the economy. By that, they set themselves off against competitors, they strengthen their autonomy of price determination and they enjoy greater opportunities for gain.

Growth will then, if left to the self-regulating forces of the market and to the policies that protect and promote them, not necessarily benefit all sectors of the economy and of society. It must be expected that differences in the gain of benefits, differences between industries, between firms and people that are due to differences of power will determine further development, further growth. By that, growth will promote the further process of concentration of capital in the economy.

This growth could go on without eliminating chronic unemployment; it may even increase it. This may be acceptable to individual firms since it may help them to lower wages and reduce costs of production, to increase their profits, investments and growth. On the other hand, this development could lead to increasing polarization of the economy and of society.

Therefore, growth in itself is not the solution. It is not just the question of production vs. distribution, the question of the size of the cake as opposed to its share. It is not just the question of how much is produced, but also what is produced and how it is done.

If what is produced is determined by producers who succeed in "guiding" demand to make it absorb what they produce, wasting scarce resources is not precluded by the workings of the market. If "how production is organized" is determined by capital in the short-term interest of profit maximization (by flexibilizing labor, lowering wages, introducing "work on demand," etc.) and not by distributing work optimally to the hands available (by reducing working hours, by introducing job-sharing, etc.), the long-term interest of optimum utility for society cannot be obtained.

The process of innovation has continually accelerated its pace. The compulsion to innovate has steadily grown and become more urgent due to deregulation and the opening of frontiers, the globalization of the economy. Deregulation and globalization, however, mainly serve the big and the strong; and even the fastest runners in most cases are sooner or later absorbed by them and help to expand their sphere of activity.

In its first phase deregulation is directed mainly toward the workplace in the plant; it is used to enforce the flexibility of labor and its mobility.

Given the background of heavy unemployment, growing job insecurity and weakened union power, it is possible to eliminate regular working hours and stable employment, to reduce wages, to lower the minimum wage or to eliminate lower limits altogether. It is possible to reduce the number of jobs by making the still employed take over the work of those fired (on top of their own work).

By deregulation, the employer tries to transform labor into a sort of raw material whose input in production, just like that of any other material, causes only direct costs and is furnished "just in time." When this occurs, labor is robbed of its role as a factor of production, a factor exercising a productive and creative role in the economy. It loses its claim on a "fair" share of the added value and of its growth. This evolution eventually could be dangerous for the social system on which the market economy rests. Even in the absence of a socialist alternative, the absence of which has greatly favored the rise to prominence of neoliberalism, complete disregard of the aspirations of the wage-earner cannot but eventually cause grave problems both on the factory floor and in the political arena.

Labor is indissolubly tied to the person who exercises it, is tied to man. It cannot be switched on and off at will without encroaching on the life of man. Moreover, labor is not only an element of the sphere of direct production; it is an element of every economic activity of man, be it that of a laborer, a professional worker, an employee, a civil servant or even a manager.

The new concept of work as a raw material, therefore, degrades not only the worker, but everybody who does work. It risks forcing the worker into opposition to the system not only on account of the conflict concerning distribution, but also on account of his status as a part of productive and creative mankind, refusing to be regarded as a mere input.

Deregulation now does not limit itself to the sphere of direct production, to the sphere of the worker; in its second phase it is directed against the middle classes, their traditionally protected incomes (their rents) and their safe positions. The old middle classes (small shopkeepers, tradesmen, professionals and agriculturists), having lost their protection by law, regulations and custom, either lose their positions altogether or can maintain them partially under much worsened conditions and under the permanent threat of losing them definitely.

But even the new middle classes (employees, middle management, junior executives and even civil servants) are not spared. They are increasingly made redundant by economy drives of the state, towns and communities as well as of private enterprises, favoring not only slender production but also slender administration. According to a *New York Times* Special Report, neither their incomes, nor their conditions of work, nor their positions are safe anymore; they have lost the feeling of security that regular work used to give them and also have lost faith in their future and in the future of a better life for their children.[129]

As long as work, in terms of time spent on it and in terms of remuneration, represents the greater part of the life, activity and livelihood of the concerned — so long as it provides the greater part of their incomes — conditions of work and the distribution of its fruits are of major importance to every worker. This is not only true for the "working classes," but also for a great part of those whose income from capital is inferior to their income from work and those whose old age is not secured by pension funds.

It is, however, the middle classes who to a great extent have up to now furnished the loyal basis of the economic, social and political system of the market economy. To lose their support could eventually cause grave problems for the maintenance of the Western democratic system of government and society.

Whatever the outcome of this evolution, in the meantime measures could be taken to counteract the always greater concentration of power and its exercise by the "producers" (big business) and to strengthen the position of "labor" (in its widest sense) and of the consumer in the face of this power. Power can be checked by counter-power, and this could be generated in response to failings of the economic system, failings that prevent it from responding to basic needs, to basic interests of important layers of society. If the position of wage-earners and of consumers was strengthened, they could develop centers of counter-power against the "producers."

The first priority should be the struggle against unemployment. By fighting unemployment (and not the unemployed), by sufficient creation of new jobs and by lifting the threat of job insecurity, the bargaining position of wage-earners could be considerably strengthened. As long as heavy unemployment persists, the position of the wage-earner is much too precarious for him to resist successfully the pressure of employers on working conditions and wages. The first objective of wage-earners and of their organizations should be the reduction and elimination of unemployment. Their unions should realize that they, in the interest of their members, should care as much for the unemployed as they do for their working members. The notion of preserving their status, the effort of giving priority to preserving the level of their wages, should cede precedence to the effort in favor of creating jobs.

This, to be really effective, will require the reduction of working hours and the sharing of jobs. Without job-sharing, a significative diminution of unemployment will hardly be possible, at least not in Western Europe where the downward flexibility of wages is not unlimited.

It is probably unrealistic to expect employers to accept these measures without a certain lowering of wages. In this case, priority should be given to the reduction of working hours and job-sharing, and a certain sacrifice should be demanded of those still employed. In the interest of solidarity with the unemployed, and of their own well-considered, long-range interests, it should be possible to demand and expect such a sacrifice to be accepted. After all, what could be the counter-power of wage-earners if it is not based on solidarity?

If the daily working hours were reduced to, say, 6 hours and this were accompanied by job-sharing, very considerable numbers of new jobs could be created. A general introduction of work in two shifts (of 6 hours each), where before only 8 hours per place of work was in use, would very rapidly create a great number of new real workplaces. And this could be introduced not only in industry. Why should banks, shops and other services not be open 12 hours a day? Why could the building trades not make better use of their heavy and costly equipment by employing it 12 hours a day instead of 8?

To the wage-earner, this would offer an important gain of leisure, better job-sharing also in the home and a welcome opportunity for the aged to gradually fade out of employment. Wage-earners would gain time for extra-economic activities, and also for improving the general and professional level of their capabilities.

This would cause a certain loss of income, which, however, depending on the individual wage level, must not go beyond a low percentage of the wage (*e.g.*, between 2 and 8 per cent).

The employer, in introducing this system, would profit both from a higher productivity of labor and from a better utilization of his equipment, a higher rate of depreciation and a more rapid replacement and modernization of old equipment. These advantages are of great importance to improving his competitiveness and his profits. At the same time, capital requirements for investment in workplaces would relatively diminish, as would, in all likelihood, capital interest. This could permit employers to raise hourly wages, the exact rate to be negotiated between organizations of employers and of wage-earners.

The remaining difference between the daily earnings of the wage-earners (lower because of reduced working hours and only partially compensated by higher hourly wages) should at least partially be covered by direct subsidies of the government. This government could do out of economies realized by the diminution of unemployment payments and out of the increase that more direct and indirect taxes would bring, an increase due to higher income and higher consumption of the newly employed. This should on balance keep the expenses of government within tolerable limits.

The wage-earner should be able to accept a limited reduction of his income since besides the gain in leisure and quality of life, he would also gain security in his job and a better outlook for himself and for his children. Moreover, it can be expected that under full or very high employment, wage-earners would be in a better position to resist excesses of deregulation and obtain a "fair" share of the value added by their work and of its increase due to higher productivity.

The other part of the population whose position must be strengthened in the face of the "producer" is the consumer.

One important measure to obtain this should be steps taken to improve their information, to raise the level of their consciousness and knowledge of the mechanics of the market economy and of the efforts of suppliers to manipulate them. In the face of the immense offer on the market and of overwhelming supplier publicity as the main source of information of the consumer, an enlightening and seriously informative (counter) publicity should be introduced. This should be based on scientific analysis and control of the quality of commodities and services offered on the market and of their price. It should present exhaustive comparisons of the diverse commodities (and services), of their qualities and their price.

Such research could be accomplished by scientific institutions and by departments of universities where the essential objectivity of their information must be guaranteed by their independence from industry and other suppliers. This information, to carry weight and have effect, should be published in form and volume comparable to that of the publicity of the suppliers.

To finance at least a part of these very expensive measures, specific duties could be levied on all forms of publicity, be they on the radio, on TV, on advertisements and posters, and also on other electronic media. To a certain extent, proceeds from a tax on added value could be used.

As for products protected by patent, there should be created commissions charged with control of their pricing and costing. Such commissions could be composed of representatives of the government and those representing producer and consumer organizations. These commissions should see to it that prices reflect seriously established costs or that deviations be properly taxed.

These and other measures could help to make profits again a residual item, a result of market imperfections, as they were considered by neoclassical and other economists, and not a rightful gain to glorify. After all, profits are either taken out of the added value that could just as well be attributed to labor or taken out of the pocket of the consumer, who in most cases is not even aware of it.

Apart from these measures, there is the general macroeconomic frame of the economy, the fiscal and monetary policy of the government and its orientation toward or against monetarism, toward or against big business, that exerts an influence on the direction in which the economy develops.

In view of the globalization that opens every national economy to world finance, the possibilities of any single government are limited. Regional groupings or superpowers may find more scope for policies that counteract the dictates of the "market" and may even orient this dictate to their own advantage.

Favoring growth or rigor, demand or supply, employment or downsizing remains a basic option that can influence the direction of future development. This also depends on relative power.

All these measures may not in themselves change the "course of history." They could, however, encourage people to look for new ways, for new solutions, and not capitulate before the omnipotence of the market.

8

THE PROCESS OF CONCENTRATION IN THE ECONOMY

The pursuit of gain is the motor that drives the process of accumulation; the concentration of capital is the result and profit is both its fruit and also the fuel that drives the motor.

Helmut Arndt writes in his book *Die Konzentration in der Wirtschaft* (The Concentration in the Economy) : "Under concentration originally...only the concentration of production [leading to] bigger and more capital-intensive enterprises, under elimination of smaller ..in particular artisan workshops..was understood."[130]

Arndt then explains the notion of concentration by quoting Karl Marx, who "knows two meanings of the concept of concentration" :

1. Concentration that depends directly on accumulation or rather is identical with it; and
2. Concentration of capital already formed, abolishing their individual independence by an altered distribution, a centralization that follows an expropriation of a capitalist by a capitalist"[131]

Arndt also cites Werner Sombart, for whom concentration is only the concentration of production in big factories. Sombart considers growth not to be concentration in *"the proper sense."* It is true that growth in itself is not identical with concentration; overaverage growth, however, leads to concentration.

We have seen that investing profits results in capital accumulation, which permits continued internal growth as well as accelerated growth by mergers and acquisitions. As such, growth serves the trend toward concentration. Sombart distinguishes between "concentration in *the broader sense*" — representing an increase of the share of the total production by the "higher classes of factories," without restricting "the living space of the small"— and "concentration *in the narrow sense*," being "the growth of the share of big factories at the expense of the smaller."[132]

It is open to question if these distinctions help to understand the process and nature of concentration. It is precisely growth (which Sombart excludes) — growth of factories and enterprises — that is an essential condition of that process. Furthermore, in real economic life, there is no clear-cut distinction between his "concentration in the broader and in the narrower sense."

Arndt also cites J.M. Blair, who writes that "[when] the physical volume of production has increased at a faster rate than has the number of establishments, then obviously concentration has been occurring." But the fast growth of big units in relation to the growth of small ones also signifies concentration to him. Blair points to relative growth as an indicator of concentration.[133]

Then Arndt cites G. Rosenbluth, for whom concentration is "the degree to which a small number of firms account for a large proportion of an industry's output," meaning that it is a question of market share.

We want to show, using statistical data gathered from industrial enterprises in the United States, that the process of concentration, corresponding to the definitions of Blair and Rosenbluth but also in the sense of Karl Marx (*i.e.*, of progressive accumulation), continues to make headway.

In the two decades before the "oil shock" of 1973, *i.e.*, between 1954 and 1974, the United States experienced strong and continuous growth of the economy, growth accompanied by an even stronger growth of the leading industrial (but also commercial and financial) corporations. According to *Fortune* magazine,[134] revenue, profit, assets and the personnel employed by the 500 leading U.S. industrial enterprises grew as follows :

GROSS SALES (in billions at current prices)	1954	$136.8
	1974	$834.0
This represents an annual (nominal) growth of :		9.5%
Inflation during this period was 80%, or on a per annum basis		3.0%
The real annual rate of growth, therefore, was :		6.5%
The yearly average rise of profits was (nominally) :		8.7%
Assets rose (nominally) per annum by :		9.2%
The number employed by these corporations increased :		100.0%
Rising annually by		3.4%
The "Fortune 500 Corporations" employed this percentage of persons active in industry :		74.0%
The share of these firms out of the total output of industry rose from 1954 to 1974 from 50.0% to :		66.6%
During this period the U.S. gross national product grew by :		25.0%

These data show that for the two decades between 1954 and 1974, the growth of the "Fortune 500 Corporations" surpassed by far the growth of all United States industry and that of the economy as a whole, resulting in a pronounced concentration in the economy.

Since 1974, stronger-than-average growth has not been realized by *all* the "Fortune 500 Corporations," but principally by the leading companies in each industry. Table 1 shows the growth of revenue of some leading industrial companies from 1974 to 1993 (and 1996) and compares it with the average growth of the "Fortune 500 Corporations" and with that of the GNP of the United States.

We have selected a number of leading industrial firms, one or several of each important industry, to illustrate the growth of leading corporations. For "Food" and "Pharmaceuticals," more firms have been chosen because of their importance as producers of consumer goods. We have taken 1974 as a basis for comparing the evolution of revenues, assets and employees with 1993 and have added 1996 to bring it up to date.

TABLE 1

Revenue of 36 leading industrial United States corporations in the years 1974, 1993 and 1996 in billions of dollars (at current prices); growth in $ and % from 1974 to 1993

Company	Revenues			Growth	
				In $	In%
	1974	1993	1996	74-93	74-93
1	2	3	4	5	6
General Motors	31.55	133.65	68 37	102.1%	323.6
Ford Motor	23.62	108.52	46 99	84.9	359.4
General Electric	13.41	60.82	79 18	47.4	381.9
Motorola	1.37	16.96	27 97	15.6	1138.7
Texas Instruments	1.57	8.52	11.71	7.0	445.9
IBM	12.68	62.72	75.95	50.0	394.3
Hewlett-Packard	0.88	20.32	38.42	19.4	2204.5
Du Pont	6.91	32.62	39.69	25.7	371.9
Dow Chemical	4.94	18.06	20.05	13.1	265.2
Monsanto	3.5	7.90	9.26	4.4	125.7
Philip Morris	3.04	50.62	54.55	47.6	1565.8
RJR Nabisco	3.23	15.10	17.06	11.9	368.4
Procter & Gamble	4.91	30.43	35.28	25.5	519.3
Colgate	2.62	7.14	8.75	4.5	171.8
Pepsico	2.08	25.02	31.65	23.0	1105.8
Coca Cola	2.52	13.96	18.55	11.4	452.4
Anheuser Busch	1.40	11.51	10.88	10.1	721.4
Heinz	1.44	7.10	9.11	5.7	395.8
CPC International	2.57	6.74	9.84	4.2	163.4

1	2	3	4	5	6
Campbell Soup	1.[illegible]7	6.59	7.68	5.1	346.9
Kellogg	1.[illegible]1	6.30	6.68	5.3	524.5
Quaker Oats	1.[illegible]3	5.73	5.20	4.5	365.9
Johnson & Johnson	1.[illegible]4	14.14	21.62	12.2	628.9
Bristol-Myers	1.[illegible]9	11.41	15.07	9.8	616.4
Merck	1.[illegible]3	10.50	19.83	9.2	691.7
Americ. Home Prod.	2.[illegible]5	8.31	14.09	6.2	302.4
Abbot Lab.	0.[illegible]7	8.41	11.01	7.6	987.0
Pfizer	1.[illegible]4	7.48	11.31	5.9	383.1
International Paper	3.[illegible]4	13.69	20.14	10.7	351.9
Caterpillar	4.[illegible]8	11.62	16.52	7.5	83.8
Gillette	1.[illegible]5	5.41	9.70	4.2	336.0
Xerox	3.[illegible]8	14.98	19.52	11.4	318.4
Eastman Kodak	4.[illegible]8	20.06	15.97	15.4	336.2
Goodyear	5.[illegible]6	11.64	13.11	6.4	121.7
MMM	2.[illegible]4	14.02	14.34	11.1	377.6
R.R. Donnally	0.[illegible]5	4.39	6.60	3.9	366.7
Fortune 500	833.[illegible]5	2,370.00		1536.05	184.0
GNP	1,477.[illegible]4	5,374.00		4896.46	331.0

Table 1 shows that the revenue of almost all the leading corporations has grown more than the average of the "Fortune 500 Corporations." Apart from hi-tech companies such as Motorola, Texas Instruments, Hewlett Packard or those having made important mergers and acquisitions (*e.g.*, Philip Morris, Pepsico), almost all pharmaceutical firms have grown twice as much (or more) than the GNP.

Growth of assets (Table 2) has been particularly strong for hi-tech companies (Motorola, Hewlett Packard, Texas Instruments and Xerox), for companies that made important mergers (Philip Morris, RJR Nabisco, Pepsico) and for pharmaceutical firms (Johnson & Johnson, Bristol Myers, Merck, Abbot Lab.). Growth largely exceeds not only that of the "Fortune 500 Corporations" but also that of the GNP.

TABLE 2

Assets of 36 leading industrial United States corporations in the years 1974, 1993 and 1996 in billions of dollars (at current prices); growth in $ and % from 1974 to 1993

Company	Assets			Growth	
				In $	In %
	1974	1993	1996	74-93	74-93
1	2	3	4	5	6
General Motors	20.47	188.20	222.14	167.73	819.2
Ford Motor	14.17	198.94	262.87	184.77	1304.0
General Electric	9.37	251.51	272.40	242.14	2583.8
Motorola	1.07	13.50	24.08	12.43	1161.7
Texas Instruments	0.95	5.99	9.36	5.04	530.5
IBM	14.03	81.11	81.13	67.08	478.1
Hewlett-Packard	0.65	16.74	27.70	16.09	2475.4
Du Pont	5.98	37.05	37.99	31.07	519.6
Dow Chemical	5.11	25.51	24.67	20.40	399.2
Monsanto	2.94	8.64	11.19	5.70	191.9
Philip Morris	2.65	51.21	54.87	48.56	1832.5
RJR Nabisco	3.13	31.30	31.29	28.17	900.0
Procter & Gamble	3.65	24.94	27.73	21.29	583.3
Colgate	1.36	5.76	7.90	4.40	323.5
Pepsico	1.38	23.71	24.51	22.33	1618.1
Coca Cola	1.54	12.02	16.16	10.48	680.5
Anheuser Busch	0.93	10.88	10.46	9.95	1069.8
Heinz	0.99	6.82	8.62	5.83	588.9
CPC International	1.35	5.06	7.87	3.71	274.8
Campbell Soup	0.82	4.90	6.63	4.08	497.6
Kellogg	0.51	4.24	5.05	3.73	731.4
Quaker Oats	0.78	2.82	4.39	2.04	261.5
Johnson & Johnson	1.41	12.24	20.01	10.83	768.1
Bristol-Myers	1.04	12.10	14.69	11.06	1063.5

1	2	3	4	5	6
Merck	1.24	19.93	24.39	18.69	1507.3
Americ. Home Prod.	1.24	7.69	20.79	6.45	520.2
Abbot Lab.	0.82	7.69	11.13	6.87	837.8
Pfizer	1.68	9.33	14.67	7.65	455.4
International Paper	2.73	16.53	28.25	13.90	509.2
Caterpillar	2.93	14.81	18.73	11.88	405.5
Gillette	0.99	5.10	10.44	4.11	415.2
Xerox	4.46	38.75	26.82	34.29	768.8
Eastman Kodak	5.06	20.33	14.44	15.27	301.8
Goodyear	4.17	8.44	9.67	4.27	102.4
MMM	3.02	12.20	13.36	9.18	303.9
R.R. Donnally	0.37	3.65	4.85	3.28	886.5
Fortune 500	833.95	2,370.00		1536.05	184.0
GNP	1,477.54	6,374.00		4896.46	331.0

Table 3 shows that assets have grown much more than revenue; that means that relatively more assets are required (*i.e.*, capital) to generate revenue in 1993 than in 1974. It can also be seen that capital required for investment in capital goods has grown disproportionately. Capital as the scarce factor of production has become even more scarce. Its strong position as a scarce factor compared with labor has been further strengthened.

Table 4 shows that most big industrial corporations (apart from those in hi-tech industries and those that have made important acquisitions) have considerably reduced their working force from 1974 to 1995 while increasing both their revenues (Table 1) and their assets (Table 2).

Since growth in most cases is also due to innovation, we gather that innovations have had a strong bias toward economizing labor and not toward economizing capital; this is in spite of the fact that capital is the (relatively) scarce factor of production, a contradiction that the economy of the market has not been able to resolve.

TABLE 3

Growth in per cent of Revenue and of Assets of the 36 Corporations from 1974 to 1993

Company	Revenue	Assets
1	2	3
General Motors	323.6	819.2
Ford Motor	359.4	1304.0
General Electric	381.9	2583.8
Motorola	1138.7	1161.7
Texas Instruments	445.9	530.5
IBM	394.3	478.1
Hewlett-Packard	2204.5	2475.4
Du Pont	371.9	519.6
Dow Chemical	265.2	399.2
Monsanto	125.7	191.9
Philip Morris	1565.8	1832.5
RJR Nabisco	368.4	900.0
Procter & Gamble	519.3	583.3
Colgate	171.8	323.5
Pepsico	1105.8	1618.1
Coca Cola	452.4	680.5
Anheuser-Busch	721.4	1069.8
Heinz	395.8	588.9
CPC International	163.4	274.8
Campbell Soup	346.9	497.6
Kellogg	524.5	731.4
Quaker Oats	365.9	261.5
Johnson & Johnson	628.9	768.1
Bristol-Myers	616.4	1063.5
Merck	691.7	1507.3
Americ. Home Prod.	302.4	520.2
Abbot Lab.	987.0	837.8

1	2	3
Pfizer	383.1	455.4
International Paper	351.9	509.2
Caterpillar	183.8	405.5
Gillette	336.0	415.2
Xerox	318.4	758.8
Eastman Kodak	336.2	301.8
Goodyear	121.7	102.4
MMM	377.6	303.9
R.R. Donnally	866.7	886.5

This process leads us to an ever greater advantage of capital-intensive production over labor-intensive production and an advantage of capital over labor, an advantage of the First World over the Third World.

This advantage finds its expression in the level of wages paid to labor. Since, however, labor is not only a factor of production, but also, as consumers, an important factor of consumption, lowering wages reduces labor's capacity to consume and lowers demand while supply (production) is increasing.

This also is a contradiction that the economy of the market finds difficult to resolve.

Table 5 shows the evolution of market share, an indicator of the degree of concentration in the economy, and illustrates the continuing trend toward concentration at the top in most industries. We can see, that as a result, 17 out of 36 industries show increasing market shares among the top firms and only four industries show a decreasing share (from 1987 to 1996). We also note that the number of industries where No. 1 controlled 20% or more of the market has risen from 10 out of 21 industries in 1987 to 15 industries in 1996, and that the number of industries where the Nos. 1-3 controlled 50% of the market or more has risen from 7 to 12. So, all in all, we do not see any reason to doubt that the trend toward greater concentration prevails.

TABLE 4

Number of Employees Per Corporation (in thousands) for the years 1974, 1993 and 1996, and the Evolution between 1974 and 1996 in %

Company	Employees			Evolution in %
	1974	1993	1996	1974-96
General Motors	747.3	710.8	547.0	0.87
Ford Motor	464.7	322.2	371.7	0.80
General Electric	404.0	222.0	239.0	0.59
Motorola	51.0	120.0	139.0	2.73
Texas Instruments	65.5	59.0	59.9	0.91
IBM	292.4	267.2	268.6	0.92
Hewlett-Packard	28.9	96.2	112.0	3.88
Du Pont	136.9	114.0	97.0	0.71
Dow Chemical	53.3	55.4	40.3	0.76
Monsanto	60.9	30.0	28.0	0.46
Philip Morris	38.0	173.3	154.0	4.05
RJR Nabisco	32.5	65.5	79.7	2.45
Procter & Gamble	50.0	103.5	103.0	2.06
Colgate	43.6	23.0	37.9	0.87
Pepsico	49.0	423.[illegible]	486.0	9.92
Coca Cola	31.8	34.0	26.0	0.82
Anheuser Busch	12.2	43.3	25.1	2.05
Heinz	32.2	37.7	43.3	1.41
CPC International	42.5	38.9	55.3	1.30
Campbell Soup	32.9	45.9	40.7	1.23
Kellogg	17.0	15.2	14.5	0.85
Quaker Oats	25.4	20.2	14.8	0.58
Johnson & Johnson	54.3	81.6	89.3	1.64
Bristol-Myers	29.7	49.5	51.2	1.72
Merck	27.0	47.	49.1	1.82
Americ. Home Prod.	45.7	51.4	59.7	1.31
Abbot Lab.	22.8	49.7	52.8	2.32
Pfizer	39.5	40.5	46.5	1.18
International Paper	52.7	72.5	87.0	1.65
Caterpillar	80.1	51.3	57.0	0.71
Gillette	33.1	33.4	44.1	1.33
Xerox	101.4	97.0	86.7	0.86
Eastman Kodak	120.7	110.4	94.8	0.79
Goodyear	154.2	90.1	88.9	0.58
MMM	83.6	86.2	74.3	0.89
R.R. Donnally	11.6	34.0	38.0	3.28

TABLE 5

Market Share of the No. 1 and of the Nos. 1-3 of their Industries in the years 1987, 1993 and 1996 in %

Industry	No. 1			Nos. 1-3		
	1987	1993	1996	1987	1993	1996
1	2	3	4	5	6	7
Aerospace	14.0	20.1	20.5	38.4	50.9	56.2
Beverages	31.7	37.5	41.5	75.6	75.7	83.5
Building Materials Glass	17.2	18.7	22.9	39.7	53.2	65.5
Chemicals	22.4	20.1	21.9	37.9	36.2	38.8
Computers Office Equipment	48.6	40.0	35.2	65.7	62.3	62.0
Electronics Electrical Equipment	20.1	30.2	36.7	42.7	44.4	56.3
Food	11.2	22.7	12.5	24.5	38.9	30.5
Forest and Paper Products	10.[illegible]	12.6	16.8	28.9	32.8	38.5
Industrial and Farm Equipment	15.1	16.1	15.5	29.1	39.5	32.3
Metal Products	16.5	15.7	19.1	37.9	39.1	45.5
Metals	15.3	16.7	20.2	39.3	34.4	38.1
Mining, Crude Oil Production	12.9	41.7	20.7	35.4	62.2	54.8
Motor Vehicles and Parts	45.3	40.4	36.6	89.8	86.4	81.9
Petroleum Refining	21.3	24.6	26.4	45.1	47.4	52.2
Pharmaceuticals	12.7	15.2	17.0	31.2	38.7	44.4
Publishing	12.9	12.1	14.8	32.2	32.4	32.8
Rubber and Plastic Products	39.4	42.7	42.9	66.5	65.7	58.1
Scientific, Photo and Control Equipment	28.2	22.[illegible]	23.4	70.1	54.0	55.1
Soaps, Cosmetics	46.4	60.3	58.0	70.7	82.4	80.3
Textiles	19.[illegible]	13.4	20.0	46.3	38.1	47.8
Tobacco	47.3	50.7	79.3	94.8	88.7	92.9

9

THE EVOLUTION OF THE RATE OF PROFIT

The theory of the "falling rate of profit" is based on some of the oldest "laws" formulated by economic theoreticians.

It was David Ricardo who discovered some 200 years ago that the growth of population required an increase in the production of grain. In a fully developed country, this could be achieved only by extending cultivation to lands of lower yield or by a more intensive exploitation of land already cultivated. Both of these measures would increase the cost of production and cause the price of grain to rise. If the level of real wages for labor is maintained, *i.e.*, if it rises with the increase of the price of grain, the profit of capital, being the difference between cost and return, must fall. Ricardo also realized that increasing returns could be obtained in manufacturing. In view of the overwhelming importance of agriculture in the economy of his time, the "race" between increasing returns in manufacturing and diminishing returns in agriculture could not be won by manufacturing and would therefore result in a fall of the rate of profit in the economy.

John S. Mill, following his master Ricardo in this argumentation, even declared that diminishing returns in agriculture and mining were the most important proposition in political economy. He maintained that if this law were different, nearly all phenomena of production and distribution of wealth would be other than they are. Karl Marx reformulated the law of the falling rate of profit and defined it as the law governing the evolution of the capitalist economy and causing eventually its breakdown.

Marx based his analysis on the law of value (the "labor theory of value"). For Marx, profit was the result of surplus value created by labor and appropriated by capital. He distinguished between constant capital (machines, installations, raw materials) and variable capital (labor) and called the relationship of constant capital to variable capital the "organic structure" of capital.

Surplus value was the difference between the value of labor (*i.e.*, roughly the cost of labor) and the value of the product of labor. With the increase of the share of *constant* capital in relation to *variable* capital due to the accumulation of capital (the reinvestment of profit), the rate of surplus value in terms of *total* capital must necessarily fall and with it the rate of profit.

This concept was shared by many Marxists even in our time and was the basis of their appraisal of the prospects of the capitalist system. (It was so for Ernest Mandel but not for John E. Roemer.) They considered the fall of the profit rate as almost synonymous with the decline of the capitalist system.

For the neoclassical economists, it is the evolution of the cost of production that determines the rate of profit. They maintained that with the increase of production of an enterprise beyond a certain point, variable cost (meaning mainly cost of labor) would be rising since the productivity of labor beyond this point was declining and also because of the rising cost of labor due to increased demand for it. With that reasoning, profit, as the difference between cost and return, is bound to fall. Under conditions of perfect competition, where price is supposed to establish itself on the level of marginal cost, profit is completely eliminated.

The fall of the profit rate and the eventual elimination of profit meant that the accumulation of capital would cease and the limits of growth would be reached (see Chapter 6).

It was Alfred Marshall who discovered that for "decreasing cost industries," the elasticity of supply of a commodity, conforming to the law of "increasing returns," was theoretically infinite (over long periods). This implied that there were no limits to the growth in the size of firms but he held this to be incompatible with the maintenance of competition in industry. However, he suspected that an individual producer would couple his supply curve not with the general demand curve for his commodity in a wide market, but with the particular demand curve of his own special market.

This aspect was then, in the context of the theory of the market, developed by Joan Robinson and E.H. Chamberlin into the theory of imperfect or monopolistic competition.

By combining decreasing cost with imperfect competition, we arrive at the conclusion that the profit rate of the individual firm is not condemned to fall and that the size of firms is not subjected to absolute limitations. We have also maintained that the evolution of the economy was not determined by its average rate of profit and/or its tendency to fall, but by the profits of the leading firms. These profits, for most of them, continue to increase, a proposition illustrated by the table at the end of this chapter.

It is, however, not only the falling rate of profit, but also the theory of the equalization of the profit rate that must be rejected. Because competition was thought to regulate the market, it was also thought to be evident that the market provided for an equalization of profit rates.

For Walras, this is what the "General Equilibrium" represented, and for Karl Marx, it was evidence he never questioned, even if it posed great theoretical problems for him.

It must be surprising that the theory of the equalization of profit rates was not confronted with data based on economic reality. The marked differences in the rate of profit between industries and individual enterprises — which, moreover, maintained themselves over the years — did not provoke a revision of this theory. This is perhaps due to the fact that it would have meant abandoning the idea that competition regulated the formation of price; rather than giving this up, the theoreticians ignored reality.

A look at the table of 36 corporations (Table 6) shows profits in terms of revenue and in terms of assets for the years 1974, 1993 and 1996. Taking into consideration the great volatility of profits, we see that these have been largely maintained and even increased (and this even before the age of the preeminence of "shareholders value").

Some of the companies profits have grown spectacularly (*e.g.*, Ford Motor, General Electric, Philip Morris, Coca Cola, Anheuser Busch, Bristol Myers, Abbot Laboratories). Significant diminutions have been rare and carry the mark of specific problems experienced by the particular firm (IBM, Texas Instruments, Monsanto, RJR Nabisco, Merck, International Paper, Goodyear). Most of them have recovered in the succeeding years.

The same is true if we consider profits in terms of assets. Because of the important rise of assets, the rate of profit is nevertheless generally lower, indicating a relatively lower profitability of capital investments. This trend has probably been reversed lately (see "shareholders value"). In any case, it has not reduced the volume of profits.

It is also difficult to find in these figures an indication of a tendency toward equalization; and this is true as much for industries (*e.g.*, food and pharmaceuticals) as for individual firms (*e.g.*, Pepsico and Coca Cola, Philip Morris and RJR Nabisco).

In times of high unemployment and of great accent on shareholders value, profit rates will reflect these factors and tend to rise while wages fall.

This table shows that 21 out of the 36 firms have increased their profits per reveaue, while 14 have increased their profits per asset. These firms may not be "representative" (whatever that may mean), but they are at the top of their respective industries, and most of them are leading their development.

We may assume that the above-average results from these firms can be traced to the strength of their position in the

TABLE 6

Rate of Profit of Revenue and Assets for 1974, 1993 and 1996. Evolution of the Respective Profit Rates from 1974 to 1996

Company	In % of Revenues			In % of Assets			Evolution of	
							Revenues	Assets
	1974	1993	1996	1974	1993	1996	74/96	74/96
1	2	3	4	5	6	7	8	9
General Motors	3.0	1.8	2.9	4.6	1.3	2.2	0.97	0.48
Ford Motor	1.5	2.3	3.0	2.[illegible]	1.3	1.7	2.00	0.68
General Electric	4.5	7.1	9.2	6.[illegible]	1.7	2.7	2.04	0.42
Motorola	5.2	6.0	4.1	6.6	7.6	4.8	0.79	0.73
Texas Instruments	5.7	5.5	0.5	9.[illegible]	7.9	0.7	0.09	0.09
IBM	14.5	(12.9)	7.1	13.[illegible]	(10.0)	6.7	0.49	0.51
Hewlett-Packard	9.5	5.8	6.7	12.[illegible]	7.0	9.3	0.71	0.55
Du Pont	5.8	1.7	9.2	11.[illegible]	1.5	9.6	1.59	0.86
Dow Chemical	11.3	3.6	9.5	10.[illegible]	2.5	7.7	0.84	0.71
Monsanto	9.2	6.3	4.2	11.0	5.7	3.4	0.46	0.31
Philip Morris	5.8	6.1	11.6	6.[illegible]	6.0	11.5	2.00	1.74
RJR Nabisco	9.6	(1.0)	3.6	9.[illegible]	(0.5)	2.0	0.38	0.20
Procter & Gamble	6.5	(2.2)	8.6	8.[illegible]	(2.6)	11.0	1.32	1.26
Colgate	4.5	2.7	7.3	8.[illegible]	3.3	8.0	1.62	0.91
Pepsico	4.2	6.3	3.6	6.[illegible]	6.7	4.7	0.86	0.75
Coca Cola	7.8	15.6	18.8	12.[illegible]	18.1	21.6	2.41	1.70
Anheuser Busch	4.6	5.2	10.9	6.[illegible]	5.5	11.4	2.37	1.65
Heinz	4.4	5.6	7.2	6.[illegible]	5.8	7.6	1.64	1.17
CPC International	3.9	6.7	5.9	7.[illegible]	9.0	7.4	1.51	1.01
Campbell Soup	5.8	0.1	10.4	10.[illegible]	0.2	12.1	1.79	1.16
Kellogg	7.1	10.8	8.0	14.[illegible]	16.1	10.5	1.13	0.74
Quaker Oats	3.2	2.9	4.8	5.[illegible]	5.9	5.6	1.50	1.10
Johnson & Johnson	8.4	12.6	13.4	11.[illegible]	14.6	14.4	1.59	1.25
Bristol-Myers	7.5	17.2	18.9	11.[illegible]	16.2	19.4	2.52	1.69
Merck	15.9	20.6	7.6	17.[illegible]	10.9	7.1	0.48	0.42
Am. Home Products	12.5	17.7	13.4	20.[illegible]	19.1	9.1	1.07	0.44
Abbot Laboratory	7.1	15.6	17.1	6.[illegible]	18.2	16.9	2.41	2.52
Pfizer	8.8	8.8	17.1	8.[illegible]	7.0	13.2	1.94	1.65
International Paper	8.7	2.1	1.5	9.[illegible]	1.7	1.1	0.17	0.11

1	2	3	4	5	6	7	8	9
Caterpillar	5.[illegible]	5.5	8.2	7.8	4.1	7.3	1.46	0.94
Gillette	7.[illegible]	5.3	9.8	8.9	5.7	9.1	1.40	1.02
Xerox	9.[illegible]	(0.3)	6.2	7.4	(0.3)	4.5	0.67	0.61
Eastman Kodak	13.[illegible]	(7.5)	8.1	12.5	(7.5)	8.9	0.57	0.71
Goodyear	3.[illegible]	3.3	0.8	3.8	4.6	1.1	0.27	0.29
MMM	10.[illegible]	9.0	10.7	10.0	10.4	11.4	1.04	1.14
R.R. Donnally	6.[illegible]	2.5	(2.4)	7.8	3.0	(3.3)	0.72	0.72

economy, that the relative superiority of their power finds its expression in their relatively superior results.

In view of this, the question of whether the rate of profit in the economy is falling or not is beside the point from the perspective of the economy: the evolution of the economy is driven by the leading firms and their above-average results, which in the majority of cases continue to rise.

10

LIBERALIZATION AND GLOBALIZATION

Liberalization can be distinguished between its operation in a national market and its impact on international markets. In terms of national markets, liberalization found its first high mark with the famous (or infamous) Manchester-Liberalism of the last century. This form of liberalization mainly served the interests of the owners of capital, but also had the effect of invigorating the economy and making it perform better. Eliminating restrictions on economic activity furthered competition and resulted in a "survival of the fittest"; the most efficient members of the economy prevailed. With that, the entire economy was meant to be lifted to a level of high efficiency and productivity, benefiting society as a whole.

The promoting competition, monopolistic price fixing and exploitation of consumers should be eliminated. This basic arguments, going back to Adam Smith, cannot as such be contested; moreover, it has, to a certain extent, been borne out by history. The development of the British economy in the 19th Century, for example, is a case in point. It was this development that led to the predominance of the British Empire in the world economy and to its military and political hegemony over the world.

Still, even at that time, this evolution did not promote the welfare of all it mainly benefited the upper classes of society — The particular British symbiosis of the aristocracy and the upper layers of the bourgeoisie. The mass of the population, in particular the working classes, suffered the full weight of capitalist oppression and exploitation. They were recruited from farm laborers and small farmers, who were driven from their land by big aristocratic landowners. They flooded into towns in search of a livelihood. There they faced extremely long working days, child labor, ruthless exploitation of women and wages on or below the level of mere subsistence.

Significantly, changes in these conditions did not occur because of the automatic functioning of the free market. It resulted from the struggle of the emerging working classes through their trade unions and political movements. Together, these organizations slowly raised the standard of living of professional workers then of laborers, and finally of the mass of the population in general.

INTERNATIONAL LIBERALIZATION

The elimination of barriers between national economies defines international liberalization. The promotion of free trade and the unhampered flow of goods, services and capital is leading to globalization of economies, markets and production. At the same time, the opening of worldwide markets has led to the globalization of enterprises.

The ideas favoring free trade go back to David Hume and his theory of "relative advantages," and to David Ricardo, who showed that everybody had to gain from the free exchange of goods and services. History has shown, however, that the development of the real economy did not produce these positive results. In real economic life, the exchange of goods is not an exchange between equals, but an exchange between more and less powerful entities. This leads to an unequal distribution of advantages resulting from the exchange.

This has been particularly true in the exchange between the economies of the first world and those of the third world, even after the collapse of the colonial empires. The highly developed economies of the West have benefited from the exchange to the detriment of the less development economies of the countries of the South. This exchange was, and still mainly is, based upon an exchange of raw materials and the products of cheap labor (products with little added value) for goods requiring capital intensive production, high tech advances, and services that have a high degree of added value. The result of this exchange is a high rate of profit.

This first world/third world exchange furthered the rise of powerful international corporations capable of exploiting the world markets and benefiting from globalization. The globalization of liberalized markets, under the given circumstances of one-sided superior technology, superior capital equipment, and superior capital power, has firmly established the unequal relationship between the first and third worlds. It has strengthened the hold of some companies over the markets of the world and has contributed to maintaining the developing countries in a state of permanent dependence, impeding their efforts to pursue their own autonomous economic, social and cultural development.

Institutions such as the World Trade Organization (WTO) and the International Monetary Fund (IMF) — controlled as they are by Western countries (and Western ideas) — serve as powerful instruments to further the drive towards liberalization. Liberalization fosters globalization and globalization then embraces the whole world, its production and its markets.

Since superior power dominates inferior power in an open market, since this domination results in greater profits being extracted from these markets, since these profits reinforce superior power ever further, a trend is established by which the powerful grow always more powerful, the big always bigger. Under these circumstances, the exploitation of the weaker is firmly established, and a reversal of this trend — without a basic change of these circumstances — cannot be considered to be a realistic perspective.

It is true that we live in one world and that the third world and its development not only depends on the first world, but that the latter also depends for its development on the opportunities offered by the third world. If, however, the terms of these relationships are determined unilaterally by the West to serve their own specific interests, they will not offer developing countries a real chance to further the autonomous development of their economies and societies, a development that can lift them up to the status of equal partners from current relationship of dependence. The functioning of the markets under the terms of liberalization and globalization as imposed by the IMF and WTO make an escape from this dependence highly improbable.

SUMMARY AND CONCLUSION

This book has offered a critical discussion of the theory and reality of the economy of the market.

Starting from the price of commodities and of the factors of production as well as from the process of price formation, it looked at various theories of price and value, and sets against them the author's view of price and its formation.

After a short presentation of Polanyi's model of the market economy in Chapter 2 and referring to Max Webster's definition of power as the chance to prevail even against resistance, price is shown as not only an expression of value, whether this be understood as a cost of production or as evaluation by the consumer, but also as an expression of the relative power possessed by the contracting parties, *i.e.*, the relative superiority of the power of one party over the other in the process of exchange. Then the classical and neoclassical theories of price were analyzed in terms of the reality of the market economy; we demonstrated that the essential assumptions of these theories — such as the purely rational behavior of the consumer in the market (a behavior that cannot be influenced by the supplier) as well as free and perfect competition — are not valid for the most part. In short, they cannot help us understand the functioning of the economy in the real world.

Starting from production — the supply of commodities and services — we explained that increasing fixed costs determine the pricing behavior of the producer, or supplier, in the market. The tendency toward product differentiation and enhancement of company image, which finds its prominent expression in the creation of branded commodities and results in the displacement of price competition by quality competition, is reinforced by rising fixed costs (cost of depreciation, interest on capital, cost of administration, etc.). Since variable costs — the cost of raw materials, of energy, of supplies, of direct labor, etc. — rise at about the same rate as output (production), increasing output spreads fixed costs over a greater number of products. This reduces the costs of each unit. However, the producer normally can sell his increased output in the market — given a certain level of demand — only if he reduces his price. Under the condition of price competition, a continuous rise of output thus tends to result in a continuous lowering of prices. Price competition is accordingly intensified and can eventually lead to price wars, where not only profits are reduced, but the very existence of a firm can be threatened.

To counteract this process, the producer tries to avoid *price* competition and replace it with other types of competition — *quality* competition in various forms : product design, presentation, packaging, service, sales promotion, advertising, marketing, etc. This enables the producer to prevent the consumer from making precise, rational, calculated comparisons of his products with those of other producers, or at least, to render this more difficult. At the same time, quality competition interacts with product innovation. This causes an enormous increase in the variety of commodities offered for sale on the market and enormous differentiation in the supply of commodities.

As a result, the consumer has a problem finding his way among the available choices on the market and becomes ever more dependent on advice and information to make his choice among the multitude of commodities offered in the market. The advice and information are provided by the producer through advertising. For the consumer, it becomes an indispensable aid; for the producer, however, advertising is designed to promote sales.

Advertising does this by giving a product a unique image, thus reinforcing product differentiation and making it more difficult for the consumer to compare products rationally. On the other hand, advertising tries to enhance the value of the product in the eyes of the consumer. It offers additional utility — fictitious utility — which is paid for by higher prices. And finally, advertising tries to awaken new desires in the consumer and in many cases actually creates the demand for the commodity supplied.

In this way, advertising becomes an instrument of power in the hands of the producer, an instrument for manipulating the consumer. For the consumer, a rational overview of the market is no longer possible; he is unable to make a calculated comparison between the commodities offered, unable to arrive at a rational decision on his purchases.

The market actually becomes an accumulation of countless individual markets, where the producer is a monopolist, controlling supply and at the same time using advertising to create and shape demand. Free or perfect competition thus becomes imperfect, and this in turn becomes "power-determined" competition. The market economy becomes a system where power prevails and thereby gains more power.

This discussion was followed by an analysis of the question of whether power or economic law determines the economic process of the market economy. The question is important; the answer determines whether intervening in the economic process is possible and makes sense.

If economic science matches the pattern of "natural science" (as was postulated by Böhm-Bawerk and also by Friedman), no interference in the market may seem justified. However, to establish such a comparison is highly problematic since social science deals with human behavior, and human behavior is neither completely rational nor transparent, nor completely predictable and constant.

On the other hand, even the natural scientist is not prevented by his knowledge of the laws of nature from intervening in a natural process or from using his knowledge of these laws to obtain certain desired results and to create new realities that would not have come into being without his intervention. Besides, an economic law — such as the law that price is determined by supply (determined by marginal costs) and demand (determined by marginal utility — is valid only under very precise, very restrictive conditions. These conditions involve the existence of a perfect market, full employment and other conditions that in real economic life are only rarely fulfilled.

The same holds true for the law of distribution, *i.e.*, the law that determines the share of the social product that the factors of production (capital and labor) obtain. It is held to correspond to the "increment of product that is due to its participation in the process of production" (Böhm-Bawerk). This law also presupposes perfect competition, full employment and a closed market.

As a result, it can be said that in real economic life, power cannot only make use of economic laws to further its interests; it can also modify these laws by shaping and manipulating supply and demand. Interventions in the economic process are therefore possible and can make sense (at least to those who know how to intervene).

The book then examined the different conflicts or confrontations in the economy, especially the "classical" confrontation between the producer and the wage-earner — the class struggle — and the confrontation between one producer and another and the fight over (and against!) the consumer — the competitive struggle. The results of these confrontations express the relative strength of the contracting parties, or a "hierarchy" of power. This determines the extent of exploitation — on the one hand effected through wages (the price of labor) or on the other through the price of commodities and services.

The notion of a society as a class society (a consequence of the confrontation between capital and labor) could therefore be complemented by the notion of society as a pyramid of power. When seen as a pyramid of power, it becomes a society of exploitation, where exploitation is effected through price.

The two traditional classes — the bourgeoisie and the proletariat — find their place on this pyramid, as do the "middle classes" — small businessmen, the free and independent professionals, craftsmen, civil servants, salaried employees, farmers — who, in accordance with their relative position of power, enjoy protected incomes and participate in the process of exploitation through the price they are able to obtain for their work. The position of the individual agent on this pyramid is determined by his respective relative power and finds its expression in the level of his income.

Thus we find on this pyramid agents who exploit more than they are exploited, as well as those who are victims of twofold exploitation — unskilled workers, many part-time wage-earners, a large part of the female workforce, foreign labor and more. These victims are doubly exploited — through their wages and through the price they have to pay for the commodities and services they need.

From this view of society operating under a market economy, we can conclude that power is not constrained by the automatic function of a self-regulating economy and that power at best can be kept in check by countervailing power — associations, trade unions, consumer organizations, citizens organizations, political organizations and the like.

From this point on, the book looked at the dynamic nature of the market economy. It was seen as the result of the combination of science and technology and their application to the improvement of economic performance. The mechanism of the competitive market economic system with its drive and compulsion to accumulate capital creates the need to innovate and invest. The problem, however, is that growth and wealth are not necessarily synonymous, that growth can be achieved at the expense of wealth, and wealth can increase at the expense of further growth.

It has become clear that growth does not automatically generate wealth for all; rather growth, left to the automatic mechanism of "power-determined competition," takes place at the expense of certain strata of the population — and of their working and living conditions.

As for the prospects of future development of the economy — keeping in mind that prospects are not prognoses — it can be said that power-determined competition, if unhindered, can lead to greater and greater concentrations of power and that the market economy does not possess a regulating mechanism to constrain this process and lead to a state of equilibrium.

On the basis of examples taken from statistics of industrial firms in the United States, we indicated that the process of concentration is continuing. The statistical material presented showed that the growth above the average of leading firms is related to their above-average profits and that it results in further growth of profits. Growth of revenue, even at constant or lower rates of profitability results in an increase in power.

An excellent illustration of this process is given by certain high-technology firms. Companies such as Intel and Microsoft are not only able to earn high profits because they dominate their markets, but they also use their profits to continue their technological advance and maintain their superiority and domination. They do this by investing great portions of their profits in continued development, continued expansion, either by using their own creations or by absorbing promising developments of other companies. In these cases, it is obvious how profits result from dominance and how they serve to reinforce that dominance.

For the future of the market economy, it is irrelevant whether the *general rate* of profit rises or falls. This future will be determined by the evolution of the leading firms, by *their* dynamics and *their* profits.

In summary, we have shown :

- The rise of fixed costs leads producers to increase their output in a quest for increasing returns.
- Increased output leads to tougher price competition and to lower pricing.
- To counter this, price competition is replaced by quality competition.

- This leads to a fragmentation of the market, to imperfect competition and finally to power-determined competition.
- Competition, instead of restraining power, becomes an instrument to strengthen the powerful.
- Power-determined competition reinforces the trend toward ever greater concentration of capital and power.

CONCLUSION

To sum up our analysis of price and its function in the market economy, we conclude that the price of commodities (and services) in the market economy occupies a key position in the control of the economy.

According to established theory, price has the following functions :

- Coordination (of supply and demand)
- Information (on relative scarceness)
- Control of performance (of the efficient use of scarce goods and of the means of production)
- Distribution (of the social product, the added value, of income)

Under the real conditions of an industrialized market economy, the established theory must be rejected. We found :

1. Price is an expression of relative power.

   Relative power, the gradient of power between the parties in the economy, finds its expression in price. This is true of consumer goods and services as much as of the factors of production : labor, land and capital, of wages, rent and interest.

   The impact of power can be found in the intercourse of the producer with his suppliers and financiers, as well as in the relations between capital and labor, and in those between the producer and the consumer, where it finds expression in the wage and in the price of the commodities supplied.

2. Free competition, which is meant to neutralize the effect of power on price, in real economic life is either "imperfect competition" or "quality competition" between different goods and services, where it is not easy to compare and quantify quality, with the result that this finds uncontrolled expression in price or it is price competition that serves to conquer or defend markets.

   None of these forms of competition necessarily produces rational economic results, produces prices based on marginal productivity or marginal utility; they are strategies in a battle fought by using instruments of power (*e.g.*, control of supply, control or manipulation of demand), the results of which (prices, wages, quantities) reflect the relative power of the parties.

3. Free competition becomes "power-determined competition." This development takes place under the pressure of continuously rising fixed costs and of their rising share in total costs, a consequence of ever more capital-intensive and more highly organized production. Production becomes more capital-intensive because technological progress increasingly replaces labor by capital and at the same time creates forms and magnitudes of organization that make "administration" (planning, organization, coordination, work preparation, control of performance and quality, etc.) grow at the expense of direct labor.

   The pressure of fixed costs causes production to expand constantly to achieve a maximum of reduction of piece costs. As a consequence of this expansion, the producer is forced to lower his supply price ever more to render possible the sale of his increased output.

4. The producer tries to defend himself against this vicious circle by developing strategies aimed at the creation of protected markets for his products, markets that are not exposed to price competition.

Through product differentiation, through the creation of branded products, through the use of advertising, by developing a company image and by public relations, the producer creates qualities that are not quantifiable, qualities that are seen as attributes of his products and as a criterion on their value, this limiting the ability of the consumer to make rational and calculated price comparisons with competing products.

5. This does not mean, however, that competition is abolished, it is shifted from price to quality and is fought out in the media by a prominent presence on the market, on the sales shelf, on posters, in newspapers and magazines, on radio and TV, and in the mailbox, through advertising, sponsoring and PR activities.

   In the course of this development, advertising as an instrument of information becomes an instrument for manipulating the consumer; in employing it, the producer tries to enhance the value, the expected utility of his product, its acceptable price in the eyes of the consumer, as well as to increase the quantity the consumer is prepared to buy at this price.

6. Thus price loses its function of coordinating supply and demand (which is now achieved by sales promotion and marketing).

   Price loses its function of informing consumers about the value of products (of the real value behind the fictitious value created by advertising) especially since price in many cases is no longer an expression of value but rather is meant to establish an impression of the value of a commodity and is so interpreted by the consumer.

   Price also loses its function of controlling performance, controlling the efficient use of scarce goods and of the means of production (but it furnishes proof of the efficacious use of advertising since this finds its expression in the price level accepted by the consumer).

But price does not lose its function of distributing the social product, of the distribution of incomes. This function, however, is exercised under conditions where power dominates, where instruments of power are used, and not under conditions where power is constrained by competition.

7. Since price expresses relative power and since competition does not neutralize differences in power, the price of equivalent products may differ in accordance with the degree of power possessed by the producer.

Since price maintains its function of distributing incomes, profit — the rate of profit of the producer — is higher or lower according to his degree of relative power. There is no equalization of the rate of profit since high rates of profit do not attract competition as much as capital (in the form of participation, of credits, etc.) the mobility of capital being much greater than the mobility of production.

This serves to further strengthen the position of power for powerful enterprises. It is this rate of profit and these total returns that finance the development and further expansion of powerful firms.

What is claimed to make for an equalization of the rate of profit is not a fact established by data, but a theoretical construct based on the assumption of perfect competition.

8. Insofar as price competition is eliminated, relative power, the hierarchy or gradient of power between the parties on the market, can affect the formation of price without hindrance and result in a distribution of incomes that favors the powerful.

This triggers off an evolution that makes the powerful more powerful, the big ever bigger. Thus the accumulation of capital and the process of concentration in the economy are driven further and further.

9. Since the market economy is not in a position to control this evolution through its own mechanism, through its own laws of functioning, this evolution being precisely the result of this very mechanism and of its dynamics; since the market economy, as a result of power-determined competition, can necessarily guarantee neither efficient performance nor optimum allocation of scarce resources, so that neither the factor of production "capital" (for example, rampant speculation in real estate, on financial markets, etc.) nor the factor of production "labor" (for example, growing chronic unemployment) is by necessity employed at optimum levels; since competition does not lead to neutralization of power and of the powerful, but to their reinforcement; since this evolution can be considered to be undesirable both economically and socially, carefully planned interventions in the mechanism of the market are necessary to counteract this evolution.
10. If the need to intervene in the mechanism of the market (whether by action or by counteraction) is accepted as a basic principle, this could lead to the elaboration of suitable methods and plans for preventing undesirable developments and promoting those that are desired.

FOOTNOTES

1. Polanyi, Karl, *The Great Transformation,* Beacon Press, Boston, 1957, pp. 68-69.
2. Blaug, Mark, *Economic Theory in Retrospect,* p. 40
3. *Collins, Dictionary of Economics,* London and Glasgow, 1988, p. 304
4. *Ibid.,* p. 118
5. Blaug, *op. cit.,* p. 197
6. Blaug, *op. cit.,* p. 294
7. Blaug, *op. cit.,* p. 325
8. Blaug, *op. cit.,* p 297
9. Blaug, *op. cit.,* p 305
10. Collins, *op. cit.,* p 381
11. Robinson, Joan, *Contributions to Modern Economics,* Oxford, 1978, p. 174.
12. Chamberlin, Edward H., *The Theory of Monopolistic Competition,* Cambridge, USA, 1932, p. 5-.
13. *Ibid.,* pp. 205-6
14. Böhm-Bawerk, *Zeitschrift für Volkswirtschaft, Sozialpolitik und Verwaltung,* Vienna, 1914, p. 205.
15. *Ibid.,* p. 206
16. Quoted by Böhm-Bawerk
17. Böhm-Bawerk, *op. cit.,* p. 207
18. Böhm-Bawerk, *op. cit.,* p. 208
19. Böhm-Bawerk, *op. cit.,* p. 209
20. Böhm-Bawerk, *op. cit.,* p. 210
21. Böhm-Bawerk, *op. cit,* p 211
22. Böhm-Bawerk, *op. cit,* p 213
23. Böhm-Bawerk, *op. cit.,* p 215
24. Böhm-Bawerk, *op. cit.,* p. 217
25. Böhm-Bawerk, *op. cit.,* p. 219

26. Böhm-Bawerk, *op. cit.*, p. 221
27. Böhm-Bawerk, *op. cit.*, p. 222
28. Böhm-Bawerk, *op. cit.*, p. 224
29. Böhm-Bawerk, *op. cit.*, p. 226
30. Blaug, *op. cit.*, p. 427
31. Blaug, *op. cit.*, p. 428
32. Böhm-Bawerk, *op. cit.*, p. 227
33. Böhm-Bawerk, *op. cit.*, p. 229
34. Arndt, Helmut, *Markt und Macht,* Tübingen, 1973, p. 3
35. *Ibid.*, p. 4
36. *Ibid.*, p. 4
37. *Ibid.*, p. 4
38. *Ibid.*, p. 5
39. *Ibid.*, p. 7
40. *Ibid.*, p. 8
41. *Ibid.*, p. 9
42. *Ibid.*, p. 9
43. *Ibid.*, p. 24
44. *Ibid.*, p. 24
45. *Ibid.*, p. 45
46. *Ibid.*, p. 46
47. Arndt, Helmut, *Konzentration in der Wirtschaft,* Dunker & Humbolt, Berlin, 1971.
48. *Ibid.*, p. 108
49. *Ibid.*, pp. 109-10
50. Lerner, A.P., *The Concept of Monopoly and the Measurement of Monopoly Power,* "The Review of Economic Studies," Cambridge, June 1934, p. 50.
51. *Ibid.*, p. 157
52. *Ibid.*, p. 161
53. *Ibid.*, p. 166
54. *Ibid.*, p. 166
55. *Ibid.*, p. 166
56. *Ibid.*, p. 166
57. *Ibid.*, p. 167
58. *Ibid.*, p. 168

59. *Ibid.*, p. 168
60. *Ibid.*, p. 169
61. *Ibid.*, p. 169
62. Blaug, *op. cit.*, p. 46
63. Blaug, *op. cit.*, p. 93
64. Blaug, *op. cit.*, p. 106
65. Schumpeter, J.A., *Capitalism, Socialism and Democracy*, Allan and Unwin, London, 1943, p. 27.
66. *Ibid.*, p. 24
67. Roemer, John E., *Analytical Foundations of Marxian Economic Theory*, Cambridge University Press, Cambridge, 1981.
68. *Ibid.*, p. 52
69. *Ibid.*, p. 53
70. *Ibid.*, p. 153
71. *Ibid.*, p. 160
72. *Ibid.*, p. 154
73. *Ibid.*, p. 159
74. *Ibid.*, p. 157
75. *Ibid.*, p. 161
76. Blaug, *op. cit.*, p. 570
77. Blaug, *op. cit.*, p. 426
78. Blaug, *op. cit.*, p. 427
79. Blaug, *op. cit.*, p. 428
80. Rostow, W.W., *Theorists of Economic Growth — From David Hume to the Present*, p. 19.
81. *Ibid.*, p. 20
82. *Ibid.*, p. 23
83. *Ibid.*, p. 23
84. *Ibid.*, p. 31
85. *Ibid.*, pp. 29-30
86. *Ibid.*, p. 35
87. *Ibid.*, *p.* 35
88. *Ibid.*, p. 39
89. *Ibid.*, p. 55
90. *Ibid.*, p. 56
91. *Ibid.*, p. 55

92. *Ibid.*, p. 56
93. *Ibid.*, p. 57
94. *Ibid.*, p. 59
95. *Ibid.*, p. 36
96. *Ibid.*, p. 36
97. *Ibid.*, p. 37
98. Marx, Karl, *Manifesto of the Communist Party,* and Friedrich Engels 1847, p. 5.
99. Marx, Karl, *A Contribution to the Critique of Political Economy*
100. Schumpeter, *op. cit.*
101. Schumpeter, *op. cit.*, p. 26
102. Schumpeter, *op. cit.*, pp. 33-34
103. Hicks, J.R., *Classics and Moderns,* Oxford, 1983, p. 117
104. Rostow, *op. cit.*, pp. 160-61
105. Rostow, *op. cit.*, p. 167
106. Rostow, *op. cit.*, p. 168
107. Rostow, *op. cit.*, p. 171
108. Rostow, *op. cit.*, p. 171
109. Rostow, *op. cit.*, p. 172
110. Rostow, *op. cit.*, p. 173
111. Rostow, *op. cit.*, p. 234
112. Rostow, *op. cit.*, p. 235
113. Rostow, *op. cit.*, p. 235
114. Rostow, *op. cit.*, p. 236
115. Rostow, *op. cit.*, p. 237
116. Schumpter, *op. cit.*, pp. 81-82, 84
117. Schumpter, *op. cit.*, p. 134
118. Schumpter, *op. cit.*, p. 132
119. Schumpter, *op. cit.*, p. 134
120. Blaug, Mark, *Economic History and the History of Economics,* p. 194
121. *Ibid.*, p. 229
122. *Ibid.*, p. 219
123. *Ibid.*, p. 219
124. *Ibid.*, p. 220
125. *Ibid.*, p. 222

126. *Ibid.,* p. 223
127. *Ibid.,* p. 227
128. *Ibid.,* p. 229
129. "The Downsizing of America," a *New York Times* special report, 1996
130. Arndt, *op. cit.,* p. 3
131. Arndt, *op. cit.,* p. 4
132. Arndt, *op. cit.,* p. 5
133. Arndt, *op. cit.,* p. 6
134. *Fortune* Magazine, April 1975

BIBLIOGRAPHY

……., *A Collins Dictionary of Economics,* Macmillan Press, London, 1987.

……, *The New York Times Special Report : The Downsizing of America,* Times Books, Random.

House, New York, 1996.

Arndt, Helmut, *Markt und Macht,* J.B.C. Mohr (Paul Siebeck), Tubingen, 1973.

Arndt, Helmut, *Wirtschaftliche Macht,* C.H Beck, Munich, 1976.

Balogh, Thomas, *The Irrelevance of Conventional Economics,* Weidenfeld and Nicolson, London, 1982.

Blaug, Mark, *Economic Theory in Retrospect,* Cambridge University Press, Cambridge, 4th Ed., 1985.

Blaug, Mark, *Economic History and the History of Economics,* Wheatsheaf Books, Brighton, 1986.

Böhm-Bawerk, Eugen von, *Macht oder okonomisches Gesetz,* Zeitschrift fur Volkswirtschaft und Sozialpolitik, 23.Band Wien, 1914.

Chamberlin, Edward Hastings, *The Theory of Monopolistic Competition,* Cambridge, Harvard University Press, Cambridge, USA, Eighth Edition, 1962 (1932).

Chamberlin, Edward Hastings, *Monopolistic Competition and General Equilibrium,* Cambridge, Mass., USA, 1940.

Chamberlin, Edward Hastings, *Towards a More General Theory of Value,* New York, Oxford University Press, 1957.

Friedman, Milton, *Price Theory,* Aldine Publishing Company, Chicago, 1962.

Glastetter, Werner *Konjunktur — und Wachstumspolitik,* Meyers Forum, — B.I. Taschenbuchverlag Mannheim, 1993.

Harcourt, G.C. (editor), *The Microeconomic Foundations of Macroeconomics,* London and Blasingstoke, Macmillian Press, 1977.

Hawke, G.R. Economics for Historians, Cambridge University Press, Cambridge, USA, 1980.

Kaldor, Nicholas The Scourge of Monetarism, Oxford, New York, University Press, 1982.

Kaldor, Nicholas, Economics Without Equilibrium, University College, Cardiff Press, Armonk, New York, 1985.

Kalecki, Michal, *Studies in Economic Dynamics, Allen* & Unwin, London, 1943.

Kalecki, Michal, *Selected Essays on Economic Planning,* Cambridge University Press, New York, 1986.

Kalecki, Michal, "Collected Works Volume 1," *Capitalism, Business Cycles and Full Employment,* Clarendon Press, New York : Oxford University Press, 1990.

Kleinewefers, Henner, *Reformen fur Wirtschaft und Gesselischaft, Campus* Verlag, Frankfurt / New York, 1985.

Lerner, A.P., *The Concept of Monopoly and the Measurement of Monopoly Power,* The Review of Economic Studies, London, June, 1934.

......., *The New Palgrave : A Dictionary of Economics,* Macmillan Press, London, 1987.

Niehans, Jurg, *A History of Economic Theory,* Johns Hopkins University Press, Baltimore and London, 1990.

North, Douglas C., *Structure and Change in Economic History,* W.W. Norton & Company, New York, 1981.

Parker, William N. (editor), *Economic History and the Modern Economist,* Basil Blackwell, Oxford, UK, 1986.

Patinkin, Don, *Money, Interest and Prices,* Harper & Row, New York, 1965.

Polanyi, Karl, *The Great Transformation (1944)*, (1957 Suhrkamp Verlag Frankfurt), Beacon Press, Boston, (1957).

Robinson, Joan, *The Economic of Imperfect Competition* (1933), Macmillan, London, 1961.

Robinson, Joan, *Essays in the Theory of Economics Growth*, Macmillan, London, 1962.

Robinson, Joan, *Contributions to Modern Economics*, Basil Blackwell, Oxford, 1978.

Roemer, John E., *Analytical Foundations of Marxian Economic Theory*, Cambridge University Press, 1981.

Roemer, John E., *A General Theory of Exploitation and Class*, Cambridge, Mass., USA, Harvard University Press, 1982.

Rostow, W.W., *Theorists of Economic Growth from — David Hume to the Present*, Oxford University Press, New York, Oxford, 1990.

Salin, Edgar / Jacques Stohler (Herausgeber), *Notwendigkeit und Gefahr der Wirtschaftlichen Konzentration*, Kyklos Verlag, Basel, 1969, J.C.B. Mohr (Paul Siebeck) Tubingen.

Schumpeter, Joseph A., *History of Economic Analysis*, Oxford University Press, New York, 1954.

Schumpeter, Joseph A., *Capitalism, Socialism and Democracy*, George Allen & Unwin, London, 1943.

Steedman, Ian Paul Sweez et al., *The Value Controversy*, Verso Editions, London, 1981.

Timmerman, Manfred et al., *Die okonomischen Lehren von Marx, Keynes, Schumpeter*, Verlag W. Kohlhammer Stuttgart, Berlin, Koln, Mainz, 1986.

Tobin, James (editor), *Macroeconomics, Prices, and Quantities*, Essays in Memory of Arthur M Okun, Basil Blackwell, Oxford, Wash., D.C., Brockings Institution, 1983.

INDEX

A

Abbot Laboratory, 129, 131, 132, 134, 139, 140

Accumulation, 61, 66, 86, 90, [illegible]-97, 106, 110, 125-26 137

Acquisitions, 125, 129 131

Advertisements, 124

Advertising, 3, 6, 15, 22, 26, 29, 32-34, 47, 55-57, 60-62, 112 1[illegible]7, 154

Aerospace, 135

Age, 46

Agriculture, 81-83, [illegible]8-89, 91, 109 117

Allocation, 19, 25, 62, 72, 74-75

American Home Products, 129, 131, 134, 141

Anheuser-Busch, 128 130, [illegible], 13[illegible], 139-40

Arbitrage, 105

Arndt, Helmut, 21, 33, 45, 125

Art, 89

Artisan, 93

Assets, 127, 128, 130, 131, 139

Associations, 150

Austrian School, 72

B

Banks, 80, 122 (See also Credit, Finance)

Barter, 1

Bazaar, 60

Behavior, 18-19, 21-22, 145

Berlin, 45

Beverages, 135

Big companies, 77, 79

Billboard, 62

Birth rate, 44 (See also Population)

Blair, Jim, 126

Blaug, Max, 8, 19, 43, 103

Böhm-Bawerk, Hugen von, 35-45, 72, 79, 148-49

Bonus of power, 61

Bourgeoisie, 91, 103, 106 149

Boycott, 38

Brands, 30, 60

Bristol, Myers, 129, 130, 132, 134, 139, 141

British, 83, 95

Building materials, 134

Building trades, 122

Businessmen, 104

Buyers, 3 (See also Consumers, Customers)

C

Calculus, 20

Campbell Soup, 129, 130, 132, 134, 140

Cantillon, Richard, 104

Capitalism, 94, 100
Capitalists, 93, 97, 106
Capital, 11, 14,15, 20, 25-26, 28, 36, 43-44, 51-52, 64-68, 70, 82, 109
  Formation, 83
Capital intensive, 125
Cartels, 6, 38, 63 (See also Monopoly)
Casson, Mark, 105
Caterpillar, 129, 131, 133, 134, 141
Chamberlin, Edward H., 6, 30, 50, 138
Change, 84, 94, 111
Chemistry, 91
Children, 87, 110, 120, 123
Choice, 10
Circular flow, 98
Civil servants, 119, 150
Clark, J.B., 43
Class struggle, 68-71, 149
Classes, 87, 97, 120
Classicists, 20
Climate, 85
Club of Rome, 117
Coca Cola, 128, 132, 134, 139-40
Colgate, 128, 130, 132, 134, 140
Collins, 24
Comfort, 87
Commodities, 1, 5, 8, 18, 22, 25, 28, 47, 54, 60, 63, 82, 94
Communist Manifesto, 91
Comparative advantage, 82
Comparisons, 28, 66
Competition, 1, 3, 5-6, 9-10, 20-23, 37, 59, 75, 92, 102, 109, 115, 146, 148 (See also Power)
Concentration, 61, 110, 118, 125, 133
Concessions, 64, 77
Conclusion, 152
Conditions, 62
Conflicts, 149
Confrontation, 4, 63, 149
Consciousness, 92, 101
Constant capital, 92, 137
Constitutional, 4
Constraints, 84
Consumers, 7, 22, 26, 47, 60, 73, 98, 121, 154 (See also Buyers, Customers)
Consumption, 82, 86, 113-14
Contract, 10
Contradictions, 94
Control equipment, 135
Corporation, 53, 79
Cosmetics, 135
Costs, [illegible], 15-21, 24, 46, 57, 61, 89, 95, 97, 146-47
Counter-power, 46, 87, 121
Counter-publicity, 123
CPC International, 128, 130, 132, 134, 140
Craftsmen, 150
Creativity, 100
"Creative destruction", 26
Creditor, 4
Credit, 78, 80, 100, 115 (See also Banks, Finance)
Customers, 59 (See aso Buyers, Consumers)
Cycles, 100, 112

D

Debtor, 79

Decision-makers, 104

Decreasing returns, 109

Demand, 3, 6, 8, 10-11, 14-24, 35, 40, 50, 57-58, 61, 64, 78, 86, 109, 134, 147

Demand curve, 23

Demographic, 90 (See also Population)

Depreciation, 14, 48, 122

Deregulation, 118-20, 123

Design, 60, 147

Despotism, 87

Development, 82, 107

Dexterity, 84

Differentiation, 29-31, 33, 59

Discount, 80

Displacement, 59, 93

Distribution, 36 62-64, 110, 120

Divergence, 56

Dow Chemical, 128, 130, 132, 134, 140

Du Pont, 128, 130, 132, 134, 140

Duties, 124

Dynamics, 7

E

Eastman Kodak, 129, 131, 133, 134, 141

Ecology (See Environment)

Economic laws, 35, 39 (See also Laws)

Economic reality, 25, 39

Economy of market (See Market Economy)

Education, 97, 110 (See also Training)

Effective demand, 17, 20

Efficiency, 3, 67, 75

Elasticity, 28, 53, 57, 61, 137

Electrical equipment, 135

Electronics equipment, 135

Employees, 127, 135, 150 (See also Workers)

Employers, 42, 44, 64 (See also Big companies)

Employment, 108, 119, 122 (See also jobs)

Energy, 147

Engels, 91

Enjoyment, 44, 47

Entrepreneur, 6, 100-7

Environment, 46, 117

Equation of Homogeneity, 50 (See also Homogeneous)

Equilibrium, 20-21, 24-27, 31, 34, 46, 52, 86, 98, 105 109, 116, 138

Equimarginal, 19

Equipment 43 (See by type)

Ethics, 94

Evolution, 98, 128, 151

Exchange, 1, 2, 67

Exhaustion, 117

Expectations, 113

Expenses, 78 (see also Costs)

Exploitation, 4, 43, 45, 68-72, 82, 106, 149

Exports, 82, 113

F

Factories, 125

Factors of production, 20-21, 25, 35, 73-75, 146

Failure, 112, 116

Families, 87

Farm equipment, 135

Farmers, 150
Fashion, 46, 60
Fear, 60
Female, 150
Fermentation, 82
Fertility, 86
Fictitious utility, 48 (See also Utility)
Finance, 100, 106 (See also Banks. Credit)
Financier, 5, 78
First World, 85
Fish pond, 97
Fixed cost, 14 (see also Costs)
Flexibilization, 114-15
Food, 116, 127, 139 (See also Agriculture)
Forces of nature, 91
Ford Motor Co., 128, 130, 132, 134, 139-40
Forest products, 135
Fortune, 127, 129-31
Free competition, 61
Free market, 6
Free University of Berlin, 45
Friedman, 148
Frugality, 82

G

Gain, 2, 125
General Electric, 128, 130, 132, 134, 139-40
General Motors, 128, 130, 132, 134, 140
General Theory of Exploitation and Class, 4
Germany, 35
Gillette, 129, 131, 133, 141
Glass, 135
Globalization, 63, 118, 124
Goodyear, 129, 131, 133, 134, 139, 141
Gossen, 18, 47
Grain, 89, 136
Great Depression, 116
Gross National Product, U.S., 127
Growth, 65, 83-85, 90-91, 93, 108-111, 113-19, 124, 150
Gutenberg, 50

H

Habit, 55
Heinz, 128, 130, 132, 134, 140
Hewlett, Packard, 128, 129, 130, 132, 134, 140
Hicks, J. R., 95
Hierarchy, 149
Historical school, 35-36, 38
Homogeneous, 23, 43, 49, 69, 75 (See also Equation of Homogeneity)
Hours, 63, 118-19, 121
Human capital, 98
Human will, 42
Hume, David, 81

I

IBM, 128, 130, 132, 134, 139-40
Ignorance, 87
Imitation, 29
Imports, 82
Income, 18, 46, 73, 84
India, 82
Industrial equipment, 135
"Industrial reserve army", 36, 93
Industries, 24, 85, 137

Infant mortality, 44 (See also Population)

Inflation, 127

Influence, 115

Information, 3, 11, 21-22, 25, 32, 75, 79, 123

Innovation, 98-101, 111-13, 118, 131 (See also Invention)

Inputs, 104

Instruction, 15

Interest, 14, 66, 78-79, 85, 99, 121

International Paper, 129, 131, 133, 134, 139, 141

Invention, 84, 104, 106 (See also Innovation)

Investment, 84, 96-98, 100, 110 113

Invisible hand, 25

J

Jaffe, William, 75

Jevons, William, 50

Job-sharing, 118, 121

Jobs (See Employment)

Johnson & Johnson, 129, 130 132, 141

Judgement (See Decision-makers)

"Just" wage, 43

"Just in Time", 76, 119

K

Kellogg, 129, 130, 132, 134, 140

Keynes, John Maynard, 5, 116

Knowledge, 3, 23, 96

L

Labor, 2, 5, 11-15, 20, 35, 42 49, 63 66, 68, 74, 80, 87, 109, 124, 147 (See also Unions, Worker)

Laborer (See Worker)

Labor-intensive, 134

Land, 11, 36, 82-83, 93

Landlord, 4, 82

Landowner (See Landlords)

Large corporations (See Big companies)

Law of Value, 69-72

Laws, 61, 85, 110, 136, 148

Leisure, 19, 122-23

Lerner, A.P., 53, 60

Liberty, 87

Limited liability, 104

Limits (See Constraints)

"Limits of growth", 109

Location, 54

Losses, 113

Luxury, 82

M

Machinery, 48, 83, 97

Magazines, 61

Malthus, Thomas, 44, 85-88, 93, 116

Management, 26, 100, 120

Manchester, 17

Mandel, Ernest, 137

Manipulate, 123

Manufacturing, 83, 89, 109, 136

Man, 116-17

Marginal

- Costs, 16
- Product, 105
- Productivity, 38, 43, 67
- Utility, 2, 17-22, 37, 40, 72, 95
- Values, 19

Market

- Clearance, 25

- Economy, 1, 10-11, 81, 91, 108, 110, 119, 146
- Mechanism, 26
- Share, 126
- Transparency, 21-22, 25
- Wage, 66

Marketing, 3, 6
Marshall, Alfred, 95-98, 137
Marx, Karl, 67-72, 91-94, 106, 110-11, 125-26, 136-38
Maximum utility, 4
"Means of production", 91
Measurement, 53
Menger, Carl, 17
Merchandising, 106
Merchant, 82
Merck, 129, 131, 132, 134, 139, 141
Mergers, 126, 129
Metal products, 135
Metals, 135
Micro-economics, 95
Microsoft, 151
Middle classes, 120, 150 (See also Classes)
Mill, John S., 136
Minimum wage, 119 (See also wages)
Mining, 89, 109, 135
Miser, 82
MMM, 129, 131, 133, 134, 141
Monetarism, 124
Monetary policy, [illegible]0
Monetary stability, 78
Money, 11
Monopoly, 3, 6, 25, 31, 33, 40, 42, 44, 50-51, 53, 59, 61, 99, 106, 116
Monopsony, 3, 50-51, 77
Monsanto, 128, 130, 132, 134, 139-40
Moral, 86
Motor vehicles, 135
Motorola, 128, 130, 132, 134, 140

N

Natural
- Law, 36, 39, 42, 45-46
- Price, 4, 14, 89
- Science, 148

Navigable, 91
Needs, 46-47 (See also Wants)
Negotiated, 65, 122
Neo-classical, 1, 4, 9, 19, 49, 58, 61, 7[illegible], 74, 98, 105, 108, 124, 137, 1[illegible]6
Neo-liberalism, 119
New York Times, 120 (See also Newspaper)
Newspapers, 61
Noneconomic variables, 88

O

Office equipment, 135
Oil, 12[illegible], 135
Omnipotence, 25
Omniscience, 25
Open market, 80
Optimization, 20
Organic structure, 92, 111, 115
Organization, 7, 15, 61, 102, 111, 153
Output, [illegible], 25
Ownership, 3, 91

P

Package, 31
Paper products, 135
Part-time, 150
Partners, 59
Patent, 3, 31, 124
Pension, 120
Pepsico, 128-31, 133, [illegible]9-40
Perfect
    Competition, 20-23, 25, 30, 41, 92
    Knowledge, 23
    Market, 46
Perspectives, 116-17
Petroleum, 135 (See also Oil)
Pfizer, 129, 131, 133, 34, 141
Pharmaceuticals, 127, [illegible]5, 13[illegible]
Philip Morris, 128, 13[illegible], 13[illegible], 34, 139-40
Photo Equipment, 135
Pigou, Arthur C., 6
Planning, 112, 116
Plastic products, 135
Pleasure, 60
Polarization, 118
Political, 4
Polanyi, Karl, 11-12, 46
Pools, 38
Poor, 83
Population, 65, 84-89, 109, 123
Posters, 124
Powerlessness, 51
Power, 2-3, 8, 35-48, [illegible]9, 7[illegible], 7[illegible], 96, 115, 148
    Bonus, 52
    Scarcity, 3
Power, determined competition, 34, 58, 148, 150
Price, 1-2, 4, 10, 12, 17-18, 27, 33, 35, 39, 41, 44, 47, 59, 72, 89, 99
    and Competition, 7
    of labor, 64, 72
    to utility, 60
Price law, 40 (See also Laws)
Private ownership, 68, 91, 103
Private property, 10 (see also Private ownership)
Process, 97, 111, 118
Procter & Gamble, 128, 130, 132, 134, 140
Producer, 5, 20, 43, 59, 63-65
Production, 14-17, 20, 27, 89, 93, 117, 146
Productivity, 63, 122
Professional, 112, 150
Profit, 1-2, 4, 6, 10-12, 19-20, 53, 60, 63, 75, 84, 89, 92, 109, 117, 125, 151
Prognoses, 151
Progress, 112
Proletariat, 149 (See also Class struggle)
Psychological, 87, 93
Public relations, 15, 56
Publishing, 135
Pyramid of power, 149

Q

Quaker Oats, 129, 132, 134, 141
Quality of life, 116, 123
Quality, 21, 28-29, 46, 69, 102, 123, 147

Quantities, 15, 33, 40, 57

R

Radio, 61, 124

Railways, 91 (See also Transportation)

Rare, 65

Rate of profit, 109, 136-37

Raw materials, 99, 116, 147

Real estate, 111

Real-life, 75

Reality, 25

Redundancy, 44

Refining, 135

Regulations, 80

Reification, 71-72

Reinvestment, 82

Relationships, 9

Reliability, 22

Religious, 86

Rent, 12, 88

Research and development, 15, 26, 109

Reserves, 80

Resources, 20, 25-26, 62, 108

Respectability, 87

Retailers, 29

Revenues, 128

Ricardo, David, 65-66, 88-90, 116, 136

Rich, 83, 90

Risk, 84, 103, 105

RJR Nabisco, 128, 130, 132, 134, 139-41

Robinson, Joan, 6, 29-30, 50-51, 58, 60, 97, 138

Roemer, John E., 4, 69-71, 137

Rosenbluth, G., 126

Rostow, W.W., 81, 83-84, 88, 95, 115

R.R. Donnally, 129, 131, 133-34, 141

Rubber products, 135

S

Sraffa, 50-51

Salesmanship, 29

Sales, 3, 15, 22, 32, 59, 77, 127

Satisfaction, 18, 21, 47, 55, 61

Saturation, 18, 26-27, 102

Savings, 78, 82, 93, 97

Scarcity, 3-4, 40, 114

Schmalenbach, Eugen, 26

Schools of Economic thought, 1

Schumpeter, Joseph, 21, 26, 94, 99-103, 106, 111-13, 116

Science, 89, 108, 111

Scientific equipment, 135

Scientific institutions, 123

Security, 86

Self-regulating, 22

Selling, 57

Services, 1, 3, 28

Shareholders value, 139

Shares, 6, 135

Shopkeepers, 120 (See also Retailers)

Shops, 122

Similarity, 55

Size, 25-27, 61, 76, 118

"Slender production", 76-77

Small businessmen, 150 (See also Shopkeepers)

Smith, Adam, 4, 14, 61, 64-65, 83-86, 83, 104, 108

Soaps, 135

Social power, 38
Social relations, 38, 70
Social science, 148
Social-Security, 63
Sombart, Werner, 125-25
Soviet Union, 117
Specialization, 76
Speculation, 115
Sponsoring, 57
Sports, 106
Stagnation, 96
Standards, 114
State (government), 35, 56, 53, 80, 95, 116, 120
Stationary state, 95
Statistics, 151
Status, 116
Steamships, 91 (See also Transportation)
Stimulants, 86
Strikes, 36 (See Unions)
Structures, 102
Subsidies, 122
Subsistence, 44, 64, 84
Substitutability, 55
Subsupplier, 76
Summary, 151
Superiority, 2
Supplier, 5, 60, 76
Supply, 3, 6, 8, 10, 14, 17, 20-40, 44, 54, 64, 73-74, 108, 146, 149
Supply curve, 15
Surplus value, 67, 110 (See also Value)

T

Taste, 46
Taxes, 115, 123
Taxpayers, 26
Teams, 112
Technology, 48, 61, 98-99, 109, 150
Telegraphs, 91
TV, 61, 124
Texas Instruments, 128, 130, 132, 134, 139-40
Textiles, 82, 134
Theme, 7
Third World, 76, 85
Tobacco, 135
Trademarks, 6, 31, 56, 58, 60
Trade, 10, 27, 82, 106
Training, 15, 110 (See also Education)
Trees, 97
Trend, 52
Triffin, Robert, 50
Trusts, 38

U

Unemployment, 8, 25, 80, 114, 116-19, 121, 123, 139
Unions, 45, 49, 67, 121, 150
United States, 151
Universities, 123
Unskilled, 150
Utility, 1, 60, 67 (See also Marginal utility)
Utilization, 122

V

Value, 1, 14, 18, 40-42, 6[illegible], 146 (See also Marginal value)
Variable capital, 92, 137
Vienna, 17, 35
Von Thünen, Johann Heinrich, 105

W

Wage fund, 36, 64

Wige-earners, 4, 15, 52, 63-64, 72, 76, 113

Wages, 12, 36, 63, 80, 109, 121-22

Walras, Lèon 17, 20-21, 72-75, 99, 105, 132

Want, 18, 81

Wealth, 86-87, 89, 96, 108, 150

Weber, Max, 3

Western Europe, 25, 117, 121

Workers, 36, 84, 150

Work, 19 (See Labor, Unions)

World Trade Organization, 27

"Wrong signals", 75

X

Xerox 129, 131-33, 141

Saṁrakṣikā Series
No. 1

General Editor
Sucha Gopalakrishnan

Saṁrakṣikā Series

The Saṁrakṣikā Series is the compilation of the papers presented during the seminars organized by the National Mission for Manuscripts. The seminars provide an interactive forum for scholars to engage with ideas related to the manuscript heritage of India and promote a discourse around the knowledge content of Indian manuscripts, relocating the past within the thoughts, debates and cultures of the present.

Indigenous Methods and Manuscript Preservation

Indigenous Methods and Manuscript Preservation

Editor
Anupam Sah

National Mission for Manuscripts

NATIONAL MISSION FOR MANUSCRIPTS
New Delhi

and

D.K. PRINTWORLD (P) LTD.
New Delhi

Cataloguing in Publication Data — DK
[Courtesy: D.K. Agencies (P) Ltd. <docinfo@dkagencies.com>]

Seminar on Oral Traditions and Indigenous Methods of Preservation and Conservation of Manuscripts (2005 : New Delhi, India)
Indigenous methods and manuscript preservation / edited by Anupam Sah.
xvii, 252 p., 23 cm. — (Saṁrakṣikā series ; no. 1)
Papers presented at the Seminar on Oral Traditions and Indigenous Methods of Preservation and Conservation of Manuscripts, held at New Delhi in February 2005.
Includes bibliographical references.
Includes index.
ISBN 8190402900

1. Manuscripts, Indic — Conservation and restroration — India — History — Congresses. I. Sah, Anupam, 1968 –61
II. Title. III. Series: Saṁrakṣikā series ; no 1.

DDC 011.31 22

ISBN 81-904029-0-0
First published in India in 2006

Published by:
National Mission for Manuscripts
Indira Gandhi National Centre for the Arts Building
No. 5, Dr. Rajendra Prasad Road
New Delhi - 110 001
Phone: (011) 2338 3894; *Fax:* 2307 3340
E-mail: director.namami@nic.in

and co-published by:
D.K. Printworld (P) Ltd.
Regd. Office: 'Sri Kunj', F-52, Bali Nagar
Ramesh Nagar Metro Station, New Delhi-110 015
Phones: (011) 2545 3975; 2546 6019; *Fax:* (011) 2546 5926
E-mail: dkprintworld@vsnl.net
Website: www.dkprintworld.com

Printed by: D.K. Printworld (P) Ltd., New Delhi.

Preface

THE National Mission for Manuscripts was established in February 2003 by the Ministry of Tourism and Culture, Government of India. With India's manuscript collection estimated at almost five million, the Mission, through nation-wide networking of institutions, is in the process of locating, documenting and digitizing this textual heritage of the country. Further, the Mission has also been engaged in the conservation and preservation of manuscripts; and rendering accessible their knowledge content through lectures, seminars, school programmes, and further, through bringing out critical editions of significant texts. The Mission has a mandate of creating a first of its kind National Electronic Catalogue of all the manuscripts.

The practice of writing, preserving and worshipping the "word" has been an age long tradition in India. Over centuries the "written word" — the manuscript, has been the vehicle of cultural legacy from the past, on various aspects of Indian philosophy, culture, politics and science. A tradition that saw *vidyā* as the only real *dhana* can now legitimately take some pride in the fact that the world has come to recognize knowledge as the key resource for change. In an attempt to reconnect with the Indian knowledge systems, the National Mission for Manuscripts began a Seminar Series called "Saṁrakṣikā." The Series seeks to bring to a common platform the theories, methods, experiences and cultures around the manuscript heritage of the country. This is the first volume of the Series, a compilation of the papers presented during the first National Seminar organized by the Mission in February 2005. In collaboration with the Indira Gandhi National Centre for the Arts, the Seminar "Oral Traditions and Indigenous Methods of Preservation and Conservation of Manuscripts" presented various aspects of manuscript preservation, and a series of technical sessions to bring together the textual, methodological and practical aspects to the same platform. Along with the Seminar, the Mission had also put together an exhibition to showcase these techniques.

The first of the Saṁrakṣikā Series, this Seminar was devoted mainly to conservation, a crucial aspect in manuscript studies, and one of the most significant activities of the Mission itself. The Mission has been involved in organising workshops for imparting conservation training to a vast range of students and professionals. Through nation-wide Manuscript Conservation Centres and a larger network of Partner Centres the Mission has a sharp focus conservation methodology and research. Sustained in India through centuries, these systems include traditional techniques of preparing various types of writing surfaces and inks, ways of preservation and storage of manuscripts. For centuries, holders of manuscript collections in India have used various natural organic and inorganic materials for protecting and treating their manuscripts. Due to the advent and widespread availability of synthetic chemicals, changes in the social, agrarian and living systems and other factors, the oral traditions, practices and knowledge systems of traditional methods of conservation of manuscripts have fallen into disuse.

To highlight the traditional systems of conservation of manuscripts, the National Mission for Manuscripts has now brought together this collection of papers on indigenous methods, materials and practices for conservation of manuscripts. The Seminar was an effort at bringing together a group of people who shared their experiences and ideas, and formulated a plan of action for the revitalization of that knowledge. It was also an effort to formulate recommendations related to exploring the efficacy of these age old techniques as well as explore oral traditions related to manuscripts. The papers in this Volume will reflect various ideas, questions and suggestions which came up in course of the Seminar. They deal with a wide range of themes — preparation of writing materials, making of inks, the use of plants, herbs and fruits in preservation of manuscripts, the effect of environment on manuscripts, and a range of indigenous practices of manuscript conservation.

This book is perhaps the first such attempt of its kind to enhance knowledge relating to the conservation of manuscripts in India through indigenous methods. We hope that it will contribute to the Mission's attempt in protecting India's rich and vast manuscript heritage.

Dr. Sudha Gopalakrishnan
New Delhi, 2006

Contents

Preface
SUDHA GOPALAKRISHNAN vii

Acknowledgement xv

Key to Transliteration xvii

Introduction
ANUPAM SAH 1

Keynote Address
C.P. AGRAWAL 7

1. Learning and Aphasia: Reflections on India's Oral Traditions
G.N. DEVY 13

2. The Sacred Thread
HEATHER BROWN 23

3. An Introduction to the Traditional Practices for the Control of Bio-Deterioration of Manuscripts
K.K. GUPTA 35

4. Indigenous Conservation Practices for Palm-leaf Manuscripts in India
C.N.K. ALAHAKOON 61

5. Traditional Method of Sāñcīpat Making and Preparation of Ink in Ancient Assam
BHUPEN GOSWAMEE 73

6. Sāñcīpat Tradition: A Study in the Majuli Island of Assam
UTPAL DAS 83

7. Scientific Analysis of Traditional Indigenous Methods of Manuscript Preservation
SUDHENDU MANDAL
SANJAY KUMAR MAITI 105

8. The Use of Turmeric in the Preservation of Manuscripts
S. SUBBARAMAN 119

9. Traditional Methods of Conservation of Paper Manuscripts: As Gleaned from Two Persian Texts
IMTIAZ AHMAD 125

10. Awareness and Practices of Manuscript Preservation in Ancient and Medieval India: A Review of Literary Evidence
SHREENAND L. BAPAT 135

11. Traditional Practices and Palm-leaf Manuscripts in Tamil Nadu
V. JEYARAJ 143

12. Manuscript Conservation in the Śaivite Maṭhas of the Erode District of Tamil Nadu
C. Maheswaran 151

13. Indigenous Practices and Materials for Conservation of Manuscripts in Libraries
S.K. Das 159

14. Palm-leaf Manuscripts and Indigenous Conservation Practices at the Saraswati Mahal Library, Thanjavur
P. Perumal 169

15. The Manuscripts of the Tawang Monastery
Maltesh Motebennur
Nawang Phuntso 177

16. Manuscript Conservation Methods Employed at the Rampur Raza Library
W.H. Siddiqui 185

17. Paper Making at Sāṅgāner: Changes Over Time
Ritu Jain 193

18. The Jain Approach to the Conservation of Manuscripts
Jitendra B. Shah 205

19. Kadata of Karnataka: An Introduction
Usha Suresh 213

20. Indigenous Methods of Conservation of Manuscripts in Manipur
K. SUSHILA DEVI 219

21. Decline and Revival of Forgotten Manuscript Traditions
ANUPAM SAH 227

The Contributors 237

Index 243

Acknowledgement

THE National Mission for Manuscripts expresses its gratitude to the Ministry of Tourism and Culture for providing it with a platform for engaging in various activities relating to manuscript documentation and preservation.

We wish to thank the Indira Gandhi National Centre for the Arts for collaborating with the Seminar on "Oral Traditions and Indigenous Methods of Preservation and Conservation of Manuscripts." We specially thank Ritu Jain, Conservator, IGNCA, for her assistance during the seminar. We are grateful to the participant institutions, delegates from the Manuscript Resource Centre-s as well the Manuscript Conservation Centre-s for contributing and facilitating the compilation of these papers. We would also like to express our gratitude to the chairpersons of the various sessions and to the scholars and experts who presented the papers. Anupam Sah, the editor for this volume of the Series has helped in the coordination and organization of the seminar and its compilation, editing and publication. We would like to thank him for his support.

The organization of the Seminar was possible because of the support staff of the National Mission for Manuscripts. The Mission acknowledges the contribution of D.K. Rana, Sanghamitra Basu, Gitanjali Surendran, Neha Paliwal, Neeraja Gopi, Shibani Murlidhar, Samir Krishnamurthy, Prabhat Kumar Das, Abdul Razique, Kakul Fatima, Anurag Arora, Yashaswini Chandra, Reena Rawat, K.K. Thapliyal and J.P.S. Tyagi.

We also offer our thanks to the volunteers from the National Museum Institute and to the Gandhi Smriti, India International Centre, Indian Institute of Public Administration, Indian National Science Academy and Janpath Guest House for their logistical support during the Seminar.

We thank the team at Alpana Khare Graphic Design and D.K. Printworld (P) Ltd. for their help in bringing out this Volume.

Key to Transliteration

VOWELS

अ *a*	आ *ā*	इ *i*	ई *ī*	उ *u*	ऊ *ū*
(but)	(palm)	(it)	(beet)	(put)	(pool)
ऋ *ṛ*	ए *e*	ऐ *ai*	ओ *o*	औ *au*	
(rhythm)	(play)	(air)	(toe)	(loud)	

CONSONANTS

Guttural	क *ka*	ख* *kha*	ग *ga*	घ *gha*	ङ *ṅa*
	(skate)	(blockhead)	(gate)	(ghost)	(sing)
Palatal	च *ca*	छ* *cha*	ज *ja*	झ *jha*	ञ *ña*
	(chunk)	(catch him)	(john)	(hedgehog)	(bunch)
Cerebral	ट *ṭa*	ठ* *ṭha*	ड *ḍa*	ढ* *ḍha*	ण* *ṇa*
	(start)	(anthill)	(dart)	(godhead)	(under)
Dental	त *ta*	थ *tha*	द *da*	ध* *dha*	न *na*
	(path)	(thunder)	(that)	(breathe)	(numb)
Labial	प *pa*	फ* *pha*	ब *ba*	भ *bha*	म *ma*
	(spin)	(philosophy)	(bin)	(abhor)	(much)
Semi-	य *ya*	र *ra*	ल *la*	व *va*	
vowels	(young)	(drama)	(luck)	(vile)	
Sibilants	श *śa*	ष *ṣa*	स *sa*	ह *ha*	
	(shove)	(bushel)	(so)	(hum)	
Others	क्ष *kṣa*	त्र *tra*	ज्ञ *jña*	ळ* *ḷ*	ॠ* *ṝ*
	(kṣatriya)	(triśūl)	(jñānī)	(play)	

अं (ं) *ṁ anusvāra* (nasalisation of preceding vowel) like *saṁskṛti*

अः *visarga* = *ḥ* (aspiration of preceding vowel) like (*prātaḥ*)

ऽ *Avagraha* consonant #'consonant (like:- *ime 'vasthitā*)

Anusvāra at the end of a line is presented by m (म्) and not ṁ

* No exact English equivalents for these letters.

Introduction

OVER millennia, India's knowledge systems had been nurtured through the medium of speech — spoken, heard, remembered and developed. Subsequently the written word manifested itself in various forms and developed through a profusion of media. The imagery of words was itself complemented with diagrams and illustrations. Much of what has come down to us in the written form through manuscripts and spoken medium through oral traditions is sacred, both in content as well as in the physical form. These are relevant today as much for their historicity and aesthetic appeal, as for the knowledge contained in them.

In the first week of February, at the cusp of winter and spring of 2005, in New Delhi, under the umbrella of the National Mission for Manuscripts, traditional practitioners from different parts of India demonstrated how paper was created from plant fibres, ink was prepared, pigments were ground and manuscripts created. At the same time, a group of librarians, archivists, historians and conservators were invited to come together and deliberate over three days on oral traditions as well as on the methods, materials and techniques of conserving manuscripts through minimum dependence on synthetic chemicals, relying more on plants and their products.

There was a need for such a deliberation at this stage when the National Mission for Manuscripts is surveying and documenting manuscripts throughout the length and breadth of India. With libraries and repositories shouldering the responsibility of conserving their already large collections, there is now a movement to encourage and empower individual collectors in villages and towns to look after their manuscripts themselves. The use of local practices and medicinal plants to help conserve local manuscript heritage is more easily understood and accepted in villages and small towns than the use of "chemicals." It is also perhaps safer as well as economically easier for the ordinary people in possession of manuscripts to use them. The reality that many custodians of manuscripts prefer their sacred manuscripts not to be "defiled" by the use of synthesized chemicals also precipitated the organization of *Saṁrakṣikā*, this seminar on "Oral Traditions and Indigenous Methods of Preservation and Conservation of Manuscripts." The seminar lasted three days and the exhibition on the same theme lasted a week.

The presentations were accompanied by group discussions with interventions in between. A set of recommendations was framed during the course of the seminar. Papers were presented both in Hindi and in English. Those in Hindi were translated into English for this publication, while the interventions were transcribed from the recordings.

The keynote address in this volume is based on the lecture by O.P. Agrawal in which he provided an introduction to the variety of traditional conservation practices in India and hoped that the deliberations lead to a systematic research and testing of traditional conservation practices and materials before advocating their efficacy. K.K. Gupta gives an overview of the various plants that have been identified for their insecticidal properties that could be applied also for the material conservation of manuscripts.

Complimenting the written manuscript tradition, Jyotindra Jain stresses on the nature and importance of the oral tradition and says that it must be preserved in its oral form so that it can continue to be a document of culture right up to contemporary period. G.N. Devy, however, eschews the distinction of written and oral traditions as two different categories especially as speech is domesticated in writing. He brings forth the element of pictographic writing/oral tradition and observes that metaphysical leanings of different cultures must be considered as they affect our interpretation of respective written and oral traditions. That a vast number of our people have remained "illiterate" and yet have a vast amount of knowledge with them should remind the National Mission for Manuscripts that the relations between knowledge and script, truth and script and speech and script should be considered in our diverse cultural contexts. Interventions at this stage touch on issues concerning the use of indigenous terms and whether indigenous populations are willing or are able to preserve their traditions.

Heather Brown stresses the importance and possibilities of the collaboration and cooperation in both the specifics of "conservation" and in the broader interconnected strands of "preservation" that included preservation microfilming and digitization. Ms Brown suggests that microfilms produced and stored to rigorous standards could outlive in practicality the digitized version of our manuscripts.

Shreenand Bapat's paper deals with the literary evidence of manuscript conservation practices in ancient and medieval India. V. Jeyaraj, P. Perumal and C. Maheshwaran explain how Palm-leaf manuscripts have been preserved through natural means in Tamil Nadu. An introduction to the manuscripts of the Tawang monastery in Arunachal Pradesh is provided by

M. Motebennur and N. Phuntso and this is followed by a paper by Anupam Sah on the revival of the forgotten manuscript traditions. Ritu Jain's paper traces the changes to the paper-making traditions of Sanganer. S. Mandal and S. Maiti's paper dwells on the scientific analysis of India's indigenous methods of manuscript preservation.

J.B. Shah provides insights on the approach of the Jain community in India to the preservation of manuscripts and of the knowledge contained in it. The tradition of conservation is inherent in their way of life, in the Jain *Dharma* and is explained through examples in this article. Article by Usha Suresh provides an insight into the lesser-known *kadata* that is peculiar to the state of Karnataka in south India. Manuscript formats similar to the *kadata* can also be seen in South-East Asian countries.

The presentation by C.N.K. Alahakoon from Sri Lanka traces the vast array of natural materials and processes used for conservation of the Palm-leaf manuscripts in Sri Lanka. In Majuli, an island in in the north-eastern state of Assam, lives Shri Buddhindranath Barpathak who still practises and teaches the art of creating the *hāṅsī pat* manuscripts made from the bark of the *agaru* tree. With the help of Mr Barpathak, Bhupen Goswami has prepared the article on *sāñcī* (*hāṅsī*) *pat* making and preparation of ink peculiar to Assam. Mr Utpal Das, a research scholar from Assam follows with a paper that gives an introduction to the history of Assamese manuscripts and then after an interview of the locals, analyses the reasons for the disappearance of the *sāñcīpat* manuscripts and offers some solutions. K. Sushila Devi's article on the manuscripts of Manipur and their conservation also brings to light the fact that the traditional scholar was engaged in all stages of the production of the manuscripts. The practice of "burying for preservation" is also explained in this article.

Imtiaz Ahmad's article draws our attention to two Persian texts that devote a major portion of their contents to tools and techniques of penmanship and also provide bits of information on ensuring the longevity of the manuscripts. W.H. Siddiqui examines in his article the development of writing and its spread in the Islamic world. He then introduces the conservation practices at the Rampur Raza Library, an important repository of Islamic manuscripts.

The papers and their respective interventions are followed by a set of recommendations on the following topics:

(i) Research on traditional practices and materials for conservation of manuscripts,

(ii) Documentation of traditional practices of conservation and oral traditions related to manuscripts preparation,

(iii) Application of traditional conservation practices and research, and

(iv) Revival of traditional manuscripts making, technology and writing traditions.

The variety of papers in this volume containing a large wealth of information is the first effort of its kind to concentrate on India's strength in the area of manuscript conservation. This volume could be of interest to professionals as well as to the lay reader. Each article could be a seed waiting for someone to help it sprout into an activity that will contribute to carry on our manuscript and oral traditions further into the future with us, nurturing them perhaps through yet more millennia to come.

Rampur **Anupam Sah**

Keynote Address

O. P. AGRAWAL

THIS seminar aims at studying the traditional methods and products which have been used in our country over centuries, even millennia, in conserving cultural property. This cultural property is not a single item, neither are manuscripts of a single type. They can be on Palm-leaf, paper, bamboo leaf, *hāṅsī pat* and other material. Cultural property includes other artifacts and even buildings, created in different periods and different styles in various places. None of this can escape the harshness of the elements and other agents which are often termed as factors of deterioration.

One of these factors of deterioration is insects, and these devour a variety of materials, especially wood and paper. Then there is fungus that attacks almost all types of manuscripts, except birch bark. There is an instance of a birch bark having been repaired using paper, and after some time, due to improper care the repaired manuscript was attacked by insects which destroyed only that portion of the manuscript that had been repaired using paper. The rest of the birch bark was left intact. Is that an indication of birch bark itself being an insect proof material, and could it be used to help conserve manuscripts?

Amongst other factors of deterioration, climate affects all materials in a profound manner. Not only large wooden sculptures and architectural timber are affected resulting in cracks, but the delicate manuscripts too contract and expand with changes in relative humidity in the atmosphere. The constant variation in relative humidity brings about a change in the dimensions of the manuscript. When a manuscript folio is pasted on board or some other support, it cracks apart when the board expands or contracts. Light causes fading of the inks, while atmospheric pollution, both natural and man-made, darkens some pigments, especially lead pigments. Improper storage, incorrect handling and careless transportation damage our cultural property even more.

Conservation of cultural property deals with the control of these deterioration factors and the removal of their negative effects on these objects. In order to conserve, we often need to use chemicals many of which are toxic, costly and not easily available. Even the commonly used para-dichlorobenzene and naphthalene balls are toxic to some extent. What is the alternative to the use of these chemicals? This is what we have to examine during this Seminar. It is in this context that the use of indigenous products and practices takes relevance, and it is not only Indian materials and practices but also those of other countries that we should study and adopt.

Some studies were undertaken (by O.P. Agrawal) in 1979-1980 for UNESCO and the results were published in the book, *Appropriate Technologies in the Conservation of Cultural Property.* One of the articles (by O.P. Agrawal) is printed in that book under the title of "Appropriate Indian Technology for the Conservation of Museum Collections." In this study, information was collected on insecticides and fungicides that have been traditionally used for the preservation of materials.

The first indigenous insecticide that comes to mind is from the neem tree, margosa, which has been used for millennia for its medicinal properties. This tree is very common and the neem leaf has been used widely. Neem seed is again more potent than the leaf. The oil of neem tree is very effective for the conservation of wooden objects. To illustrate the use of neem leaves, there is this incident to narrate, V.S. Agrawal an official of the Archaeological Survey of India in the 1980s once visited the Central Museum in Jaipur and wanted to inspect the condition of a carpet stored in a wooden box for the last 25 years in the *tośakhānā*, the royal store. The box was opened and heaps of dry neem leaves removed from it. To his amazement he found the carpet in a very good condition and attributed the absence of damage to the large quantities of neem leaves placed with the carpet in the box.

There are other materials such as *Ghoḏa bac* or sweet flag, which have been used at the Oriental Research Institute in Baroda for almost 35 years, and are still being used for the preservation of collections. Tobacco, black cumin, pepper, camphor, turmeric and other natural products have been commonly used since ages in India, so have fungicides such as the phenolic fumes of *ajvāin* carum been used.

The use of these materials has been propagated by word of mouth, by use and by example. Decades ago children were told that snake slough and the colourful peacock feathers help one to learn better if they are placed within the pages of the school text book. Whether the children believed it or not, they often placed the peacock feathers within the books and when one observes these books, they are still intact with no signs of insect induced damage. Did this happen due to the presence of a copper compound or a sulphate, in the colourful peacock feather? Is the snake slough poisonous? These are questions that need to be addressed. As the practice of much of this traditional knowledge is diminishing, there is need to document these before they disappear altogether.

Traditional materials and practices must be explored even for other purposes such as adhesives, consolidants, detergents and cleaning agents for use in conservation. While flour paste that is generally prepared is not very flexible when it has dried, wheat grains after being soaked in water, when squeezed, release a milky fluid that when heated and made into a paste is very flexible. Tamarind seed paste is weak, flexible and has been used as an adhesive as well as a consolidant in miniature and even wall paintings. It is now important to start thinking in terms of research. *Rīṭhā*, soap nut is slightly acidic and has been used for centuries in India for washing silks and woolens. *Śikākāī* or Acacia Concinna has been extensively used for washing silks and woolens as well as hair. For cleaning metals, the pulp of *imlī*, tamarind, has proved very effective as it contains tartaric acid and tartarates. In order to prepare the Palm-leaf manuscripts for writing on, various oils are applied such as those of *gingili* or *til*, mustard, lemon grass and citronella, wood oil in Thailand and *dummela* oil in Sri Lanka. Other preservation practices are those of hanging palm leaves in kitchens where they are exposed to fatty vapours and smoke, cleaning with hot sand and baking in kilns as is done in Thailand.

During this Seminar it is expected that the speakers will share their various experiences of use of such traditional practices and materials. This should then lead to systematic and scientific research which should be multi-disciplinary, involving conservators, chemists, entomologists, botanists and others. It is necessary to take this research forward, assess the shortcomings, pursue the positive results, and thoroughly test the products before putting them to use and advocating their efficacy.

Interventions

A.S. Bisht: Many of the conservation professionals from India have been abroad for training at some point of their professional career. We learnt many conservation processes, and looking at the West, we brought in the use of various chemicals to preserve our cultural heritage. While there has been an emphasis on the use of chemicals, the resultant environmental pollution due to these chemicals was hardly ever considered in the past. The chemicals used by custodians of collections and by conservators were never considered toxic. As time passed, the problems which accost our cultural heritage have, however, remained. It is thus very important for us to analyze natural products with the view of solving our problems in conservation. If not, it is doubtful if it will ever be done in future.

Jyotindra Jain: When I was asked to chair this session, I thought that I would not have much to contribute as this would concern with technical preservation of manuscripts. One sees now that the scope of the Seminar includes the conservation of the oral traditions along with the material conservation of the manuscripts. I congratulate the organizers of this National Seminar, for keeping in sight the other rich side of texts and manuscripts, which does not have a material form but resides in narratives, folklore, mythology, and in the cultural documents contained in oral traditions.

I would like to say a few things about oral traditions, its nature and importance. In the context of Vedic tradition, for example, there is a question of remembering, memorizing and preserving the text in its purity. This idea of purity leads to an idea of authenticity and then to an idea of tradition and the preservation of the traditional text. When we talk of preserving a certain Vedic rendition in its purity and therefore allowing only a certain community, certain individuals to recite in a certain manner, under a certain guru, so that the purity is not lost, what is important in that is the idea of preservation in purity.

When comparing this with tribal and oral traditions, I feel that the merit lies exactly in the opposite; the idea is not only to preserve the tradition in the original form but also to listen to the various renderings that occur. Each version that one gets is extremely important because by doing a comparative study of versions of renderings we arrive at a better meaning and a better understanding of the subject.

The prominent Hindi writer Shri S.S. Vatsyayan once gave a series of three lectures at the South Asia Institute in Heidelberg University where Dr. Sontheimer, one of the foremost scholars in oral traditions also worked. Dr. Vatsyayan talked of the problems of transformation of oral traditions in writing, and how when an oral tradition is put to writing it comes to an end, by becoming like an object in a museum, out of context. Oral tradition by its very nature can circulate anywhere; it is continuously on the move and a document of culture right up to the contemporary period.

1

Learning and Aphasia
Reflections on India's Oral Tradition

G.N. DEVY

Abstract

This paper discusses the place of oral compositions in literary traditions of modern Indian Languages by focusing on the nature of oral textuality and the modes of conservation of those texts. It also addresses the relationship between the written and the oral, including the interchange of textual features between the two. The wealth of oral scripts and texts in India is phenomenal. It is necessary to think of ways and means of conserving these texts for the purpose of their dissemination since oral traditions are facing the danger of aphasia in our times. The aim of this discussion is to draw up tasks and the strategies to accomplish the tasks from a national perspective.

Introduction

We are standing at a precious moment in the intellectual history of India, and there are a number of questions that are bothering me. I am here to raise these questions before the audience and not the answers that I have arrived at. I felt interested in oral traditions and during the initial days I thought that the issues in oral traditions would be philosophically, if not historically, relatively simpler and less complex than the issues found in written literary traditions. However very soon this illusion was broken and I realized that in oral traditions, the transactions are as complex. Going a step further, I realized that it is not possible to think of written and oral tradition as two different terms at all.

Speech and Writing

This fact that written and oral traditions are not different was brought to my notice by a pair of illiterate entertainers from Maharashtra who performed an interesting feat of translation. These two stood two hundred feet apart from each other, a distance visually clear but not orally so. I whispered in the ear of one of them, sentences in Sanskrit, Marathi, Hindi, Gujarati, and a French visitor whispered a sentence in French. This person then used his fingers and palms to signal and the person on the other side spoke out precisely the same sentences. They said that their families have been practicing this knowledge for the past 400 years. In their non-scripted transmission there was sound. In their transmission that did not use orthography, there was a great ability to interpret sound in almost orthographic terms. What was spoken was written as well.

This brought me back to something that is a common sense observation but one that I had forgotten since I went to school. All writing is speech. Speech not only precedes writing, but speech also lives and is domesticated within writing. Some critics of English literature told me that Indian poetry is very sentimental. I tried to figure out if Indian sentiment is more sentimental than the sentiment in English poetry. I concluded that it would be stupid to attempt any such comparison. I came to the conclusion that the linguistic devices within the poetic tradition in India, that are more sensitive to the speech traditions and speech habits of the audiences, perhaps bring about some of those elements.

Written and/or Oral Traditions

A.K. Ramanujan, who I admire, said at one place that in India everybody knows the *Mahābhārata* because no one reads it. Whether the *Mahābhārata* is written or whether it belongs to the oral tradition is a difficult question for me to answer. We know that at some stage it becomes a collection of heroic tales. It comes from an oral tradition, from many traditions; it then gets consolidated as a text, and then gets authenticated and standardized. Then again, we think in terms of folk *Mahābhārata*, tribal *Mahābhārata*, and then we compare. Within our society, is then the existence of the *Mahābhārata* "activity," the *Mahābhārata* "culture," a written or an oral tradition? I cannot answer this question with any degree of confidence even now.

Prof. Jyotindra Jain has worked on Pithora paintings. These are made by illiterate *Ādivāsīs* in Gujarat and in parts of Madhya Pradesh, and these painters are called *lakhara,* the ones who write. Is this Pithora image a painting, or can we also call it writing? Is it a pictographic writing tradition? Are there some traces of pictographic scripts in these images that developed in this country and were left behind after the decline of Buddhism? It is difficult for me to say whether the awareness of writing is there in the painting, even though it is clear to me that the painting does write the history of the people as well as the cartographic description of the people. The painting is like the map of the area, with the Narmada in the South and the hills in the North with the river flowing. Is it an oral tradition? There is of course the oral narrative, and in fact there are several narratives that keep changing. Once again I do not know whether it is an oral or a written tradition.

Metaphysical Attitudes

I am raising and presenting these rather childish and simple observations to point out the fact that our entire metaphysical attitude to this world, to the meaning of the world and to the truth of this world has remained different from that of others. This has affected our relationship with the written and the oral differently than that metaphysical attitude available elsewhere, such as in China where a scholar like Jiang Ro argues that the distinction between truth and reality does not exist in the Zen School of Chinese Metaphysics. What the mind perceives as existing and what really exists, that 'Truth' and 'Reality' distinction, is infact the same. In the West what is truth is understood very differently than as is understood in various Indian traditions.

Truth by Writing

I do not know if in other countries too, in a court testimony, one has to say aloud after touching a written text that one will tell the truth and nothing but the truth. Is 'Truth' achieved by writing alone; if the thing is not written then it is not the truth? This is a problematic thing for us. Therefore, I think we need to look at the question of manuscripts in this Country very differently.

Historical Realities of the Indian Subcontinent's Scripts

In this Country there have developed a variety of scripts that are competing with each other, but not conflicting. A very large number of scripts are available in Indian traditions including those that have disappeared. There are some scripts that are used in schools while some are not used. There are languages without scripts, languages with a notion of scripts different than the ones written on paper or rock, but which have an awareness of orthographic representation of the language outside of the spoken word. These are far too many and the creation of such a range of scripts, allowing so many languages to exist, coexist, intermingle and yet not destroy each other, is an admirable fact. Therefore, these historical realities of our metaphysical bents should be necessarily considered by the National Mission for Manuscripts.

Concluding Remarks

It would not be enough to just document our manuscripts digitally or in print or record in whatever format we have at our disposal. (I put ten tribal languages in print and still curse myself for that. It created social impacts that I had not foreseen. This, however, is not the right time to talk of print capitalism, illiteracy and poverty.) In this Country there are, according to the 1971 census, almost 110 languages, each one is spoken by more than 10,000 individuals and only twenty of them are listed. One feels it is necessary first to challenge the established contemporary notion of aesthetics. We have to begin with a new National, not nationalistic, sense of aesthetics that has to be brought centre stage in our intellectual discourse. Subsequently, we have to see why and how such a vast number of our people have remained illiterate, and yet have such a vast amount of knowledge with them. The relation between Knowledge and Script, between Truth and Script, Speech and Script, all these relationships are problematic for us differently than elsewhere. My humble submission at this juncture, when the oral and written traditions are being seen as one part of a larger spectrum, is that we must make an effort to make a larger beginning.

Interventions

Anupam Sah: Working in the field of conservation, and when working with traditional craft skills and with craftsmen, one sees that the terminology used often has Latin, German, Italian and English elements. While this practice is perfectly fine, the exclusive use of these, and a complete non-use of traditional and local terms may also create a divide between the traditional progenitors of these art forms, our craftsmen and those of us who document them and present them at such venues and seminars. When we do not use the local terms, often most of us err when forcing English equivalents of these local terms into our vocabulary. We also often err because of our shallow understanding of occidental terminology. At the same time, the actual practitioners are also unable to share the platform with us. They often feel their art form itself is inferior, its material and technology and nuances not considered worthy of being expressed in their local language. Language is a subtle but powerful medium to effect change and development. Would it be worthwhile to also start using our traditional and local terms when writing and reporting our work?

G.N. Devy: Those who do not know these traditional terms feel comfortable with them. A villager is comfortable in my speaking English with Dr. Jain, but perhaps I may not be comfortable talking the village language with that villager. Most Indians are bilingual and they tolerate, celebrate and relish the bilingual situations of communication. Turning someone's lack of language into a knowledge opportunity for oneself and this has often been done by us, is a social sin and should be avoided.

There is a danger in developing Indian terms as such, especially because we have many languages and no one Indian language. Linguistically, it would be impossible to have one term. The use of such terms could also actually nurture a mindless nationalistic pride with political connotations. We know what the Orientalists did with terms by bringing about a difference in their spelling and local pronunciation. We have now got into the habit of using these terms and we tolerate them now.

Ratna Basu: When we talk of terminology we tend to either not understand, or to misinterpret and misrepresent when we are not able to use the categories used by the local practitioners themselves. When we look at English terminology, the kinds of categorizations that have come are very definitive in terms of how the English looked at their own literary history and their genre distinctions as they exist. In addition, when dealing in the social context were categorizations of a socio-political management, and having borrowed the same structure of thought and also of running the political distinctions and tensions and conflicts in the categories and having laid certain rules, in which we used the same structures and linguistic categories, we do sometimes then are not trying to understand. We insist that the categories have to be universal and have to be understood. But what is being understood is not the same as is being conceived or perceived by the members of the local community themselves in relation to their heritage. I wonder if we can come to a definitive conclusion. This remains a burning issue.

G.N. Devy: I do not disagree with you. For different fields, however, it works differently. In the case of written music, of more recent origin, our vocalists trained in the Indian way are comfortable with categories and they can use terms like *rāga* and *tāla* even when talking in English. In computers, for example, we have to use terminology developed in Japan and America. Any field that has developed its indigenous contemporary philosophy will have earned the right to devise a set of terms for its contemporary use, not till then. We have to earn the right to use our own terminology by developing a philosophy for our discipline. This itself would change from discipline to discipline. This is why the dialogue between allopathic medicine and Āyurveda has been a very difficult dialogue. In fact, they were two monologues rather than a dialogue, and that has been so because the contemporary philosophies of these two systems are not available with us now.

O.P. Agrawal: The terminology that we are discussing is that which is used to describe a certain practice. I suggest we use the local terms and give an equivalent term in English or Hindi or any other language. In Japan too they use their local terms and give an English equivalent. If we stop writing and reporting our work using local terms, then other than not being able to express ourselves correctly, we may even forget one day the terms actually used by the practitioners.

Maltesh Motebennur: Do we need to educate our *ādivāsīs*, the aborigines, and if we do then will their oral traditions be affected?

G.N. Devy: Before we begin to educate our *ādivāsīs*, we must learn from them, otherwise we would be doing to them what Macaulay did to us. There was this film in which a man was trapped in a cave and as a journalist needed a story, the trapped man was kept there. Let the *ādivāsīs* decide what is good for them. If it helps them in their life, they will carry that tradition forward. These traditions do not always need an artificial respiration. I do not think I will preserve their tradition thinking that if I do not do it, the tradition will disappear. Rather I would preserve it if I feel that there is something in it to learn from.

Jyotindra Jain: Are the *ādivāsīs*, the tribals, really in a position to decide for themselves? They are not two static entities, the tribals and the non-tribals. If we bring forms of administration, forms of education, information through television or through other forms, and then they develop aspirations for other jobs is there any possibility left for us to say that they can decide? I think they are not in a position to decide.

G.N. Devy: There is cause for concern and one can worry a lot. In three centuries of our history of the onslaught of colonization and enslavement, the *ādivāsīs* have remained where they were because of their innate strength.

Jyotindra Jain: In our democratic aspirations we strive to incorporate them in the mainstream. For the British, the *ādivāsī* communities were peripheral and therefore were left as they were by default. If they are asked today, they would definitely opt for good concrete housing, fine jobs and many other things perhaps leaving many of their traditions, written and oral.

2

The Sacred Thread

HEATHER BROWN

Abstract

This paper deals with the importance of using traditional methods preservation in conjunction with the modern techniques to achieve a result, or "hybrid solutions." It further addresses the important role that the librarian has to play in terms of recording what has been conserved, microfilmed digitized etc. It also touches upon the role of the mission in this regard as well as other issues including the importance of copyright issues and handling and treatment of the manuscripts themselves.

Opening Remarks

In contrast with the majority of papers at this conference that will deal with specific examples of indigenous conservation techniques, this paper is essentially an overview. From this broader perspective, it uses the analogy of the "sacred thread" to identify the complex and interlinked strands that can contribute to the preservation of India's heritage.

Background to Analogy

The sacred thread, *Upavīta*, is an integral part of traditional Indian culture. The thread is symbolically the prerequisite for obtaining knowledge, especially spiritual knowledge. It is like a "passport" for knowledge, linking the knowledge of the past and present with the educational future.

India's Heritage

India's cultural heritage is extraordinary. Dating back to the time of the Vedas, the knowledge covers a vast range of subjects from architecture to Ayurvedic medicine, *yoga* and philosophy, literature and drama, economics to applied sciences. India is often called the "land of origin" as the excerpt from the following poem expresses:

Origin

What name is given to origin;
the first steps walked,
the first spoken thought,
the first written word,
the first fire?

So distant has the wind blown
from the land of first light.
To its land of origin,
the wind cannot return,
where all knowledge was revealed
and walked with holiness.

To origin is given the name Bharat (Brown, K 2003)

It is this extraordinary knowledge from the 'land of origin' that needs to be preserved. This is expressed succinctly in the following words by Sri Prabhakar Keshav Sardeshmukh Maharaj: *"Money does not last. Empires disappear. Nothing else but knowledge lasts eternally."*

Ultimately this heritage is part of the memory of the whole world. UNESCO has a well established "Memory of the World Register,"

<http://www.whc.unesco.org/nwhc/pages/home.pages/homepage.htm>

India's potential to add to manuscript collections to this register is vast — and simultaneously the preservation needs are high.

Traditional Conservation Techniques

This conference highlights the importance of traditional techniques in preserving Indian cultural heritage. Using the analogy, they are like a strand in one of the sacred threads. These are techniques learnt from and based on nature. Examples in the area of preventative preservation include using leaves of the Neem tree to repel insects as well as red cloth and traditional chalk drawings (Perumal & Wheeler 1997). Traditional techniques such as these need to be gathered together and showcased to the world.

There is also the potential to work in collaboration with modern techniques; linking strands to achieve results that have even more far reaching implications. This concept is not new. There are parallels in a number of other fields. To give two brief examples: In the area of environmental research — traditional conservation practices in Karnataka are informing new biodiversity research (Gokhale 2004); while in the area of cancer research, the "Bharatiya Sanskriti Darshan Trust" is an example of successful collaboration between modern medicine and Āyurveda (BSDT 2005).

Similarly, the field is ripe as collaborative research is needed for its potential to integrate traditional conservation techniques with "modern" approaches — especially in the area of preventative preservation. One of the more fruitful areas could be that of IPM (Integrated Pest Management).

Collaboration and Cooperation

All of these link with the trend for new alliances across the world. UNESCO's *Memory of the World* program has as its foundation the concept that "we cannot do it alone," especially the new field of digital preservation. With like-minded organizations like "Ausheritage," there is good potential for collaboration and cooperation in the research of traditional techniques — and it would be heartening to see this as one of the outcomes of this conference. The protection of India's intellectual property rights is another important strand — particularly in the area of Ayurvedic medicinal formulae and techniques.

Preservation, Conservation and Reformatting Roles

Along with conservation's role in preserving the original or "artefact," it is important to see the whole interconnected picture. Conservation techniques together with traditional techniques are a vital part of the overall preservation picture.

IFLA (the International Federation of Library Associations) has defined preservation as an interconnected thread of many strands: The term "includes all the managerial and financial considerations, including storage and accommodation provisions, staffing levels, policies, techniques and methods involved in preserving library and archival material and the information contained in them."

IFLA Principles for the care and handling of library material
<http://www.ifla.org/VI/4/news/pchlm.pdf>

In comparison, IFLA's definition of conservation is of one specific strand of:

> "Specific practices taken to slow the deterioration and prolong the life of an object by directly intervening in its physical and chemical make up. Examples would be repairing damaged bindings or de-acidifying paper." The role of conservation therefore is in preserving the original or the artefact through techniques such as stabilising, protecting, cleaning etc

Along with conservation's role, it is important to see the other strands in the whole interconnected preservation thread. Especially significant is the complementary strand of reformatting or copying — microfilming, digitizing etc. This strand is of key importance when the originals are crumbling and turning to dust. The strand of preservation microfilming has the advantage of long life expectancy, while the strand of digitizing provides widespread access, but the thread is frail and needs constant replacement. Combining these two strands provides a new, more flexible, accessible and longer lasting hybrid thread. This hybrid approach also has parallels with the linking of traditional and modern conservation techniques.

The National Mission for Manuscripts

The National Mission for Manuscripts has a pivotal role in linking and coordinating the threads, in identifying what is available and systematically describing the manuscripts. In this work librarians play a key role in building databases, making connections and helping avoid duplication.

There is also a future need for "resource description" for "preservation metadata" — recording not only the existence of individual manuscripts but also their physical condition and conservation treatments. This could also be linked to existing surrogates — reformatted copies that have been microfilmed, digitized etc. This is a sphere ripe for further research and development and India has the potential to lead an IT revolution in this area.

The Next Stages

The next stages involve three key strands that are closely intertwined: cooperation, priorities and research.

Cooperation is needed to determine priorities at local, national and international level. For example, should the strategies be providing protective "enclosures" such as the red cloth covers, or conservation treatments akin to intensive first aid, or reformatting through microfilming and digitizing, or indeed a combination of all or some of these?

Research is also needed to test traditional techniques and link them with modern approaches such as integrated pest management. Collaboration with like-minded organizations can also assist in promoting the research through international literature. The work of Mr. Perumal is a classic example. It was through collaboration with Mr. Wheeler from the V&A Museum that Mr. Perumal's work was published in a journal that has been widely circulated through the international preservation community.

All of these tasks are difficult; indeed they are of "Himalayan" proportions. Time is running out and the manuscripts are crumbling and turning to dust. The scale of preservation issues requires national and global cooperation, but in many cases human behaviour has not evolved to a level at which this cooperation would be possible. In the words of Abby Smith from the Council of Library and Information Resources (CLIR): "***Cooperation*** is hard; ***Coordination*** is divine." (National Library of Australia, Web Archiving Conference, 2004.)

However, to return to the analogy, is not the thread, after all, the sacred thread — a passport for knowledge? India, as the "land of origin" has the potential: to coordinate and collaborate, nationally and internationally, to link the strands of the sacred thread from the traditional past, with the strands of the present, and join them in new collaborative and innovative ways so that knowledge is preserved for the future.

Origin

What name is given to origin;
the first steps walked,
the first spoken thought,
the first written word,
the first fire?

So distant has the wind blown
from the land of first light.
To its land of origin,
the wind cannot return,
where all knowledge was revealed
and walked with holiness.
To origin is given the name Bharat.
To truth, teacher.
To all things, God.

So blow wind
until all knowledge is fulfilled
and stillness sits upon the Earth
and all walk with holiness
and eternity flows
in the river of silence.

Interventions

Jyotindra Jain: In the last 25 years, one has noticed that the volume of cultural property in India on an average is diminishing. I find that museums are headless and no directors are appointed for years. Working within this field, when I hear of preservation and when I talk of preservation, my own words sound hollow. I hope one day we do a conference on that and address the real issue of how to deal with the mass of cultural property that we have and which we are losing with each passing day. It is the kind of administration that is more harmful than these insects and other factors of deterioration. I hope what I say will be heard.

S.C. Panda: Are you satisfied with what India has achieved in terms of work in the field of conservation?

Heather Brown: In India though there has been a lot of activity in the field of conservation of cultural property, not much is known of it outside of India. This is one of the issues of collaborative research. The first place of publication of your work should of course be within your own country, but I do beg you to share your work more widely. A lot of Indian studies are only reflected in Indian journals and not in international publications. We should perhaps disseminate more widely.

Maltesh Mottebennur: Is microfilming not outdated? Is it really helpful in comparison to digitization?

Heather Brown: That microfilming is outdated is one view. In my own professional view, the life expectancy of microfilm that has been produced to rigorous standards is estimated to about 500 years if it is stored correctly and it is this storage that might be a problem in India. The life of digital information is transient. Some debate the life of a CD to be ten years. To compound things further, the software and hardware change in a matter of a few years. In my library and in other libraries in the world, the conservative solution is to microfilm, as the preservation base and digitize for access and then you get the best of both worlds. To read the microfilm, even in the future all one will need is a simple magnifying glass, while our great grandchildren may pick up a CD, that may have become obsolete by then, and question what that might be, and they may not be able to read it.

Ratna Basu: Do you think that dissemination of knowledge and acceptance of others' point of view and getting articles published in international journals is the only issue, when maybe the other publication has a political agenda of its own? It is not that it is not known what the other has done but the problem is the acceptance of the others' work.

Heather Brown: That is why we need collaboration and that is why I recommend like minded institutions and people to work together. What often blocks collaboration is simply politics. There will be friends and colleagues who are supportive. There are ways of collaborating and sharing. A lot of politics is simply jealousy. We must find ways around negative issues

A.S. Bisht: Technology is changing fast and so are practices, even though many Indian traditional means of conserving cultural property have remained the same. Have the indigenous techniques in Australia remained as they were or have they changed?

Heather Brown: That area still needs research. We are just beginning to understand the sophistication of our original people. Research has just started especially in Bush medicine and most of this is oral traditions. Some links of Bush medicine go back to Āyurveda.

P. Perumal: Many of us do work, but cannot write due to our language constraints. Due to collaboration with Mr. Wheeler, my work has been disseminated to the Western world.

Heather Brown: Your paper was so well presented that the National Library of Australia and IFLA approached the V&A for permission to reproduce it in the microfilming training materials and your paper has now gone all over the Asia Pacific region to Japan and elsewhere, and that is part of collaboration and dissemination.

Vipul Shah: When we talk of our manuscripts and knowledge in our manuscripts, we feel proud of our inheritance. When we think of preserving, however, we only think in terms of Western methods like digitization and microfilming. Why do we not simply apportion a small part of the budget and reproduce the manuscripts in the traditional manner and techniques. All these systems of microfilming and digitization are part of an unsustainable model.

With digitized material, anyone can access the matter. Knowledge should not go to anyone and everyone without any checks. Manuscripts should be utilized for the purpose they were created and not just frivolously. For example, manuscripts dealing with spiritual texts should be used as such, but people read them not with the intention of becoming pious but instead they use them for material gains.

Heather Brown: We need to look at priorities because as a preservation manager there are some items in my library that do not need extensive treatment. So we microfilm them to the highest standard and store the microfilm in the best possible conditions. We are digitizing without thinking of the other alternatives. Yes, access should be restricted.

References

Bharatiya Sanskriti Darshan Trust (India) — Cancer research project www.ayurved-wagholi.org

Brown, Heather, Training in Preservation Microfilming, Module 2 Preservation Canberra: National Library of Australia 2003 www.nla.gov.au/preserve/trainmat.html

Brown, Kelvin, "Origin," *Collector of Words*, Vol. II, Adelaide: Score Sounds, 2003.

Gokhale, et al., *Prioritising Traditional Conservation Practices for Karnataka*, Centre for Ecological Sciences, Indian Institute of Science, Bangalore: Newsletter Issue 4, 2004.

http://wgbis.ces.iisc.ernet.in/biodiversity /newsletter/issue4/

IFLA International Federation of Library Associations www.ifla.org

IFLA Principles for the care and handling of library material, www.ifla.org/VI/4/news/pchlm.pdf

Li, Zuzao, "The Traditional and Modern Preservation of Library Rare Books and Precious Rare Material in China," *International Preservation News*, (19 July), 1999, pp. 8-11.

National Library of Australia Web archiving conference 2004 www.nla.gov.au

National Mission for Manuscripts (India) www.namami.nic.in

Perumal. P and Wheeler, Michael. *Traditional Practices for the Control of Insects in India*, April 1977, pp. 8-9.

UNESCO Memory of the World

whc.unesco.org/nwhc/pages/home.pages/homepage.htm

3

An Introduction to the Traditional Practices for the Control of Bio-Deterioration of Manuscripts

K.K. GUPTA

Abstract

Care of manuscripts was a major concern in the past and efforts were made to protect them from the different agents of deterioration. One of the most important of the deterioration agents was biological growth. India has a history of using herbs and other natural products effectively against the activity of bio-organisms. These products were apparently non-toxic to humans. The methods used to save the manuscripts were based on experience and knowledge of herbs and other natural materials and these practices were passed down to later generations. Gradually these practices went into oblivion in favour of modern and readymade materials. Most of the modern materials used today to counter insect attack are relatively drastic and toxic. It is therefore important to re-evaluate the traditional materials which are in use and to explore the possibility of using them with some modifications, if required. Conventional insecticides, at the same time, should not be too readily dismissed in favour of non-chemical methods as it is better to work with products which have a long history and for which a lot of information, particularly about their advantages and disadvantages, is available. This paper deals with some traditional materials and practices that have the potential of being used for the protection of manuscripts from bio-deterioration.

Introduction

Care of manuscripts was a major concern in the past and efforts were made to protect them from various agents of deterioration. One of the most important of these deterioration agents was biological growth. The methods used to save manuscripts were based on experience and knowledge of herbs and other natural materials. These practices were passed down from generation to generation. With the advent of the Portuguese, British and French colonists in the Indian Subcontinent the traditional practices like using Neem leaves to protect crops and stored grains came to be regarded as backward and created a stigma. This led to the abandoning of these ecologically sound practices in favour of modern readymade chemical products imported from the west. Centuries of knowledge and wisdom accumulated in the minds of people based on the trials and errors of generations were threatened slowly but surely. Most of the modern materials used today are relatively drastic in action and toxic. Various methods are being used in different museums, archives and other manuscript repositories. These methods aim at killing the bio-deteriogens while some aim at deterring their growth or repelling them from their storage or display areas.

The materials used to combat the bio-deteriogens have their advantages and disadvantages. The toxicity of these materials to humans is one of the greatest disadvantages. Not only are they a potential health hazard for those who use them but the use of the right lethal dose for the insect is also very vital. Too heavy a dose would unnecessarily expose the custodians and others concerned to toxicity, while too less a dose is not only ineffective but also increases the resistance of the bio-deteriogens against these chemicals. Lately, some methods such as creating an atmosphere of low oxygen, increased temperature as well as deep freezing have been developed. These, however, need special equipment and trained persons, and are rather expensive for a permanent use for large collections of manuscripts. Conventional insecticides however should not be too readily dismissed even in favour of non-chemical methods such as heat cold, gamma radiations as it is better to work with products that have a tested history and about which a lot of information as regards their advantages and disadvantages is available. It is important, however, to re-evaluate the traditional materials used and to explore the possibility of using them with some modifications to increase their efficacy, if required.

Summary of Practices for Preservation of Manuscripts

India has a history of using herbs and other natural products against the activity of bio-organisms, and these products were very effective and were apparently non-toxic to humans. Various practices were followed to preserve manuscripts from decay often in conjunction with natural products. Manuscripts were often stored in kitchen lofts, where smoke due to various materials used in cooking kept the insects away. The storage boxes were made of hard wood with insect repellent properties. The manuscripts were wrapped in yellow or red cotton cloth. It is perhaps for this reason that red leather and cloth is common in India to wrap books and manuscripts. Combination of *Acorus calamus*, cumin, cloves, pepper, cinnamon and camphor was used as an insect repellent for six months, though it had to be replaced after six months or so. Peacock feathers and snake slough have often been found kept in old books perhaps for their insect-repellent property. It was also a common practice to rub citronella oil on Palm-leaf manuscripts to increase flexibility and to deter attack by insects.

Turmeric has also been used as an insect repellent by rubbing its paste on the palm leaves and by dyeing the binding cords and the cloth covers. Dried leaves from a neem tree were sometimes placed between the covers of the book to deter booklice. It has been believed that the insecticide present in the leaves is at its maximum potency at spring time, when the tree is in full flower and the leaves are of red colour. The Palm-leaf manuscripts are stored in closed wooden cupboards, with several sachets containing a variety of dried leaves and spices, such as neem leaves, sweet flag, cloves and pepper corns for keeping the insects away. The smoke produced on burning camphor oil has been found to be very effective as an insecticide and a fungicide. In southern India, leaves of *Vitex Negundo, nochi* are burned to repel mosquitoes from houses. Fumes of *ajvān* obtained by its burning, has often been used as a fungicide and an antiseptic in Indian homes. *Havan* performed as a religious activity also has similar action though more effective as a number of herbs is burnt in it. Dried tobacco leaves have been used in India to protect woollen clothes against insect attack. A mixture of camphor and clove has also been used to repel insects from textile and manuscripts collections. Smearing a mixture of mud and cow dung is still used to purify and sanitize areas. Colourful geometric designs known as *Rangolī* in Northern India and *Kolam* in the South are said to help keep insects away especially when red ochre is used in the colourful mixture. There are many more practices which either had been or are still used in different parts of the country, but because of the availability of ready made materials, lack of knowledge and of confidence in their long-term efficacy, they are dwindling away.

Fig. 3.1: Vitex Negundo

Fig. 3.2: Azadirachta Indica

Fig. 3.3: Pyrethrum

Fig. 3.4: Nicotiana Tabacum

Fig. 3.5: Cinnamomum Zeylanicum

Fig. 3.6: Acorus Calamus

Fig. 3.7: Annona Squamosa

Fig. 3.8: Allium Sativum

Fig. 3.9: Trachyspermum Ammi

Fig. 3.10: Consolida

Fig. 3.11: Piper Nigrum L.

Fig. 3.12: Curcuma Longa L.

Fig. 3.13: Achillea Millefolium

Fig. 3.14: Mentha Arvensis

Fig. 3.15: Zingiber Officinale

Action of Natural Insecticides and Insect-repellents

Many of the natural materials mainly of plant origin have the property of eradicating insects. Their main property responsible for this is the aroma they possess. The word "aromatherapy" means "treatment using scents." It refers to the use of essential oils that have aromatic essences extracted from plants, flowers, trees, fruit, bark, grasses and seeds, which enter the body by inhalation, absorption or consumption. The essential oils are complex mixtures of natural substances made by plants viz., ketones, terpenes, esters, alcohols, aldehydes and hundreds of other molecules. The essential oils' molecules are small and they penetrate the skin easily and enter the blood stream directly. A concentrate of essential oils is non greasy and evaporates quickly. The oils are used as pesticides either to repel or to kill certain insects. It is fairly common for two or more oils to be used in the same commercial product. However, some botanical pesticides can be quite toxic to humans, e.g. Methyl Salicylate (oil of wintergreen) which is commonly used as a food flavoring can be quite toxic in large doses.

These materials act as insecticides or insect repellents with various action mechanisms.

Vaporizers

Vaporizers are insect repellents used normally in the form of mats that are heated or lit electrically or otherwise to release an aroma. Essential oils are non-toxic insecticides with just two or three drops of the oil on a mat. Smoke from burning camphor helps to remove moths.

By definition, an insecticide is a substance that performs a biocidal action on insects due to the nature of its chemical structure. For example, if we kill an insect using a cyanide killing jar we can say that cyanide has an insecticidal effect.

However, we cannot say the same about water if it is used to kill the insect, since that mortality cannot be attributed to water's chemical structure or properties. Most plant species contain compounds that allow the plants to be used as insect deterrents rather than as insecticides. This means that in some way these compounds inhibit normal development in insects. This can be done in different ways which will be briefly described below.

Insect Growth Regulators

The growth regulator effect may be seen in several ways. Some compounds inhibit the proper metamorphosis of the insects. These may force the insect to go through an early metamorphosis, so that development takes place at a time not favorable for the insect. Some molecules have been observed to alter hormones related to metamorphosis so that insects suffer malformations and die.

Feeding Deterrents

Feeding deterrence is perhaps the most studied mode of action for plant derivatives used for insect pest management. Strictly speaking, a feeding deterrent is a compound that once probed by the insect causes it to stop feeding and starve to death. Many compounds exhibiting this action are terpenes.

Repellents

The use of plants as repellents is an old practice and this has been done using compounds having bad odour or irritant effects, as is the case of garlic and hot peppers. Guatemalan and Costa Rican natives used to "paint" containers or sprinkle them with garlic powder before using them to store corn or beans to prevent the grain from being damaged by insets and also to keep away rodents.

Confusants

The presence of certain chemical compounds in plants is a sign for insects to find their food source. The monarch butterflies feed on plants that are highly poisonous and they locate them because of the presence of the poisonous compound. One way to use this characteristic in pest management is to set up traps by spraying them with infusions of certain plants that are more attractive to insects.

Resistance

Resistance is the ability of the insects to withstand an insecticide. Most insecticides of botanical origin are extracts containing a group of active ingredients of diverse chemical nature. From the point of view of resistance, the short residual life of plant insecticides may be considered as a positive attribute, since there will be a very low probability that two extracts would always be identical. Even if all the same compounds are found in the extract, concentrations almost always will be different. Generally speaking, insect resistance takes longer to develop to a mixture of natural active compounds than to any one individual component. This may be because it is more difficult to detoxify a compound complex than a single molecule.

Natural is not Always Non-poisonous

It would be a big mistake to consider products of plant origin including botanical insecticides, harmless merely because they are natural. There are a large number of plant products which are highly toxic. Ancient history mentions that Socrates was sentenced to death by making him drink a diluted extract of hemlock. There are a number of plants containing substances that are toxic to humans, including plants as common as almond trees, some bean species, garlic, strawberries and apples, among others. We must therefore not forget that the toxic potential of a molecule is the nature of its chemical structure and not its origin.

Advantages and Disadvantages of Botanical Insecticides

Advantages

- Most of these plants, the botanical insecticides, are known by the common farmer
- Often these plants also have other uses, like medicinal applications
- Many of these products act very quickly, inhibiting insect feeding
- Most of these compounds are not toxic to human beings
- Most of these compounds are not very expensive
- Resistance to these compounds is not developed as quickly as with synthetic insecticides
- They generally do not require special equipments and precautions

Disadvantages

- Most of these products are not truly insecticides since many are merely insect deterrents and their effect is slow
- They are rapidly degraded by UV light so that their residual action is short
- Not all plant insecticides are less toxic than the synthetic ones

- They are not necessarily available throughout the year
- Most of them have no established residue tolerances

The Properties of an Ideal Insecticidal Plant

- It should be a perennial plant
- It should have a wide distribution and be present in large numbers in nature
- The plant parts, the leaves, flowers or fruits, to be used should be removable
- Harvesting should not mean destruction of the plant and that would mean avoiding the use of roots and the bark
- The plants should require small space, reduced management and little water and fertilization
- The plant should have additional uses (for example medicinal use)
- The active ingredient should be effective at low rates

Natural Materials with Potential to be Used for Heritage Preservation

Some substances in the plants and the animals are chemical substances, which are not directly beneficial for their growth and development but are the parts of their defense systems against certain damaging insects or bacteria. Since they have the required properties, such plant and animal products could be used as external insecticides or insect-repellents. Some of the natural materials that have the potential of being developed into useful products for protecting manuscripts from bio deterioration are listed below.

Neem

The neem tree (*Azadirachta indica*) is regarded as one of Mother Nature's gift to the world. In India, it is commonly found in house compounds in both villages and cities. Sushruta, the Indian scholar, in the fifth century BC recommended it as a "*kṛmihara*," an agent effective against insects. In the times when the Vedas were composed the Neem was called the *Sarva Roga Nivāriṇī*, one that could cure all ailments and ills, and is still regarded as such. The Neem tree originated in India, but about 200 years ago when ships began travelling the world, the tree was carried to all parts of the globe. So today we have several varieties of Neem trees, such as Indonesian, African, Mauritian, Burmese, Philippine etc as well as the original Indian. As a pesticide, the oil from neem seeds is believed to break the life cycle of pests and deters them from feeding and/or hatching. Studies have shown that active compounds in the oil inhibited the secretion of hormones into the blood, inhibiting the moulting and reproductive function in insects. In Africa, Asia and Latin America, leaves of the neem tree (*Azidarachta indica*) are sometimes burnt, producing an unpleasant odour, or hung dried inside houses.

Neem oil is known to be active against over 400 insect pests. It is believed to be particularly active against chewing and sucking insects such as caterpillars and beetle larvae. Neem oil is extracted from the tropical Neem tree, *Azadirachta indica*, contains insecticidal properties that are composed of a complex mixture of biologically active compounds. The best known of these is *Azadirachtin*, its J form being most active against insects. Other active ingredients include *Nimbin*, *Nimbidin*, and *Salannin*. The greatest concentration of these ingredients is found in the kernel of its seed. Its various active ingredients act as repellents, feeding inhibitors, egg laying deterrents, growth retardants and direct toxins. It is believed that because of a large variety of active ingredients, insects will have great difficulty developing immunity because if they become immune to one molecule, the others will have their effect. It may also be because it adversely affects the insect's hormone system. And so no insect will be able to become immune, because its hormone system is essential for every bodily function. Significantly, insects develop resistance in each subsequent generation, and as insects dosed with Neem cannot breed, there are no subsequent generations in which resistance can develop.

Neem is affective against insects in various ways, namely:

- disrupting or inhibiting development of eggs, larvae or pupae
- preventing the moulting of larvae
- repelling larvae and adults
- disrupting mating and sexual communication
- deterring females from laying eggs
- poisoning larvae and adults
- feeding deterrent
- blocking the ability to swallow by reducing the motility of the gut
- preventing metamorphosis, thus preventing insects from maturing into adults
- It has very low toxicity for mammals

Its active ingredients, however, biodegrade rapidly in sunlight.

Neem seed oil and leaf extracts have also been used for centuries to prevent fungal infections in the tropical regions where neem is found. Use of neem-based powder and neem smoke makes the area dry, and kills the fungus. Neem extracts are some of the most powerful antifungal plant extracts found in Indian pharmacopeias against certain fungi (Khanna and Chandra, 1972). It has been found that the compounds gedunin and nimbidol found in the neem leaf, control several fungi.

Pyrethrum

The pyrethrum plant, *Chrysanthemum Cinerariaefolium*, contains several active substances that are toxic to insects. Almost all it's insecticidal activity lies in the flowers and comes from a mixture of six chemical constituents — *Pyrethrin I, Pyrethrin II, Cinerin I, Cinerin II, Jasmoline I* and *Jasmoline II* collectively called "*Pyrethrins.*" *Pyrethrins*, which are esters with insecticidal properties, act both on the central nervous system and in the peripheral nervous system causing repetitive discharges, followed by convulsions, paralysis and death. The active material can be extracted with a solvent from the dried flowers and stems. Dried pyrethrum flowers, ground to a powder, or the extract obtained from them, are used to produce insect-repellent sticks and coils. The coil is placed on a suitable stand and the free end is lit. The most important characteristic of these compounds is their irritating effect, which causes the insect to stop feeding as soon as it encounters a treated surface. Pyrethrum acts as a contact poison with rapid knock down effect on a wide range of insect species. It disturbs the insects, forces them to move out of their hiding places. Its repellent action towards insects even in very low concentrations makes it very useful. It is one of the safest insecticides because of its low mammalian toxicity, and so causes no significant harm to human health. It is highly unstable in light, moisture and air.

Nicotine

Nicotine is an alkaloid obtained from some plants in the *Solanaceae* family, particularly tobacco, *Nicotiana tabacum*. This compound is not found free in the plant but in the form of *Maleates* and *Citrates*. Nicotine is prepared commercially by the steam distillation of tobacco waste in the presence of alkali. It is a colourless and odourless liquid that darkens and develops a disagreeable smell on exposure to air. Nicotine is essentially a non-persistent contact insecticide. Nicotine activity causes the production of new nerve impulses which cause convulsions and death. An important new class of insecticides, commonly known as neo-nicotinoids, is the synthetic copy or derivative of the nicotine structure. Sprays containing free Nicotine or Nicotine Sulphate are employed as contact poison.

Rotenone

Rotenone is a flavonoid extracted from the roots of two plants, *Derris spp.* and *Lonchocarpus spp.* Rotenone contains insecticidal constituents, collectively designated as *rotenoids*. It is a contact and ingestion compound which acts as a repellent too. Its mode of action involves the inhibition of the electron transport at the mitochondrial level thus inhibiting insect metabolism. Insects poisoned with Rotenone intoxication causes a drop in oxygen consumption, respiratory depression and ataxia leading to convulsions in the insects, and finally to paralysis and death by respiratory arrest. Rotenone is much more toxic than nicotine but has little effect on humans or other warm blooded animals. A recent research, however, has linked rotenone to nerve damage, and so the extracts derived from this plant are not necessarily very safe.

Cinnamon Bark (Cinnamomum zeylanicum) Madagascar Darchini, Nagkesar

Cinnamon Bark oil is extremely strong antibacterial and antifungal in nature. The essential oil of cinnamon bark is dominated by the two *Phenylpropanoids Cinnamaldehyd* and Eugenol. Cinnamon Leaf oil is far less sensitizing than Cinnamon Bark oil, but is a powerful broad spectrum anti-infection and anti-fungal. The aroma is similar to a blend of cinnamon and clove (because of its high Eugenol content).

Sweet Flag

Sweet Flag, *Acorus Calamus* or *Ghoḍā Bac* is an uncommon but widespread semi-aquatic plant, having a branched and aromatic root or rhizome. Both the leaves and rhizome are psychoactive, due to the presence of *Asarones*. It is commonly known as sweet flag. The aromatic leaves used to be placed on the floors of medieval churches and houses as effective air-fresheners and insecticides. The Chinese also traditionally used it as an insecticide. Dried powder of the root has been used for getting rid of household pests.

Karañja

Seeds of *Karañja, Pongamia glabra,* contain bitter and dark coloured oil (*Pongamia oil*), which contains toxic flavonoids including *Karañjin* and *Pongamol* alkaloid. The oil possesses insecticidal and anti-bacterial properties because of the presence of alkaloids. Field trials of mixtures of neem (Azadirchata indica) and *Karañja* Oil (pongammia glabra), have shown excellent results against several families of pests.

Cassia

Cassia's chemical constituents should make it a powerful germ killer, and a possible dermal toxin, easily absorbed into the skin. *Cassia, Cinnamomum cassia* and *Cinnamomum aromaticum* blend with citrus, wood and other spices.

Seetaphal

The leaves and seeds of Seetaphal, *Annona squamosa*, have very powerful insecticidal properties. The custard apple genus contains several tropical species that produce large, aromatic, sweet-tasting fruits; these include the Sweet-sop, the Soursop, and the Cherimoya.

Cedar Wood

Cedar trees belong to the pine family. The genus produces fragrant, durable, red-coloured wood. The *Deodār cedar, Deodār,* occurs in the Himalaya and is an important timber tree in India. The name "cedar" is also applied to other conifer trees with fragrant wood. Cedar wood oil is often used in mothproofing, and may contribute to the control of certain other insects. Cedar works best in confined spaces such as clothes storage bins, but had little effect in other applications.

Because of its insect-repellent aroma, this has been used for making cloth chests. It is also excellent for preparing insecticide blends.

Citronella

Oil of Citronella is volatile, liquid oil derived from dried cultivated grasses. Oil from the citronella plant is widely used as a repellent. Industrially produced citronella is an active ingredient in some commercial repellents. Citronella is about as effective in repelling some insects as the chemical repellents, but its effect lasts for only about an hour. Citronella oil is an insect-repellent but its effect is very brief. It is sometimes prolonged by mixing the volatile repellent with animal fat or oil to reduce the rate of evaporation. Citronella oil is not expected to cause harm to humans, pets or the environment.

Garlic

While Garlic oil, *Allium sativum ophiascordon, Ampeloprasum, Sativum sativum*, is not exactly considered an essential oil by purists, but it has been considered an organic pesticide for some time. Garlic exhibits antibacterial, antifungal and insecticidal qualities. Garlic oils kill pest insects. When it is combined with oil, it becomes a very effective insecticide. Some studies also suggest that a garlic oil spray also has fungicidal properties. Good results have been seen with a garlic and neem oil combination against insects.

Clove

Clove, *Syzgium Aromaticum*, is a tropical tree of the *Myrtaceae* family, and is an aromatic material. The oil is obtained from cloves by repeated distillation.

Ajvāin

The essential oil of *ajvāin, Trachyspermum ammi* is dominated by thymol, though a-pinene, p-cymene, limonene and γ-terpinene, have also been found. It is known as Carum, *Ajowan* also.

Myrrh

Myrrh, *Commiphora myrrha*, an aromatic gum resin, is obtained from a tree in Africa and Arabia. Myrrh consists of a mixture of resin, gum, and the essential oil myrrhol, which produces the characteristic odour. It has a bitter and pungent taste. The gum resin is used today as an antiseptic in mouthwashes and toothpastes.

Costus

Costus, *Saussurea lappa*, is known locally as Kuṭh or Kuṣt The root of the plant Costus contains the alkaloid *Saussurine*. According to Sir R.N. Chopra, the roots of Costus were used to protect woolen fabrics from insects. Costus is an herbaceous plant, grows in Himachal Pradesh, and yield an essential oil on steam distillation and *resenoids* when extracted with solvents.

Sandal Wood

True sandalwood, *Santalum album* is a tree widely cultivated in southern India and is locally known as *Chandan*. The articles kept in boxes made of sandalwood are not affected by insects. It has been found to contain a compound which has pronounced hormone activity, disturbing the physiological process of developing insect larvae. Sandal wood dust is commonly used as an insect repellent. The dust is traditionally kept in cupboards used for storage of textiles etc. It also acts as a humidity buffer.

Nirgaṇḍī

Nirgaṇḍī, *Vitex Negundo*, is a shrub found almost throughout India. After being dried in sun, the leaves of the shrub are inserted between the bunches of Palm-leaf manuscripts to keep the insects away.

Vetiver Zizanoides Linn

Locally known as *Khus*, this is a densely tufted perennial grass with branching roots. It is found almost in all parts of the country. Its roots and oil are both used as insect repellents.

Sabadilla

This is a compound that can be obtained from seeds of a plant known as *Schoenocaulon officinale* (*Liliaceae*). Seeds of this plant have been shown to have high concentrations of alkaloids which impart its toxic properties. The mode of action is disruption of neuron cell membranes causing reduction of nerve activity, paralysis and death. The ground seeds are one of the plant insecticides with the lowest mammal toxicity, but that is not the case with their isolated alkaloids which are both highly toxic.

Larkspur

Larkspur, *Sonsolida*, is an anti-parasitical, insecticidal plant, some species of which contain poisonous alkaloids such as *Aconitine*. Delphiniums are also called *larkspurs*, but the true *larkspur* belongs to another, related genus.

Black Pepper

Black pepper, *Piper nigrum L*, known as *Gol Mirchī* or *Gulkī*, contains about 3% essential oil, whose aroma is dominated by *Monoterpenes hydrocarbons*. *Sesquiterpenes* make up about 20% of the essential oil. *Phenylether* are found in traces. Higher terpenes are less volatile and therefore of less importance. Loss of monoterpenes due to bad storage conditions makes it less effective. The most important odorants organoleptically in black pepper are *linalool*, *α-phellandrene*, *limonene*, *myrcene* and *α-pinene*. The musty flavour of old pepper is attributed to the formation of heterocyclic compounds (*2-isopropyl-3-methoxypyrazine*, *2,-3-diethyl-5-methylpyrazine*).

Canola Oil

Canola oil is an edible vegetable oil obtained from the seeds of two species of rape plants, *Brassica napus* and *B. campestris* of the family *Cruciferae* (mustard family). It is used to control insects. Canola oil is considered safe for human consumption. Canola oil repels insects by acting as an insect irritant. Canola oil appears to have no adverse effects on humans or the environment.

Catnip Oil

Nepatalactone, the essential oil in catnip, can be used as a very effective mosquito repellent. The researchers believe that catnip repels mosquitoes by an irritant reaction.

Cottonseed Oil

Cottonseed oil is generally considered the most insecticidal of the vegetable oils. Several commercial products are available that contain cottonseed oil; however this oil is not generally available for widespread use.

Peacock Feathers

While the feathers are attached to a peacock, they leave aromatic accretions, which spread throughout their feathers. When the feathers are detached, the residual aroma acts as insect repellent. The feathers therefore have been found placed within old books for this insect repellent property.

Turmeric

Turmeric, *Curcuma longa L*, is known as *Haldī*. It is an erect, perennial herb, of the ginger family. Turmeric contains an essential oil, which contains a variety of *sesquiterpenes*, many of which are specific for the species. Most important for the aroma are *turmerone* (max. 30%), *arturmerone* (25%) and *zingiberene* (25%). It is found in many parts of India. It has been a common practice to rub a paste made from turmeric into palm leaves that imparts to it a slight yellow colour, but endows it with an insect repellent nature. The active principal is alkaloid.

Snake Slough

Snake Slough is charged with an aroma liberated by the male snake probably to entice the female, while it is on the body. Normally it gets rid of the slough after the end of the mating season. The slough is collected from the bushes and trees. Pieces have been found kept in old books, perhaps because of their residual inset-repellent aroma.

Black Cumin

Black cumin, *Nigella Sativa Linn*, is cultivated in many parts of India where it is known as *Kālā Jirā* or *Mungrelā*. The seeds are stated to contain 0.5 % to 1.4% of an essential oil and a saponin like glucoside, melanthin. It was a common practice to scatter the seeds between the folds of linen and woolen clothes to protect them from insects. Sometimes the seeds were mixed with camphor powder and sprinkled between the folds of textiles

Microbial Insecticides

Microbial insecticides are products containing microorganisms or their byproducts that result in insect diseases. Like botanical insecticides, they are of natural origin and have similar advantages and disadvantages. However, unlike botanicals, microbials have no effect on mammals. In fact, any given microbial will kill only a very limited group of insects.

Bacillus Thuringiensis

Bacillus Thuringiensis (BT) is probably the most common microbial "active ingredient." It is a naturally occurring, soil borne organism that paralyzes and destroys the stomach cells of insects that consume it, especially larvae of flies and moths. At present BT is the only "microbial insecticide" in widespread use for insect control. Bacterial agents, however, are effective in controlling insects in the larvae stage only, and because of the very selective nature of microbial insecticides, users must know what pest they want to target, and ensure a proper selection.

Ryania

Ryania is a stomach poison, which will cause an insect to undergo a long period of inactivity before its death. Its residual period is longer than other botanicals. More attention has been given to this insecticide in recent years.

Catnip

Catnip deters flea beetles, aphids, Japanese beetles, squash bugs, ants and weevils. It repels mice quite well. Sprigs of mint spread around the house deter mice and ants.

Wormwood

It is an excellent deterrent to most insects. The two best varieties for making insect spray are Silver King and Powis Castle. Silver Mound is great as a border plant and is the most toxic wormwood.

Yarrow

Yarrow, *Achillea millfolium*, has insect repelling qualities and is an excellent natural fertilizer. A handful of yarrow leaves added to the compost pile really speeds up the reactions. It may increase the essential oil content of herbs when planted among them.

Mint

Mint, *Mentha Arvensi* is commonly known as *Pudīnā*. In its natural form the mint plant leaves are used to repel cockroaches. *Transpulegol* is said to be the active principal causing irritation to ants and cockroaches.

Red Squill

It is obtained from the bulbs of red variety of *Urginnea Maritime*, a native Mediterranean species. Used against rodents from ancient times, the toxic substance, a glucocide, has little effect on human beings.

Ginger

In China, *Zingiber officinale Roscoe*, ginger root and stem are used as pesticides against aphids and fungal spores. The characteristic aroma of ginger is due to a volatile oil present in a concentration of 1% to 3%. The volatile oil of ginger root was capable of inhibiting the growth of bacteria in a closed chamber,

Apart from the above mentioned materials, there are several other natural products of plant or animal origin, which are either being used in different parts of India, where they grow or have suitable properties for eradicating the insects or fungal infection. These include *Tulasī* (*Ocimum sanctum*), Basil (*Ocimum basilicum*), Capsicum (*Capsicum annuum*), Goldenseal (*Hydrastis canadensis L.*), Eucalyptus (*Eucaliptus globolus*), Laserwort (*Sapohsnikobia divaricata*), Myrobalan (*Phyllanthus emblica*), Palmarosa (*Cymbopogon martinii motia*), Saffron (*Crocus sativus L.*), and many other citrus and herbal oils. These natural materials have been found to be effective in many cases, but they also seem to have failed in some other cases. Since it has been observed that their efficacy significantly increases by introducing some surfactant, preparing their mixtures and by adding some synthetic chemicals, these need to be re-evaluated preparing new recipes accordingly.

Conclusion

Though natural materials from plant and animal origin are not always sufficient to eradicate insects and fungal growth, they should not be dismissed in favour of other synthetic materials. Efforts instead should be made to exploit their relatively non-toxic characteristics and ability to resist the development of resistance, by addition of some other non-toxic material or using their mixtures.

Interventions

Jyotindra Jain: I am wondering that when insects get used to certain types of synthetic insecticides, why would they not get used to the natural insect repellents? In my farm I noticed that the Neem trees were eaten up by white ants and since then I have begun to question the efficacy of our traditional systems.

K.K. Gupta: There is a need for research even for those systems of ours that have been used for centuries.

Vipul Shah: When we evaluate our traditional systems, we evaluate from modern parameters. Why can we not go to the original thought behind the system? For example, when we undertake a fast in India, we do it for the development of our soul, our *ātman*. When someone says that the fast is good for health, then we are evaluating it from a much lower level.

When preserving the manuscripts using a scientific approach and attitude, we forget that the basic thing is about maintaining the purity of the *grantha*, the *cetanā* of the *grantha*.

The manuscript has been created by someone who has written it with purity of mind and body and with reverence. This same manuscript is being treated by us using cheap chemicals not considered *pavitra* or spiritually pure in any way. The *prāṇa,* life force of the manuscript should be kept alive. Let us not evaluate things only from modern parameters.

Why understand water only as H_2O? Scientifically all the waters will be of the composition H_2O, yet the quality of river water is different form that of rain water which in turn is different from tap water or bottled water. Therefore I believe we are doing injustice by evaluating and certifying traditional systems by modern parameters.

K.K. Gupta: Traditional systems are not always so effective. There is need to modify them a bit if necessary.

V. Jeyaraj: When the anti-insect ingredients present in natural products evaporate, they are prone to attack. When the seeds or leaves are used instead of the synthetic chemical, they may serve the same purpose of preserving our materials. Therefore we should use what can be available. Use traditional and synthetic products alternately if necessary.

T.C. Saikia: What natural products can tackle fungus?

K.K. Gupta: Smoke of neem and *sat-ajvāin.*

Maltesh Mottebenur: Is there any method to tackle rodents?

K.K. Gupta: Rotenone is used for repelling mice and rats.

A.S. Bisht: In conservation and in this Mission of preserving the manuscripts, there is no one-time treatment. Manuscripts need continuous care and watch. Most of the damage happens in the store because of not keeping it in order. More than the insects and light and climate it is we and only we who are responsible for damage suffered by our collections. We often do not do our duty as we are supposed to do. We should have collective responsibility to keep our documentary heritage in a good state of preservation.

To control the proliferation of insects there was once propagated the application of radiological control. Gamma rays were bombarded on the manuscripts. The insects then could not multiply. What we do is use available technology. We must manage with what we have. Insects are after all living creatures and we should create an environment by which insects eat something else instead of our manuscripts. It is therefore all about preventive conservation. We must use knowledge properly with our head and our heart. We must not unduly just keep searching and researching over and over again.

Saroja Bhate: There are advantages and disadvantages of using traditional as well as modern materials and technology. We need to study those cases especially where traditional methods and systems have failed. Though I am not a champion of traditional systems, I must relate that we have cases where traditional methods have been used successfully to preserve collections as at the Bhandarkar Institute in Pune. For the last 70 years the collection is in a good state of preservation.

K.K. Gupta: Yes, we need to see both the advantages and disadvantages very critically.

Shreenand L. Bapat: The climate of Pune too helped to keep the manuscripts in a good condition. The efforts of the workers and the custodians of the collection, cannot be ignored either.

4

Indigenous Conservation Practices for Palm-leaf Manuscripts in India

C.N.K. Alahakoon

Abstract

In Sri Lanka the art of writing has been in existence since the fifth century BC. The prolific use of Palm-leaf manuscripts and their production helped education to flourish and libraries to be established in Sri Lanka. A strong awareness of conservation of manuscripts along with their proper preparation and care was built up by the clergy as well as by the students, and because of this, traditional organic written records from the thirteenth century are still present in a relatively good condition. This paper discusses the different indigenous methods and materials that were applied during the preparation and conservation of Palm-leaf manuscripts in Sri Lanka. Many of these methods are practiced even today.

Introduction

Every country has its own methods of preserving writings for a long period of time. In Sri Lanka though the art of writing has been in existence since the fifth century BC, the oldest Palm-leaf manuscript available today in Sri Lanka is the *Cullavagga* which belongs to the thirteenth century CE. Being organic in nature, palm-leaves are susceptible to decay and disintegration over time. This may have happened due to lack of proper maintenance, unsuitable storage techniques and unsatisfactory environmental conditions. The Palm-leaf manuscripts serve as authentic and important primary sources of knowledge and information and should be preserved and conserved. While today there are numerous synthetic chemicals and pesticides manufactured that are used also for preservation and conservation of cultural property, it can be assumed that earlier the technical skills involved in the process of preparation of manuscripts has helped these manuscripts to last for more than seven centuries. The use of herbs and local techniques are not hazardous for humans and neither for the manuscripts' materials. At the same time, these methods do not need much expertise, tools, equipment and money. It is therefore the necessary starting point in this study to identify the indigenous methods that have been and are still used to preserve the Palm-leaf collections in various parts of the country.

Traditional Processing of Palm-leaves

Since ancient times the palm leaves have been prepared as a support to write on. Normally the best writing support is prepared from the unopened leaf bud of young palms. After the midribs are removed, these leaflets are coiled into loose rolls. These coils are then boiled in water for three to four hours, often with the addition of tender pineapple leaves (*Ananas comosus*),[1] raw papaya (*Carica papaya*) and its leaves,[2] leaves and fruits of *Beli* (*Aegle marmelos*), *keppetiya* leaves (*Crotolaria retusa*) or *Pinna* leaves (*Clerodendrum phlomidis*) or *Bombu* leaves (*Symplocos cordifolia*).[3] To monitor the completion of the boiling process, some paddy is placed in the container before boiling and when the rice splits. When the pieces of papaya can be made into pulp easily with fingers or when the

Fig. 4.2: Carica Papaya

Fig. 4.2: Alstonia Scholaris

Fig. 4.3: Cocos Nucifera

keppetiya leaves come off the branches, the palm leaves are considered sufficiently boiled. The use of these leaves as additives is said to enhance the durability of the Palm-leaf in addition to "brightening" its colour. The rolls are then taken out and hung out in single strips in gentle sun for three days or more until dried and stiff, taking care not to expose them to the sun's full heat.

At this stage, the procedure adopted for processing the leaves is according to the needs of the library or the scribe. These dried leaves are then exposed to dew for two or three nights and the leaf turns supple, light in weight, strong and durable. If there is then no immediate demand or only occasional future demand, the strips are tidily rolled into big reels and put into a store, that could be a loft in the kitchen, for later completion of the process when required.[4] This system is effective for prevention of insect attack on the Palm-leaves.

When required, the rolled leaves are taken out of the kitchen loft and smoothened and polished by repeatedly running them over a smooth surface of a wooden log which is a metre long piece of either the Areca nut palm (Arica catechu), Rukattana (*Alstonia scholaris*) or *Gadumba* (*Trema orientale*). A long pole of *Walla* wood (*Gyrinops walla*),[5] often used as a mortar to pound spices in a pestle, is also be used for the purpose.

The next step is to assemble all the leaves as a bundle and then perforate them with a heated iron rod to pass the cord for tying the bundle. The leaves are then cut according to the required size. The edges of the palm-leaves which are tightly pressed together are singed with a hot iron rod to remove the irregularities of the leaf-edges. The end of this rod is sometimes wrapped with a bit of cotton rag soaked in coconut oil and set alight. The gentle flame singes the edges of the leaves and it is believed that this process prevents the formation of mildew on the leaves and protects them from insect attack.

The Palm-leaf bundle covers are good quality wooden boards made of hard wood such as that of Ebony (*Diospyros ebenum Koen*), *Gammalu* (*Pterocarpus marsupium*), Iron wood (*Mesua ferrea*), *Val Sapu* (*Michelia nilagirica*), *Milla* (*Vitex altissima*), *Jak* (*Artocarpus integrifolia*),[6] Teak (*Tectona grandis*), and Toon (*Cedrela Toona*)[4] and there is mention also of *Kenda* wood (*Maccaranga peltata*) being used for preparing the covers. The bundle of leaves is pressed with these two flat wooden cover boards and tied with a cord. The material of the cord was unbleached cotton or the fibres of the Wild Hemp or *Niyanda* (*Sansevieria Zeylanica*). The boards prevent curling of the leaves at the edges and also protect them from chipping and abrasion. To prevent the cord from slipping through the cover, the cord is attached to a perforated old coin, a decorative bead, crystal, a carved piece of ebony or ironwood or engraved horn, ivory, silver, copper or brass disc that could sometimes be even of gold or studded with gems.

Writing on the Palm-leaf

The normal writing instrument used is a steel stylus, the *Panhinda*. The stylus is made to suit the work. Its shape, length, and weight are balanced to give the scribe the physical ease in plying the tool. Five distinct features of the *Panhinda* are (i) *chatra* or sunshade — the edge of this is a sharp blade or a fine saw for trimming the leaf or cutting it; (ii) *Patra* or leaf — this is a flat part, shaped like a leaf and is generally decorated; (iii) *Nāla* or tube is generally ribbed or beaded; (iv) *Gaṇḍa* or ball is always a smooth rounded part; (v) *Lekhanīya* or the writing point is always steel. These five distinct parts have fixed proportions according to a rule and for *chatra, patra, nāla, gaṇḍa* and *lekhanīya*, the proportions of the dimensions are four, two, three, one and ten respectively; for the whole *panhinda*, the proportionate measure is twenty. Scribes often cut a notch in one thumbnail to form a lever for the stylus to move on.[7]

Traditional Inking Method

The writing on the Palm-leaf was always scratched with a stylus and the faintly visible letters need to be inked. This inking is done with lampblack. The lampblack is made by burning waste cotton or rag and mixing the ash with what is commonly known in Sri Lanka as resin oil. Most temples use this method to prevent cracking or splitting of the leaf due to dryness from age. This method is used in Sri Lanka and India.[8] The cotton (*Gossypium herbaceum*) leaf is also sometimes burnt and the dust is mixed with resin and this thick mixture is applied gently with a piece of rag and then cleaned with a piece of cloth1. Another method is to cut to pieces and burn the branch of the *Gadumba* tree (*Trema orientale*) after having removed its bark. The charcoal is sieved and this fine charcoal powder is then mixed with *Dummala* (Resin) oil. This black ink was rubbed over the incised leaf, then it was left to dry and after that the leaf surface was cleaned with powdered *Dahaiya*, rice bran, that removes the excess black ink off the leaf surface.[5] Other than the rice bran or rags, after applying the mixture, sifted *Kurahan* (*Eleusine coracana*) is also used to wipe away the excess oil off the leaves. This helps to prevent the leaves from getting stuck.

Traditional Oiling Methods

From ancient times, a variety of oils have been applied on palm-leaves in Sri Lanka by the following methods.

(i) The powdered charcoal of the *Gadumba* tree (*Trema Orientalis*) is mixed with boiled resin oil and Mee oil

(*Madhuca longifolia*) and applied on the leaf. Resin oil is distilled from the following mixture: 2/3 of resin dug out from fields and 1/3 of resinous roots such as Kekuna (*Canarium zeylanicum*) and *Divul* or Wood Apple (*Feronia limonia*).[1]

(ii) In some of the areas in the country especially in the central part of the island, this oil is prepared by mixing *Dummala* (resin) oil and *Kekuna* oil that is distilled from the seeds of *Canarium Zeylanicum*.

(iii) Two varieties of fossilised roots are used for this purpose. The resins come from fossilised roots of plants which are dug out from paddy fields, river beds or swampy lands such as *Hal* (*Vateria Copallifera*) and *Dun* (*Doona Zeylanica*). The resin oil is effective to maintain the texture of the Palm-leaf in good condition and it also acts as an excellent preservative against attacks by insect pests.[9]

(iv) There is another traditional formula for making oil for preservation of palm-leaves. It is a heavily guarded secret and not easily divulged. According to it, *Devacāru* (*Erytroxylum monogynum*) roots, *Divul* (*Limonica accidissima*) roots, *Goraka Maliyam*, a resin from the *Garcinia cambogia* tree, and distilled *Dummala* (resin) are mixed together to get an aromatic oil. This mixture is excellent for preventing the leaves from becoming brittle with age and the strong aroma keeps insects away.[5]

(v) *Athdemata* (*Gmelina arborea*) roots and *Savendara* (*Vetiveria zizanioides*) roots are also used for the preparation of oil.

(vi) In the absence of *Dummala* oil, *Dudu* oil (*Gelastrus paniculatus*) is also used for oiling and inking the manuscripts. This oil is brown in colour. Sometimes when these two oils are not available, finely powdered plumbago is also applied by rubbing it using a piece of rag.[10]

(vii) To avoid brittleness, splitting and loss of flexibility of the Palm-leaves, *Pāngirī*, Citronella oil is also used and it is known to have insect repellent properties.

(viii) In the process of oil distillation, some people mix *Kekuna* oil (*Canarium Zeylanicum*) or *Dorana* oil (*Dipterocarpus glandulosus*) instead of resin oil.[3]

Traditional Oil Distillation Process

Two methods of oil distillation process have been used in Sri Lanka and are still practiced in the South Eastern province of the country. These two methods are:

(i) Take two new clay pots of the same size. Bury one of them in the earth keeping the mouth of the pot a little bit above the ground. Half fill the second pot with resins that have been dug out from around the roots of certain trees. On the top of this layer, place pieces of *Agil* wood until the pot is almost full. Cover the mouth of the pot by using a *Pol Matulla* (*Cocos nucifera*) and turning this pot over, place it mouth to mouth over the buried one. Seal the rims of the two pots with clay before firing it. Firing is done by placing the firewood around the upper pot and setting it alight. When the resins are heated, they strain through the *Agil* wood and drops of the distilled resin fall into the buried pot. This resin oil is used to ink the manuscripts. This method of oil distillation is still practised in the south-eastern Province especially in Anuradhapura district of Sri Lanka. Most of the indigenous medicine men and the other elderly manuscript scribes know only this most traditional method.

(ii) The second method of this Palm-leaf ink making process is the one which we commonly know from the past. In this method a new clay pot is taken and a hole, one inch in diameter is made three to four inches below the rim of the pot. A Bamboo (*Bambusa*) or Papaw (*Carica papaya*) stalk, ten inches long is fixed into the hole. The outer surface of the pot is thickly coated with cow dung and clay. *Hul* and *dun* resin is placed in the pot and then water is added in the ratio of 10:1 by weight. The quantity of *hul* taken is more than that of *dun*. It was customary to dig the fossilized roots on Wednesdays or Saturdays as these days were considered auspicious for this purpose. The mouth of the pot is covered with a coconut shell and a thick clay layer is applied to seal the air gaps. The pot is put on a hearth and heated over a strong flame. Resin oil drips out from the open end of the bamboo or papaw stalk. First, brown coloured oil is collected and after some time an oil that is greenish-black in colour comes out.

The use of these oils has been an effective method to preserve Palm-leaf manuscripts. The existence of the copy of the *Cullavagga* in the National Museum, Colombo and of the copy of the thirteenth-century *Visuddhimagga* in the University of Peradeniya in an excellent state of preservation bear ample testimony to the effectiveness of this oiling technique. On the other hand, the monographs on paper of a later period have disintegrated and perished.

Traditional Storage Methods

Some of the traditional methods which have been adopted by the custodians of manuscripts and are still in practice are mentioned below.

(i) If there is no immediate requirement of the processed Palm-leaf or only for an occasional future demand, the strips are tidily rolled into big reels and put into storage in kitchen lofts for later completion of the process. By this method the leaves can be preserved for a long time without being affected by insects, fungi or mildew.

(ii) The bundle of leaves is placed between two stiff flat wooden boards. This prevents warping and physical damage to the leaves.

(iii) The Palm-leaf bundles are kept in closed boxes or chests and never have they been found to be kept in open racks or shelves.

(iv) Some of the repositories and private collectors keep branches of *Kohomba*, *Margosa* (*Azadirachta indica*) with the manuscripts and it acts as a very good insect repellent. Its use has been widely recognized since ancient times.

(v) Leaves of the *Keppetiya* (*Croton retusa*) tree are dried in mild sunrays and kept along with the bundles of the manuscripts. This helps to protect the Palm-leaf manuscripts against any kind of insect attack.

(vi) Dried *Savendara* (*Vetiveria zizanioides*) roots also protect the manuscripts from insect attack. Its sweet aroma acts by repelling insects.

(vii) Fumigation has also been used to prevent damage from fungus and insects in early days in Sri Lanka. Few drops of *Kohomba, Margosa* (*Azadirachta indica*) oil is put on to a burning charcoal tray and the aromatic fumes are employed as an insecticide and fungicide.

(viii) Another natural product is *Pāṅgirī* oil (Citronella oil) which is applied in the storage boxes and cupboards and is a good insect repellent.

(ix) From time to time, the manuscripts are oiled using *Dummala* (resin oil) and the strong aroma prevents silver fish from attacking the folios.

(x) Wrapping the manuscripts in decorative and coloured cloth protects them from dust, insects and humidity.

(xi) When transporting a manuscript, a narrow cotton cushion with a strap is used to protect the manuscript from damage in transit.

Concluding Remarks

The above mentioned plants and their products — oils, seeds, powders etc. have been recognized and used since ancient times as insect repellents and as preservatives in Sri Lanka. Moreover, over centuries users in Sri Lanka have been very much concerned about the safe handling of the manuscripts. One author mentions:

> Given an opportunity to examine an *Ola* [Palm-leaf] book, old or new, it is always advisable to be extremely careful when separating the leaves, which may be in a sound condition or might have been rendered brittle from lack of periodical oiling, so as not to injure [the leaves] by mishandling them.[8]

Though there are numerous synthetic chemicals used for the preservation and conservation of palm leaves today, we must also note that the traditional notions and methods of preservation of manuscripts covered all aspects of the material and these traditional methods helped to enhance the durability of palm-leaves for such a long time.

Interventions

T.C. Saikia: What is rice bran? How is it used?

C.N.K. Alahakoon: It is sprinkled on the inked manuscript folio and then wiped off with a cloth. It takes away the excess ink off the surface of the folio.

S. Mandal: It will be useful to have all botanical names of the local species mentioned in the presentation.

P. Perumal: Is there any ratio for making holes in the Palm-leaf manuscripts?

C.N.K. Alahakoon: The holes are made according to the size and according to the subject. For example, in *Jātaka* and in Buddhism commentaries, the holes are a little bigger. The holes are placed in the following manner: Fold in three parts and then in four parts. Two pairs of creases are formed. Perforate in between the creases.

Anupam Sah: One may also refer to Anand Kentish Coomarswamy's book, *Mediaeval Sinhalese Art*, in which he guides the perforation of the cord holes, as mentioned by Ms. C.N.K. Alahakoon using the Sanskrit rule:

> *ayamena caturbhāgaṁ, tribhāgaṁ punareva ca* ।
> *ubhayoḥ sūtra-madhyena, tathā kuryāt chidra-lakṣaṇam* ॥

S. Mandal: Are we destroying fossils for the sake of these traditional resin distillation systems?

C.B. Patel: Many of the traditional systems are the same in India. What is the oldest Palm-leaf manuscript available in Sri Lanka?

C.N.K. Alahakoon: The thirteenth-century manuscript, the *Cullavagga*, is in the National Museum, Colombo.

References

1. T.G. Piyadasa, "Libraries in Sri Lanka: Their Origin and History from Ancient Times to the Present Time," *Studies on Sri Lanka*, Series No. 1, (1985): 21-31. India: Sri Satguru Publications.
2. Sanda Lalith Ranasinghe, "Pukola Pot Liyana Pansalaka Hinda," *Silumina 8* (18 June 2000).
3. Saroja Wettasinghe, *Palm-leaf Manuscripts: With Special Reference to the Colombo Museum Collection*, Research paper submitted as course work for M.Sc. in Architectural Conservation of Monuments and Sites, University of Moratuwa, 1986, 5-11.
4. Andreas Nell, "Sri Lanka Palm-leaf Manuscripts Books," *Sri Lanka Observer Annual*, 1932: 29-31, Colombo: Lake House.
5. Sirancee Gunawardana, Palm Leaf Manuscripts of Sri Lanka, Ratmalana: Sarvodaya Vishva Lekha, 1997, 33-38.
6. W.A. De Silva, "Catalogue of Palm-leaf Manuscripts in the Library of the Colombo Museum," *Memoirs of the Colombo Museum*, Series A. No. 4, vol. I, Colombo: Sri Lanka Government Press, 1938, xxiv.
7. Anupam Sah, "Palm-leaf Manuscripts of the World: Material, Technology and Conservation," *Reviews in Conservation* 3 (2002): 15-24.
8. Andreas Nell, "Palm-leaf Manuscripts or Ola Books," *Sri Lanka Today* 3 and 4, (March-April 1954): 39-40.
9. C.N.K. Alahakoon, *Management, Conservation and Preservation of Palm-leaf Manuscripts: A Research Study Based on Selected Collections in Sri Lanka*, M.L.S. thesis, University of Colombo, 2003, 157.
10. K.D.G. Wimalaratne, *Pustakala Dravya Samrakhsanaya Saha Pratisamskaranaya* (Conservation and Preservation of Library Materials), National Library Services Board, Colombo, Sri Lanka, 1989, p. 63.

5

Traditional Method of Sāñcīpat Making and Preparation of Ink in Ancient Assam

BHUPEN GOSWAMEE

Abstract

Of all the various kinds of manuscripts, the Sāñcīpat variety is characteristic of Assam. This paper traces the production of the Sāñcīpat manuscripts and describes the process involved in its preparation. Inherent in the preparation of the manuscript is the secret of its longevity. This paper addresses aspects of the tree, the processing of the bark, the preparation of the ink and storage of the manuscript

Sāñcīpat and its Antiquity

Sāñcī, pronounced as *Hāñcī* is the name of a tree commonly known in Assam as *Agaru* tree, and *pat* means the "Sheet(s)" for writing on. The *pat* are prepared from the bark of the tree. Based on the literary account[1] available in *Harṣacarita*, written by Bāṇa, it may be presumed that manuscripts were written

---

1. It is stated in Bāṇa's *Harṣacarita* that Bhasarvarma, the king of Kāmarūpa (the ancient name of Assam) sent several presentations including a *sāñcīpat* to Harṣavardhana Śīlāditya, the king of Kannauja.

on *Sāñcīpat* in Assam as early as the seventh century CE, however no collections of this period have so far been recovered or reported from any part of the country. On the basis of the collections of *Sāñcīpat* manuscripts available in India, the antiquity of its use as a writing material goes back to CE 15-16. A *tāntrika* work, *Ārya Mañjuśrīkalpa,* also mentions the use of *Agro-valkal* which means, bark of *Agaru* tree.

The Agaru Tree and its Uses

Sāñcīpat is prepared from the bark of the *Agaru* tree that belongs to the family of *Thymelaeuceae*. It is known as *Agar* in Hindi and Gujarati, *Aggalicandanam* in Tamil, *Agru* in Telugu and *Agaru* in Assamese and Bengali while its botanical name is *Aquilaria malacensis Lamk.* Previously it was known as *Aquilaria agallocha Roxb*. Description of this tree is found in the book *Flora of Assam* written by Kanjilal. The *Agaru* is a large evergreen tree with white flowers and grows in the areas of Karbi Anglong, Hojai, Lanka, Dakhin kol or South Kamrup of Assam and in some parts of Meghalaya and Tripura. It grows well in hilly regions. Unfortunately, the destruction of forests has minimized the growth of *Agaru* tree in the region. Some modern researchers have planted this particular species of tree in different places of Assam such as in the H.K. Baruah Regional Botanical Research Centre of Guwahati University which is the largest botanical garden of North East India.

Once the tree is 15-20 years old, it tends to get infected with fungus, and from that fungus infected wood an essential oil is obtained that is used in perfumery and medicine. The costliest cosmetics like *Atar* and *Agaru* scent are made of this oil. The Government of India is exporting a large quantity of *Agaru* trees from India to the Arab countries for preparing these valuable cosmetics. In case the *Agaru* tree is not infected by fungus, no such aromatic oils can be obtained from it. The bark of the tree is used to prepare the *Sāñcīpat* manuscripts.

Preparation of Sāñcīpat

The *Agaru* bark cannot be used in its natural state for writing and painting, and therefore, to make it suitable for the purpose, it has to undergo a particular processing indigenous to Assam for centuries.

Step 1 An *Agaru* tree of not less than 15-16 years of growth and with a minimum 30-35 inches of girth is selected for its bark, as the bark of immature trees is less thick and may easily be infested by insects.

Step 2 The selected tree is measured about 4 feet above the ground and the bark around the trunk is marked and incised with a knife.

Step 3 From above this incised portion the bark is removed in strips 6 to 15 feet long, and 3 to 27 inches in breadth as required. The strips are removed off the trunk in an upward motion. The bark below the 4 feet mark around the trunk is not removed as this portion is very much uneven and not suitable for writing.

Step 4 These strips are rolled up separately with the inner white part of the bark outwards, and the outer green part inside.

Step 5 The rolled strips are dried in the sun for some days until they dry up well.

Step 6 When these have dried, the bark is cut into pieces of convenient sizes, normally 9 to 27 inches long and 3 to 18 inches broad or of any other size as needed.

Step 7 The pieces are then immersed in water at least for three days.

Step 8 After three days these are again dried well in the sun.

Step 9 Thereafter, the bark is boiled in water in a big iron pan to extract the alkali and to kill any worms and insects if they may be present.

Step 10 Once the boiled pieces have been cooled, the hard green outer layer of the bark becomes soft and easily separable.

Step 11 The outer layer is removed carefully and the surface is scraped smooth with a knife.

Step 12 These are then dried again in the sun at least for half an hour, and when perfectly dry, rubbed with a piece of burnt brick made of sand and potter's clay.

Step 13 A paste prepared from *Matimah* (*Phascolus radiatus*) is then rubbed in.

Step 14 The smooth bark is then dyed yellow by means of arsenic sulphide (*Haital*) and also by vermilion (*Hengul*).

Step 15 The dyed bark is dried in the sun.

Step 16 The bark strips are then rubbed again as smooth as marble.

Step 17 The strips are now ready for use as a sheet to be written upon with a specific Assamese ink.

Preparation of Assamese Ink

The ink that was used in old Assamese manuscripts was made of peculiar ingredients available in Assam, the formula of which is known to men of the older school. The chief characteristic of Assamese ink is its ability to tenaciously stick on the glossy surface of the *Sāñcīpat*. Its durability has been proved in the old manuscripts where the ink has not faded though the folios have deteriorated. The basic ingredients of Assamese ink are *Kehraj* plant (*Verbesina prostrata*), unripe green *Silikha* or *Harītakī* (*Terminalia citrina*), cow urine, a piece of rusted iron heated in the fire, a phosphorent extract from large earthworms, dew drops and ash of cooking iron pot.

Step 1 The *Kehraj* plant is taken out from the ground along with its roots, washed and its juice is extracted by grinding it manually. The extracted juice is kept in an earthen pot.

Step 2 Green *Silikha* or *harītakī* is ground and its juice is also extracted and mixed with the juice of *Kehraj*. This attributes a specific colour and permanency.

Step 3 Equal quantity of cow urine is mixed with the above juices.

Step 4 This solution is heated in an iron pot. While heating, a large quantity of froth forms but gradually the froth subsides and the liquid turns thicker or denser.

Step 5 A piece of rusted iron is heated on the fire until it becomes red hot and then it is plunged into the above solution. This makes the solution darker in colour.

Step 6 This solution is then filtered with a cotton cloth to remove the unwanted elements.

Step 7 Two or three large earthworms (*Bonda kechu*) are taken out from the earth and a bit of salt is sprayed on them. A white bright liquid, which probably is phosphorus, seeps out of the earth worm. This phosphorent liquid is mixed with the already prepared ink in equal quantity. This will bring a special sheen and permanency to the ink.

Step 8 At this moment and later on too, the ink may turn quite dense. It becomes very important to dilute it with the addition of dew drops. These dew drops are collected in a specific manner.

Process of Collecting Dew Drops

Dew forms usually in the months from October to December. During these months dew is collected from the open fields by a specific method. A large sized, clean and starch-free cotton cloth is stretched flat with the help of four wooden or bamboo posts in an open field for the night. A piece of small, clean and round pebble is placed on the middle of the stretched cloth. A clean pot is placed on the ground beneath the pebble. In the morning, the pot will be full of clean water of the dew. This water is the equivalent of today's distilled water.

Step 9 If the ink is found to be light in colour, smooth ash of iron cooking pots may be mixed with it. Then of course, the ink is to be filtered again with the help of cotton cloth to remove the unwanted elements from the ashes.

Step 10 The ink is now ready to write with and it is stored in the *Mahīcuṅga*,[2] an inkpot made of bamboo.

---

2. *Mahīcuṅga*: *mahi* = ink; *chunga* = long pot.

Writing Instrument

Before the advent of modern pens, writing instruments were prepared from a fern that is known in Assamese as *Dhekiya*. This "fern pen" is very smooth and suitable for writing on *Sāñcīpat*. The "fern pen" is put inside the ink pot made of bamboo. To prevent the nib of the pen from becoming blunt by touching the bottom of the ink pot, a bunch of human hair is put inside the inkpot so that the nib of the pen may rest on this soft cushion.

In this way, *Sāñcīpat* and Assamese ink were prepared to write manuscripts in Assam.

Indigenous Conservation Methods

The process of *Sāñcīpat* making has in itself the elements of preventive conservation. Modern paper making processes use chemicals that add an inherent self destructive mechanism in the paper. On the other hand the destructive elements are removed from the *Sāñcīpat* during its very preparation. For example:

- Mature bark is taken as the immature bark is prone to insect attack
- The sun-drying process eliminates possible fungus growth
- Submerging the sheets in water after sun-drying makes the sheet long lasting
- Boiling the sheets involves the process of destroying the insect eggs, larvae and other unwanted elements
- The folios were coloured with *heṅgul* (red lead or minium) and *haitāl* (yellow arsenic). Use of *heṅgul-haitāl* makes the manuscript more attractive on the one hand

and prevents the manuscript from being attacked by worms and insects

- In the centre of the *Sāñcīpat* folios, a hole is made for the folios to be secured together with a cord so that no folio can be missed or lost. This hole is known as *Nābhirandhra*
- Two thicker folios, little bigger than the manuscript folios are used as covers at both the sides of the body of the manuscript. Wooden pieces are also used as covers. Manuscripts without wooden covers are kept in wooden boxes specifically made for the purpose
- The manuscripts are normally wrapped with red cloth. It is said that red colour is insect repellent. In the absence of red coloured cloth, white cotton cloth is dyed yellow with the juice of turmeric. Turmeric is known to have insect repellent properties. Skins of goat, deer and snake have also been used as manuscript covering materials. A small manuscript titled *Guṇamālā* by the Vaiṣṇava Saint Śaṅkaradeva is preserved in the Museum of Bengenati Satra of Majuli and it is protected with six ivory pieces
- In some places of Assam, the manuscripts are preserved above the bamboo made ceiling of the kitchen or in the cowshed
- Tobacco is also rubbed on the sides of the manuscripts. Green neem leaves are placed along with the manuscripts. Tobacco and neem leaves prevent insect attack.

With the help of all these indigenous methods of conservation, manuscripts dating as far back as the fifteenth century have been preserved in different repositories of Assam.

Acknowledgement

The author has deep reverence for Shri Buddhindranath Barpathak, the octogenarian from Majuli Island who still in this old age practices the art of making *Sāñcīpat* manuscripts and teaches this skill to others with the hope that this dying art form will survive. The oral descriptions and demonstration by Shri Barpathak have helped the author to write this article and the author records his appreciation of this sharing of knowledge.

References

Barpathak, B.N., *Description of Sāñcīpat and Assamese Ink Preparation*, Personal communication, 2004.

Bhuyan, S.K., "A Note of Assamese Manuscripts," *Descriptive Catalogue of Assamese Manuscripts*, ed. H.C. Goswami, Calcutta, 1930.

Das, Narayan and Rajbongshi, Paramananda, *Asamiya Sanskriti Kanika*, Guwahati: Chandra Prakah, 1996.

Das, Jugal, "Sastriya Chitrakala," *Asamiya Sanskriti*, ed. H.P. Neog and Lila Gogoi, Guwahati: Assam Sahitya Sabha, 1975.

Gait, Sir Edward, *A History of Assam*, Calcutta, 1967, 428.

Goswami, Jatindra Nath, "Sankari Kristi," *Asamiya Sanskriti*, 1975.

Kanjilal, *Flora of Assam*, Volume IV: Nycataginaccae to Cycadaceal, 1940, 112.

Neog, Maheswar, *Purani Asamer Chitrakala*, n.d.

Sarma, Benudhar, *Hatelikha Puthi*, n.d.

Sarma, Harendra Nath, *Descriptive Catalogue of Art Objects*, Purvabharati Museum, Nalbari, 1987.

Sarma, Satyendra Nath, ed., *Descriptive Catalogue of Assamese Manuscripts*, K.K. Handiqui Library, Gauhati University, 1999.

The Wealth of India: A Dictionary of Indian Raw Materials and Industrial Products, vol. 1, A: Raw Materials, Council of Scientific and Industrial Research, New Delhi.

6

Sāñcīpat Tradition
A Study in the Majuli Island of Assam

UTPAL DAS

Abstract

Assam has a long history of art, culture and literature. The materials used in writing literature as a medium are unique and splendid. *Sāñcīpat*, *tulāpat*, Assamese ink and use of colours have immense historical value. Majuli — the largest river island of the world still has the legacy of making traditional *sāñcīpat* a dying art form based on which once upon a time Assamese literature bloomed into its full extent. Lack of public awareness and disinterest on the part of State Governments as well as owners of these historical documents, have been contributing to the great loss of this unique tradition of *sāñcīpat* making. The revival of this technique will certainly help Assam literally, culturally and socio-economically.

Introduction

ACCORDING to the noted historian Dr S.K. Bhuyan, "One of the vast means of conserving and transmitting Hindu civilization and culture was through *pothīs* or manuscripts, elucidated by the verbal comments and explanations of the learned . . . almost every Assamese family had in its possession a cluster of Assamese manuscripts. . . Sanskrit classics and commentaries are also to be found in the libraries of Assamese families." As learning bloomed in this part of the world, it attracted scholars of other countries like, "Hiuen-Tsang, Kabīr, Śaṅkarācārya, Caitanya, Guru Nānak, and Guru Teg Bahādur, who visited Kāmarūpa to imbibe the culture of the country and to give the best they had to give." The translated version of Bāṇa's *Harṣacarita* by Cowell and Thomas (Chapter VII, p. 214) talks about the King Bhāskaravarman, the ruler of Kāmarūpa in the seventh century who presented "Volumes of five writings with leaves made from aloe (*agaru*) bark and of the hue of the ripe pink cucumber" to the friend Harṣavardhana of Kanauj.

The Past

Assam has a rich history of art culture and literature. The *Caryāpada*, a form of songs/poetry related to the preachings of the Buddhist religion are the first instance of written literature found in Assam. These *Caryāpadas*, in Assamese language are believed to have been written between eighth and tenth century CE on *sāñcīpat*, a type of paper made out of bark of Sāñcī tree. In fourteenth century, a pre-Vaishnavite literary age could be traced after a dark period of about four centuries after *Caryāpada*. Hem Sarasvati's written works can be considered as the first systematically written literature of that age.

The Assamese literature from fourteenth century to the end of eighteenth century comprises of Vaishnavite literature and literature of the Ahom Age. Mahāpuruṣa Śrīmanta Śaṅkaradeva's works namely *Kīrtana, Daśama, Rāma-vijaya, Pārijātā-haraṇa, Patnī-prasāda, Kālīya-damana, Keḷi Gopāla, Rukmiṇī-haraṇa, Haricandra-upākhyāna, Bhakti-pradīpa, Ajāmilar-upākhyāna, Balichalana, Guṇamālā, Bhakti-ratnākara, Nimi-Navasiddha-saṁvāda* are the biggest contribution to the Assamese literature. The works were mostly on *sāñcīpat* and *tulāpat*. Sometime *Bhūrja-patra* and bamboo stretches were also seen in use. The literature in the Ahom Age is famous for the emergence of historical literature, i.e. *burañjī*s (chronicles). The *Purani Asomor Burañjī* is believed to be the oldest *burañjī* of Assam.

Though the practice of painting in ancient Assam is mentioned in *Harṣacarita* by Bāṇabhaṭṭa and in the account of Hiuen-Tsang early in the seventh century, however the golden era of painting in Assam was initiated by Śaṅkaradeva. The Satras or the Vaishnavite monasteries were the nerve centres of drawing and painting in ancient Assam. Śaṅkaradeva showed his extraordinary talent in illustrating the vision of seven heavens in the painting *Sāt Baikuṇṭha* on *tulāpat*, the paper made of cotton, for his drama *Chihnyatra Daśamaskandha Bhāgavata*, written by Śaṅkaradeva, which was found at Balisatra in Nagaon district is an excellent example of a vividly illustrated religious book. Paintings that are found on the pages of *Bhāgavata Purāṇa* show the artistic and skilful application of local colours. Colours like green, red, yellow and blue were used extensively. In some pictures, the four boundaries were decorated with the drawings of flowers and creepers; book containing such pictures are called *Latakata pothī* (creeper curved book). Some significant paintings are found in the book like, *Darrang Raaj Bangshavali* (genealogical details of the royal family of Darrang) compiled and painted by Suryakhori Doivagya in seventeenth century; *Hastividyārṇava* by Sukumar Borkath, *Śaṅkhacūrda-badh* by Kaviraj Chakravarty, *Gīta Govinda* and *Lava-Kushar Yuddha* by Harihar Bipra. According to Dr Maheswar Neog the pictures contained in the hand-written book *Kalki Purāṇa* authored by Ghanashyam Khargharia Phukan in the nineteenth century marks the end of the history of Assamese fine arts.

Nature of Ancient Writing Materials of Assam

We hereby see that various writing materials were used to write *pothīs* in Assam. The best way to understand how to care for or to preserve collections is to study the nature of the materials, their history, technology and manufacturing principles. But as the old literature on the history of writing materials is very rare, it becomes difficult to know the exact nature of manufacturing them.

From the eighth century *Caryāpada* to the early nineteenth century Ahom age literature, three types of paper materials were used in Assam. These are namely *sāñcīpat, tulāpat* and *Bhojpat* or *Bhūrja patra*. Sometime thinly sliced *bamboo stretches* were also used as leaf of book.

Sāñcīpat

Sāñcīpat is made from the bark of *sāñcī* or *agaru* tree or aloes woods (*Aquilaria agallocha*) which are processed through a tremendous laborious process of curing, seasoning and polishing the raw slices and conditioned with many things for dazzle and durability. The 9-27 inches long and 3 to 18 inches broad with 1 mm thick pieces are put into cold water for about an hour, and the alkali is extracted, after which they are dried in the sun for half an hour. When perfectly dry, they are rubbed with a piece of burnt brick. A paste prepared from *matimah* (*Phaseolus radiatus*) is rubbed on the back and further dyed yellow by means of yellow arsenic orpiment (*haṅgul/haital*). This is again followed by sun drying, after which the strips are rubbed as smooth as marble to be ready for use. These processes were followed to enhance the ability of the leaves to retain the ink permanently. The centre of each leaf was perforated for the fastening string to pass through. Leaves thicker than those used in the body were used as covers. These *pothī* were very carefully preserved, wrapped up in pieces of cloth, enclosed in a wooden box, and were handed down as heirlooms from father to son.

Tulāpat

The *tulāpat* leaves were made by pressing cotton. Not much is known about the process of making this paper. The use of *tulāpat* increased from the middle of the Ahom Age. "They were used for inferior manuscripts, for letters, for private documents, and for official orders, for records of revenue grants, judicial trails, and dispatches," but, these does not mean that leaves of *tulāpat* were not long-lasting as we have seen records in *tulāpat* made 300 or 400 years ago are still in good condition.

Bhojpat

Bhojpat were a type of big leaf usually used as plates in feast, processed, dried and used as leaf of books. Uses of thinly sliced bamboo stretches as paper leaf were limited.

Assamese ink

The preparation of Assamese ink was peculiar in nature. The ingredients as well as the formula, are indigenous and known to men of the older school. The chief characteristics of Assamese ink are its durability and tenacity to glossy and slippery surface. The durability of the ink is such that though the folios of some manuscripts have crumbled due to insects or by humidity and dampness, the ink has not apparently faded. Importantly enough, the point of view of preservation is that there was a regular process of reviving faded script written by inferior ink, but with the passage of time, the technique has now become obsolete and forgotten. The Assamese ink was the product of the distillation of the extract of *Terminalia citrina* (*silikha*) and the urine of bulls. The root of goose quill or reed was sharpened to use as pen for writing.

Dyes

In the paintings, yellow, green and red colours were prominently used. Occasionally, the use of blue colour is also seen. The formulae of colours have now been practically forgotten. The dyes of permanent nature, locally made from yellow orpiment (*haṅgul/haital*), indigo, carbon of earthen lamp, *Terminalia citrina* (*silikha*) extract, chalk (*khaḏīmāṭī*), egg yolk, the viscid substance of *Outenga* (a kind of acid fruit) seed and gum from tamarind tree.

The Present

With the advent of British in Assam, modern printing technology ushered in and thereafter writing materials such as paper and ink initiated in literature writing, which were mostly imported into Assam from outside.

Every old, well-known Assamese family still possesses a *vaṁśāvalī* or genealogical history which are potential source of history, culture, lives and career of the bygone era. The study of Assamese manuscripts or *pothī*s provides an excellent opportunity to understand the evolution of Assamese language and scripts. Unfortunately the treasures hidden in Assamese manuscript have not yet been fully brought to light primarily due to numerous difficulties attached to the manuscript hunting process. The first individual attempt to collect Assamese manuscripts was made by Rev. Nathan Brown between the years 1840 and 1850. In his attempt, he could collect as many as 18 manuscripts of historical importance which were latter on deposited at the American Baptist Mission at Guwahati and finally to the Kamrup Anusandhan Samity during 1925.

Another individual attempt was made by Sir Edward Gait in 1895 and followed by some other sporadically. Though the effort of Sir Edward Gait was recorded in his *Progress of Historical Research in Assam*, published in 1895, the actual number of manuscript he collected is not known. The first serious and successful attempt to collect manuscript was in fact made by Paṇḍit Hemchandra Goswami between 1912 and 1914 when he was deputed for the purpose by Sir Archdale Earle, Chief Commissioner of Assam and Lt. Col. P.R.T. Gordon, the Hon. Provincial Director of Ethnography, Assam. Paṇḍit Goswami could collect as many as 233 manuscripts, of which 156 were in Assamese and 77 in Sanskrit which were subsequently handed over to the Kamrup Anusandhan Samity for preservation. Later on he compiled a descriptive catalogue of the same entitled, *Descriptive Catalogue of Assamese Manuscripts* (1930).

There are a few government repositories of manuscripts in Assam, namely, Kamrup Anusandhan Samity (1912) (presently Assam State Museum); Department of Historical and Antiquarian Studies (1928); Anundoram Borooah Institute of Language, Art and Culture (1990); Silchar Normal School (1908); and Krishna Kanta Handiqui Library of Gauhati University (1958). Besides, there are 665 *satras* (Vaishnavite monasteries) in entire Assam (along with innumerable numbers of personal libraries/collections) acting as repositories of *sāñcīpat* and other manuscripts. Be it governmental or non-governmental, it is seen that there is no coordination or sincere efforts in their activities as some are engaged either to a certain extent in manuscript collection or acting simply as store houses without proper preservation or some of them have stopped playing any role to fulfil their objectives set earlier.

It is observed in a simple survey conducted by me and one of my friends that the physical condition of *sāñcīpat* preserved in the above-mentioned repositories are deteriorating every passing day as virtually no scientific methods are in use with them barring one or two instances. The government officials who are engaged in these particular activities and are trained outside the State as sponsored candidates, either perform their responsibilities very lightly or face stiff negligence from the part of their higher authority, adding fuel to the fire of deterioration of manuscripts.

Like government-owned repositories, the existing 665 *satras* (Vaishnavite monasteries) in Assam where much of the original manuscripts written by Mahāpuruṣa Śaṅkaradeva, Mādhabadeva and other Vaishnavite *gurus* are reposed, also stated to be the same in condition. The physical condition of manuscripts of private or family-owned collections are deplorable, as virtually nothing is being done for the treatment of age-old manuscripts owned as family heirloom.

Discontinuation of Sāñcīpat Making Tradition

From the seventh century CE to the nineteenth century, the entire Assamese literatures produced during these 1200 years was totally written on indigenously made *sāñcīpat* using naturally produced local ink. The literature produced during this period is the backbone of the Assamese identity, Assamese language and Assamese history, culture and heritage. But, it is a matter of great apprehension that once on which the entire literature of a nation or a race was written or existed is of no use today. Why so is it that an indigenous manuscript making technique has fallen to total disuse. To understand this, with the advice of Dr Anupam Sah, Coordinator (conservation), I did communicate with ten (10) persons of various sections of the society of the Majuli island, asking four questions to all of them. Amongst the interviewee:

- Dr Pitambar Deva Goswami, Satradhikara or the Head of the Auniati Satra (Vaishnavite Monastery)
- Mr Budhindra Nath Barpathak of 85 years of age and is said to be the only living person who still holds the legacy of making *sāñcīpat* on his own effort in the Auniati Satra
- Two scholars from two Satras namely Auniati Satra and Uttar Kamalabari Satra
- Two lecturers from Majuli College
- Two students from the Majuli College
- one businessman, and
- one social worker

The Majuli island selected for this purpose was on the basis of three factors:

1. Out of 665 *satras*, as many as 33 *satras* (earlier there were 66 *satras* in Majuli) are in the Majuli island with the historically unique Auniati Satra which is the largest and said to be one of the oldest ones which attract hundreds of domestic tourist every year.
2. The 33 *satras* along with traditional households of Majuli island possesses more than 4,000 numbers of manuscripts written on *sāñcīpat* and *tulāpat* which are believed to be the original copies of literature produced during fifteenth century CE, which have immense literary, historical and religious value.
3. Most importantly, from the point of view of conservation, Majuli island holds the unique tradition

of making *sāñcīpat* manuscript with indigenous technique where Mr. Budhindra Nath Barpathak, is said to be the only living person who still holds the legacy of making *sāñcīpat* on his own effort in the Auniati Satra.

Reason for the Loss of Indigenous Sāñcīpat Making Techniques Today

The response to the questions were:

- Easy availability of machine-made paper at the door-steps
- The indigenous method of making *sāñcīpat* is too expensive
- Rarity or non-availability of raw materials such as Sāñcī Tree (*agaru* tree or aloewood or *Aquilaria agallocha*), *hiṅgul* (Mercuric Sulphide), *haital* (orpiment or Arsenic Sulphide)
- The indigenous method of making *sāñcīpat* is too laborious and time-consuming

Analysis of Responses

All the above answers are too significant. There are also some historical and socio-political reasons for the loss of this indigenous *sāñcīpat* making technique. From the seventh-century king Kumar Bhāskaravarman's reign to the last Ahom king Jogeswar Singh's reign till 1825, the entire literature produced during these 1200 years was dominated by making of *sāñcīpat*. A technique that ruled 1200 years suddenly disappeared from the world. There is no evidence of a single literature produced on *sāñcīpat* after the Yandaboo Treaty in 1826 by which British entered into Assam. Machine-made paper and printing technology appeared in Assam only in 1836 when two missionaries namely Rev. Nathan Brown and Oliver Cutter established the first printing press at Sivasagar during 1836. Some of the reasons are as follows:

One of the most immediate reasons for the sudden disappearance of *sāñcīpat* techniques is the invasion of Burmese into Assam. Burmese reign of terror and tyranny lasted from 1817 to 1826. During this period, Men, women, children, babies were killed brutally; the king with other royal families along with nobles and their subjects fled into the hills and jungles of other valleys and large numbers died of disease and starvations; rights and records of property and manuscripts were thrown into wells and rivers and were burnt down. The Ahom royal libraries which were once production centres of *sāñcīpat* and literature on it, were set on fire; a large number of *pandits*, nobles, subjects of both sexes were taken to Myanmar as slaves. The Myanmarese incursions in Assam depopulated the country and removed all traces of civilization. The literary society of Assam was total by fragmented and could not recover again. With the loss of huge part of our civilization, we lost our innumerable valuable literature on *sāñcīpat* and the indigenous *sāñcīpat* techniques as well.

With the advent of the British in Assam, modern printing technology was ushered in and thereafter writing materials such as paper and ink were initiated in literature writing, which were mostly imported into Assam from outside. Assamese society, which had just started reuniting itself after the Myanmarese massacre, was left no other option but to accept the easily available machine-made paper at their doorsteps. Though missionaries showed their interest in collection of manuscripts during the British rule, they never tried to revive the traditional process of manuscript making.

Lack of interest on the part of government, NGOs and also from the present generation is another factor that is contributing to the loss of the *sāñcīpat* making process.

Ignorance about *sāñcīpat* and the techniques of making it, is another factor for its deplorable state. Religious as well as social taboos are the main reasons behind this ignorance. *Sāñcīpat* and related activities were always under the control of a limited section of the society. The mass have never been allowed to participate in such activities.

Threats Before Majuli

The problem of Majuli island is multiple in nature. From the point of view of importance, both geologically and culturally, it is about to be declared as a world heritage site by UNESCO. The problem, the Majuli island is facing today is threatening its very existence. Every year, we are loosing our cultural items in different forms. As per information available, almost 10,000 manuscripts have already been lost from the island in many natural disasters like flood, fire, etc. Worried by the situation, the Auniati Satra has opened its various branches at different places outside the Majuli apprehending possible shifting of its main base with all property, if any natural calamity strikes in future.

The largest river island of the world, Majuli is shrinking by a few meters every year due to erosion caused by the mighty river Brahmaputra. Majuli had originally an area of 1256 sq km (485 sq miles). But due to constant annual erosion, it has been reduced to only 929 sq km. It is feared that if preventive measures are not taken early, Majuli may disappear from the world geography along with the rich cultural heritage that developed many century back.

Like annual festivals, floods occur every year in the Majuli which cause enormous damage to lives and property. The remaining age-old cultural items such as *sāñcīpat*, rare documents, paintings, artefacts, stone and wooden sculpture of historical value are always in danger as many of them have already been washed out in the perennial flood.

Majuli is geographically cut-off from the mainland. Road, railway or airways, all three modes of communication are not available. Majuli is connected with the mainland only by ferry service; that too gets disrupted during monsoon due to heavy rain and flood.

The telecommunication services are also disrupting and not free from hazards. Majuli frequently remains cut-off from the mainland.

The inroads of IT in respect of microfilming, CD-Rom, digitalization, etc. of manuscripts are pressing need of the moment, but no institution including the government is coming forward to accomplish this task.

Thousands of local as well as foreign visitors including research scholars of various fields visit various *satra*s in Majuli, yet, a well equipped guest house to attract foreign as well as domestic tourist; or a documentation centre for the research scholars; or a scientific archive for preservation of cultural and historical materials is not available in any *satra* on the Majuli island.

*Satra*s need fund to run various traditional activities including preservation and conservation of *sāñcīpat* manuscripts, rare documents, paintings, artefact, stone and wooden sculpture of historical value along with running their Toles (schools). The collections of fund from visitors is not enough for various activities or to initiate a new venture on its own.

How these Problems could be Addressed

Summary of Responses

The government, various institutions related with the subject, NGOs and the public as well should come forward to save Majuli and its cultural heritage in whatever way they can.

Cultural, religious and educational conferences and meetings should be held regularly.

Ministers, influential persons and political leaders, scholars and learned persons should be invited regularly to make them aware of the situation.

Analysis of Responses

Looking at the vastness of problems facing Majuli today, anybody will be clueless as to how to address the pressing problems. I think, the existing 66 *satras* can do wonders for not only preservation and conservation of cultural materials but also for keeping age-old identity of the island intact.

Participation in various cultural programmes such as *Bhaona* (Vaishnavite drama), *Borgit* (Vaishnavite songs) outside Majuli and in various places of the country and inviting participation of others for the same inside the Majuli may help in bringing it in contact with national-level organizations, both government and NGOs.

Exhibition of cultural items, such as *sāñcīpat* literature, and making of *sāñcīpat*, at various book fair, trade fair, inside and outside the State, would make people understand the value of it.

Conducting academic conferences and seminars in Majuli relating to the ancient literature may attract academicians and scholars form inside and outside the State, in which might spreading the knowledge of *sāñcīpat*.

Government should declare all 665 *satras* as tourist sites (and place them in their websites to attract foreign tourist and scholars) without interfering the religious sentiments of the custodians. The Department of Tourism should come forward with various projects including guesthouse for foreign and domestic tourists and encouraging the locals in such ventures.

The Ministry of Culture should certainly come forward with minor projects like setting up small museums and documentation centres wherever possible to attract scholars from various fields.

How Sāñcīpat Making Process can be Revived in Assam

It is obvious that we cannot let the existing *sāñcīpat* manuscripts which have immense cultural, historical and literary value die in our hands. The death of *sāñcīpat* manuscripts mean the death of our literature, culture and history. The best way to care and preserve our *sāñcīpat* materials is to understand the importance and nature of it and revival of the *sāñcīpat* making techniques. The following interviews with the inhabitants of Majuli as mentioned above might throw some light on this vital aspect.

How the Sāñcīpat Makers of Majuli can Revive the Craft

Summary of Responses

- Setting up of schools or training centres at the *satras* to educate young generation regarding the rich value of *sāñcīpat* and techniques of manufacture
- Plantation of abundant *sāñcī* trees for easy availability
- A perennial source of fund is needed to run such ambitious programmes

Analysis of Responses

My observation suggests that ignorance about *sāñcīpat* as well as its production techniques may be treated as one of the main constraints of the present generation. Efforts have to be made to make the people aware of their culture, so that the present generation can come forward to revive the forgotten tradition of *sāñcīpat* making. To strengthen my point I would like to state the result of the simple bibliographic survey conducted by me recently on the topic "Literature on Traditional Manuscripts in Barak Valley of Assam since 1906," in three districts of Assam, namely Hailakandi, Cachar and Karimganj in southern Assam. I started bibliographic search from the year of 1906, as it is believed that consciousness of manuscripts in this valley started with the establishment of Silchar Normal School in 1906, where few scholars of this region started collecting *sāñcīpat* manuscripts to make Silchar Normal School a repository-cum-research centre of the same. The search of literature of 98 years (from 1906 to 2004) reveals an astonishing fact as tabulated below:

No. of Articles on MSS.	*No. of Journals on MSS.*	*No. of Books on MSS.*	*No. of catalogues on MSS in Article form.*	*No. of catalogues on MSS in Book form.*
16	NIL*	1	2	1

* The journal *Akhar Britta*, vol. 5 (1), 1995 was a special issue on *sāñcīpat* MSS.

The fact observed in the survey indicate that the study of manuscripts or the research activities related to the traditional manuscripts are as low as negligible. The situation in other parts of Assam seems to be no better. It only indicates the poor knowledge level and lack of popularity of traditional manuscripts amongst the present generation.

Another observation is that the syllabus of the degree honours course of Assamese literature and Bengali literature offered respectively by Gauhati University and Assam University has a paper on ancient literature. As already stated, from seventh century CE to nineteenth century CE, these 1200 years of Assamese literature and tenth century CE to eighteenth century, these 800 years of Bengali literature are totally based on manuscripts. The paper on ancient literature in the degree course of the above-mentioned universities encompasses manuscript-based literature of the above periods. But it is really surprising to know that the honours students of the said paper are not acquainted with *sāñcīpat* manuscripts though they are studying manuscripts-based literature in that paper. Maximum numbers of students do not even know how *sāñcīpat* looks like! This is because there is no live demonstrations of *sāñcīpat* manuscripts in the classroom. As a result, students of literature remain ignorant and do not understand the value and importance of manuscripts and the origin of their own literature. So I would like to suggest:

- As educational institutions are the most effective organization in inculcating values among students, class room demonstration of *sāñcīpat* manuscripts, their making process, script and languages used in *sāñcīpat* may work wonders to the students of honours class of various fields, such as, literature, language, history, museology and tourism study. At least 15 marks relating to "various types of manuscripts" will surely enhance their knowledge on manuscripts interest in further research and study on the topic

- Department of culture should come forward with incentives/rewards/citation for outstanding research work in this dying art form
- Training centres or schools can be established in all 665 *satras* to train new generation on *sāñcīpat* making techniques and a collaborative tie-up of these centres with colleges and universities may yield better result in bringing consciousness and knowledge development
- A project on plantation of *sāñcī* or *agaru* tree or aloes wood (*Aquilaria agallocha*) can be initiated in all 665 Satras to become self dependent on *sāñcī* bark. Plantation of *sāñcī* tree also has environmental advantages which might prevent recurring erosion and flood at a place like Majuli
- Covering all the above aspects, the Department of Culture and Tourism may initiate a project at Majuli to train people on *sāñcīpat* making techniques along with other indigenously produced writing materials, so that the process of *sāñcīpat* making may be revived. In the training along with *sāñcīpat* making techniques, writing techniques of Assamese scripts on *sāñcīpat* may also be taught. The National Mission for Manuscripts, independently or in collaboration with UGC, may initiate a crash course on Assamese and other scripts written on *sāñcīpat*
- Such a kind of project is possible only when a perennial source of fund is available to the *satras*; as a model project, N.M.M. may come forward for initial funding, at least for initial few years
- The project should include not only making of *sāñcīpat*, but should also incorporate new ideas on *sāñcīpat*, other non-traditional market-viable products such as

greeting cards for all seasons and occasions, paintings on *sāñcīpat* using traditional colours, etc.

Improvement in the Quality of Life at Majuli Due to Revival of the Sāñcīpat Traditions

The summary of the responses received is as follows:

- *Sāñcīpat*, would be the media to spread Assamese *saṁskṛti* all over the world
- The efforts of Mahāpuruṣa Śrī Śrī Śaṅkaradeva and Śrī Śrī Mādhavadeva, undertaken 500 years ago, will yield result, as the world will come to know about them, their activities, literature, *satras* and of course about the Vaisnavite movement
- It may be a means of employment generation in the locality
- Economical benefit to the *satras* and to the business community, as well as various products of *sāñcīpat* origin and raw materials needed for *sāñcīpat* making may ultimately turn into a big market

Analysis of Responses

The revival of the old techniques of making *Sāñcīpat* may have enormous influence on the socio-economic conditions of Assam. Assam will not only be known as literally and culturally developed state, but soon would also be able to penetrate the national and international market with its eco-friendly natural products. The *satras* may soon turn up into financially self-dependent organizations the socio-economic condition of the inhabitants in and around *satras* may rapidly change:

- One big advantage the *satras* have today is the typical mindset of much of the religious Assamese people.

The bulk of the Assamese people are religious in nature and they still do not prefer to perform their rituals with printed books. Religious books or books on rituals and rites of machine made paper are not allowed in many families even today. *Satras* can take advantage of this situation by producing literature on rites and rituals on *sāñcīpat* and let these out for marketing with the same respect and sanctity

- Many scholars and researcher want original works of Śaṅkaradeva and Mādhavadeva for their study and research purpose. *Satras* can develop multiple copies of such original works of Mahāpuruṣa on newly-made *sāñcīpat*
- Universities and colleges can use these newly-made *sāñcīpat* copies of original works for demonstration and research purpose
- They can be sold as children books with figures and portraits
- Traditional paintings using natural colours *haṅgul/haital* can be developed for marketing
- Entrepreneurship may grow with the revival of *sāñcīpat* techniques. Production of greeting card using *sāñcīpat* with natural or combination of natural and artificial colours with traditional style of scripts may even have potential to penetrate into the billion dollar international market of greeting cards. The advantage of *sāñcīpat* origin greeting cards will be its natural look; eco-friendly, bio-degradable and everlasting quality — say 500 years! If properly channellized, the revival of *sāñcīpat* making techniques may have the potential to revive the socio-economic condition of Assam

Conclusion

The discussion cited above aims to receive attention from the scholars and those engaged in national duties in preservation and conservation of traditional manuscripts. Majuli being the epicentre of cultural heritage of Assam has the potential to survive on its own without much interference. Revival of *sāñcīpat* making techniques may bring new dimension into its life, socially and economically as well, which will ultimately help to preserve its rich cultural heritage.

References

Bhattacharjee, Pulin Bihari, "Silchar Normal School Rakhita Prachin Pothīr Tālikā" (A Bibliography of Ancient Manuscripts Preserved in Silchar Normal School), in *Smaranika*, 6th Conference of Cachar-Banga Sahitya and Sanskrit Sanmilan, Silchar, 1984, pp. 50-59.

Bhuyan, S.K., *A History of Assam 1681-1826* CE, Delhi: D.K.F. Trust, 1933, p. 262.

———, *Anglo Assamese Relations 1771-1826*, Guwahati: Lawyer's Book Stall, 1949, p. 641.

Das, Utpal, "An Orientation to the Importance of Preserving of Historical Materials of Assam," Seminar Paper on Social Role of Media and Building up of a National Information Resources Centre-cum-Archives for the North-East, Media Trust, Guwahati and RRRLF, Kolkata, 21-22 September 2004.

Gait, Edward, *A History of Assam*, Guwahati: LBS Publications, 1950, p. 390.

Goswami, Hemchandra, *Descriptive Catalogue of Assamese Manuscripts*, Calcutta: University of Calcutta, 1930, p. 274.

Hunter, W.W., *A Statistical Account of Assam*, vol. II, London: Trubner & Co, 1879, p. 490.

7

Scientific Analysis of Traditional Indigenous Methods of Manuscript Preservation

SUDHENDU MANDAL and SANJAY KUMAR MAITI

Abstract

From ancient times, India and her neighbouring countries have been a rich reservoir of varied forms of manuscripts. The diversity of the manuscript wealth of India is mainly governed by their geographical availability, cultural influence and religious background. In India, the basic ingredients of manuscripts were derived from nature and were mostly of plant origin. An in-depth study of the science of Manuscriptology will reveal the remarkable ingenuity and outstanding sense of preservation of our intellectual ancestors from the moment of manuscript preparation up to their storage. The present paper makes an investigative approach into the traditional Indian manuscript preservation techniques as practised in National Library, Kolkata and has analysed the effectiveness of the ancient trends in the light of modern science and their applicability in the present-day modern preservation systems.

Introduction

SINCE time immemorial man has succeeded in leaving behind the records of his activities for future generations. The manuscripts are the hand-written records of man, which served as the vehicle of intellectual thoughts and ideas reflecting the knowledge and wisdom of our ancestors. Ancient rare manuscripts are a priceless treasure for any country to possess, and they are one of the most accurate sources to trace the cultural legacy of a nation. India and her neighbouring countries, from very ancient times, are the richest reservoir of varied forms of manuscripts. The literary heritage of India is very old and the various types of ancient manuscripts of our country serve a pivotal role in fostering the great literary heritage and religious culture of our country.

Diversity of Writing Materials in India

The great majority of the manuscripts collections, which constitute our precious national heritage on the Indological and oriental literatures are scattered in the temples, monasteries, Jain *granthabhāṇḍāras*, libraries, archives and even under the possession of individual private collectors. The diversity of writing materials is mainly governed by their geographical availability, stage of technological development, cultural influence and religious background.[1] India, from the very beginning was rich in her natural resources and the basic ingredients of the manuscripts were mostly derived from nature and were predominantly of plant origin.

In India as well as in the countries of South-East Asia which were enlightened by India's cultural influence, the bulk of manuscripts were produced on palm leaves before the advent of paper. Writing was made by incising and subsequent inking with lampblack on the leaves of thicker and shorter length of palmyra palm (*Borassus flabellifer Linn. Fam. Palmae*), as was the prevalent traditions of Orissa and south India, or it was written with ink on the thin, flexible, delicate, longer leaf of talipot palm (*Corypha umbraculifera Linn. Fam. Palmae*) available mostly in western India and Bengal. Studies indicate that flexible talipot leaves have greater durability then leaves of palmyra palm. The Palm-leaf has a long tradition of use up to thirteenth century and later in various parts of India, whereas in south India this tradition prevailed up to nineteenth century having a lasting decisive influence. This governed the shape of the Indian manuscripts in "*punthi* format," which became the norm for most of the Indian manuscripts. Besides Palm-leaf, two types of important bark manuscripts flourished: (i) the inner bark of the Himalayan birch or *bhūrja-patra* (*Betula utilis Linn. Fam. Betulacease*) which were abundant in Kashmir and north-western Himalayas mostly between the eleventh and sixteenth century. In the north-eastern states, especially in Assam, *sāñcīpat* or aloes (*agaru*) bark (*Aquilaria agallocha Roxb. Fam. Thymeleaceas*) manuscripts, better termed as *ahom punthis* were used from the sixth century.[4] The birch bark is glossy reddish white in appearance with knot streaks, multilayered and joined by nature gum. While aloes bark is much tougher than birch bark, it has a thin, fibrous and even textured surface. With the introduction of paper following the Muslim conquest in India and subsequent manufacture, supply and use of indigenous papers from rags (tulot paper), hemp fibres, etc. since thirteenth century onwards there was a gradual decline in the existing manuscript tradition and a gradual switch-over to the paper-based manuscripts in *punthi* format. Besides these, manuscripts on cotton cloth containing charts, multi-coloured texts are also countered[14] in western Indian libraries.[5] Thus, the learned tradition of India was mostly preserved in the medium of Palm-leaf, birch bark, *sāñcīpat*, cotton cloth and indigenous paper-based manuscripts. However, various other writing materials like copper-plates for legal transactions were used elsewhere for durability and black cotton cloth (*koditam*) impregnated with tamarind seed extracts were used for keeping accounts in Karnataka of south India.

Preservation Strategies Adopted in Earlier Days

The art of preservation is as old as human civilization itself. Our forefathers had judiciously selected the basic materials for writing from nature and were quite aware of the unsuitability of these organic materials in Indian tropical climate. Hence, they resorted to various means of processing, which they adopted through their time-tested experience, with great ingenuity for making those materials suitable for writing and imparting durability to them against various deteriorating agencies. Most of our traditional knowledge and experience were lost with passage of time, while some literary evidence gives us scope of rediscovering our valuable traditional experience.

Diversity in Processing Techniques as a Primary Step in Preservation

The preparation and processing of the writing materials often involved elaborate, laborious process requiring much time and patience. The processing techniques were of diverse types varying from place to place. In various parts of India particularly in Orissa, the flexibility of the palm leaves through seasoning was achieved by a number of ways like sun drying, burying in mud, sometimes exposure to kitchen smoke, drying in grain stores under paddy heaps or by boiling in hot water and subsequent application of turmeric (*Curcuma longa Linn.*) paste.[6,7,8] Sometimes, the leaves were buried in damp sand followed by treatment with turmeric solution in sour boiled rice and finally polishing the leaves with a smooth stone or conch shell.[9] The south Indian tradition was the application of gingili oil or *til tel* (*Seasamum indicum*) over the shade-dried leaves for flexibility[2] besides other special types of processing. Curcumin, the chief constituent of turmeric imparted the colour to the manuscripts and the essential oil of turmeric is supposed to have insect-repellent properties. The birch bark sheets were made durable by moderate degree of processing. This was done by smearing it with oil and then polishing, so as to make it fit for writing.[2] The birch bark has been reported to be insect-resistant by its very nature, probably due to the presence of essential oils and methyl salicylate as a constituent.[17] The aloes bark is aromatic in nature and is reported to be seasoned by alkaline treatment of the peeled bark with subsequent application of protective "*matimah* paste" (*Phaseolus radiate*). The bark was made insect-resistant by dyeing with orpiment (yellow arsenic sulphide; As_2S_3) and also by treatment in sulphur fumes. The indigenous paper-based manuscripts were generally of rough surface texture sized with yellow arsenic and an emulsion of tamarind seeds (*Tamarindus indica*) acting as a smoothening agent. The universal custom of applying orpiment was not only for colouring the manuscripts but also for protecting them from insect attack. Manuscripts were also made of rag-based white Kashmiri papers. Paper documents made from rag and hemp fibres sized with rice gruel without orpiment were susceptible to insect attack. The cotton cloth manuscripts were generally prepared by impregnation with rice or wheat starch paste and polishing them with stone.[5]

Use of Durable Inks in Writing

As writing ink being the prime requirement for intellectual activities, the preparation of writing ink was done carefully with an eye towards preservation. The traditional methods of preparing ink were always aimed at preparation of durable quality ink. Various formations of ink were reported in several literature[6,7,9,10] for writing on various types of manuscripts. For writing on the talipot palm leaves, ink was prepared from lampblack obtained from the soot of *kesadura* plant (*Verbesina scandens*) or seasamum oil and sometimes adding various other materials and vegetable gums. The ink for the birch bark manuscripts was generally prepared by boiling the almond shell charcoal with cow's urine[5] (*Urina bovis*) and for *sāñcīpat* manuscripts by distillation of fruit of *silikha* (*Terminalia chebula*) with bull's urine.[14] Such inks were of indelible nature, still retaining their glaze. The ink for the paper manuscripts were prepared by mixing lampblack with coffee-coloured infusion of roasted rice, sugar, *kesadura* juice and acacia gum for extra gloss.[10] All these indicate how the ancient writers thought about the techniques of preserving their ideas for centuries to come.

Preventive Binding and Storage

In ancient times, our intellectual ancestors realized the utility of recovering the manuscripts from external damage. The manuscript leaves were protected by keeping them in between two seasoned wooden boards generally of *śāl* (*Shorea Robusta*), *segun* (*Tectona Grandis*), jackfruit (*Artocarpus Integrifolia*), *neem* (*Azadirachta Indica*),[11, 12] etc. or other forms of covers acting as guards and tied up with cotton thread round the whole bundles. The finished pile of palm leaves were normally strung on a cord through pre-bored holes. This practise helped to retain the manuscripts in position. The seasoned woods never changed their shape. Sometimes the inner textual portions were protected from insects and external damage by a few blank leaves placed over the first and below the last folio of the manuscript. Sometimes thicker barks were used as covers for sāñcīpat manuscripts.[4]

As sunlight and dust had devastating effects on the well-being of collections, stringent protective storage measures

Fig. [illegible]1: Tamarindus Indica

Fig. 7.2: Terminalia Chebula

were adopted to protect the manuscripts. The most conventional practice which remained unchanged for centuries was wrapping the manuscripts in red, yellow and sometimes in white cotton cloth and occasionally in silk cloth.[12] The practice of wrapping the manuscripts in cloth controlled air circulation, protected the manuscripts from dust and humidity and prolonged their life by excluding the UV fractions of light. Silk has been reported to be immune to worms and red is believed to be an auspicious as well as a repelling colour for the insects.[12] The yellow cloth covers in turmeric preparations were also used for the same reason.

It was a common practice in the ancient Indian temples and monastic libraries to store the manuscripts in pigeon-hole type wooden cupboards. Particularly in the Jain *grantha-bhāṇḍāras*, the manuscripts were preserved in insect-repellent enclosures to give the documents the first line of defence against the threats from the external deteriorating agents. It also produced a suitable microclimate around the documents to check fluctuations of temperature and humidity.[14,15]

Care in Handling and Housekeeping of Manuscripts

The manuscripts were carefully handled and placed on the beautifully decorated wooden book cradles or book supports to minimize wear and tear at the time of reading. They were treated with high esteem, sometimes placed near the household deities and often prayers were made to them.[7] Periodically sun-drying of manuscripts in the month of Bhādrapada, i.e. in August, helped in retarding the mildew caused due to dampness.[-6] Some other practices like dusting, cleaning and air drying of manuscripts periodically or on special occasions like *Vijayadaśamī* or *Sarasvatī Pūjā*,[6] practice of exposing the documents in kitchen smoke[,16] or on raised bamboo platforms to eradicate the white ants were also reported. All these practices are supposed to be effective measures against insect attack.

Traditional Insect Control Measures

Plants are "nature's chemical factories," providing a wide range of phytochemicals mostly aromatic essential oils, alkaloids, resins, etc. Our ancestors had discovered and utilized such plants having insect-control properties. It was the common ancient practice of keeping dried aromatic/bitter plant parts of *ghodā bac, neem, nisinda, aśvagandhā*, black cumin seeds, camphor, etc. in cloth sachets near the manuscripts or in between the manuscript bundles and storing them in the boxes made of repellent woods like *neem*, sandalwood, camphor, agarwood, etc. thereby ensuring a constant repellent environment around the manuscripts.[2, 13, 13] Sometimes, the treatment with aromatic oils of repellent plants like lemongrass, turmeric (used as paste), and camphor, etc. for imparting flexibility to the manuscripts also made them insect-resistant. The insect-repellent plant materials commonly employed for manuscript preservation along with their important constituents are presented herewith.[17, 23]

Various other materials derived from plants and animal sources like tobacco leaves, *pandri* grass, black pepper, clove, cinnamon bark, peacock feather, etc. were applied in various ways to check the menace of insects [2, 11, 12, 24]

Traditional Building Design

To adapt to harsh climatic conditions, the buildings were specially designed to provide passive climatic control and thereby maintain a natural air-conditioned environment. Sometimes, the library buildings were made on high grounds to check natural disasters. The repositories were built in the

Table: Plant Materials used for Control of Insects

S.No.	Name of the Plants & their families	Parts used	Important Constituents
1.	*Neem* (*Azadirachta A. Juss: Fam. Meliaceae*)	Leaves/woods	Bitter limonoid compounds like Azadirachtin, Nimbin, Nimbidin, Salnnin
2.	*Ghoḍā vaca* (*Acorus calamus L. Fam. Araceae*)	Rhizome	b-Asarone, Calamene, Calamenol, Methylisoeugenol
3.	Camphor (*Cinnamomum camphora* (L.) *J.S. Presl; Fam. Lauraceae*)	Resins/Woods	(+)- α-Pinene, bisalboline, Cineol, Terpineol, Caryophyllene
4.	*Aśvagandhā* (*Withania Somnifera Dun; Fam. Solanaceae*)	Roots/Leaves	Bitter alkaloids Withanine, Somniferine, Withananine.
5.	Black Cumin (*Nigella sativa L: Fam. Ranunculaceae*)	Seeds	Toxic glycoside Melanthin.
6.	*Nisinda* (*Virex negundo L; Fam. Verbanaceae*)	Leaves	Alkaloids
7.	Sandalwood (*Santalum album L: Fam. Santalaceae*)	Heartwood	a-and ß- Santalols (sesquiterpene-alcohols), Santalal, Satalone, Santene.
8.	Agarwood (*Aquilaria agsllocha Roxb.: Fam. Thymelaeae*)	Bark/Woods	Agarol
9.	Lemon grass (*Cymbopogon flexusus Nees Sleud.* (*wats*); *Fam. Gramineae.*)	Oil	Citral
10.	Indian Wormwood (*Artemisia absinthium L.: Fam. Compositae*)	Woods	a-and ß-Thujone Phellandrene
11.	*Haldī* (*Curcum L.: Fam. Zingiberaceae*)	Rhizomes	Curcumin (colouring matter), α-Phellandrene, Termerones, Zingiberine

interior part of the temples and monasteries in such a way that the thermal and hygroscopic properties of the buildings and their contents were favourable for maintaining good stable indoor climate and for protection against sunlight and storms.[11] Sometimes, the manuscripts were protected in the underground rooms attached with the temples.[5]

Preventive Disinfection of Environment

Our forefathers had the deepest sense of air purification which may have a relation with manuscript preservation. The burning of incense and aromatic plants like *deodār*, sandalwood, agarwood and their products, exudations of Indian frankincense or *guggul* and like materials were the essential parts of worship and religious ceremonies in Indian temples, monasteries, etc. where the libraries were mostly attached with. These materials not only maintained religious sanctity, but are also supposed to disinfect the environment.[25]

Effectiveness and Applicability of the Traditional Methods

From the foregoing discussions it is quite obvious that the traditional means of preservation are a wide spectrum of preventive preservation techniques against various agencies that threaten the collections. A few traditional practices seem contradictory to the modern preservation ethics like sun drying of documents,[9,6] using acidic turmeric paste,[26] possible contamination and migration of resinous products from wooden covers to the manuscript leaves,[13] damage of manuscripts by the binding cords, etc. Apart from these contradictions, the traditional practices provide a number of compatible, environmentally sound, non-hazardous, cost-effective and time-tested means that can be effectively employed in the Integrated Pest Management of underdeveloped libraries scattered everywhere in our country, which are lacking in funds and infrastructure. Such organizations may benefit by adopting the easily accessible and practical traditional method of preservation. The National Library of India has a sizeable collection of various types of manuscripts which have been well-preserved by employing a few of our traditional preservation means along with modern methods with success.

Conclusion

The world of document preservation is gradually becoming more and more technology-oriented. We have been gradually shifting from our inherited natural methods to the world of synthetic chemicals by deploying more and more funds, infrastructure, etc. The problem of manuscript preservation, however, still persists. It is, therefore, high time to think of the problems underlying the present preservation trends very seriously. Our traditional preservation methods may be the alternative means to safeguard our heritage for posterity and their application should be encouraged.

Notes

1. Albertine Gaur, *Writing Materials of the East*, The British Library, 1979.
2. O.P. Agarwal, *Conservation of Manuscripts and Paintings of South-East Asia*, London: Butterworth, 1984.
3. Jane. Turner, ed., *The Dictionary of Art*, vol. 15, London: Macmillan, 1996.
4. R. Dasgupta, *Eastern Indian Manuscript Paining*, Bombay: Taraporevala & Sons, 1984.
5. Kastoor Chand Kasliwal, *Jaina Grantha Bhandars in Rajasthan*, Jaipur, 1967.

6. B.K. Padhi, "Preservation of Palm-leaf Manuscripts in Orissa," *Conservation of Cultural Property in India*, 1974, 7, 61-65.

7. J.P. Das, *Chitra-pothi: Illustrated Palm-leaf Manuscripts of Orissa*, New Delhi: Arnold-Heinemann, 1985.

8. Subhas Pani, *Illustrated Palm-leaf Manuscripts of Orissa: A Selection from the Orissa State Museum*, Orissa State Museum, 1984.

9. M.M. Cakravartti, "Notes on the Language and Literature of Orissa," *Journal of the Asiatic Society of Bengal*, LXVI (1-4) (1987): 317-48

10. B. Mukhopadhyaya, *Administration of Manuscript Libraries with Reference to Sanskrit*, Sanskrit College Res. Ser. CXXVII, Calcutta.

11. B.K. Datta, *Libraries & Librarianship of Ancient and Medieval India*, New Delhi: Atma Ram & Sons, 1970, p 248.

12. O.P. Agrawal, "Appropriate Indian Technology for the Conservation of Museum Collections," *Appropriate Technologies in the Conservation of Cultural Property*, 1981.

13. Y.P. Kathapalia, *Conservation and Restoration of Archive Materials*, UNESCO, Paris, 1973.

14. P. Coremans, "Climate and microclimate," *Conservation of Cultural Property with Special Reference to Tropical Conditions*, UNESCO, Paris, 1973, 27-40.

15. J. Hanus, et al., "Influence of Boxing Materials on the Properties of Different Paper Items Stored Inside," *Restaurator* 16(4), (1995): 194-208.

16. K.V. Sarma, "In Quest of Early Manuscripts/Collections Dealing with Science & Technology in India," *Indian Journal of History of Science*, 32(2), (1997): 161-72.

17. C.K. Atal and B.M. Kapur, ed., *Cultivation and Utilisation of Aromatic Plants*, RRL, Council of Scientific and Industrial Research, Jammu, 1982, 815.

18. *The Wealth of India, (11 Vols): Raw Materials*, Council of Scientific and Industrial Research, New Delhi, 1984-1976.

19. R.N. Chopra, R.L. Badhwar and S. Ghosh, *Poisonous Plants of India*, second edn., ed. U.N. Dhar, Calcutta, 1965.

20. R.N. Chopra, S.L. Nayar and I.C. Chopra, *Glossary of Indian Medicinal Plants and its Supplements*, Council of Scientific and Industrial Research, New Delhi, 1956.

21. M.S. Swaminathan, S.L. Nayar and I.C. Chopra, *Plants and Society*, London: Macmillan, 1989.

22. National Research Council, *Neem: A Tree for Solving Global Problems*, Washington DC: National Academy Press, 1992.

23. B.S. Parmar and C. Devakumar, *Botanicals and Biopesticides*, New Delhi: Westvill Publishing House, 1993.

24. W.J. Plumbe, "Preservation of Library Materials in Tropical Countries," *Libraries Trends*, 8(2), (1959): 291-306.

25. Frances Kennet, *History of Perfume*, London: Harrap, 1975.

26. D.J. Lee, L. Bacon and V. Daniels, "Some Conservation Problems Encountered with Turmeric on Ethnographic Objects," *Studies in Conservation*, 30(4), (1985): 184-88.

8

The Use of Turmeric in the Preservation of Manuscripts

S. SUBBARAMAN

Abstract

There is a long tradition in India of the use of turmeric as a prophylactic. It has been proven that it contains antiseptic properties. It is common that turmeric is one of the materials used for seasoning palm leaves and preparing them for writing. Paper too may be treated with turmeric, and owing to its use in the past many old manuscripts have remained free from fungal attack, even under conditions of high humidity. This paper proposes to highlight the distinct properties that make it such an effective preservative material for manuscripts.

Introduction

IN administering and taking medicine for different ailments, it is sometimes found that while the drug serves its main purpose of curing the disease, there are certain undesirable side effects, and therefore, one has to be careful of taking such a drug. Similarly, we have to adopt a cautious approach in the use of chemicals for conservation procedures. The chemicals may in the long run have an adverse effect on the valuable materials subjected to treatment, and they may even prove hazardous to the people handling them. This is the reason why a chemical has to undergo rigorous testing for ascertaining its short- and long-term effects, before it is approved for use in conservation.

The use of natural products in place of chemicals can therefore be proposed. For instance, for the prevention of insect attack on Palm-leaf manuscripts, if a natural product like *neem* leaf or sweet flag is found to be effective, it is better to use it rather than a synthetically produced chemical substance. The natural product is much less likely to have an adverse effect on the Palm-leaf as well as on humans. It is in this context that indigenous techniques of preservation assume importance since these techniques make use of natural products. This paper deals with one such product, turmeric.

What is Turmeric?

Turmeric (Botanical name: *Curcuma longa Linn.*) is a perennial herb of the ginger family (*Zingiberaceae*). It grows to 2-3 ft. in height with a short stem and tufted leaves. The rhizomes, which are short and thick, constitute the turmeric of general usage. The plant is a native of South Asia and is grown on a large scale in India and South-East Asian countries.

Curing and Preparation

The rhizomes, which are brownish yellow in colour, consist of a central bulbous portion bearing a number of finger-like lateral offshoots. The bulbous and finger-shaped parts are separated, freed from adhering dirt and fibrous roots and subjected to a process of curing and polishing. The curing involves cooking the rhizomes in boiling water until they become soft. This may take a few hours. The cooked rhizomes are allowed to cool gradually and spread out in the open to dry. The dried rhizomes are polished either by hand-rubbing or rotation in a mounted drum. The length of dried rhizomes may vary from one to three inches in length. Turmeric is usually sold in the market in the form of powder that results from grinding the rhizomes.

Traditional Uses of Turmeric

The use of turmeric dates back nearly 4000 years to the Vedic culture in India where it was used as a culinary spice, medicine and also had some religious significance. Some of the uses of turmeric are:

1. *Culinary Use*: Turmeric is used extensively in the East and Middle-East as a condiment and culinary dye. It is used in curries and curry powders, rice dishes and added to chutneys and pickles.

2. *As a Dye*: It is also used for dyeing wool, silk and unmordanted cotton to which it imparts a yellow shade in an acid bath. It is sometimes used in combination with other natural dyes like indigo and safflower to impart different shades.

3. *As an Indicator*: Turmeric paper is a reagent in the British Pharmacopoeia for testing alkalinity. In the alkaline medium it turns from yellow to reddish brown. It is also used as a test for alkaloids and boric acid.

4. *Medicinal Use*: In Indian systems of medicine, turmeric is used as a stomachic, tonic and blood purifier. Mixed with warm milk, it is said to be beneficial in common cold. The juice of the fresh rhizome is used as an anti-parasitic for many skin ailments. Turmeric paste is applied externally on open wounds as it is said to have antiseptic properties. *Curcumin* in turmeric has been

shown to be active against *Staphlo coccus aureus* (pus-producing infections). It is an antacid and in small doses it acts as a carminative and appetizer.

5. *As a Cosmetic*: In parts of Asia, turmeric water and paste is applied as a cosmetic to lend a golden glow to the complexion. Indians as well as Indonesians apply turmeric on their bodies as part of their wedding ritual.

Uses of Turmeric in the Preservation of Manuscripts

1. In certain regions, particularly in Orissa, turmeric paste is applied on the surface of Palm-leaf when processing and preparing it for writing.
2. In paper manuscripts, every third or fourth folio is sometimes found to be coated with turmeric. We can see examples of such manuscripts in the Saraswathi Mahal Library of Thanjavur, in Tamil Nadu.

Manuscripts so treated are found to be protected from fungal attack.

Chemistry of Turmeric

1. Analysis of Indian turmeric has given the following values:

Moisture	13.1%
Protein	6.3%
Fat	5.1%
Mineral matter	3.5%
Fibre	2.6%
Carbohydrates	69.4%

Carotene 50.0 I.U./100g.

(Calculated as Vitamin A)

2. Steam distillation of the dry rhizomes yields 5-8 per cent of an essential oil, with a density of 0.929 and refractive index of 1.5054. It consists mainly of *Turmerone*, a *Sesquiterpene* (58 per cent). The other major constituent is *Zingiberene* (25 per cent), another *Sesquiterpene* found in ginger. Smaller quantities of *d-phellandrene* (1 per cent), *d-sabinene* (0.6 per cent) *Cineol* (1 per cent) and *borneol* (0.5 per cent) have also been identified.

3. A *ketone* and an alcohol identified as *p-tolymethyl carbinol*, have been obtained from the volatile distillate.

4. A crystalline colouring matter, *Curcumin* (0.6 per cent), with melting point 180-183 degrees celsius, is obtained from turmeric. This has been identified as *Diferuloyl methane* and it dissolves in concentrated Sulphuric Acid giving yellow colouration.

Concluding Remarks

The phenolic character of curcumin probably accounts for its germicidal property, and therefore its usefulness as a preservative for Palm-leaf and paper manuscripts includes its ability to inhibit fungal growth. The essential oils in turmeric, consisting of *Turmerone* and *Zingiberene*, which are of the Terpenoid group, also contribute to its preservative properties. While its yellow colouration may render it unsuitable for general use as a preservative, turmeric certainly has some specific applications in the preservation of manuscripts in a very effective manner.

Interventions

Vipul Shah: How do we know that the natural product is up to the standard?

Dr. Subbaraman: The chemical constituents will have to be ascertained first to verify if the material is up to the standards.

Ratna Basu: Cupboards or cases can be washed with turmeric water or a paste can be applied too. The wrappers can be washed in turmeric water too. We are employing this practice and getting good results.

A.S. Bisht: Over the years the use of turmeric has been propagated. Even today, we are only mentioning the fact that the material can be used. What about the process and the method of introduction of the material? That must be given thought to also at the same time

S. Bapat: Is turmeric paste acidic?

A.S. Bisht: Why get scared of acidity. It is the scale that is important. Some acidity may even help to preserve paper. Turmeric solution in water has been used in the past

9

Traditional Methods of Conservation of Paper Manuscripts
As Gleaned from Two Persian Texts

IMTIAZ AHMAD

Abstract

Our forefathers devised simple ways and means to ensure the preservation of manuscripts. Some of these methods are now broadly referred as "conventional" methods and are still in use. In this connection, one particular text is of immense value and interest. It deals with the tools and techniques of penmanship and describes the different types of papers, ink, and pen used for writing of manuscripts and also the method involved in their preservation. It is in this context that the quality of the different types of papers and ink involved in the preservation of the written texts is highlighted. It also spells out the conditions in which books should be kept to ensure that they remain safe from insects and also the vagaries of nature. The aforesaid information may enable us to unravel some of the secrets of preservative methods and techniques used in the seventeenth and eighteenth century which are cheaper and convenient. The treatment of existing manuscripts with the materials mentioned in the book may help in improving their longevity and endurance.

Introduction

Manuscripts constitute the intellectual and academic heritage of any country or society. They preserve the traditional wisdom and learning of yore. India, with its hoary and glorious past is perhaps the largest repository of such manuscripts in a number of languages, written on a variety of materials, such as Palm-leaf, birch, cloth, leather and paper. Paper manuscripts, in India, have a direct relation with the medieval period. The Turks brought the use of paper as a writing-material to India in the thirteenth century. Thereafter, Persian and Arabic texts, written by hand on paper, in an increasingly large number and variety came to be composed. Most of these texts related to history, religion, philosophy, literature, sciences and other branches of learning. Invariably, these were richly decorated and illuminated. The tradition continued with vigour till about the close of the eighteenth century. The coming of the printing press ushered in a totally different situation. However, the manuscripts for their calligraphic beauty and the ornamental decorative techniques, as well as their basic subject-content, still enjoy great importance not only among scholars and connoisseurs but also among the general people.

Two Persian Texts

Referring back to the developments in the thirteenth century, one may say that the period heralded a sort of revolution in North India. Together with the writing of books on paper, there also developed the varied ancillary arts of decoration, illumination, binding and gilding of books. This, in turn, gave rise to crafts such as manufacture of paper, ink, making of pens, use of natural dyes and their extraction, manufacture of gum and resin, making of leather-sheets for the purpose of book-binding, etc. Many such techniques, and the experiments made in that connection have been recorded by perceptive observers. Consequently, we have had some interesting Persian texts that deal with the details of such crafts and techniques. At the same time, they also shed valuable light on the materials used for conservation and preservation. The present paper draws attention to two such Persian texts, the *Bayāḏ-e Khuśbuī*[1] and the *Tuḥfat al-Wurūd*.[2] Though not exclusively devoted to the techniques of conservation, both devote a major portion of their contents to the tools and techniques of penmanship. In that context, they also provide sporadic but useful information on the ways and methods of ensuring a long life for the manuscripts; in other words, their preservation and conservation.

Bayāḏ-e Khuśbuī

The *Bayāḏ-e Khuśbuī* was written earlier and is larger in content than the *Tuḥfat al-Wurūd*. It was written in the seventeenth century and it deals mainly with the household/establishment of the nobles. In the eight chapter of the Manuscript, the Chancery or Department of Writing is mentioned. There is a detailed description of the manufacture of paper, its colouring, decoration, the use of various ingredients, etc. The text is yet to be edited and published.

Tuḥfat al-Wurūd

The *Tuḥfat al-Wurūd* is a relatively later work, though it too was written in the seventeenth century. The author 'Abd al Mun'im was a professional calligraphist who shared his experiences of making pens and ink used in writing. The

---

1. *Bayāḏ-e Khuśbuī*, unpublished text, Aligarh Muslim University (AMU) microfilm.

2. *Tuḥfat al-Wurūd*, unpublished text, personal copy.

description given by him of the techniques and ingredients of making ink which does not easily fade out nor washes out with water and also the information given by him about the different types of inkpots and the effect they have on the storage of ink make interesting reading. Unfortunately, this text is also yet to be edited and published. But, significantly, the ingredients and techniques mentioned in both texts are purely indigenous. This makes the two texts particularly important for our purpose.

Relevance to Preservation

It is a well-known fact that the ravages of time, natural factors, human neglect — or more seriously, mishandling — have taken a considerable toll and many manuscripts face the challenge of deterioration, mutilation or even extinction. It is our responsibility to see that these problems are overcome and the wisdom of the past that has survived till the present is preserved for posterity. The National Mission for Manuscripts is seriously engaged in this most daunting task. However, the challenges and the determination are not new. Our forefathers too devised ways and means to ensure the preservation of manuscripts. Many of the simple — often crude by modern standards — methods adopted by them were, nevertheless helpful in fulfilling the desired objective. These methods are now broadly referred to as "conventional" or "traditional" methods and some of these are still in use. Our experiences in this venture have made us realise the efficacy of some of these methods and also the need to perpetuate the same.

In this connection, the aforesaid texts are of immense value and interest. They deal with the tools and techniques of penmanship and describe the different types of papers, ink and pen used for writing manuscripts and also the method for preparing these and the ingredients used in the process. They shed valuable light on the qualities of different types of papers and ink which helped in the preservation of the written texts. They also spell out, in some instances, the conditions in which books should be kept to ensure that they remain safe from insects and also the vagaries of nature. They are useful because they present before us an idea of the in-built mechanism for preservation of manuscripts. The use of special care in making of paper and ink and its storage so that it contributes to the perpetuation of the life of the manuscript makes interesting reading. Some of the techniques and ingredients mentioned in these texts may provide new opportunities and possibilities in the work of conservation and restoration of damaged manuscripts. Moreover, they also enable us to have a better appreciation of the care and concern shown by the bygone generations for preservation of the written word. They also offer a possibility of comparing the existing traditional methods and techniques with the past background outlined in these texts.

Conservation Related Observations in the Persian Texts

The present paper deals with the contents of the above-mentioned texts and explores the possibility of the use of similar techniques which are cheaper and convenient. The treatment of existing manuscripts with the materials mentioned in these texts may help in improving their longevity and endurance.

We may now take a more detailed look at the contents of the two texts. A beginning may be made with the *Bayāḏ-e Khuśbuī*. As mentioned earlier, the eighth chapter of the book deals with the techniques and ingredients of the manufacture of paper. Some of the ingredients used for colouring the paper include saffron, lemon oil, pomegranate-oil, cinnamon, apple-peels, *sabza* (possibly grass) and salt.[3] There is also a passing reference to the fact that these ingredients give the paper better lustre, enable a more accurate drawing of designs and floral patterns for decoration and ensure their longevity. Unfortunately, the exact manner in which this works has not been discussed at length. This lacuna does, in a way, affect the utility of the information but it also invites attention to the possibility of exploring the possible use of these ingredients and techniques for the purpose of conservation of manuscripts.

The account in the *Tuḥfat al-Wurūd* is somewhat more detailed. It focuses mainly on the making of pen and ink and the proper storage of ink. It comments upon various types of inkpots and the impact they have on the quality of the ink. To quote some of these observations:

> . . . the ink turns white in an inkpot made of stone and its blackness is wasted [*sic*]. Similarly in coloured inkpots the ink turns white and camphor-like. If you write with such ink the brightness of the script is lost. Similarly in the inkpots made of white glass black-ink loses its colour and shine. In the case of wooden inkpots, the ink tends to dry and the flow of writing is obstructed. . . . Inkpots made of porcelain or copper are far better. For one thing, they do not absorb much ink. Even if the ink gets dried you can lighten it by mixing a small quantity of water. More importantly, ink kept in such inkpots does not lose its glaze or lustre easily.[4]

The technique for making ink makes interesting reading[5] even though the process by itself appears quite cumbersome. It is

3. *Bayāḏ*, op. cit., 236 ff.
4. *Tuḥfat*, op. cit., f. 24 ff.
5. Ibid., f. 36 ff.

advised that one should take a small, clean piece of unstarched white-cloth, dip it three times in indigo-leaf extract and dry it in shade. He should then make a wick of it and burn it in a glazed lamp (so that the oil may not be absorbed by it), fill it with mustard oil and burn the wick in the lamp in a cool and shaded place where the breeze is not very strong. The lamp should be covered by a hemispherical mud-cover. The soot should be allowed to settle on the inner side of the cover. It should then be collected and tied up in a white-cloth. It should be dipped in wine and kept inside a paste made of gram-flour. After a short while, it should be placed, for about two hours, under the ashes of an extinguished bonfire, preferably during the night. It should be allowed to cool for sometime. The covering of gram-flour and cloth should then be removed and the paste carefully dissolved in water. The quantity of water may be determined as per need. The resin of the Neem-tree should be separately obtained, boiled in water in an iron vessel. It should then be mixed with the ink and the settled particles carefully drained out. A pinch of alum, cinnamon and salt should be separately boiled and the extract mixed with the ink. It should be stored in proper ink-pots. It may be added here that in an earlier context, the author has cited porcelain ink-pots as the best for storage of ink.

Concluding Remarks

The aforesaid information may, perhaps, enable us to unravel some of the secrets of preservative methods and techniques used in the seventeenth and eighteenth centuries. This, in turn, may give us a better perspective on the conventional methods of preservation. This may also enable us to check whether these techniques and ingredients are still in use. As we all know, calligraphy, though a dying art is not yet extinct. Many of the *madrasas* still teach the art. It may be ascertained whether it is possible to employ similar techniques now for making ink and paper, besides pen — the techniques for which have also been discussed in the *Tuḥfat al-Wurūd*, but left out in the present presentation, so as to ensure the endurance of these works. An attempt should also be made to locate other identical texts, especially those that may enable us to unravel the techniques used for making paints and colours that were employed for decoration and illumination of books. One can also perhaps explore the details about preparing the covers used for the books. It is interesting to note that the quality of the leather used in many of these covers is very good and it has endured for several centuries.

More importantly, when it comes to the restoration or retouching of the old, damaged or worn out texts, can these techniques and components be of effective help? Can they contribute not only to the restoration but the future conservation of the written heritage? Possibly, a two-pronged strategy may be adopted in this regard. On the one hand, such texts, and there must be several more besides those mentioned in this brief presentation, should be taken up for a careful study, editing and translation. On the other hand, experimental attempts may be made to employ these methods for our present needs as far as the conservation and repair of old paper-written manuscripts are concerned. The Mission may, perhaps, at a later stage examine these possibilities for it is important not only to preserve the written word but also the tools and techniques of penmanship that produced those records.

Interventions

Shreenand L. Bapat: Is the paper of Samarkand and Bukhārā really better than the Indian paper?

Imtiaz Ahmad: I would say yes. Two things are mentioned in the text, that the Persian paper has longer life and greater endurance. The paper of Central Asian origin survives for a longer period. The texture is suitable for writing well. The *Kitāb al-Haśā'iś* is a manuscript that is more than 1000 years old. It describes 350 medicinal plants and herbs and is replete with coloured sketches with comments on the medicinal qualities of the plants and herbs. Keeping in mind this fact of its age, we observe that even today the ink is firm and colours are intact. This reflects on the quality of the paper too.

Vipul Shah: There is the practice of keeping silk cloth in the ink pot so that the tip of the pen will not break.

Imtiaz Ahmad: Very valid point but it has not been mentioned in these two texts. It is, however, a very good point.

Ratna Basu: In the *Abhilaṣitārtha-cintāmaṇi*, in the Commentaries of the *Kāmasūtra* by Vātsyāyana and in several *Lekhapaddhati*, it is mentioned that when neem-leaf juice is boiled in an iron pot, the proportion should be carefully maintained. If the content of iron is higher, then it will damage the paper. Therefore, do not make the concoction out of proportion or it will char the paper.

Imtiaz Ahmad: Neem juice and other solutions are even mentioned in earlier texts and this goes on to show the continuity in the system till as recent as the seventeenth century.

10

Awareness and Practices of Manuscripts Preservation in Ancient and Medieval India

A Review of Literary Evidence

SHREENAND L. BAPAT

Abstract

The Indian tradition of learning has predominantly been an oral tradition. As writing was popularized, coping and recopying of texts became the most important way of protecting content, and was considered by some modern day scholars as the only way to preserve manuscripts. There have been, however, some reflections on the preservation of manuscripts and documents in ancient and medieval Indian Literature, the Aśokan edits, the *Arthaśāstra* of Kauṭilya, Purāṇa's Dosabodha and the medieval saint literature, to name a few. Though the purpose of these texts was not to describe preservation as such, they contain references to the concept and process of conservation. These references are important links to the practice of conservation in ancient India. This paper, with the help of textual data, attempts to highlight the knowledge, awareness and the practice of Manuscript preservation in ancient India.

Introduction

The ancient Indian tradition of learning was predominantly an oral tradition. Just as the Vedas along with their Aṅga's were transmitted orally from generation to generation in a formal manner, the epics and the Purāṇa's were disseminated informally through the bardic tradition before they were written. A Kṣatriya therefore, a person who had "heard" much *vis-á-vis* a "well-read" person of the modern times. It seems at least some adherents of the oral tradition looked down upon the practice of writing and this is reflected in a verse that counts "reading from books" in the list of hindrances to learning.[1] This confrontation between learning "by heart" and writing seems to have not lasted long as we find in the *Atharvaveda* a clear reference to replacing the books safely into the boxes whence they were taken.[2] This verse reflects the consciousness of contemporary learned society regarding preservation of scriptures. This consciousness is also reflected from Kauṭilya's advice for construction of a separate building for archives, wherein the official records of the state would be reposited[3] as also from Aśoka's sermons being inscribed on rock for durability.[4] Similarly, Kaṭāhaka the hero of the *Kaṭāhaka-jātaka* (believed to have been canonized in the first century BCE), has been said to be a *Bhāṇḍāgārika*, record-keeper.[5]

1. *dyūtaṁ pustakaśuśruṣā nāṭakāsaktireva ca* ।
   striyastandrī ca nidrā ca vidyāvighnakarāṇi ṣaṭ ॥
2. *yasmāt kośād udabharāma vedaṁ tasminnantaḥ avadadhma enam* ।
   — *Atharvaveda* 19.72.1
3. *akṣapaṭalamadhyakṣaḥ prāṅmukhamudaṅmukhaṁ vā* ।
   vibhaktopasthānaṁ nibandhapustakasthānaṁ kārayet ॥
   — *Kauṭilīya Arthaśāstra* 2.6
4. *iyaṁ dhammalipi lekhāpitā kiṁti ciraṁ tiṭheya iti*. Edict 2.
5. *seṭṭhiputte lekhaṁ sikkhante eva dāso pi so phalakaṁ vahamāno gantvā teneva saddhiṁ lekhaṁ sikkhi gaṇanaṁ sikkhi . . . kaṭāhako nāma . . . bhāṇḍārikakamma.*

Early Literary Evidence for Manuscript Preservation

The earliest evidence of materials for covering and binding together folios of manuscripts goes back to the third century CE. The *Rāyapaseṇiyasutta* mentions the use of *Kambi*, *Ḍorā*, *Granthī* and *Chādana* (wooden boards, cord, knot and covering cloth respectively) for the purpose.[6] Similarly, the Simhalese tradition of Buddhist learning has recorded an interesting account of Upāli, who had brought to Ceylon a manuscript of the Vinaya from India in 489 CE.[7] The account speaks for a practice of marking a red dot on the opening folios of manuscripts on every New Year day. It is reported that the manuscript possessed 975 dots when it arrived in Ceylon. The manuscript should thus be "dated back to" 486 CE. Perhaps it could also be inferred from this citation that the people were aware of the concept of "antiquity" of manuscripts.

Deterioration of Manuscripts

Rājaśekhara the author of the *Kāvyamīmāṁsā*, a work on Sanskrit and Prakrit poetics, has referred to several causes of loss of a text. The causes include: (i) careless storage; (ii) sale (to a careless person); (iii) giving away; (iv) owner's withdrawal from a place; (v) insects; (vi) fire; and (vii) water (disaster).[8] The same author has further mentioned that the owner's poverty, intoxication or calamity, neglect, misfortune, and trusting wicked or untrustworthy persons are the causes

6. . . . *patra, kambi, ḍoro, garanthī, lipyāsana, chādana, śṛṅkhalā, masī, lekhanī, akṣara.* — p. 50

7. J. Takakusu, "Pali Elements in Chinese Buddhism: A Translation of Buddhaghosa's *Samantapāsādikā*, A commentary on the Vinaya Found in Chinese Tripiṭaka," *JRAS*, 1896, pp. 415-39.

8. *nikṣepo vikrayo dānaṁ deśatyāgo'lpajīvanam* |
truṭiko bahnirambhaśca prabandhacchedahetavaḥ || — 10.53

of loss of a scripture.[9] Rājaśekhara has further prescribed the use of boxes, wooden covers for manuscripts and has also advocated the need of having well-plastered walls in the room where the poet would compose[10] and this room would have also been the manuscript repository.

Ritual Worship of Manuscripts

There has been and still prevails the practice of worshipping manuscripts at regular intervals. That scholars were aware of the possible degeneration of the manuscripts occurring through this practice and that this practice was frowned upon by some and also considered not easy to be done away with is evident from Subhāṣita that opposes this practice by saying: "(if at all a manuscript has to be worshipped), the manuscript should be worshipped with dry and insect-free flowers and ointments. If at all it has to be given a bath of water, its image falling in a mirror (kept behind the manuscript for the purpose) should be given the bath,"[11] Various other famous Subhāṣita also advise to take care of manuscripts.[12]

---

9. *dāridryaṁ vyasanāvagatiravajñā mandabhāgyatā* ।
duṣṭe duṣṭe ca viśvāsaḥ pañcakāvyamahāpadaḥ ॥ — 10.54

10. *tasya (kaveḥ) saṁpuṭikā saphalakakhaṭikā, samudgaka, salekhanīkama-ṣībhājanāni tāḍpatrāṇi bhūrjatvaco vā salohakaṇṭakāni tāladalāni susaṁmṛṣṭā bhittayaḥ satataṁ saṁnihitāḥ syuḥ* — 10.60.

11. *gandhairnirudakaiḥ puṣpaiḥ kṛmikīṭavivarjitaiḥ* ।
darpaṇe pustakaṁ dṛṣṭvā secayet pūrvavad ghaṭaiḥ ॥

12. *tailādrakṣejjalādrakṣecchithilavandhanāt.*
mūrkhahaste na dātavyamevaṁ vadati pustakam ॥

saṁbhūṣyaṁ sadapatyavat parakarād rakṣyaṁ ca sukṣetravat ।
saṁśodhyaṁ vraṇitāṅgavat pratidinaṁ vīkṣyaṁ ca sanmitravat ॥

badhyaṁ baddhayavadaślathaṁ dṛḍhaguṇaiḥ smaryaṁ harernāmavan ।
naivaṁ sīdati pustakaṁ khalu kadāpyetad gurūṇāṁ vacaḥ ॥ etc.

Practice of Writing and Storage of Manuscripts

Rāmadāsa, the saint from Maharashtra in the seventeeth century CE has written a chapter on the practice of writing. As regards preservation, he has referred to (i) the use of strong paper; (ii) the paper being burnished well; (iii) boards of imported* wood for storage; (iii) strong silk threads; (iv) pieces of cloth for covering; and finally (v) red coloured wax-treated cloth in order to avoid the entry of moisture in the manuscripts.[13] The Rājavyavahārakośa, dated 1677 CE, a lexicon of Raghunathpant Hanmante, a minister of Shivaji the Great, has mentioned the use of cord, covers, hard boards, cloth covers and finally wooden boxes for safe storage of the official records of the State.[14] Pliny too has reported the "use of citrus oil for preservation of books against moths."[15]

Preservation of the Contents of a Manuscript

By preservation of the scriptures, the tradition may perhaps also imply the preservation of the written matter, and maybe not necessarily that of the physical form of the manuscript. There are numerous references to preservation of the ink, in the case of manuscripts and of the paint in the case of paintings.

---

* Burmese teack?

13. *Natural History*, vol. IV Book XIII.

14. *ghaṭya kāgada āṇāve. japona nemasta khaḷāve. lihiṇyāce sāme asāve. nānāparī. sūnyā kātaṇyā jāgāīta. khaḷi ghoṭāḷe tāgāīta. nānā suraṁgamiśrita Jāponi ghyāve.* — 19.1.14-15

    tāgaṭī itiśryā karāvyā. baṁdarī phaḷyā ghoṭāvyā. nānācitrīṁ citārāvyā. ucaṁ citreṁ. nānā gopa (gopha) nānā bāsane. meṇakāpaḍe sinduravarṇeṁ. peṭyā kulupeṁ japaṇeṁ. pustakāraṇeṁ — 19.1.19-20

15. *āhuḥ kāgalasūtraṁ tu tailakhṁ nāma kovidāḥ. jilīdo lekhabandhaḥ syād bastanī nāma veṣṭanī. jñeyaṁ jilīdapuṣṭaṁ tu pṛṣṭhapatraṁ vicakṣaṇaiḥ. tathā veṣṭanavastraṁ tu rumālaḥ parikīrtitaḥ. peṭārā peṭakaḥ jujdānaṁ nāma saṁcikā.* — *Lekhanavargaḥ*, 110-11

Some such references are (i) The *Citrasūtra* of the *Viṣṇudharmottarapurāṇa*, of the fifth century CE, mentions the use of the juice of *Mataṅga* and *Dūrvā* for preservation of the paint. It further says that the paint in such an illustrated work does not get lost even if it is washed with water[16]; (ii) The *Lekhapaddhati*, a medieval text, prescribes a manner for preparation of ink that is "harder than diamond";[17] (iii) The Dāsabodha of Rāmadāsa refers to the handwriting not getting lost even when the paper is lost.[18]

Durability of the Paper

The late Rajendra Lal Mitra referred to hand-made paper for its strength and longevity as compared to the newly introduced "English foolscap (machine-made) paper" in his letter written to Capt. J. Waterhouse, Secretary of the Asiatic Society, Calcutta, on February 15, 1875. He has also cited the

---

16. *mātaṅgadurvārasapaṭṭabaddhaiḥ saṁstambhitaṁ citramudārapuccham* |

dhautaṁ jalenāpi na nāśameti tiṣṭhatyanekānyapi vatsarāṇi | — 40.30

17. *maṣyāmnāyaḥ. ubhayorapi maṣyormahārāṣṭrabhāṣayā ḍeralīti prasiddhasya riṅgaṇīvṛkṣasya vanaspativiśeṣasya satkatakasya phalarasasya madhye prakṣepe satejastvamakṣikābhāvādayo guṇā bhavanti . . . bhaplūvaghūgha(?)rasena ekaikaṁ kṣiptvā sarvāṇi patrāṇi hā(ā)hana. kophali (āhatakopari?) mardante. tadanantaraṁ pisāśvatthābhidhaṁ tavakṣīlā(rā)parṇāmacūrṇaṁ madhye muktvā tanmānenāmbu pūryate. pacāccūrṇaṁ vinā dvitrāṇi dhāvanī(nā)ni nītārya(ya) nītārya(ya) prakṣālyante. tadanantaraṁ vilomajjvalā payasīṁhai(?) pīlū ca syāditi . . . khāṇḍa bola anai lakkhāresa kajjala bajjala anai trambārasa. bhojarāja misi nipāi pānauṁ phāṭai misi navi jāi. bolasya dviguṇo gundo gundasya dviguṇā maṣī. mardayedyāmayugmaṁ tu maṣī vajrasamā bhavet.*

18. *bhovateṁ sthaḷa soḍūni dyāve. madhyeṁci camacamita lyāhāveṁ. kāgada jhaḍatāṁhi jhaḍāveṁ. nālageci akṣara.* — 19.1.11

prevalent Bengali practice of keeping the manuscripts on the wooden lintels of the houses for safeguarding them from insects.[19]

It seems in the unfathomed mass of literature one may find immense material on this topic of indigenous practices of preservation of manuscripts. This paper is a small attempt to draw the attention of the scholars to the ancient and medieval literature that refers to preservation of manuscripts.

Interventions

Dr. Imtiaz Ahmad: These references are very useful and I am thankful to Mr. Bapat for making this effort to compile them and place them before this audience.

---

19. Manuscripts written on country paper sized with yellow arsenic and emulsion of tamarind seeds . . . white arsenic is rarely used for it, mucilage employed in such cases being acacia gum. Ordinary paper sized with rice gruel, but such paper attracts damp and vermin of all kinds . . . silver fish . . .

    . . .The superior appearance and cheapness of European paper has of late induced many persons to use it, instead of the country arsenicized paper, writing pothis; but this is a great mistake, as the former is liable to be rapidly destroyed by insects (He has cited here examples of European paper of 1830 *vis-á-vis* manuscripts of the Fort Williams of 1801). . . . This fact would suggest the propriety of Government records in Mufassil Courts being written on arsenicized paper instead of ordinary English foolscap which is rapidly destroyed by climate and also by white ants. . . . Ordinary yellow paper (with turmeric) is not proof against attacks of insects. — R.L. Babu Mitra to Capt. J. Waterhouse, Secretary, *Asiatic Society*, February 15, 1875 (in A.E. Gough (ed.), *Papers Relating to the Collection and Preservation of the Records of Ancient Sanskrit Literature*, Office of the Superintendent of Government Printing, Calcutta, 1878, p. 15.

11

Traditional Practices and Palm-leaf Manuscripts in Tamil Nadu

V. JEYARAJ

Abstract

Many Palm-leaf manuscripts have been preserved in institutes, libraries, and *mathas* in Tamil Nadu. Traditionally, seasoned Palm-leaf manuscripts were made available for writing both in the scholarly circles and by common folk and were freely available. Natural liquids like oil, milk, turmeric, lime, red ochre etc, were used in the preservation of manuscripts. Siddhā medical practices were also used in the preservation of manuscripts. This paper deals with the herbal and natural materials used during preparation, storage, and handling of Palm-leaf manuscripts.

Introduction

A lot of Palm-leaf manuscripts have been preserved in institutions, libraries and *maṭhas* in Tamil Nadu. Traditionally Palm-leaf manuscripts were made available for writing for scholars, administrators and common folk. Seasoned palm-leaves were available in the shops for this purpose just like paper is available in shops today. In the preservation of manuscripts, Siddhā medical practices were also in vogue in the ancient past. The Siddhā Medical Practitioners are trying to find out the ancient methods of preserving the manuscripts by searching for new information in the available Palm-leaf manuscripts. This paper deals with herbal and other natural materials used in the preparation, storage and handling of the Palm-leaf manuscripts.

While parchment and Bhūrja Patra, (birch bark) were common in North India, palm-leaves were the main writing support in South India. Leaves from the Country Palmyrah (*Borassus flabellifer*), Śrītāla (*Corypha Umbraculifera*), and Lanthar Palmyra (*Corypha Utan*) were the ones used for writing, and sometimes illustrations were also made on them. In the preparation of Palm-leaf manuscripts itself, preservative methods were adopted right from the seasoning stage itself.

Methods of Seasoning the Palm-leaf Manuscripts

Seasoning is a process by which the leaves are able to withstand the effects of the environment, thus prolonging the life of the leaves. There are many methods of seasoning depending upon the environment, availability of local resources etc. The tender leaves that are four to five weeks old are cut into the required size and dried under shade or buried under marshy water. Some other methods of seasoning are:

- Boiling the leaves in water, milk or turmeric solution
- Baking the leaves in steam
- Keeping the leaves buried in wet sand
- Keeping the leaves in a moist haystack
- Applying Gingeli oil and allow the leaves to absorb the oil

Such seasoned palm-leaves are then inscribed by a metal stylus.

Method of Writing and Inking

Palm-leaf manuscripts were written either by stylus or by brush using ink. The inscribed letters are of the colour of the leaf and therefore difficult to read. The essence of Kadukkai (*Terminalia Chebula*) or green leaves of Kovakkai plant (*Coccinia Grandis*) was applied on the inscribed portions to make them appear black and easily legible. From early times, soot mixed with vegetable gum has been used as ink. Iron gall inks obtained from the seed of the gall fruit, containing tannin and iron oxide, have also been used. Commercial inks are being used these days for inking the manuscripts.

Re-inking the "Faded" Text

Frequent handling as well as heat and microbial activity obliterate the ink, and when this "fading" happens, there is a need for the manuscript text to be re-inked. This is done again by rubbing into the incised text Kadukkai essence, Kovai plant leaves or lampblack mixed with oil.

Use of Oils for Preservation of Palm-leaf Manuscripts

When Palm-leaf manuscripts become dry, various oils are applied as softening agents to impart flexibility to the manuscript folios. These oils are extracted from plants and some of these oils are also employed as insect repellents and to counter fungi. The mostly useful oils have been listed below:

- Cedar wood oil
- Citronella oil
- Lemon grass oil

- Olive oil
- Eucalyptus oil
- Sandalwood oil
- Turpentine oil
- Palm-leaf oil

Traditional Preservation with Herbs

Various parts of plants and their products such as oils, flowers, bark, seeds, resins, roots and leaves have been used traditionally in the preservation of Palm-leaf manuscripts. Many of these natural materials are insect repellents and are kept dried whole or in the powdered form along with the manuscripts. Ghora bach (*Acorus calamus*) is very effective as are Ginger, sandalwood powder, powdered seeds, leaves and roots of *Tephrosia Vogeli*. Leaves of Neem (*Azadirachta indica*), Tobacco (*Nicotiana tabacum*), *Tulasī* (*Ocimum basilicum*), Adhatoda (*Adhatoda Zeylanica*) and Chrysanthemum (*Chrysanthemum cinerariaefolium*) have been extensively used by the ancients to protect the manuscripts from deterioration.

At the Saraswathi Mahal Library, Thanjavur, the following are pulverized after drying under shade and kept in small cloth sachets in between the bundles of the manuscripts:

Black cumin	1 Part
Cinnamon bark	1 Part
Sweet flag	1 Part
Pepper	¼ Part
Cloves	¼ Part
Green camphor	little bit

Fig. 11.1: Acorus Calamus

Termite attack has been known to be controlled by the application of the decoction of *Karinjottei* (*Samadera indica*), and of *Sotrukathazhai*, Aloe vera.

Care of Manuscripts Through Rituals and Proper Storage

Annual rituals in homes and institutions involve the application of either a paste of coconut leaf juice and wood charcoal or turmeric on the manuscripts. During *Vijayadaśamī*, the Palm-leaf manuscripts are removed from their storage and bathed in the rays of either the rising sun or setting sun in order to counter insect and microbial activity.

Traditionally Palm-leaf manuscripts were kept in the kitchen lofts where the smoke from the cooking fires safeguarded them from insects and fungi. It is common practice to protect the Palm-leaf manuscripts from physical damage, dust, moisture and distortions by placing them tightly between wooden planks. Red silk or cotton cloth are considered a protection against insects and therefore the manuscripts were kept bundled in them. Cords dyed yellow with turmeric were used to avoid fungal and insect attack. Cloth was dyed red using a solution of turmeric and lime in order to protect manuscripts from insects.

Conclusion

Traditional methods of preservation of Palm-leaf manuscripts are time tested and also friendly to the environment. Generations before us have found various materials for preservation of our collections. These must now be studied for their efficacy in today's context. Many synthetic materials have today replaced the herbal remedies. Whether we use herbal or synthetically produced materials for the control of biological activities, the very same materials should never be used continuously. The materials should be changed in order to avoid the insects developing immunity to them. Extensive research is needed to find out the contents of various herbal materials, which can control insects and fungi acting on our manuscript collections.

References

Agrawal, O.P., ed., *Conservation of Manuscripts and Paintings of South-East Asia*, London: Butterworths, 1984.

———, *Preservation of Art Objects and Library Materials*, India: National Book Trust, 1993.

Gupta, C.B., "Preservation of Palm-leaf Manuscripts," *Conservation of Cultural Property in India*, 7, (1974).

Harinarayana, N., *The Science of Archives Keeping*, The State Archives, Government of Andhra Pradesh, Hyderabad.

Jeyaraj, V., *Care of Archival Materials*, Thanjavur Maharaja Serfoji's Saraswathi Mahal Library, Thanjavur, 1999.

———, *Care of Records* (Tamil), Government Museum, Chennai, 1997.

Joshi Binduvasini, R., "Preservation of Palm-leaf Manuscripts," *Conservation of Cultural Property in India* (1989).

Kathpalia, Y.P., *Conservation and Restoration of Archival Materials*, UNESCO, Paris, 1973.

———, *Conservation and Restoration of Library Materials*, UNESCO, Paris, 1983.

Nair, M.V., "A New Method of Relaxing Brittle Palm leaves," *Conservation of Cultural Property in India*, 18-20, (1985-87).

Sah Anupam, "Save Palm-leaf Manuscript Heritage," INTACH, Indian Council of Conservation Institutes, Lucknow, 2001

Sarkar, N.N., "Non-chemical Methods in Library Management," *Conservation of Cultural Property in India*, 28, (1995).

Sharma, Govind, *Recent Advances in Conservation of Manuscripts*, Vrindavan Research Institute, Vrindavan, 2004.

Singh, R.S., *Conservation of Documents in Libraries, Archives and Museums*, New Delhi: Aditya Prakashan, 1993.

Thangavelu, S., "Palm-leaf Manuscripts and their Preservation," *Proceedings of the Silver Jubilee Seminar on Conservation of Cultural Property*, 1991.

Uniyal, C.P., "Preventive Conservation of Archival Materials — Some Rather Ignored but Vital Aspects," *Conservation of Cultural Property in India*, 28 (1995).

12

Manuscript Conservation in the Śaivite Maṭhas of the Erode District of Tamil Nadu

C. MAHESWARAN

Abstract

A pilot study conducted at various Śaivite *maṭhas* of the Erode District of Tamil Nadu has revealed that for centuries the authorities of these *maṭhas* have adopted certain indigenous conservation practices, employing various indigenous materials — especially organic in nature — in their efforts to conserve the priceless treasure of the manuscripts in their custody. As these religious *maṭhas* are usually not open to the public in addition to the advent and availability of synthetic chemicals, this indigenous knowledge system has remained a secret. In this paper, the author highlights the indigenous practices of both preventive and curative methods of conservation such as fumigation and softening that are carried out periodically with locally available materials of organic origin in the 17 Śaivite *maṭhas* established in the *tāluks* of Perundurai, Bhavani, Kangeyam and Dharampuram of the Erode District. The details of such indigenous practices and materials used can be applied in the field of conservation and cultural heritage.

Introduction

Śaivism, the cult wherein Lord Śiva is worshipped as the prime deity, flourished in the state of Tamil Nadu in the medieval period, when several *maṭhas* were established at various places in the state. While western Tamil Nadu has 51 Śaivite *maṭhas*,* the Erode District in this region is host to 17 of these Śaivite *maṭhas*. As these *maṭhas* are often inaccessible to the general public, society remained unaware of the indigenous knowledge system in existence and being practised at the *maṭhas*. In this paper, therefore, an attempt is made to highlight the indigenous practices of both preventive and curative conservation techniques that are carried out periodically with the locally available indigenous materials, especially of organic origin, in the Śaivite *maṭhas* that have been and are functioning in the *tāluks* of Perundurai, Bhavani, Kangeyam and Dharapuram of the Erode District.

Maṭhas as Repositories and Custodial Centres of Manuscripts

These *maṭhas* served not only as religious centres but also as resource centres where varied subjects such as literature, grammar, philosophy, astrology and medicine were taught and these are documented in manuscripts, especially Palm-leaf manuscripts. These centres have tried their best to conserve the priceless treasures of Palm-leaf manuscripts in their custody, by employing indigenous materials and methods. The information that could be gathered from the seventeen Śaivite *maṭhas* of the Erode District point to a surprisingly low numbers of manuscripts in the following five *maṭhas* considered to be repositories of Palm-leaf manuscripts.

---

* *Maṭha* is a type of monastery belonging to a Hindu religious order. The *maṭhas* ususally have a temple, administrative unit, residential facilities and also schools of religious learning.

(i) Srilasri Sivasamaya Paṇḍita Guruswamigal Maṭha, Sivagiri (Kangeyam Tāluk) [15 bundles]

(ii) Sivathiru Kanagagiri Paṇḍita Guruswamigal Maṭha, Pattali (Gobichettipalayam Tāluk) [3 bundles]

(iii) Sivathiru Kodumudi Paṇḍita Guruswamigal Maṭha, Keeranoor (Dharapuram Tāluk) [2 bundles]

(iv) Sivasri Navarathna Nayaga Paṇḍita Guruswamigal Maṭha, Bhavani (Bhavani Tāluk) [1 bundle]

(v) Sri Manickavasaga Swamigal Thirumadaalayam, Koonampatti (Perundurai Tāluk) [yet to be enumerated]

Indigenous Conservation Practices in the Śaivite Maṭhas

In these *maṭhas*, the Palm-leaf manuscripts are stored within a characteristic cane box known as *Oalaichuvadi petti* (Lit. box of Palm-leaf manuscripts). This cane box is woven in a manner that leaves small gaps ensuring ventilation to the Palm-leaf manuscripts kept in it. The bundles of Palm-leaf manuscripts are stacked inside the box in a characteristic way to avoid overcrowding and to minimize the load of one bundle over the other. Every year during *Navarātri* celebrations the bundles of Palm-leaf manuscripts kept in the cane box are unpacked and subjected to "general cleaning." The various steps involved in this general cleaning are the following:

(i) Dusting with a soft cotton cloth.

(ii) Rubbing extracts of leaves (such as of palmyra palm; coconut; ivy or gourd).

(iii) Fumigation with frankincense fume.

(iv) Keeping the manuscripts between boards made of teak wood and tying this assembly with turmeric-soaked cords uniformly distributed over the boards. The bundle is then wrapped in a coarse red-coloured cloth.

(v) These manuscripts are kept with sachets of a powdered mixture of shade-dried black cumin seeds, cinnamon, sweet flag, black pepper, cloves and green camphor.

Other than this general practice of storing the Palm-leaf manuscripts in cane boxes, those manuscripts that are referred to frequently are kept in typical wooden hangers known as *Oalai thookku* (lit. Palm-leaf hanger) or *Chuvadi thookku* (lit. manuscripts hanger).

It may be worth mentioning that during rituals, fumes of frankincense, camphor, incense sticks are present around the manuscripts as are chrysanthemum flowers and leaves of basil, and these are known to have insect-repellent properties.

Indigenous knowledge systems are often passed down successive generations. Indigenous conservation practices are usually employed without an awareness of the scientific principles involved. While these practices, especially that of the "annual general cleaning," help in conservation of manuscripts by the use of materials essentially of vegetal origin, often the manuscripts are preserved because of good housekeeping as well as of some inherent medicinal properties of the manuscripts' materials.

Concluding Remarks

These Śaivite *maṭha*s are keen to employ indigenous organic materials, especially of vegetal origin, to preserve their manuscripts. These indigenous practices and materials could be put into wider application in the field of conservation of cultural heritage after careful scrutiny and testing for effectiveness. As there is today a marked decline in the employment of indigenous practices and materials in these *maṭhas*, there is need to gear up the use of our traditional systems of conservation.

Acknowledgement

The author wishes to record his deep sense of gratitude to Shri M.A. Siddique, I.A.S, Director of Museums, Government of Tamil Nadu for having permitted the author to participate and present this paper at this seminar.

Notes

1. For the complete list of the Śaivite *maṭhas* of the Erode District of Tamil Nadu, please refer to Table I.
2. For the preparation of the powdered mixture with insect-repellent properties, please refer to Table II.
3. The indigenous materials of organic origin used in the conservation of manuscripts at the Śaivite *maṭhas* of the Erode District are listed in Table III.
4. According to Sri Balamurugan Esana Sivachariyar (belonging to the Srilasri Sivasamaya Paṇḍita Guruswamigal Maṭha, Sivagiri) the workshop on Preventive Conservation of Manuscripts conducted by the INTACH ICCI Bangalore Centre under the aegis of the National Mission for Manuscripts has revived the spirit of conservation of manuscripts in their *maṭha* (Personal Communication).

References

Jeyaraj, V. & P. Perumal, "Indigenous Methods of Conservation of Manuscripts," *Proceedings of the Workshop for the Trainers on Preventive Conservation*, Government Museum, Chennai, 2004.

Maheswaran, C., "Preventive Conservation: Documentation (Mimeo)," *Workshop for the Trainers on Preventive Conservation of Manuscripts*, Government Museum, Erode, 2004.

Pushpa, M.N., "Plants used in the Indigenous methods of Preventive Conservation of Manuscripts," *Proceedings of the Workshop for the Trainers on Preventive Conservation of Manuscripts*, Government Museum, Chennai, 2004.

Table - I

Śaivite Maṭhas of the Erode District of Tamil Nadu

Sl. No.	Name of Maṭha	Locality
1.	Sivathiru Navarathna Nayaga Paṇḍita Guruswamigal Maṭha	Bhavani, Bhavani Tāluk
2.	Sri Maanickavaasaga Swaamigal Thirumadaalayam	Koonampatti, Perundurai Tāluk
3.	Srimadhu Aanda Subramaniya Paṇḍita Guruswamigal Maṭha	Perundurai, Perundurai Tāluk
4.	Srimadhu Aadhi Saiva Puranthira Paṇḍita Jagathguru Swamigal Maṭha	Saathamboor, Perundurai Tāluk
5.	Srimath Moovaendha Paṇḍita Guruswaamigal Maṭha	Vellode, Perundurai Tāluk
6.	Sivathiru Kodumudi Paṇḍita Guruswaamigal Maṭha	Keeranoor, Perundurai Tāluk
7.	Sivathiru Kanagagiri Paṇḍita Guruswaamigal Maṭha	Pattaali, Gobichettipalayam Tāluk
8.	Srilasri Sivasamaya Paṇḍita Guruswaamigal Maṭha	Sivagiri, Kangeyam Tāluk
9.	Srimadhu Maanicka Naayaga Chandhrasekara Paṇḍita Guruswaamigal Maṭha	Kodumudi, Kangeyam Tāluk
10.	Sivathiru Meenakshi Sawa Puranthara Paṇḍita Guruswaamigal Maṭha	Kadaiyoor, Kangeyam Tāluk
11.	Sivathiru Kulasekara Paṇḍita Guruswaamigal Maṭha	Muthoor, Kangeyam Tāluk.
12	Papramaeswara Paṇḍita Guruswaamigal Maṭha	Moolanoor, Kangeyam Tāluk
13.	Sivathiru Chandhrasaekara Paṇḍita Guruswaamigal Maṭha	Vellakoil, Kangeyam Tāluk
14.	Sivathiru Kanagasabaapathi Paṇḍita Guruswaamigal Maṭha	Valliyerachal, Kangeyam Tāluk
15.	Srimath Aana Sivasubrahmaniya Paṇḍita Guruswaamigal Maṭha	Avalpoondurai, Kangeyam Tāluk
16.	Sivathiru Uthama Paṇḍita Guruswaamigal Maṭha	Kangeyam, Kangeyam Tāluk
17.	Para Para Paramaeswara Paṇḍita Guruswaamigal Maṭha	Alangiyam, Dharapuram Tāluk.

Table II
Preparation of a Powdered Medicinal Mixture as Disinfectant/Insecticide/Insect-Repellent

Ingredients	Quantity
Black Cumin seeds	1 Part
Cinnamon bark	1 Part
Sweet Flag	1 part
Cloves	¼ Part
Black Pepper	¼ Part
Green Camphor	25 gms

Method of Preparation of the Powder

All the above indigenous ingredients are dried in the shade and then pulverized separately, one at a time. Each powdered ingredient is then put together and mixed thoroughly. 5.0 grams of this mixture is then packed into cloth sachets of four inch dimensions. Such sachets packed with medicinal powder are kept between the bundles of Palm-leaf manuscripts and on the shelves.

Table - III
Indigenous Materials of Organic Origin Employed in Conservation of Palm-leaf Manuscripts at the Śaivite Maṭhas of the Erode District of Tamil Nadu

Sl. No.	Common Name	Botanical Nomenclature	Part(s) used	Utility
1.	Sweet Flag	*Acorus calamus*	Rhizome	Insecticide/Insect-repellent
2.	Adhatoda	*Adhatoda vasica*	Leaves	Insecticide/Insect-repellent
3.	*Margosa*	*Azadirachta indica*	Leaves	Insecticide/Insect-repellent
4.	Ivy gourd	*Coccinia grandis*	Leaves	Softening agent / Insecticide/ Insect-repellent
5.	Cinnamon	*Cinnamomum zeylanicum*	Bark	Disinfectant
6.	Turmeric	*Curcuma longa*	Rhizome	Disinfectant
7.	Chrysanthemum	*Chrysanthemum cinerariaefolium*	Capitula of flower	Insecticide
8.	Clove	*Eugenia caryophyllata*	Flower bud	Disinfectant
9.	Black Cumin	*Nigella sativa*	Seed	Disinfectant
10.	Tobacco	*Nicotiana tabacum*	Leaves	Disinfectant/Fungicide/ Softening agent
11.	Sweet basil	*Ocimum basilicum*	Leaves	Softening agent / Insecticide/ Insect-repellent
12.	Black Pepper	*Piper nigrum*	Dried fruits	Fungicide/ Insecticide
13.	Myrobalan	*Terminalia chebula*	Dried fruits	Softening agent
14.	*Khus-Khus*	*Vetiveria zizanioides*	Rootlets	Packing material
15.	Palmyra palm	*Borussus flubellifer*	Leaves	Softening agent
16.	Coconut	*Cocos nucifera*	Leaves	Softening agent

13

Indigenous Practices and Materials for Conservation of Manuscripts in Libraries

S.K. Das

Abstract

The Paper describes the various factors of deterioration of Birch bark, Palm-leaf and Paper manuscripts and measures to control them and describes the techniques which could be deployed for reinforcing fragile and brittle sheets by indigenous practices and materials.

Introduction

Birch barks, Palm-leaf, Paper have been used by men since very early times for writing. As a result, a number of documents and manuscripts have been produced in all parts of the world. Today all these works constitute the written heritage of mankind and are invaluable for understanding the history and evolution of each period and region. It is obligatory on our part to protect and conserve this heritage as long as possible.

Manuscript Collection of the Asiatic Society

The Asiatic Society was founded on 15th January, 1784 by Sir William Jones (1746-1794). Manuscript collection of the Society is varied and rich, and covers most of the Indian languages and scripts as well as several Asian ones. It appears that the number of manuscripts amounts to a little over 47,000, out of which there are 1000 bundles of Palm-leaf manuscript and 4 bundles of Birch Bark and 1 volume of Parchment manuscript. The materials used for the manuscripts are clearly varied-palm and palmyra leaves, birch barks and paper of various grades.

There are manuscripts on leaves and books using vegetable dye as ink. The oldest item of this kind is a late Gupta script text on *Tantra Kubjikāmata* (Palmyra) from the seventh century CE. There are some rare treasures in the Society's collection. Some of them are *Aśṭasahasrikā Prajñāpāramitā* (Palmyra), an illustrated Pali Buddhist text in the Newārī script of Nepal from the eleventh century CE, Emperor Shah Jahan's biography *Pādśāhnāmah* with his autograph, and *Jami'al-Tawārīkh* a sixteenth century illustrated manuscript relating to the history of Chenghis Khan and his descendants, the Hungarian scholar Alexander Csoma De Koros's *Sanskrit-Tibetan-English Dictionary* (1830) in his own handwriting and an illustrated Burmese *Rāmāyaṇa* and Persian *Mahābhārata*. There are some more, like a volume on astronomy(1497) in Latin, the first Bengali Grammar (1778) by N.B. Halhead, an illuminated manuscript of the *Holy Qurān* and the *Gulistān* which are said to be first copies from the original manuscript.

Condition of its Collection

On invitation, Dr. O.P. Agarwal visited the Asiatic Society, Kolkata during 1984 when the Conservation Laboratory of the Society primarily started. He reported "Due to years of neglect and negligence, this most precious collection is today in a pathetic state."

Causes of Deterioration

The cause of deterioration was not only neglect and negligence; there were other factors (external and internal) also which damaged such materials. They are dust, light, heat, humidity, acidity, gaseous, pollution insects, fungus, rough handling and improper storage. Paper, Palm-leaf and birch bark are perishable materials. They can be torn out, burnt, water damaged, stained by dust and dirt; attacked by biological and micro logical agents. The deterioration is more in libraries and archives of tropical countries due to climate changes, insects and pests etc.

Preventive Measures Taken by the Society

Prevention is better than cure. So regular cleaning of manuscripts by soft brush and vaccum cleaner, wrapping of Manuscripts bundle by acid free handmade paper and red salu (cloth), to save them from dust and insects, is being done in the Society. The light in its ultraviolet range has high energy to deteriorate cellulose fibers by photo oxidation. It fades works of art. In this case a project has been taken by the society to use reflected light. Heat causes brittleness. Excessive heat beyond 32 C speeds up processes of degradation, discoloration and the evaporation of the natural oil present in Palm-leaf and birch bark causing loss of flexibility. Humidity beyond 70% permits moulds to grow and flourish. It causes paper to swell and pigment layer to peel off. So temperature 22° C to 24° C and relative humidity at 55% to 60% have been controlled by 24 hours air conditioning system in the stack area of the Society. It is advisable that if an air-conditioning system is not available in any Library then chemicals like Silica Gel or Calcium Chloride (2-3 Kilograms for a room of 20-25 Cubic metre space capacity) is the best answer in moist climatic conditions and damp buildings. Circulation of air in the stack area is essential to eliminate pockets of stagnant air, which encourages growth of micro-organisms and other injurious pests.

Prevention Measures Currently in Use by the Asiatic Society

There are so many biological agents which deteriorate the organic materials like paper and Palm-leaf. But Birch bark is generally not affected by insects except termites. Insects may be classified in two groups viz. surface feeder and inside feeder. Silverfish, cockroaches, book lice, crickets and termites, Termites are surface feeders and cause extensive damage to manuscripts. They are controlled by spraying of "PIP" insecticide (liquid and readymade, turpentine oil and 2% Pyrethrum mixed). Naphthalene bricks are also used as insect repellants. Some of the safe insect repellants are: Neem leaf dried in a special way, Red Sandal wood and Tobacco leaves. Book worms in manuscripts are controlled by putting them in the fumigation chamber for at least twenty one days and the dose is five kilograms P.D.B/ 1000 cubic feet space. At present Ethoxide gas is used in the vacuum Fumigation chamber for complete sterilization of insect infested volumes in the Asiatic Society, Kolkata. Future programmes involve the installation of a freeze dryer, for complete eradication of insects without using any insecticide which is harmful to human beings.

Menace caused by rats/mice can be effectively controlled by poisoning and trapping. Poisons are always used with baits which are spread over places frequented by rats/mice. Dry bread and cheese have been quite effective as a bait base. Some of the good rat poisons are Zinc Phosphide (3-5%) and Arsenic Oxide (10-15%). The best way is to use baits in traps.

Fungus or mildew infested manuscripts may be treated by fumigating in a Thymol fumigation chamber. The doze used is 1 ox/16 cubic feet space for 12-14 days. A 40 watt bulb is required to melt and evaporate the Thymol in the fumigation chamber otherwise fungus affected areas can be sprayed with 5% Thymol in Methyl alcohol.

Accidental Causes of Deterioration

There are so many accidental causes to deteriorate the Manuscripts such as flood, fire, leakage of roof, busting of drainage pipes etc. Fire is also a greatest accidental agent which damages Library materials in a very short time. It is therefore, imperative that precaution and prevention against fire must be taken. Inflammable products should be stored outside the library building. The Carbon dioxide fire extinguishers must be kept in conspicuous place. The drainage pipes should be regularly inspected for blockage or leakage. Flood and other natural agents deteriorate the paper and other library materials. In such a situation manuscripts should be removed to drier surroundings where humidity can be controlled.

Documentation Before Treatment

Before the treatment of manuscripts the following documents are necessary:

1. Photography before and after treatment.
2. Preparation of history sheet;

   These sheets are used as record of information collected from manuscripts when they are received for treatment. Before starting the treatment, the physical conditions of the manuscripts as apparently visible is recorded on the same sheet.
3. Proposed treatment i.e. methods and materials should be recorded before treatment.

De-acidification

Acidity does not affect the Palm-leaf and birch bark manuscripts to the same extent as it harms the paper manuscripts. Paper becomes acidic from a number of different causes such as acid from polluted atmosphere, acid sizing like alum, acid pigments like Verdigris and inks specially Iron Gall ink. Acidity causes loss of strength by hydrolysis of cellulose molecules. So de-acidification is essential for neutralization of acid. De-acidification does not strengthen paper but it stops further deterioration by acid hydrolysis. There are three types of de-acidification which are maintained by the Conservation Laboratory of the Society such as:

i) Aqueous method

ii) Non aqueous method

iii) Gaseous method

Before de-acidification of paper manuscripts, we test the ink, whether it is water soluble or not. If ink is soluble in water then we adopt non-aqueous method for de-acidification of manuscripts. 2% solution of $Ba(OH)_2$, $8H_2O$ in methanol is applied on the sheets of manuscript with a brush or a spray. Sometimes we de-acidify the manuscripts in the Ammonia de-acidification chamber using Ammonia and water, the proportion being 1:10 and the time required is 4-5 hours. After exposure in Ammonia fumes, the manuscripts should be exposed in fresh air for 12-14 hours to dispel excess Ammonia. But this process is transitory.

The Curative Measures of Brittle and Fragile Paper Manuscripts are Mending, Repair, Lamination, Encapsulation etc.

There are various techniques of restoration, both conventional and modern. Method of restoration depends on likely use of the document. Restoration always aims at maintaining the originality of the document. Following is a brief discussion about the types of restoration in vogue, today:

(a) *Full Pasting*: Brittle documents/Manuscripts, which are written on one side, may be strengthened by pasting a rag acid free handmade paper at the back using Dextrine or *Maidā* paste or CMC paste. The size of the paper for full pasting should be slightly larger than the size of the document to be pasted over. After the paste has dried, the oversize hand made paper is trimmed with a pair of hand scissors to the size of the document keeping a margin of 2-3 mm all around to safeguard the edges of the document when in use.

(b) *Tissue Repair*: Toned sheets of any documents/manuscripts on which writings have not faded but show only slight deterioration can be reinforced with Tissue paper by using CMC paste or dextrin paste.

(c) *Chiffon Repair*: Chiffon or fine transparent silk gauze is used for repairing extremely fragile ink corroded or insect damaged documents/manuscripts. Before undertaking repair with Chiffon, all the patches pasted on the document/manuscript should be removed. Dextrine paste is used in the process.

(d) *Sizing*: The slightly brittle portions can be put back to work by using gelatin, methyl methacrylate, paralite, methyl cellulose etc. in presence of water.

(e) *Lamination*: Manuscripts which have lost strength due to Bio-chemical deterioration can be strengthened by lamination. This process should be applied after de-acidification of manuscripts.

Solvent lamination is the best method of lamination, which can be done with lens tissue paper, cellulose Acetate Film and acetone. But imported tissue paper and cellulose acetate film are costly foreign materials and sometimes these are not available easily. It is not possible for a small library to procure and use these materials for restoration of manuscripts. It is, therefore, suggested to adopt chiffon and country made tissue paper (free from acid, waxy and oily constituents) for lamination and polyester film for encapsulation of manuscript. The polyester film is cheap and easily available in the market.

(f) *Encapsulation*: The document or manuscript in this process can easily be encapsulated with the help of Polyester film without using any chemical or heat and pressure. It can easily be handled and is completely reversible in nature without disturbing the document or manuscript. The manuscripts may be sealed with the help of double sided adhesive tape or using high frequency ultrasonic welding machine to avoid atmospheric pollution and the bio-deterioration and also imparts strength to the document.

Restoration of Palm-leaf Manuscript

Two types of Palm-leaf manuscripts are seen in libraries (i) *Tāla* (ii) *śrītāla*. Tala Palm-leaf is thick and coarse, written on by a metallic stylus using charcoal dust for distinct writing. *Śrītāla* Palm-leaf is thin, flexible like paper and written on by carbon ink with a reed pen. Insects easily attack both the palm leaves. Their excreta jam the Palm-leaf manuscript bundle. Due to prolonged fluctuation of relative humidity and temperature, the Palm-leaf manuscripts loose their natural oil and the leaves become brittle and fragile. To lubricate them and retain the flexibility, we use citronella oil on both the sides of each Palm-leaf manuscripts. Cintronella oil also acts as insect repellant. Broken portions may be repaired using extra Palm-leaf with fevicol. Treated Palm-leaf manuscripts can be encapsulated by polyester film or it may be strengthened by Chiffon lamination.

Restoration of Birch Bark Manuscripts

Birch bark is an inner layer of Birch tree and it is composed of several layers with natural gum and woody knots. As is naturally salted i.e. salt of salicylic acid is present there, insects do not attack it. It has natural stain so it cannot be bleached. It is available in 3 × 4 size and of Himalayan origin and is still available in Kashmir. Carbon ink is used for writing on it.

After a considerable time the natural gum loose their adherence and the layers get separated. Separated layers can be fixed using 2-3% CMC paste or thin *maidā* paste by fine brush. After joining the separated portions, it may be lubricated by using citronella oil on both sides of the Birch bark manuscript. After that the Birch bark sheet can be encapsulated by using polyester films and it can be handled easily.

Air-condition: Ideal air condition system reduces the Bio-chemical deterioration.

Manuscripts on paper decay continuously under normal temperature & humidity. Lowering of temperature slows down the chemical activity and thus reduces the rate of decay of the materials. Manuscripts stored in an air conditioned system at 55% RH and 22° C temperature with incoming air filtered off the acidic gases and dust, will difficult to maintain the manuscripts for more than a few centuries.

Conclusion

It is well known that regarding preservation of documents, manuscripts etc. rapid developments are taking place in Western Countries. India is a tropical country. Its conservation problems of Library materials are more critical than that of Western countries. In spite of that, India is also gradually moving ahead in the field of conservation work by indigenous practices and materials.

Hence the Conservation Laboratory Division of the Asiatic Society, Kolkata is in progress in the same field through its various performances of conservation work. In day-to-day preservation work, different types of new methods, modern techniques etc. which have already been adopted by few pioneer institutions. like the National Archives of India, National Museum in New Delhi, NRLC and INTACH in Lucknow are regularly followed by the Asiatic Society, Kokalta . Today hopefully, the said pioneer institutions will give us some guidelines on indigenous practices and materials for conservation of manuscripts in the libraries in India.

Acknowledgement

The author expresses his deepest sincere gratitude to the organizations of this Seminar for their kind permission of presenting this paper.

References

Agarwal, O.P., *Conservation of Manuscripts and Paintings of South-East Asia*, London: Butterworth, 1984.

Cunha, George Martin and Cunha, Dorothy Grant, *Conservation of Library Materials*, 2nd edn., vol. I, 1971.

Preservation of Archival Matetials, National Archives of India, New Delhi.

14

Palm-leaf Manuscripts and Indigenous Conservation Practices and Material Used at the Saraswati Mahal Library, Thanjavur

P. PERUMAL

Abstract

This paper deals with the indigenous practices and materials used in the Saraswati Mahal Library in Thanjavur. The Library has more than 25,000 Palm-leaf Manuscripts and 24,000 paper manuscripts. This paper deals with the various techniques employed by the library to preserve these manuscripts.

Introduction

We find a large number of Palm-leaf manuscripts in various Indian libraries today. The Saraswati Mahal Library at Thanjavur in Tamil Nadu has more than 25,000 Palm-leaf manuscripts and 24,000 paper manuscripts. The leaves of palm-trees were used as a writing material because palm trees grew abundantly in India and South Asian countries and were the cheapest and the most easily available material that could be used as a writing support. Palm leaves, if well treated and carefully maintained have a reasonably long life even in hot and humid tropical regions where the climatic conditions generally have an adverse effect on their durability. It has been observed that it is difficult to preserve Palm-leaf manuscripts for more than 500 years unless we have devices to control temperature and humidity and protect the manuscripts from insects.

Types of Palm Leaves

Though there are various types of palm trees, only the leaves of the following three types were used commonly for purposes of writing:

(i) *Corypha Umbraculifera*

(ii) *Borassus flabellifer*

(iii) *Corypha Utan*

The palm tree *Corypha umbraculifera* is known as Śrītāla or *Talipot*, and it grows in the humid coastal areas of South India, Ceylon, Malaysia, Andaman and Thailand. It is also called *Talapana, Coondalpana* or *Talipenai*. The leaves are broad and long, the surface is smooth and thin and these leaves are more flexible than the leaves of the other types. *Borassus flabellifer* is known as Palmyra and it grows in a climate that is comparatively dry. The Palmyra flourishes in South India and its leaves are thick and are not longer than two feet. The third variety is *Corypha Utan*, known as *Lontar*, and it thrives in Burma and Thailand. Its leaves have a blend of the Talipot and Palmyra palm leaves. The *Lontar* leaves are long, broad and thick and most of the Burmese manuscripts were written on these leaves.

Writing on Palm Leaves

For writing on palm leaves, five-to six-month old leaves are collected, separated by cutting away the mid rib and dried in the shade. After drying, the leaves are cut into a convenient length for writing and the surfaces are burnished. Two small holes are made for passing the cord to tie the bundle of leaves. The holes are placed in such a way that they divide the leaves more or less in three equal parts. Writing on palm leaves is done in the following manner:

(i) One method is to inscribe on the leaves with a stylus;

(ii) The other method is to write with ink on leaves using a bamboo pen or brush. For incising the writing, palm leaves have to be processed to soften the surface of the leaves before a stylus is applied on them. The stylus or *śalākā* made up of iron, steel, brass, with a pointed tip and sometimes embellished with bone and ivory is used for writing. One type of metal stylus has the pointed tip at one end and a sharp knife on the other end.

When incising the writing, the seasoned leaves are supported on a rigid surface or on the fingers of the left hand while incisions are made using the right hand to hold the stylus which rests on the thumb of the left hand for support and to prevent it from slipping. The incised leaves are given a two fold treatment for assuring the clarity of script. Turmeric paste is applied on the surface of the leaves of the manuscripts that are sacred and therefore kept in puja, worship. A mixture of vegetable juice of *Kovai Elai* (*Cocina indica*) and lamp soot prepared using castor oil was applied for rendering the incised writing clear. Nowadays lamp soot mixed with some volatile oils like Citronella is used for this purpose. In North India the palm leaves have been written with ink by using pens or soft brushes as the North Indian scripts are angular and such incisions would tear the leaf.

The Palm-leaf bundle

After writing, to avoid damage by insects, the leaves are arranged, strung and then placed between two planks of mango, bamboo, or teakwood. To hold the manuscript in position, the end of the cord that runs over the manuscript bundle to bind it in place is fastened to a device made of a Palm-leaf piece with the mid rib intact and it resembles the beak of a parrot. If the manuscript has more than two hundred folios, when the cord cannot hold them easily without damaging them, a small rod of copper or bamboo called *Nārasam* is pierced into the other hole of the manuscript bundle to hold the leaves in place. Other than wooden boxes, manuscripts were stored on a plank of wood called *Thooku* that was hung in the kitchens. Earthen urns with covers or bamboo cases with covers were also used to store manuscripts

Preservation Techniques

From ancient times several indigenous materials were used for preservation. The people were aware of the four basic factors leading to deterioration, namely, dust accumulation, direct sunlight, heat and humidity. To overcome these problems, manuscripts were usually covered with red coloured silk or cotton cloth which offered some protection from dust, light, heat and humidity. Red coloured cloth was used as it by its very colour acted as a repellent to insects and perhaps this also explains why red lines were drawn in front of the houses in the winter months, to prevent insects from crawling into homes. This is possibly the reason why the spines of books were bound with red coloured cloth or leather in most of the Indian libraries. Since turmeric has germicidal properties, paste or water treated with it was applied to the leaves to prevent fungal attack. Most of the manuscripts in the Saraswati Mahal Library have been treated with turmeric paste too. Plants like *kovai* that have been used for inking the text of manuscripts are bitter and are endowed with insect repellent qualities. The inking in addition also seals the stylus engraved manuscript surface from absorbing moisture. In practice it is found that the unblackened (uninked) manuscripts are destroyed faster than the inked manuscripts.

The Saraswati Mahal Insect Repellent Formulation

Many local materials like dried *Margosa* leaves, tobacco, camphor, black cumin, sweet flag, snake slough and peacock feathers have been used as insect repellents. The Thanjavur Maharaja Serfoji's Sarasvati Mahal Library at Thanjavur uses a mixture of the following spices in the powdered form to protect its manuscripts from insect attack. This formulation has been mentioned in the indent book of the librarian, Kuppa Bhatta, who served in this Library in 1882.

Black cumin	4 parts (1 kg)
Sweet flag	4 parts (1 kg)
Cloves	1 part (¼ kg)
Pepper	1 part (¼ kg)
Bark of cinnamon	4 parts (1 kg)
Camphor	(20 grams)

This powdered mixture is wrapped in a small cloth and such bundles are kept in the cupboards as insect repellent. This mixture is effective for six months, after which it has to be replaced with a freshly prepared mixture.

The administrative report of this Library published in 1921-22 mentions the preservation activities in the following manner:

> "The disinfectant vegetable mixture made in the Library is being applied to Palm-leaf manuscripts. The mixture makes the writing clearly visible and also strengthens the leaves. According to the recipe, found in the old records of the Library, of the disinfectant powder, the vegetable extracts are purchased; dried and small quantities of it are tied up in cloth and placed in the books and manuscript shelves. About 550 such packets have been made and kept in the shelves."

It is also mentioned that the manuscripts were dusted, cleaned and exposed in the shade to light and air. Use of the juice of the Dhatura leaves, and placing of dried *Margosa* leaves between adjacent manuscripts and books was prevalent. Citronella oil has also been used for Palm-leaf preservation from 1922-23. Because of the continuous steps taken for the preservation of manuscripts and books, the collection of this Library is in a good condition. If the good health of the manuscripts in the Sarasvati Mahal Library is an indication of the benefits of using indigenous preservation materials, then it might be important to scientifically analyze the local materials for their efficacy in a large scale conservation of manuscripts.

Interventions

Anupam Sah: What wood do you suggest to make boards to keep manuscripts in place?

Mr. P. Perumal: In Tamil Nadu we use seasoned teak, jackfruit wood

Fig. 14.1: Ingredients used in the insect repellent formula at the Saraswathi Mahal Library

Anupam Sah: Your paper is based on the composition that has four-five ingredients. Is it being used in this form because the ingredients have been traditionally used or is it based on your own studies and tests?

Mr. P. Perumal: No, we have not tested the efficacy of any ingredient. We are using the components because this mixture was prescribed. We did not question it. I do think, however, that just the component Sweet flag (*Acorus Calamus*) would be enough. There is need for researching this composition itself.

15

The Manuscripts of the Tawang Monastry

MALTESH MOTEBENNUR and NAWANG PHUNTSO

Abstract

This paper presents a brief history of the region near Tawang, the monastery and its library. The paper then introduces the manuscript collection and the indigenous method of the preparation of the paper. The objective of this article is to raise interest so as to bring about a conservation of the collection as well as a revival of the traditional paper making techniques amongst the Monpa and Sherdukpen tribes of Tawang and West Kameng districts of Arunachal Pradesh.

Introduction

The Tawang Monastery is one of the largest Buddhist monasteries in Asia and is located in Arunachal Pradesh in India. On the request of Mr. Anupam Sah, who had earlier rushed to the Monastery with an architect colleague Mr. Janhwij Sharma, to convince the monks not to demolish their wooden library for a cement concrete structure, a visit was made to this region to identify persons who could still make the traditional paper using the indigenous techniques. At the same time, the manuscript collection of the Tawang Monastery was examined. This paper introduces the monastery, the collection and the method of preparing local handmade paper.

Arunachal Pradesh

From where the mountains rise stretching northwards from the plains of Assam to the boundaries with China, lies India's farthest North-Eastern State of Arunachal Pradesh. Once referred to as the North East Frontier Agency (NEFA), Arunachal Pradesh is the largest among what is grouped as the Seven North-Eastern States or "The Seven Sisters." It is a vast land, austere and lovely, covering an area of 83,743 square kilometres and straddling the Eastern Himalaya like an intervening belt of green shadowed in perpetual rain and mist. From its meeting point with Bhutan in the West, the State stretches 1,030 kilometers eastwards descending from the northern boundary into the thickly forested slopes of the Patkoi hills, thus forming a triangular border with Bhutan, China and Myanmar. The area's remote geographical location, its inhospitable terrain, and the reported ferocity of its people left it outside the sphere of early explorations and evoked a very mixed reaction from those who first encountered it. The state is home to twenty five major tribes spread across 3,649 villages, most of which are located in remote valleys and hilltops.

As with most places in the mountains, though life is harsh, there is a measure of security. This remote Frontier State has now to catch up with the rest of the world, conforming to the new rules of change that are sweeping the land. Tribal society in the deep interiors is not entirely as picturesque as we like to imagine it. Even though one has to struggle in order to survive, the locals have established for themselves a way of life that is in harmony with the environment that surrounds them.

The Road to Tawang

Following the road to the district headquarters of Bomdila, one is struck by the air of worship and prayer. A pathway is lined with prayer flags that flutter in the cold, clear air. These are the tall *Ganzen Tsemo Lungdar*, with the emblem of the wisdom sword and the crown of sun and moon suspended over the eternal wheel. Following the Tibetan calendar, these are erected after the completion of every twelve-year cycle. A *Rimpoche*, reincarnate lama, is consulted and according to the year of birth, a particular mantra and type of flag is prescribed. The main flag is colour coded according to the corresponding zodiac sign and to these are attached strips of cloth. The colour blue corresponds with the sky and water, white stands for clouds, red for fire, green for living things, trees, plants and yellow for the earth.

Among the Monpa and Sherdukpen tribes of Tawang and West Kameng districts, Lopon Rimpoche is the local name for the Indian monk, Padmasambhava, who is believed to have established Buddhism in this area sometime in the eighth century. The West Kameng region of Arunachal is devoutly Buddhist and daily life is closely interwoven with religious practices. Among the Monpa and Shredukpen tribes there are seven and nine places respectively hallowed by the visit of Padmasambhava. These are places where the great master is believed to have sat in meditation and the impressions that he has left of his presence are revered and cherished to this day.

Beyond the soft rain and mist of Bomdila, on the road to Tawang lies the fortress town of Dirang-Dzong. The old fort is a four storeyed structure that was built in 1831 to function as an administrative centre under the direct control of Tawang monastery. A senior monk called a *Dzongpen* whose main duty was to collect taxes for the monastery was deputed to run it. Legend has it that the construction of the fort was fiercely resisted by the men of twelve leading households of this village that opposed the authority of the Tawang monastery being imposed on the freedom of the people of Dirang. In the ensuing armed struggle all the twelve men were brutally killed. Today, the fort stands in the old village as silent testimony to the brave men who fought for the freedom of the Monpas of Dirang village that still practices the pre-Buddhist Bon religion and perform rituals of the older Nyingmapa Buddhist sect.

The Tawang Monastery

According to local legend, more than four hundred years ago, a great monk, Lodre Gyatso, or Mera Lama as he is popularly known, travelled to this area in search of a site for a new monastery as a centre for the reformist "Yellow Hat" or Gelugpa sect of Mahayana Buddhism. He sat down on a hill to pray for guidance and when he looked around again he found that his horse had wandered off. Following the horse's hoof prints, Mera Lama came upon the palace of one of the local kings, Gyalpo Kala Wangbu. He at once perceived this as a divine sign that this was to be the chosen site. In another version, the horse, on reaching the present site of the monastery refused to go any further and instead began to strike the earth with his hoof. In recognition of the part played by the horse that led him to the site, Mera Lama called the chosen place "Ta-Wang," (Ta-horse, Wang-chosen). The full name of the monastery is Tawang Ganzen Namgye Lhacheh, which translates as "The celestial paradise of the divine site chosen by a horse."

The Library Collection

The library of the Tawang Monastery is a wood and stone structure and is known as the *Par-khang* or the *La-khang*. The manuscripts are stored on the first floor. Each manuscript is carefully wrapped in cloth, placed between wooden boards and then each bundle is placed in long pigeon-hole shaped wooden storage along the walls. The monk custodians treat the manuscripts with reverence.

Kan-gyur: In the Tawang monastery library, there is one set of 200 volumes of hand written *Kan-gyur* written after the establishment of Tawang monastery. Another set of 200 volumes of *Kan-gyur* written in gold and silver inks is also available in the monastery and these were written in Tibet much before the establishment of the Tawang Monastery.

At the Tawang monastery the *Kan-gyur* is read twice a year, once during the winter and once again during summer, to seek the blessings of Buddha, to ward off evil, for good luck, to secure a good harvest and for keeping away diseases. Other than at the monastery, individuals also read the *Kan-gyur* in their respective villages. Besides the above manuscripts, there are many other documents related to Buddhist studies not just in the Tawang monastery but also in its branch *gompas* and other village *gompas*.

Ten-gyur: There are about 300 volumes of *Ten-gyur* in the library.

The Manuscripts

The *Ten-gyur* manuscripts are mainly the teachings of scholars, disciples and *ācāryas** like Asank, Baru Bandhu,

---

* Teacher.

Dig Nag, Acharya Tsonkhpa of Tibet and others. The *Ten-gyur* is read in the Tawang monastery when there are natural calamities like flood, drought, epidemic diseases, earthquake, heavy snowfall etc. The *Kan-gyur* scripts are the teachings of the Buddha and contain more than a hundred volumes with each volume containing 400-500 pages. Some of the volumes of the *Kan-gyur* are *Bum, Nyiti, Gyetong, Choido, Felchin, Kontsek, Gyui, Nyangdey, Zungdui* and *Dulwa*.

The manuscripts are written in the Bhodi alphabets whose development is attributed to Thonmi Sanpota, Personal Secretary to the King Songtsen Gombu, the first Dalai Lama of Tibet. He wrote in a number of religious Buddhist scripts, *Pecha*, and documented the teachings of Buddha and of other *ācārya*.

Paper Making Techniques

Many of the manuscripts are written and block printed on paper made from the fibres of a local shrub *shugu-sheng*, of the Rhaphnus species, that grows in the Mon region of Tawang and West Kameng Districts of Arunachal Pradesh as well as in the Tsang area in Tibet. This local hand-made paper is still produced in the Mukto area of Tawang District. This paper, unlike other factory produced paper, is tough and does not get damaged easily.

For writing the scripts on local paper, inks are known to have been imported from *Gyana* (China). A type of ink was then produced in the Mon area too. The Monpa people burnt Pinewood and collected the soot on the inner surface of an earthen pot. The soot was mixed with castor sugar or *miśrī*, plant gum, deep roasted barley and water. This mixture is thoroughly mixed and kept for at least for a week before it is used.

For writing with this ink, a simple type of pen made from *sik*, a small species of bamboo found in Rahung areas of West Kameng District and Tawang was used by dipping into the ink. For writing on the local handmade paper, three to five sheets of such papers were pasted together with the help of local plant gum, animal *Klih* from the Gall Bladder of animals and also wild spice, *Yerr*. The purpose of using the bitter *Klih* was to protect the manuscripts from attack of insects and fungus. The ink is also fast and does not easily get damaged with moisture. It takes a scribe one day to write a page of the size 70 cm by 15 cm. Other than the black ink, texts are also written using gold, silver and other colours that were made with pigments brought in from nearby Bhutan. In the present day, modern paints are being used for writing manuscripts. Some traditional scribes are still present in and around Tawang District. One of these scribes is Shri Lungten residing in Shyo village.

Concluding Remarks

The monastery collection has had its share of problems related to the conservation of the manuscripts. Other than damage by the elements, there have been reported instances of removal of some ritual articles and manuscripts. It is time that thought is given to save and revive traditional monastic values as well as the related collections. The Tawang Monastery being out of the way for most institutions and individuals is a challenge for those who really wish to conserve its heritage.

Interventions

Vipul Shah: In Nepal and Bhutan, on the pretext of "reviving" this skill of paper making, the local paper makers are being forced to use caustic soda. The traditional method is to pass water through wood ash to produce a mild alkaline solution. What is the status there in Tawang?

Maltesh M.: No, here the few paper makers that are there still use the traditional method of passing water through wood ash and no synthetic chemical is used.

Vipul Shah: Does the ink spread? Do they size the paper or use orpiment on it?

Maltesh M.: No the ink does not spread. I suppose using the wood ash solution provides the sizing to the paper. No orpiment is used on it either.

Ratna Basu: What is the ink made of? Sometimes gall bladder is used to make ink.

Maltesh M.: Pine wood is burnt, the soot is collected. It is then mixed with *mīrī*, castor sugar, burnt barley and then kept for a week. Water is then added to it along with the gall bladder of a bovine. The gall bladder, the bile helps to protect the inked portions of the manuscript from insect attack.

References

Dai, Mamang, *Arunachal Pradesh — The Hidden Land*, New Delhi: Sky Printers, 2003.

Tiziana and Gianni Baldizzone, *Tribes of India*, New Delhi: Bookwise India, 2002.

url: www.arunachaltourism.nic.in

16

Manuscript Conservation Methods Employed at the Rampur Raza Library

W. H. SIDDIQUI

Abstract

The paper examines the development of writing and the spread of libraries in the Islamic world. It then explains the various methods by which the manuscripts in the Rampur Raza library, one of the major libraries of Islamic collections, have been taken care of since its establishment in 1774.

Introduction

There has been awareness about the storage and preservation of manuscripts and books from the very beginning, at least since setting up of libraries started in the Islamic countries. Before the discovery of paper making, books and records were written on stone, terracotta plaques, bark of trees, palm leaves, animal bones and skins. Except for relatively permanent materials like stone and terracotta, all other materials that were used for writing were perishable, and hence, very few specimens of such materials have survived. Those that have survived are in a very bad state of preservation and they require priority treatment.

It is surprising that Islamic scholars who had written lakhs of books, treatises and research papers on different subjects such as History, Geography, Religion, Biographies, Chemistry, Physics, Geology, Zoology, Botany, Medicine, Astronomy, Astrology, Mathematics, Algebra and Geometry, have only casually referred to the early Islamic libraries and their collections. Moreover, they have not recorded how the manuscripts were looked after and what methods were adopted for their preservation. Some awareness, however, can be observed when we find mention of how the librarians used to keep the manuscripts in wooden and iron boxes and later in wooden almirahs. I may briefly mention some of the ancient Islamic libraries and their history.

Development of Writing

The Arabs had developed writing before the advent of Islam. There were seventeen persons in Quraiś who knew the art of writing. A few women also practiced writing. The Jews had already learnt the art of writing at Medina before the birth of the Prophet Muhammad.[1] They used to write on stone and animal skin. The necessity of reading and writing was emphasized in the *Qurān* for copying the message of God. Side by side, the sayings of the Prophet (*Ḥadīth*) were also written on the bark of trees, bones and animal skins.[2] During the days of the Prophet there were writings like the Arabic version of *Qurān*, the letters of the Prophet, didactical poems in praise of the Prophet and certain written agreements between Muslims, Jewish and Christian kings.

---

1. Hafiz Ahmed Ali Khan Shauq, *Tārīkh-i-kitāb Khānah-i Razā*, ed. W.H. Siddiqui, Rampur, 1998, p. 41.
2. Hafiz Ahmed Ali Khan Shauq, *Khāzinah Futūḥ al-Buldān-i Balazari*.

Spread of Libraries

Though there have been no separate chapters in history books of the Arabs on libraries, with the extension of Islamic influence and establishment of new States, the writings and collection of books became very popular.[3] The Caliph Manṣūr of Baghdad got hundreds of books of Latin and Sanskrit translated in Arabic. Caliph Hārūn Raśīd established a great institution of research and translation, which he named *Bait'ul Hikmat*. It had two sections, one of which housed the library and the other was the bureau of translation from different languages such as Sanskrit, Persian, and Latin etc. Yaḥyā, the Minister of the Caliphate invited great *Pandit*s from India and appointed them for translation work. Caliph Mamun also followed the same path. Ibn Abil Jāriś was the binder of the *Kutub Khānah* (Library) of Māmūn,[4] which later became a popular interest of the ministers and noblemen who then began to establish their own libraries. Muhammad Abd al Malik Zayāt, the Minister of Wāthiq Billāh, used to spend Rupees 10,000 per month on translation of books.[5]

There were four lakh volumes in the library of Ḥākim Mustansir (d. AH 332 / CE 943-944), the Caliph of Andlas (Spain) and he had appointed his agents for purchasing books, i.e. manuscripts from Spain, Syria, Egypt, Persia and Khurasan. The library of Nūḥ bin Manṣūr, King of Bukhārā, was very famous. About it Avicina wrote that the books on philosophy seen by him in that library were not found in other libraries. He described the library as a big house in which there were

3. Hafiz Ahmed Ali Khan Shauq, op. cit., p. 48.
4. Rasacil Maulana Shibli Shauq, op. cit., p. 48.
5. Ibid.

several rooms and every room housed books on various subjects including science. There were several large wooden boxes in which books were kept on top of each other.[6]

Azadu'd-Daula Delmi had also established one very impressive and big library. The building of the library was very large and had many rooms and every room had almirahs standing by the walls and every almirah was three yard wide and as tall as a human and was decorated in golden designs. There were separate rooms for particular subjects, with distinct list of books.[7] The Library of the Fatmid king of Egypt was exceptional and it had no equal elsewhere. It was housed in the royal palace and had forty separate apartments with books on different subjects and there were eighteen thousand books on philosophy. The specimens of celebrated scribes namely Abū Muqla and Ibn al-Bawwāb were also preserved in the wooden boxes.[8] All these libraries belonged to kings and ordinary persons could not benefit from them. However, it was Sāpūr bin Ardṣīr who established one *Dār al-'Ulūm* in AH 382 / CE 992, and bequeathed many books for the use of the general public. In AH 395 / CE 1004-1005, the Fatmid king Bin Amīr Allāh established a king's library in Egypt, for the use of the general public where copying of books was allowed and paper, pen and inkpots were provided to scholars free of cost.[9] With this, libraries began to be built for every *madrasah* and mosque. Eventually, a large number of *madrasas* and libraries were established by the Sultans and Mughals in India.

---

6. Rasacil Maulana Shibli Shauq, op. cit., p. 50.
7. Ibid.
8. Ibid.
9. Ibid.

Care of Manuscripts and Books in the Rampur Raza Library, Rampur

The Rampur Raza Library was established at Rampur in CE 1774-1775. The books were very carefully kept in wooden almirahs and were periodically verified by the emperors, noblemen and *kitābdārs* (librarians) as is evidenced from their seals and autographs on the overleaf of manuscripts. Besides the *darugāh* (superintendent) of libraries, there were large numbers of employees who took care of books and adopted indigenous methods of preservation including good practices such as those of cleaning the manuscripts regularly. Particular manuscripts such as that of the *Holy Qurān*, were kept in *Juzdān* or stitched silken or cotton cloth. The manuscripts were and are still are kept at the Raza Library in airtight iron almirahs which were specially designed and manufactured by Godrej in the twenties. There were *Waraq gardans* (dusters) who used to look after every folio of the manuscript and clean it with a soft white cloth. During the period of the existence of the Nawabi State of Rampur, the Raza Library had more than fifteen *Waraq gardans* whose task was to clean the manuscripts and books regularly. A few of them are still working at the Raza Library. The manuscripts and books were dried in the sun if moisture was noticed in the almirahs.

The manuscripts and books were taken out from the almirahs and kept on clean carpets and the attendants cleaned the folios of the manuscripts and pages of books from morning till evening. The manuscripts and books which were found to be attacked by insects were manually cleaned and exposed to the sun for removing the insects. The manuscripts and books that were infested by insects were kept away in separate almirahs for protecting the remaining manuscripts and books. Brittle and damaged manuscripts and books were handed over to the menders and book binders for proper repair and binding. By this process the manuscripts and books were saved from dust, insects and damages. It is because of this regular care that a large number of old books have survived for centuries and have come down to us.

For the safety of manuscripts and books, besides peacock feathers and snake skins, dried neem leaves were also kept in the folios of the manuscripts. Later pieces of alum also began to be placed in the almirahs for the safety of manuscripts and books. In Rampur Raza Library there were proper arrangements for repairing damaged manuscripts and books. The menders repaired the damaged margins by pasting suitable papers. Repairs were also made in patches on the main text of the manuscripts by pasting transparent thin paper with paste specially made for the purpose. Damaged folios were removed from their "windows" and pasted on separate paper as is evidenced from the rare manuscript of *Dīwān-i Bābur* written in Turkish language. Illustrated manuscripts were also repaired with special thin papers and saved from further damage. The pasting material (*leī*) was prepared using *maidā,* mixed with powder of copper sulphate and mixture of alum. *Maidā* was mixed in water, and then the powder of copper sulphate was added into the pot and put on the fire. The solution was stirred by a wooden spoon for some time till the paste was prepared. Later the use of copper sulphate was stopped and alum was used for better pasting without the onset of yellow patches.

Continuation of the Conservation Tradition

There has been a separate binding section in the Rampur Raza Library for more than a hundred years, which has always repaired damaged bindings and also provided new bindings when required. If the leather of the binding was damaged it was removed and healthy leather was used for this purpose. The old system of preservation and binding of manuscripts and books in the Rampur Raza Library continued until 1995 when a Conservation Laboratory was established in the Library and scientific conservation work started. The Rampur Raza Library continues its tradition of taking care of its exquisite collections.

7

Paper Making at Sāṅgāner
Changes Over Time

RITU JAIN

Abstract

Sāṅgāner has been a centre of paper-making for centuries. Over the years, however, the quality of paper has changed and the number of families involved in the craft has decreased. This paper traces the changes that have taken place in its way of making.

THE very topic of the seminar reminds us of the extraordinary statement given by a great literary master:

> I have traveled the world twice,
> Met famous saints and sinners,
> The old stars and the hopeful beginners,
> The kings and the queens,
> The writers and the poets,
> The maters and the cooks,
> All in one library ticket,
> In the wonderful world of books.

Who will deny the universality of this wonderful statement! We all agree to this. One thing which is quite essential is the preservation of our tangible and intangible attributes of culture for the use of present and future generations. It is an alarming issue. We all agree to apply the techniques and materials of so-called modern or the scientific world to preserve and protect the heritage including books, manuscripts, paintings etc. But we should not forget that ours is a beautiful country where large numbers of tribes and indigenous communities have been residing since time immortal practicing their own rituals, cultures, social norms, behavioral patterns and religious beliefs. The essence of plurality is in fact the power of India.

It is true that Palm-leaf and birch bark dominated as support for writings by the saints and the learned class but the situation completely changed after the advent of paper. And what would we do without paper? Imagine the feel of paper on which delicate miniatures were painted, the paper on which our vast cultural knowledge has been penned down with so much effort and care. From this thought arose my desire to explore the nearly 1000 year heritage of paper artisans in India and to establish the fact that the Japanese were not the only masters of this great craft and that very good quality paper was being made in our country.

History

Noor Mohammed's papermaking forebears, following the will of their Mughal lords, entered Rajasthan in 1500's when Akbar conquered the Punjab and his army chief, Mansingh, shifted Noor's ancestors from Sialkot to Tijara, north of Jaipur. Singh was honored by the creation of a special sheet produced in Sialkot that came to be known as Mansinghi paper. Noor's predecessors continued to move, propelled by drought and water shortages. Over 200 years ago, Maharaja Jai Singh, builder of the Pink City, sent Noor's ancestor's to Sāṅgāner, a village south of Jaipur, giving them use of the Saraswati River for paper making.

In Sāṅgāner every man of a paper family is related in one way or another. Since men, women and children participate in various aspects of paper making, unity is considered advantageous. Women used to prepare the fibers before electric beating machines were adopted. They usually live together in the Muslim section of the town; they share the same blood, the same clan name, and the same craft skills. Training and the passing on of these skills is achieved effortlessly within the family and reinforced in an environment humming with villagers engaged in similar activities As a result, traditional Indian papermakers with Arabic roots belong to families self-contained now for many centuries.

Kāgẓī sheet makers were men of stamina, able to endure repetitive labour, lifting against the tremendous weight of water with every sheet, hands always wet, bodies standing in earthen pits or squatting above another pit for countless beck breaking dips.

Paper Material

Analysis of paper fragments indicates that primarily linen fibre or linen rag and starch size were the first ingredients. There is almost complete absence of physical evidence of paper's earliest days. The earliest known Jain manuscript on paper is dated 1229 (*Karakasambardhocyota*, Lalbhai Dalpatbhai Institute, Ahmedabad). Paper was mostly made from Linen, Jute, Sunn, Hemp, Gunny bags and even fishing nets. Elderly people still remember going as little boys to the market with his grandfather to buy old bullock carts bags. In the earlier days fibres were carefully picked up and sorting of impurities was done by hand. Before fibres were submitted to pounding, they were sometimes fermented after being washed. The bacteria fostered by this method help to pre-digest, break down and soften the fibres, fermenting is an old method that apparently has its roots in earlier oriental tradition. Circular troughs sunk into the ground form pits for fermenting, called often lies outside the papermaker's hut.

Cleaned raw material was mixed with a carbonate of soda called *Sajjī*, and left to soak in the pits for two to four days. One record indicates that *sajjī* comes from two wild plants, *kangan khar* (*Panicum italicum*) and Gora lana which grows in brackish soils. A detailed explanation of *sajjī* appears in Dard Hunter's book *Paper Making by Hand in India*.

> . . . Workers cut the plant of the *kangan* in autumn and allowed them to dry. In the mean time a circular hole about 5 feet broad and 3 feet in depth was dug in the ground; at the bottom of this excavation was buried one or two earthen wares, the bases of the jars being level with the bottom of the pit. With a pointed tool a worker pierced numerous holes in the protruding portions of the jars, making it possible for any liquid to run therein. A fire was started within the excavation and heaps of the dried millet (*chena*) plants were thrown on the flames until the collected mass of vegetation had been consumed. The liquid expelled from the plants was flowed through the small pierced holes into the sunken jars. The residue was finally stirred and covered with earth, which assisted in the cooling process. In a few days time the earth was thrown aside and the workers had a mass of crude unpurified potash for their labour."

Besides the pits in which the wet pulp ferments, heaps of wet, retting fiber were often left to break down for several days under sun on *cabūtrās* (platform). The sun naturally bleached the fibres, which were also rubbed across rough *cabūtrās* in order to further break them up. Duration of fermentation varied according to the seasons and was usually two to nine days, with heat increasing the rapidity of the process. But extra exposure also resulted in deterioration of the pulp, it becoming moldy and yielding inferior paper.

Often after fermentation the pulp was washed, beaten and the process repeated again. The process of fermenting, washing and beating was repeated five or six times at intervals of four or five days, until the mass was absolutely white and thoroughly broken.

The hardness or softness of sheet is first a reflection of the fibres used and second of how long they are beaten. For example linen experts its own quality in the sheet giving it a crisper look while cotton rag gives a softer appearances, similarly the longer they are pounded the harder or crisper is its appearance in the sheet.

One of the most difficult parts of preparation of pulp was the breaking down of fibres. This required substantial strength. One *Kāgzī* recalled that those who pounded fibers had "ribs of the width of four fingers" and another claimed "they would eat curd with 25 *capātīs* at one time."

Wooden trip hammers, called *dhenkī*, with a pivot post and stone or pounding cap at one end, once roared thunderously as they macerated fibers placed in a well under the pounding pulp they were still used in India during the first part of this century, although none can be found today. It was moved up and down at the opposite ends, pounded by both men and women. The process of beating by hand led to a gradual breakdown of fibres and resulted in long stronger fibers that ultimately resulted in a paper with better strength and texture.

Making the sheet on a grass mould is the high point of the entire process, the metaphysical moment of creation when the craftsperson gains the satisfaction of seeing the motion of the hands turn a slush of fibre and water into a finished, well made sheet of paper.

Simply a combination of a rigid wood support, a flexible, handwoven reed mat and two removable sidebars, this lightweight tool, called a *cāparī*, has changed little during centuries of use. The quality of paper depends, not only on its raw material, but also on the mould and the way it is moved by the artisans, it must be well constructed and free of clogged fibres, sag, or dislodged reeds. Moreover, the quality of the shake given to the mould during sheet making determines how well the fibres bond and how evenly they scatter to form a sheet of uniform thickness. The materials for these moulds used to be inexpensive and easily available locally. Despite their use by Indian craftsmen for over 600 years, however they succumbed to the intrusion of heavier Western woven-metal moulds. Today, artisans still using the *cāparī* are numbered.

The traditional grass mould is weaved by knotting the vertical threads weighted by terracotta spools. Traditional horsehair threads used in the past have often been replaced by cotton thread or nylon filament.

With *cāparī* in hand and the pulp prepared, the paper maker is ready for the moment of truth-fabrication of sheet.

In Erandol, Khuldābād and other regions the vat person stood waist deep in an earthen pit, sheet making in another sunken pit in front of him while in Sāṅgāner, the artisan squats above a sunken pit, creating sheets by bending forward with a rather back-breaking scoop.

The paper maker holds the *cāparī* in both hand on either end, and it is dipped into the vat filled with pulp and water. Once balanced evenly across the horizontal axis, the mould is lifted up to the surface of the water. As it is raised, the suction is broken and for an instant before the water drains, the mould is guided into a back and forth, and sideways shake which orders the fibres, the grass mat and the wooden support, bearing the newly formed layer of pulp, are for a second placed back down against the water in a quick floating motion. This detail of forcing the water against the grass mat makes it easier to remove sheets. Two sidebars are then taken away, and the grass mat is lifted from its wooden rest and turned over to release.

Papers made from traditional fibers were stacked one fresh wet sheet atop another and could later be separated for drying. Since contemporary use of cotton cuttings does not supply enough mucilage to prevent sticking, today cloth is interleaved between the stacked sheets.

Indian papermakers, working from such positions, could produce 175-500 sheets per day.

Most *kāgẓī* in their eighties or older describe the *"Do Pānī kāgaẓ"* or the double dip paper made to prevent sticking and to create a stronger sheet. In manager, one old elder recalls of making 500 sheets daily of these two-dip paper. This type of special paper is no longer made, and even the traditional single sheet, made by the hands of an individual artisan on a grass mould, is becoming an endangered art.

Drying of Paper

Wet sheets of every hue and quality were brushed onto the smooth plaster or lime washed outer walls of buildings to dry under the warming sun. Traditionally fresh sheets were stacked over one another and covered by rock weights that gradually force the water out; sometimes the weights are progressively increased. Finally, the sheets are peeled apart so that they can be dried. Papers dried this way become flat and smooth like the building and are peeled when the water has evaporated. Warm temperature effortlessly assists the process. Brushes used to feather stoke sheets onto drying walls are called *kūñcī* or *bowarā*. Sometimes they are made from a soft date palm frond or other fibers not quite as exotic as those of a brush Dard Hunter saw in Nowshera in the thirties made from the wispy beards of goats.

Wall drying is almost obsolete today with each year departure from tradition seems to be gaining an ever faster momentum though at least one family in Sāṅgāner still uses walls in a humble narrow alley between buildings.

Sizing

Many materials were used for sizing in India. In one of the larger semi-traditional mills in Sāṅgāner, a huge pot over an open fire relentlessly breaks down animal skin into a clear, glistening viscous liquid for sizing. Some Sāṅgāner sheet makers add starch sizing to the pulp as it is being beaten creating an "internal size" which prevents bleeding from any surface.

Hand Polishing the Paper Sheets

Today no one hand polishes paper except for a few rare individuals. The loss is dramatic considering that paper was still hand polished as recently as the 1930's. Polishing

implements were often beautiful and reveal surprising variety. Perhaps most common are the agate, quartz with exceptionally smooth surfaces called *goṭā* or *batte*. The feel of each of these tools in unique yet all have a grand, worn, touch-of-the-hand feeling and although hard, their silken must have eased the efforts of those who sat hour after hour, week after week, rubbing on an endless succession of paper sheets. As the worker tediously rubbed the agate back and forth over the paper's surface he occasionally brought the stone in contact with his hair, thus adding a small amount of oil to the agate burnisher. Both sides of the paper were vigorously polished this way. A poet describes in verse, the subtleties of polishing:

> That paper must be polished so
> That no creases appear in it
> The board for polishing should be wiped clean
> With a stone hand, but neither hard, nor softly.

A sloped wooden polishing board called *ghoṭlī* was often used for burnishing.

Under the pressure of growing commercial demand and for product diversification, hand made paper manufacturing units are using waste cotton rags that are cut into bits with the help of choppers after sorting. These are then cooked in open digesters with a low percentage of alkali and washed. Cut and dusted rages are beaten, with or without bleaching. The material is washed by means of washer drums followed by further beating. Wet sheets are lifted by the vat man with the help of wire mesh frames, either by dipping the same into traditional vat containing pulp or by pouring measured quantity of pulp into the mould held in the improved type paddle operated univat containing water. Coucher transfers the wet sheet to the sloth napkin or woolen felt by mild pressing of the mould. This lifting and couching process continues till a post of wet sheets interleaved with cloth/felt is made. The post is then pressed under a hand operated screw press or a small power operated hydraulic press after sizing paper is plate glazed between zinc? G.I. sheets and passed to and fro under heavy mechanical pressure through a small power, operated calendaring machine.

The paper has changed and so have the processes of papermaking and the paper makers. India is now emerging as a powerful supplier of commercial handmade paper due to advantages like plentiful raw material, an unending labour force, a penchant for color and variety and an unbroken craft tradition. The children, mother, father, uncle, aunt, grandparents at Sāṅganer all interact in an active lifestyle based on shared craft goals. They still make paper, though changed over time. . .

References

Aggarwal, O.P., *Conservation of Manuscripts and Paintings of South-East Asia*, London: Butterworth and Co., 1984.

Soundria Alexandria, *Gift of Conquerors*, Mappier, 1999.

Clapperton, R.H., *An Historical Account of its Making by Hand from the Earliest Times Down to the Present Day*, Oxford: Shakespeare Head Press, 1934.

Dutt A.K., "Paper making in India," *The Paper-maker* 24 (2 October, 1995): 11-19.

Emerson, H.W. *Monograph on Paper Making and Paper Mache in the Punjab*, India, 1907-08.

Gupta, C.B., "Conservation of Paper Palm-leaf, Birch bark, Parchment and Vellum Manuscripts in Libraries," Calcutta Seminar on Conservation of Library Material, January 1932.

Guy John, *Palm-leaf and Paper*, National Gallery of Victoria, Melbourne, 1982.

Hunter Dard, *A Paper making Pilgrimage to Japan*, Ohio: Mountain House Press, Chillicothe, 1932.

Jonathan, A., Hill, *Papermaking by Hand in India*, New York: Pynson Printers, 1939.

Lakshmi, A., "Handmade Paper in India," *The Paper-maker* 26, no.2 (1957): 31-37.

18

The Jain Approach to Conservation of Manuscripts

JITENDRA B. SHAH

(TRANSLATED FROM HINDI BY ANUPAM SAH)

Abstract

The Jain community in India is particularly sensitive to the preservation of manuscripts and the knowledge contained in it. The article discusses the tradition of conservation of manuscripts inherent in the Jain *dharma* and this tradition of conservation is illustrated through various examples of manuscript preservation effected by the Jains.

Introduction

We have been hearing about the traditional methods of conservation. Dr O.P. Agrawal too explained such methods in his keynote address. Even though most of the technical subjects have been talked about, I will try to place in front of you some of my thoughts related to the subject of conservation of manuscripts. In Jain *dharma*, there is a long history of manuscript preservation. As far as I know, the largest collections in India would be of Jaina manuscripts. There are numerous collections in Gujarat, Maharashtra and Rajasthan.

Today, in Ahmedabad alone, there exist lakhs of Jain manuscripts. In Pāṭan, Khambat, Jaisalmer, Jamnagar, Baroda, there are thousands of manuscripts, in a good state of preservation. These manuscripts are preserved well and the main reason for that is the tradition of Jain *dharma* to conserve manuscripts as well as the knowledge contained in them.

Jñānācāra

According to Jain *dharma*, knowledge is taught as *śruta-bhakti*,[1] as *ācāra*,[2] to a *śrāvaka*[3] even if the *śrāvaka* is uneducated. There are five *ācāra* in Jain *dharma* and the first of them is *Jñānācāra*.[4] According to this, the duty of any *śrāvaka*, even if uneducated, is to conserve knowledge and wisdom. One of the techniques followed by every Jain individual is that of *Pratikramaṇa*. Every evening the misdeeds committed are discussed. Each follower of Jainism expresses devotion and asks for forgiveness in case any wrong has been committed towards any of the 84 lakh *yonis*.[5] There are five *pratikramaṇa* and one of them addresses "knowledge," "means of knowledge" and the "knowledgeable person." Forgiveness is asked to atone for any "sins" that may have been committed knowingly or inadvertently in the form of touching manuscripts with the foot, mishandling, obliteration of ink using moist finger tips, using manuscripts as pillows. There is an aura of devotion that permeates the attitude of the Jain community towards their manuscripts.

---

1. That which one hears with devotion
2. Conduct
3. A practitioner of knowledge
4. Conduct with respect to knowledge
5. It is believed that there are 84,00,000 living entities in the world

Muni Śrī Puṇyavijayajī

Muni[6] Śrī Puṇyavijayajī is one of the first *muni* who has been active in the field of preservation of manuscripts in the contemporary sense. More than five lakh manuscripts that were dispersed in collections in Pāṭan, Khambaṭ, Ahmedabad, Jaisalmer were catalogued and published by him. According to him, other than maintenance, we must also protect manuscripts against disasters both natural as well as State emergencies for which we must have a system to protect our collections. As an illustration, he mentions that during the period of Kumārapāla, about 950 years back, there was a change of power and Ajayapāla took charge of the throne. In order to remove all memories of Kumārapāla, he ordered for all the manuscripts related to the previous king to be destroyed. Vāgbhaṭa, the Royal Minister, knowing that the *granthabhāṇḍāra*[7] will be destroyed, had the entire collection moved to Jaisalmer where he knew that the manuscripts will be safe.

Community Efforts

In a more recent incident, in 1947 at the time of the Partition, Gujranwala, a Jain centre with 20,000 manuscripts fell in the geographical boundary of the newly carved nation Pakistan. When the possibility of partition loomed, the realized that *śrāvaka* it would be impossible to transport 20,000 manuscripts to India at this time. They transferred the manuscripts into cupboards and placed them in the cellar and built a wall around them and a floor above them. The *śrāvaka* returned to India but there was lot of pain of having left the manuscripts behind.

---

6. Sage
7. A repository of manuscripts

At that time they did not know what to do and it was not possible at that time to venture to retrieve the manuscripts due to the political situation. Afterwards, when the situation improved, Sristhi Kasturbhai Lalbhai of Ahmedabad who established the Lalbhai Dalpat Bhartiya Sanskriti Vidyamandir, the L.D. Institute, and a gentleman named Dharmavira of Delhi brought the whole collection from Gujranwala in Pakistan. This collection is now housed in the B.L. Institute of Indology situated in Delhi.

Sometimes there are other disasters, such as the earthquake that took place in Kutch. As various buildings including the *granthabhāṇḍāras* were destroyed, it became the duty of the members of the Jain community to retrieve the manuscripts, and they did not fail in their duty. Youth groups were organized and they brought back cupboard-loads of manuscripts from the earthquake affected areas to Ahmedabad. It is clear that the buildings themselves must be able to take care of themselves and thus safeguard the property and lives within them. When people themselves are being affected, saving manuscripts may seem like an absurd thing to do. However if a group is taking care of people, others can take care of other things, including manuscripts. Safeguarding our collections is our duty, it is a mission.

There are so many manuscripts that have been written over the years. Every Jain *śrāvaka* educated or illiterate must have a book written atleast once in a lifetime. This has been a practice for the last 1500-2000 years and the creation of manuscripts is thus a continuing process for the Jain community.

Local Treatment

Haldī, ghodā bac, aśvagandhā, tobacco are used to preserve manuscripts and I will not repeat them. One of the problems we face is that the custodians of manuscripts in the *granthabhāṇḍāra*s are not trained to protect the manuscripts in a formal manner. There is a need to educate these people. Some manuscripts get stuck and such manuscripts are then immersed in rivers by some to save the manuscripts from inadvertent disrespect. In our traditional system, Muni Puṇyavijaya advised us to spread a fine powder on the folios whose ink has turned sticky due to the binding media having absorbed moisture. The folios do not stick then. To separate the folios that are stuck, the manuscript could be kept in a moist earthen pot. The moisture causes the manuscript inside to separate. It needs patience. When all the pages have been separated sprinkle *gulāla*[8] or any other fine powder. To protect the edges against damage, we keep the folios between slightly larger wooden boards and then cover the bundle with cloth. The best, of course, would be a teak box preferably hollowed out so as to avoid joins and gaps. However this option may not be possible today due to the high cost and the diminished availability of teak wood.

References in Manuscripts

The method to bind manuscripts is illustrated in Jaina manuscripts that say, *the manuscripts should be tied like an enemy is tied*. This firm tying procedure protects the folios from the elements. We often find the following verse written on the Jaina manuscripts, *Protect me from water, protect me in the cupboards, protect me from loose binding and don't give me in the*

8. A coloured powder.

hands of the foolish. Who do we call foolish and who not? Perhaps in this context a foolish person is the one who does not care for the value of a manuscript and disrespects it. There is an instance when a scholar requested a Jain *muni* for a manuscript and began turning the manuscript pages roughly. The *muni* immediately took the manuscript back and told the scholar that the manuscript is not for him to study. Another verse exhorts, *Protect from fire, from water, from rodents. . . the manuscript has been written with a lot of effort, the neck, back and tongue of the scribe have contorted with the effort of writing the manuscript, so take due care*. The scribes write with such effort and we too must be sensitive to it and take care that we treat the manuscripts with due respect.

Concluding Remarks

In villages one of the major problems is that while many do not know how to look after the manuscripts, they will not part from them either. The key to taking care of manuscripts, I feel, is devotion to them and for their intrinsic value. We have been able to incorporate it into the system of the community in relation to the *granthabhāṇḍāras*. In the monsoons, as the manuscripts are not supposed to be moved, they are not issued. After the rains, the *granthabhāṇḍāras* are opened. On the occasion of *Pañcamī*,[9] members of the community purify themselves, fast, remain in one place and express devotion to "knowledge" by taking care of the manuscripts by dusting them, checking for insect attack and other damages, exposing them to fresh air and light and then rebinding them if required. This is also known as *Jñāna Pañcamī kā Pūjan*, the Worship on *Jñāna* (Knowledge) *Pañcamī*. There is a continuous preservation process and the creation of new

9. The fifth day after the new moon as well as after the full moon.

manuscripts too. This is a small introduction to the way the Jain community looks after its manuscripts and I hope that this lecture complements the technical aspects that have been so lucidly discussed by the knowledgeable speakers before me.

Interventions

Shreenand L. Bapat: In the monsoons those four months were those when the Jain priest did not move out. Today that might not be the case. What happens now?

J.B. Shah: Is it done today too. The manuscripts are taken out beforehand and the stores are closed. The folios are wrapped carefully.

Shreenand L. Bapat: *Sādhus* are not allowed to keep personal possessions. Can a *sādhu* take a manuscript with him?

J.B. Shah: In the monsoons the *sādhus* would remain in one place. During the non-monsoon months, manuscripts are issued to them and after using them the *sādhus* returned the documents through any *śrāvaka* they may come in contact with. This has been a very reliable system and is extensively used.

19

Kadata of Karnataka
An Introduction

Usha Suresh

Abstract

Kadata or *Kadita*, also known as "black-book" is a type of manuscript little known outside the State of Karnataka in India. The author briefly introduces *Kadata*, its technology, dispersion and its importance as a source of historical information. The *kadata* of the Sringeri Maṭha have been prominently discussed in this article. The need for conservation of the *kadata* collections is being addressed and much more needs to be done.

Introduction

Inscriptions, monuments, coins, foreign accounts legends, traditions, literary works, palm leaves and paper records are important source materials that shed light on the political, economical, social and religious conditions of Karnataka of the past. *Kadata* or *kadita*, though relatively unknown, is another important source material that throws light on different aspects of medieval and early modern history. The existence of *kadata* goes back to the fourth century BCE and they have been widely used in medieval and early modern times. The *Epigraphica Indica* mentions a stone inscription of about the first quarter of the eight century CE that refers to a *Kriyācirika*, a deed of purchase written on a piece of cloth. *Kadata* is also known by other names like *pat*, *paṭkā* and *karpasika-pat*.

Technology

Buhler in *Indian Paleography* has noted that the Indians used to write letters on well-beaten cotton cloth. D.C. Sircar in *Indian Epigraphy* writes that according to historians, the mercantile community of the Mysore region is stated to have prepared their account books with sheets of cloth seasoned with a paste made out of the powder of tamarind seeds and afterwards blackened with charcoal. *Kadata* is a long sheet of cloth covered with a paste made of ground tamarind seeds and charcoal powder, well burnished with a smooth stone, dried, and folded in the form of a book of about two to three hundred pages that opens out like an accordion. Soapstone was employed to write on the *kadata* by the *Saṁbhoga* who used to register the records relating to land transactions. Sometimes while dispatching messages from one place to another, a sheet of *kadata* was rolled and inserted in the hollow of a piece of bamboo. *The Manual of the Administration of the Madras Presidency* mentions that a *Kadata* is a folded cloth seasoned with black-ink and used as an account-book in Kannada.

Dispersion

R.Narasimhachar, in his early twentieth century writing, states:

> In the Sringeri Maṭha there are several cart-loads of *kadatas*, nearly 200 years old, stored in two or three big rooms. A careful examination of these *kadatas* is likely to reveal several interesting facts with regard to the history of the Matha, and it is earnestly hoped that the authorities of the Matha will arrange for this examination before the *kadatas* are lost or destroyed by white ants.

Besides Sringeri, there are other places in Karnataka, where *kadatas* are preserved. The Keladi Museum and the Vīraśaiva Maṭha in Simoga District also possess *kadatas*. About 250 *kadatas* of Yalanduru Jagirdar near Mysore, are preserved in the Mysore Divisional Office of the Karnataka State Archives. The microfilmed rolls of the Śṛṅgerī *kadatas* are available in the Karnataka State Archives, Bangalore. The Oriental Research Institute of Chennai, Śrī Mañjeśvara temple in Kerala, Śrī Gokarana Partagal Maṭha in Goa and Kāśī are some other places where *kadatas* are preserved. There are about 205 *kadatas* that contain *nirupas*[1] and *binnavaṭṭales*,[2] and these are more important from the historical point of view. Such records registered in the *kadatas* number around 15,000. Other than these, there are about 548 *kadatas* that contain matters related to accounts.

Historical Records

The records throw light on political, administrative, religious, economic and social conditions from the fourteenth to the nineteenth century of the Sringeri Dharmasaṁsthāna in particular and Karnataka in general. According to the records in the *kadatas*, temporal powers like the Ādil Śāhīs of Bijapur, Mughal officers, Nizāms of Hyderabad, Haider Ali and Tipu Sultan of Mysore, Vijayanagara, Keladi, Marāṭhās, Wodeyars, the British and several chieftains made endowments to the Maṭha and respected the presiding elders, the *Jagadgurus*, over the ages. There are over 18 letters written in 12 *kadatas* that help to throw light on the correspondence between the Sringeri Maṭha and the Marāṭhā Ruling Houses like Peśwās, Ghorpaḍes, Sindhiās, Holkars, Bhosales and Pawārs and

1. Orders.
2. Letters of respectful communication and petition.

various sprincipalities in India. There are about 60 records spread over 15 *kadata*s that inform about the correspondence between the Sultan of Mysore and the Sringeri Maṭha and about 160 records spread over 43 *kadata*s that establish the close contacts between the Sringeri Maṭha and the Wodeyar dynasty of Mysore.

Thomas Munro, collector of the Canara District in 1800, states that *Saṁbhoga*s of the Canara District used black-books for several centuries to register *paṭṭā*s relating to land and land-revenue accounts. It appears Munro himself used such *Kadata*s while reintroducing the land-revenue system of the Vijayanagar period (CE 1336-1565), in the Canara District.

Generally, the records in the *kadata*s are dated in Śālivāhana Śaka era while the *binnavaṭṭaleṣa* issued by Haider and Tipu are in *Hijri*. Besides these, the *Kali* and Christian years are also used. Many records are in the Kannada language and script while there are some in Sanskrit, Marathi, Tamil, Telugu and Persian languages though the script of all of them is Kannada. The records in different languages point out the Śrī-Maṭha's contact with various principalities in India.

The above cited examples are but a few illustrative records from the *kadata*s of the Sringeri Maṭha. As mentioned earlier, there are about 15,000 records registered in 205 *kadata*s, besides the account books. It is in this context that one can well imagine the fund of historical information stored in these *kadata*s.

Concluding Remarks

While examining and conserving some *kadata*s of State Archives, it has been observed that they are better preserved than any other documents of the same period. In the meantime, a sincere attempt is being made these days to conserve *Kadata*s, palm-leaves and other paper records by the Sringeri Maṭha under the guidance of the Bangalore Centre of the INTACH, Indian Council of Conservation Institutes and the Regional Conservation Laboratory, Mysore.

In order to undertake an intensive drive for the conservation of *kadata*s, it is proposed by the Karnataka State Archives in collaboration with Regional Conservation Laboratory Mysore, to undertake a project as well as to organize a seminar using the services of experts in the field to throw light on the following:

1. History of *kadata*s
2. Survey, documentation and status of preservation of *kadata*s
3. Material and technology of *kadata*s, and
4. Conservation of *kadata*s

Interventions

Tej Singh: I am happy to know that work is being done at the Sringeri Maṭha with the help of INTACH, Indian Council of Conservation Institutes and the National Research Laboratory for the Conservation of Cultural Property.

Shreenand Bapat: These are State records. Are there any seals or stamps on them?

Usha Suresh: Not state records, only matha records. They are not in the possession of our archives. They are essentially account matters.

G. S. S. Rao: Any document coming from the Mysore Maharaja to Sringeri was copied faithfully on the *kadata*. The original document remains elsewhere. With the passage of time, as the originals have been lost, only the *kadata* remain that were there only for the *maṭha*'s reference. As the matter has been accurately copied, the *kadata* become most important as sources of information.

Saroja Bhate: From the point of view of historical importance, *Kadata* are very useful. In fact, we know more from *kadata* than from inscriptions. There are no paper letters or records as the Vijayanagar endowments were all recorded on the *Kadata*. These aspects are well known to historians. It is the technical aspects related to conservation etc. that must be given more consideration.

20

Indigenous Methods of Conservation of Manuscripts in Manipur

K. SUSHILA DEVI

Abstract

This paper touches upon the various natural plants and materials used for conservation of Manuscripts especially in Manipur.

INDIA is a land of rich heritage. Compared to the other countries of the world it is richest in terms of manuscripts. In spite of the enormous diversity of languages and cultures; we are one in terms of our manuscripts. We have manuscripts in different scripts and languages, but in writing and structure, the manuscripts are very much alike. It proves that our civilization is made up of different colours strung together in one thread.

We are the richest in terms of manuscripts but to preserve such rare and priceless antique articles, we must use certain methods. It is not only for our own benefit but for the benefit of our future generations. Our forefathers used different plant products and their extracts for preservation, which are more friendly to our health and surrounding.

Everything has its durability. But by using certain methods and plants extracts it can be made more durable and the life span of the material can be made longer. Some of the plants or animals products used as preservative and methods are mentioned below.

Use of Cow Urine

The writing materials should be first dipped in the urine of cow for 5 to 6 hours. The urine penetrates the writing materials and makes it more durable. The alkaline nature of urine makes the material disliked by the insects and worms, thus helping in preservation. Further, the process can also be used to make the existing manuscripts waterproof.

Uses of Neem Leaf or its Fruits (*Malia Indica*)

Either Neem leafs or fruits are first boiled with water thoroughly to extract the alkaline contents. After the solution has cooled down, it is filtered through clean thick cloth or cottons. The filtered solution is smeared in the writing or already written materials as Neem is a natural insect repellent.

Uses of Tulsi Leaf (*Ocimum Sancum*)

Tulsi leaves should be kept between folios of the manuscripts to prevent insects from attacking the manuscripts and to make it more durable.

Uses of Oxalis Leaf (*Oxalis Retriculatus*)

The use of oxalis leaf is also a very convenient method. The plants are found in abundance in nature. First of all, it should be burnt very slowly without producing much flame. The smoke coming out of the raw burning of the oxalis leaf is a preservative. The smoke is introduced in the manuscripts once, which makes them free from the attack of insects and worms for more than ten years. So the process should be repeated after 10 to 11 years.

Uses of Marigold Leaf (*Tezecta Indica*)

The petals of Marigold flower are used as preservatives by keeping them in between the folios of the manuscripts. Marigolds have a natural tendency of repelling insects and warms.

Use of Tobacco Leaves (*Nicotine Tobaccum*)

Solution of Tobacco leaves is very useful. The solution of tobacco leaves in water is smeared in the manuscripts or the dried leaves are placed in between the folios. The benefit is tremendous as the insects are repelled from the manuscripts.

Use of Red Cotton Cloth

Manuscripts should always be wrapped in red cotton cloth because red colour is a natural repellent of worms and insects.

Use of Wooden Plank

Manuscripts should always be covered from both sides by a wooden plank, a bit larger than the manuscripts. It makes the manuscripts safe and prevents them to come in sudden contact with fire in case of fire accident. Lastly the wooden planks should be tightened with a thick cotton string.

Mode of Keeping Manuscripts

The manuscripts should always kept in a rack, which should be at least 4 to 5 feet above the ground level. After preventive measures are done, the manuscripts should be placed in racks. It prevents the manuscripts from coming in contact with water vapours, which causes damage

Room for Keeping Manuscripts

The manuscripts should be kept in a well ventilated room free from moisture. The room should not damp and should be kept clean, dry and airy.

Writing Materials

According to late Pandit Achouba Ng. Kulachandra Singh the material used for manuscripts is varied and rich. Papers of various grades, palm leaves, barks of *Kona* and *Tengna* (leaves resembling Palm-leaf), *Agor*/birch bark, *bhūrja patra* and, *meitei* leather for *sading puya*. *Meitei Che* are seasoned and polished before they are used. We have little information about *Meitei Che* prior to the reign of Khagemba.

Indigenous paper technology flourished in ancient and medieval Manipur. A thick type of *Meitei Che* is found to have been manufactured and used for writing *puyas*, horoscopes, almanacs and records of information and secrecy. *Meitei Che*/ paper is thick and hard. It is softened by the rubbing of Kinghkin (*costus specious*) for the purpose of writing. There is a need to revive this technique.

There are many illustrated manuscripts like the map of Kangla, Paphal, Subika, Subika Laishaba, etc, which are important from the point of view of calligraphy, colour and glimpse of fine arts.

Papers and manuscripts are made into a bundle of folios. A single folio of a complete treatise does not constitute a separate bundle. Some other written folios of a separate treatise are placed next to that of a single folio. Thus, we find that often several works (chronicles, literature, astrology, music, etc.) are tied in one and the same bundle. The damaged part of a manuscript page can be rewritten with the help of a great *Pandit/Maichou* who is aware of the text.

Normally a *Pandit* is engaged in all the stages of book production, comprising the preparation of *Meitei Che, Agar Bak* writing, making the hard wooden cover and binding the bundle with a *Meitei* Cloth. It shows the multiple functions of a scribe. It does not involve division of labour relating to collection, preservation copying the manuscripts, book binding with leather and needle.

The *Salai*s/*Sib*s and other clans believe that the careless keeping of genealogical manuscript is said to have been the cause of accidents, ill luck and the shortening of life span.

Technique of Preserving Rare Manuscripts

The *Salai*s never give the sacred *puya*s to the hand of non-Meiteis. The collection and preservation of manuscripts are made by the *Meitei* inhabitants of Myanmar, Cachar, Takhel and Tekhao/Assam.

They have deep reverence for the *puya*s, therefore, many of the people are not trained enough in this field, which involves the understanding of the *Lairol*. The manuscripts remain in the custody of *Pandits*, where they are preserved. Many of them fall pray to insects. This proves fatal for their preservation as they are lost to the world of scholars. The practice of burying the damaged manuscript has naturally destroyed some of them.

Method of Conservation Adopted by the *Loi*/Scheduled Castes

The practice of preserving manuscripts among the Scheduled Castes/*Lois* viz. Sekmai, Khurkhul, Leimaram, Phayeng, etc.

is similar to that practiced by the people of Burma and Myanmar and is very interesting. Manuscripts were preserved underground by a practice, according to which the leaves are wrapped in *Leihoura* leaves (they look like plantain leaves), which can resist the attack of white ants and insects. The underground heat and moisture cannot harm this leave.

A type of black varnish called *Khe* (which grows in the Kabow Valley), is obtained from the juice of Kheu tree/*melanor how writta,* is is applied on the bundle in order to make it waterproof. The *Lois* belonging to the South Eastern side of the valley are in the habit of burying the book bundle in the cremation ground of their forefathers and old relatives with their ashes.

Need for Revival for Literary and Sacred Purposes

In the opinion of late W. Yumjao, the ruler was the custodian and responsible for the preservation and safety of the places where manuscripts and things of archaeological values are buried under the ground. The rulers would spread the rumour that if it is unearthed the ruling prince would die early. So any request for unearthing a place was flatly refused by the Mahārājā and his *Pandit* Loisang. The superstition is attributed to the fact that they were greedy and were eager to possess the precious material buried underground including Manuscripts for their own interest without serving the purpose of preservation.

It is urged that documentation of damaged manuscripts, making old descriptive catalogues and Indigenous methods should be preserved before it is too late. It is the duty of the State Archives to authenticate them through experiment and to encourage the use of manuscript for the benefit of the public.

The section on the manuscript must be developed into a full fledged library through acquisition and preservation. The Department may venture to publish a bulletin in bi-lingual containing printed rare and unpublished manuscripts from Assam, Myanmar, Arunachal, Sikkim and Bengal.

It must continue the camps, workshops, seminars for training the people of this part of India which are increasingly popular as in these years. In the light of the present circumstances of resource scarcity, constraints in infrastructure, ecological uncertainties of scientific alternatives, building up on traditional or indigenous practice constitute a practical means of meeting our essential needs.

Periodic Reading of Manuscripts

The manuscripts should be read periodically as they are a source of knowledge. If damages are found, then preventive measures should be taken up.

We in the present generation have used organic and inorganic chemical as preservatives. Some of the chemicals are Ketone, Thiamol, Copper Sulphate, Silica gel etc. Besides they are hazardous to health and are not available in remote parts of the country. On the other hand, the use of such chemicals needs scientific knowledge, but the methods are hardly understood by the common people.The indigenous practices of preservation are friendlier to our health and surrounding eco-system and are easily practicable.

Today our age-old manuscripts, the rare priceless antiques should be taken care of and preserved for the future. We are indebted to our forefathers for keeping and preserving such priceless and rare manuscripts. The educated youth of the present generation, do not realize the importance of manuscripts. At present, the manuscripts are not thought of seriously, except by some interested persons. If such practices continue then the rich heritage will surely be in a state of ruin.

Lastly, I would like to make an appeal to all, that without these age-old manuscripts no one can make a research successful, in the field of either arts or science. Paper making technique did not progress beyond a certain stage on account of influence of modern paper. Writing was less in use in earlier times. Paper making style could not survive here while in other parts of India and the world it was fast advancing because of Sheer necessity and state support. This created the impression that paper and paper making came to Manipur from outside.

21

Decline and Revival of Forgotten Manuscripts Traditions

ANUPAM SAH

Abstract

Revival of an art form such as forgotten manuscript traditions involves various tangible and intangible aspects. It is pertinent to understand how different manuscript traditions evolved while some fell to disuse. The components of a revival effort are many and need to be considered together. A possible approach to initiate the revival of the manuscript traditions is outlined along with some real benefits of such an exercise.

Introduction

While working to conserve manuscript collections, we find that the art of creating manuscripts, their materials and tools and the intangible aspects associated with the process have been forgotten. The people who created and those who can still create exquisite manuscripts have been largely ignored. Yet another art form lingers on the edge of the endangered human practices. Manuscript writing traditions progressed over centuries from writing and inscribing on stone tablets, metal sheets, leaves, bast, and paper prepared by hand and then eventually on paper manufactured on machines. Today many thoughts are typed by authors directly on the computer and printed digitally. This article introduces the elements of traditional processes of creation of a few types of manuscripts, the reasons why the traditions began to cease and were replaced by others. The components of a manuscript revival are outlined along with a possible approach. The article concludes with an idea of the network benefits and brief concluding remarks.

The Body and Soul of a Manuscript

Support

Other than stone, metal and proteinaceous surfaces such as parchment and vellum, manuscripts in India have predominantly been prepared on surfaces made of plant material. The plant material has either been used very close to its original form such as in *Bhūrja Patra*, birch bark, *Tāla patra* or palm leaves, or it has been processed as in the case of *Hāṅsī pat*, the bast of *Agaru* tree and palm leaves too. Through a more vigorous intervention, plant fibres have been beaten to pulp to form sheets of handmade paper, the surface of which is smoothened and burnished to make it suitable for use as a writing support. Other supports such as those of a *Kadata*, have been prepared using a cotton cloth base on which was applied a smooth ground of chalk and plant gum binder. The shapes of manuscripts vary from loose or bound folios to accordion shaped or long scrolled documents.

Inks

The ink can be made of pigments usually of earth and mineral origin. Vegetable origin "pigments" are essentially dyes precipitated on white inert powders. Sometimes dye-based inks have been used too. The pigments are often made into a concoction with ferruginous elements and vegetal additives. This is often tempered with a binder.

Text and Illustrations

The text can and does relate to a variety of subjects ranging from poetry, grammar, treatises, to land and revenue records. The text can either be surface written or it can be incised into the surface of the writing support, and then inked in. The illustrations accompanying the text can be diagrams by the scribe or they can be sketches and painted images supporting the text and drawing inspiration from it.

The Process of Writing

The action of writing itself is a very personal process imbued with various feelings that can be of quietude, spirituality, exhilaration or intense emotion or also of pure detachment. It is the complementary involvement of the mind and the physical body in order to manifest thoughts into writing. It is a process that both emanates and is actualized by the being.

Environment

The manuscript making process leads to a creation of micro environments both at the community as well as the individual level. Besides the creation of an environment of working together and a creation of an ambience where the communities are involved, is also the creation of the individually energised space that contains the scribe writing meditatively as well as the space of the reach of the scribe's mind.

Purpose of a Manuscript

The process of creation of a manuscript can broadly encompass aspects of education, communication, record keeping, selfless service as well as conscious efforts to earn temporal or spiritual merit.

Human Interactions with the Manuscript

The contents of a manuscript as well as the body of the manuscript are an inter-phase between a human being and a human creation. Interactions with manuscripts can be in the form of reverence, ritual worship, a desire to glean knowledge, repetitive use or a glancing reference. The reading itself of the contents can be imbued with a variety of emotions and can manifest as silence, loud announcement, whispers, personal or community singing in folk style or in well laid out chanting rules.

The Outer Covering

The tendency for safekeeping of the manuscripts has resulted in a variety of covers, binding methods and containers. These, like the texts can be simple and effective or gloriously embellished and visually arresting and can be made of a variety of materials such as wood, metal, bone, ivory or cloth.

Thoughts on revival of manuscript traditions must then take into consideration a revival of many components and not just fabrication of handmade paper. The thought on revival brings to the fore a hint that something passed away, that it died. Did our manuscript traditions really die? If they did, then why?

Decline / Evolution of the Manuscript Traditions and their Revival

The common refrain that one hears is that the advent of modern manufactured paper sounded the death knell of our glorious manuscript traditions. Perhaps our manuscript traditions have never died; perhaps they have organically evolved into other effective manifestations of human expression. Then again, manufactured paper was just another element that contributed to the evolution of our writing traditions.

With human progress in time, the materials in use for imparting education, effecting communication, as well as record-keeping changed over the decades. For centuries privileged children learnt to handle a *lekhanī,* a *parhinda* or a metal stylus to incise letters on a Palm-leaf. With time, chalk and slate made inroads into primary schools as well as institutes of higher learning. Pencils at one time were for slightly older children and for those who could economically afford them. Ink pots and fountain pens were a sign of graduating to higher standards of schooling, but that too gave way to the ball pen and that in turn has evolved into a plethora of gel pens and micro tipped ink cartridge writing instruments. With the advent of white boards and markers and electronic projections, even the black boards are being supplemented and may eventually be completely replaced. The varieties of paper that came into the markets nurtured a change in the writing instruments too.

Along with our traditional writing techniques and manual calligraphy, came adherence to rigorous self-discipline, sincere effort and the praise and the admonitions of the teacher. Changing social perceptions had their effect on the relationship between the teacher and the student.

Our requirements changed and to illustrate it with the subject of record keeping, we have seen that our volumes of records increased dramatically. Our filing systems changed as did our storage and retrieval systems. From shelves to compactors and now to digital discs, these movements of human requirements affected the way we created our manuscripts too.

Communications on scrolls adapted to the evolving postal system. Very important have been the changing tastes and preferences of the users, us. Introduction of standardized formats such as aerogramme, inland letter and postcards and the mechanical, electronic and digital medium today have created another genre of manuscripts, where the hand that can also write now creates alphabets through a machine. Some can do it better and more skilfully than others. That too is a skill and perhaps an art. The mind is still involved as it was centuries ago.

Going by the assumption that our manuscript traditions never died but evolved into other effective means of expression we may say that our manuscript traditions have been forgotten during the ensuing evolution of human activity. Many of us may acknowledge that memories of human progress run deep and true, and when that is the case, it is only a question of reviving our memories and reliving them in order for them to manifest again as beautifully as in the past. The manuscript traditions when revived would again be a tangible expression of human effort to connect time and again with our own past even as we endeavour to link our effort to human progress into the future.

Components of a Revival

Revival of the manuscript traditions would include both the tangible and intangible components. Some of these components are those mentioned as the body and soul of the manuscript in the opening paragraphs of this article. The basic ones can be listed as:

- Revival of the physical material and technology associated with manuscript traditions
- Identification of the practitioners, teachers and students
- Revival of the rituals and traditions that accompany the use of the physical components
- Revival of the skills and numbers of practitioners
- Revival of the teaching methods by which the skills and the processes of the tradition can be imparted
- The patrons and the end users
- The positioning of the pure revived form and its adaptation and modification by contemporary society
- The context within which the revival effort is made
- The context within which the revived tradition will be practiced
- Sustenance of the revived tradition
- The legal and moral realm of intellectual property rights

A Possible Approach

Some of the steps that would be necessary to undertake a Revival exercise can be summarized as follows:

- Identification of patrons with whose support the process can be conducted over an initial period of one or two years
- Identification of a coordinator well versed in material and technology of manuscripts and with experience in working with communities on similar efforts

- Documentation and research of the material and technology of the forgotten traditions. Testing formulations for their authenticity and durability
- Establishing faith with the old practitioners and assuring each other of working together to revive the tradition
- Identification of practitioners of varied age groups including old practitioners with memories of the tradition, and young ones, skilled and with the ability to absorb the tradition
- Establishment of a project school where the pure form of the manuscript tradition can be pursued and disseminated
- Creation of attractive exemplar "sample" manuscripts and the processes that can be displayed and used to advocate the first signs of "revival"
- Identification of strategic partners to showcase the process and product to catch the imagination of the public and policy makers
- Creation of a demand: The creation of a demand for the manuscripts. The demand can be for paper, the inks, the tools or the materials as well as the finished manuscript. The created manuscript would be in demand not only for the finished product but also the manner in which it has been created. The various avenues to incorporate the revived tradition in daily lives and on special occasions should be explored
- Consider systems that ensure a fair livelihood to the practitioners and encourage a growth of the tradition

- Document the process and disseminate the results and improve the process for future related activities

Benefits and Concluding Remarks

Events and actions are intrinsically interrelated. The revival exercise and the final results can help in the creation of such schools of learning for other crafts too. This itself can spawn a major livelihood movement that also develops self esteem and pride in local skills and traditions. A variety of ancillary products and employment opportunities can develop. It can lead to the creation of heritage nuclei in various parts of the country and those can then be levers for socio-economic development. Manuscripts writing is an arm of the education traditions and could be networked with national education systems to encourage learning at the primary level and encourage research based on primary sources at a higher level.

Manuscript preparation is closely linked with our natural vegetation and can result in a regeneration of local green covers in order to provide a controlled source of species that have by now become very sparse and almost extinct in their natural environments. Rural development, empowerment of women and of the physically challenged can all be incorporated at their local levels in this exercise. Even the Incredible India Campaign is probably waiting for something like this to happen.

We go to great lengths to preserve the endangered Mountain Quail. The Edelweiss is a protected flower. Thousands raise a cry to preserve a local monument. Let us then give one try to revive at least some forgotten human traditions also, perhaps our manuscript traditions, to begin with.

The Contributors

G.N. DEVY former Professor of English at the Maharaja Sayajirao University of Baroda, set up the Bhasha Research and Publication Centre in 1996, and the Adivasi Academy at Tejgadh in 2000, with a view to creating a national corpus of adivasi languages, literature and arts. He has received the Sahitya Academy Award, the SAARC Writers Foundation Award, the Prince Claus Award and Gunther Sonthiemer Award. His publications include "After Amnesia," "Of Many Heroes," "In Another Tongue," "Painted Words" and "Indian Literary Criticism." Prof. Devy writes in English, Gujarati and Marathi. He is currently Professor of Humanities at the Dhirubhai Ambani Institute of Information and Communication Technology.

HEATHER BROWN is currently Preservation Manager at the State Library of South Australia. In collaboration with the National Library of Australia and IFLA, Ms Brown has developed microfilming training materials which have been distributed throughout the Asia Pacific region under the auspices of IFLA-PAC with the aim of better preservation of heritage materials through high quality microfilming techniques. Heather delivers training courses in reformatting for the Singapore National Archives.

K.K. GUPTA is Consultant Coordinator, Conservation with the National Mission for Manuscripts, New Delhi. As Assistant

Chemist at the National Museum, New Delhi, he has over 38 years, worked extensively on the conservation of antiquities and works of art in the Museum. He has also given training to researchers and specialists at the National Museum and later in Japan, through a UNESCO programme. Mr. Gupta was also Editor of the journal *Conservation of Cultural Property in India*, for five years. He has written many articles as well as a book "Restoration of Oil Paintings."

C.N.K. Alahakoon is a Senior Assistant Librarian managing the special collections at the University of Peradeniya, the oldest university library in Sri Lanka. She has a Masters Degree in Library and Information Sciences from the University of Colombo, with a specialization on "Management of Conservation and Preservation of Palm Leaves in Sri Lanka."

Bhupen Goswami has a Masters Degree in Library Science. He has had over 33 years experience in various university libraries. He was the Academic Counselor of the BLIS and MLIS programmes of IGNOU, teaching the elective paper, "Preservation and Conservation of Library Materials." He is presently the Librarian of K.K. Handiqui Library, Guwahati University, as well as Coordinator of the KKHL MRC and the KKML MCC for the National Mission for Manuscripts.

Sudhendu Mandal is the Director of National Library, Kolkata. He has been a Professor of Botany at the Viswa Bharati University.

Dr. Sanjay Kumar Maiti is presently the Library and Information Assistant at the Preservation Laboratory of National Library, Kolkata where he has been attached since 1989. He holds Masters Degrees in Physiology and Library Sciences. He is presently enrolled for masters in Library Science. He is an Associate Fellow of the Indian Institute of

Chemists and a life member of the Indian Association for the Study of Conservation of Cultural Property (IASC).

S. Subbaraman retired as Superintendent Archaeological Chemist, Archeological Survey of India. He was responsible for the conservation of monuments in South India, including Ajanta and Ellora. He has a Masters Degree in Chemistry, and has received higher training at the Central Institute of Art Restoration, Rome and the British Museum Research Laboratory, London. He has worked on the conservation of paintings in World Heritage monuments like the Ajanta Caves, Brihadeshwara Temple, Tanjore, etc. He set up the Conservation Laboratory of the Indian Museum, Kolkata, heading it for nine years. He is now Director of the INTACH Chitrakala Parishad Art Conservation Centre, Bangalore.

Imtiaz Ahmad is presently Director of the Khuda Bakhsh Oriental Public Library, Patna. He has taught in the Department of History, Bhagalpur University and Patna University. He is a member of the Indian History Association for the Study of History and Archaeology, Bihar Research Society and Bihar Itihas Parishad. He is presently engaged in editing the Comprehensive History of India, Vol. XI (jointly with Prof. Shireen Moosvi). He is at present writing a biography of Bahadur Shah Zafar and working with Prof. Irfan Habib on a volume on the Delhi Sultanate for the People's History of India S eries. Apart from this he has authored two books and over 50 articles on Sufism and Bihar.

Shreenand L. Bapat has a Post-Graduate Degrees in Sanskrit and Archaeology. He is currently working on his Doctoral degree. He has been trained in the conservation of manuscripts at INTACH-OACC, Bhubaneshwar. He has written extensively and has numerous radio programmes to his credit.

He has worked at the Bhandarkar Oriental Research Institute as Assistant Curator. He is presently on deputation with the Tilak Maharashtra Vidyapeeth as a Lecturer in Indology.

V. Jeyaraj is a post-graduate in Chemistry and History and a Doctorate in Analytical Chemistry concentrating on the study of metal antiquities and their conservation. He has been involved in the conservation of museum objects since 1978. At present he heads the Conservation and Research Laboratory, Government Museum, Chennai. He is the President of the Indian Association for the Study of Conservation of Cultural Property, New Delhi and Coordinator of the Manuscript Conservation Centre, Chennai.

C. Maheswaran is the Curator for Anthropology at the Government Museum, Chennai. He graduated in both Linguistics and Anthropology and has earned a Doctorate in Linguistics. He is a specialises in tribal studies in Tamil Nadu and has authored many books and papers related to Anthropology and Paleology. He is presently involved in the refurbishment of the Anthropology Gallery at the Government Museum, Chennai.

S.D. Das is the Conservation Officer of the Asiatic Society in Kolkata. He has worked as the Assistant Chemist in the National Library, Kolkata, as the Head of the Conservation Unit.

P. Perumal is a conservator, trained under a UNESCO sponsored conservation course at NRLC, Lucknow and ICCROM sponsored international Japanese paper conservation course in Japan. He received the Nehru Foundation Fellowship and interned for three months in libraries and museums in the United Kingdom. He is presently researching on the "History and Development of Manuscript Conservation" at the Tamil University, Thanjavur. He has conducted conservation training courses for more than two hundred librarians and delivered lectures in seminars and workshops. He has published several research articles on the conservation of books and manuscripts. He is a member of Indian Association for Studies on Conservation, New Delhi and presently Editor of the IASC journal.

Motebennur Maltesh is presently working as Assistant Librarian in Arunachal University, Rono-Hills, Itanagar, Arunachal Pradesh, India. He did his Masters in Geology and Library Sciences from Karnataka University, Dharwad and NEHU, Shillong, Megahlaya. He has taken keen interest in automation and modernization of Arunachal University Library. His current interests lie in the preservation of rare Buddhist manuscripts of Arunachal Pradesh.

Nawang Phunsto belongs to the Monpa tribe of Aruanchal Pradesh from Tawang. He graduated in Geography from Arunachal Pradesh in 2002 Presently he is working as a Research Scholar in the Department of Geography, Arunachal University. He is working for the preservation and conservation of Bhoti (Tibetan) script and for other heritage issues in the Tawang area. He is the Secretary of a local NGO in Tawang.

W.H. Siddiqui is Former Director with the Archaeological Survey of India. He is presently the Officer on Special Duty of the Rampur Raza Library, Rampur.

Ritu Jain was In-Charge of the Conservation Laboratory of the Indira Gandhi National Centre for the Arts. At present she is working for the Parliament Library. She has a Masters Degree in Art Conservation from the National Museum Institute, New Delhi and has received training in Japanese

Techniques of Paper Conservation from TNRICP, Tokyo. She is also involved in imparting training on preservation, conservation techniques and has initiated workshops on awareness for cultural heritage and its preservation amongst the school

J.B. Shah has been Professor, and has lectured widely on Indian religion and philosophy. He is presently the Director of the L. D. Institute of Indology at Ahmedabad.

Usha Suresh is the Director of the Karnataka State Archives at Bangalore. She has coordinated a number of projects and has also helped organise various training workshops on preventive conservation.

K. Sushila Devi is at present Director-in-Charge of the Manipur State Archives and Project Coordinator of MRC, Manipur. She has a Doctorate degree from Manipur State University. She has presented radio and TV programmes on the archival movement in Manipur and is actively engaged in archival campaigns.

Anupam Sah is an art conservator-restorer, heritage conservation strategist and trainer in the application of both preventive and curative conservation techniques. He has helped establish and run conservation laboratories, numerous conservation projects and training programs in India with his conservation teams. He has served as resource person for the conservation of cultural heritage to various national, local and international organizations. Anupam has worked for the Indian Council of Conservation Institutes, a unit of INTACH as a member of its Board of Directors At present he is the Director of Uttranchal Institute for Conservation Research and Training, Nainital. He is a recipient of the 1999 Sanskriti Award for Social and Cultural Achievement.

Index

Acacia Concinna, 10

ācāra, 206

acid/acidic, 10, 88, 114, 121, 123-24, 161, 164-67

additives, 229

Adhatoda, 146

adhesives, 10

Aegle marmelos, 62

agaru, 4, 73, 74, 75, 84, 86, 92, 100

Ahom, 84-87, 92-93

ajvāin, 9, 38, 50, 58

alkaline, 184, 220

Aloe vera, 147

archives, 36, 103, 136, 148, 167-68, 215-17, 224

Arica catechu, 63

aromatic, 39, 48, 49, 50

Arsenic Sulphide, 92

Artocarpus integrifolia, 110

Arunachal Pradesh, 3, 177, 178, 182, 184

ash, 65, 77, 78, 184

Asiatic Society, 116, 140-41, 159-60, 162, 168

Assam, 4, 73-75, 77, 79-81, 178, 223, 225

aśvagandhā, 209, 112

Atharvaveda, 136

bamboo, 7, 68, 78-80, 85-87, 112, 171-72, 183, 214

bark, 4, 7, 107, 109-10, 112, 144, 146, 157-162, 164, 167, 185-86, 194, 204, 222, 228

bast, 227-28

Beli, 62

Bengal, 107, 116, 225

Betula utilis, 107

Bhādrapada, 111

Bhāṇḍāgārika, 136

bhūrja patra, 85-86, 107, 144, 222, 228

bind/binder, 172, 187, 190, 209, 228-29

birch, 7, 107, 109, 110, 126, 144, 159-60, 161-62, 164, 167, 194, 204, 222, 228

black-book, 213, 216

boiling, 62, 79, 108, 110, 120, 144

Bombu, 62

Bonda kechu, 78

Borassus flabellifer Linn, 106

Buddhism, 15, 71, 137, 179-80

Buddhist, 84, 137, 160, 177, 179-82

Bukhārā, 133, 187

burañjī, 85

burnished, 139, 171, 214, 228

burying, 5, 103, 223-24

Cachar, 98, 103, 223

calligraphy, 131, 222, 231

camphor, 9, 37-39, 54, 112, 130, 146, 154, 157, 173

Canara District, 216

cāparī, 198-99

carbonate of soda, 196

Carica papaya, 62, 68

carum, 9, 50

cellulose, 161, 164-66

Central Asian, 133

charcoal, 65, 70, 110, 147, 166, 214

chemical, 1-2, 8, 11, 27, 35-37, 39-43, 46, 48-49, 57-58, 62, 71, 79, 112, 115, 119-20, 124, 148, 151, 161, 165-67, 184, 225

Citronella, 10, 38, 49-50, 67, 70, 145, 167, 171, 174

cleaning, 10, 27, 111, 153-54, 161, 189

Clerodendrum phelomidis, 62

Coccinia Grandis, 145, 158

cockroaches, 56, 162, 56

Coconut, 63, 68, 147, 153, 158

community, 4, 12, 19, 28, 104, 205-08, 210-11, 214, 229-30, 101

conservation, xi, xii, xiii, 2-5, 8-11 13, 18, 23, 25-28, 30, 33, 58-59, 61-62, 71, 79-80, 90-91, 95-96, 103, 115-17, 119-20, 125, 127, 129-30, 132, 135, 151-52, 154-55, 148-49, 151, 153, 155, 158-60, 61, 72, 79, 164, 168-69, 174, 177, 183, 185, 190-91, 204-05, 213, 217-19, 223

consolidants, 10

Corypha umbraculifera Linn, 107

Corypha Utan, 144, 170

cotton, 37, 63-65, 70, 77-78, 80, 85, 87, 107, 109, 110-11, 121 147, 153, 172, 189, 197, 199, 200, 203, 214, 220-21, 228

crafts, 18, 198, 126-27, 235

Crotolaria retusa, 62

Cullavagga, 61, 68, 72

cumin, 9, 37, 54, 112, 145, 154, 157-58, 173

curing, 86, 119-20

custodian, 2, 11, 37, 59, 69, 97, 181, 209, 224

darugāh, 189

detergents, 10

deterioration, 3, 5, 7-8, 27, 30, 35-36, 43, 90, 128, 137, 146, 159, 161, 163-67, 172, 197 devotion, 206, 210

dew, 63, 77-78

dharma, 4, 205-06

Dhekiya, 79

dhenkī, 198

digitization, 3, 30, 32

disaster, 94, 112, 137, 207-08

documentation, 5, 95, 97, 155, 163, 217, 224, 234

drying, 79, 86, 108, 111, 114, 140, 171, 200-01

durability, 63, 71, 77, 86-87, 107-08 136, 140, 170, 219, 234

durvā, 140

duster, 189

dyes, 88, 121, 126, 228

earthquake, 182, 208

earthworms, 77-78

education, 21, 61, 229, 231, 235

Egypt, 187-88

environment, 50, 53, 59, 112, 114, 144, 147, 178, 195, 229, 235

Epigraphica Indica, 213

extract, 41, 46-47, 76-77, 87-88, 128, 131, 153, 174, 219-20

faith, 234

feather, 9, 37, 53, 112, 173, 190, 201

flexible, 10, 27, 106-07, 166, 170, 198,

folios, 70, 77, 79-80, 87, 137, 145, 172, 189-90, 209, 211, 220-22, 228

folklore, 11

frankincense, 153, 154, 114

fungicides, 8, 9

fungus, 7, 46, 58, 70, 74-75, 79, 161-63, 183

Gelugpa sect, 180

ghodā bac, 48, 112, 209

ghoṭlī, 202

gingili, 108, 10

Gora lana, 196

granthabhāṇḍāra, 207-10

gum, 50, 88, 107, 110, 126, 141, 145, 167, 182-83, 228

H.K. Baruah Regional Botanical Research Centre, 74

haṅgul, 86, 88, 102

hāṅsī, 4, 7, 73

hāṅsī pat, 4, 7

haital, 76, 79, 86, 88, 92, 102

Haldī, 53, 209

handmade, 161, 165, 178, 183, 203-04, 228, 230

harītakī, 77

Heidelberg, 12

heṅgul, 79

heritage, 2, 11, 19, 23-25, 43, 59, 90, 94, 96, 103, 106, 115, 126, 132, 148, 151, 154, 159, 183, 194, 219, 226, 235 *hiṅgul*, 92

horoscope, 222

illumination, 126, 132

illustrated manuscripts, 160, 190, 222

illustrations, 1, 144, 207, 229

imlī, 10

immerse, 76, 209

incise, 65, 75, 145, 171, 229

Indian Epigraphy, 214

Indian Paleography, 214

indigenous, 2-4, 8-9, 19, 23, 31, 61-62, 68, 75, 79-80, 87, 90, 92-93, 105, 107, 109, 120, 128, 141, 151-55, 157, 159, 168-69, 172, 174, 177, 189, 194, 219, 222, 224-25

inks, 8, 109-10, 145, 164, 181-82, 228, 234

inscription, 213, 218

insecticidal, 2, 39, 43-44, 46-50, 52, 53

insects, 2, 7, 25, 30, 24, 33, 35-41, 43-47, 49-51, 53-55, 57, 59, 66, 69-70, 75-76, 80, 87, 110-12, 125, 129, 137-38, 141, 145-48, 154-55, 158, 161-62, 165-67, 170, 172-73, 183-84, 189-90, 210, 220-21, 223

INTACH, Indian Council of Conservation Institutes, 217

intangible, 193, 227, 232

intellectual property rights, 233

iron, 63-64, 76-78, 131, 133, 145, 164, 171, 186, 189

Iron gall, 145, 164

Islamic, 5, 185-87

jackfruit, 174, 110

Jain, 4, 15, 18, 21, 30, 57, 106, 111, 115, 195, 205-11

Jñānācāra, 206

Juzdān, 189

kadata, 4, 213-18, 228

Kadukkai, 145

Kāgẓ, 195, 197, 200

Kāgẓī, 195

Kan-gyur, 181-82

kangan khar, 196

Karinjottei, 147

Kāśī, 215

Kehraj, 77

keppetiya, 62, 63, 69

Kerala, 215

kesadura, 110

Kheu, 224

Klih, 183

knowledge, vii, viii, ix, 1, 3, 4, 10, 14, 17-18, 23-24, 29, 31-32, 35-36, 38, 59, 62, 81, 96, 99-100, 106, 108, 135, 151-52, 154, 194, 205-06, 210, 225, 230, 232

Kovakkai, 145

Kṣatriya, 136

Kutub Khānah, 187

L.D. Institute, 208

lakhara, 15

languages, 13, 16-18, 99, 126, 160, 187, 216, 219

Lanthar, 144

leaf, 3-4, 7, 9-10, 25, 36, 38, 43-44, 46, 48-49, 51, 53, 55-56, 58, 61-72, 80, 84, 86-87, 106-10, 112, 114, 116, 119-20, 122-23, 126, 131, 133, 143-49, 152-54, 155-62, 164, 166-67, 169-74, 185, 190, 194, 204, 213, 217, 220-22, 224, 227-28, 231

lekhanī, 137, 231

lemon grass, 10, 145

libraries, 2, 31, 61, 72, 84, 89, 93, 106-07, 111, 114-17, 143, 148, 159, 161, 166, 168-69, 172, 185-89, 204

light, 4, 8, 24, 29, 42, 46, 58, 63, 78, 88, 97, 105, 111, 127, 129, 161, 172, 174, 210, 213, 215, 217, 225

literary evidence, 3, 108, 135, 137

longevity, 5, 73, 125, 129, 130, 140

loss, 52, 67, 83, 92-94, 137-38, 161, 164, 201

madrasas, 188, 132

Mahābhārata, 15, 160

Majuli, 4, 80-81, 83, 91, 94-97, 100-01, 103

maṭha, 143, 151-52, 154, 155, 157, 213-18

Manipur, 4, 219, 222, 226

manufacture, 62, 189, 222, 227, 230-31

Manuscriptology, 105

manuscripts, 1-5, 7-8, 10-11, 16-17, 32-33, 35-38, 43, 51, 57-58, 59, 61-62, 67-75, 77, 79-81, 83, 87-90, 92-95, 97-99, 103, 106-07, 109-12, 114-15, 119-20 122-23, 125-30, 132, 138-39, 141, 143-48, 151-55, 159-64, 159, 177, 181, 183-87, 189-91, 194-95, 204-11, 213, 222-28, 230, 232-35

Margosa, 9, 69-70, 173-74

Marigold, 221

Mataṅga, 140

matimah, 76, 86, 109

medicinal, 2, 9, 26, 42-43, 117, 121, 133, 154

medieval, 3, 48, 116, 125, 135, 140-41, 152, 213, 222

Meghalaya, 74

Meitei, 222-23

memories, 207, 232, 234

metaphysical, 3, 16, 17, 198

microfilming, 3, 27, 28, 30, 32-33, 95

mineral, 122, 228

miniature, 194, 1[illegible]

missionaries, 93

moisture, 46, 122, 139, 147, 173, 183, 189, 209, 222, 224

monsoons, 95, 210-11

mosque, 188

muni, 207, 209-10

Muni Śrī Puṇyavijayajī, 207, 209

Museum, 8-9, 12, 30, 36, 28, 68, 72, 80-81, 89, 97, 116, 215

Muslim, 107, 127, 186, 195

mustard, 10, 53, 131

narrative, 15, 11

National Library, 72, 105

National Library of Australia, 29, 32

National Library of India, 115

National Research Laboratory for the Conservation, 217

neem, 9, 25, 36, 38, 44-46, 48, 50, 57-58, 80, 110, 112, 117, 120, 131, 133, 162, 190, 220

New Delhi, 1, 81, 116-17, 148, 168, 184

Nicotine, 47, 221

Nicotiana tabacum, 47

Nicotine Tobaccum, 221

nut, 63, 10

Ocimum sanctum, 56 220

oil, 10, 38-39, 44, 46, 48-53, 55-56, 63, 65-68, 70, 74-75, 108-10, 112, 123, 130-31, 139, 143-46, 161-62, 166-67, 171, 174, 202

oral tradition, 1, 3, 5, 11-15, 20, 31, 135-36

orpiment, 86, 88, 92, 109, 184

orthography, 14

Outenga, 88

Oxalis, 220

paddy, 62, 66, 108

painting, 10, 15, 75, 85, 88, 95, 101, 102, 115, 139, 148, 168, 194, 204

Palm-leaf, 3-4, 7, 10, 33, 51, 61-66, 68-72, 107, 116, 122-23, 126, 143-49, 152-54, 159-62, 164, 166-67, 169-70, 172, 174, 194, 204, 222, 231

palmyra, 106-07, 144, 153, 160, 170

Pāṭan, 206, 207

pandri grass, 112

panainda, 64-65, 231

Panicum italicum, 196

papaya, 62, 68

paper, 1-5, 7, 13, 16, 23, 27, 32, 36, 52, 61, 68, 72-73, 79, 84-88, 92-93, 99, 102-03, 105-07, 109-10, 116, 119, 120-30, 132-33, 135, 139-41, 143-44, 151, 155, 159-69, 175, 177, 182-86, 188-90, 196-204, 213, 217-19, 222, 226-28, 230-31, 234

patrons, 233

pen, 79, 88, 125-27, 129-30, 132-33, 166, 171, 183, 188, 231

penmanship, 5, 125, 127-28, 132

pepper, 9, 37, 38, 40, 52, 112, 146, 154, 173

Persian, 5, 125-27, 129, 133, 160, 187, 216

Phascolus radiatus, 76

phenolic, 9, 123

pictographic, 3, 15

pigment, 1, 8, 161, 164, 183, 223

pineapple, 62

Pinna, 62

Pithora, 15

plant, 1-2, 39-43, 46-49, 51-52, 55-57, 66, 70, 77, 105-06, 110, 112, 114, 116, 120, 133, 145-46, 155, 173, 179, 182-83, 196, 219-20, 228

poisonous, 9, 41, 52, 116

polishing, 86, 108, 109, 120, 201-02

pollution, 8, 11, 161, 166

powder, 40, 46, 48, 54, 65, 70, 121, 146, 174, 190, 209, 214, 228

practitioners, 1, 18-20, 233-34, 144

pratikramaṇa, 206

preservation, 2-5, 8-12, 23, 25-28, 30-32, 37, 43, 59, 62, 66, 68, 71-72, 87, 89, 95-96, 103, 105, 108-09, 112, 114-15, 119-20, 122-23, 125, 127-29, 131, 135-37, 139-41, 143, 145-48, 168, 172, 174, 185-86, 189, 191, 193, 205-07, 210, 217, 219-20, 223-25

preserve, 3, 11-12, 37, 59, 62, 68, 70, 86, 97, 103, 124, 126, 132, 135, 154, 169, 194, 209, 219, 235

process, 51, 62-63, 67-68, 69, 73, 78-79, 86-88, 94, 97, 99, 100, 108, 120, 124, 129, 130, 135, 144, 164, 165-66, 190, 196-98, 201, 203, 208, 210, 220, 227, 229, 233-35

processing, 62-63, 108-09, 122

Prophet, 186

protect, 35-36, 38, 51, 54, 64, 69-70, 111, 146-47, 159, 170, 173, 183-84, 194, 207, 209-10

pulp, 10, 62, 196-201, 203, 228

Purāṇa, 85, 135-36

purity, 11-12, 57

puya, 222-23

Quraiś, 186

Qurān, 160, 186, 189

rain, 95, 178-79, 210

Rampur Raza Library, 5, 185, 189-91

Rīṭhā, 10

Re-inking, 145

recommendations, 2

record, 17, 61, 81, 87, 93, 105, 132, 136, 139, 148, 155, 163, 174, 185, 196, 213-18, 222, 229, 231
  record-keeper, 136
  record-keeping, 231

red, 25, 28, 37-38, 49, 56, 77, 79-80, 88, 111, 137, 139, 143, 147, 154, 161-62, 172, 179, 221

Regional Conservation Laboratory, 217

relative humidity, 3

religious, 38, 85, 91, 94, 96-97, 101-02, 105-06, 114, 121, 151, 152, 179, 182, 194, 213, 215 repellent, 37-40, 43-44, 46-47, 49, 51, 53-54, 57, 67, 69-70, 80, 109, 111-12, 145-46, 154-55, 172-73, 220-21

research, 2, 4-5, 9-10, 25-26, 28, 30, 31, 33, 47, 57, 72, 74, 89, 95, 98-100, 102, 148, 186-87, 215, 217, 226, 234-35

revival, 4-5, 83, 97, 101-03, 177, 224, 227-28, 230, 232-35,

revive, 93, 97-98, 102, 183, 222, 234-35,

Rhaphnus, 182

rhizomes, 120-21, 123

ritual, 102, 122, 138, 147, 154, 180, 183, 194, 230, 233

sacred, 1-2, 23, 25, 29, 171, 223-24,

sajjī, 196

sāl, 110

Samadera indica, 147

sāñcī, 4, 73, 84, 92, 86, 97, 100

sāñcīpat, 4, 73-75, 77, 79-81, 83-86, 89-103, 107, 110

sandalwood, 51

Saraswathi Mahal Library, 122, 146, 169, 173

satra, 80, 85, 89, 90, 91-92, 94-97, 100-02

scribe, 63-65, 68, 183, 188, 210, 223, 229

script, 3, 13, 15-17, 87, 88, 99, 100, 102, 130, 160, 171, 216, 219

scroll, 232

Seasamum indicum, 108, 110

seasoned, 109-10, 143, 145, 171, 174, 214, 222

seed, 5, 9-10, 39, 44, 46, 48-49, 52, 54, 58, 66, 70, 88, 108, 109, 112, 145-46, 154, 214

Shorea robusta, 110

shugu-sheng, 182

Sialkot, 194

Siddhā, 143-44

Śirākāī, 10

silkha, 88, 77, 110

Simoga, 215

sizing, 164-65, 184, 201, 203

skill, 18, 62, 81, 184, 195, 232, 233, 235

smoke, 10, 37, 38-39, 46, 58, 108, 111, 147, 220

snake, 9, 37, 54, 80, 173, 190

soap, 10

Soapstone, 214

Sotrukathazhai, 147

South-East Asian, 4, 120

speech, 1, 3, 14, 15, 17

Śrāvaka, 206-08, 211

Sri Lanka, 4, 10, 61, 65, 67-68, 70, 72

sritāla, 166

Śṛṅgerī, 215

starch paste, 109

sticky, 209

storage, 8, 26, 30, 36-37, 49, 51-52, 62, 69-70, 73, 105, 110, 128-31, 137, 139, 143-44, 147, 167, 181, 185, 231

stylus, 64-65, 145, 166, 171, 173, 231

sun-drying, 79, 111

support, 8, 62, 111, 144, 169, 172, 194, 198-99, 226, 228-29, 233

surface written, 229

sweet flag, 9, 38, 48, 120, 146, 154, 173, 175

Symplocos cordifolia, 62

Takhel, 223

Tāla patra, 228

talipot, 106-07, 110, 170

tamarind, 10, 88, 108-09, 214

tangible, 193, 227, 232

Tawang Monastery, 3, 177, 179-83

teak, 64, 153, 174, 209

techniques, 1, 5, 23, 25-27, 31, 32, 62, 92-94, 97-98, 100-03, 105, 108, 110, 114, 120, 125-32, 152, 159, 164, 168-69, 172, 177, 182, 194, 206, 222-23, 226, 231

Tectona grandis, 64, 110

Tekhao, 223

temple, 65, 106, 111, 114, 215

Terminalia chebula, 110, 145

Terminalia citrina, 77, 88

terminology, 18-20

termite, 147, 162

test, 11, 28, 121, 164, 175

texts, 5, 11, 13, 32, 107, 125-29, 132, 133, 135, 145, 160, 173, 183, 230

Tezecta Indica, 221

Tibet, 181, 182

Tijara, 194

til, 108, 10

tobacco, 9, 38, 47, 80, 112, 146, 162, 173, 209, 221

Toles, 95

tools, 5, 62, 64, 125, 127-28 132, 196, 198, 202, 227, 234

toxic, 8, 11, 35-37, 39, 41-42, 46-48, 52, 55-57

traditional, 1, 4, 5, 7, 10, 12, 18, 23, 25-29, 31, 35-37, 57-59, 61-62, 65-69, 71-73, 83, 91, 93, 95, 98-103, 105, 108-09, 112, 114-15, 121, 125-26, 128, 129, 143, 146-47, 155, 177, 183-84, 195, 199-201, 203, 205, 209, 225, 228, 231

training, 11, 32, 97, 100, 195, 100, 225

translation, 14, 187, 132

tribal, 12, 15, 17, 21, 178

tulāpat, 83, 85-87, 91

Tulasī, 146, 56

tulot, 107

turmeric, 9, 38, 53, 80, 108-09, 111-12, 114, 117, 119-24, 143-44, 147, 153, 171-73

tying, 63, 153, 209

UNESCO, 8, 25, 25, 33, 94, 148

urine, 77, 88, 110, 220

Vansavalī, 88

varnish, 224

Vedic, 121, 11, 12

vegetable, 52-53, 110, 145, 160, 171, 174, 228

Verbesina prostrata, 77

Verbesina scandens, 110

vermilion, 76

Vijayanagar, 215-16, 218

Waraq gardans, 189

waterproof, 220, 224

West Kameng, 177, 179, 182-83

wheat, 10, 109

white ants, 57, 112, 214, 224

wood, 7, 37, 49, 51, 63-64, 66-67, 74, 86, 100, 139, 153, 162, 172, 174, 181, 184, 198, 209, 230

wood oil, 10

worship, 114, 138, 171, 179, 210, 230

writing, 3, 5, 10, 12, 14-16, 18, 20, 61-62, 64-65, 73-75, 79, 83-84, 86, 88, 93, 100, 106-10, 115, 119, 122, 125-27, 129-30, 133, 135-36, 139, 143-45, 159, 165-67, 169-72, 174, 182-83, 185-87, 194, 210, 214, 219-20, 222-23, 226-29, 231, 235

yellow, 37, 53, 76, 79-80, 85-86, 88, 109, 111, 120-21, 123, 147, 179-80, 190